Journeyman

AN AUTOBIOGRAPHY

Ewan MacColl

Re-edited, and with an introduction by
PEGGY SEEGER

Manchester University Press
Manchester and New York
distributed in the United States exclusively by Palgrave Macmillan

The names of a number of people who appear in this book, especially in the early days, have been changed to avoid hurting their feelings.

Copyright © Peggy Seeger 1990, 2009

The right of Peggy Seeger to be identified as the editor of this work has been asserted by her in accordance with the Copyright, Designs and Patents Act 1988.

First edition published 1990 by Sidgwick & Jackson

This edition published 2009 by Manchester University Press
Oxford Road, Manchester M13 9NR, UK
and Room 400, 175 Fifth Avenue, New York, NY 10010, USA

Distributed in the United States exclusively by
Palgrave, 175 Fifth Avenue, New York,
NY 10010, USA

Distributed in Canada exclusively by
UBC Press, University of British Columbia, 2029 West Mall,
Vancouver, BC, Canada V6T 1Z2

British Library Cataloguing-in-Publication Data
A catalogue record for this book is available from the British Library

Library of Congress Cataloging-in-Publication Data applied for

ISBN   978 0 7190 7935 1   *hardback*
ISBN   978 0 7190 7936 8   *paperback*

This edition first published 2009

Typeset in Plantin
by Servis Filmsetting Ltd, Stockport, Cheshire

Printed in Great Britain
by CPI Antony Rowe Ltd, Chippenham, Wiltshire

Contents

List of illustrations		vii
Introduction by Peggy Seeger		ix
Acknowledgement		xiii

Part One (1915–1940)

1	Early Days and Hogmanay	3
2	One in Three Million	23
3	Front Doors and Back Entries	32
4	Unnatural Habitat	51
5	Lodgers and Friends	60
6	The Gang	69
7	The Tangenital Mind	95
8	Happy Days?	105
9	Mother, Meg and May	120
10	Limbo	130
11	On the Broo	140
12	Big City, Big Geordie	152
13	Politics, Prurience and Fresh Air	168
14	New Comrades	178
15	Agitprop	188
16	Theatre of Action	201
17	Living in London and Dreaming of Moscow	213
18	Megaphones to Microphones	224

Contents

Part Two (1945–1989)

19	Theatre Workshop	237
20	On the Road	251
21	Enter Alan Lomax	260
22	Into the Folk Revival	277
23	Radio Ballads	301
24	Singing and Song-Writing	328
25	The Joy of Living	342
26	Time Steals on and Steals	361
	Epilogue	366
	Key to references in notes	376
	Notes	378
	Index	383

List of Illustrations

Plates appear between pages 146–7 and 274–5

Coburg Street, Lower Broughton, Salford, 1915. Courtesy of the Trustees of the National Library of Scotland

Coburg Street residents, 1915. Courtesy of the Trustees of the National Library of Scotland

William Miller, Ewan's father

Jimmie Miller (Ewan MacColl) at 12 years old

The boys of Grecian Street School, Salford 1923. Jimmie is sitting in the front row, second from the right

Coburg Street, Salford, 1959, before demolition in the 1960s

Ewan MacColl, aged 21

The Canal, Salford, where Ewan nearly drowned

The Red Megaphones, Ewan's Agitprop Group, during a May Day demonstration at Preston in 1932

Ewan as the Puppetmaster in his own play *Uranium 235* in London 1949

Part of Theatre Workshop Co. at their first home in Kendal 1945

Joan Littlewood, Ewan's first wife

Jean Newlove, Ewan's second wife and mother of his children Hamish and Kirsty

The programme for Ewan's play: *Landscapes with Chimneys* 1951

Ewan as the Street Singer in *The Threepenny Opera*, Sam Wanamaker's West End production, which opened at The Royal Court in 1956

Peggy Seeger at 19 years of age in 1954

The Ramblers, Ewan and Peggy's first group, in 1956–57

Peggy, Ewan and their son Neill in 1959

Betsy Miller in 1961. Photo by Danny Seeger

Ewan at The 'Ballads and Blues club' at The Princess Louise in London, 1957–58

Ewan with his early singing partner, Bert Lloyd

Ewan with Fitzroy Coleman. Photo by Colin Dunn

List of Illustrations

During the making of *Singing the Fishing* at South Shield, 1961

Charles Parker on board *the Honeydew* recording a fisherman

Ewan interviewing a fisherman

Ewan and Peggy on tour in Toronto in 1960

Ewan and Peggy at Newport Folk Festival in 1960

Ewan and Peggy playing in Havana, Cuba, in 1968

Hamish MacColl, Ewan and Jean's son

Ewan, Peggy, Neill and Calum at The Singer's Club, London, in 1980

Neill MacColl on a session for the album, 'Two', with Kathryn Williams in 2008

Calum MacColl in the studio

Kirsty MacColl, who died in an accident on 18 December 2001

Kirsty MacColl, with her father Ewan

Kirsty MacColl, with her godmother, Joan Littlewood, and her mother Jean

Kitty MacColl in 2007. Photo by Alan Boyd

Peggy Seeger in 2005. Photo by Martin Rosenbaum

Ewan with folklorist and catalyst Alan Lomax in 1988

Ewan accepting his first honorary degree at Exeter University in July 1986

Introduction by Peggy Seeger

Re-reading this beautifully written book, this compelling narrative of a passionate life lived to the full, has reminded me of just how interesting a person Ewan MacColl was. It has renewed yet again my love for him, my compassion, tenderness and respect. And what an apt title, indicating an interim period of growth and skill – for every human life is but a learning experience, a work-in-progress.[1]

Part One: (1915–1940). The scene is set in a Scots enclave (his extended family) in the slums of a northern English industrial town. As Ewan rummages with a sense of wonder through the treasure-chest of his childhood, he questions his memory in the way that children endlessly question adults. As the story progresses the lens widens to include Salford and its inhabitants and the questions give way to dialogues. Trying to understand the structure of his surroundings and put its chaos into order, he calls up the people in his past to help him, making them stand still so that he can remember as much as possible. When he was writing this section he would come downstairs after a long stretch of work, astonished at the detail of the memories that were flooding into his consciousness after a hiatus of threescore years. 'It's all there in my brain, Peg! Faces, smells, what their voices sounded like! I remember whole conversations . . .!'

School and (un)employment teach him that he is at the bottom of the economic heap and at a very early age he joins the vanguard of the working-class movement. The Salford newborn rides gunshot as poverty and politics give him a rough-and-tumble ride into boyhood, teenage and early manhood. The writing is lively and immediate. Part One is a cornucopia of small vignettes and tableaux. If you want to understand Ewan MacColl, this section will do.

Ewan blanks out five or six years of his life before he begins Part Two (1945–1989). In this part he also blanks out appropriate and sympathetic mention of his second wife (Jean Newlove[2]) and the birth of several of his children – omissions which I failed to notice when typing the manuscript. But World War II . . .?

Ewan said that what he did during World War II wasn't necessary to the book. It was a chapter in his life that he wanted to forget. He loathed war. He despised the army, the food, the shouting, the regimentation, the hierarchy, the robotic marching, the violence, the mass killing. There was some part of him that was bitter, ashamed or just downright bloody-minded – but that period was a closed book and that was that. I kept it closed too. Ben Harker's 2007 biography *Class Act: The Cultural and Political Life of Ewan MaccColl*, which probes many of the omissions in *Journeyman*, manages a 7-page chapter on this period.[3]

In Part Two of *Journeyman* (post World War II), the joy and excitement of work replace the sense of wonder, and the world replaces Salford. Gone are the questions, for now Ewan has answers. He has become a man with a purpose, a crusader.

The writing style reflects this arrival into adulthood. It is more literary, more matter-of-fact. The narrator's voice is assured and strong and has gradually absorbed and overridden the other more tentative forms of dialogue and tableaux. Has the brain taken over from the heart (and the genitals) as the main guiding organ or has Ewan, no longer a plaything in the hands of Fate, finally got the three organs in balance? One thing is certain: he is hot on the trail of ideas ('Ideas are the most important thing, Peg!') which he will put at the service of the working – class movement and leftwing politics, first in theatre and then in the folk revival. The battle leaves the streets and the enemy is now large sections of humanity: the rightwing, the fascists, the police, the traitorous Labour Party.

The primal adversary, of course, was always the Establishment. Ewan was in the news a great deal when MI5 opened its files on the role of the BBC in blacklisting left wing artists in the 1940s and 1950s. The Independent Newspaper headlined 'Radical MacColl tracked by MI5 for decades' (5 March 2006). Well, I certainly hope we were snooped on by the professional snoopers (even if they often get it wrong – the above article carried a disastrous picture of me with Joan Littlewood's name under it)! As the USA song goes: 'You ain't done nothin' if you ain't been called a Red'. By their enemies shall ye know them – and by your enemies (as well as your friends) shall ye define yourself.

Of course Ewan knew he was blacklisted from very early on. Of course we knew who went to bat for him and who didn't – but it wasn't a matter of much discussion between us. But then we ignored many outside influences and issues and were often ignored in return. We were busy! In retrospect, I feel we were too absorbed in our work, too single-minded and tunnel-visioned even though many of those visions laid important groundwork for the UK folk revival as it is today: centred on UK folk traditions.

Part One is fascinating. It appeals to the senses, to our 'inner child'. It is heavy with newness, hormones, farts, dramatis personae, the weather, the streets, with life-before-maturity. Part Two is equally intriguing and very different. It appeals to the grown-up mind. It is of special interest to me as it consists largely of life after Peggy met Ewan. Herein lies the working partner I lived with for thirty years, the hopes we had, the things we talked about, the projects we worked on, the people we worked with. Here's the man who came 150% alive when involved in a theatre production, writing a song or working with a singer or actor. Here is the man who could enhance your singing performance by using theatrical techniques, who could transform ideas into action, and jokes into songs. His joy and enthusiasm in the work are like a water table that bubbles up over and over throughout the sober pages of Part Two.

Hence we come to the final two chapters, documenting the period from 1987 to 1989. Ewan drops his public persona and takes an almost child-like pleasure in playing with words and feelings. These chapters, laced with macabre humour, put me in mind of the delirium that would sometimes come upon him when he had a high fever; and of his last two days, spent in hospital; and of the final scene of his last play, *The Shipmaster*, written in 1979. In this apocalyptic play, the old Scots sea captain, a master craftsman of sail, has lived past his time, into the era of steam locomotion. He's penniless, jobless, impotent and broken, he howls out his love for sail, women, life and the ocean. He rages against machines, man and death. Like the sea captain, Ewan is furious, he is asking questions and not afraid to reveal his vulnerability, insecurity and weakness. In the Epilogue he drifts in and out of logic, moves back and forward in Time, travels hither and yon in writing style as the words fall over one another in their haste to get on the page. It all pours out: his deep, abiding love and tenderness for me and our children, his devotion to music and mountains, his farewell to life. It is almost with relief that as an old man of 74 he can weep again. These closing chapters of *Journeyman* are pure emotion, a heart-rending reawakening of the innocence of childhood – just in time for death.

Ewan's knowledge of English language and literature never ceased to impress me. He ends *Journeyman* with a re-make of 'Lament for the Makaris' ('Lament for the Poets', William Dunbar. 1460–1520). Along with Dunbar, he not only faces his own demise ('Timor mortis conturbat me' – fear of death confounds me) but acknowledges Death as complicit in his soon-to-come reunion with deceased friends: Joe (Heaney), Bert (Lloyd), Moe (Asch), Bertrand (Bronson) and Vance Randolph. He knows he is dying. Fear, Love and Laughter are singing him out but he's making sure that Ewan MacColl writes the text and tune

The bookends (Part One and the two closing chapters) are, to me, the most poignant sections of the book. Ewan has allowed us to see right into the darkest, most insecure part of his soul and into the part that is filled with blindingly radiant light. Here is a man who was a walking encyclopaedia, whose skin could barely contain the passion he felt but whose mind was constantly telling him 'Be logical, be logical – emotions will betray you. Hold back, hold back, don't let them see how vulnerable you are . . . !' And no one did. Not even me, until he handed me that last chapter to put onto the computer.

Ewan died young, a young mind in an old and besieged body. I am glad he died when he did. By 1988 the heart tremors were coming frequently and getting more and more severe, a kind of daily death. How would he have managed had he become bedridden or wheel-chair bound? Would his gallant heart have survived the death of his daughter, Kirsty? How would his optimism have ridden the catastrophic fall of his beloved Soviet Union or the Westernisation of China?

I am sorry he did not live to see his children bringing up their own wonderful children. I am sorry he did not live into the more terracentric and tolerant person that he was beginning to become, for he softened and opened out more in his old age (I comment on this at length in my introduction to *The Essential Ewan MacColl Songbook*). I am sorry he did not live to see some of his songs entering the national folk repertoire. And I am sorry for all those creations that were waiting to emerge from that tireless song-factory in his head. Yes – he died too young, too soon.

It was a pleasure to read the book again, to have him with me once more. Our children refer to him affectionately as 'the old fella' and 'the auld bugger' (used as a term of affection among us) and we all have our stories to tell about our life with him. Every year at noon on the anniversaries of his birth and death (25 January and 22 October), a group of friends gather at the oak tree that was planted in his memory in Russell Square in London. They come happed up against England's eternal damp, bringing bottles of whisky and glasses, stories and memories. They exchange folklore and real-lore about MacColl the Journeyman who was really a Master Craftsman. The empty bottles and drained glasses are held upside down over the roots of the sturdy little tree. Not a drop is wasted.

Peggy Seeger, Boston, USA

Acknowledgement

Ted Power, of Brighton, has not only instigated and undertaken the re-editing of this book but he has sought out additional visual materials (photos, Salford maps, etc). He has also edited IN original material which had been edited OUT of the first edition. We are grateful for his imagination and his painstaking attention to detail. We are also indebted to Peter Cox, who supplied the final edit of Chapter 23, Journeyman's account of The Radio Ballads project. Peter's recent work Set Into Song 4 (Labatie Books 2008) sets out to value the efforts of ALL members of the team responsible for the groundbreaking Radio Ballads which first hit the airwaves in summer 1958. Ted felt it appropriate to turn to Peter, who has done very detailed research, for help and advice. We are also grateful to Sheelagh Neuling for her interest in the text and useful suggestions. We would like to acknowledge the kind assistance of Valerie Moyses and Felicity Roberts who look after the Ewan MacColl/Peggy Seeger Archive at Ruskin College Oxford. A special thank you is due to Kitty MacColl not only for scanning the illustrative content from prints in the family album but also for her advice in choosing those photos. Thank you too to Hamish MacColl for scanning and supplying pictures of his mother, Jean, and late sister, Kirsty. Finally we would like to acknowledge the assistance of Emma Brennan and Reena Jugnarain of Manchester University Press. Emma has seen the re-edited manuscript through from the beginning, while Reena has offered valuable guidance on proof-reading and the organisation of the much improved index.

(On behalf of PS and EM)

Part One
(1915–1940)

1

Early Days and Hogmanay

My memory works in strange ways, that is when it works at all. There are times when even my children's names elude me so that I have to grope like some comic-book caricature of an absent-minded professor through the names of all of them until I find the right one. On other occasions the name of a casual acquaintance, one which has lain forgotten in some dusty recess of my memory, will come leaping unbidden straight into the forefront of my mind.

Sometimes, out of the corner of my mind's eye, I catch a fleeting glimpse of a mosaic floor showing a faded and almost indecipherable pattern, a kind of three-dimensional jigsaw puzzle in reverse which reveals more and more of its secrets as the pieces are prised out. One by one they come, loosening the pieces around them until finally the entire design becomes clear.

A small piece chosen at random: a late afternoon on the edge of changing into a steel-blue evening. I have come from school, entering the house by the back door. On the scullery mantelpiece I find a tablet of Melrose which I rub on the chapped skin on the inside of my thighs. I can hear my mother singing in the front room. That is how we refer to the one comfortable room in the house: the front room. The two bedrooms are for sleeping in; they each contain a bed and a cheap chest of drawers. The scullery is for working in; it has a cement floor which, according to my mother, 'breathes damp'. It has a sink with a cold-water tap where we wash, a copper used for boiling clothes, a huge mangle for wringing them out and a gas-ring on which we make our porridge and boil the water for our tea.

The front room is where everything happens. We eat there and entertain friends. It is the centre of our social life. The table, which is its main item of furniture, has many uses. We take our meals on it. I draw and write and play games on it after the evening meal has been cleared away. My father sits at it when he writes up his notes for the union branch or when the branch holds its meetings at our house. My mother uses it for doing her ironing on and for baking. I love to come home from school when the house is full of the smell of baking, of fresh barm cakes, fatty scones, treacle scones or bread. Today it is a different smell, one that I like well enough, the smell of steamy hot linen.

The gas is not yet lit and my mother is working by the light of the fire. Her back is to me and she hasn't seen me yet. The clothes-rack is filled with white sheets which look deep crimson in the firelight. I stand there hypnotised by the smooth backwards-and-forwards glide of the charcoal-iron and the monotonous rise-and-fall of the melody of 'My Boy Willie'. Her head is bent over the table and the firelight catching her auburn hair makes it look like spun copper.

My earliest memory is of this fire-lit room. How old was I? One, one and a half, two? Certainly no more than two. My mother is standing naked in a large tin bath in front of the fire. She bends over and picks me up and sits me in the bath at her feet. I am entranced by the sight of that rosy flesh and when she steps out of the bath and begins to comb her waist-length hair I am filled with a tremendous sense of wonder. I seem to remember that my Auntie Mag was there and that she too was naked. Yes, I can see them clearly as they stand there drawing their combs through their hair. Two young women enjoying their nakedness. A truly erotic moment.

It must have been about the same time we saw the Zeppelin.[1] It could even have been the same night. I always found it thrilling to sleep in the same bed as my two cousins, John and Willie. I remember this particular night very clearly. We had been amusing ourselves by bouncing up and down in the bed and we were just about ready to fall asleep when we heard the guns. We jumped up and Willie, the oldest among us, turned the gas-light off. We crowded at the window in breathless excitement and looked at a sky across which clouds scudded, shrouding then revealing the moon's white face. A few puffs of cloud showed where the anti-aircraft shells were bursting. Then we saw it! An awesome sight, a huge silver cigar-shaped form gliding from behind a cloud. The sound of the ack-ack guns was louder now and the puffs of cloud were all round the Zeppelin. And now come long probing fingers of white light, tentatively searching like the fingers of a blind person, but failing to find the Zeppelin. It just glides on and on until we cannot see it. We lie down, snuggling up to each other, for it is a cold night.

Now why do I suddenly remember a thing like that? It's not as though it influenced me in any way or changed the course of my life. It is completely irrelevant. But then what is relevant? Is it really true that we carry around in our subconscious – or unconscious – mind memories of everything that has ever happened to us? Everything? Is that all I am, then, a snapper-up of unconsidered trifles, a walking junkyard of forgotten incidents and discarded ideas?

Of the four children my mother bore, three died in infancy. I was the survivor and, consequently, especially dear to her. From the time I was born until I went to school at the age of five, I was with her constantly and during my next nine years of school she continued to play a dominant role in my life. In different circumstance she might have become one of those over-protective mothers who smother their children under heavy layers of love. But we were dirt poor, and poverty and over-protectiveness rarely go hand-in-hand. Nevertheless I was pampered just a little, given rather more attention than those among my contemporaries who were members of larger families. For example, my mother accompanied me to school on my first day there, actually held my hand until we came to the gate of the playground where she kissed and embraced me. Then, as if this disgraceful exhibition of emotion wasn't shameful enough, she stood at the railings of the schoolyard and waved to me as I was ushered into the building. This behaviour elicited scornful comment from my classmates and several months were to elapse before they ceased to regard me as a mother's boy.

I suppose that first day at school is, for everyone, a momentous occasion for it is the point at which you take the first few faltering steps in the journey towards a personal identity. Every day for four or five hours you are outside the orbit of your mother's presence, developing new emotional ties, extending your world. Only hunger, pain or fear remind you that she can be had for the asking. Your relationship with your father is important too, but it's on a different level from that which you share with your mother. For five-and-a-half days of every week your father is away working in the foundry or the pit or the factory, but your mother is always within call and her function is to soothe your pain, feed your hunger, banish your fears and to provide you with as much love as you are prepared to take. Why then do I find it so difficult to write about her? What can I say that will do justice to her memory? Which particular facet of her character should I dwell on? Her courage, her indomitable courage . . . her patience, her need to create order out of chaos . . . her fierce temper, perhaps, or her even fiercer spirit of independence . . . her humanity . . .? My picture of her is, I suppose, compounded of all these things.

I think that my mother's remembrances of the past must have been fairly near the surface of her mind for she spoke of them frequently.[2] Indeed, she was the *shenachie* of the entire Hendry clan and of my father's family as well. Anything I know about my grandparents I learned from her. She was born on 3 March 1886, in Flemings Close, Auchterarder, Perthshire, the sixth of ten girls in a family of fourteen children. Betsy was her given name. Her mother, Isabelle Christie (Tibby to her husband) had been a farm servant before she married. My mother always referred to her as 'Auld Eezie'. In the same way she always referred to her father as 'Auld Jimmy'. But it was for Auld Eezie that she reserved her affection:

> It wouldnae hae mattered if the hoose had been like a pigsty, she would just sit doon on the corner o' the fender and sing awa' to hersel'. And read! She could read tae a band playing. She'd read onything. It was novels mostly, but she'd read onything. And she was a marvellous howdie. Ye ken whit a howdie is? A midwife. She was marvellous. We lived away in the country. And she used to go for miles around tae a' the farmer's wives, bringing the bairns hame. I never remember her charging a penny for ony o' the wark she ever did. It was sheer love and good nature.

My mother's marriage certificate gave her father's occupation as 'stillman'. Earlier he had worked as a weaver in a tweed mill, had been a barber and a general labourer. Drink, according to Betsy, was his downfall. 'He could sup oot o' a shitey cloot.' Certainly as a young man he had been somewhat wild.

In Auchterarder, once a year, they used to hold a celebration and they used to licht a bonfire in the middle o' the toon. My father was aye there, of course. (This by the way was lang before I was ever thocht o'.) He was only seventeen at the time. Well, men with flambeaus . . . ye ken what a flambeau is? It's a long pole wi' a licht at the end o't, and men wi' they lichted sticks used to walk all around this bonfire. There were always policemen there to see that nae accidents happened, I suppose. However, my faither got into a dispute wi' a policeman. My faither was a great big strong fellow and this policeman was going to arrest him, so he just took him by the scruff of his neck and flung him in the bonfire. They had a job to get him oot but eventually they did and he was all right. But my faither ran for his life and he went to Hamilton and enlisted and his faither and mither never saw him for twelve years. He was twelve years in the colours and five in the reserve. Oh, he was a real king-and-country man was Auld Jimmy. Just gie him a couple of pints and he'd start reciting:

> When war was declared on Russia,
> The first of it I heard
> As a soldier I enlisted
> In the gallant Ninety-Third.

At times when he was half-seas over he'd line us weans up ootside the wee hoose we lived in and he'd drill us. Left turn! Right turn! And he'd hae a wee stick ower his shouther in place o' a rifle.

I never tired of hearing these stories. They were a source of constant delight to me, and when all other childish pleasures palled I would try and coax my mother into talking about the past. 'Tell us the story of Auld Jimmy and the dancing bear,' I would plead. That was my favourite of all the Auld Jimmy tales. His Indian service entitled him to a quarterly pension which was paid out at Perth. After collecting it he would find a congenial pub and sit there drinking until closing time or until the publican grew weary of his martial recitations. After the pub had closed he would set out on the fourteen-mile walk to Auchterarder.

> . . .Well, the nicht was gey warm. It was summer, ye ken and what wi' the drink and the heat my faither suddenly felt awfu' weary. Well, there was this plantin' . . . ye ken whit a plantin' is? It's a wood, a plantin'. Well, he jeuks through a hole and lies doon against the wa'. Well, he was awfu' hot in the nicht, steaming hot and once he half woke up, feelin' that something was licking his face. Well, he maybe thocht it was a coo that had strayed intae the plantin' so he just turned awa' and gaed to sleep again. But in the mornin' just after dawn time he feels the licking again, on his hand this time. Well, he turned ower and he sees it's no' a coo but a big brown bear. Y'see, in they days pedlars aften had dancin' bears and they would dance for pennies or for as much as folk could afford to gie them. But my faither

-6-

wasnae thinkin' o' that and wi' a roar he's up and lowpin' through the wa' and rinnin' doon the road wi' the bear and the man after him. The daft auld bugger thocht he had the D.T.'s.

Dancing bears, mid-summer bonfires . . . the very warp and weft of romance. My mother's descriptions of her childhood were so vivid, so rich in delicious detail that her Scotland became more real in my mind than the place I was living in. And to add to my splendid vision there were those beautiful early 19th-century engravings in the two large handsome volumes of the complete works of Robert Burns which had pride of place in the glass case in the front room. Even now, some sixty-five years later I have only to close my eyes to see the dream village where my grandfather was chased by the dancing bear and where my mother, grotesquely clad in the castoff finery of the laird's wife, had once walked to school, eager to parade her finery.

I must have looked a real comedian. Imagine it, there were these shoes that were at least three sizes too big for me. And spats! Think, o' that, spats! I was wearing the laird's spats, and a silk dress wi' a bustle that must hae been made for a very tall woman. It was my mither's Auntie Margaret, y'see. She worked up at the big hoose as a cook or something and she used to send us big hampers o' claes. I think they must hae thocht a lot o' her to gie her a' they fine things. Certainly the laird or maybe his son thocht highly of her for they sent her hame wi' a bairn. Ay, they were gey partial to the Hendry women. Years later my eldest sister Belle worked at the castle and they got a bairn on her as well. That was Jimmy Stewart, Belle's wee laddie that I had the bringin' up o' until Belle went aff to Australia.

Looking back over the years I think I must have been something of a trial to my mother with my endless questions about the past. No detail was too insignificant, no event too prosaic. My appetite for my mother's stories was insatiable. I never tired of hearing about her forays into the strawberry field at Flemings farm or about the battles fought on the road to school in defence of Agnes and Mary-Anne. And there was the time she had been made to stand up in front of the entire school and recite 'The quality of mercy is not strained' from *The Merchant of Venice,* stage directions and all. It was only years later that I realised that the words 'Enter Portia dressed as a doctor of law' was not part of the actual speech. She could still recite the entire speech right up until the day of her death at the age of ninety-six. I must confess that as a child I was unmoved by Portia's famous speech and preferred 'Curfew shall not ring tonight', a melodrama which never failed to fill my eyes with tears.

She had another favourite monologue which was even more effective. I have forgotten the title (if I ever knew it) but it was a harrowing tale of a woman who takes her child to the railway line and lies down there determined to end it all only to be rescued at the last moment by a stranger, who turns out to be her long-lost husband. Banal? Not as far as I was concerned at the age of five or six. I could believe in that monstrous railway engine thundering down the track. I had often climbed onto the parapet of the railway bridge on Frederick

Road and lain there enveloped in the cloud of steam and smoke of charging locomotives.

I could believe too in a grief so intense that one would wish to die like the woman in the monologue. It was all so real, part of the fascinating world I was discovering, a world in which the past and the present fused into a single reality. When my mother told me that Auld Jimmy had once, on the road between Perth and Auchterarder, encountered a ghostly regiment of mounted cavalry or had slept by the side of a dancing bear or had thrown a policeman into a bonfire, I felt flattered that such a heroic figure was related to me. I never for one moment doubted the reality of such incidents, nor did I doubt that they belonged to a reality called Scotland which I could enter through my mother's head. It was all real, the dressing up in the laird's spats and the dress with a bustle, picking young turnips in the fields on the way home from school and eating them raw, making whistles out of hollow reeds, of being part of a large family of brothers and sisters all of whom featured, in one way or another, in my mother's stories.

'It was a wee hoose', my mother said, 'but it was aye fu' o' music, especially on a Sunday morning for the laddies were a' bandsmen. Jock played the cornet, Andra the trombone, Jimmy the bass drum and Tam the euphonium.' Euphonium! How I loved that word. I used it constantly. In the middle of a game of marbles I would tell my opponents that my Uncle Tam played the euphonium. Or hearing a playmate tell of a friend whose brother played a bugle in the scout band, I would say, 'It's not as hard to play as the euphonium.' Snotty Tattersall, jealous of the prestige conferred on me by my uncle's mastery of this impressively named instrument, conjured up out of the blue an uncle of his own who, he said, played the tuba which, he argued, was bigger than the euphonium. 'Bigger but easier to play,' I countered and so confidently did I make this claim that the tuba suffered immediate relegation.

'The tuba sounds like farting,' someone said – an observation which met with considerable support and led to Snotty being greeted for a week or two afterwards with remarks like 'How's your farter?' and 'How's your uncle's farting tube?'

According to my mother, Jock was a gifted performer on the cornet and had won prizes for his playing at competitions all over Scotland. He was something of a rebel too and in his love of books he took after his mother. Indeed, a book cost him his job and won him a degree of notoriety.

Jock was a great reader. The books were never oot o' his hand. He had a pal who was a minister, the free-kirk minister. He and Jock were bosom pals. It was him that lent him that book, y' know, it was ca'd *The Devil on Two Sticks*. We heard afterwards that it was forbidden, that book. They got to know where he was working and he was sacked frae his work for it. He was a moulder. Of course, my mither had to read it. It was a terrible thing to bring any books like that intae where my faither was. He was terribly strict aboot anything like that. He forbid this book to stay in the hoose. Anyway, a' they that could read, read it. And then it was gien back to the free-kirk minister. I dinnae ken whaur he got it, but he got it.

It wasn't until the mid-seventies that I discovered that *The Devil on Two Sticks* was by the French writer Le Sage (1668–1747). Throughout my childhood years I envisaged the events surrounding the forbidden book taking place in Flemings Close where summer bonfires, dancing bears, phantom cavalry and suchlike commonplaces were the order of the day. But I was mistaken. Some time before, the family had left Auchterarder and made their way to Stirling from whence, after a few weeks' stay, they had moved on to Denny.

My faither had a good job in the mill', said my mother, 'and he lost it through drink. They gied him plenty o' warning but he couldnae resist the bottle and when they found him asleep at his loom that was the end o't. Well, nobody would employ him so we packed up oor things and loaded them on a cart and walked tae Stirling. That's the truth, we walked a' the way; eight bairns and my faither and mither, walking the roads like Tinkers, sleeping where we could.

Auld Jimmy's drunkenness appears to have been accepted by his wife and children as a natural phenomenon. Certainly my mother's references to it were generally good-natured; after all, the family's stock of humorous stories were all born out of his drinking habits. When those habits ceased, the source of the stories dried up and family life changed for the worse.

The worse thing that ever happened in oar hoose at hame was when he went teetotal. He couldn't bear the name o' drink. Oh, no! Onybody that took a drink was no good. No good at all. Everybody should turn teetotal because my faither had turned teetotal. The man I married was awfu' fond o' my mither and we used to go along and see them every weekend. And Will used to tak' a wee bottle o' whiskey, a half mutchkin they ca'd it, tae my mither. And she had to hide it. Would you believe it? She had to hide it. My faither would hae disowned her if he had known. He was a warrior! He was as hateful after he was teetotal as he was a cheery, good-natured faither when he was drunk. He was as thrawn and as aggravating after he got teetotal as he'd been easy-going before.

My mother's references to her father in his teetotal stage are far from affectionate. In her softer moments she generally referred to him as a 'bloody auld swine'. She recalls how on her fourteenth birthday she was sent into service in the house of a Presbyterian minister, 'the Reverend Goodhall, as drucken a man as you could meet in a week's march'. Her father had arranged for her employment there as the 'slavey', the name given to the most menial female servant in a hierarchy of menials.

It was sheer slavery. I was up in the mornings at five o'clock cleaning oot the fires and bringing in the hods fu' o' coal. I could hardly lift them. They should hae thocht black burnin' shame, for I was just a wee lassie. Every heavy, dirty job that was to be done, I had tae dae. The minister wasnae a bad man, I think he just drank hissel intae a stupor so he wouldnae hae to listen to his wife. What an awfu' bitch that woman was. She thocht she was a cut above the rest o' us. She'd twa bairns and she'd brocht them up to believe that the sun shone oot o' their arses. The laddie was aboot ten years auld and she said that I should ca' him 'Master

John', the wee puke. The lassie wasnae sae bad, but bad enough. My sister Belle was the housekeeper there and she was a bobby-dazzler and no mistake, a real tyrant. You talk about slavery! That was slavery.

Her three years' term of hard labour at the Goodhall's provided the foundations for her social outlook, an outlook which recognised that society was composed of two classes, one of which preyed upon the other. If those three years were marked with humorous incidents, she had forgotten them. She certainly never mentioned them, indeed she never spoke of that episode in her life without bitterness. For her, I am sure, it was a time without hope, a bleak desolate time in which kindness had died.

Any affection she had felt for her father during childhood also died in this period. Not only had he sold her into this appalling household but he had pocketed her wages throughout the three years she was there. When she returned home and told him that she had left the Goodhall's employment he ordered her to return and apologise to her erstwhile employers. When she refused he threatened to thrash her. She responded by threatening to break the poker over his head and she must have been very convincing for he abandoned his threat and was content merely to call her names and accuse her of ingratitude and lack of respect for her elders.

The following day my mother went to Falkirk where she found a job as a pawnbroker's assistant. Compared with her experience at the Goodhall's this new job was 'sheer luxury. I didnae ken I was born!' And she was good at it – so good that in the course of the next two years she was often left to run the shop herself. It was during this period that she met my father.

One day there was a young fella come in and he handed me a pawn-ticket. He said, 'I want to take this oot.' 'Oh, ay.' Well, it was for a gold medal. So I went to the safe and got this gold medal out and told him the price. I think it was twenty-five shillings with the pledge-money and the interest. So he got the medal in his hand and he says, 'I've nae money. Can I have it till the weekend?' I said, 'No, ye cannae.' Well, I got talking to him and he told me the tale and I said, 'A' richt, but you'll be sure to come in with the money at the weekend.' 'Ay.'

However, he got the medal and he did come in at the weekend. After that he used to stand ootside the shop and wait for me till I closed the shop every nicht and eventually we started to walk oot regular. At that time he had a chum ca'd Davie Cunningham – he was a marvellous fiddler – and another yin ca'd Archie MacNeillage. He was a piper, and we used to go into a wood just at the side of where I lived, a crowd of us, and we used to sing while Davie Cunningham played the fiddle. It sounded marvellous through the trees. Then Archie would gie us a few lilts on the bagpipes. That went on for a long time, until we got married. And then we had other fish to fry.

In the spring of 1910 the entire Hendry family pulled up its roots and emigrated to Australia; all, that is, except my mother and her sister Maggie. None of the family appears to have been assiduous in the matter of writing letters, but once or twice a year there would be an exchange of notes and an occasional postcard saying that this or that sister or brother had got married. Then came the First World War, the war to end wars, and Jock, Tam, Jimmy and Andrew found themselves in France with the Australian Expeditionary Force. They spent their overseas leaves with us and though I couldn't have been more than two-and-a-half years old I still remember them. At least I remember Jock. He gave me two regimental badges which, for the next twenty years, lay in a drawer full of buttons and odds and ends. He had suffered a slight wound in the July offensive at Ypres. In his cocked Australian bush hat and his khakis he cut a very dashing figure and more than one young woman in our neighbourhood cast what my mother called 'sheep's eyes' at him.

My father was born in 1884 in Camelon, near Falkirk, Stirlingshire, the second of four children born to William Miller and Elizabeth Stratton. He was ten years old when his mother died and from that time on life was, as he put it, 'just sheer bloody hell'. That was all I ever heard him say about his childhood. My mother would occasionally refer to 'Auld Will' but he always refused to be drawn and would quickly steer the conversation into safer channels. Betsy, however, had no inhibitions about laying Auld Will's faults on the line and subjecting them to a thorough airing and beating, particularly when my father was bent double with asthma and fighting for a breath. She blamed his father and 'that cruel bitch he made stepmither tae his weans. God forgie me but if there's a hell, I hope she's still burning in it.' This was apparently the classic stepmother of the folktales, a cruel, vindictive young woman determined to eradicate the memory of her husband's previous marital relationship. Jock, the eldest son, was just a few weeks short of fourteen, the school-leaving age, so she ignored him and concentrated her violent attentions on my father, his nine-year-old brother, Alec, and Lizzie, a delicate eight-year-old girl child. Jock left home on the day he was fourteen years old and went to Glasgow where he found work as a pork-butcher's assistant. And now the stepmother could give full reign to her violent nature without fear of interference. Lizzie, being the weakest and most defenceless, caught the brunt of her ill nature. She was beaten regularly and cuffed about the head so violently that she became deaf, a condition from which she never recovered.

My father, at the beginning of his thirteenth year, developed asthma and bronchitis. Alec ceased to speak in the house and spent as much time in the streets as he could. After a particularly brutal assault on Lizzie, my father, (who by then was twelve-and-a-half years old) faced up to his stepmother and threatened to stab her with a kitchen knife if she persisted in ill-using his sister. He apparently convinced her that his intentions were serious and for a time the beatings ceased. Inevitably, however, they began again and confrontations between my father and his stepmother became frequent occurrences. At fourteen my father left school and started work in the foundry at Smith and Wellstood's as an apprentice iron moulder. This meant that Alec and Lizzie were unprotected all the time he was away at work and the beatings and stand-up battles became more frequent. One day my father came home from the foundry and found Lizzie cowering in a corner of the bedroom in a state of abject terror. Her lip was bleeding, one of her eyes closed and she appeared to be completely deaf. He ran downstairs and discovered his stepmother in the kitchen. Without a word he crossed over to her and punched her in the face. She began to scream. My grandfather, newly returned from the foundry, came running in and interposed himself between the two. According to my mother, he stood there wringing his hands and bewailing the fact that a son of his had raised his hand to a woman. 'The bloody auld hypocrite!' But Will just stood there glowering, and he said 'if that woman ever lifts a finger against Lizzie again, I'll kill her, so help me God!'. Then he turned and walked out.

Later on that night, his father, rather shamefacedly, suggested that it would be better for everyone concerned if my father found somewhere else to live. He did so the same night, after repeating his threats about what he would do if his stepmother resorted to violence just once more against Lizzie and Alec. She never did; apparently my father's threats had their effect. Alec went to live with an aunt in Perth a few weeks later and Lizzie left her father's house on the day she was fourteen. My father and grandfather continued to work in the same foundry for the next three or four years but they ignored each other and indeed never spoke to each other again.

> She was a cruel monster o' a woman', my mother said, 'but Auld Will was the real culprit. It was a' his fault, the blame was his. He was fair besotted with the bitch and he never lifted a hand to stop her torturing they weans, never even opened his mouth, the auld swine. Just look at your dad. Cannae get a breath and a' because that dirty auld brute hadnae the guts tae tak' the back o' his hand to that apology for a woman.

My father must have heard her for my mother's voice, even in old age, was penetrating. Her whispers could reduce a children's film matinee to silence. But he would let her diatribes pass without comment. He never talked about his childhood, not even about those days before his mother died. Was the pain too deep, the hurt beyond repair? I have often suspected that the cruelty and violence of his stepmother were things he had come to terms with. What really hurt and festered was his father's betrayal, the fact that he apparently didn't care enough about his children to want to protect them.

To the outside world my father presented a picture of a whole man, talented, courageous, outgoing and popular. But there was another side to his character, a side which in the course of time became pre-eminent: the vulnerable side where the nerve-ends were exposed to every shock and tremor. I was about ten or eleven years old when I first became aware of this aspect of his personality. It was one of those Salford winter days when the sky is the colour of gun-metal. My father came home from work in the early afternoon. He was very drunk and quite incoherent. After a time he sobered up and told the terrible story of how his apprentice had died screaming in agony when a bogie had overturned and covered him with its load of molten iron. For months afterwards my father's nightmares kept me awake at night. I would wake up in the small hours at the sound of his voice moaning and crying out in anguish while my mother tried to comfort him.

I would have liked to comfort him too but I didn't know how. Physical demonstrations of affection between fathers and sons were not common in the working class circle in which I grew up. I can only remember the one time, throughout the whole of my childhood, when my father embraced me. It was in the summer holidays. July or August and it is a great adventure for me to take a hot lunch to my father who is working at Hodgkinson's foundry. It is an awesome, exciting place. The glare of the open furnace bathes everything in a fiery glow, the heaps of sand on the floor, the iron rails with the bogies on them and the giant ladles. And there is the noise, the scream of compressed air from the fettling room, the sustained roar of the furnaces, the clank of metal and the rattle of steel chains as the overhead gantry lowers its grab for a tub of newly tapped molten metal, Then a hooter sounds. 'Stand back there', says my father as he pushes me against a wall, 'don't move!' And suddenly the air is filled with a swirling mass of yellow cloud. For a minute or two I am convinced that I am choking to death. As it begins to clear, the moulders and their apprentices appear like devils struggling through the flames of hell. One of them pulls me to him and gives me a quick hug. His shirt smells scorched. It is my father though he looks different here in the foundry. That hug makes me feel strangely jubilant.

One small embrace. Not much to last a lifetime. There were no endearments either. My memory may be at fault here but I don't remember my father ever once uttering an endearment to me. And yet I sensed in him a deep and passionate nature. Was it shyness or embarrassment that inhibited him, was it that appalling Scottish macho mentality that equates love with weakness? Perhaps. And yet I, too, find difficulty in communicating my feelings to my children. I have five of them, two daughters and three sons. I not only love them all but, for most of the time, I like them too. And yet, when we meet a good deal of our conversation is about trivialities. Is it inevitable that children and parents grow further and further apart with the passage of time? Do we distance ourselves from our parents in order to become ourselves? Is such distancing part of the survival process?

My father's introduction to revolutionary politics began during his apprenticeship when he came under the influence of a pattern-maker who appears to have been a follower of Bakunin. It wasn't, however, until several years later that he was moved to act on his burgeoning political beliefs. He was working in Paisley at the time, as a blacksmith, when he first heard John MacLean speak and was fired with revolutionary zeal. He had saved up a few pounds in the bank, enough to live on for a few weeks. So he left the smithy and joined MacLean's entourage of young men and stumped the country for several weeks proclaiming MacLean's vision of a Scottish Workers' Republic. When his money gave out he returned to the foundry at the Carron Iron Works where he had served his apprenticeship. At the same time he threw himself into trade-union activities and became a tireless campaigner for a single union that would break down the craft boundaries which separated the various categories of foundry work. As was to be expected, he wasn't popular with the management and it wasn't long before he found himself out of a job.

His life at this period didn't only consist of political activities. He was, after all, a young man with an appetite for life. He was becoming known as a singer and he was courting my mother who at this time was working in the pawnbroker's shop in Falkirk. Her father viewed him with a good deal of disfavour.

> My faither couldnae stand Will's opinions. They were like a red rag tae a bull. He was a real man for the bosses, my faither, a fair lickspittle to the gentry. Thought the sun shone oot o' Lord Strathallan's airse.' The memory of her father never failed to make her bridle. Even when she had passed the ripe old age of ninety-four, the mere mention of his name was enough to revive all the indignation of the past. 'He was an auld swine, but your faither was a match for him.

They were married in 1908. My father was twenty-four and my mother twenty-two years of age. In the two years that followed his marriage, my father was sacked from three or four different foundries because of his union activities and it became fairly obvious that there was no future for him in Scotland. Burnley, in northeast Lancashire, was his next base, working in the foundry of a firm specialising in textile machinery

During my childhood my parents spoke often of Scotland and their life there. They were exiles and still regarded themselves as visitors rather than settlers in this new land. I loved their stories – they were jewels embellishing my childhood with visions of a magical landscape in which my father and mother walked in a cloud of music. 'In the summer in Campbell's wuid we'd sing and Rab Watt would mebbe play his melodeon. Will could sing like a lintie . . .' For a child who had never been out of Salford it was an evocation of Paradise.

The pay was poor, so after a few weeks he moved on again to Warrington and found work in the foundry of an automobile plant. My mother was still living in Bonnybridge recovering from a miscarriage. Her sister Maggie, who had married a pipe-moulder from Falkirk and gone to live with him in Salford, wrote to my mother that there was work to be had there and accommodation for the asking. My mother wrote to my father suggesting that he find work in Salford, which he did. She joined him there two weeks later. Once again my mother became pregnant and once again she miscarried. Almost immediately afterwards she developed pneumonia and almost died. The doctor frightened my father almost to death by warning that my mother was in danger of becoming a consumptive and needed a warmer climate.

In the next two or three weeks my parents made their plans. My father would go to Australia where there was plenty of work for skilled moulders, and there he would earn enough to pay for my mother's passage over and for somewhere to live. And so in the summer of 1912 he began the six-week voyage to Australia. He found work right away in a foundry on Cockatoo Island and at the same time found himself up to the neck in a union battle which had been on the boil there for some time. He wrote enthusiastic letters to my mother and managed to supplement his wages by busking at the Sydney races. Then, eight months from the day he left, my mother received a telegram saying that he was on his way home. It would seem that the unrest in the foundry had finally erupted in a strike and the emigration officials suddenly decided that my father's entry permit had been due to a mistake. He was deported. Later he would joke about it, but he always regretted losing the chance to settle there. It must have been fairly soon after his return that I was conceived. A few months later, the First World War started. I was born on 25 January 1915.

I have thought of him often since I began to write these notes. The memory of him evokes both pride and regret. Pride because he was so transparently honest (indeed his honesty bordered at times on self-destruction) and because he never deviated from his belief in the revolutionary destiny of the working class . . . and because he could sing like a lintie. I regret that I never tried to get closer to him, that I never told him how moved I was by his singing. I regret that he died without realising more than a tiny percentage of his potential. Sometimes I'm floundering in the trough of the night and I hear his voice and a few notes of a song. In the moment between sleeping and waking I seem to be on the threshold of some momentous discovery; but the moment passes and the promised revelation fades into the light of morning. There are times when I dream that he is my son. I try to speak to him but compassion has rendered me mute. My eldest son Hamish sometimes reminds me of him in the way he walks or sits in a chair. My youngest son, Calum, also has certain of his characteristics. But then, so many things remind me of him. The smell of bluebells, for instance.

How old was I? Three . . . four? Has the war ended yet? We are in Heaton Park or somewhere near it, walking in a grassy glade bordered by trees that had bark which was smooth to the touch – beeches, sycamores perhaps. There was a shallow stream hidden in the long grass and I fell into it. I sit in a patch of bluebells while my mother dries my feet. I have never seen bluebells before. Their smell is overpowering and I am filled with wonder. My mother scolds me a little but her heart isn't in it. My father takes me on his shoulders but after a few steps puts me down. His asthma is troubling him and he finds it difficult to breathe. There is a one-armed man with us, short and black-haired like my father. There is a woman too, young and vivacious. I seem to remember that she laughed a lot. My mother tells me that they work in a circus. The man takes me on his shoulders and gallops around the glade with me. Then he climbs a tree and hangs from one of the branches pulling a monkey-face. Afterwards he does a handstand and executes a few somersaults. I am enraptured. He takes me on his shoulders again and we leave the park. Opposite the park gates there is a large pub and they go in, leaving me sitting on a wooden bench outside. It seems to me that they stay in the pub a long time. My mother comes out several times to see that I am all right but I feel very resentful. The young woman comes out and puts her arms round me. She is wearing perfume that I like very much. Finally they come out and we make our way to the tram stop.

The drink has made them merry and there is a good deal of joking and laughter. The tram is one of the open-topped kind so we climb the stairs and sit in the rounded stern. 'Give us a song, Will,' says the one-armed man, and I notice that my father's asthma has gone. He begins to sing and soon the entire car-load of passengers is listening. I am overcome with embarrassment and try to pretend that I am not with them. The one-armed man who appears to have an insatiable appetite for the songs of Robert Burns, applauds loudly after each rendition and then suggests another title: 'The De'il's Awa' wi' th' Exciseman', 'Afton Water', 'Willie Brewed a Peck o' Maut', 'The Silver Tassie'. My father is in full flight now and the entire tram is spellbound by his performance. Only *I* am not amused. Indeed, I am mortified with shame and sit there wishing that I had the magical power to make my father disappear into thin air.

Why should that day stand out so clearly in my memory? Was it the one-armed acrobat who made such a deep impression on me, or was it the sharp blue revelation of the bluebells? Perhaps it was the combination of the two – but most of all it was the shame I felt at seeing my father singing on the top of a tram. Had he sung with less feeling, less pure passion perhaps I wouldn't have minded so much but he sang with his entire being, poured his soul out on the top of a Salford tram.

Singing and politics were the two great passions of my father's life and I sometimes find it difficult to remember that he had a life outside these two activities, a life of which I knew practically nothing. The foundry claimed most of his day and if I didn't understand exactly what went on there then I knew enough to paint pictures in my head from overhearing talk between my father and mother. And there were the endless discussions about union matters between my father and his mates who often called round at weekends and there were the occasional union meetings in our kitchen. One of them sticks out in my mind. I had been playing football in the back entry and, suddenly feeling hungry, rushed into the kitchen to get a piece of bread-and-jam. Half-a-dozen men, including my father, are seated round the table. One of them is banging his fist on the table and speaking in angry tones. He stops when he sees me and for a split second the scene is held like a still photograph. Then my father half-rises from his chair and indicates the door with his thumb. I get out quickly. I can remember the sun shining and the cries of my companions as they raced up the entry after the ball. Why am I so sure that it was a spring day in the month of May? I don't know, but I'm sure I'm right. It was midday too, and that's strange. My father and his mates should have been at work unless . . . of course. That's it. It was a strike-committee meeting.

I remember riding on his shoulders to a political rally in Stevenson Square a year or two later and I can remember the sea of faces but not much else.

Time, however, has not blurred the memory of an event which took place on my eighth birthday. For some reason or other I wasn't at school and had been to the cinema with my mother and Mrs Drummond. We arrived home to find the front door locked, an unusual occurrence. My mother prised the window open and helped me to climb through. My father was lying on the floor, drunk. I opened the door and let my mother in. She stood there looking down at him and said, 'Oh my God, he's lost his job!' I ran to the kitchen and returned with a large jug of water which I threw in his face. He sat straight up with a wild look in his eye and then let out a roar of rage. 'Ye young whelp! I'll hae the hide off your back for that!' I raced out of the house convinced that he was close on my heels. I came back later, slinking in by the back door and expecting the worst. 'He's sleeping it off upstairs,' my mother said. 'You must never do that again, son. He's been a good faither to you. Never lifted a hand to you since the day you were born.' And it was true. Only once in my life did my father ever strike me and that was three or four years later. The neighbourhood was buzzing with the rumour that a boy had drowned in the Irwell. I had failed to come in for my evening meal and my parents were convinced that I was the drowned boy.

Death by drowning was not exactly a daily occurrence in our district but both the river and the canal claimed their annual toll of victims and, for a time at least, the scene of the tragedy would be out of bounds to us. Mere Woods, the Seven Arches and the canal bank were permanently out of bounds but we went there just the same. Mere Woods belied its name. The mere had been filled with rubbish and the entire area was an enormous dump of old slag heaps, half-buried hulks of broken and rusted machinery, hillocks of cement and lime and overhanging banks of willow-herb, brambles and scurvy grass. The real fascination, though, was the river. In the town, where it ran between the walls of factories and by the ends of streets, its banks were man-made. But here it ran wild, racing over boulders and pebbles here and swirling there in foam-topped eddies. The foam was brown and dirty white with the consistency of whipped cream. It ran wild in a dozen mad tributaries heavy with poisons spewed from a dozen mills and factories. It was full of treacherous currents and one summer's day during the school holidays I saw two brothers drown in it. One of them, attempting to retrieve a tennis ball, had slipped and been carried away by the current. His brother had tried to save him and the two of them had drowned. We carried the news to their mother who ran screaming into the street.

Even more dangerous were the Strawberry Hills. Surely there was never a more inappropriate name for such a bleak place. We called them the Mucky Mountains. They were a cluster of low, clay hillocks lying at the back of Strangeways Prison. Utterly devoid of vegetation, they served as a dumping ground for the rusting frames of old bicycles, perambulators, bedsteads and heaps of broken crockery. The clay never seemed to dry out and sliding down the slippery clay slopes on a sheet of corrugated iron was a favourite pursuit of generations of Salford children. As the troughs between the hillocks were often full of rainwater one had to be both careful and lucky. Even so, there were deaths there every year. One summer four children were drowned.

How old was I? Nine. . .ten? Younger? It is Saturday, a fine spring day. Mr Drummond has given us a bunch of white narcissi which he has grown on his allotment. Their perfume is strong enough to make itself felt above the smell of the shoulder-of-mutton roasting in the oven. I am reading Jack London's *Martin Eden* which my father has picked up at a second-hand bookstall on Pendleton market. I mean I was reading it but I got sidetracked by listening to my dad. He seems to be working his way through his repertoire of songs.[3] I have noticed before that there are certain pieces which he only sings on special occasions. 'MacGregor's Gathering' is kept for party socials at Hyndeman Hall; tearjerkers like 'A Long Time Gone', monologues like 'The Stowaway', old music-hall numbers like 'The Saftest o' the Faimily' and Harry Lauder songs are kept for the pub. Burns' songs, duets sung with my mother or sometimes with my Auntie Mag (like 'Huntingtower', 'The Beggar Laddie' and 'The Rowan Tree') are sung mostly at home, at Burns nicht gatherings and Hogmanay. His Saturday (and sometimes Sunday) afternoon sessions include these latter pieces and a whole host of songs, ballads and fragments, some of which only get sung once in a blue moon, as my mother would have said. Today he's in fine fettle. He stopped off at The Cross Keys on the way home from work and had a couple of pints, 'just enough to oil the dry parts', as he puts it. He's still wearing his moleskins, his working trousers and the sleeves of his striped union-shirt are rolled up showing forearms pitted with innumerable tiny circular white marks, the healed scars of molten metal burns. He is sitting with his feet up on the hob with his right hand cupping his ear as he sings the tale of 'Glasgow Peggy'. He abandons it after a couple of verses and falls to whistling. Then he starts singing again.

> I'm sitting on the stile, Mary,
> Where we sat side by side,
> On a bright May morning long ago
> When first you were my bride.

I slip out of the kitchen into the front room. There are certain songs that act on my tear glands and this Irish exile's song is one of them. My mother is sitting by the fire reading *The Red Letter,* a weekly women's magazine which I collect every Thursday from Spencer's the newsagent. 'It's just a lot of nonsense,' she says, but she likes to read it. 'It generally has a good murder or two in it. There's nothing like a good juicy murder to keep your spirits up.'

> The place is little changed, Mary,
> The sun shines bright as then;
> The lark's loud song is in my ear
> And the corn is green again.

Damn! I have to choke back the tears. It's almost as bad as 'The Stowaway'. That really tears me up inside. There it's the story itself, the idea of that boy facing up to the brutal captain who wants to hang him from his yard-arm. But the song's different somehow. Maybe it's that little dip in the tune in the middle of the first line. It's something else, something in my father, in the way he sings it, a kind of naked longing. I am moved in spite of myself.

'Dad's in good voice,' I say, trying to sound casual.

'Ay, he's a bonnie singer is your faither. Braw.'

Perhaps it was only in song that he allowed his passion to surface. No, I don't think that's entirely true. I remember the way he sat by the fire and wept when he heard of the death of Lenin. He was inconsolable for days afterwards. And I remember the fury that shook him when the General Strike was betrayed, the bitterness with which he cursed the right-wing leaders of the T.U.C. Generally his hatred was reserved for institutions like the church and the capitalist system. With individuals he was more tolerant, content to dismiss those of whom he disapproved as 'evolution's failures'. Winston Churchill he hated with every fibre of his being, regarding him as an enemy of the working class. For Snowden, J.R. Thomas and Walter Citrine he had only contempt and usually referred to them as 'pimps' or 'shit-eaters'. He expressed a passion and a hunger for life when he sang and it made no difference whether he was singing to himself or for an audience. It was, however, at Hogmanay that he really came into his own, for with us Hogmanay was an orgy of singing.

The preparation for it began at the beginning of December when my mother would embark on the annual pickling of onions and red cabbage, and about halfway through the month she would bake black bun and shortcake. All this, of course, depended on my father being in work. Round about the 27th of December the preparations would be speeded up enormously and from then until Hogmanay itself the house would never be free of the smell of baking and cooking. There were herrings to be pickled, potted-heid and ham-and-beef rolls to be made, a ham to be boiled and a dozen loaves of bread to be baked. On 30 and 31 December the house had to be cleaned out from top to bottom so that it 'shone like a new pin'.

Then it was New Year's Eve, the most important festival of the Scots calendar. But it wasn't Hogmanay yet. That wouldn't begin until the first guests arrived. My mother would busy herself polishing the kitchen range (which had already been polished) and at about half-past-eight my father would go off to The Cross Keys and The Royal Archer to check on his friends and make sure that they weren't doing the heavy drinking yet. He would return with half-a-dozen of them, workmates and wives and the half- and quarter-bottles of whiskey would be put on the table. While the drams were being poured out the men would be lighting their pipes or filling them with dark plug-tobacco while the women would sit there looking rather prim and uncomfortable. Then my father would propose the first of many toasts: 'To absent friends. Weel may they thrive.'

Invariably, someone would add 'to them that's awa'', which my father would cap with 'and to the lass that made the bed for me'. And then he would start pouring the beer from one of the half-dozen jugs brought earlier from the off-license at the end of the street and the real steady drinking of the evening would begin, for these were beer drinkers, men who worked in the dry heat of the foundry or the engineering shop. Then my mother, understanding the needs of drinkers, would bring in the pickles and the ham and a brisket of beef and the ham-and-beef roll and bread and butter. And the men would compliment her on the sweetness of the beef and ham and the women would praise the baking and ask the recipe for the ham-and-beef roll. I would stand there half hidden in the folds of the curtain which hung in the doorway between the front room and the kitchen hearing the rise-and-fall of voices talking about people I didn't know and events which had taken place in a land I had never seen.

Then my Auntie Mag would arrive, sometimes accompanied by her husband, Tammy Logan, and my cousins John and Willie. Immediately there was a change of tempo, a new mood. Maggie wasn't one for serious conversation about the merits of this or that union leader or, indeed, of political topics in general. Parties and booze-ups were her natural element and parties, as far as she was concerned, meant plenty of laughter, booze and singing.

'Gie us a sang, Will,' she would say.

'You sing, Maggie,' my father would answer.

'Ay, I will when I've had a few.'

'What'll I sing then?'

'Onything as lang as it's lively.'

'Ay, come on, Will,' his mates would urge.

'Quiet, quiet everyone,' my aunt would say, ignoring the fact that she was the only one making a noise. 'Order please!'

And my father would begin:

If it wasn't quite a mile it was three-quarters of a mile,
When a man's old safety bicycle broke down,
He twisted all his wires and he punctured all his tyres,
And he fell upon the roadside like a clo-o-o-wn.

'For God's sake, man!' Maggie expostulated. 'No' that kind o' a song. Gie us a proper song.'

'He's makin' a fool oot o' ye, Mag,' my mother explained.

'He'd better no',' said Maggie, but the gleam in her eye softened when she heard the opening notes of Robert Tannahill's philosophical drinking song:

This life is a journey we a' hae tae gang,
And care is the burden we carry alang
Though heavy be oor burden and poverty oor lot,
We'll be happy a' thegither ower a wee drappie o't.

Halfway through the verse my mother came and sat next to my father and sang the song right through with him. The chorus sounded beautiful with everyone singing at the top of their voices and one or two singing harmonies:

Ower a wee drappie o't, ower a wee drappie o't,
We'll be happy a' thegither ower a wee drappie o't.

'For God's sake,' Maggie said, 'ye'd think this was a wake.' And she'd sing:

Awa' ye wee daft article,
Ye arenae worth a particle,
For common sense it tak's to mak' a man;
Ye're no' the size o' tuppence
And your income's only thruppence,
Ye mebbe think you'll get a wife
But ye'll no' get Mary-Anne.

This would be a signal for anyone who could hold a tune to contribute a song or a snatch of a song to the proceedings. Then suddenly somebody would call for quiet and everyone would sit there listening for the sound of the bells from the Pendleton church ringing the new year in. My mother would grab me and I'd find myself standing holding hands with her and my father and everyone would be singing 'Auld Lang Syne'.

I'd be packed off to bed again after that. If the weather was cold then I'd probably find a coarse linen bag in my bed filled with bran and heated in the oven. Or if there was no bran in the house there would be a loose shelf taken from the oven and wrapped in a blanket. And I would lie there listening to the singing and the excited rise-and-fall of voices and sometimes I would creep out of bed and down the stairs and sit listening on the bottom step while my parents sang duets like 'The Beggar Laddie' and 'Huntingtower' and 'The Spinning Wheel' and my Auntie Mag would sing 'The Cruel Mother' and Jock Sinclair would recite 'Holy Willie's Prayer' and Jock Muirhead would sing 'Jamie Foyers'. Then someone on their way out to the toilet in the backyard would catch sight of me on the stairs and I would be whisked off to bed again and would fall asleep with the songs still ringing in my ears.

The morning of New Year's Day was always an exciting time. For one thing, several of my parents' friends had stayed the night, sleeping on chairs or on the floor. My aunt had shared my mother's bed and my father had slipped in beside me. And there was the special New Year breakfast with oatmeal porridge and mealy puddings and black puddings and bread toasted at the fire. And for those that needed it there was a dram to start the day right. Then the menfolk were sent off for a walk while my mother and Mag set about 'reddin' up the hoose'. On these occasions I usually accompanied my father and his friends as far as The Cross Keys or The Royal Archer and was then sent off to play.

My father would return home after the pub closed, cheerful but tired and would go up to his bed for a couple of hours' sleep. Meanwhile, my mother and her sister would be baking a great pile of treacle-scones and fatty cakes for the renewal of festivities and emptying basins of their shivering mounds of potted-heid, and all to the accompaniment of a constant stream of gossip about friends and neighbours, news about the family in Australia and comments about Tammy's shortcomings. From time to time visitors would drop in with a bottle and take and offer a dram. My mother, having no head for alcohol, generally refused, but my aunt, (who refused nothing) tended to become so quarrelsome after a while that my mother would persuade her to lie down for a couple of hours.

At dinnertime my mother served us with bowls of ham-and-lentil soup from a huge black cast-iron pan and when two or three of last night's guests turned up, they too must have their bowls of soup. More and more would keep dropping in until, at about nine o'clock, the room would again be full of moulders with their wives and sweethearts and it would be like New Year's Eve all over again with the singing and reciting, the talking, the joking, the laughter. 'Hogmanay nicht aye lasts the week,' my mother would say. Well, that was a slight exaggeration, but it certainly never lasted less than three nights and often as many as four. It was an orgy of good fellowship, a feast of singing and good talk. I remember how desolate I felt when it came to an end, and then I would lie and hear my father wheezing as he laced up his heavy boots and dressed for the foundry. Then his steel-shod bluchers would ring briskly on the paving stones as he walked up the street and out of my hearing.

These, of course, were the Hogmanays of the good times when my father had a job. They lasted up until 1928 or 1929 when my father's brother Jock died of a heart attack. He had become the owner of a butcher shop in Glasgow and for Hogmanay he generally sent us a hamper with sausages, black and white puddings, spiced beef and pork, sometimes a saddle of venison and always a bottle of whiskey so that even in the harsh year of 1926 when my father was involved in a prolonged strike we still managed to celebrate Hogmanay. In the three years that followed the strike he was in and out of a job a good deal and by 1930 he was driven to seek work outside his trade. He managed to find casual labour from time to time but it never lasted long and by 1931 he had become just another reject among three million other rejects.

2

One in Three Million

When I first began to think back on my early days I could scarcely recall my father except in the most generalised way, as a kind of presence, a collection of political opinions, beliefs, prejudices, epithets and aphorisms. Then I would see him for a very brief moment, walking, sitting, raising a glass of beer to his lips or singing; subliminal images almost, here and then gone. But they build up a series of pictures, incidents, some small, some large – none without significance.

How old am I? Eight . . . nine? That would make it 1923 or 1924. Surely it was later than that! I must have been nearer ten. I seem to think that the incident marked a new stage in my life. Furthermore, I feel sure I felt that at the time. Sunday – and I remember it as late spring.

We are walking along Market Street, my father and I. We have walked all the way from home, up Lower Broughton Road, down Blackfriars Road, through Greengate, past the Flat-Iron Market and over Blackfriars Bridge and across Deansgate. Town (for us, Manchester is 'town') is almost deserted. The shops are all closed, the roads empty of traffic. Lockhart's Café is closed too, though there is a door open with a notice saying that the Clarion Debating Society is meeting upstairs. It is our destination. We are going to hear a lecture on Haeckel's *Riddle of the Universe* which will be followed by a debate. My father regards such activities as an important part of education. There are about thirty people present, mostly men. Among them I recognise Dick France and Sannie Wylie and a man called Savage whose wife runs a fish-and-chip shop and who smells of grease. A man stands up and begins to speak. I doze off. When I wake up the man has finished speaking and a young man in the audience is on his feet talking. Someone shouts for him to sit down but he goes on speaking. I understand very little of what is being said but I like the way the young man rolls out his words. And fine words they are: big words, important words. As we leave, a man at the door hands us a duplicated sheet of paper advertising a rally of the Clarion Cycling Club. I fold mine up carefully and put it in my pocket intending to show it to my mother when I get home.

I am not suggesting that I remember all this in sequence – I don't. There are just short, disconnected flashes of memory. Chairs making a dull squeak as they are moved across mottled cream linoleum; a man sipping water from a glass in between sentences; a young man with closely cropped hair speaking from the floor and . . . perhaps I'm confusing several occasions. That young man with the cropped hair: wasn't he one of a group of young men, all with such hair, who came to a meeting addressed by a bloke called Casey who claimed to have invented a new approach to thinking? Yes, he wrote a book called *Thinking* and went around the country lecturing on it. That must have been 1929 or 1930. I was in the Young Communist League (YCL) by that time and some of the bright young lads of the movement were there, all set to demolish Casey during the discussion period. Their fine-spun arguments, however, were interrupted by a group of young men. They wore grey collarless shirts, dark grey trousers made of coarse material and big boots. From time to time they shouted, 'What about Thea von Harbou?' and 'Smash the machine! Smash the machine!' On being asked to defer to the chair they rose in a body and stamped out without another word. They have stuck in my memory all these years. Five or six young men trying to convert Fritz Lang's *Metropolis* fantasy into a reality.

That lecture, too, was held in a café on Market Street, next door to the Market Street Cinema. Actually, I accompanied my father to Lockhart's Café for a whole series of debates and began to take pleasure in the cut-and-thrust of argument. I don't know that I learned a great deal but I did come to recognise that argument can be as much a sport as football and I learned that knowledge is a kind of power.

How old am I? Seven . . . eight . . . nine? A Saturday in summer. It's about half-past-one. One of those hot days when the street fills with children playing, women gossiping, men sitting on their doorsteps still in their working clothes. Our next-door neighbours, the Caldwells, have been quarrelling for the last half-hour and now the house will no longer contain them. Mrs Caldwell runs into the street screaming, pursued by her husband, Arthur. He catches her by the throat and begins to beat her. At that moment my father appears, walking down the street. He's been putting the finishing touches on a job at the foundry. He carries his jacket over his arm. My mother rushes up to him crying, 'For God's sake, Will, stop him! He'll kill her!' My father races towards Arthur and spins him round by the shoulder. 'Hit a woman, would ye?' Arthur tries to push my father away. My father responds by leading with his left to Arthur's chin. It's a terrific blow and Arthur goes down like a felled tree. The neighbours come running to assess the damage and my father and mother go into the house. After a moment I follow them. My father is sitting by the table in the scullery, white-faced and shaking.

'What in the name o' God did I need tae dae that for?'

'He'd hae killed her,' my mother says.

'Not he', says my father, 'he wouldnae hurt a fly. He's a' mouth.'

'He was in a rage.'

'She probably deserved a' she was gettin.' He's really angry now. 'That'll be the last time I ever stick my bloody nose intae ither folk's affairs.'

'I'll go and see if he's all right,' says my mother. She goes and after a few minutes comes back with our neighbour.

'I'm bloody sorry, Arthur. I just dinnae like to see a woman gettin' battered. All the same, I shouldnae hae hit ye like that.'

'It's all right, Bill. No offence taken. It's that bugger. She's driving me mad. She was on the bleedin' town again last night. I come home from work and t' bloody kids 've not 'ad a bloody bite since last night, and then it was only a few bloody chips. Honest to Christ, I'll swing for that bastard.' Tears gush from his eyes as my mother slips a cup of tea into his hand. My father is overcome with remorse.

'I'd a couple of drinks in me, Arthur. I just wasnae thinkin' richt.'

When I go out of the house a group of my friends are standing by our front door. I have become very important suddenly. One of them says, 'Your dad must be dead strong.' I admit it, loftily. This is fame and it feels good.

Dead strong! Yes, that is how I choose to remember him, strong and active, dominating his environment by physical strength or by the use of his voice. And yet there were times when he would sit crouched in a chair fighting for breath, or I would come downstairs in the morning to find him bent over a steaming bowl inhaling the rank fumes of the latest asthma cure. Our house was never quite free of the smell of those sputtering herbal cigarettes which were supposed to bring relief to those devastating chest complaints. Sometimes I would lie in bed and cover my head with the sheet so as not to hear the dreadful paroxysms of coughing. They went on and on and on until it seemed that his entire body was being torn apart. And yet as soon as the attack was over he became my 'dead strong' father again. When I was still a small child he would be off to work before I got up in the morning and I would lie there in the darkness hearing the clatter of his boots on the pavement. I got so that I could tell whether he had asthma or not by the noise his boots made. If he was free of asthma, the sound of his footsteps was brisk and precise, but if he was in the throes of an attack or beginning to undergo one then the sound was indecisive and the pace slow. If the attack was severe there would be a pause between every twelve or fourteen steps. For all that, he was an active man. He walked everywhere and I don't ever remember him choosing to ride on a tramcar or a bus except when he was with my mother or with friends who refused to walk. Even our Sunday morning excursions to Whitefield and Bessie's o' t' Barn were taken on foot. Often he would go on walking for eight or nine miles carrying me on his shoulders for the greater part of the journey.

How old . . .? Six . . . seven? I am in the throes of a prolonged illness, a gastric condition which makes it impossible for me to eat or drink without vomiting. 'Bile', my mother calls it. I have gone through all the familiar stages, ordinary vomiting, green vomit and now black. 'The black bile,' my mother whispers to Mrs Drummond when she waddles into my sickroom. I can't sleep. The gas has been turned low and I can hear its wheezing filling the room. There is a ring-board hung on the wall at the foot of the bed, a flimsy, gaudily painted, lozenge-shaped board with small hooks set into it. There are a number of small rubber rings hanging from the hooks. I throw the rings with my mind and imagine each one of them landing on the appropriate hook. Irritated, I turn my head so that I won't have to look at it. My father is sitting in a chair under the gas-light. His face is in shadow but I can see that he has fallen asleep. He had been reading Gene Stratton Porter's *Girl of the Limberlost* to me and I must have dozed off for . . . for how long? He's still wearing his moleskins and working clothes. He's spelling my mother who has gone to lie down on top of the bed in the next room. He'll be wearing the same clothes when he goes off to the foundry in the morning. The gas-light falling on his hair makes it look shiny like a gypsy's hair. He looks young, his face is heavy with sadness and I am suddenly overcome with sadness, too, at the thought that I must die. For Doctor Curran has told my mother that there is nothing more he can do for me. For almost a week now I have been surviving on a spoonful of brandy whipped up with white of an egg. But now I cannot even keep that down and he has advised my mother to send for a priest. In our street they say, 'First the priest, then the coffin.' I whimper, 'I don't want to die.' My father opens his eyes and crosses to the bed. 'You're no' gaun to die, son. Me and your mither'll no' let you die.' He takes my hand in both of his. I want to cry but I am too weak.

He was still a young man (at least in *my* mind) until about 1930. He would have been forty-six years old then. My calculations may be wrong, of course, or perhaps my memory is at fault. I think 1926 might be a more accurate date.[1] That was a rough year, the long strike of the iron moulders and the betrayal of the General Strike took a lot of the bounce out of his walk. It was a period of intense activity. As the foundry shop steward, he was involved in every aspect of the strike. Up at the crack of dawn and off to the picket line, every day. And meetings! Strike meetings, union branch meetings, trades-council meetings, solidarity meetings with other unions. We saw him at bedtime and between meetings or when he came off the picket line to have his bruises dressed with compresses of comfrey leaves. Once a week he would find time to accompany me and my mother to the pit heaps at Pendleton or Pendlebury or Agecroft to search for scraps of coal. In the three years that followed we were, according to my mother, 'just hanging on by the skin of our teeth'. In the spring of 1927 he was fired from the foundry where he had worked for almost five years and in the months that followed found it increasingly difficult to find work. Or rather, difficult to hold a job down for more than a couple of weeks.

'Could ye no' keep your mouth shut just till we get straight?' my mother would say. My father protested that he hadn't put a foot wrong. 'Then why in the name o' God can ye no' haud on tae a job?'

It was a cry from the heart and one which I was to hear with increasing regularity as our position became more and more desperate. It wasn't that my mother disagreed in any way with my father's politics, but there were times when the sheer weight of her responsibilities drove her to the brink of despair.

Yes, she understood that he was one of three million, that unemployment was a disease of capitalism, but it didn't alter the fact that we didn't have enough to eat.

My father felt that unemployment reduced him as a man; and as a skilled worker he felt humiliated and cast out from the fellowship of his mates. My mother sympathised but at the same time she felt that it was unjust that she should be the one who was forced to battle for the family's survival. And battle she did – she was indomitable. Every morning she was up and away out of the house by half-past-four, hurrying through the dark streets or riding the clattering tramcar with its load of early shift-workers and scrub-women. By the time the first office workers were arriving at their places of work, she had put in four hours heavy toil and was hurrying across the city to do another five or six hours of washing and cleaning. 'Brute work' is how she described it in her later years, and indeed that is how I saw it as a twelve-year-old boy. Small wonder then that occasionally her bitterness and despair exploded in furious denunciations which generally culminated in a paroxysm of tears. Quarrels which were less inflammatory were daily occurrences; or rather, my mother would try to quarrel, haranguing my father and trying to goad him into retaliating. There was a pattern to these engagements. She would launch her opening sallies, which would be received in silence or with murmurs of agreement from my father.

'Ay, Bet,' he would say. 'Ay, Bet,' and there would follow a furious monologue in which their past life together would be reviewed and his character shredded. His silence would whip her into a rage of invective. When it became unbearable, my father would interrupt it with a remark signalling his imminent departure.

'For God's sake, woman, haud your tongue and gie your mouth a rest!' And he'd reach for his cap and leave the house. If he had enough money for a pint he would go to the pub at the end of the street and if he was without money then he'd go for a walk until she cooled off. I hated these rows. I learned to sense them before they started and I would cringe in anticipation. Afterwards, my mother would feel sorry and tell me about how she had met my father in the pawnshop and she'd enumerate his many virtues. One day my Auntie Mag suggested that my mother would have done better to marry a man like her Tammy.

'Tammy!' Incredulity sent my mother's voice right to the top of its range. 'Tammy! That big saft bap's no' fit to tie Will's bootlaces. He's ony bloody road for tuppence. Will's worth ten o' him.'

'Ay, and the rest,' said Mag agreeably.

'And I'll tell ye something else.' My mother was in full spate now. 'Will's never lifted a hand to me since the day we met and that's mair than you can say for that big drink o' water *you're* married tae.'

'That was a while back, Bessie. If he tried it again, I'd tak' a knife tae him. I'd open the bugger up.' And the conversation settled down to comfortable sisterly gossip.

It wasn't long after that exchange that my aunt called round with some interesting information. Her husband Tammy, now a foreman in a pipe-moulding foundry, had seen a list of names of men who should not be employed in the industry and my father's name headed the list. A short time afterwards my father applied for a job in the foundry at Metropolitan-Vickers where moulders were being hired for a big casting destined for the Soviet Union. He was told to report for work the next morning. He did so only to be informed that a mistake had been made and there was no work for him. The blacklist was working efficiently.

It was in the next three or four years that the iron entered into his soul. He smiled less, sang less and gave up drinking altogether. He had never been a particularly heavy drinker but he had always enjoyed the conviviality of the pub and the company which was part of drinking. At The Cross Keys or The Royal Archer he could be sure of finding men like himself, moulders and pattern-makers who had come down from Denny, Bonnybridge and Falkirk to work in the Lancashire foundries – men like Sanny Wylie, Jock Sinclair, Jock Muirhead, Ted Kavanagh and Will Strachan. But a man needed to be able to stand his round if he was to keep his self-respect, and who could do that on the dole? So he stopped going to the pub. In any case, men with jobs don't fancy hanging around with the unemployed. Why should they? There's something about an unemployed man, an unemployed *craftsman* in particular, a kind of furtiveness. He has the demeanour of a dog that expects to be beaten. Not that my father's beaten – not yet. He spends a good deal of his time and energy fighting cases before the unemployment tribunals. He has become something of an authority on unemployed rights and he wins more cases than he loses. But it seems to me that some of the zest for the struggle has gone out of him. He spends most of his mornings in the reading room of Peel Park library, leafing through the newspapers. I often see him there, flanked on either side by Jock Sinclair and Jock Muirheid, both of whom have also been consigned to the scrap heap.

For many years I forgot what it felt like to be unemployed – and by *unemployed* I am not referring to short idle periods between jobs but to the interminable, sustained condition of apartness which is the lot of those who exist only as statistics in a government department which spends much of its time playing word games with the object of finding euphemisms to describe the jobless. But now I am constantly reminded of it by those boxed talking heads, those bland rubbery faces which smile and smile and smile in countless darkened rooms while trampling the truth to death.

I always associate the Peel Park reading room with unemployment and my father's sudden transformation into an old man. It had a smell of newsprint, disinfectant and unwashed bodies, the smell of the early morning queue of shuffling, hawking, spitting, coughing, hopeless men outside the Albion Street Labour Exchange, the smell of despair, of poverty. But the reading room was warm and if you were patient and waited long enough you might get a place near one of the radiators. There were long leather-topped tables, too, at which one could sit and read *The Textile Mercury, The London Illustrated News* and *The Architectural Review.* The chairs there were always occupied by old men who appeared to have died. Occasionally an attendant would come and rouse them by clapping his hands and saying, 'Come along, now, this isn't a doss-house.' The sleepers would blink their eyes, cough, turn a couple of pages of the journal they were pretending to read and then relapse into their customary coma. One day while walking through the park on my way home from the library I found myself following close behind my father and, for the first time, noticing how changed he had become. His broad shoulders had assumed the stoop of defeat. His hair was shot with iron-grey streaks and his skin, which had given him the swarthy hue of the southerner, had turned ashen. The biggest change, however, was in his walk. Gone the brisk, purposeful step that I had always associated with him. It had been replaced by the slow saunter of the permanently unemployed. As I drew closer to him I noticed that I topped him by a couple of inches and I experienced a sudden fierce surge of protectiveness.

That strip of decayed concrete which wound its broken way through Peel Park is one of the most vivid visual images of my past. A path crumbling into tarry gravel at the edges with potholes filled with scummy water. Wooden forms with the bottle-green paint peeling off, plaster nymphs and dryads with nipple-less breasts and Victorian hairstyles and an improbable dancing faun whose nose has been painted red. Almost half-a-century later while watching Renais' *Last Year in Marienbad* I was transported back to that Salford scene. That long shot of the formal garden in which time seemed to have been frozen took me back to that other scene of frozen time with the plaster of Paris maidens smiling their vacant smiles forever and ever. And there was that other time when I forgot my unemployment card and turned back to get it. I hurried back through the park, sweating under the early summer sun. I must have been fifteen years old, maybe sixteen.

As soon as I open the back door I know there is something wrong, something out of place, something different. Gas! It's the smell of gas. I check the gas-ring but nothing seems to be out of place there. Then I notice that the door which closes off the kitchen from the front room is closed. That is really odd, for it is never closed from one year's end to the next. I try to open it but there is something stopping it. I push with all my weight and open it wide enough for me to slip through. The smell of gas is much stronger here so I move the coats and newspapers which have been used to block up the door and then I rush through the kitchen and open the back door as wide as it will go. Back in the living room I notice that the blind is drawn down so for a moment I don't see the pile of old coats on the floor or the length of rubber tubing which has been used to connect the heap to the gas-fitting. When their significance bursts upon me I hurl myself at them and begin tearing them away. The gas-mantle has been carefully removed and put on the mantelpiece. I am filled with an uncontrollable rage as I turn off the gas-tap. 'You can't die!' I shout, 'You can't die. For Jesus' sake, don't die! Please, please, don't die! You can't! You can't!' I go on shouting even while I'm opening the front door and raising the blind and then I stand there helpless saying over and over again 'What shall I do, what shall I do?' In a complete panic I rush out of the house and start banging on the Caldwell's front door. There is no reply but I know Arthur Caldwell is on night-shift this week and has probably been asleep for three or four hours by now. I open the door and run to the bottom of the stars shouting Arthur's name. When he doesn't answer I run up the stairs and bang on his bedroom door. He appears immediately, buttoning up his trousers as he follows me into our front room. In a moment he is down on his knees with his ears to my father's chest. 'He's still breathing. Let's get him out into the open.' Together we drag him through the kitchen and into the back yard where Arthur, sitting astride him, begins to knead his chest, breathing curses with every press of his hands. 'Buggers . . . buggers. . . buggers . . . don't. . . give . . . a sod . . . not . . . one . . . bloody . . . sod . . . what the bloody . . . hell you . . . do a daft . . . bloody thing like . . . this? . . . Come on . . . me old cock! . . . Don't let the . . . bastards . . . get you . . . down. . . That's it, that's it. See? A cup of char's what you need.' He goes into the kitchen to make a brew of tea, leaving my father sitting on the kitchen doorstep his hands hanging limply between his knees and the tears running down his face. And I stand there, helpless, consumed by love and anger and shame at the thought of being so powerless.

In the bitter winter of 1947 I received a telegram from my mother telling me that my father was dying. At that time, Theatre Workshop was on tour in South Wales and I hurried back to my parent's cottage on the Derbyshire-Cheshire border. They had moved there in the summer of 1935. It was a rather tumble-down old place with enormous oak beams and a rear window through which one could see the lights of half-a-dozen cotton towns below. There was thick ice on the road up to the cottage that night and the wind howled and moaned as it caught up snow as fine and dry as caster sugar and sent it swirling and eddying around my feet.

'Thank God you've come', my mother said, 'there's not much time left.' I climbed the stairs to the tiny room where my father was lying – my parents' bedroom. There was no mistaking the fact that death was already upon him. He seemed to have shrunk, to have become a youth again. What had happened to those broad shoulders, those muscular arms? His head was sunk in the pillows. The hair which had been so black and lustrous was now predominantly grey and the brown skin of his face was now only a transparent film through which you could see the white flesh. His eyes were closed and I thought he was asleep or unconscious. I sat in a chair by the side of the bed and took his hand in mine. I sat there for what seemed a long time hearing only the ticking of a clock and the occasional dry rattle of snow on the window panes. I felt my hand growing stiff but when I attempted to disengage it from his he turned his head and looked at me with eyes which seemed to be looking at some distant landscape. My mother slipped into the room, as if some extra-sensory perception enabled her to see through doors.

She bent over him and whispered, 'Will.' 'Ay, Bet,' he said, the words barely audible. Then suddenly his hand gripped mine and he pulled me towards him, speaking. This time I couldn't catch the meaning of his words. My mother bent over him as his lips began to move again. 'Ay, Will', she said, 'ay,' and she smoothed his pillow. 'He wants you to sing.' she said.

I remembered that other time with Jock Sinclair. The thought of raising my voice in that room of stillness and death shocked me. And what could I sing? What is an appropriate song for someone who is dying? I searched desperately through my mind for inspiration and found myself singing:

Ye banks and braes and streams around the castle o' Montgomery,
Fair are your woods and fair your flowers, your waters never drumlie;
Their summer first unfaulds her robes and there it langer tarries,
'Twas there I took my last fareweel o' my sweet Highland Mary.

My throat was so dry that the last two lines of the song of the song were a hoarse whisper. 'I think he'll sleep now,' said my mother, and I made a move towards the door but at that moment he raised his head from the pillow, looked wildly round the room and then fell back again. Those lines in MacDiarmid's poem on the death of his father came to me at that moment and, indeed, I have never heard them spoken since without remembering my father's last panic-stricken look at the world:

And I thocht o' the last wild look ye gied
Afore ye deed.

That's just how it was. I sat there for a long time and wept.

Four days later he was cremated at the Stockport crematorium. The snow-banks were pitted with the pockmarks of recent rain and gave the cemetery the appearance of an abandoned junkyard. Snow lay like dirty soapsuds on the tops of headstones and hung like sullied plumes of ostrich feathers from the branches of dispirited trees. The oak-panelled interior of the chapel smelt of chrysanthemums and furniture polish. There were just three of us there, my mother, Joan Littlewood and me, to see his clay make its last short journey.[2]

3

Front Doors and Back Entries

We are apt to talk about childhood as if it were a single unified experience made up of random encounters and bounded on the one hand by infancy and on the other by puberty. It is nothing of the kind. At least, that is not how I remember *my* childhood. I see it as having been composed of three distinct periods each with its own influences, loyalties and rules of behaviour.

The first period covered five years, from the time I first became conscious of those huge faces peering down at me from all kinds of angles until my first miserable day at school. During that half-decade it was my mother who influenced me most directly and, to a lesser extent, my father. In the course of time my Auntie Mag and Uncle Tam and Alice Drummond, Sanny Wylie, Jock Muirhead, Jock Sinclair, Will Strachan and other friends of my parents also came to exert some influence. In short, adults were the main influence in my life and the place where they exerted their influence was in the rooms that I slept in, ate in, breathed in and from which I conducted my slow discovery of the world. Those four rooms, my bedroom, my parents' bedroom, the kitchen-cum-scullery and the front room were the true centre of the universe and the all-knowing, all-powerful beings who inhabited it had been put there to protect, serve and amuse me.

All that changed when I went to school. Up until then I had trusted my mother and now she had betrayed me, abandoned me in a kind of open-topped cage filled with shouting, yelping, screaming, threatening wild animals who either raced past me as if I wasn't there or who pulled faces at me and taunted me with being a mammy's boy. It was an important stage in my development and it certainly marked a shift of loyalty. *She* who had deserted me in my hour of need deserved no loyalty. And it was all her own fault. Wasn't it? Well, wasn't it?

During the next six or seven years I discovered that my home was not the centre of the world and neither was the school, though that represented a large chunk of new territory. The real centre of my world now was the street. I don't think any of us who lived there ever gave the street its proper title. Other streets in the neighbourhood were referred to by their names and indeed street names

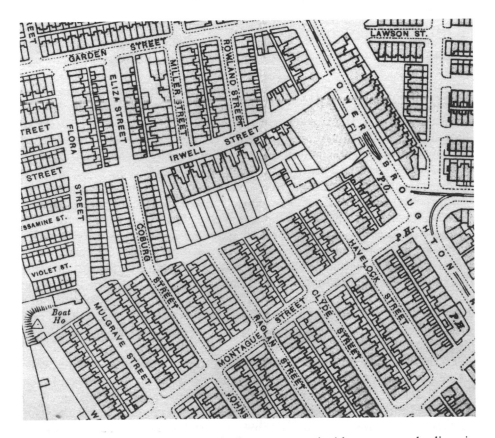

were often used to identify a particular person as in 'the woman who lives in Mulgrave Street at the house with the yellow blind', or 'the young red-haired woman in Irwell Street'. If there was more than one family with the same name then the street name would be used in conjunction with it as in 'the Miller Street Joneses', or 'the Raglan Street Andertons'. Their namesakes who lived in our street were simply 'the Joneses' and 'the Andertons'. 'Our street' – that is how we referred to it. Or as '*t*' *street*.

It was divided into an upper and a lower half, separated from each other by a paved area open to pedestrians and cyclists and closed to heavy traffic by two five-foot high granite posts. It was known as 'the square' and, in addition to separating the two halves of 'our' street, it was also the boundary between Flora and Mulgrave Streets. At its centre it opened into two alleyways, one of which separated the back yards of the lower end of 'our' street from the back yards of Flora Street, while the other separated the back of Mulgrave Street from the back of the upper end of our street. Each half of the street consisted of two rows of terraced houses facing each other across two strips of pavement and a roadway laid in granite sets. There were twenty-four houses in each of the two terraces in the lower end of the street, where I lived, and all of them were identical: forty-eight smoke-blackened, brick-built, two-story dwellings, ninety-six identical windows, forty-eight sandstone doorsteps and window sills reduced to an off-white or a pale ochre by repeated scourings with white and brown stone.

The interior layout of the houses was simplicity itself: two downstairs rooms separated from each other by a small landing from which a narrow flight of steep wooden stairs led to two upstairs rooms. The main downstairs room, known to most families as 'the front room', opened directly on to the street. There was no hallway or lobby and one could, without experiencing any discomfort, stand with one foot in the street and the other in the front room. It was the living room, in the exact sense of the words. Its centre-piece was a cast-iron kitchen-range, for in this room the family's meals were cooked and eaten. It was where gatherings were held, where weddings and funerals were celebrated, the room to which you were confined if you were ill or if the weather was bad. A doorway situated at the back of the room led to the kitchen-cum-scullery. This contained a small fireplace, a copper for boiling clothes and an alcove leading to a place under the stairs known as 'the coal-hole'. Next to the copper was a shallow, sandstone sink with a single cold water tap. There was also a small gas-ring attached to a gas bracket by a rubber hose. A door set in the back wall of this kitchen led into a paved yard in which stood the privy. A wooden gate some six-and-a-half feet high led into an alley which everyone called 'the back entry'.

The houses in the upper half of the street differed from ours in three respects: they were entered by a hall or lobby; they possessed a bay window; and their kitchens and sculleries weren't combined and consequently meals could be cooked and eaten in the kitchen proper while the front room became a parlour reserved for ceremonial occasions. These physical differences gave rise to differences in social attitude.[1] Those who dwelt in the upper half of our street were said to regard themselves as 'a better class of people' who 'kept themselves to themselves'. 'Fur coat and no drawers,' was Mrs Drummond's verdict. This was my world then, my street and the half-dozen streets and alleys around it.

From twelve to fourteen was the final phase of childhood. Once again the centre of your universe changed and now school was the focal point of all your thoughts and activities. As for the street – well, it was just two rows of houses past which you walked on the way to and from school. And the gang? Strange the way it had disintegrated after the fight between Killus and Tolly. It had been the most important thing in your life right from way back. It had never occurred to you that there might come a time when it no longer existed. And then suddenly all gone like water down the drain. Once or twice you slipped out of the house and sauntered to the end of the street in the hope of seeing Woodsy or one of the others. Dave Gair waved from across the street and shouted that he was off to some sports centre or other. That was it – everybody is suddenly going their own way. You too. These days you're off, as soon as you've had your tea, to meet Izzy Schneider or Barlow in the park or else to play cricket on Spike Island with Dave Bamber and some of the other lads.

It's really a transition period. A transition towards what? The question fills you with a kind of dread. Towards . . . the end of childhood. There was a time when you thought that was just a matter of changing from short trousers to a pair of long pants – longies, you called them. How you longed for longies! But now you know it's a much more serious matter. The matter of a job, of knowing that you need to know more than you know to get a job. You get a sudden lurch in the stomach when you think of it. A job! Office boy, brew-lad, dog's-body, hey you! What's the point of thinking about it? Fill the time in with as many of the last pursuits of childhood as you can. Childhood? Talking with Meg Patterson and her friends, learning how to clothe your most serious thoughts with flippancy, cheering yourself hoarse when Alec James gets the ball at his feet and weaves his way past Arsenal's centre-half, desolated when May Petrie announces her departure.

The last days of childhood. Yes, the period of preparation, of apprenticeship for the adult world. I can still remember the trepidation and eagerness with which I embarked on this part of the journey. I have only to think back to relive the breathless excitement of discovering girls and friends with whom I could talk about books and politics.

How old am I? Four or five? I must have turned four for I can read. It's one of those hot spells that we occasionally get in July or August. The street has been baking all day but now it is cooler. There is a gentle warm breeze which occasionally wafts the smell of bleach from the river two streets away. Evening. People are home from work and the evening meal has been eaten and cleaned away. Women sit on their doorsteps fanning themselves with rolled-up news-papers and exchanging desultory gossip with a next-door neighbour. Here and there a man sits smoking his pipe or drinking a glass of beer, too weary to walk to the pub at the end of the street. There are five of us, boys and girls, sitting on a doorstep and singing from *The Bumper Song Book*. Or rather, we are trying to sit – five is too many to squeeze onto the step but everyone wants to be as near the book as possible. We take turns to sit next to Elsie Cray who is turning the pages of the book (which is only fair as it was her mother who provided the two pennies which were needed for its purchase). Song after song we race through, for we are all determined to show that we know the words and can sing the song faster than our neighbours. 'Where do you work-a, John? On the Delaware Lackawan. Oh, what do you do-a, John? Oh, I push, I push, I push.' Or, 'Shepherd of the hills, I hear you calling. Shepherd of the hills . . .'

How did we know the tunes? From whom did we learn them? This was before the days of radio or television and the films were silent. Yet we seemed to know all the tunes. Yes, of course we learned them from each other. But how did those who taught the rest of us know them? From their parents, perhaps, from older brothers and sisters. I learned 'Shepherd of the Hills' from a pierrot troupe on the South Pier at Blackpool.

It must have been when I was four that I first began to realise the impor-tance of the street. 5 November 1919: a tremendous bonfire in the street and a clothes-line stretched between the bedroom windows of the Johnston's and the Paul's. And a 'guy' hanging from it dressed in a German soldier's tunic and spiked helmet. Everyone was out in the street. There were bottles of beer and tin trays of treacle-toffee and fudge. Somebody brought a piano out and soon everybody was singing 'There's a Long, Long Trail a-Winding' and 'Blighty is the Place for Me'. And the fireworks were shooting out trails of coloured sparks and blue and green and red fireballs and Little Demons going off with a loud bang and rip-raps shooting this way and that, sputtering and crackling like pistol shots. And then the guy catches fire and a cheer goes up and we are all racing round singing:

On the croft, on the croft where the Kaiser lost his horse
And the eagle on his hat flew away;
He was eating currant buns when he heard the British guns
And the sly little bugger run away.

Later that night there was a bit of a row when three or four over-enthusiastic older lads tried to push the piano into the fire. My mother often recalled how Arthur Caldwell staggered out of his house carrying a chest of drawers which he hurled onto the fire. It was, I think, one of her most carefree Salford memories.

The fifth of November was an important date in our calendar and the prepa-rations for it usually began early in October, though the last week in September was not considered too early to begin collecting wood for the fire. This was a serious business and involved every child in the street. No-wood-no-fire was the rule and we (and indeed every street gang in the locality) ranged far and wide looking for wood. There were no copses, thickets, woods or common lands within miles of us, no trees except those stunted hawthorns and hollies in the public parks. Wood as far as we were concerned meant man-made things like doors, fences, window-frames, furniture and packing crates. Our hunger for wood was insatiable. No rickety fence was safe from our depredations, no door loose on its hinges was exempt. We attacked ruined buildings like flocks of vultures and picked them clean of floorboards, doors and posts. We haunted the loading bays of factories on the lookout for broken crates and boxes. We roamed the industrial wasteland of Trafford Park. This was where 'the big stuff' was to be found and street gangs from far and wide explored it in search of treasure. And treasure there was in plenty: all kinds of wonderful things like a dump of thousands of blue glass rods of various lengths; or a small mountain of black rubber discs; or the piles of shining ball-bearings which supplied every street for miles around with much prized steelies. And every so often you would come upon a giant wooden beam. Once we discovered a forgotten dump of hand-grenades from the First World War. We took more than a dozen of them and had a great time pulling the pins out of them and throwing them off Peel Park bridge into the Irwell. Some of them were no longer 'alive', but those that were made a very satisfactory noise. The hand-grenade boom came to an end when an eleven-year-old boy in a street not far away from ours blew his hand off while wrestling with a rusty pin. Our most spectacular wood prize was a railway-sleeper that we found on a railway-bank near Eccles. We hauled it with ropes for almost four miles while scouts went ahead sending warnings back of patrolling coppers and roving gangs in West Pendleton and Hanky Park.

The storing of the wood was of prime importance. It had to be as safe as possible and in a place convenient to the spot where the fire would be lit. The back yards were the obvious place since they were overlooked by kitchens and guarded by a locked door at night. Doors and walls could be climbed, of course, and they *were* – frequently. Indeed, the raiding of a neighbouring street's wood-pile was one of the great and memorable bonfire-season treats. 1920 was the last time a bonfire was lit in the street. That year, sparks from the blaze set the Bury's front bedroom on fire and the fire engines had to be sent for. From that time on, our November fifth celebrations were held in our back entry.

The lighting of the fire was generally done by the gang leader with the rest of the gang yelling instructions and advice. As soon as the fire had reached a respectable size, the fireworks would begin, mostly bangers, Roman candles, Volcanoes and the occasional rocket. It wouldn't be long before the old folk came out and everyone would sit around on crates and boxes destined for the fire. Then potatoes would be roasted in the red embers at the edge of the fire and trays of treacle toffee and freshly baked parkin would appear. The fire would get bigger and bigger and every time fresh wood was thrown on it a great rush of sparks would go funnelling into the air and, tired by this time, you would sit hypnotised by the pulsing red heart of the fire, hearing the burning wood crackling and sputtering and whooshing as the streams of resin boiled into tongues of flame.

From time to time the intense heat would crack the paving stones under the fire and hurl them in splinters high into the air. By ten o'clock the street would be clear of children and for an hour or sometimes two, the fire would be given over to those we called 'the big lads', the eighteen and twenty year olders. They would sit round talking and occasionally singing snatches of current hits. For some odd reason, those of us whose bedroom windows overlooked the back entry considered it important to be able to report on the 'big lads' and the next day Galty would say, 'I looked out of the window at eleven o'clock and they were still there.' Then Edwin Caldwell would say, 'I looked out at twelve o'clock and they were still there.' And Woodsy, or somebody else, was bound to say that he'd seen 'em at one o'clock and then everyone would start shouting and yelling daft things like 'I saw 'em at a hundred o'clock!' Then you'd spend half-an-hour picking up the spent carcasses of Roman candles and Fiery Clusters and whatnot. You'd hide what you found in the gang's hiding place and at the week-end you'd take them to Peel Park bridge and throw them in the river and throw stones at them. For months afterwards, the bleached white paving stones in the back entry bore testimony to our great bonfire.

Though I can't remember very much about my earliest years I still carry in my mind the memory of unconnected incidents and happenings, a kind of personal gallery of very vivid miniatures. May Day, for example. I still remember my first May Day. The first of May was a milestone in the year and it was celebrated as a working-class festival. Different age groups honoured it in different ways. We, the children, paid homage in the old way, with a maypole and songs. Strictly speaking, the maypole wasn't really a maypole at all but a broom-handle decorated with coloured paper streamers. The preparations for the ceremony began in mid-April and were the exclusive province of the girls who would be busy making skirts, blouses and cloaks of coloured tissue paper to be worn on the great day. Others would be collecting empty cigarette packets for the silver foil which lined them. This was taken out and used for covering the cardboard crowns made for the queen and her consort. The girls were generally between six and eight years old; the consort – the only male role in the drama – was a boy of three or four. At five you were considered to be too old and in any case wouldn't have condescended to take part in such a sissy affair. But at three or four you were proud to be chosen for such an honour. I have a clear picture of myself standing in the Livesey's back yard and being dressed by the girls. 'Dressed' meant having items of tissue-paper clothing pinned to your real clothing by girls who were excited at having a real living doll to play with. And I can remember my own excitement as we made our entrance into the street clutching our paper streamers attached to the maypole. We moved down the street stopping outside each house to sing our May song:[2]

> We come to greet you here today
> And we hope you will not turn us away,
> For we dance and sing in a merry ring our Maypole lay.
> For we all, for we all,
> Bright are the roses, bright are the stars,
> Happy the birds that fly in the air;
> Happy the fishes that swim in the sea,
> For we all, for we all,
> As happy, as happy can be.
> Last year we had a maypole, it was a pretty sight
> For gentle . . . [here the May Queen is named]
> Was crowned the Queen of May.
> With hearts and voices calling
> Our gentle little queen,
> For gentle . . . [queen named]
> Was crowned the Queen of May.
> This our May, bright and gay,
> Listen to our happy lay,
> We can dance, we can sing,
> Fol the rol, de rol dol dol dol,
> Happy news we bring.

My recollection of that moment is extraordinarily clear. Elsie Hewitson, the Queen of the May, is holding my hand for I keep wanting to stop to admire my handsome yellow tissue-paper robes and Dot Dow keeps pushing me in the back. I can still hear the song, and not only the song but the voices singing it, the heartbreakingly pure voices of children enacting a dream. I heard it again thirty-three years later. I was visiting friends in a street not far from Salford docks when I came upon a group of nine small girls carrying their broomstick maypole. Their costumes were a little more elaborate than those worn in my young days but the song was unchanged and the voices were the same. I have seen many festivals and celebrations but none of them have moved me as much as that Salford maypole. Is it still a feature of Salford's street life or has it been buried by the sludge of television, Dallassed and quiz-gamed out of existence?

It wasn't only the girls who celebrated May Day. The lads too, all those who had reached the mature age of five and over, had their traditional ceremony. Maybe the tradition was more debased than the girls' but it was, nevertheless, a tradition. The girls' maypole ceremony looked back in time to a magical world of natural beauty, a world of birds and fishes and roses. The boys were catching glimpses of the festival of Chronos, of Saturnalia, celebrated by the lighting of bonfires, dancing and the singing of lewd songs. 'Time for blackies,' someone would say – blackies being the local name for guisers – and a group of boys, most of whom were between seven and ten years of age, would appear dressed in the most outlandish way they could devise. Some would wear old coats back to front and inside out with ruined bowlers, shawls, policemen's helmets, kadies (old straw hats) and babies' bonnets. Others might rise to enormous bombazine skirts or dresses, relics of departed grandmothers, dresses with bustles, flannel bloomers topped with elaborate corsets, button-up boots, lace bonnets, hats trimmed with artificial flowers and assorted fruits. Some might wear combinations of men and women's attire, Dad's bluchers, an old silk petticoat and a steel helmet, a memento of the war. Costume was obviously a matter of personal taste and initiative. Custom, however, demanded that everyone's face be covered with a thick layer of blacklead, the stuff used for cleaning and polishing stoves and kitchen grates – hence the name 'blackies'. Some of the more traditionally minded blackies achieved the same effect by rubbing their faces with bacon fat and applying a liberal helping of soot. Like the girls, we sang outside every house in the street and collected pennies wherever we could. Our repertoire consisted of popular hits of the period with a few changed street rhymes to pep things up a bit.

In the twenties, and even in the thirties, May Day was an official public holiday marked by street parades and demonstrations. These were grand affairs with thousands of people taking part. First came the brass and silver bands, followed by the members of trade-union branches walking behind their union banners proclaiming UNITY IS STRENGTH, UNITED WE STAND – DIVIDED WE FALL, SOLIDARITY AND STRENGTH and WORKERS OF ALL LANDS UNITE.[3]

A river of banners flowing down Blackfriars Road followed by another brass band playing 'England Arise' and then a karni-band playing 'Felix Kept on Walking', their kazoos sounding like amplified comb-and-paper music. Then the funny men and women dressed to look like apes and beer barrels and clowns and skinny versions of circus strongmen. Another kazoo band dressed like the pierrots you see on the pier at Blackpool and then a mixed choir seated on a brewer's dray drawn by four beautifully groomed horses. Behind them walked the girls and young women in their Whitsun finery, many of them garlanded with spring flowers.

Then a cheer goes up from the crowds lining the route. It's the horses! Thousands of them . . . well, dozens at least: Clydesdales, feathered Shires, magnificent Percherons, Belgians and Suffolk Punches groomed to perfection, their manes and tails braided with coloured ribbons, their brasses shining like gold and the paintwork on their carts fresh and sparkling for the occasion. Teams of four came first, then pairs, then singles. The brewers' drays, followed by the railway carts, followed by the Co-op carts and then the coalmen who always got a special cheer on account of their having removed the last trace of coal dust from their wagons and transformed them into things of beauty. After the heavy stuff there would be the bread vans, the grocery vans and the milk floats with their gleaming churns decorated with sprigs of hawthorn blossom. Inevitably the children lining the pavement would break ranks and rush to the vans and floats begging for rides.

In the afternoon the Labour Party would hold a meeting in the Town Hall Square or in one of the public parks. The platform would generally be one of the Co-op coal carts that had been in the procession earlier that day but now the sideboards would be draped with Labour Party banners. Ben Tillet, our local M.P., was often the main speaker. He was popular and always drew a big crowd. More often than not the Independent Labour Party (ILP) held its own meeting and it too usually attracted a fairly big audience, particularly if Jimmy Maxton or Fenner Brockway was speaking. My father moved among the crowd meeting old friends. I sat on his shoulders like a young prince bored by his subjects' enthusiasm. (Memory is a truly extraordinary phenomenon. While I was writing the above I suddenly beheld a picture of myself riding on my father's shoulders; it was a mere momentary glimpse but it was sharp and clear. I was wearing a sailor's suit and my father, in a suit of rough brown cloth, was shaking hands with a large man whose thick red moustache and magnificent watch-chain suggested power and dignity. A publican? A trade-union official? A member of the council perhaps?)

I suppose I must have played in the streets with children of my own age during my pre-school years. One thing is quite certain: there was no way that a boy of four or five would have been accepted as a companion for six and seven year olds. A boy of eight or even seven would be eligible for membership of a street gang dominated by boys of eleven or twelve but those who were five or younger were still babies and any attempt on their part to run with the gang was discouraged. Girls were more tolerant and I have vague memories of being 'on' in various girls' games and of sitting in a circle of girls singing:

Poor Mary sat a-weepin', a-weepin' a-weepin',
Poor Mary sat a-weepin' on a bright summer's day.[4]

And it was the girls who taught us to play hopscotch and how to make our spinning tops go whizzing round as if they had a life of their own. And they taught us how to plait both single and triple strings and how to weave wool on a cotton-spool stuck with gramophone-needles. They taught us to sing 'The big ship sails on the alley, alley, O' and 'Here comes a duke a-riding' and 'Sam, Sam, the dirty man' and scores of the kind of rhymes and songs used in skipping games. I distinctly remember a big girl named Marion Openshaw teaching me to roll my first wooden hoop. Hoops were seasonal toys. No chaffinches, thrushes or sweet-tongued blackbirds sang spring carols in our street, no, indeed. The hoop-man was our true spring's harbinger, a jaunty little man wearing a crownless straw hat on a head as bald as an egg. The upper part of his body was encased in a wooden frame hung with hoops of all sizes, large ones for the ten-year-old girls and small ones for boys and girls under five. After that age boys graduated to a 'garf', a steel hoop which one guided with a short hook made of galvanised iron. Wooden hoops were for girls and babies, you were told, and the garfs made such a satisfactory clatter as they rolled along the streets. They were bought at the ironmongers which, let's face it, was a dreary kind of place. It wasn't like buying a wooden hoop from a man who had no crown to his hat, who could whistle like a bird and who, if you'd begged him, would unharness his hoop frame and do a clog-dance on the pavement and top the performance with some cartwheels.

Going to school would make all these street games accessible to me – it would introduce me to the joy of being part of a group, a member of a gang, a prime spirit in a collection of prime spirits. The streets meant freedom, the chance to try your skill at climbing walls, to test your nerve by clambering to heights that were considered dangerous, to demonstrate your growing strength by shovelling manure at the coalyard. As for loyalties, they would be divided between the members of the gang and your parents. Your home would still be the place where you fed and slept but it would no longer be the place where you played. That function disappeared with the crayons and the colouring books. Of course, you still loved your mother and father, but you didn't want to be with them all the time. It was enough to know that they were somewhere around in the background ready to give a hand when it was needed. It was a ready-made, bread and butter kind of thing. Not like the love you felt for the gang or for Jenny Glover or Dot Pringle.

I was ill a great deal during my early childhood and seem to have spent months either lying on my back or recuperating. My problem was gastritis, a crippling stomach complaint which kept me off school for weeks at a time. The attacks generally occurred without warning, producing vomiting so violent and so prolonged that it reduced me at times almost to a skeleton. Little appears to have been known about diet at the time but it soon became obvious that there were certain items of food which could put me on my back for weeks on end. Bacon, lamb-chops, eggs, oranges, beef, etc., were among the things I had to avoid and, naturally, these were the things that I longed for the most. So I lay upstairs and counted the patterns on the wallpaper, vomited and pined for the food which would make me vomit. And called for my mother forty times a day. On one occasion my bed was brought down to the kitchen but the smell of food cooking and clothes drying made it impossible for me to stay there so I was taken back upstairs.

Dr Curran came to visit me in his beautiful old shining black Beardmore cabriolet with its gleaming brass sidelights and leather upholstery. He was a large, slow-moving Irishman who always smelled strongly of brandy and tobacco and who wheezed like an old pair of bellows. He had a large, gold Hunter watch which he held at arm's length as he took my temperature. He had a stethoscope which looked like a short trumpet. It was made of ivory and had faded coloured flowers painted or engraved around its mouth.

It was while I was recuperating from these dreadful bouts of sickness that my taste for reading was born. Many of the stories I read then became part of my delirium. One of them, Hans Anderson's *Girl Who Trod on a Loaf*, affected me so deeply that for weeks afterwards I would wake screaming in the night.

Most of my earliest memories are of incidents and events associated with summertime. In the summer the street came alive, particularly when the schools had broken up for the summer holiday period. I seem to remember long, dreary afternoons when nothing happened. Boredom, irritability, dissatisfaction with that stupid Meccano set; and who wants to play with plasticine? 'What can I do, mam? What can I do?'

Mondays were different. Monday morning was washing-day and almost all the women in the street would have their coppers lit and their washing boiled, scrubbed and dollied by eleven o'clock. Then they would peg them out on the washing lines strung across the back entry. That was a social time, a time for gossip and jokes and sometimes quarrels. But regularly at two o'clock in the afternoon I would accompany my mother and our next-door neighbour Mrs Drummond and her son Alfred to the Vic on Blackfriars road. The Vic, or Victoria, to give it its proper name, was a late Victorian theatre which had specialised in what my mother referred to as 'blood-and-thunder nichts'. It had also served as a variety theatre and was now a cinema with two changes of programme each week. It had a powerful smell compounded of urine, disinfectant and dust. It cost threepence to sit in the stalls and the noise of hundreds of juvenile voices demanding to know what was written on the screen was loud and continuous. Scenes from *Broken Blossom* and *The Four Horsemen of the Apocalypse* still occasionally disturb my sleep, mixed up with glimpses of Richard Barthelmess tortured by thirst as he staggers across a desert of sand.

My mother and her friend preferred watching the misadventures of Potash and Perlmutter. Only comedies featuring Wallace Beery and Raymond Hatton were held in higher regard.

Mary Drummond was a stout, easy-going country woman who had grown up in a Shropshire farming community, as English as my mother was Scots. 'She's no' ower particular when it comes to cleaning the hoose,' said my mother, 'but by God she can bake.' She baked all her own bread, barm cakes and currant loaves. Her pork pies had pastry which melted in the mouth. Her husband, George, was a brass-moulder, a balding, thin-faced, slow-speaking Cheshire man with the kind of moustaches that became popular again in the 1970s. He suffered from what his wife called 'nervous dyspepsia' which caused him to break wind often and thunderously. So impressed were his workmates by the frequency, volume and variety of his anal bombardments that they honoured him (and his productions) with a plaque, a shining brass medallion with a moulded relief of what at first sight appeared to be one of those puffing cherubs that are sometimes seen on old maps. A closer examination revealed that the 'cherub' lacked eyes, nose and mouth, these having been replaced by a long, deep fissure, the edges of which had been rounded with loving care, as had the Gothic script which ran round the rim of the plaque:

TO OUR GEORGE. CHAMPION FARTER OF SALFORD AND PROBABLY THE WORLD.

The legend on the obverse side was more lofty in tone:

IN MEMORY OF GEORGE DRUMMOND, WHOSE FARTS CLEARED COX'S FOUNDRY OF RATS, MICE AND OTHER VERMIN. FROM HIS GRATEFUL WORKMATES, SALFORD, LANCS., 1921.

How proud Mrs Drummond was of that medallion! She showed it to her neighbours one Monday morning when the washing was being hung out. Their screams of laughter brought me running to the back door. There must have been a dozen women all whooping and screaming with laughter as the medallion was passed round among them. That raw, uninhibited sound of women's laughter was one of the most characteristic and unforgettable sounds of my childhood. Whenever we heard it we would pause for a moment and listen intently, unsure as to whether the sound was laughter or screams of pain, hatred, defiance or mockery. The difference was one of nuance.

The street-picnics were always occasions for plenty of such laughter. They were annual affairs organised by the women. Only women and young children took part in them. The preparations for them began months in advance. One or two women would be delegated to collect weekly subs (subscriptions) and finally a charabanc and driver would be hired and we would assemble outside Hill's paper shop on Lower Broughton Road, the women laden with baskets containing raincoats and sandwiches, tins of sardines, corned-beef and crimson-skinned polony sausage. The children compared buckets and spades. Oh, the joy of boarding that magnificent chara and being allowed to sit next to the window for the first part of the journey (later we would change places with the Drummonds so that Alf could look out of the window). The wonder of it all! Fields, trees, villages and open space – and there were bottles of sarsa-parilla and dandelion and burdock to drink and Vimto and ice-cream soda! At the back of the chara there was a crate of Guinness which the three fat women occupying the back seat regarded as their own. Naturally, Mrs Arkroyd was there and Mrs Godwin, though strictly speaking she had no right to be on the picnic as she didn't live in our street but in the next one over. She was a known bruiser, however, with a formidable reputation and no one cared to challenge her on this June morning.

Blackpool, Morecambe or New Brighton was our destination and on arriving we would make our way in small groups to the nearest beach. There we would plonk ourselves down for the day and our mothers would argue the pros and cons of hiring a deck chair. Threepence seemed an awful amount of money to pay just to sit down. Still, it's only once in a way. They would sit down with a sigh, enjoying the unaccustomed luxury of the deck chair while we played with our buckets and spades and collected spent matches to make railings for our castles. If the sun shone and the weather was fine the day of the street-picnic could be a foretaste of paradise. Even the long walk along the beach or prom-enade to find a public lavatory couldn't spoil it. If it rained the day could be pure, unadulterated torture for our mothers. Trailing round the streets of a strange town with a frustrated child or children with only a shilling or two in your purse was a miserable way of spending what might be your only holiday of the year. It was difficult to convince even the youngest member of the family that the tram-shelter in which you were eating your sandwiches was an exciting place. Still, there were compensations. I remember on one occasion, going with my mother and Mrs Drummond and Alf into the hall of mirrors in Blackpool. I can still hear the screams of laughter with which they greeted the sight of their distorted reflections. Each new impossible image brought forth louder screams and finally Mrs Drummond laughed so much that she wet her drawers. They were still laughing when they boarded the coach for the homeward journey. This always followed a set pattern. At first there would be plenty of loud laugh-ter and ribald exchanges as the different groups described their experiences. After a time this would give way to the singing of old favourites like 'Daisy, Daisy', 'Nelly Dean', 'Just Plain Folk' and similar pieces. Then one by one the children would drop off to sleep, their hands sticky with Blackpool rock. Then one or two mothers would nod off and then a few more until, at last, only the driver and maybe a woman or two would be left awake.

There were works' picnics as well. My mother used to dread the time when the works' picnic came round. 'The annual booze-up', she called it. It gener-ally took place early in July. 'Poultice time' was another of my mother's names for it and she always arranged to have plenty of comfrey leaves in readiness for the poultices she was sure would be needed. On the fatal day she would see my father off with stern warnings about what would happen to him if he came home scarred, maimed or wounded in any way. A dozen times during the day she would look up from whatever work she was engaged in and say 'I wonder what he'll be like the nicht when he comes hame?' Her misgivings were not ill-founded for my father nearly always returned from these foundry outings the worse for wear.

Many of the kids in our neighbourhood never went away on holiday at all. Only those who came from families with few children could hope for a holiday at the seaside. More often than not those hopes were unfulfilled. Nevertheless, summer was always an eventful period. The street came alive in the summer particularly in the school holidays. On Saturday and Sunday mornings there were the charabancs that passed along Blackfriars Road and Lower Broughton Road bound for seaside resorts. A small band of us, half a dozen or so, would make our way to points along the route and, as the coaches rolled past we would chant 'Mouldy pennies, mouldy pennies!' and some of the passengers would throw pennies or halfpennies and we would go chasing them as they rolled along the gutters.

And from morning till night there would be an almost continuous procession of street performers, both men and women. And singers: soloists, duos and even choirs. Yes, I remember two choirs, one a group of Welsh miners and the other a band of five unemployed fishermen from Grimsby. There were escapologists who had themselves put into strait-jackets with hands and feet bound with rope and chains, which attached the feet to the back of the neck. Looking like trussed chickens they would be bundled into the kind of sack that is used to carry the mail and there they would lie on the granite cobble-stones twitching and shaking; then a hand would appear, then the shoulders, then, with a tremendous effort, the whole body would be free of the sack. It was like watching a moth emerge from its cocoon. There were tap-dancers, step-dancers, clog-dancers, Punch-and-Judy men, spoons players, bones (rickers) players, barrel-organists with and without monkeys, men and women with performing dogs, musical-saw players, harmonica players, trumpeters, whistlers, jugglers and penny whistlers. There were even tumblers and acrobatic troupes performing for pennies on the street at that time.

Then there were the food vendors, the fruit and vegetable sellers and fish-mongers.[5] In the winter hot pies could be bought from a horse-drawn van equipped with a tin oven heated by a paraffin stove. And a woman sold pea-and-lentil soup and peas-and-cabbage with ham-shanks served piping hot from a converted ice-cream van. In summer the ice-cream cart and the hokey-pokey van were never far away: 'Hokey-pokey, penny a lump, the more you eat the more you trump!' we would shout as soon as we heard the familiar two-toned bell. The ice-cream cart was greeted with 'I scream, you scream, we all scream for ice-cream.' Men pushed handcarts round the streets selling brushes, linoleum, rugs and candy. Then there was the rag-and-bone man, whose wailing cry could be heard three or four streets away: 'Ragbone! Ragbone! Pots for rags! Bring out your rags! Ragbone!' He was a fierce-looking man whose face was set into a permanent scowl. The 'pots' which formed part of his sales pitch were cups and saucers which he exchanged for old clothes. Sometimes instead of crockery he gave goldfish, which generally died before the day was over. When he ran out of pots or goldfish, he bartered his stock of brown and white stones. These were used by housewives for whitening the paving stones immediately outside their front door and for 'creaming' their front door steps and window-sills. He came every week, as did the greengrocer and the fishmonger. The chair-mender, with his melancholy two-note cry consisting of an interval of a descending fourth, came twice a year at the most. The knife-grinder did the same and the man who welded broken pots and pans came regularly at the end of Whitsun week.

The hawker we called 'the song-man' was welcome above all others. It was generally in high summer that he came and sometimes just before Christmas. He sold songbooks with the words of all the current popular songs in them, twenty-five quarto sheets of cheap paper with three or four songs to a page with a hand-drawn cover with the words *The Bumper Song-book: 101 Hit Songs*. It was crudely produced and on some pages the print was so faint that it could be read only with difficulty. But for us it was the holy book and he who sold it to us was regarded as a kind of high priest. It was partly his appearance. He was a tall man with hair down to his shoulders and great staring eyes. He wore an overcoat the bottom of which almost reached to the ground, and whereas most of the street traders entered the street at one end and exited by the other, he walked down the street, then up again and then did a third lap at high speed. And all the time he would be chanting his wares. Chanting is not quite the right word. There were too many pitch changes for a chant and yet it wasn't exactly singing either. More than chanting, less than singing or perhaps a mixture of both. The words of his chant-song/song-chant consisted of the hundred-and-one titles of the song-book. Each ten or twelve titles were delivered without punctuation or pauses for breathing. At every seventh or eighth step he would turn round in a small circle and then continue on his way. It was an enthralling performance and for days afterwards we imitated it.

The hawkers with carts and vans and the entertainers always worked in the middle of the street, that is, on the cobblestones or (to be more accurate) the granite sets. You didn't *have* to go out and watch the escapologist wrestling with his chains or listen to the man singing 'Danny Boy'. You could, if you wanted, ignore the Welsh choir and the rag-and-bone man. But the door-to-door hawker couldn't be ignored – maimed and disfigured ex-soldiers from World War I begging or selling laces and collar-studs; gypsies willing to read your hand or selling clothes-pegs or artificial flowers; kite-sellers and women selling tablecloths and linen handkerchiefs; bug-fat workers with salves that would keep insects away in summer and cure bronchitis in winter; chair-menders and firewood sellers, chimney-sweeps and photographers. They knocked at your door and if you didn't answer they knocked again and they kept on knocking till you were finally forced to open the door. 'They're a damned nuisance!' my mother would say. But more often than not when she opened the door and was faced with some poor wretched fellow human being, she would invite him in for a cup of tea and a freshly baked scone or tea-cake. With the club-man or rent-man it was a very different matter indeed.

In our street you were considered to be well off if you bought your clothes and shoes from a shop rather than through a clothing club. The method of operation of such clubs was simplicity itself. A door-to-door salesman – the club-man or tally-man – called on you and showed you a catalogue from which you were asked to choose the items you wished to purchase and for which you undertook to pay a certain amount of money each week until the cost of the items had been met. The weekly payment could be as little as threepence and as much as half-a-crown. I don't remember my mother ever paying more than a shilling a week into such a club. When your payments had reached the agreed amount you were given a ticket to present at a local clothing warehouse and there you were fitted with clothes or shoes in your price-range. Naturally, there was little choice in either style or quality. Most people, even when they were buying club clothes, were aware of the fact that the material was inferior and the workmanship shoddy, but they were caught between the jaws of poverty and necessity and it was generally agreed by those who were at the base of the social pyramid that the clubs were 'handy'.

Then there was the 'never-never' system, the instalment plan. This differed from the club system in two respects: first, the interest charged by the instalment system was much greater; secondly, the goods ordered were received on an initial down payment. The collector who called for the weekly instalment was always called 'the HP-man' irrespective of sex. Like the rent-man and the tally-man, the hire-purchase man was regarded as an enemy. He or she, you reasoned, had talked you into buying blankets or a chair or a dresser and now you couldn't keep up with the instalments. You seemed to have been paying off the debt forever.

Finally there was the club-man. Everybody in the street had a club-man. However hard-up you were you tried to keep up with the payments to the club-man, for he carried in his little book the symbols which guaranteed a respectable burial. The dread of being buried in a pauper's grave still haunted my parents' generation. It was this dread which gave rise to Burial Clubs and Friendly Societies – and so every Monday the club-man came round and registered your payment in his little black book and then signed his name in the folded pink card which you kept in an old biscuit-tin along with your marriage-lines, birth certificates, insurance policies and rent-book.

By the time you were four years old you had learned that you and your family were living in a state of siege. You only had to catch a glimpse of the rent-man or tally-man walking towards you and you were off, running home to your mother with the news that danger was approaching. If she had enough money to pay the required instalment then it was safe enough to return to the game you were playing. If not, she locked the door and you hid with her under the stairs until he had passed.

Callender, the rent-man, was a sinister-looking Scot, middle-aged, middle-sized and with a pale face that wore a permanently baleful expression. From a distance this commonplace little man with his bowler hat and leather rent-bag looked harmless enough but I swear that when he appeared on his rounds a hush fell over the street. At close quarters he was terrifying. Even strong-armed boozers like Pisser Arkroyd quailed when confronted by him. Perhaps it was his eyes which made him look so fearsome. They were light grey and the skin round them always looked red and sore. I was afraid of him even when I was protected by a locked front door and it wasn't his eyes that made me afraid. It was because he moved in an aura of barely-contained ferocity. To a woman who was two weeks in arrears he would say, 'Two weeks nearer the poorhouse.' That was the nearest he ever came to cracking a joke. At three weeks the unfortunate woman would be subjected to a basilisk-like glare which would be held until the woman had to hold on to the door handle to stop herself collapsing. Then the awful words would come: 'How long will it take you to get your things together?' Or, 'Better start packing.' No tears, no excuses, no impassioned stories of sick children or lost jobs could move him. He was implacable. Years later when I saw pictures of the matchstick dead of Auschwitz and Buchenwald, I asked myself what kind of people could commit such foul deeds. I thought of Mr Callender.

Every woman in the street both hated and feared him. Everyone, that is, except my Auntie Mag. She would often come and stay with us for a couple of days at a time after a quarrel with Tammy. Her first confrontation with the rent-man was a memorable event. My mother had spoken about him so my aunt had the advantage. My father was on short-time at the foundry and we were behind with the rent. When the dreaded knock on the door came, Maggie said, 'I'll see to him.' She opened the door and stood there, a short, somewhat round-shouldered young woman peering through pebble-lensed glasses.

'The rent,' Callender said.

'What about it?'

'There's two weeks' arrears.'

'There's three weeks now,' said my aunt.

Callender switched on his basilisk glare but he had met his match. Generally women who couldn't pay the rent made their apologies and explanations in hushed voices so that their humiliation could be endured in comparative privacy. Not so my Auntie Mag. Her opening salvo was delivered in a voice that could be heard with ease by anyone living within a hundred yards of us: 'Is there something wrong wi' your eyes? You're standing there like a constipated collie dog straining to hae a shite!'

It is difficult to look sinister or fearsome or dignified in the face of such a greeting. The rent-man grew red in the face and his famous glare gave way to a look compounded of horror and bewilderment. Giving him no time to assert his normal manner, Maggie turned and yelled to my mother, 'Bet, there's a daftie oot here and he's wanting some opening medicine. Quick, bring oot a bucket!'

'Now just a minute,' Callender began.

'You havenae got a minute,' said my aunt. 'In aboot twenty seconds ye'll be needin' tae put yoursel' through the wringer so bugger off and tak' your wee bag wi' ye.' As Callender scuttered along the pavement, Maggie fired her parting shot from the middle of the street. 'You're a bloody disgrace to the country that bore ye! So ye are!' The assault over, she came back into the house to be given a cup of tea and be complimented by my mother.

'You were in good form, Maggie.'

'Ach, he's just a wee man!'

'Let me know when I can do the same for you.'

'I'm haein' a bit trouble wi' an insurance man. Thursday's his day.'

'I'll be roond.'

And indeed she would, and she would deal with the insurance man just as efficiently as my aunt had dealt with the rent-man. This way they had of dealing with each other's debtors continued right through my early childhood; and while my mother could be every bit as formidable as my aunt, I doubt whether she derived the same amount of enjoyment from the encounters. Maggie loved them. She was a natural-born street fighter, a sworn enemy of officialdom and the mere sight of a man with a collecting-book was like a call to battle.

The hawkers, street-performers, beggars, rent-HP-tally- and club-men were, so to speak, regulars. They came year after year. The musicians might play different instruments, the acts of street-performers might change and the HP-man or the club-man might wear a different face occasionally but their functions remained constant and unchanging.

More frequent visitors were the horse-drawn vans and carts. Almost all the deliveries at that time were made by horse-drawn vehicles. The bread came in a lightweight van drawn by a single light horse, a Cleveland Bay. We knew the names of all the different kinds of horses. We pestered the drivers with questions about their type, sex and eating habits. The milkman brought his milk in churns carried in an open cart which looked like a smaller version of a Roman chariot. It was drawn by a Welsh pony much given to snorting and shaking its head. Its name was Mabel and when we saw it all dolled up in the May Day procession we greeted it with cheers. There was a coalman whose cart was pulled by a patient Clydesdale which would allow us to walk between its legs. The two other coal carts that delivered in our street were drawn by Shires, as were most of the railway carts. The pub at the bottom of the street was served by a brewer's dray pulled by a team of four Suffolk Punches while the off-licence at the top end had its deliveries made by a wagon drawn by two Percherons.

There were pigs too, yes, pigs! Three streets away from us there was a short alleyway, a cul-de-sac in which there was a single-story building in which pigs were killed and prepared for the pork butchers. Every two or three weeks a drove of young pigs would go scampering and snuffling through the back streets followed by a swineherd and his dog with a horde of children following behind, all the way to the killing shed. Once the pigs had passed inside we would become silent and wait for the squealing to begin. Afterwards, if we were lucky, a knifeman would distribute handfuls of newly killed pigs' tails among us. These were highly prized trophies and could be bartered for cigarette-cards, marbles and other valuable artefacts. Our immediate use for them, however, inclined more towards art than commerce. We would tuck them into the flies of our shorts and allow them to hang out like little pink penises. The sight of several small boys walking along the street with these delicate appendages was enough to halt passers-by in their tracks. It was a satisfying moment when we detached our pseudo-members and raced off waving them in the air and shouting, 'Fooled you! Fooled you!'

With the end of summer came the end of my solitary childhood experience. For five years I had been like a neutron searching for a nucleus, like a cub unconscious of the pack. I had been living through my parents, eating, hearing, seeing and thinking through them. Now it would be different. I was soon to be part of a nucleus called 'the gang' and another one called 'school'.

4

Unnatural Habitat

Three of the four schools which served our district were within ten minutes walking distance from my home. One of them, St Boniface's, was a Roman Catholic school. The other two, St Andrews and Ascension, were Church of England establishments.[1] The four or five Catholic children in our street all, of course, attended St Boniface's. Only three went to Ascension which was so 'high church' that in comparison St Boniface's seemed like a secular institution. The rest, apart from me that is, went to St Andrews.

It was a single-story brick building dating from the 1880s. Its interior consisted of three small classrooms where infants were taught and a large open-plan teaching area where children between the ages of eight and fourteen received their education. Overlooking the entire assembly was a raised platform large enough to accommodate Mr Driscoll, the headmaster, whose drinking and gambling habits were well-known to every man, woman and child for miles around. The school day began with the singing of hymns and was followed by the rhythmical chanting of multiplication tables. The hymn-singing appears to have lacked strict supervision and parodists had a fairly free hand in providing interesting substitutes for the stanzas printed in the hymn books. The shuffling of feet, the coughing, the opening and shutting of desks was a signal for Mr Driscoll to terminate his first snooze of the day and begin the day's labours.

I never actually saw the St Andrews headmaster go through his daily drill but I frequently heard it described and saw it imitated by dozens of juvenile mimes. Indeed, Mr Driscoll's alcoholic exploits were so well charted and so frequently enacted by his charges that they became part of the folklore of the neighbourhood. It was a matter of dispute as to whether his first drink of the school day coincided exactly with the combined voices of Standard Three intoning 'three times five is fifteen' or whether 'three times seven' was the exact moment. Everyone, however, was agreed that it was taken from a stoneware Stephen's Ink bottle which was kept in the bottom right-hand drawer of his desk. As the arithmetic lesson lumbered on its way, Mr Driscoll busied himself taking empty Guinness bottles from the drawers of his desk and packing them neatly into two oilcloth shopping bags. This done, he would point at a boy nearest him in the class who would then hurry to the desk, take the shopping-bags and the money wrapped in a note listing the day's purchases and race to the nearest off-licence. Mr Driscoll was man of few words and was generally content to express his needs by gestures, belches and the lip-smacking which followed the emptying of each of his innumerable glasses of Guinness.

Mr Driscoll's days were regulated by the opening and closing hours of the off-licence, by the hour at which Joe Fairclough, the bookie's tout, started taking the day's bets and by the time the early edition of *The Evening News* arrived with the day's racing results. Promptly at eleven o'clock in the morning the finger would point again and an eager messenger would rush forward and depart bearing a shilling, or sometimes a half-crown, wrapped in a scrap of notepaper bearing the name of the day's chosen horse. Thereafter, the various classes would proceed uninterruptedly with their lessons while the head gave his attention to the columns of the sporting chronicle. A further bet would be placed early in the afternoon and soon after three o'clock the racing edition of *The Evening Chronicle* would be on his desk. A lost race would be signalled to the assembly by the rapid opening and closing of the drawers of his desk, by the slap of his cane on the desk-top and by the prolonged clearing of his throat. A 'win' would cause him to leave his platform and move among the desks of his captive audience, patting a head here and a shoulder there.

It was generally agreed that he only ever really became animated when he sat down at the school piano during the singing classes. It was because of his efforts and musical taste that half the kids in our district ran about the streets singing choruses from light operas by Offenbach, Messager and Weber. The fairies' chorus from *Oberon* is an unlikely street song, but it was a huge favourite with us and became a regular item in the repertory of back-entry singers, and it was a not uncommon sight to see half-a-dozen boys and girls ensconced in the dustbin niches of our back entry singing 'Who is Sylvia?' or 'Blow, Blow, Thou Winter Wind'.

Mr Driscoll's exploits were the subject of a certain amount of hilarity and a good deal of scandalised gossip. My father waxed wroth at the mere mention of his name. Education was, in my father's eyes, a matter of supreme importance for he believed that the workers would, as soon as they were educated, rise up and destroy the capitalist system. He was very naive as far as education was concerned. Driscoll was obviously resigned to the fact that the entire education system was, as far as the children of workers were concerned, a hoax, a deliberate attempt on the part of the authorities to keep the rabble in a state of blissful ignorance. If he had ever been aflame with ideals, those flames had guttered out a long time ago. He had found refuge in silence and the waters of forgetfulness.

If Driscoll was a burned-out fire, Mickey Thomas, who taught the thirteen and fourteen year olds, was a volcano in constant noisy eruption. He was a small, skinny Welshman who spoke in a high-pitched singsong voice and substituted p's for b's, c's for g's and t's for d's. He lived with his mother and his clothes were almost as ragged as those of his pupils. The patches on the seat of his trousers were a source of constant merriment to those who found it impossible to believe that anyone who had authority over them could be as poor as they were. They hazed him constantly, roused him to a pitch of fury so that he threatened them with outrageous punishments in a voice like a strangled scream. His delighted pupils repeated and embellished his performance in the schoolyard, in the square, on the croft, in battles with hostile gangs. His threats were absorbed into the repertoire of street cries and the winter nights rang with them as the clog-shod runners of St Andrews raced down the back entries and alleyways. 'I preak your pack, lad!' was a favourite threat. 'I smash every pone in your pody', which was generally followed with 'I'll make you learn to read or die in the attempt.'

He came to school on a bicycle and night after night discovered that his tyres had been deflated or his valves removed or his pump-connector had disappeared. On these occasions he would be surrounded by a crowd of interested pupils, eagerly awaiting his furious denunciations. Once he discovered that the wheels of his bicycle had been stolen and, unable to find words to denounce his tormentors, burst into angry tears. Most of the boys present were abashed at the sight and the girls turned on them and said they ought to be ashamed. 'Poor Mister Thomas', they said, 'it's a shame.' But shame or not, it didn't prevent those same girls, on their last day of school, from overpowering him, taking down his pants and thoroughly lathering his private parts with a gooey mixture of axle-grease and red ink. Poor Mister Thomas indeed!

My father's loathing of religion was all-embracing. He showed the same antipathy to priests and parsons that some folk show to spiders and snakes. As far as he was concerned, they were all hypocrites and part of the conspiracy to keep his class in perpetual bondage. No church school, therefore, for me. There was a school two-and-a-half miles away, a state school with no ties with the church and that, my parents decided, was the place for me.

I was five years old when my mother took me by the hand and walked me there on the first morning. She left me at the school gates and no sooner had she disappeared than a ferocious young bully called Horace Evans snatched the new cap off my head and kicked it into the air. When I complained tearfully I was punched for my pains. Then he was joined by a pugnacious six-year-old called Stanley Barlow and the two of them danced round me taunting me for being the kind of boy who needed to be shown the way to school. For the next few weeks (or was it months?) I was their whipping post. Every day to and from school they waited for me and jeered and taunted as they pinched, smacked, punched, cuffed and tormented me. One day, driven beyond endurance, I turned and hit back at Horace Evans. Immediately my schoolfellows formed a ring and I was forced to take off my jacket and do battle with my enemy. To my astonishment, I beat him and had to be pulled off him. He ran off blubbering while I, intoxicated with victory, turned and offered to fight Stanley Barlow as well. He refused the challenge, whereupon I gave him his kadins – three light ceremonial blows symbolising his defeat. The following morning, Horace Evans called for me and we walked along together. On the way we were joined by Stanley Barlow and we made our way to school. I had made friends, my first school friends – and I had learned a valuable lesson.

At school I was entering into a host of new relationships – but in the street I was in a kind of no man's land. Six weeks or so ago I had been welcome to join in the girls' games. But not now. Not only was I unwelcome but my new-found male pride would not have permitted me to take part in feminine play. At the same time, I was not always welcome to join the boys. I was too young. From time to time I would be allowed to run after a ball or retrieve a kite from a lamp post, but as soon as some exciting exploit was embarked upon I was told to clear out. I don't remember how long this state of affairs lasted – several months certainly, perhaps a year. During this period I spent many of my weekends with my cousin John Logan.

When my mother referred to them collectively as 'the Logans' there was an element of implied criticism. 'Ay, they're a queer lot, the Logans,' she would say, looking meaningful. Even Maggie, her sister, was not free from the Logan taint; after all, she had married one of them. The degree of taintedness varied according to the degree of discord or amity existing between our family and theirs at any given moment. When my mother referred to her sister as 'Mag', then it meant they were on good terms; when 'Maggie Logan' was used then they were at odds.

The Logans had left the north two or three months before my parents and for a year or two had lived in several different districts of Salford. In between they dossed down in our house.

John Logan was my particular friend. He was my senior by eighteen months but from the time we were infants we were close friends, in spite of the fact that we lived several miles apart. It was mostly at weekends and during holiday periods that we met. Up until I was five years old our weekend meetings depended on my parents' being free to take me visiting, but once I began going to school I was considered mature enough to travel alone on the tramcar to Patricroft. So on a Saturday morning, or sometimes on Friday night, I would set off with my carfare clutched tightly in my hand and my toothbrush in the breast pocket of my best jacket. On Sunday evening I would return home again. Occasionally the procedure would be reversed and John would visit me. During the summer holidays we spent entire weeks in each other's company, exploring the industrial wastelands that bordered the Ship Canal or doing the dangerous things we'd been warned against doing on abandoned factory sites or on the decaying locks of old canals. Armed with bottles of sharp, green liquid made with crystals from a lucky-bag, we crept on tiptoe past haunted houses, heard the crump-crump of Nasmyth's thousand-ton steam hammer that could strike an egg without breaking the shell, raced along forgotten tow-paths past half-submerged barges and rusting locomotives.

Unnatural Habitat

A high point in the long and sometimes tedious summer holidays were the excursions known as 'the poor children's outings'. These were annual affairs organised by various charities and sponsored by local branches of the Loyal and Ancient Order of the Buffaloes, or by the Oddfellows. The assembly point was the tramcar-depot in Eccles. The noise of several hundred small boys and girls, unrestrained by either parents or schoolteachers, sounded like a gigantic gathering of migrating birds. We all wore our tickets pinned to our jackets or blouses and distracted charity workers herded us into our appropriate groups. Everyone had a tin drinking mug; some carried it on a string around their necks, others had it attached to a belt or a piece of string which tied round their waist. Suddenly the tramcars appeared, a dozen or so of the open-topped kind. Within a matter of minutes we had boarded them and were off, singing:

We're off for Canaan's shore,
We're off for Canaan's shore,
We're off for a trip on the hallelujah ship
And we're never coming back any more.

It was a noisy trip. We sang and in between songs we cheered. If a pedestrian waved at us we cheered. If a dog barked we cheered. If we passed another tram we cheered. In fact, we seemed to be riding on a sea of cheering.

Worsley was our destination. Or was it Monton? I'm not sure that I ever knew. I couldn't have been more than six years old at the time. I do know, however, that I was wearing a new suit which had been bought through Mr Glendinning's clothing-club. Whichever it was, Worsley or Monton, it was a pleasant enough place, a large field bordered on three sides by trees and on the fourth by a wooden fence with a stile leading to a path on the other side which wound through a downward sloping meadow to a farmhouse. Two long trestle-tables had been erected at the entrance to the field and as we passed through the gate we were each given a bun and an orange and had our tin mugs filled with milk.

Afterwards there was an egg-and-spoon race, a three-legged race and a fat man with a bald head and a very red face led us in community singing. He taught us the words of 'Ilkla Moor Baht 'at', 'The Quartermaster's Store' and 'The Nottingham Poacher'. My cousin John disappeared during the singing and came back bursting with excitement. He had been exploring and had discovered a pig called Fat Lizzie. Furthermore, he had found a short cut to it where one would be safe from the prying eyes of the farmer. Half a dozen of us wriggled our way to the back of the choristers and, crouching low, ran for the stile. Once over it we skirted along the top of the field and then dropped down to a stream. It was about eight-foot wide and quite fast-flowing. 'Now', said John, 'this is the secret way. So follow me.' We did so, stooping low in the long grass like Indians hunting buffalo. After a hundred yards or so we came to John's secret bridge, a narrow plank. We crossed it, or rather, the others did. I tried to and fell in for the plank was not only narrow but slippery with mud.

The water was apparently about twelve feet deep and I would have drowned had it not been for my cousin who grabbed me by the hair and pulled me to safety. A farm labourer who came by took me to the farm kitchen where I sat, wrapped in a blanket, by the fire while my clothes were dried. I went home none the worse for my adventure, having bound John by an oath not to say a word about my near drowning.

A few days later, my mother found a wet handkerchief in the breast pocket of my jacket and threatened me with terrible punishments if I didn't tell her what had happened. I think I might have brazened it out had it not been that the suit had shrunk and no longer fitted me. I confessed the whole sorry business and later wished I hadn't as for months afterwards I never left the house without a stern admonition to stay away from water. Poor Betsy – she had borne five children and I was the only survivor.

I think the fear of drowning haunted the minds of most mothers in our neighbourhood, certainly during the summer holidays – and not without cause. We could run through the square and down the short cul-de-sac of Worral Street and find ourselves by the side of the River Irwell. An even shorter run would take us to the ten-foot brick wall behind which lay the canal, an early 19th-century ditch lined with decaying factories, dead and dying cotton-mills and abandoned brickyards. Its cobbled towpath was a favourite haunt of lovers whose desperate need for privacy rendered them impervious to the smell of chemicals, bilge and rotting garbage. In the few-and-far-between scorching days of summer, bands of naked youths would risk death by poisoning and break through the foul scum with the crawl and trudgen. Unwanted kittens were disposed of there and the inflated carcasses of dead dogs made splendid targets for stone-throwing enthusiasts. Occasionally a defeated citizen of the damnable town would use it to put an end to an intolerable existence.

John would spend what seemed to me to be an inordinate amount of time combing his hair and plastering it down with a sickly-smelling grease. He had flaming red hair which was naturally wavy and he was rather vain about it.

I think I must have been about ten or eleven when I began to notice that our weekends were assuming a different pattern. For one thing, we were spending a lot more time with John's friends than was customary; I felt that I had been demoted. I was no longer John's best friend but someone who was not so much accepted as a member of the inner circle as someone to be tolerated.

John had developed into a strong and stylish swimmer and just after his fourteenth birthday was chosen as a reserve in the county water-polo team, so our weekends together became less frequent. When we did manage to meet we spent a lot of time listening to gramophone records of pop singers like Morton Downey and Sophie Tucker. John had already decided that we were going to become a famous singing duo and set about persuading me to learn songs from Layton and Johnstone records.

'But I know plenty of songs already,' I protested.

'Old stuff,' said John. 'You've got to keep up with the times.'

When we felt that our material was sufficiently polished we allowed ourselves to be persuaded to get up and sing in front of my father and a few of his cronies. They were bewildered but polite, all but Jock Sinclair, who said, 'If that's music then I'm the Shah of Persia.'

John now had a new circle of friends, mostly swimmers like himself, fourteen and fifteen year olders, strong and well-built and, for the most part, radiating the kind of confidence which borders on arrogance. During the week they met at the baths where they exchanged gossip in the changing room and trained for the Saturday matches and competitions. On Sunday evening they congregated at the Cross and, secure in numbers, joined the Monkey Parade.

This preliminary mating ritual was, in the pre-Second-World-War period, a common phenomenon throughout Britain. As a method of making contact with the opposite sex it was, to say the least, tentative. The routine was simple enough: groups of two or more youths would saunter along a thoroughfare and try to engage in conversation groups of two or more girls who were parading along the same thoroughfare in the opposite direction. The conversational gambits were generally uninspired, consisting of the kind of clicking sounds that are used to encourage a horse to go faster, or remarks like 'Going far?' or 'Fancy a walk?' The response to these and similar overtures might be a toss of the head or a burst of laughter or a mocking 'Does your mother know you're out?' Occasionally – very, very occasionally – a girl (or girls) would show themselves willing to talk and the two groups would coalesce and the boys and girls would pair off but never for more than a few minutes. They would walk along together desperately searching for something to say but would always fall back on stock witticisms, the flip talk of embarrassed adolescents. Sometimes arrangements would be made to meet the following evening but the girls never turned up. It was all part of the ritual. Afterwards the group would walk along in a kind of glory, dizzy with success as they sang the praises of this or that particular girl.

It was after one of these inconclusive encounters that John waxed lyrical about his ideal girl. He had met her a few weeks before at a swimming gala. She was the daughter of a prosperous accountant and had recently become the British breast-stroke champion. My cousin had, apparently, made a good impression on her and had been invited to her home for tea. His voice was heavy with admiration when he described the visit. 'You should see that place!' he said. 'When you go in the front door there's a square hall with walls panelled with dark wood. And there's a little room off it. And do you know what it's for? It's for washing your hands! Imagine that – a room specially for washing your hands!' When he launched into a eulogy of middle-class girls I felt bound to protest but he brushed my arguments aside with descriptions of smooth skin and shining hair. 'It's all that good food,' he said. 'It stands to reason. It'll be a middle-class girl for me when I get married. They're so healthy.'

Our last time together occurred when I was fourteen and a half. I had been spending the weekend at his house and on the Sunday morning had watched him playing water polo at the baths. In the evening, a cousin of his, Nancy, had called with a friend to visit her uncle. After tea, Tam and Maggie went out leaving us to entertain the two girls. John contrived to get me into the kitchen and in great excitement whispered that this was our chance. We would offer to take them home and I would partner Nancy and he, the friend. I was excited at the prospect for Nancy was a pretty seventeen year old and she seemed to like me. At the wasteland above Irlam o' th' Heights, we paired off and arranged to meet in half an hour at the half-way house.

It was a moonlight night in early April and I walked with Nancy until we were screened from the road by a bank of last year's rosebay.

'Let's lie down,' I said.

'It's cold,' she said.

'I'll keep you warm.' I took off my coat and laid it on the ground.

She sat down, smoothing her skirt and carefully removing the navy blue straw hat she was wearing. She had pale gold hair and lying there in the moonlight she looked as if she was made of transparent silver. In an odd kind of way I felt that I could see her skull through the skin of her face. It made her seem heartbreakingly defenceless. I lay by her side with my arm under her head and we kissed. After what seemed a long time I crept my hand under her blouse and fumbled with her brassiere, half expecting her to brush my hand aside. Instead she eased herself up and undid the clasp.

'They're small,' she said.

'They're nice,' I said, hoarsely, feeling the nipples harden under my fingers. By this time I was rigid with desire and trembling, partly with passion and partly with cold. I began to stroke her legs, venturing a little higher with each caress until, at last, my fingers were inside the leg of her cami-knickers, feeling the slightly coarse thatch of pubic hairs. And then something strange began to happen. I was suddenly conscious of the two of us in that desolate landscape of scurvy grass billowing down to that valley of slums, factory chimneys and pithead gear. It looked ghostly in the moonlight like her fragile skull and the blue tributary of her heart pulsing in her throat. I felt such compassion for her and myself and all of us that I wanted to weep and I knew couldn't go on. If she had resisted or shown that she was eager it might have been different, but she was so passive, so unresisting. It was as if she had already reconciled herself to accepting whatever life did to her without complaint. Acting on a sudden impulse, I stood up, filled with a kind of impatience. 'Come on', I said, 'let's go. They'll be waiting for us.'

'What happened?' she said.

'Nothing happened.'

'Was it something I did?'

'No. I'm cold.' I was shivering violently. We walked back to the road in silence. I was still big with desire and she must have noticed it for she stopped and said, 'Why didn't you?'

'I don't know,' I said miserably.

'How old are you?'

'Turned fourteen.'

'I thought you were older,' she said.

John and I walked Nancy and her friend home to Weaste and then John got a late night tram to Peel Green. 'See you soon,' he said as the tram moved off.

5

Lodgers and Friends

In those early years of the 1920s my father always seemed to be surrounded by a host of friends and our front room saw many convivial gatherings. They generally took place on a Saturday night after the pubs had closed. They were spontaneous affairs for the most part, with maybe a dozen guests, mostly my father's workmates and their wives and perhaps two or three drinking cronies. Not that these were just drinking sessions. Someone would bring three or four bottles of beer and the company would sit and drink and talk and argue and then someone would say, 'Gie us a song, Will.' I used to lie in bed listening to the drone of conversation and the hypnotic rise-and-fall of my parents' voices singing the tale of 'The Beggar Laddie'. Sometimes I would fall asleep hearing the voices raised in argument. I always knew when Sanny Wylie was there. He was a member of the Freethinkers Society and always spoke in a slow, reasonable way that often infuriated his opponents. He was a moulder but his real talent lay in inventing things, mechanical things and gadgets which would improve a machine's performance. He lived in Failsworth on the other side of Manchester and once or twice we visited them and stayed the night. At six o'clock the next morning (it was a Sunday) the entire family – father, mother and six or seven children – trooped off to the local swimming bath, taking us with them.

Another couple who often came to the Saturday night sing-songs was Davie Muirhead and his young bride, who blushed rosy red every time any man other than her husband spoke to her. Fred Nightingale was a frequent visitor as well, one of the few Englishmen accepted into this circle of exiles. He earned his living as a pub pianist and was rumoured to write songs and patter for a famous comic. He was a pleasant, smiling man who smoked cigarettes, a freakish habit in that company of thick-twist smokers. Occasionally the evening would be enlivened by the arrival of Bill Wallace with a bottle of whiskey and some small gift for my mother.

Bill was our lodger, the first of a succession of lodgers. Most of them were working men or left-wing political organisers, the exception being Bill. He was a commercial traveller who worked for a textile firm and who was frequently away for a week or ten days at a time. My mother would sometimes refer to him as 'a real gentleman' but more often he was 'a gallus bugger'. My father brought him home one night after a riotous session at The Slip Inn, a Manchester pub where my father sang occasionally. Wallace, a Scot of Scots, had been hypnotised by my father's singing and refused to be parted from him. He slept that night on the floor in front of our kitchen fire where my mother discovered him the next morning. It says a great deal about Wallace that he was able to charm my mother out of her angry mood, for she had very little tolerance for my father's sporadic drunken sprees. But Wallace, as she often said, could charm the birds oot o' the trees. So he became our lodger and shared my bedroom. He had matching luggage of deep brown leather and silver-backed hairbrushes and a shaving brush with a handle made of deerhorn. His hair spray smelt of tangerines and his tweed suits gave off a superb aroma of whiskey and cigars. I remember him as a tall man, with close-cropped ginger hair, trim moustache and a tracery of pale blue veins showing like streams and rivers on the contours of his face. He walked like a man playing the pipes and, indeed, he once brought home a set of great Highland bagpipes and entertained the entire street by walking up and down the pavement playing 'Killiecrankie'. Above all, he loved to hear my father sing and would sit there for hours listening as he wept for the fate of Patrick Spens and his drowned mariners. I used to wait at the end of the street and meet him so that I could be carried on his shoulders along the pavement and into the house. Whenever he came back from one of his 'selling jaunts' as he called them, he would greet my mother, holding her at arms' length, with the words: 'Here she is, the fair maid of Perth.' He was a heavy drinker and an obsessive gambler and my mother often scolded him on both counts.

'You're a daft bugger, Bill Wallace.'

'So I am, Betsy, so I am.'

'Why do you do it?'

'Habit, Betsy. Just habit.'

'It's a bloody bad habit.'

'It's worse than that, lassie. Could ye lend me a pound?'

'Now, where in hell would I get a pound in the middle o' the week?'

'Ah, well. If ye dinnae ask, ye dinnae get.'

For me, he was no commercial traveller, he was Alan Breck come to life. 'A wild yin,' was how my father saw him, a big, wild hielan'man 'wi' no' an ounce o' harm in his hale body.' And what was he doing in this dark, satanic slum with his tweeds and silver-backed hairbrushes?

He left us after a year or so, leaving no address. According to my father, he was 'on the run frae a woman he'd been thick wi'.' His bed in our back bedroom was now occupied by Boston Dunn, a tall, lanky young man from Falkirk. Now in his second year as a journeyman-moulder, he had come down from Scotland 'on spec', meaning that he didn't have a job but hoped to get one. He accompanied my father to the foundry where he worked and got a job there. He was politically active but, unlike my father, did little union work. Two or three nights a week he attended Communist Party meetings and at weekends canvassed the party newspaper round the streets. On Sunday mornings he would potter about in his shirt-sleeves, cleaning his tools, polishing his working boots and washing his hair. And all the time he would be going through his repertoire of 'heartbreakers', richly embellished with portamento, glottal sobs and scoops, the stuff and fibre of pub-tenor style. My father disliked his singing intensely and would constantly interrupt him with insulting remarks such as 'Are ye in pain, laddie? That's a terrible bloody noise you're making.' To which Boston would reply, 'You're oot o' date, Will. This is the way they sing these days.'

He was always late for his meals. Even when he'd been in the house all day he would still be late. My mother would call him and tell him his meal was on the table. 'I'll be down,' he would call. After five minutes or so my mother would call him again. 'Are ye coming?' 'Anon,' he would cry. This annoyed my mother intensely and she would shout to him at decreasing intervals and finally he would arrive. 'Mr Anon' was my mother's name for him. One day he had just answered her final call when there was a knock on the door and before we had time to answer it three or four big plain-clothes detectives burst into the room. At the same moment Boston appeared. One of the policemen asked if he was Boston Dunn.

'Who's asking?' said Boston.

'Is your name Boston Dunn?'

'Ay,' said Boston.

'We've a warrant here for your arrest,' the detective said and before we knew what was happening they had handcuffed him and bundled him out of the house. It all happened so quickly that they were gone before anything could be said or done.

'Oh, my God!' my mother cried. 'What are we coming tae? Detectives in the hoose!' My father tried to comfort her but she wouldn't be comforted. 'It's all your fault', she said, 'you brought him into the hoose.'

'You didnae object.'

'You'll no' be content till we're oot in the street!'

My father went off to the police station to try and find out what Boston was charged with. He came back later in the evening with the news that our lodger had been distributing an illegal newspaper to soldiers in the local barracks.

'You mean they needed a' they big dees tae arrest a man for gien oot a few newspapers?'

'That's about the strength of it.'

'They'll no' keep him inside, surely.'

'He'll be lucky if he gets oot in the next twa-three years.'

'Ye cannae mean it.'

'I mean it all right. They'll charge him wi' treason or incitement tae mutiny. As sure as fate they'll send him doon.'

My father's guess was a little off the mark. In actual fact they contented themselves with charging him with a perfectly ordinary misdemeanor for which the judge sentenced him to six months' imprisonment.

And then there was the man with the gun. If I ever knew his name I have forgotten it. I was, I think, about six or seven years of age when he came to us. I don't know whether my father knew him or whether he had seen the postcard advert in the local newsagents. I remember that he slept a lot and seemed to work at odd hours. I also remember that he was a very big and very silent man. He would sit at the table over his dinner without speaking a word. I don't think he was with us more than two or three weeks, but I do remember the occasion of his going. My mother was upstairs making the lodger's bed when suddenly she exclaimed, 'Oh, my God!' My father went to the foot of the stairs and shouted, 'What's wrong?'

'Come up,' she said, and he went up quickly with me at his heels. My mother was standing at the bedhead holding back the pillow.

'What's wrong?' said my father.

'Look.' And then we saw it, a large, sinister-looking pistol, black and menacing against the sheet.

'A gun!' said my father.

'Ay, a gun – and what's it daein' here?'

'No, how the hell would I ken that?'

'Will', my mother said earnestly, 'the man could be a murderer.' My mother, like many working-class women of the period, was something of an authority on murder and could list most of the notorious murder cases of the last half-century. Within ten minutes or so she had my father almost convinced that our lodger was a mass-murderer and that we were the next on the list for the gun.

'You'll gie him his notice the nicht,' she said.

'I'll dae that,' said my father. 'He'll need to find somewhere tae gang.'

'Well, he's no' staying here!'

That evening at the dinner table we were so quiet that the man was driven to comment on it. 'Something wrong?' he said.

'That gun under your pillow is what's wrong,' my mother said.

'Sorry about that,' the man said. 'I forgot to put it away. I was going tomorrow morning anyway.' He left the next morning and that was the last we saw of him.

Our next lodger was the man who stuttered. My father, for some reason, called him The Presser. His real name was Geoffrey something, the first Geoffrey we had ever known. It was a name my father couldn't bring himself to pronounce in the presence of its owner. I don't know why but the name embarrassed him. To my mother he would sometimes utter the name as if he was savouring a not altogether pleasant new taste. 'That's a gey fancy name for a bloke without a trade,' he said, for Geoffrey was employed as the manager of a small gentleman's outfitters and that, in my father's view, was not a respectable way of earning a living. On the other hand our lodger was a freethinker and knew Esperanto and, more important, he owned a well-thumbed copy of Paul Lafargue's *Right To Be Lazy*. I think my father would have been able to over-look Geoffrey's job had it not been for his stutter which was one of the worst cases of its type I have ever heard. He was all right until he encountered a *y*, a *w* or a *t* and then he would gag and wrestle with the offending letter until his face grew purple and his entire body would contort with the strain. This used to terrify my father who was convinced that at any moment Geoffrey would collapse and die at his feet. He made a point, therefore, of limiting conversa-tions to 'Good morning' and 'Good night', but even these simple sallies were abandoned when it seemed that our lodger was in danger of strangling on the *g*'s involved in his response. From that time on my father avoided all unneces-sary contact with Geoffrey, which was not a simple matter in the confines of a small terraced house.

And yet in many ways Geoffrey was a model lodger. He was quiet, neat and, to use my father's description, 'as clean as a Whitsuntide virgin'. More impor-tant, he brought a breath of the modern world into our house in the form of gadgets and devices which none of us had seen before. The most noteworthy of these was a rowing machine on which he used to exercise at weekends. It was a noisy contraption and the first time it was used it brought most of our neigh-bours to their front doors under the impression that Arthur Caldwell had finally gone over the top and was demolishing his home from within.

Geoffrey's second-hand Dictograph machine was also the subject of much animated discussion. He used it in conjunction with a gramophone on which he played Italian language discs, for he was ambitious and spent hours working at adding Italian to his other accomplishments. At the first sound of the gramo-phone my father would leave the house saying it was painful enough to have to listen to someone strangling on the English tongue without subjecting oneself to even greater torture in a foreign language. His most successful gadget was a combined trouser-and-tie-press. To say that our neighbours were impressed by this extraordinary machine was to minimise its effect; even my father, who was rarely at a loss for words, was silenced by it. When Geoffrey was finally moved to another branch of his firm our relief at being spared from witnessing his titanic battles with consonants was tempered with regret at no longer being in touch with a man who was, so to speak, a bridge between us and the new technology.

Our lodgers came and went. Sometimes they stayed for a year or more but gen-erally they were gone after a few months. My father's workmates, too, tended to move on, sometimes after a few months, sometimes a few years. They would be laid off or fired or find jobs in other towns. Some of them joined the ranks of the unemployed, some gave up and went back to Scotland. One or two emigrated to Canada, and Davie Muirhead and his wife went to New Zealand. In the end there was only Jock Sinclair left. He lasted up until 1927. He had been a friend of my father's since the time they were both apprentice moulders at Smith and

Wellstood's. Jock, like my father, had played an active role in the struggle to combine workers in the various foundry trades and occupations into a single iron-founders' union. He had worked in the same foundry as my father and drank in the same pubs. They were both members of the Workers' Arts Club and, when they were unemployed, signed on at the same Labour Exchange. Jock was possessed of a sardonic turn of mind and a gift for argument which made him both admired and disliked. In his mid-forties he contracted tuberculosis of the lungs and spent fourteen months in hospital. When he came out it was to find that he no longer had a job. His face, which had always been somewhat sallow, was now as white as if it had been bleached and made him look singularly malevolent. His patience, too, had suffered and he did nothing to hold his biting tongue in check. Among his friends he was renowned as a Burns scholar and his stay in hospital had enabled him to add to his considerable knowledge of the poet's works. So now, in addition to being able to recite many of the longer poems, he could quote extensively from the bard's correspondence. In his final years he added Dunbar's *Twa Marriet Wemen and the Wedo* to his repertoire. He had also committed to memory the entire *Rubaiyat of Omar Khayyam* in order to be able to confound his *bete noire*, Jack Wilson, a member of the Workers' Arts Club committee. There were those who maintained that it was his hatred of this rather inoffensive and completely ineffectual club member that kept Jock alive. He certainly never neglected an opportunity of abusing him.

His hatred was all-embracing. First of all, he hated him for his appearance, the very ordinariness of which infuriated Jock. 'He's just a lang streak o' piss,' he would say. 'Just look at the bloody great Jessie. His face has got as much expression as a shit-house door.' In his less emotional moments he would describe Wilson as being 'as daft as a make watch' or as 'an apprentice con-man trying to pass himself aff as a human being'. On Saturday nights Wilson would turn up at the Workers' Arts Club dressed in his best navy-blue serge suit and sporting a watch-and-chain and a gold Albert. 'Like a bloody pea-hen,' said Jock, convinced that the finery was just to impress people, while the watch 'is to try and kid folk that he can tell the time, whereas in reality he disnae ken whit day it is'. He found Wilson's voice particularly irritating, 'like a strangulated duck wi' the croup'. He also hated him for his even temper, which Jock regarded as a sure sign of English insensitivity: 'nice polite folk who cover their mouths when they yawn and say *excuse me* when they're cutting your balls off.'

The fact that Wilson was a member of the club committee was another cause for resentment in Jock. 'He's just there to put his hand up when the right-wing gie him the nod. A bloody yes-man, an arse-hole creeper. Committee man? I've shit better.' But it was really Wilson's literary pretensions that goaded Jock to unleash his most withering diatribes. Wilson was given to quoting *Omar Khayyam* and at socials was known to quote from *The Merchant of Venice,* always the same few lines. Jock's loathing for Wilson and all that he represented, in Jock's mind at any rate, was complete. As far as Jock was concerned,

Shakespeare (and for that matter the entire body of English literature) was just about on par with Wilson's navy-blue suit and his gold Albert. Jock's lips would curl in disgust as he spat out gobs of Shakespeare and, if Wilson tried to interject, Jock's voice would go soaring up and up, over the drone of conversation, the click of billiard balls and the noise of the three-piece band playing at the dance upstairs. And when his voice could soar no higher, he would stop and say 'Drivel. Just a load of bloody drivel. Listen!' . . . and he would launch into *Tam o' Shanter* or *Holy Willie's Prayer* and his eyes would shine like stainless steel rivets in that bloodless face while little bubbles of foam formed and burst and formed again at the corners of his mouth. For an eight-year-old boy it was both exciting and awe-inspiring to see the way a grown man could be possessed by the power of words and how a poem could fill him to the brim with love and passion. Later I was to realise how that same love could make a man blind, for it was twenty years or more before I overcame my prejudice against Shakespeare.

Jock's knowledge and love of Burns gave him a special place in my father's affections. My mother, on the other hand, disliked him intensely and said his sneering face 'gave her a grue' (made her miserable). What she really disliked was his foul language and the fear that it might corrupt the vocabulary of her sole surviving child. In spite of my mother's fairly constant criticism of his friend, my father continued to invite him round to our house and they would sit in front of the fire talking union politics and exchanging gossip about who had just come down from Falkirk or Denny or Bonnybrig. Later, when Jock was confined to his bed and slowly dying, my father took me to visit him, for 'death', said my father, 'is an important part of life.' It was part of my education, he said, to be in the company of death from time to time.

So I sat there in a creaking wickerwork chair in the corner of the room feeling the cold seep into me as I watched these two old men (old, that is, in my eyes) begin another instalment of the long ritual of leavetaking.

'Well then, how are ye keepin'?'

'No' weel. I'm wearin' awa', Will.'

'Och no, Jock. Ye'll get ower this. Ye've got ower it in the past.'

'No' this time, Will. I'm at the hinder end.'

My father fumbles for his pipe and then remembers that one doesn't smoke at the bedside of a dying friend. 'Have you got plenty to read?' he asks.

'Ach, I cannae be bothered.'

'Would ye like me to read to ye?'

'No' the nicht.'

I am conscious of the clock ticking away. When are we going to leave? I am cold and the chair creaks.

'Mebbe', the dying man says, 'ye could sing a song or twa.'

'Whit'll I sing?'

'Onything.'

My father clears his throat, looks up at the ceiling and very softly sings:

Lang hae we pairted been,
Lassie, my dearie
Noo we are met again,
Lassie, lie near me.

This song and others of the same type have always bored me, but now I am moved to tears and my heart is sore in my breast. I hang my head down so that my tears won't be noticed, and then wipe them away with the sleeve of my jersey. The song finishes and after a moment, Jock says, 'There wasnae onybody that could match him. Was there?'

'No', says my father, 'there wasnae. He was a poet-and-a-half.' I am afraid to move for fear the creaking of the chair should suddenly destroy the moment.

'Gie us 'Eppie Morrie',' says Jock, suddenly brisk.

'Will it no' disturb them doonstairs?' says my father.

'No, go on! Dying man's privilege.'

My father launches into the ranting lilt of the defiant Eppie:[1]

Four-and-twenty hielan' men cam' fae the Carron side
To steal awa' Eppie Morrie, for she wadnae be a bride,
    A bride, she wadnae be a bride.

Then oot and cam' her mither then, it was a moonlicht nicht,
She couldnae see her dochter for the water shined sae bricht,
    Sae bricht, the water shined sae bricht.

I have heard my father sing this song many times but this is the first time I have listened to the words, really listened, and I am stirred.

Haud awa' frae me, Willie, haud awa' frae me,
Before I'll lose my maidenheid, I'll try my strength with thee,
    With thee, I'll try my strength with thee.

Jock lies there with a smile just touching his lips which look as if they've been carved out of alabaster. 'She was a gallus lass,' he says.

'Ay', my father agrees, 'she was that.'

After a moment, Jock makes a weak gesture with his hand towards me. 'Can the laddie sing?'

'Oh ay', says my father, 'he's a bonnie wee singer.' After a moment he says to me, 'Will you no' sing us a song?'

'I can't think of one.'

'Come on', he says, 'you'll think of one.'

Reluctantly I cross over to the side of the bed. My mind is a complete blank. In desperation I begin to sing:

The deil cam' fiddlin' through the toon
And he danced awa' wi' the exciseman,
And ilka wife cried, Auld Mahoun,
I wish ye luck o' the prize, man.

'No' bad,' says Jock.

For the rest of the visit I sit quietly, conscious of the fact that I have done something valuable and learned something very important, though I am not sure what I have learned. I have seen a man dying. His body is certainly dying and that is a fact. His mind, however, is far from dead and that, too, is a fact. Furthermore, I saw him mouthing the words of 'Eppie Morrie' and that is another fact. What, then, do these songs mean? What is the source of their power? I don't know, but I have learned that they possess some unique quality – and that is an important fact.

6

The Gang

The street was our universe and our university. It was the place where we slept and dreamed and ate and collected our inheritance. It was where we fought and discovered love and friendship, acquired the skills which would help us to survive. The heavy stone with which you pounded fragments of brick and glass to powder was your first tool, that broomstick maypole gave you your first taste of ritual drama.

The street was our stage, our race track, our gymnasium. It was our jungle, our prairie, our untamed ocean. It was anything we wanted it to be. It bore no trees, no flowers, no autumn harvest or fruit or vegetables, but it observed the seasons with games and pastimes. In the square at the bottom of the street we played 'footer' (football) until we were driven off by irate housewives fearful for their windows. So we would adjourn to the back entry and continue the game there. In summer we played cricket with wickets drawn in chalk on a gable-end of the street or on the wall of someone's back yard. Sometimes we would play 'vault the horse' or 'piggy', an ancient game which was played with a short length of wood (the piggy) about an inch in diameter and sharpened at both ends and a flat stick about eighteen inches long. You struck one of the sharp ends of the piggy with the stick so that it catapulted into the air where you hit it with all the force you could muster. On the croft we played duckstone, another traditional game, one involving strength and the ability to throw straight. Using small boulders and bricks you built a column some three feet high and then from a distance of twenty or so feet away you attempted to knock it down by hurling large stones at it.

In the spring we played marbles with *clays, glassies* and *steelies* (ballbearings of all sizes and much prized). Then there were the hoops and garfs and whip-and-top days when the pavements would be alive with scores of round-tops and peg-tops whirring away across the flagstones. We drew circles in coloured chalk on the flat surface of the tops so that when they spun they made beautiful designs. Some of the girls were so expert with their whips that they could capture their spinning tops and throw them eight or ten yards along the street so that they would land still spinning.

The girls had a much larger repertoire of games than we had, particularly ring games.[1] I think one reason for this is that many of them had younger brothers and sisters and were expected to keep them entertained. The ring games were mostly simple ones and could easily accommodate a couple of toddlers. The skipping and ball-bouncing games, on the other hand, were often complicated and called for much manual skill from those who took part in them. Many of them involved the exercise of verbal skills too; for tongue-twisting rhymes and nonsense rigmaroles delivered at tremendous pace often accompanied the skipping games.[2] The boys' games tended to rely more on physical strength and speed. Our ball-bouncing games were certainly much simpler than the girls' and there were fewer of them. Football and cricket were, of course, the main ones. There was ball catching – that helped you to develop the skill needed to become a good fielder in a game of cricket, but there wasn't much else. Tip-it, perhaps – that was a game for two players who stood opposite each other, maybe eight or nine feet apart. Midway between the two players, a coin was laid on the ground. The players then bounced the ball at each other while attempting to hit the coin or turn it over. A hit, or tip, scored ten points; a turn-over doubled the score.

The lamp posts which stood at both ends of the street were not lit during the summer months. They did, however, come in for a great deal of use particularly by the girls. They were made of cast-iron and were not unattractive. Their nine-foot high fluted columns supported a diamond-shaped glass-and-metal box which was there to protect the gas mantle from wind and rain. Just underneath it and attached to the post proper was a metal arm, put there to facilitate the cleaning and repairing of the lamp. It also provided the girls in the street with a marvellous swing. A rope, one of those yellow straw ones which were used to secure orange-boxes, was thrown over the arm of the lamp post. A loop would be made in the other end of the rope and a girl would sit in it while her companions pushed her round and round the post until all the slack had been taken up. Then she would be released and would go spinning back round the lamp post, screaming with pleasure.

Most of the girls were good at string games, too. The making of cats'- cradles and more intricate string structures was an annual craze. The street, normally full of cries and yells and noise of all kinds suddenly became quiet as dozens of boys and girls attempted impossible feats with a three-foot loop of string. Most of us could achieve the simple structures but it was the girls who were the real experts. We watched in bafflement as their nimble fingers slid among the loops, double loops and unloops of the string. Then the craze would pass and we would collect string for another purpose, for plaiting into whips, short-handled whips which could be made to crack like pistol shots. They were usually about five feet long to begin with but as you became more adept at their manipulation they grew longer and longer. When you reached the point where you could whip a piece of paper out of a friend's hand at twelve feet you were regarded as a person of some importance. Tolly Godwin could do it at fifteen feet – but then he could do anything.

Nut-ships were another craze. Any hard-shelled nut could be made into a nut-ship, but walnuts were best, almonds were more difficult. Walnuts could be opened with a knife into two halves, but almonds were used whole and the shell had to be rubbed down on a rough wall or pavement until they were just the right shape, and that could take hours of patient and sometimes painful rubbing. After fashioning the hull of your nut-ship, you then had to file a small groove at its sharp end. A needle-file was ideal for this part of the operation and in a street like ours, where almost everyone had a father or brother who owned tools, getting the right tool for the job was no problem. Into the groove you fitted a matchstick to serve as a jib-boom which you made fast with a blob of hot candle-grease. Another blob served to anchor a second matchstick, your main and only mast. After you had threaded paper sails onto it you were the owner of a fine square-rigged ship, more like an East-Indiaman than a clipper but a fine craft all the same. And seaworthy, you hoped. You found out after the first heavy fall of rain when it went sailing gaily down the gutter.

And there were tanks too, wonderful self-propelled tanks made from bobbins (cotton reels), half-an-inch of a candle with a hole cut around where the wick had been, a rubber band and a matchstick. To see these small, Leonardo-like contraptions moving inexorably across the pavement was to experience the ecstasy of creation.

Right at the top end of the upper part of our street was the off-licence-cum-dairy. Its proprietor, Mrs Ollerenshaw, was a tall, thin, faded woman who disapproved of drinking. Nevertheless, she did a thriving trade in beer and stout and, according to my father, knew more about looking after the stuff than most pub-keepers in the district. A counter ran round three sides of the shop. Behind one side there was a large milk churn with different-sized dippers hanging from its rim, a gallon can of cream and a marble slab with a round of yellow butter on it. On the opposite side of the counter there were two beer pumps with porcelain handles and behind them were rows of beer bottles. It was always spotlessly clean. Mrs Ollerenshaw's passion for cleanliness was so well known that women who sent their children for a quarter of butter or a gill of milk would warn them to wipe their shoes before entering the shop. If you forgot to do so, Mrs Ollerenshaw would fix her pale blue eyes upon you and say, 'Haven't you forgotten something?' It was rumoured that she closed her shop in wet weather to prevent mud being carried in from the street.

At the bottom end of the upper part of the street was Mrs Strickland's front-parlour shop. It was the kind of shop you ran to if you suddenly needed a loaf or some cheese or half-a-pound of bacon, but there was no choice. There was only one size of loaf, one kind of cheese (Cheshire) and one cut of bacon. There was a large notice on the back wall which read NO TICK. She was a small, plump widow with pleasant features but a sharp tongue. Her shop was at the entrance to the square and she lived in a perpetual state of anxiety that one of us was planning to kick a ball through her window.

The shop which meant most to me and my contemporaries was Fenton's, at the top end of our half of the street. 'The toffee-shop' we called it, a veritable Aladdin's cave filled with bottles of boiled sweets, creamy whirls, chocolate logs and Meltis bars. The window revealed boxes of wigga-wagga, swaggering dicks, gob-stoppers, blackstrap spinach and laces, aniseed balls, Victory-V Gums, kayli (sherbert), bobby-dazzlers, treacle toffee, Devon caramels, peanut crunch and coconut ice. Sometimes there would be licorice root which, when you chewed it, turned your mouth and lips bright yellow; and there were dried pods of carob (locusts, we called them) which we chewed until our tongues were saffron-hued. In the space between the toffees and the glass there were the lucky bags and novelties, none of which cost more than a penny.

Lucky bags were a favourite buy. They were filled with all kinds of wonderful things: wrist-watches made of chocolate and licorice, little sachets of kayli which you sucked through a licorice tube and in which you might find a lucky charm in the form of a tiny white-metal pig or a sheep or a milkmaid carrying a yoke with two buckets. Some of them had dolly mixtures in them, rings, propellers, swanee-whistles and buzz-saws. The propellors were two-bladed pieces of tin with a small hole in the center, which allowed it to fit onto a metal skewer where it rested on a small tin collar. With this you pushed the propeller off the skewer and it would go sailing through the air, often to a considerable height. The buzz-saws consisted of a circular tin disc about three inches in diameter. In the centre of the disc were four holes through which you threaded some tough string in such a way that you were left with loops about twelve inches long on each side of the saw-blade. You put a hand into each loop and by rhythmically tightening and slacking the string the disc could be made to rotate rapidly. There were also one-wheel cyclists which, with the aid of a short length of thin twine, could be made to race round the rim of a plate. Put-and-take also invaded the lucky bags. It was a national craze in the early 1920s, a game of chance played with a hexagonal miniature spinning-top each of the six sides of which bore a number. The players took turns in spinning the put-and-take and whichever number was uppermost when it stopped revolving was the player's score. Whoever finished with the highest number, won the game. Simple, crude and obsessive. Our put- and-take tops came in lucky bags. They were generally moulded in white metal, though a few were made of brass. These were highly prized by the older lads who played pitch-and-toss on the croft. They were said to be lucky.

The street-toys were all popular. Some, like the buzz-saws and the propellers, were simple; others, like the one-wheel cyclist, were ingenious. But they all cost money, a penny or a ha'penny. Not large amounts, but wages were low, unemployment widespread and pennies were not easily come by. Still, there were cigarette-cards and they didn't cost anything. These cards and the collecting of them played an important role in the life of my generation. The tobacco companies vied with each other in issuing new sets of cards. Each packet of ten or more cigarettes had its card tucked neatly between the silver paper and the cardboard of the pack. They were issued in sets of fifty and included

'Famous Cricketers', 'Footballers', 'Railway Locomotives', 'Sailing Ships', 'Wild Flowers', 'Do You Know?', 'Household Hints', and 'Cries of London'. They were generally well printed and often superbly designed and to get a complete set of any one of them took patience and perseverance.

The bulk of your collection was got by accosting strangers in the street with 'Got any cigarette-cards, Mister?' As you became older and more independent you worked the main roads and the cinema queues. There always came a point when you lacked two or three of a set. Then you looked around for someone who had duplicates of the ones you were after. If the owner was willing, you swapped; or, if you were a gambler, you played 'siggies' for them. Siggies was a game of skill. You leaned one of your cards (the 'Jack', or 'leaner') up against a wall at the point where it met the pavement. Then the players stood at the kerb and flicked cards alternately at the Jack. Whoever succeeded in knocking it down took all the cards on the ground. In another version of the game, the Jack was laid flat on the ground while players attempted to cover it, or cover part of it, with a flicked card.

There always came a time during the summer holidays when the street was overcome by a kind of lassitude. You had played all the games and you were tired of the park. Kersal Moor was too far away and it was too hot anyway. It was then that the coloured chalks usually appeared and soon the flagstones in the square would begin to fill with the work of dozens of artists and designers. My particular efforts were neither original nor accomplished. I confined myself to pictures of clipper ships, three-masted, four-masted or schooner-rigged, all sailing through the same storm. I was about average or perhaps a little lower than average. We had two artists, however, of outstanding talent: Tolly, the leader of our street gang, and Janet Taylor, who lived next door to the off-licence at the top-end of the street. Her pictures were the more imaginative of the two. She painted landscapes which were like the landscapes of dreams, forest glades full of strange plants where incredible butterflies and gaudily hued birds flew and hovered. Tolly drew portraits of patrician-looking women with long hair and perfect features, of men with reptilian eyes, of leopards and tigers. He drew humorous cartoons, too, in which we, his friends, figured. Sometimes people on the way home from work would make a detour in order to look at the drawings and see what was new. Their fame aroused envy in the breasts of neighbouring gangs, particularly the Miller Street Mob who, one year, broke through our defences and pissed all over Tolly and Janet's creations. For two or three years afterwards we mounted a not very efficient guard over our art works but there was no way we could protect them from the rain. One heavy shower was enough to obliterate them. Time after time we came onto the street in the morning to find that our art exhibition had gone, leaving only one or two red or blue chalk smears.

'Rain, rain, go away, come again another day,' we chanted. But we were small children then and still believed in magic. By the time we were a few years older we had learned how to wait out the rain without having to go back home. Home was all right as a place in which to sleep or to have your meals, providing they didn't take too long. But other than that, it was a place to be avoided, particularly in the summer. The street, the square, the croft: *those* were the places where everything was happening. Let's face it, if you were the kind of person who went running home every time there was a spot of rain then you would probably find when you came out into the street again that everyone else had gone off on some marvellous adventure. So rain or no rain, you stayed with your pals. If you were in the square or the back entry when a sudden shower came on, you raced for the 'alcoves'. These alcoves were meant to facilitate the removal of dustbins from the street's backyards but only one or two of them still served that purpose. The rest provide us with shelter. So we sit there perched in holes like little owls, a long line of us stretching halfway down the back entry. Someone starts to sing and within seconds we all join in:

> In Miller Street, in Miller Street
> They never wash their dirty feet,
> They're growin' spuds and sugar-beet
> Inside their dirty ear-holes.[3]

And when that was finished another voice would pipe up, eager to be heard:

> He's a ragtime soldier, ragtime soldier,
> Early on parade every morning,
> Standing at the corner with a rifle in his hand . . .

And now that the military theme was established:

> Ar-soldiers went to war, ar-soldiers fighting,
> Ar-soldiers stuck their bayonets up the Germans'
> Ar-soldiers went to war . . .

And song would follow song until the rain stopped or until hunger sent us racing back home for tea.

The making of wheelboards could occupy several days of the summer holiday period. We used them all the year round but the actual building of them usually took place in the week before the autumn school term began. For the classic wheelboard you needed two matched pairs of baby-carriage wheels with axles and body-brackets attached, a stout wooden plank four or five feet long, several feet of strong cord, three feet of 1/16th wire and some nails. The collection of these components might take two or three days and visits to a number of waste-tips. You attached the wheels to the plank using wire and the body-brackets so that the axle overlapped the plank by three or four inches on each side. Both ends of the cord were then attached to ends of the axle and could be used to steer the 'machine'. Downhill, the wheelboards could achieve truly amazing speeds and many a notable race took place between the ace drivers of these hand-cobbled speedsters.

'What shall we do?' It's a question that gets asked a dozen times a day. Nobody fancies football or cricket or any other of the usual games. 'Why don't we raid the Miller Street Gang?' someone suggests, but no one is interested.

Several other half-hearted suggestions are turned down and then Tolly, in his usual take-it-or-leave-it fashion, says he is going to look for fossils at the Pendleton pit-heap. We are suddenly enthusiastic at the thought of the 'specimens' waiting to be found. After a brief stop at Fenton's to buy some wigga-wagga, we proceed on our way. Wigga-wagga is an exceedingly chewy toffee which dyes your tongue a wonderful olive-green. We compare tongues frequently as we continue on our journey. Lying on the parapet of Frederick Road railway bridge, we spend a happy half-hour spitting on passing goods trains. Killus spots a policeman approaching and we are down in a trice and racing down the road, Tolly's steel-rimmed clogs striking sparks from the pavement.

The pit-heap is fascinating. 'Specimens! Specimens!' we shout and go racing up the heap in our excitement. 'Come back!' Killus shouts, and we go sliding down again. 'That copper could have followed us,' says Killus. We feel menaced and speak in whispers. 'Somebody'd better dog out,' says Tolly. 'We'll flip for it.' We form a ring and swing our arms chanting 'Flip, flap, flo-bang.' On the word *bang* you place one hand on top of the other, palm up or palm down. If there are more palms down than up, then all palms down are out, and we chant 'flip, flap, flo-bang' over and over until only one person remains. This time Seghead is the odd one out. 'Right', says Tolly, 'you're dogging out.' Seghead obviously feels that fate has dealt unjustly with him. 'What about *my* specimen?' 'Don't worry', we assure him, 'we'll give you one of ours.' We spread out and begin to search. We have been going for about half an hour when Biff Jarman lets out a yell. He has found his specimen, a six-inch length of a tree branch with bark, turned into grey slate. Now our appetite has really been whetted and we return to our labour with redoubled enthusiasm.

We hear another yell. This time it is Seghead and he is pointing to the top of the heap where two men are standing and waving their arms at us. We pretend to ignore them, but when they begin to come towards us we take to our heels and run. After about a hundred yards we stop and look back. The men have returned to the top of the heap. When they see that we have stopped they make threatening gestures and take a few steps towards us. We retreat a short way and stop again. 'Let's hide,' someone suggests; and we do so, behind the wall of the pit offices. We communicate in whispers again. 'Let's wait', Tolly says, 'perhaps they'll go.' Every few seconds someone peeps round the corner and reports that the men are still there. Finally Dub Carey, who is renowned for his eyesight, reports that the men are carrying steel rules.

'They're probably there for the afternoon,' he says. We move off disconsolately, having been robbed of the chance of finding the greatest specimens of all time.

'There's a pit-heap at Agecroft,' says Tolly. 'There's one at Swinton', somebody else says, 'and that's straight up the road from here.' It's about two miles. As we walk we discuss the possibility of finding a specimen of a fossil the like of which has never been seen before. Should we sell it or give it to a museum and become famous? The general consensus is that we should sell it and become rich enough to buy a ship which we could use to explore the world looking for fossils. Seghead is still grumbling about the fossil he never had the chance of finding when we reach the Swinton colliery tip. Biff Jarman is dogging out this time since he already has a specimen. The rest of us spread out and begin to comb through the most recently tipped heaps.

Within ten minutes both Killus and Bill Woods have found specimens – not so impressive as Biff's perhaps but well worth having. The rest of us continue our search, convinced that we are on the threshold of a momentous discovery. But that discovery is never made for a few minutes later our defences are breached by the enemy in the shape of a fierce-looking man with a big stick who threatens to put his boot up our arses if we don't move off quick. So we move and when we can no longer hear his voice we stop and discuss our next move.

'I think we ought to get back home,' says Killus.

'It's all right for you', someone says, 'you've already got a specimen.'

'Anybody know the time?' asks Dub Carey. Nobody does, and suddenly it is important for us to know. A woman passes and Seghead calls to her, 'What time is it, Missus?'

'It's about quarter to five.'

'Jesus Christ!' says Woodsy. 'Me ma'll kill me.'

'Come on', Killus says, 'let's go.'

Only Tolly doesn't move. 'I'm going to Agecroft,' he says. 'I came to find a specimen and I'm going to find one.'

'You're daft,' says Killus. 'Anyway, the rest of us are going home. Come on.' All except Tolly are undecided. 'I'm going,' Killus says. 'I'm coming as well,' Biff says. Nobody blames him for that. Everyone knows his old man is very handy with his fists and Biff gets knocked about quite a lot. But with Killus it's different; all he'll get is a bit of a talking-to.

'For the last time,' Killus says, but nobody makes a move except Biff.

The two of them go off.

'How do we get to Agecroft?' says Seghead.

'I know a short cut,' says Galty. His uncle works as a stoneman at Agecroft so naturally he's a bit of an expert. 'Follow me.' After about half-an-hour it becomes obvious that we are well and truly lost. Seghead's really beginning to flag and his muttered comments about Galty's uncle are not going down too well, at least not with Galty, who tends to be touchy about his family ever since his younger brother was sent to an approved school. When we hear a church clock strike six, we decide (or rather Tolly decides) to abandon the search for Agecroft and make for home. By this time we are all agreed that our misfortunes are all Killus' fault. It's a long walk home and we are tired and dispirited. All except Tolly, his steel-shod clogs ringing confidently on the pavement. In an odd way that bright clickety-click is what keeps us going.

On those days towards the end of the summer holidays when nobody could think of any new or exciting ways of spending time, we generally finished up by playing in the coalyard. It lay behind The Acrobats' house at the corner of what everyone called 'the croft'. On one side it was bounded by a brick wall and on the other by a high wooden fence which had been patched and re-patched so many times and with such a variety of materials that scarcely any of the original building material remained. Just inside the gates of the yard was a tiny wood-and-tarpaper shack known as 'the office'. At right angles to it were stables for two horses and beyond them the three coal stacks, one for small-coals, one for cobs and the third for best coal. On the other side there were miscellaneous piles of junk and, in the corner, the muck pile, a magnificent heap of horse manure which sometimes reached a height of seven or eight feet.

If you lived locally, that is anywhere within three- or four-hundred yards of the depot, coal was not delivered to you. You had to come and collect it yourself. At the yard your coal was weighed and loaded into a small but incredibly heavy wooden bogie with three-inch steel wheels and a long steel handle with which to pull it. That was our job. It needed two of you to pull the bogie though three was a better number, two to pull and one to ride on top of the coal. In the heat of the summer, Dirty Sam the coalyard man would get out the hair-clippers and we would gather to watch the horses being shorn. After that we would line up and before the day was finished almost every boy in the district would have a shorn head. I only once experienced the horse-clippers. My mother was furious and forbade any further shearings.

It was the muck pile, though, which had the greatest attraction for us for in the hot summer days the manure swarmed with small white maggots and we would descend on them armed with empty tobacco tins, cocoa tins and jam jars. In between filling our tins with the maggots we would take prodigious leaps from the top of the wall on to the bed of steaming, sweet smelling horse-shit.

Kersal Moor was about three miles away from where we lived. It was a place favoured by lovers and children. Often on fine days during the summer a big group of us would go from the street and spend the day there playing cowboys and Indians, pirates, smugglers, explorers and looking for lost golf-balls. There was a small stream which flowed between the bottom of the moor and a water meadow and in the late spring thousands of tiny frogs bred there. We would spend hours catching them and then put them into pillar-boxes that we passed on the way home. For some reason or other frogs were regarded as insensate creatures; perhaps it was because they lacked teeth or claws or poisoned glands that we treated them with such casual cruelty.

On the whole, animals were treated with kindness in the street. Families who owned dogs or cats lavished a great deal of love and affection on them. Sick sparrows and pigeons were nursed with great solicitude and those with leg injuries were brought to Mrs Turnbull who lived next door to The Cross Keys. She was clever with birds and used to fit them with wooden legs made of matchsticks.

When I was small, I had little or no identity of my own. I was my father-and-mother's child. Yes, I played in the street with other children and in the square and on the croft. I even went as far as Kersal Moor a couple of times but I wasn't part of a group, of a gang. The children I played with had no identities either; they, too, were merely their parents' children, though they later became members of the gang, 'our gang', The Square Gang', just as I did. The initiation ceremony which resulted in the formation of the gang was a tremendously important moment in my life, a truly significant stage in my development, for at that moment I suddenly became aware of myself and the world around me in a completely new way. It happened, I think, at Whitsuntide. We were playing on the croft and I recollect that at some point in the late afternoon my companions became rather secretive and stopped what they were doing to peer through cracks in the fence. When I asked what they were looking at they put their fingers to their lips and made a number of signs with their hands, none of which I understood. Eventually Tolly whispered, 'We're going over for an MC,' and he quickly clambered over the fence. The rest followed suit with me in the rear. Crouching behind the nettles, we reconnoitred the wasteland. 'Now', said Tolly, 'for the MC,' and he crept forward and returned a few seconds later with half a dozen dock leaves which he distributed all round.

'What's an MC?' I enquired. 'A midnight crap,' said Tolly and, dropping his short-pants, squatted down. The rest of us followed suit and a few minutes later we rose and surveyed the steaming offerings we had just laid at the invisible god of mystery. Following his example, we wiped ourselves with the dock leaves. 'Now we're a proper gang,' said Tolly. 'And from now on everyone who wants to join'll have to do a midnight crap.' 'Mine's the biggest,' said Killus. 'Mine smells the worst,' boasted Biff Jarman. We climbed back onto the croft and performed the final part of the ritual. 'We've all got to swear we'll keep the MC secret,' Tolly solemnly declared. One by one we spat on our hands and drew our fingers across our throats saying 'God's honour'. For the first time in my life I felt important. I was equal among equals. I possessed a secret my parents didn't know anything about. Before the MC we had been a motley crew of children who had come together because we lived in the same neighbourhood and had been born at roughly the same time. But now everything was changed, we had come together because we had *chosen* to do so, we had *chosen* each other. I was beginning to have an identity.

That initiation ceremony added an extra element to all our games and pastimes, transformed them into quests, tests, explorations and adventures of all kinds.[4] Furthermore, you were aware that your position in the gang was dependent upon your skill and daring in running, jumping, climbing, fighting and doing all the things you need to do in order to survive in the street. Everything suddenly became part of your apprenticeship for . . . what? What kind of a job? You didn't know, but whatever it was you would be competing with adults who had more experience than you and you would be expected to move quickly and if you found yourself working in a foundry or a mill or an engineering shop then you had to be sure-footed or you might find yourself being chewed up by the gears of a bloody big machine. So you learned to regard the street as a kind of workplace where the lamp posts were tools, as were the granite posts which barred the way to wheeled traffic through the square.

They were about four an a half feet high and about four feet apart. And there came a time in your life when you had to climb them and stand upright on the arched top of one of them. Once this had been accomplished you felt that a new stage of your life had been reached. The next stage was to leap from one post to the other without coming off. These two stages could occur any time between the ages of five and nine. You were generally about eleven or twelve by the time you arrived at the third stage, which involved vaulting over one of the posts. Once you had achieved this you could stand with 'the big lads' and pretend to understand all the dirty jokes or you could join in the rhythmic chant which greeted Hip-and-Gee-Whoa's progress across the square as she limped her way to the off-licence.

After the square posts you were ready for gateposts. In Lord Street, along which I walked on the way to school, there was a row of decayed houses many of which bore signs advertising cheap lodgings. They had probably been rather grand establishments at one time but now they were in an advanced state of decrepitude with their stucco peeling off in tatters and their gardens abandoned to trash and rubbish of all kinds. But they still had their gateposts, their stone gateposts topped with spheres, domes, cupolas, rosettes, cones, heraldic lions and *fleur-de-lis*. The test was to see if you could travel the length of the street running along the walls and jumping from one impossible gatepost to the next. You needed a good eye and sound sense of judgment for you were sometimes jumping from one extreme slope to another with only an inch or two clearance for your feet; or you balanced on a sharp stone pinnacle and jumped to another pinnacle. Once you became good at it you would occasionally do it wearing a blindfold.

From jumping to climbing was only a short step. Walls are a challenge. You climb a three-foot wall and it becomes vital for you to find a higher one. And so it goes on. In our street one summer, climbing became the craze. Someone noticed that the bricks in the gable-end of the street had lost some of their mortar. Before long we were all busy trying to scale the wall. It was tough on the fingers but before long several of us had mastered the technique. I believe I was the first of my mates to actually reach the roof. Getting down was more difficult and the contradictory advice given by those below didn't help. In the course of the next few days, half-a-dozen of us scaled the wall and soon we were going up and down that gable as if it was a three-foot fence.

But the time came when the gable wasn't enough; there had to be other walls. So every expanse of brick became a challenge. There was one wall in particular which cried out to be conquered and that was the eighteen-foot wall on Trafford Road behind which lay the docks. Every child in Salford must have tried at some time or another to slip through the dock gates but if any had succeeded the news hadn't reached us. The docks were a magnet. Behind that wall lay all kinds of riches. Trafford Road was a fair distance from our street, at least three miles, and the route lay through the territory of numerous street gangs, some of which had fearsome reputations. Furthermore, the wall was in much better condition than our gable-end; the bricks were smoother and the mortar between them was still intact.

We reconnoitred the wall and chose a spot behind a wooden advertisement-hoarding which would give us a little cover. Then we began the job of scraping out mortar for handholds. Our tools were the sharpened ends of umbrella spokes. The low handholds were comparatively easy to make; the high ones were incredibly difficult. The scraper had to support himself with the tips of the fingers of his right hand gripping a 3/4-inch ledge of brick while hacking away at the mortar with his other hand. You could only manage two or three minutes at a time, then you came down and someone else took over. There were other interruptions too. Every time one of the lookouts whistled you shinned down as quickly as possible and hid behind the hoarding. If it was a 'special' signal (meaning it was a copper) then you cleared off until the law had passed. It took us about a month to reach the top of the wall. By that time autumn was well advanced and our passion for the wall was almost spent. The fifth of November was approaching, bonfire night, and we had to concentrate our energies into getting a good supply of wood.

Then the word reached us that a cargo of Canadian apples had started unloading at the docks. The time had come. The assault on the wall should take place immediately. That night, eight members of The Square Gang, armed with poles, sped through the unfamiliar territory of Cross Lane and the streets behind Oldfield Road. Most of us were wearing plimsolls. Tolly, our leader, was, as usual, wearing clogs and their steel-shod rims made a discreet approach impassible. Killus and Dub Carey – who were to dog-out for us – had brought their wheels. Seghead and Biff Jarman each carried lengths of rope: Seghead's was tightly wrapped around his middle, a thirty-foot length of half-inch manila which he had 'found' in a builder's yard during his summer holidays; Biff's was two lengths of clothesline doubled and carried over the shoulder like a Swiss mountain-guide. It was dark when we arrived at the wall and after seeing the copper pass on his beat we began the assault.

As the champion climber, I had to make the first ascent. I was followed by Chick Lowrie. Then a rope was thrown to us and after exhorting those on the other end not to let go, we descended. Dave's father had once worked on the docks and Dave had pumped him during the last few weeks and now had a fairly good knowledge of the topography. The grapevine had yielded the fact that the apple cargo was being unloaded at Number Nine Quay. Dave led the way and, sure enough, got us to the right place without any fuss. There was the ship with lights shining through a couple of the portholes and, even more important, there were a dozen or so barrels stacked in front of the warehouse door. We tiptoed over to them. They were apples all right, you could smell them. The barrels were of two sizes and of a rather crude construction. The large size was quite beyond our combined strength but the smaller size, while still heavy enough, was manageable. We turned one on its side and gave a tentative push. It made a noise like someone treading on nutshells. At that moment a man appeared on the deck of the freighter. We froze and held our breath, expecting to see the deck fill with the enemy. But he merely walked to a gap in the bulwarks and, after urinating into the water, went below again.

Without a word, we began to push the barrel. I remember it making a fantastic amount of noise but maybe most of that came from the beating of my heart. We covered the two- or three-hundred yards from Number line to the wall in what must have been record time, over railway lines, through pools of stagnant water, under parked railway wagons. When we arrived at the wall we were so breathless that we had to wait a good three of four minutes before we could whistle for the rope. Biff appeared above us within seconds of the signal and lowered the sling to us. Quickly we rolled the barrel into the sling and made it fast to the manila rope. Then we heard Spotty whisper to the others, 'Hold on, they're coming up.' From the top of the wall we could see their upturned faces and their hands gripping the rope. It took six of us to haul that small barrel up the wall and three of us to lower it to the other side. We wasted no time in loading it onto Killus's wheels. Then we were away, a heroic band of brothers intoxicated with success. Through the dark streets, ready to do battle with The Percy Street mob or the West Park Street gang, our poles at the ready, we fairly raced home with our booty. That was a heroic journey worthy to be sung of by skalds and *shenachies*. Having sworn each other to secrecy, we parted after concealing our precious barrel in a pile of wood destined to burn in honour of Guy Fawkes.

In the period approaching bonfire night there were always a couple of weeks when we made repeated journeys to the chemist's shop for a pennyworth of sulphur. Bonfire night and Hallowe'en were the two last festivals of the year before Christmas. The traditional festival of Hallowe'en was maintained only in the most vestigial form. We blacked our faces, wore our jackets inside out and went from door to door begging for pennies. Our routine was primitive. We would knock at a door and sing:[5]

We are the Salford Boys
We can shout and make a noise
We can fight and we can sing
And we can dance the polka!

One of the group, the one wearing a hat, would then step forward and say:

'Here come I, old Doctor Brown,
The cleverest doctor in the town.'
'Can you prove it?' (we would all shout out)
'I can prove it, groove it and remove it.'

Whereupon 'The Doctor' would take off his hat with a flourish and we would all sing:

> Christmas is coming, the goose is getting fat,
> Please put a penny in the old man's hat.
> If you haven't got a penny, a ha' penny will do,
> If you haven't got a farthing God bless you.

We rarely went further than our own street with this ceremony and we rarely got more than a couple of coppers. Our performance was too abbreviated to produce much response, and in any case November was a bad month. Not much money about and Christmas on the way. It was much more fun to tie the handles of two door knobs together, knock on both doors and then race off pursued by blood-curdling threats of irate householders. Another favourite trick was to loosely pack some paper into the mouth of a drainpipe and set fire to it. The wind would catch the flame and the thrumming it produced sounded alarmingly loud in the house to which the drainpipe was attached. Another simple trick was to rub your chin down a window-pane. This always produced screams of rage from within the house.

Hallowe'en, bonfire night, Christmas and New Year were the high points of our winter. When the weather became cold we made winter-warmers out of cocoa tins and wire. The making of an efficient winter-warmer was simplicity itself. With a nail or some other sharp object you pierced a number of small holes in the lid and base of the tin. You then threaded your length of wire through a hole in the bottom and anchored it with the nail. Your tin was now attached to a three-foot length of wire, your 'swinger'. All you had to do now was stuff a bit of old rag into it and set it alight. As soon as it began to flame, you blew it out so that the rag merely smouldered. You then sealed the tin and set to swinging it around your head so that the rag burned fiercely. On the cold, dark nights of January and February a winter-warmer could become a thing of beauty. If you whirled it around your head for a couple of minutes your tin would turn a rich cherry-red. Whirl it even faster and it would flame like a blow-torch and make a wonderful thrumming noise.

In very cold weather a couple of Salvation Army women, 'saldossers' we called them, would go through the streets ringing a bell and off we would race to the Salvation Army Hall at the corner of Irwell Street. It was really a converted shop with the window painted green. Inside, we sat on wooden forms and sang 'Canaan's Shore' and

> Wash me in the blood of the lambkin
> And I shall be whiter than the snow.

'Food for the soul,' said the fat cheerful lady who played the piano. 'And now, food for . . .'

'THE BELLY!' we howled and lined up at the counter for our bowls of pea-soup or sticky buns and, on one occasion, helpings of Christmas pudding. Afterwards, we raced back along Irwell Street singing:

The Gang

Wash me in the water that you washed your dirty daughter
And I shall be whiter than the whitewash on the wall.

And there were the games, night games mostly, for in between getting home
from school and having an evening meal there wasn't much time for daylight
games, maybe half-an-hour before the lamplighter came round with his lighting pole. After tea was the exciting time, for then you played games like rally-o,
which went on until the last one of you had been called in for bed. I don't know
why this particular game was held in such high esteem. It was simply hide-and-
seek played in the dark. You counted out and the 'odd man out' was 'on'. He
or she stood with closed eyes and counted up to a hundred while everyone else
found a hiding place. Then the 'on' person shouted 'ready!' and began to search
for those who were hiding. There was no lack of places where you could conceal
yourself: back doorways, dustbin recesses and scores of lavatory roofs. The area
was quite extensive for it not only encompassed our back entry but the square
and the Mulgrave Street back entry too. Often the searcher and indeed those
who were hiding would spend an entire evening cut off from their companions.

It is rally-o more than any other pastime which conjures up most vividly the
winters of my childhood. Standing in the shadow of a back doorway, feeling
the cold seeping up through your boots and the hot patches of skin where
the wind has chapped the insides of your thighs; or lying on a lavatory roof,
making yourself as flat as possible so that you won't be seen against the skyline
or suddenly revealed when a kitchen door is opened and floods the yard with
gas-light. Then a cat, patrolling its beat, prowls by and stops, tail in the air at
the sight of you. 'Go away,' you whisper and after a moment it does, skirting
you with disdain. Sometimes you wonder whether the game has stopped and
everyone gone home leaving you alone. But it is the cold you remember most
and the smell of the night wind, fresh or loaded with smells from the docks, the
close flat stink of bleach, the throat-stinging smell from Broughton Copper or
the heavy, ripe smell of the brewery. And the sounds, the complaining whine
of a tramcar climbing the slow gradient of Frederick Road, the steady clank of
goods wagons from the railway yards and, in the background, the occasional
low-pitched growl of a ship's siren.

'The sun never sets on our Empire,' said Mr Small and his pointer skittered
across the map of the world like a duck on a frozen pond. 'All the parts marked
in red', he declared, 'are ours.' It's a lie, it's a lie, it's a lie, I said, but in my
head, hoping that my eyes didn't show my thoughts. It would be even worse
if I started blushing. But I knew he was lying and I felt embarrassed for him.
Even at the age of eight I found it impossible to believe that I had a part share
in his Empire. It was an incongruous notion. Really! Was it so unreasonable
to suppose that I would be wearing socks which had been darned so often that
scarcely any of the original wool was left if I owned an empire? And all that stuff
about Britain being the workshop of the world! How could anyone say that

without blushing, when the workshop had laid off three million of its workers? You had only to walk out of our street half a mile in any direction to realise that the workshop was just an old ruin. Sure, it had once been great, that is if greatness is measured by the amount of wealth and poverty created.

It had once been a settlement on the side of a clear, purling stream until Vikings sacked it in 999 A.D. The survivors replaced the burnt thatch and made their mud-and-wattle walls a few inches thicker than the old ones and in the course of time the settlement became a village whose people paid tithes to the church and taxes to the earl who owned them. And time passed and the village became a town and the fields of wheat and barley disappeared under the new crop of mill chimneys, pit-winding gear and factories.

And, of course, there was our street and its thousands of duplicates, clones of clones derived from a glimpse of a future battery farm in some poultry farmer's nightmare. And the mines, mills, factories and the regimented rows of brick hutches needed people. So they came in their hundreds, thousands and tens of thousands, the farm-servants, the ploughmen without fields or horses, the shepherds who had become sheep, the sowers without seeds, reapers without harvests, village artisans without tools. Out of the small-holdings, hamlets and villages, from the poorhouses of rural Lancashire, Cheshire, Derbyshire; from Wales and Ireland and Scotland they came, Burke's 'swinish multitudes', Dr Johnson's 'rabble, the lazy, sottish and brutish mob'. That is how 18th- and 19th-century gentlefolk perceived us. 20th-century Tories had added the term 'workshy' to the description.

My mother used to come home from doing a day's charring in a big house and she would tell us how the lady of the house had talked about 'the workshy' and 'the won't-works' with her bridge-playing friends. Years later I asked her how she had managed to contain her temper on these occasions.

'Och!' she said, 'they dinnae ken ony better. In my younger days I'd hae flared up and breenged oot o' the hoose. But they werenae worth it. I expect they were nice enough, really. It was just that they didnae ken onything; they were just plain ignorant.'

'But surely, to *clean* for such people . . .'

'I wasnae cleaning for them. I was cleaning for you and your faither.'

Maybe that was what was wrong with Mr Small, just plain ignorance. He certainly didn't know much about his pupils or the way they lived. If he had, he would surely have avoided mentioning *our* Empire quite so often. The fact is, you could live in Higher Broughton or Prestwich or Broughton Park and know as little about what went on in Lower Broughton as about the customs and practices of Indians living in the Gran Chaco of Venezuela. Come to think of it, I expect the Gran Chaco has been studied a great deal more thoroughly than Lower Broughton, Hanky Park or Ordsall.

The fact that the sun never set on our great Empire didn't prevent it from setting in our street with monotonous regularity. Its daily going-down coincided with the visit of the lamplighter and his pole. When we were still young enough to believe that certain adults possessed magical powers, we used to cluster round the lamp post at our end of the street in anticipation of his coming. One of us would take up a position by the stone posts and report his progress across the square. Then he would appear round the end of the street and we would make way for him to begin the nightly miracle. He was a short, silent man who accepted our homage with grave dignity. He wore a ship-captain's hat with a silver badge of the corporation's arms and a black oiled coat of the type worn nowadays by fish-wardens and clerks who like their clothes to suggest owner-ship of a substantial grouse-shoot in Wester Ross. The moment when his pole entered the glass cage of the lamp was the high point of the ceremony. We would stand there with upturned faces holding our breath until the moment when the gauze mantle was suddenly suffused with light. We would then follow him to the lamp post halfway down the street and then to the one at the top of the street and all the time no word would be spoken. Then he would go into the next street and we would resume whatever game we had been playing before his arrival. What did he do for the rest of the day? Ideally, he should have retired to a cave or to the Scythian rock where his father still lay bound. I still like to think of him as one of the children of light, a priest or at least a torchbearer in the service of Prometheus. The very opposite of Innes, who was really a creature of the shades.

Innes was the district knocker-up and the most consistently irascible human being I have ever known. Perhaps it was his occupation which made him so short-tempered. Half past four in the morning is an unearthly hour at which to begin one's work, but that was when he started his rounds. He carried a long, flexible bamboo pole with which he rattled the bedroom windows of those on his list. The earliest risers would be the first to be so assaulted and if this didn't wake them it would be followed by a louder and more sustained burst of rat-tling accompanied by growls and curses from the enraged knocker-up: 'Get up, you lazy sod! Lying there stinking in your bed . . . Get up! Come on, you lazy bugger!' This would be repeated at decreasing intervals until the sleeper rose up and began hurling insults at the torturer. Occasionally my father would bound out of bed, throw up the window and join in the exchange of abuse: 'Shut up, you bad-tempered auld swine! Bugger off! Why the hell don't you go and droon yourself, you half-witted auld bugger!' When the right pitch of fury had been reached, the window would close with a crash and all would be silent again for perhaps ten or fifteen minutes, then a door would open and close, then another and another. And the sound of iron-rimmed clogs and hob-nailed boots would rattle down the street. In half-an-hour or a little less, the entire scene would be repeated, though this time the sound of clogs and hob-nailed boots would be heavier. After the half-past-six contingent had been wakened, the clogs and boots sounded like an army marching at the double. After them the clogs and bluchers gave way to the lighter sound of boots and shoes as the clerks and warehousemen got on their way. In winter, the clattering clogs and hob-nailed boots always sounded louder than in the summer months. I would lie there in the icy cold bedroom with the cold oven-shelves sending their chill through the length of old flannel in which they'd been wrapped the night before. I'd lie there dreading the moment when I would have to get up and feel the cold linoleum against my feet and I would drift off to sleep again as the reluctant dawn crept across the sky, grey and featureless or mottled like the belly of a dead mackerel.

Innes' working hours were awkward perhaps, but they were short and by eight o'clock he was finished for the day – a three-and-a-half-hour working day! Then he went to bed and slept till three, after which he got up and read the paper and quarrelled with his wife. Well, not exactly *with* his wife but *at* his wife. Mrs Innes was one of the street's official deathwatchers, a role she shared with Mrs Evans, another of our neighbours. They had taken it upon themselves to keep informed about the state of their neighbours' health and if they were seen entering a house together then one knew that the grim reaper had struck there. My father had a horror of them both and always referred to them as The Ghouls. And yet they performed a useful function in the street. They washed and prepared the dead for burial and apparently did so with great efficiency. Perhaps it was the barely restrained eagerness with which they approached the unfortunate household that provoked my father's antipathy.

The ritual of death and burial was observed with proper solemnity and pomp. After the washing and laying out of the corpse, the undertakers would arrive with the coffin and neighbours would stand at the doors, wiping their eyes with their aprons and discussing the departed in hushed voices. Then The Ghouls would let it be known that the corpse was ready for viewing. Neighbours would then call at the bereaved house and spend a few minutes at the side of the open coffin. The real ceremony of viewing, however, took place in the evening when those who had a job came home from work. Then family after family would troop round the coffin and murmur their words of sympathy. During the critical days of illness and death, and right up until the day after the funeral, neighbours undertook to shop, wash and sometimes even clean for the bereaved family.

On the day of the funeral, every house in the street would have its blinds drawn and Mrs Innes would take the wreath, purchased by the pennies contributed by neighbours, from door to door. Then the hearse would arrive, a magnificent bed of brass, steel and polished wood, enclosed in a case of glass, drawn by four glorious black horses each with a feathery black plume tossing at its head. The undertakers, too, were resplendent in black frock coats and tall hats each with its black cockade. Behind, there were three or four horse-drawn carriages for the mourners. This is what a lifetime's pennies paid into the burial society bought you: a funeral worthy of a prince. For once in your life (well, not exactly in your life) you were *somebody*.

Now the coffin is brought out on the shoulders of the undertaker's men and slid onto its metal bed. Then the wreaths are brought out and the coffin is smothered in them. Now the mourners are filling the other coaches, the women in black and the men wearing black armbands on their left arms and carrying their hats in respect. The neighbours standing at the doors weep and say, 'Isn't it lovely?' between their sobs. After the burial service the mourners return to the house of the dead and partake of a cold collation: ham and tongue with pickles and a seed cake baked by Mrs Drummond.

There were, as one would expect, variations on the routine. When Jimmy Hobbs' baby died, for instance, the viewing of the corpse was done quite differently. There was no money for a proper funeral so Jimmy lifted two wooden boards from a building site, sawed, sandpapered and fashioned them into a rough coffin for his child. The lid had a glass plate through which one could look on the tiny wizened face of the corpse. For three or four days prior to the burial the coffin stood upright by the Hobbs' front door, with a saucer balanced on top of it, into which neighbours and passers-by put their contributions towards the funeral expenses.

'What's your name?'
'Baldy Bane.'
'Where do you live?'
'Down the drain.'
'What number?'
'Cucumber.'

We lived at Number 37. On our left was Number 35 where the Drummonds lived. The Caldwells lived at Number 39. Harriet and Arthur Caldwell had brought three children into the world: Edwin, Laura and young Art, (the baby of the family). Arthur Senior, the breadwinner, was an unskilled labourer who, in spite of widespread unemployment, was rarely out of a job. He was a short, compact man, surprisingly strong, with a deep gravelly voice which sounded like a smothered shout. He quarrelled continuously with his wife and threatened his offspring with hair-raising and sometimes picturesque punishments, such as 'I'll tan your arse till you can fry sausages on it' or 'I'll break every bone in your body. I'll bash you to a pulp. I'll tie your feet round your neck and stick an orange in your mouth.' He was really the gentlest of men and my father observed on many occasions, 'They kids think the sun shines oot o' his arse.'

The loudness of his speaking voice was matched by his actions. He seemed to be constantly moving the furniture or knocking nails into this or that wall. On Saturday nights he would come home from The Cross Keys in fine fettle and after a meal of fish and chips followed by some light-hearted skirmishing with his wife he would tramp up the uncarpeted stairs and we would hear him grunting and talking to himself as he undressed. My father, lying there in the darkness, would say to my mother, 'And now comes the Saturday night serenade.' Sure enough, we would hear through the thin wall a reverberant rattle that sounded like a long roll played on a kettledrum. 'He sounds as if he's had

The west side of Coburg Street[6]
31 Arkroyd & wife ('pisser') and daughter Pattie
33 Evans (with Mrs Innes: one of street's official death watchers)
35 Drummond, George & Mary (son: Alfred = 'Killus')
37 Miller, Will & Betsy (*4th house from bottom* = top of lower end!)
39 Caldwell, Arthur & Harriet (children: Edwin, Laura & Art)
41 Shaw, Frank ('Black Catholics')
59 Farrow, Joe & Gwen (Joe was disabled at copper works; childless couple)
The east side of Coburg Street
28 Seymour (a large family living in the upper half of street opp Strickland's shop)
30 Strickland's front-parlour shop (daughter: Kathy Strickland)
32 Hewitson (Mrs Hewitson = a widow living with her son Teddy)
34 Lawson (one year only) followed by The Acrobats (Hungarian Circus Act)
36 Yearsley (living oppisite the Miller family – regular job possibly in textiles)
38 Innes (the district knocker up; wife = a death watcher, also opposite the Millers)
40 Tattersall: window cleaner with two sons: Harold and Teddy ('Snotty')
56 Livesey: furnace worker at papermill ('top' end of street – Ewan means 'bottom'!)
   The Fenton's Toffee Shop (see the Fenton girls) was also at this end of the street.
   Others in the street are Needham; Hopwood; Cray & Carmichael; Tippet

a skinful tonight,' my mother would say as Arthur relieved himself into the galvanised iron bucket he kept under the bed. My father would bang on the wall and shout, 'For Christ's sake, get nearer the bloody target! All you need is a fife and you could lead the bloody Orange Walk!'

'I'm just having a piss,' Arthur would say, apologetically.

'For Christ's sake, put the bloody thing away and let's get some sleep.' The springs of the bed would creak as Arthur lay down and sometimes, after a few minutes of silence, we would hear the hoarse whisper again: 'Will . . .? Are you awake?'

'Of course I'm bloody well awake. How the hell could I be anything else with you pissin' awa' like the bloody Niagara Falls?'

'Will . . .'

'What?'

'Piss off!' I would wait for my father's chuckle and then settle down to sleep.

Ours was the fourth house from the bottom end of the street. On our right were the Drummonds and next to them the Evanses and then the Arkroyds.

Across the street in the house opposite to the Arkroyds lived a young couple called the Lawsons. Ronnie, their boy, had inherited his parents' cheerful nature and even though he was a year younger than Duckfoot, who was the youngest member of our gang, we regarded him as one of us – well, not exactly a *member* of the gang but near enough. To celebrate his seventh birthday we were all invited to a party at his house where we drank Vimto and Tizer and ate helpings of jelly and custard and sticky buns and cream cakes. As far as I can remember that was the only time that anyone in our street held a birthday party. It wasn't long afterwards that Ronnie took ill with diphtheria and died.

The Lawsons didn't stay long in the street after that. They moved away, to Canada or New Zealand or one of those places. Their house was now occupied by a family of acrobats. That was our name for them, The Acrobats. They toured round the country with a travelling circus and in between tours stayed home 'and washed their clothes', as my mother used to say. The father of the family was a Hungarian and perhaps that is why nobody ever referred to them by name, just The Acrobats. They had a fifteen-year-old daughter, Ella, who took part in the family's acrobatic displays. There were also two small children who, when their parents were on tour, were looked after by their grandmother, a very brown and very tough old lady who rarely opened her mouth to speak and who was known to us as The Dummy. At times, the circus would be laid up or disbanded for three or four weeks and The Acrobats would return to our street and delight us all by practising on the pavement outside their house. Once during a summer break they climbed up on to the roof and ran a rope between two chimney stacks on the opposite sides of the street. When Mrs Whatever-her-name-was walked along that rope using a clothes-prop for a balancing pole, the entire street turned out to applaud. After that, the big lads took to whistling and making clucking noises whenever the lady walked down the street. One day they were doing it when The Acrobat came out of his front door followed by an enormous man who had to stoop to get through the doorway. They stood there for a moment and the whistling stopped, then they both began to walk towards the lads. They had only taken a couple of steps when the lads took to their heels and ran. They never whistled after her again. 'Just look and enjoy,' said Basher Docherty, who worked at the coalyard.

Mrs Needham was easily the most noisily patriotic individual in the entire street. My mother called her Mrs John Bull. She was an obsessive flag-waver; birthdays of the most obscure royals were signalised by the unfurling of an enormous Union Jack, and at elections the Needham's doors and windows were resplendent with the blue posters and leaflets of the Tories. She had another obsession: gambling. She played the horses. Her whole day was structured around the 2:30 at Aintree or the 3 o'clock at Irwell Castle. Bob Needham, her husband, worked for the railway as a carter. He was a keen trade unionist and treasurer for his union branch. He kept the union funds in a small, lacquered tin cash-box. In the spring of 1927, Mrs Needham opened the box with a bread knife and laid the union money on a dead-cert, an outsider guaranteed to win at enormous odds. It was a non-starter. When Bob Needham discovered that the union funds had disappeared, he 'went wrong in the mind', to use my mother's phrase. He waited until Saturday morning when his wife went out shopping and then proceeded to kill himself. He was very methodical. He cut a length of rope from a clothesline, made a noose in one end of it and fastened it around his neck. The other end he fastened to one of the rollers of the clothes mangle. After turning the handle so that all the slack of the rope was taken up, he gave it a sharp turn and broke his neck.

The people who lived in the upper half of our street didn't seem to have many children, or rather only a few of them did. There were the Finns who lived almost at the top of the street; they had two girls and a boy but they were much older than us and the girls were already working. Mike Finn had been working at Broughton Copper but lost his job during a rationalisation drive. Then there were the Glovers – father, mother, two sons and four daughters. Apart from young Harry and my erstwhile love Jenny, the rest of the Glover children were grown up.

Almost at the bottom of the street lived the Hewitsons. Mrs Hewitson had been widowed when her son Teddy was only a year old. Her husband had died for Field Marshal Haig in the Ypres salient. His widow worked hard to bring her son up decent, at first as a card-room operative in a cotton mill and then as a cleaner in St Boniface's School. She was a devout Catholic. Every room in the house had its statuettes of the Virgin, embroidered sacred hearts and even the lobby sported a crucifix. Teddy was taught to toe the religious line. In addition to attending St Boniface's school, he was up every Sunday morning for early morning mass and he rarely missed an afternoon or evening service. When he was seen wearing a surplice and gown and carrying a lighted candle in the Whit

Monday procession, his position in the gang became somewhat insecure. At first he ignored our jibes and jeers but when individual derogatory comments swelled to a mocking chorus he was forced to take action. After a week of fights in which noses were bloodied and eyes blackened, his right to be regarded as a leading member of the gang was reaffirmed.

Round about the time I was thirteen I lost contact with him. The gang was beginning to disintegrate. The older ones among us were leaving school and, if they were lucky, getting jobs and making new relationships. When I next saw Teddy he was doing battle with the police in an unemployed demonstration. I met him again several months later when we walked together on a hunger march to the Lancashire County offices in Lancaster. He told me that his mother had died and that, after Lancaster, he was to visit relatives in Sunderland. 'After that', he said, 'I'm going to Australia.'

'How're you going to manage that?'

'I'll find a way,' he said.

By this time I had become a dedicated member of the class-conscious pro-letariat and I suggested that he really ought to consider staying and playing a leading role in the struggle against the system.

'Stay here?' he said incredulously. 'In this rotten hole? You must be kidding.'

I hope he found his way to Australia. He deserved a time in the sun. There have been times when I wished that I had gone with him.

The Strickland's shop was next door to the Hewitson's and formed one of the corners of the square. Mrs Strickland's daughter, Katherine, was an adopted child who suffered from her mother's regular diatribes against the 'badly brought-up brats' whose noisy games of football in the square were, she said, driving her off her head. She complained about us endlessly to anyone who would listen and three or four times every day she would stand at the opening to the square and belabour us with shrill imprecations. We disliked her intensely and some of the dislike rubbed off, occasionally, on her daughter. The tapeworm was another black mark against Kathy. When she was about eight or nine she developed a voracious appetite and after several visits to The Abattoir she was delivered of an enormous tapeworm which Mrs Strickland proudly displayed in a jar of surgical spirit. It bore a small label with the date and dimensions of the worm. The figure of eighteen feet tugs at my memory. Could a tapeworm attain such a monstrous length? I may be imagining the length but I am not imagining the feeling of revulsion which overcame me whenever I found myself in the proximity of Kathy Strickland. It wasn't until I had left school that I realised how foolish I had been. I was coming home after a long day's work in the garage when I saw her coming towards me and suddenly realised how beautiful she was. She smiled and said 'Hello' as we passed. Years later, when walking through the National Gallery, I was suddenly struck with the realisation of having lived the first twelve years of my life in the same street as the subject of Botticelli's *La Primavera*.

These were my parents' neighbours – the men we ran after asking for cigarette-cards as they walked from the street to their places of work or the Labour Exchange, the women for whom we ran errands, in whose houses we played when it rained, whose washing we endangered with our balls and piggies, who chased us away from their windows, who swore at us and whose watchful eyes tried to keep us from harm. We heard their stories piecemeal as we played in the front rooms when the evenings were too cold and dark for us to run in the streets. We were as familiar with these instalments of domestic dramas, told at mealtimes or overheard from washday gossips as we were with our own lives . . . and what we heard, we shared with each other. We were a gang after all. One for all and all for one.

'Did you hear . . .' said Tolly.

'My mam said that Hip-and-Gee-Whoa . . .' said Seghead.

'I heard Mr Needham say that . . .' Teddy Hewitson said.

And so the tales were pieced together, anecdotes crystallised, legends created, myths born. And you yourself were becoming part of a tale, a myth, a legend which would be told at some future time by one or all of your companions. And as they told it, they would remember more and more incidents which they hadn't remembered for a long time. How Seghead once broke a broom-handle over young Callaghan's head; how Edwin Caldwell threatened to tan his mother's arse; and of the three-day battle that Tolly fought with Killus.

Tolly was my friend, my special friend. No, he was more than that. He was my *veray parfit gentil knight,* my patron saint, my idol. He lived in Mulgrave Street next to the Dows and was the youngest of five children, three girls and two boys. His father had died in a bizarre accident while working for an undertaker. He was driving a hearse drawn by a pair of horses which took fright at the demented barking of a stray dog. Mr Godwin was thrown from the high driving-seat and one of his feet became entangled with the reins. He was dragged along the road for a considerable distance and then the maddened horses turned and trampled him to death. His wife, a short, pugnacious and iron-willed woman, maintained her family by going out and cleaning a large suite of offices attached to an electrical components factory. When she had finished there she went on to the glue works where she sorted and graded bones all day.

Tolly was the runt of the family, small, compact and very fast in his movements. He was rather taciturn, but when he spoke he did so with effect. He wore clogs and, as running was his natural mode of locomotion, he could usually be heard approaching from afar. Though spare in build, there were few who could match him in a rough-and-tumble and in a race he was always first among the first. His clogs and celluloid collar were the first things you noticed. For the rest he habitually wore jerseys and short pants that were too big for him. His mother bought them at jumble sales and he wore them winter and summer until they were so full of holes that their original shape was no longer recognisable. Then they were replaced by identical substitutes.

The Gang

When I look back at myself and my childhood contemporaries I see us as a constantly moving group of boys and girls whose voices are raised in perpetual clamour, a group which forms, scatters and reforms like quicksilver, a group which asserts its identity by shouting, yelling, screaming, laughing, jeering, chanting, singing and weeping. All but Tolly. He was the quiet one. I don't believe I ever heard him cry or yell like the rest of us. He ruled by silence. This undersized, underfed child with the pinched features and the celluloid collar was our leader. He didn't need to give commands or make threats or promises. He ruled by example. His reign lasted for almost eight years, from the time we were both about five years old until a short time before we were fourteen. He lost his position by the time-honoured process of physical combat.

His opponent, Killus, had been a loyal follower for as long as any of us and if he had found Tolly's leadership irksome or oppressive at any time he had managed to conceal it. But in the course of the last twelve months or so Killus had changed. He had shot up and shed almost all his child's skin. The metamorphosis was not entirely complete but it was well advanced.

A fight in the street was always an exciting business but the battle between Tolly and Killus was in a special category. For one thing, they were friends, members of the same gang; and for another, they were both renowned scrappers and neither was expected to give any quarter. Fights were usually spontaneous affairs and the almost continuous high-pitched yelling of the spectators was generally a signal for adults to come and separate the combatants. Not on this occasion. There was a tacit agreement that the fight should be conducted in silence and, incredibly, it was. The only sound to be heard was the smack and thud of fists on flesh, the heavy breathing, the grunting of the two fighters and the occasional groan from the watchers. The fight moved backwards and forwards in the square and up the back entry until it was interrupted by the cries of women calling their children home for tea. The fight was then stopped, the fighters wiped the blood from their faces and, having agreed to continue the next day, went off to their evening meal.

After school the following day, it began again and, as on the previous evening, continued till tea-time. On the third night the fighters continued the battle until both of them were so weary that they could scarcely lift up their hands. The fourth night was decisive. They fought until darkness began to fall, both of them bruised and bloody, their hair plastered to their faces with sweat. Killus's superior weight and height were just too much for Tolly. He was a head shorter than his rival and maybe a stone lighter. His speed and agility had, at first, stood him in good stead but now he was utterly exhausted and moved like a sleepwalker. He had taken terrible punishment. His face was bruised and cut in several places – both eyes were swollen and he had lost a tooth. Finally both hands fell to his sides, a sign that he accepted defeat, but Killus was caught up in the rhythm of destruction and continued showering him with punches.

When we pulled them apart, Tolly had reached his limit. He could barely stand upright and his face looked as if it had been caught in a machine. I remember feeling anguish such as I had never experienced before. I think it was at that moment that I conceived a disgust for physical violence that has stayed with me all my life. I ran into the house and got a bucket of water and a towel and then set about trying to clean Tolly up. We were all very quiet as we helped him to cross the square to his back door. He was so tired that he had difficulty in mounting the step to his back yard. We escorted him to the scullery door, terrified that his mother would appear, but when the door opened it was Elsie who stood there framed in gaslight. It shone straight out on to her battered brother and she gave a loud cry. Then she cried, 'Savages! Bloody savages!' and pulled him into the kitchen. It was the end of the fight, the end of Tolly's reign as our leader and, had I but known it, the end of my childhood. That night I lay in bed and cried for my friend, knowing that nothing would ever be the same again.

7

The Tangenital Mind

At first the street – or rather that small section of the street which is overlooked by your front window – is your playground. From there you are never out of your mother's sight. As you get older your area of play gets bigger; it soon includes the entire street, then the back entry as well, then the square and the croft. The route to Farmer's chip-shop becomes familiar and you could find your way blindfold to the Co-op and Cooper's and Pegram's on Lower Broughton Road. It's further still to Blackfriar's Road and the Saturday matinee at the Victoria and the Tower Cinema takes you through new territory. In fact, Saturday is a busy day. In the morning you have to go to the Co-op for your mam's bread and Mrs Yearsley's shopping. It's always crowded on Saturday morning and you have to stand in line and wait your turn for the freshly baked loaves still warm from the oven. Two square loaves for us and a cottage loaf for Mrs Y. Five pounds of potatoes and a large swede, please. The potatoes come bouncing down the chute making a noise like suppressed thunder. Staggering home with two large shopping bags bumping against your knees, stopping now and then to pick off a little crust from a loaf. Lovely crisp bread, the staff of life they call it. Three ha'pence from Mrs Yearsley and now Hip-and-Gee-Whoa has given me a list of her groceries. Back again to the Co-op. No bread this time – she bakes her own. Two whole pence from her! My dad's home from work when I get back and he gives me another twopence. I'm really in the money today. I show him my fivepence ha'penny proudly and he gives me another ha'penny to make it up to sixpence. Time for lunch. Cabbage and ribs, my favourite. See if any of the rib bones can be used as rickers. 'They're the wrong kind,' says my mother. 'Beef rib bones are what you need.'

Killus and Seghead are kicking a ball round the square and three or four other members of the gang are comparing cigarette-cards. Tolly's not arrived yet. Saturday's a heavy day for him. They're a big family and he has to do the shopping for them all. It usually involves him in making three trips to the Co-op and sometimes even more. Why don't we go and fetch him, somebody suggests. It's what we would do if it was any other member of the gang. You'd just knock on the front door and ask if Seghead or Woodsy was coming out.

But nobody ever uses the Godwin's front door. Even *they* don't use it. They come and go, using the back door all the time. I expect that is why we regard them as people who live in our street. To knock on the Godwin's back door would involve walking the length of their back yard in full view of the kitchen window. The fact is, we are all afraid of Mrs Godwin. Even Tolly's afraid of her and he's really tough. Still, it's time we were off. Episode Three of *The Branded Four* is being shown today and the earlier we get there the further back we can sit. Once the lights go out people start throwing things or flicking paper pellets and if you are at the front then you're the most likely target.

We drift towards Tolly's back door. The yard door is open so we hang around in the hope that Tolly will look out of the window. Nothing happens, so after a few moments Galty puts two fingers in his mouth and produces the shrill whistle which is the gang's secret call. It does the trick. Tolly appears at the window, white-faced and sullen. We recognise the look. He's had a belting.

'It's his mam,' Diggy Dow says. 'She's been barneying all morning. Probably got pissed last night.' Tolly comes out and joins us. He has a new bruise on his left cheekbone.

'I see your ma's been at you again,' says Killus.

'Shut up.'

'It's time we were off,' someone else says.

'I can't go', says Tolly, 'no money.'

'We've got enough between us,' says Biff Jarman. There is a chorus of agreement.

'No', says Tolly, 'I don't fancy the pictures today.'

'Two serials', Tatty says, *'The Masked Rider* and *The Branded Four.'* Tolly weakens and we grab him by the arm before he changes his mind again. We're off to the Tower.

Summer excursions to the Mucky Mountains, Kersal Moor and Mere Woods serve to extend our territory even more. The visits that you make with your parents to their friends' houses don't really help you to get to know the town properly. They lack adventure, the spirit of exploration. All you get to know is the route, the particular stretch of pavement or road between A and B. When you're on your own or with the gang it's different. There are dozens of side streets to be entered, scores of back entries to be probed, all kinds of nooks and crannies to be investigated. There are walls to be climbed, gateposts to be jumped, kerbs to be hopped. There are lucky and unlucky paving stones, grids to be peered through, stones to be thrown and tin cans to be kicked. There are walls to be chalked on, gable-ends against which balls can be bounced, shop-windows to be looked at, dog-eared posters to be torn down. There is a high wall on the way to the Tower, along the top of which broken bottles have been cemented. They line the wall like a row of irregular green teeth. Automatically, you collect stones as you walk so that when you reach the wall you can spend a few minutes throwing them at the jagged glass. After all, it's only broken glass and it's been put there to hurt somebody, so we're doing that somebody a good turn by breaking it into smaller and smaller pieces. That's what I mean by knowing places, not just the route but the special qualities of each section of the route, the pitfalls, hindrances, attractions, the smells which tell you whether you are in the vicinity of a cotton mill, a brewery, a paper-mill, an engineering factory, a coal mine; the noise of metal screaming under the blade of a vertical lathe, of massed spindles turning, of a steam-hammer thumping, of steam hissing, of shunting-engines clanking, the touch of flagstones under your knees, worn brick under your hands.

We discovered the docks and, in summer, found our way to Trafford Park and the wastelands bordering the Ship Canal. Most of all, though, we discovered the park and the 'rec', as we called the Peel Park recreation ground. At first, going to the park was regarded as a major expedition, but in the course of time it became a journey that any of us could have made with our eyes closed. During the school holidays we got into the habit of going there day after day. Our route took us past St Andrews and it was always a pleasure to run along the top of the school wall led by Seghead and Tolly imitating Mickey Thomas. Then stopping on the bridge to throw stones into the Irwell and then to the rec to play interminable games of cricket or to race along the broken footpaths looking for adventure. When we reached the ripe old age of eleven or twelve we would whistle at girls and make what we considered to be witty remarks on their appearance. This one was narrow-backed, that one was duck-arsed or hen-toed. If we saw a red-head we shouted, 'Ginger, you're barmy!' To one who looked at us with disdain we shouted 'Fur coat and no drawers!' Or we'd leer and ask 'How about a slice off the joint?', to which the stock reply was 'Go on, it's filleted!'

Our knowledge of sexual matters was, to say the least, sketchy. We knew that babies grew inside our mothers' bellies, we had a vague notion of how they got there, but we were ignorant as to how they found their way into the outside world. For a time we believed that the belly button was the point of exit but that explanation gave way eventually to the knife theory. It was obvious that the midwife carried a sharp knife in her little black bag, just like a doctor, and with this she made a slit in our mother's side out of which we crawled into the world. By the time we had been at school for a few months most of us had been put right about the details.

The four-letter words did not have the same wide currency that they have today, at least not in our circle. I don't remember hearing the word *fuck*, for example, more than half a dozen times throughout my entire childhood. The first time I ever heard it used was by a woman in a street fight. It was a Saturday night and a group of us had been exploring on the far side of Strangeways and had landed up at Victoria Station. After spending some time playing with the penny printer, a machine which for the price of a penny enabled you to emboss your name on a thin aluminium strip, we were on our way home, descending the raised station approach, when we heard shouts. Peering through the balustrades down at the street below we saw two enormous women engaged in battle. They were lit by a street lamp and the scene looked for all the world as if it had been staged. A half-circle of silent spectators stood well outside the rim of light while the two women fought. They were naked to the waist and their huge, pendulous breasts swung before them like sacks of flour as they punched, kicked, raked each other's flesh with their nails and tore at each other's hair. In between their grunts and screams and the slap of fists on flesh, they called each other 'fucking whores' and 'tuppeny gets'. It was an ugly scene and it became even uglier when a passer-by attempted to interfere. Both women turned on him and in a moment he was on the ground and they were kicking him. A policeman appeared at the end of the street and the women withdrew in the opposite direction.

The next time I heard the word was from my mother and I was shocked beyond words. Betsy throughout her life had a somewhat Calvinistic attitude to sexual matters and she never, as far as I knew, used any of the four-letter words. So to suddenly hear her say 'fuck' left me paralysed with shock. The scene is burned into my memory. It is a Saturday morning in summer and my father has just come home from work and is washing in the kitchen. Tolly and I creep in the front door and hide behind the leatherette settee intending to leap up and surprise my father when he comes through for his lunch. My mother comes in and takes his tatties-and-mince out of the oven. She's telling him about the fight they've been having next door at the Caldwells'.

'What was it about this time?' my father asks as he comes in drying himself.

'According to Arthur, Old Bill accused him of messing about with Bella.'

'Christ! He must be aff his held.'

'They were making a terrible racket,' said my mother as she slid the hot plate onto the table.

'They're aye making a racket,' observed my father. They go on talking while Tolly and I crouch there, hugging ourselves gleefully and thinking how surprised they'll be when they discover that we have been present throughout the entire conversation. Then I hear my mother say something which transforms my glee into hideous embarrassment.

'Arthur was at the back door looking for sympathy. He was in a right state. Indignant! He said, before I'll stick my cock in that dirty old bag I would fuck an auld rug!'

The thought that Tolly was hearing what I was hearing filled me with shame. Terrified that she would continue in the same vein, I leaped from my place of concealment and cried, 'We're here!' Then Tolly stood up too and we stood there with foolish smiles of anguish on our faces. It was a moment of endless silence. My mother turned so white that I thought she was going to faint. 'Oh my God!' she said. My father banged his fist on the table so that the cups and saucers rattled.

'You've no right to be hiding in here!' he shouted. Then he recovered himself and quite gently said, 'Never mind, it's no' a tragedy,' and shooed us out of the room. Neither Tolly nor I ever said a word about it to each other. We were too embarrassed. Indeed, there was constraint between us from that time on.

The word *cunt* was even more rare. I only once remember it being used by one of my companions and it elicited a negative response. 'You must never use that word,' the prohibition was delivered in a thrilling whisper with all the solemnity of a religious exorcism. ''That word is an insult to your mother.' The idea of insulting one's mother was anathema. From that time on the word was taboo.

While we were at the Junior School we were probably still in a state of innocence. All that altered when we changed over to 'the big school'. The two most direct influences for change were Ernie Worth (the masturbator) and the Old Testament. About a quarter of the boys in the school were Jewish and, consequently, were not obliged to participate in the dreary religious instruction to which the less fortunate Christians were subjected. Instead, they were given Bibles and told to read the Old Testament. Naturally we were envious, but the Jewish lads took pity on us and copied out some of the juicier bits for us. As a result, our sexual terminology became distinctly Elizabethan in tone for quite a while. You no longer talked about tossing yourself off or bashing your bishop or pulling your pud, but of spilling your seed; and for a time the story of David's foreskin-gathering exploits among the Philistines was the main topic of schoolyard conversation and the source of scores of new jokes.

Books played an enormously influential role in developing my sexual awareness. *The Arabian Nights* with its nubile maidens, snowy breasts with rosy nipples peering through filmy gauzes, silken thighs parting like startled trout, eyes as dark as olives and lips as sweet as pomegranate juice . . . how I envied Haroun el Raschid! And there was an old canvas-bound copy of *Thais* by Charles Kingsley, and several orange-bound copies of short stories by Anatole France. I was entering a period when every book that came into my hands seemed to offer new sexual stimulus.

The sexual consciousness of the gang was progressing as well. One of the most radical alterations took place when I was sick in bed. I had fallen off the parapet of a railway bridge onto my head and was severely concussed. Three weeks later when I was back in circulation I discovered that I had missed taking part in a group initiation ceremony of tremendous significance. My companions talked of nothing else and what with the winks, significant gestures and veiled references to horses and bareback-riding, I had the distinct feeling that I was no longer in the gang.

It was the Fenton girls who were the cause of it all. Their father was the new owner of the toffee shop at the top of the street. There were three of them: big, blonde girls, Gloria, Stephanie and Jill. Gloria was the oldest and the leader in most things, though when it came to initiating our gang in the delights of sex, the other two needed no encouragement. Their method was original and had the virtue of combining play with education. They had come to the street in the early days of winter when the game of rally-o was in season. Our dark streets and alleys were perfect territory for such a pastime. The girls joined in for a couple of games and then Gloria pronounced it dull. It needed pepping up, she said. So the three girls made new rules. Could we say that they . . . adapted the game? With the new rules, the girls went into hiding and the boys, all of them, were 'on'. The first one to find a girl was allowed to put his hand between her legs. If he found another girl immediately afterwards then she took him in her hand and masturbated him.

Apparently this game, which the boys found so exciting, palled on the girls after a short time and they persuaded the gang to join them in breaking into the coalyard. Once inside they all stripped off and took turns wrestling with each other. There was a full moon and the scene must have been beautiful. Woodsy described it as 'weird. It was really weird.' There was some argument as to which of the girls released the old horse but there was no doubt which of them leapt on its back and rode it round the yard. It was Stephanie, a fourteen-year-old tow-haired beauty who everyone agreed was an absolute belter. Oh, to have been there on that magical night! Sheherezade's tales were fine, but this was real. And I wasn't there! Had I known what was happening, I am sure I would have risen from my sick bed and made my way to the coalyard. But I lay there while a hundred yards away a naked nymph rode bareback through a night of silver. Mrs Galt looked through her back-bedroom window and couldn't believe her eyes. There was her son, naked, with a naked girl riding on his shoulders. She sounded the alert. The Saturnalia ended abruptly with scandalised parents dragging their offspring home through the moonlit street.

For several weeks the girls were not allowed out of the house except to go to school escorted by their mother. Some of the big boys haunted the vicinity of the shop in the hope of establishing contact and some of the gang took to slipping pencilled notes under the shop door. Mr Fenton collected a number of these scrawled declarations of passion and brought them out one midday when we were playing football in the street. He walked into the middle of the game, tore the notes into small pieces and threw them into the air. Then, without saying a word, he stalked back to his shop. Whatever punishment had been meted out to the girls was effective. Were they really tamed or was their demureness merely a facade behind which their wildness still slumbered? Yes, they really did look demure, as if butter wouldn't melt in their mouths. Even when they were allowed out alone they refused to acknowledge any of their old playmates and every effort to involve them in conversation fell on deaf ears. After a few weeks we started using the shop again, always in the hope that one day the girls would be there. They never were. The following year the Fentons moved away, leaving behind a dozen thwarted adolescents with enough memories to furnish them with a lifetime's erotic dreams.

Erotic dreams were causing me some embarrassment at this time. Quite regularly I would wake up in the morning feeling the sheets wet and cold around my loins and I took to making my own bed so that my mother wouldn't see the tell-tale spots of hardened sheet. I tried taking a handkerchief to bed with me and tucking it round my private parts but it always seemed to end up around my feet. Sometimes an extraneous noise would waken me out of a dream of incredible sexual exploits and I would close my eyes and will myself back into a world where scores of ravishingly beautiful naked girls were queueing up to pleasure me. I told my cousin John about my wet dreams and he advised me to take a cold bath each morning. He was practising for two hours every day at the baths at the time so presumably he was talking from experience. Since we didn't have a bathroom and I lacked his motivation, I was forced to emulate our current lodger and stand under a hosepipe in our backyard. I subjected myself to this unpleasant morning ritual for more than a year and though my general health may have benefited from it, my dreams were just as frequent and as fruitful as ever.

During the greater part of my childhood my world was inhabited by our gang, girls and grown-ups. With the coming of puberty I became conscious of the fact that a section of the grown-ups were creatures of mystery who possessed bodies that were infinitely desirable. A mother, sitting on her doorstep suckling a child, was a common enough sight and one to which I was accustomed. As a spectacle it had always been completely without interest. But now it was different. I longed to touch those smooth breasts, to fondle them. There was one woman in particular who walked through my dreams scattering sexual largesse like one of those beautiful maidens in *The Arabian Nights*. She was a voluptuous Welsh girl who worked as a cook in the home of a rich jeweller in Broughton Park. My mother worked there as a charwoman and occasionally Ethel (the cook) would pay us a visit on her afternoon off. She was a young woman of startling beauty who wore her finery with style. She favoured bright-colour silks and soft cashmeres, expensive garments of which her mistress had grown tired. She moved in a cloud of perfume and for days after each of her visits our front room smelled 'like a whore's bedroom' (said my father). Once she came and leaned over me when I was sitting drawing at the table. She was wearing a loose flowered dress of some flimsy material and I could see down between her breasts to the curve of her belly. Her hair was touching my cheek and what with the nearness of all that flesh and the overwhelming smell of perfume I was driven almost mad with the need to touch her.

This sudden interest in women's breasts was a phenomenon which affected almost everyone in the gang. We were all roughly the same age. Diggy Dow was a bit older than most of us, and one or two were a little younger. Harry Glover was about four years younger, but then he wasn't actually in the gang, more a kind of hanger-on. He was too old to be considered one of the really small fry and too young to be a member of our gang. He was, however, no ordinary child. Not only was he small for his age but he was beautiful. Strangers passing through the street would sometimes stop in their tracks and exclaim, 'Just look at that beautiful little boy!' His four sisters were all pretty and Harry had been cast in the same mould. Physically he was without blemish but that beautiful form housed the soul of a rapacious money-lender. He hung around the fringes of the gang and made himself available whenever he was needed. He rarely took part in any of the seasonal games like marbles, for instance, and yet at the end of the season he generally managed to finish up owning everyone else's marbles. The same was true of cigarette-cards. If you were short of the one card which would make up a set you could rest assured that Harry would be able to get it for you. Not for nothing, of course. He would let you have it for hard cash or maybe in exchange for three or four dupes (duplicates). It didn't matter how many times these cards or marbles were exchanged they inevitably landed up in Harry's pocket. Throughout my adult life I have made a practice of leafing through the financial pages of newspapers looking for Harry's name. So far I have been disappointed. It is possible he has changed his name, of course. I have read somewhere that no one knows who owns Standard Oil. Could it be Harry?

The time came when neither cigarette-cards nor marbles held any attraction for us. We had discovered breasts and Harry, ever the opportunist, had discovered that there was gold in them thar hills. Friday night was shampoo night in the Glover household and the thought of four nubile beauties stripping to the waist to wash their hair in the kitchen sink was enough to rouse us to a fury. Harry fed our imaginations with little snippets of information about the private habits of his sisters and then, when we were practically bursting with desire, offered to let us view the scene from the comparative safety of the privy in the Glover's back yard. From there we would be able to look through the lavatory window across the yard to the kitchen window where we would 'see everything. Everything . . .' hissed Harry in a thrilling whisper, adding that it would only cost us a ha'penny each. We paid without demur and followed our curly-headed leader to the lavatory where we took turns standing on the seat and gazing wide-eyed at the exhilarating display of beautiful female flesh.

That, incidentally, wasn't Harry's first excursion into the realm of profitable viewing. He had established the ha'penny peep-show fee earlier in the year. His mother had just given birth to her sixth child and was experiencing some difficulty in giving suck to the infant. Harry came to us post-haste from the lying-in with the incredible story that the doctor was busy pumping milk from his mother's breasts. Jugs, pans, bowls, jars, anything that would hold liquid, were being filled with rich, creamy milk. For the price of a ha'penny he would lead us one by one up the stairs of his home to where, through a crack in the bedroom door, we could watch the whole operation in comfort. Those who could afford to pay were enormously impressed and for days kept the rest of us enthralled with descriptions of those enormous breasts spurting milk in all directions. A deprived childhood?

Although we gained some knowledge of the facts of life at a fairly early age and were familiar with birth, death and procreation, we knew next to nothing about homosexuality or any other kind of sexual anomaly. Men like Golden Royal Fairburn and the assistant who served you with butter and cheese at Cooper's grocery store were dismissed as *Jessies* but this was just a way of saying that they were soft and lacked masculine aggressiveness. They were still regarded as 'normal', that is as heterosexual males. Frankie Linley, who lived at the top-end of Orwell Street, was another matter altogether. He was a real 'homo'. Where did we learn the word? I don't know, but that's what we called him. Little Frankie the Homo.

He'd always been regarded as a little odd by the rest of us. He preferred playing girls' games until the girls refused to let him join in with them. They said he was too bossy. He was about seventeen when he first appeared on the street wearing lipstick and rouge. It was about the time when everyone was wearing plum-coloured suits and overcoats. Frankie had such a coat. He had altered it so that it fitted very tight around the waist and exaggerated the roll of his buttocks when he walked. He ignored our shouts of derision and the cat-calls of the big lads. That was when we started calling him a homo. Whenever he appeared in our street we would fall in behind him and imitate his mincing steps. My mother always spoke of him as if he was in the final stage of a terminal illness. 'That puir laddie, that puir demented thing.'

On one occasion a crowd of big lads chased him into the square, robbed him of his trousers and plastered his genitals with dye. They tried to repeat the 'joke' a couple of weeks later but this time Frankie was ready for them and produced a large kitchen knife from underneath his jacket, threatening to geld anyone who came near him. One or two of the more foolhardy lads made tentative moves towards him whereupon he rushed at them wildly brandishing his knife and they raced off in all directions. After that they left him strictly alone. He continued to paint his face and to dress in what was considered to be a thoroughly outrageous manner. He would sail down the street refusing to be intimidated by our puerile insults, the big lads' silent hatred and the grown-ups' disapproval. With his peroxided hair, his painted face with its large nose and his slightly bandy legs he should have been a figure of fun and I suppose that in a way he was – but he had a kind of absurd gallantry which lent him dignity.

Our treatment of Little Frankie, even at its worst, was nothing compared with the kind of violence that was threatened when a child was said to have been *interfered with*. Little girls were always at risk, particularly in the summer holidays, when a kind of brooding menace seemed to hang over the street. Women became short-tempered and rows were frequent. Then suddenly the street would erupt in a frenzy of shouting and the neighbours would be transformed into dervishes intent on massacre.

I was about ten years old when I witnessed one such outbreak. It was lunchtime in early summer and I was on my way home from school. Stan Barlow and Benny Underhill were there and we decided to make a detour and explore a ruined house in Lord Street. As ruins go, it wasn't very impressive. The doors had been taken away, floorboards ripped out and most of the first floor ceilings had fallen in. Nevertheless, it was a ruin and we always explored deserted buildings on the assumption that one day we would find treasure. We had reached the point where we had climbed a flight of broken stairs to the second floor and were hurling bricks into the kitchen below when we heard the noise. It was in the distance but seemed to be getting nearer every minute. At first we couldn't make out what it was. Perhaps if any of us had ever heard the baying of a pack of hounds, we might have guessed at its cause. We began to feel scared and drew together, ready to run. Then they appeared, a mob of howling women racing as fast as they could go, filling the road, bringing traffic to a halt. Many of them were still wearing their aprons and all were armed, some with knives, some with sticks, others with hammers, chisels, shovels, and whatever else they had been able to lay their hands on. I will never forget the look on their faces, the cry of primeval hatred as they swept past followed by a score or so of stragglers determined to be in at the kill. We quickly lowered ourselves to the ground and raced after them. But Benny had twisted his ankle on the way down and when he started to limp we turned back.

All the way home the streets were agog with excitement. An eight-year-old girl had been interfered with, and the women were out for blood. 'They're going to have his balls off,' a man said, a statement with which everyone agreed. The offender was said to be a Jewish professional boxer who in the short space of a morning had been transformed from a very popular local figure into a depraved sex-maniac who had interfered with scores of defenceless little girls. The enraged women had besieged the house of the boxer's mother and after smashing all the windows had been persuaded by the police to disperse. It later transpired that the boxer had been in Birmingham when the assault took place; furthermore, the victim claimed that the man responsible had worn some kind of uniform and rode a bicycle. Mr Carey rode a bicycle and there was something funny about the way he looked at you. And Needham wore a kind of uniform – and so did the postman. And what about Mr Cray and the lamplighter? Now *there* was a dark horse. It wasn't natural for a man to be so quiet. Never a word for anybody. For a few days we kept our distance from him; I think he must have missed us for when we started following him again he looked pleased.

8

Happy Days?

I can't remember much about my first school. It was generally referred to as the infant school, though I was five years old and, in street terms, no longer an infant. I learned to form my letters there with a slate pencil on a slate and the teacher read stories to us. Yes, and we were given a pair of blunt-nosed scissors with which we cut designs out of coloured paper, and we modelled pigs and snakes and crocodiles out of plasticine. It was a happy time.

It was all very different when we moved into the big school.[1] Up until this time our classrooms had been located in the girls' school. Now the boys were in a different building altogether, separated from the girls' school by Albert Park. It was made clear to us immediately that our free-and-easy schooldays were over. You stayed in the school-yard until a whistle was blown, upon which you fell in – that is, you formed ranks. At a second whistle blast you stood to attention and at a third the assembled pupils began marching into the building rank by rank, class by class. Along tiled corridors we marched and were marshalled into an assembly hall which was really a number of classrooms from which the movable partitions had been pushed back. We were made to stand there at attention with the teachers standing by the side of their classes like company commanders. Then Mr Ellerby, the headmaster, mounted the platform. He was a small grey man in a grey suit. He suffered from a nervous tic which made him look as if he was constantly winking. I had to dig my nails into the soft flesh of my thigh to stop myself from winking back at him. His habit of playing with something in his right-hand trouser pocket had earned him the nickname of Wanker Ellerby.

After winking at us several times he commenced his address: 'I am your headmaster. My name is *Mister* Ellerby. You will address me as *Sir* at all times.' He then went on to list the various prohibitions and taboos and the kind of punishments that would be meted out to anyone who failed to observe them. He concluded his admonitory address by holding up his cane and saying, 'Is there anyone who doesn't know what this is?' The silence which greeted his question was apparently to his satisfaction for we were given the order to dismiss and a teacher began to play a spirited march on the piano. Class by class, we filed out to our classrooms like convicted felons embarking on a life-sentence in a penal settlement.

There were no lessons that day. Instead there were tests to determine whether one was A or B material. I was in the B group, the 'duffers' as our new teacher called us. Her name was Miss Tate and whenever I read about the female guards in the Nazi concentration camps I think of her. Ah, Miss Tate! She was the stuff out of which Thatchers and Tebbits are made. I was keen to learn but in her presence I was struck dumb. I became dull and stupid, incapable of learning. No, that's not true. I learned a lot about fear and hatred. But those two years I sat under her contemptuous gaze were the longest and most miserable years of my whole life.

She was a well set-up matron with iron-grey hair arranged in a bun at the back of her head. When she wasn't addressing us like a sergeant-major on parade she prowled between the desks like a hungry predator. She moved in an aura of hate and menace. You could be bent over your book trying desperately to solve a problem in arithmetic and suddenly you would become conscious of her standing behind you. Her hand would rest lightly on your shoulder and after a moment her fingers would begin to dig into your flesh and the pressure would increase until it felt as if the bones of your shoulder were being crushed in a vice. Finally the pain would be such that you were forced to cry out whereupon you would be yanked to your feet and held at arm's length by this middle-aged monster who was holding a handkerchief to her nose and asking whether there was any soap and water in your home.

The week after I moved into Miss Tate's class my father led a strike at the foundry in which he worked. Somehow, Miss Tate got to know of it and from then on my fate was sealed, for she hated strikers even more than she hated the children of the poor. Scarcely a lesson passed without there being a reference made to the strike and the loathsome creatures who were taking part in it. Meanwhile the strike dragged on and after three months of it our situation became desperate.

It was the small matter of an onion which made me realise just how desperate it was. Once a week we had a drawing class and often we were told to bring an object to draw. Sometimes it was a leaf, a banana or a pen-knife. On this particular day it was an apple. But we didn't have an apple. 'There's hardly anything in the hoose', my mother explained, 'but here, tak' this onion. It'll be just as good to draw as an apple. And mind you bring it back.'

When I produced the onion at the start of the drawing lesson Miss Tate stopped in mid-sentence and walked towards me. She walked round the onion, examining it from all sides. Returning to her desk, she called me out to face the class.

'Bring that *thing* with you,' she said. I did so. 'Now', she said,
'What is it?'
'Please, Miss, it's an onion.'
'Did I ask you to bring an onion?'

'No, Miss.'

'What did I ask you to bring?'

'An apple, Miss.'

Suddenly her face was within inches of mine, absolutely contorted with fury. 'Well, why don't you do what you're told?' When I didn't answer, she took me by the shoulders and shook me. 'Have you lost your tongue? Are you dumb as well as stupid?'

'No, Miss.'

'Did you hear that? He said he's not dumb.' Several members of the class laughed nervously, dutifully. 'I'm waiting to hear why you ignored my instructions.'

'We had no apples, Miss.'

'Couldn't your mother have bought one?'

'No, Miss.'

'Why not?'

'We've got no money, Miss.'

'And whose fault is that? People who go on strike can't expect the rest of us to supply them with money, can they?' By this time her face was crimson with fury, her eyes glazed with hatred. I was cringing with fear and everyone else in the room was scared as well.

The strike finally came to an end but my torment did not. The strike and the onion were now intertwined like snakes in a Celtic brooch. They were a motif running through all my lessons. I had become thoroughly cowed, demoralised, incapable of learning anything. I played truant as often as I could. At night I lay and wallowed in delicious fantasies in which I saw her drowning, covered in stab wounds, eaten by rats. My fear obsessed me to such an extent that eventually I fell seriously ill.

When I returned to school a month or so later the situation had changed. Indeed, during the rest of the term Miss Tate ignored me utterly. It was as if I had ceased to exist. It was a little uncomfortable at first but I soon became accustomed to it. Being ignored by Miss Tate was like being on a perpetual holiday. Many years later, my mother explained Miss Tate's change of manner. I had been delirious during my illness and had ranted and raved about my teacher to such an extent that my father went to see her and told her what would happen if she continued to terrorise his son. Whatever the warning was, it was totally effective. The damage to my education, however, was less easily put right.

Just before my tenth birthday, the school underwent a complete reorganisation. Half of it became a secondary establishment with a curriculum designed to meet the needs of those considered to be the brighter pupils. The other half was the elementary school. The secondary section's syllabus now included maths as opposed to the elementary school's arithmetic, and physics and chemistry in place of 'science'. They also studied French and biology and advanced English. I was considered to be elementary school material and at first I didn't mind. Within a year, however, it began to dawn on me that I was destined to spend the rest of my life as one of the expendables. I had been pigeon-holed and from now on I would belong with the unclaimed mail.

Many of my friends had moved up into the ranks of the secondary school and within six months we were talking two different languages. Within a year, our mutual alienation was complete. Their conversation was larded with references to logarithms and anti-logarithms, to the calculus, to Chaucer and Shakespeare, to theorems and a hundred other things. Soon we were passing each other in the street with merely a nod of recognition and after a time we didn't even do that.

During the three-and-a-half years of schooling left to me I came to realise that my formal education was coming to an end. I could read and write and I understood the general principles of arithmetic. From now on, my time would be spent in improving these rudimentary skills. I was not, however, entirely without resources. The innumerable spells of sickness brought on by the terrible Miss Tate had given me lots of time for reading. My father had been bringing home second-hand books every Saturday from the time I was about six years old. They were a varied assortment, bought off a barrow in the Pendleton Market. They were mostly too difficult for me at the age of six but at ten I was able to read many of them. They included a collection of unabridged stories from Burton's *Arabian Nights; Barry Lyndon; Vanity Fair; Captain Singleton;* Edgar Alan Poe's *Stories of the Grotesque and the Arabesque;* Victor Hugo's *Toilers of the Sea* and *Les Miserables; Tess of the D'Urbervilles;* Thomas Burke's *Limehouse Nights; Freckles* and *The Girl of the Limberlost* by Gene Stratton Porter; *The Sea Wolf, White Fang, Call of the Wild, Cruise of The Dazzler* and *Smoke Bellew,* all by Jack London; *Montrose* and *Ivanhoe,* by Sir Walter Scott and *Yeast* by Charles Kingsley; *The Pit* by Frank Norris, *Jimmy Higgins* and *The Jungle* by Upton Sinclair; *Roderick Random; Barnaby Rudge;* Masefield's *Sard Harker;* Grimms' *Fairy Tales;* Anderson's *Fairy Tales;* Wilson's *Tales of the Borders;* as well as all the boys' adventure stories I could lay my hands on. And there were occasional collections of poems among the battered volumes brought home by my dad. The only two that made any impression on me at all were some appalling verses by Poe and *The Collected Poems of Thomas Hood* (particularly 'Miss Kilmanseg and her Precious Leg').

Inspired by the books I was reading, I began to write myself. Oddly enough, I chose to write poetry. It was not very good poetry. My first effort resulted in a fairly long poem to which I gave the title of 'The 151st Psalm'. It was anti-religious in tone and not a little bellicose. It contained echoes of Walt Whitman, watered-down Whitman, and ended on a note of warning. I also wrote three or four rhymed squibs for the school magazine, the first issue of which appeared about this time. I followed these with a short play which I adapted from *The Monkey's Paw*, a macabre short story by W. W. Jacobs. This won me an invitation to join the school's play-reading society which had been formed a year before and membership of which was by invitation. Its founder,

Mr Gale, taught the school-leavers class and was, undoubtedly, the most popular teacher in the entire school. In addition to being an excellent teacher he was a footballer of note who played for Bury United in the year that it won the F.A. Cup at Wembley. He was an amateur actor too and it was rumoured that he was going out with a professional actress who worked in a repertory theatre in Chester. It is quite possible, even probable, that the rumour had no foundation, but schoolteachers who are also professional footballers, good-looking and well-dressed are obviously the right raw material for legends. Certainly the play-reading society he formed was a great success and to receive one of the group's hand-printed cards inviting one to attend a reading was like being asked to become one of King Arthur's knights.

Apart from *Midsummer Night's Dream* and Maurice Maeterlinck's *The Bluebird,* most of the plays we read were one-acters selected from Harrap's annual anthologies *Best One-Act Plays of Today.* They were, I suppose, fairly mediocre examples of the well-made play but they were enormously important to me and it was through them and the play-reading society that my decision to work in the theatre first took form.

On the whole I was fairly happy during those last years at school. For one thing, I was free of Miss Tate. That was all over. Now I had some good teachers who, since most of us could read, write and add up, could proceed (unhindered by a strict curriculum) to broaden our image of the world. They had none of the teaching aids which were considered normal facilities until Mrs Thatcher and her colleagues decided to turn back the clock. What they did was to discuss ideas with us. They introduced us to books we'd never heard of. They got us to read poems with some feeling and understanding. One of them even invited a group of us to have tea at his house. Nobody that I knew had ever heard of such a thing. I ran home from school that day and changed into my Sunday suit, a real suit which had been bought in a clothing-club and which fitted me. I plastered my hair down with cold water and could barely stand still to be inspected by my mother.

Then I was off on a ha'penny tram-ride to the new estate where Mr Rushworth lived.[2] The three other invitees were waiting for me at the corner of the road. They were just as nervous as I and if any one of us could have thought of a reason to duck out I'm sure we'd have been off like hares. Mr Rushworth welcomed us in and introduced us to his wife, a pretty young woman. They were obviously very much in love and kept finding opportunities to touch each other. Once they held hands but we pretended not to notice and when he kissed her on the cheek we were struck dumb with embarrassment. Both of them, however, took great pains to put us at our ease. The food was very good, not kid-stuff like jellies and fairy cakes but meat-pie and boiled ham and tongue, what Mrs Drummond used to call *funeral fare.* There was also a potato salad with some kind of cream on it but I didn't have any as I wasn't sure that I could get it onto my plate without spilling some of it. Only Izzy Schneider seemed unfazed by it – but then he was Jewish and used to all kinds of strange food.

Mr Rushworth really seemed to be interested in what we had to say, particularly when I mentioned some of the books that I had read. He asked us what we intended to do when we left school. Izzy Schneider said he was going to be a punter and earn money playing the horses. (He did, in fact, become a professional gambler and did well at it.) Stan Barlow said he stood a good chance of being taken on as a messenger-boy at the Co-op. None of us really had much of an idea of what we were going to do. There was more than a possibility that we would finish up on the dole and even if we got a job it wouldn't amount to much. We were elementary school material destined to respond like one of Pavlov's dogs when our number was called by the clerk at the unemployment exchange or to become temporary occupiers of blind-alley occupations.

Mr Rushworth told us that this was only his second job since he came down from college. He was, he said, a socialist and a member of the Fabian Society, whatever that was. Alf Fullerton, who had been sitting silent ever since we entered the house, pointed his finger at me and said, 'His dad's a socialist, sir.'

'Really,' said Mr Rushworth.

'Have you heard of Lenin, sir?'

'Of course. Everyone's heard of Lenin,' said Mr Rushworth drawing at his pipe.

'We've got a picture of him pinned above the kitchen fireplace,' I said.

'Your father must really admire him.'

'He says he's the greatest man that ever lived', I ventured, 'even greater than Burns.'

'Burns?' he enquired.

'Robert Burns.'

'Ah, the bard!' Mr Rushworth was delighted. 'Does your father know his work?'

'His poetry? He knows a lot.'

'How marvellous!' said Mr Rushworth.

'Jock Sinclair knows more,' I said, determined to give credit where it was due.

'Jock Sinclair?'

'He's an iron-moulder like my dad,' I replied.

'I don't suppose that you would happen to know any of his poems . . .?'

'I know plenty,' said I, suddenly feeling very confident. 'There's the one about 'Death and Doctor Hornbrook'.'

'I'd love to hear it,' said Mrs Rushworth.

I started:

See here's a scythe and there's a dart,
That hae pierced many a gallant heart,
But Doctor Hornbrook wi' his art . . .

I stopped, suddenly realising where the poem was taking me. I felt myself going red in the face as I tried to stifle the laughter that was bubbling up inside me.

Mr Rushworth, mistaking the tears in my eyes for chagrin, tried to comfort me. 'Never mind, laddie,' he said. Mrs Rushworth took me by the arm and led me to the kitchen. 'Here', she said, 'have a drink of water and you'll feel better.' For the rest of the evening the words of the poem kept running through my mind and when I undressed that night before going to bed, the backs of my thighs were bruised where I had pinched them to keep from laughing. The words ran:

> But Doctor Hornbrook wi' his art
> Has made them baith nae worth a fart,
> Damned ha' 't they'll kill.
>
> E'en them he canna get attended,
> Altho' their face he ne'er had kenned it,
> Just shite in a kale-blade and send it -
> As soon as he smells 't,
> Baith their disease and whit will mend it
> At aince he tells 't.

Before we left for home, Mr Rushworth lent me *The World of William Clissold* by H. G. Wells. I had mentioned during the evening that I had enjoyed reading *The Time Machine* and *The War of the Worlds. William Clissold* would, he said, throw a different light on Wells. Alas, I found it dull reading and though I tried desperately to plough my way through it, I didn't succeed in finishing it. Loaded with guilt, I slunk round the school-yard determined to avoid any private discussion with my teacher. It wasn't that I was afraid of him, I just didn't want to hurt his feelings. I liked him and admired him enormously. I had never met anybody quite like him before. He was, I think, the first really *gentle* human being to come my way. He never shouted at us and, though he represented authority, he never tried to crush us with it. When you spoke he listened to you and let you finish what you were saying. He didn't try to make you feel small, or unimportant, or invisible, or dirty.

Miss Tate had seen us as repulsive blind worms wriggling in the slime of poverty and had spent more than three years showing us the extent of her loathing. To Wanker Ellerby we were unruly primitives, fuzzy-wuzzies, who had to be cowed and disciplined to keep them from mutiny. Mr Gale – well, he was a hero who, on the whole, treated us well; not like friends, perhaps more like loyal subjects or trusted servants. He would joke with us, praise us when we did something praiseworthy, explain things to us and delight us with his occasional attempts at mimicry. But when he was angry you kept out of his way for he could be as violent and overbearing as anyone. Mr Rushworth, on the other hand, never abandoned his sympathetic attitude towards us and treated us always with understanding and compassion. He was a lamb among wolves. How then could I possibly hurt his feelings by telling him that I found his treasured H. G. Wells dull and unbearably stodgy? The truth is, I felt that I was more in touch with the real world than Mr Rushworth was and therefore felt I had to protect him from some of the harsher aspects of reality. So I not only succeeded in avoiding a face-to-face confrontation with him, I also failed to return his book. I went into hospital to have my tonsils removed and caught pneumonia. When I returned to school a month later, Mr Rushworth had left to take up a job in a small private school in the Lake District.

His replacement was a tall, slack-bellied Midlander called Little. Someone called him 'Chicken Little' and the name stuck. It was appropriate, for when he was excited or angry he would splutter and make noises not unlike a chicken that had been disturbed on the roost. His eyes, too, which were rather protuberant, had a rather chicken-like gleam to them. Gale and Rushworth were young men in their mid-twenties, perhaps. Little must have been twice their age and had a large, grey moustache which partly covered his somewhat thick lips. He had an odd kind of laugh. Ernie Worth, who was given to making pronouncements about the sexual practices of those who taught us, said it sounded like Miss Tate being fucked by an Airedale.

Mr Little was everything that Rushworth was not. He was noisy and given to harassing boys who stammered and stuttered while attempting to answer questions. He despised those whom he referred to as the lesser races: the darkies, the gyppos, the dagos, the chinks, the greasers, the Yanks, the froggies, the hokey-pokeys, all the peoples of Asia, the Middle East and, to a slightly lesser degree, the Irish, Welsh and Scots. According to Ryan, Little had been a Black and Tan during the Troubles. He certainly never let slip an opportunity to pass an insulting remark about the Irish. Geography lessons, in particular, seemed to bring out the worst in him. He would unfurl a coloured map of the world and drape it over the blackboard. 'Look at it!' he would cry. 'Look at it! What is the prevailing colour?'

'Red!' the class would bellow.

'And what is that?' (jabbing his pointer at India).

'India, sir,' (chanted in a thrilling whisper).

'And that?'

'Burma, sir,' (intoned like a prayer).

'And that?'

'Africa, sir,' (declaimed with fervour).

'And that, and that, and that . . .' One by one he would jab each of Britain's colonial possessions, colonies, protectorates, dominions. 'And who owns them?'

'We do, sir,' (delivered in a patriotic scream).

'And never forget it! That Empire where the sun never sets is *ours*. The greatest Empire the world has ever seen. And whose is it?'

'Ours, sir!'

'And don't any of you ever forget it.' Then he would peer at the map, his nose almost touching it. 'And what have we here? I think a fly must have done it. A cheeky little fly. No, no, I see what it is now. It's what some people call The Emerald Isle but I call it the slop-bin of the world. What is it, Ryan?'

Dennis Ryan had been through the routine too many times to be anything but bored by it. 'Don't know,' he would mutter.

'What did you say? We didn't hear it, did we?' He would look around the classroom for support but there was rarely any forthcoming. 'Well', he would shout, 'did you hear him or didn't you?' The class would stay mum. When Carey or MacNamara was the butt it was a different state of affairs, but we knew Dennis Ryan's four brothers and nobody wanted to get on the wrong side of them. Indeed, most of us were waiting impatiently for the day, or maybe the night, when Mr Little would discover just how tough the Ryan brothers were. We used to argue about the length of time he would be in hospital and the walk home from school was often enlivened by fantasies in which broken ribs, fractured limbs and shattered jaws were prominently featured.

His loathing for the Irish only manifested itself intermittently, but his hatred for the Jews was constant. As the school was situated at the edge of the Jewish district and Jews made up about a quarter of the pupils, there was plenty of scope for his disgusting anti-Semitism. Not that he indulged in Hitler-like tirades or anything of that nature. On the contrary, he served his poison in small teaspoon-size doses, contenting himself with subtle insults, innumerable sly digs and what he obviously regarded as humorous quips. That was his style of attack until Izzy Schneider joined his class. Then everything changed.

Izzy Schneider was the son of a Polish-Jewish greengrocer who sold his wares from a barrow. This in itself would, in normal circumstances, have provided Mr Little with enough raw material for several terms' worth of racial slurs. But these were not normal circumstances and Izzy Schneider was not a normal pupil. For one thing, he was the biggest boy in the school – tall, heavily built and obviously a great deal fitter than Chicken Little. He was captain of the school football team and, until he became bored with the game, captain of the school cricket team. He was the fastest runner and the strongest swimmer and never came anywhere but first in the annual examinations. Chicken Little hated him with a hatred that was never far from boiling over. Most of the other teachers seemed to dislike him too. Whenever Wanker Ellerby caught sight of him, his face would fall victim to a veritable paroxysm of twitching and, pointing a quivering finger at Izzy he would shout, 'What are you laughing at?'

'Who, me?'

'Yes, you!'

'I wasn't laughing.'

'Laughing, *what?*'

'How do you mean, laughing *what?*'

'Laughing, *Sir.*'

'Oh, I see what you mean,' Schneider would say, very politely. 'You mean you want to be called *sir.*'

At this, Wanker would go purple with rage and he would scream, 'Come to my office and I'll give you something to laugh about!' and he would stalk off, a badly assembled midget, followed by an amiable, slouching Goliath.

He was easily the most caned boy in the school. Teachers vied with each other in seeing who could cane him the most often and the most painfully. Mr Gale, generally a fair-minded teacher when it came to dealing out punishment, would go berserk when confronted with Izzy's imperturbable calm. Taking three or four steps back, he would rush at Izzy and bring the cane down with enormous force on the outstretched hand. Once he gave him three strokes on each hand and, at that moment his heroic image was flawed beyond repair as far as we were concerned. Schneider gave no indication that he felt any pain but his face went paper-white. Gale was trembling when he had finished and, after a few moments, left the classroom. We tried to commiserate with Izzy but he ignored us, looking straight ahead. Later, in the school-yard during the break, we gathered round him, jockeying for position as though by being close to him we could absorb some of his strength. 'Didn't it hurt?' we asked. 'Of course it did.' He showed us his hands and the sight of those swollen white and purple weals reduced us to awed silence. I don't think Mr Gale ever used the cane on him again after that. He ignored Izzy as Miss Tate had ignored me.

Chicken Little, however, continued to punish Izzy with unabated zeal. Izzy was more than a match for him and we began to look forward to these caning interludes in which Izzy transformed a sadistic monster into a ridiculous clown – for Izzy, by the careful manipulation of his own punishment, made Chicken Little an object of ridicule to the entire school. Having decided on the reason for punishment, Little would command Izzy to stand up. Izzy would lumber to his feet, lifting the ridiculously small desk at the same time.

'Put that desk down!' Chicken Little would roar, and Izzy would sit down with the desk. 'On your feet.' Up would come Izzy – and the desk. Enraged, Chicken Little would command two nearby boys to hold it down.

'I want you out here.' Izzy would slouch to the front of the class. 'Look at me, boy!' Chicken Little would hiss, and Izzy would look him full in the face and show the same kind of interest that one would give to a fly walking on a bald head. By this time the teacher would have grabbed his cane and would be testing its suppleness by making two or three rapid swishes through the air.

'Put your hand out.' And up would go Izzy's large hand until the fingers were within half-an-inch of Chicken Little's nose. 'Get back!' Chicken Little would roar, and Izzy would take several steps backward till his back was to the door. 'Not that far, you idiot!' Izzy moved six inches closer. 'Closer!' Another six inches. 'Closer still.' And so it would go on until Izzy was back in his original position. 'Now I'm going to teach you a lesson. You've heard of Shylock and his pound of flesh? Well, now I'm going to have my pound of flesh.'

We had heard this particular routine so often that we knew the teacher's lines as well as he himself knew them and at this point in his peroration the entire class would join him in a thrilling whisper which would not have sounded out of place in a performance of *Oedipus Rex*.

'Shut up!' Chicken Little would screech at us. 'Right, Schneider. Get your hand up and no more messing about,' and he would grab Izzy's hand.

Positioning it as though it was a piece of wood he intended to split in two, he would lean back in order to get extra swing to his cane. But Izzy knew the routine, too, and before the cane had progressed far in its parabola, his hand had gone up again so that it met the cane before it had travelled more than two or three inches, thus robbing it of most of its force.

How we loved and admired Izzy for those performances! He was so calm, so supremely confident and yet completely lacking in arrogance. I don't think I ever heard his voice raised in anger or heard him utter a threat. Why, then, did the teachers hate him so? What was it in him that roused them to such a pitch of fury? His size? Did they fear that one day he would rise up like Sampson and pull their world down about their ears? Was it his stoicism, his imperturbability, his remoteness? Were they afraid that his apparent unconcern for their opinion of him might infect the rest of us and topple their absurd power structure? Was it because he never laughed at their jokes or registered pain when they punished him? Did they resent the fact that he appeared to learn without effort, without paying any obvious attention to their explanations of this or that problem? It was compounded of all these things plus the need to subdue a force that refused to be subdued. Perhaps it was merely the expression in his eyes, indifference touched with a measure of mild disbelief.

And poor Chicken Little! He wanted so much to be a big, strong, powerful leader of men. He had been to Italy on a two weeks' vacation in the summer of 1927 and had come back to Salford with a vision of himself as the British *Il Duce*. His need for admiration was as great as his need of somebody to despise like the Irish or the Jews. It was his misfortune that he chose to demonstrate his superiority on a Jewish schoolboy who was, in every way, his superior.

Every Friday afternoon during our last two years at school, we were given an hour's woodwork instruction. The 'manual class' was the official name. The woodwork instructor was a thoroughly detestable little sadist called Shield. The Shields of this world are never in short supply. There seems to be an inexhaustible supply of them waiting to fill the post of woodwork-master in innumerable schools where they appear to thrive on making life miserable for generations of schoolboys. Our Mr Shield – or rather *my* Mr Shield – is a ripe example of the species.

Each term begins in the same way. Each class, in the course of the initial lesson, is harangued by this ferocious little bantam-cock of a man. The harangue really has nothing to do with us, or, indeed, with the craft of carpentry. Its sole purpose is to rouse this disgusting little man to the point where he will achieve the maximum degree of pleasure from inflicting pain. He goes on and on until, at the very peak of his malediction, he suddenly freezes and rakes the classroom with maniacal gaze. Inevitably someone gives vent to a nervous titter and, quick as lightning, Shield pounces on the unfortunate victim, drags him out in front of the class and canes him. This is the real heart of the performance. All that has gone before has been merely preparation, a curtain-raiser before the main event. Now Shield is holding his cane like a rapier and prodding the terrified victim with it the way a lion-tamer uses his whip to prod his beasts. And all the time he hops and skips on his chubby little legs and shrieks and bespatters the boy with flecks of foaming spittle.

'Nobody laughs at me!' he screams. 'Nobody! Do you understand, you grubby little piece of offal?' The performance is mounting towards its climax as he begins his bouncing-ball routine. We watch in fascination as he bounces up and down and the entire class holds its breath as he reaches the peak of his highest jump and brings the cane down with enormous force.

When Miss Tate uses the cane it becomes an expression of her contempt and hatred of her poverty-stricken charges; Mr Gale canes out of anger which is soon dissipated; Mr Rushworth as a last, and unpleasant, resort; Chicken Little out of frustration, furious that he was not born a Mussolini who could make the trains run on time. But Shield, this monstrous midget, canes for pleasure, for sexual gratification, to compensate for his insignificant body.

His victim dealt with, Shield becomes menacingly jovial, his eyes positively sparkle as he surveys the injured canee. 'I'm sure we all feel better for that,' he declares. 'Clears the air a little, don't you think?' He smiles his dreadful smile. 'I think we understand each other now, eh? Going to behave yourselves, are you? Shield's model students, eh? One big happy family, eh?'

The second stage of what future North American double-talk experts will call *The Pacification Program* begins. 'This', he says, drawing a right-angle on the blackboard, 'is a right-angle. Anybody disagree?' The class is silent. 'Good.' He draws another angle. 'What do we call that?'

'Please, sir', I venture, eager to please, 'it's a left-angle', and as soon as the words are out of my mouth I know I have been foolish.

'Anybody agree with him? You there, is it a left-angle?'

'No, sir,' says Art Walker.

'Are you sure?'

'Yes, sir,' Art says, but less confidently.

'*Sure?*'

'Yes, sir.' Art is whispering now.

'You do realise what you're saying?' Art is silent, a bird hypnotised by a snake. 'Well?'

'Well what, sir?'

'What? WHAT?' He is bellowing now. 'Is that or is it not a left-angle?'

'I don't know,' says Art desperately.

'He doesn't know! One minute you know and the next you don't know. How do you explain this sudden lapse of memory?' He is in full flight as he turns and faces the class. 'You heard him, didn't you?' The class is mute. 'Did you or did you not hear him deny that it was a left-angle?' One or two voices are raised in an uncertain affirmative. 'Well, did you? Speak up!'

'Yes, sir.'

'Louder.'

'Yes, sir!'

'LOUDER.'

'YES, SIR!' The class has become infected with Shield's hysteria. But Shield suddenly changes tack and he sounds almost pleasant when he commands us to come to the front of the class. We do so and stand facing our classmates. He tells us to face each other. We stand there about a yard apart.

'Now look each other in the eye.' We catch each other's embarrassed glance for a moment and then look away. 'Did you hear me?' We look back again. I see that Art's face has gone white. The puckered skin at the side of his neck where he had the mastoid operation makes him look like an old man. I can feel myself blushing. It embarrasses me – I blush red when I'm scared and I become even more embarrassed at the thought of my mates knowing that I'm scared. Art's got a scab on his left knee. I've got one on my right knee and a bad scrape on the heel of my right hand. If he canes me, that's really going to hurt. Shield pokes me gently in the shoulder with his cane. 'He called you a liar. What are you going to do about it?'

I mumble, 'I don't know, sir.'

'Don't know? Somebody calls you a liar and you don't know what to do about it?' I am intimidated, confused. I am unable to speak. 'Speak up, Mister Left-Angle. Do you hear? This clown's name from now on is Mister Left-Angle. Say Hello, Mister Left-Angle!'

'Hello, Mister Left-Angle.' The class repeats it obediently but without mirth.

'Well, Walker', says the irrepressible Shield, 'have you made up your mind?' Walker does not reply. 'Well', says Shield, 'since neither of you seems to be in the mood for action, perhaps I should supply a little of my own.' He begins to prod us both with his cane, forcing us to retreat until we are standing with our backs against his desk. 'Now', he says, 'let me see your hands.' We hold out our hands while he starts bouncing gently on the balls of his feet. I close my eyes, prepared by this time almost to welcome the pain if only it will put an end to his long drawn-out baiting of us. But the cane doesn't descend. Instead, we are ordered back to our seats. It's just another of his little ploys. Every week for four full terms I am due to have a 'manual' lesson in the course of which I can expect to be singled out as the stupid clown who thinks that the opposite of a right-angle is a left-angle.

The school day started at nine o'clock in the morning. The bell would ring and everyone would stop whatever game they were playing and form ranks. On special occasions, such as the morning of a projected visit by the inspectors from the Education Committee, the headmaster would appear and we would be called to attention. There would follow a cursory inspection and this or that boy would be sent to the wash-house. On normal days, the assistant head would blow a whistle and one by one the various classes would march into the main building. The brown tiled corridors would ring with the clatter of clogs and hob-nailed boots as we advanced into the assembly-hall. There we would stand for twenty minutes or half-an-hour. For ten of those minutes we would be watching Wanker twitching and playing with himself as he told us what a collection of scoundrels and ne'er-do-wells most of us were. The rest of the time would be taken up with singing hymns and reciting the Ten Commandments and the Thirty-First Psalm. The hymns were taken at a break-neck pace and, wherever possible, in march tempo, a rhythm favoured by the diminutive Miss Pitt, who provided the accompaniment for the occasion.

Miss Pitt had arrived at the school two years after I had. Already she was the subject of many improbable legends. She was a snappy dresser with her high-heeled shoes, her tight skirts and her blouses and jumpers calculated to show off her remarkable bosom. And it *was* remarkable. Those who were in her class said that they became accustomed to it after a time but those of us who only had it pointed at then occasionally, felt threatened. The secondary-schoolers always referred to her as Gunner Pitt, but we – the elementary-school material – were less subtle and called her 'Pitt the Tit'. She was said to be an excellent teacher, though her excellence was never demonstrated to pupils other than those in the A-stream.

She was, in spite of her shapely legs, her jiggling bottom and her magnificent bosom, a rather forbidding young woman. Perhaps it was the expression on her face, which contrived to be both supercilious and menacing at the same time. Perhaps it was her way of walking with her head and shoulders thrust back (though this may have been her way of providing a counter-balance to the weight and amplitude of her forward structure). She was in the habit of spending her lunch-break in the Council School with Mr Betancourt. He was the French teacher there, a thin and impressively tall man, so tall that rumour had it that Miss Pitt could barely reach his tool without standing on tiptoe. Hyperbole was fashionable at the time.

For a pianist, Miss Pitt's lack of height was a liability. The piano stool, for instance, had to be screwed as low as possible in order that her feet might reach the pedals. This resulted in her elbows being lower than the keyboard and, more important, her breasts occasionally striking chords that were not included in the score. The low and high notes being situated at the extreme ends of the keyboard necessitated a temporary separation of buttocks and stool with the result that Miss Pitt's tight skirt was constantly rucked up above her shapely thighs, a condition which caused much jockeying for position among the older pupils. It is a great pity that Miss Pitt's choice of musical items didn't match the bravura of her performance. Had it done so, it is not outside the bounds of possibility that our school might well have become a place of pilgrimage rivalling Glyndebourne or Bayreuth.

At most schools, the final bell is a signal for an immediate exodus, a wild rush for the door. Not so with us. Miss Tate had trained us to ignore its seductive clamour. We greeted it with poker-faced inscrutability. We had been conditioned against response, we were Pavlovian un-responders. Not until teacher gave verbal permission did we put away our schoolbooks, rulers, erasers and pens. But even then we were not free; Wanker's Law had us standing rigid by the side of our desks until we received the signal to move. This would be delayed for several minutes while the classrooms down the corridor emptied. Class Three would go first, followed by Three-B and Four-A and so on. And each class would come out marching to the rhythm of Miss Pitt's piano which at times was played at such a lick that the classrooms emptied at the trot. When this happened, marchers exchanged significant glances and spoke out of the corner of their mouths: 'She's in a hurry. Got to do a bend-over job for the Frenchman;' or, 'Got to give Long Tom his oats before she leaves.' Such comments had to be uttered quickly and with no lip movement, for Wanker was standing, cane at the ready, at the end of the corridor. One's best bet was to look chastened; a smile, a whispered word could result in your being called out and caned. School was to discipline you, make you cowed, make you resigned to your empty future, content with your lot. Surely, then, it was a mistake to employ the succulent Miss Pitt, when the mere thought of her trim thighs opening to receive the lofty Frenchman could make one's imagination . . .

Ah well! Happy days!

9

Mother, Meg and May

The Tolly-Killus fight was the beginning of the end as far as our street gang was concerned. For a couple of weeks after the battle we continued to meet in the square but the heart had gone out of us; we were no longer a unified group with common aims and interests. In some strange way, Killus' fists had punched holes in our shared dream and the magic had gone. The square was no longer Sherwood Forest and Robin had been cut down. And us? We had become aimless adolescents, somewhat fearful of the future, infected by our parents' despair, waiting for tomorrow and wishing it would never come.

Then there were new friends, new allegiances, new and interesting ways of spending time. More and more of my leisure time was being spent away from the street. I had a bike now, a second-hand three-speed job that weighed a ton. Izzy Schneider had christened it 'the armoured train'. It really was heavy but on the Broughton Road croft, which we always referred to as The Fair Ground, there was nothing that could beat it. I used to go there after my evening meal and meet Joe Bamber, Pete Chandler, Doug Ross and a lad from the Ascension school called Chinny. It was a cinder-croft and perfect for dirt tracking. The idea was to pedal like mad and when you reached a good speed you jammed the back brake on hard. The result was a tremendous skid with a great cloud of grit and cinder. It really looked quite spectacular. My old armoured train was absolutely marvellous for the job. We used to do some pretty fancy tricks, too, like standing on the saddle when you were going full lick or balancing with your feet up in the air and holding on to the handlebars. On a lightweight bike it could be quite dodgy and Dave Capper broke his wrist trying to do it.

Capper was the most accident-prone individual I have ever known. He was a tall and rather ungainly boy whose clothes were always too small for him. The sleeves of his jacket rode high above his bony wrists and his short trousers rucked up into his crotch. His perpetual tugging and teasing at his shorts and the shaking of his arms, in an attempt to make his sleeves fall level with his wrists, put him into a state of continual agitation and won him the nickname Twitcher. He was a good-natured lad in spite of his irritating habits.

The first time I ever really noticed him was when a cricket ball hit him between the eyes and knocked him out during a match between our school and a team from the Central School. A few weeks later he was in hospital with a badly wounded knee. He had slipped while climbing over the railings of the Albert Park rec and one of the sharp pointed spikes had pierced his knee cap. That put him in The Abattoir for a couple of months. He'd only been back at school a week when he had another accident. He was walking along Camp Street past a house that was undergoing roof repairs when someone threw a slate down and knocked him unconscious.

He lived eight or nine streets away from me, which practically made him a foreigner. I don't think he was ever a member of a street gang. For that you had to be on call, so to speak, every minute of your spare time. A gang, like any other social unit, needs continuity and you can't have that if you spend all your time running backwards and forwards to hospitals. Twitcher had been in The Abattoir so often that he was practically on the payroll there. He must have saved them quite a lot of money in wages because almost every time I went to visit him he was hobbling round the ward dishing out bedpans, bottles for peeing in, drinking water and newspapers. He knew all the nurses by their first names and told us once that one of them, the plump little Irish one with the curly hair, used to give his balls an affectionate little tweak while she was rubbing his bum with methylated spirits.

It was perhaps because he had missed out on the street gang bit that he attached himself to that group of choice classmates who, during their final two years at school, took on the trappings of a gang. We never got to the point of having initiation ceremonies like midnight craps, though we did toy with the idea of a secret language for a couple of weeks and we developed subtle ways of discouraging would-be joiners. Occasionally we would co-opt an associate member who had something special to contribute to the group. Such a one was Dave Patterson, a small, neat well-scrubbed boy whose sister, Meg, was a pupil at the girls' council school on the other side of the park.

For years Meg had travelled the same route to school as the rest of us and in all that time I had never given her a second look. Then, one day, we all become conscious of her shining beauty and we are suddenly wrestling and butting each other like young goats in an attempt to be near her when she passes. It was as though overnight we had discovered a delightful new species. Yes, we had heard dirty jokes and seen cartoons of Jiggs and his wife but this sudden discovery of how incredibly attractive girls could be was an overwhelming experience. In the classroom we passed cryptic notes to one another containing coded instructions as to where we would meet after school, or merely carrying the word GEM in capital letters (Meg's name written backwards). During the hymn-singing assembly-period which began the school day, we exchanged information out of the corner of our mouths and planned strategies which would help us to penetrate Meg's circle of friends. Her brother, Dave, was part of one of those plans. We enlisted him by the simple strategy of allowing him to mind Izzy Schneider's jacket while Izzy was batting in a game of cricket on the rec. He was a little bewildered by the honour but accepted it with gratitude. He responded willingly to our cross-examination and told us that Meg and half a dozen of her particular friends were in the habit of walking home through the park after school.

For the next week we made daily excursions to the park, tailing Meg's group from a distance and getting a little closer each day. When they sat down on a form we spied on them from behind the rhododendron bushes and when they walked by the pond we threw stones in it from places of concealment or hurried past them, ignoring them with shrill laughter. Finally, our repertoire of clumsy overtures exhausted, we sat down and wrote a painfully formal letter to our joint inamorata and entrusted brother Dave to deliver it. The following morning he brought the reply which we read in the comparative privacy of a summerhouse in the park. It was baffling in its ambiguity. Had she or had she not understood that we were proffering the hand of friendship to her and her circle? Did she or did she not understand that we were all madly in love with her? Was she or was she not prepared to give some indication that she liked us? Would she or would she not meet with us in the park or in a place of her own choice and talk with us about . . . anything she liked to talk about? These questions, presented with great obliquity, were the subject of the second epistle carried to the loved one by David, our Hermes.

The answer to that letter was just as cryptic as the first and was obviously the work of several hands. A third letter was dispatched full of coy references to our state of mind and bearing the pseudonymous signatures we had chosen for ourselves. This was followed by a fourth letter and a fifth and, with each one, David's position in our circle became a little more elevated. It was quite extraordinary to see the way his personality flowered as his function as go-between became more and more important.

The fifth letter was our last. Our patience was all used up and writing was getting us nowhere. Abandoning all subterfuge we confronted the girls directly in the park and introduced ourselves. They were friendly and just a little bit superior in their manner. Two of them laughed a good deal and passed smothered comments on us from behind their hands. We sat down on the grass with them and tried desperately to think of things to talk about. They seemed so sure of themselves compared with us. They were about the same age as we were but they seemed older, more mature. Only Izzy appeared to be at ease in their company.

It was early spring and rather cold. I was carrying my jacket over my arm. It had been given to my mother by a woman who employed her as a charwoman. It had belonged to her husband and was several sizes too large for me. I was ashamed that these self-possessed young creatures should see me wearing it. One of them noticed that I was shivering and asked why I didn't put my jacket on. 'It's too big for him', Underhill said, 'his mam got it at a jumble sale.'

I felt too miserable to deny it but Dougie Singleton spoke up for me: 'You're talking through your hat,' he said. 'His mam goes out cleanin' and a woman gave it to her.'

'Is that right?' one of the girls asked. I tried to answer but no sound came out of my mouth. I was burning up with shame. I wanted to die there and then. Instead I leapt to my feet and raced away. I could hear them calling after me but I went on running until I felt that my lungs were going to burst. I walked the rest of the way home, seeing nothing and nobody and hating my mother for shaming me by going out cleaning. Children are hopeless conformists; they soak up the ideas and opinions of those around them and search out the dominant group in order to increase their chances of survival. When I got home I set the table for the evening meal. It was a relief to find that my parents hadn't yet come home from work. I was in no mood to have to talk to anybody so I went upstairs to the room I shared with our lodger. He was there, lying on the bed reading. He spoke to me but I didn't answer. I went back down the stairs and out into the back yard. A game of football was in progress in the back entry but I couldn't face the idea of being with my friends so I went into the lavatory and sat down on the toilet. There, in the whitewashed, brick cubicle, bare of everything but the nail which held the wad of cut newspaper, I allowed the waves of embarrassment, shame and despair sweep over me.

Afterwards, I went into the kitchen and ran cold water over my eyes. I needed time now before I met anyone I knew so I went into the back entry. The footballers had gone. It was teatime and they would be sitting down to their evening meal. I started walking towards Irwell Street but had not gone more than a few yards when my mother came round the corner. She looked so faded and tired that my heart gave a lurch and released a sudden violent storm of emotions. It lasted only a moment and then I was running towards her full of love and guilt. By the time I reached her and took her oilcloth shopping bag from her, I had resolved to abandon all thoughts of girls.

My resolve lasted until noon the following day when Izzy told me that we would be meeting the girls again after school that day.

'Not me,' I said.

'Don't be a berk', he said, 'they're good sports.' Realising how close I had come to being cast out of Izzy's circle, I experienced a moment of real panic. I was being asked to prove that I, too, was a good sport.

'I'll be there,' I said.

This time I wore my oversized jacket as an act of miserable defiance. I was suspicious, expecting further humiliation, but the girls ignored me – and I resented that, too. Once or twice, Meg caught my eye but looked away hurriedly as if embarrassed and I wondered what had been said about me during my absence. I was relieved when it was time to go our separate ways and a little taken aback when one of the girls took my arm.

'I go the same way as you,' she said. Then, while I was trying to think of something interesting to say, she said, 'Why did you run off yesterday?'

'Don't know,' I mumbled.

'It was silly', she said, 'and wrong. My ma works in a smelly old chip shop.'

I look at her out of the corner of my eye. How amazing that I hadn't noticed her before. She's much better looking than Meg Patterson. I keep stealing looks as we walk, each time seeing another item of perfection: the jet-black hair cut in a close shingle, the brown eyes flecked with little motes of gold, matching the tawny gold of her skin. 'What does your dad work at?' I asked.

'He's dead.'

I noticed the way her perfectly shaped ears lay close to her head. 'I like your ears,' I said.

'Yours stick out,' said she.

'It's not my fault.'

'Who said it was? Anyway, they're nice. Gives you something to get hold of,' and, suiting the action to the word, she took hold of my ears and pulling my head towards her, kissed me smack on the lips. 'There!' she said. 'Now we're friends.' I was so astonished that I forgot to feel embarrassed.

It was the beginning of a halcyon year, a period of unalloyed happiness. We met every day on the way to school and again on the way home. That summer in the school holidays we were rarely apart except to sleep. She was accepted by the few who were still in our street gang and would take part in the group exploits, searching the ruins of decayed houses, raiding neighbouring gangs for bonfire wood, collecting maggots in the coal-yard manure heap, wrestling, climbing trees, scaling walls, taking part in wheelboard races and doing all the things that we, the boys, did. At other times, the two of us would lie on the grass in the park and I would tell her about the books I was reading or I would recite long passages from *The Mask of Anarchy* or from Edgar Alan Poe or tell her the stories I had read in that single volume of Burton's *Arabian Nights*. I think I liked that best of all. She would lie on her side soaking up the sun and I would watch the play of emotions on her face as I spoke. Occasionally, at the end of a story that she found particularly exciting, she would hug me to her and that was as close as we ever came to having any kind of physical contact with each other – and yet I loved her deeply and was thrilled by her dark beauty.

Towards the end of the holidays our relationship underwent a violent change. Several of us had been playing games in the park but May just sat on the grass and watched us. Soon the rest drifted away, leaving the two of us alone. I could sense her unhappiness and tried to persuade her to confide in me.

'It's nothing,' she said as she began to lace up her plimsolls. Then she said, in a voice charged with misery, 'Last night I started my period.'

Uncomprehending, I said, 'Your *what?*'

Defiantly, she explained the process of menstruation and then burst into a wild fit of sobbing. 'It's so unfair! I'll never be able to climb trees again or do the things *you* do!' She was inconsolable. When her tears had stopped, she finished lacing her plimsolls and spoke the words that murdered my happiness. 'It doesn't make any difference,' she said dully. 'We're leaving here.' I was speechless with misery. I felt as if all the juices of my body had dried up. 'We're going to live at my uncle's in Cumberland. He's got a farm.' She rose to her feet and flicked the grass off her skirt. 'I've got to go now.'

'Will I see you tomorrow?'

'No.'

'Why not?'

'My mam says I've not to see you any more.'

'Why?'

'She says you're unsettling me.'

'What does that mean?'

'I don't know, but I can't meet you any more.' She took hold of my hand. Normally all her movements were beautifully coordinated, but this gesture was clumsy and she must have become aware instantly that it was false in the situation, for she turned and ran off as if pursued by a mad dog.

I passed the next three days in a haze of misery, haunting the end of the street in which she lived and occasionally walking furtively past her house. I rehearsed the things I would say to her, spoke passionately under my breath as I walked along the streets. I only caught sight of her once. It was a Sunday morning and she was wearing her best clothes. She came out of the house and, seeing me standing there, bolted back in again. That was the last time I ever saw her. It was the end of summer.

The last term at school and for me and my friends it was a busy one. It was not that we were given much work to do. Our formal school work had ended two years earlier and we had, in a way, been marking time ever since, awaiting the day we would take our place in the line of messenger boys, brew-lads, unskilled labourers and regulars of the dole queues. Mr Gale took the school-leavers' class and he worked hard to make our last term an interesting one. He read chapters from Conrad's *Lord Jim* and *Typhoon*, from Melville's *Redburn* and *Typee*, from Mark Twain and John Masefield. He organised debates between us and the class below ours. One of them was called 'Can Animals Reason?' I defended the proposition, bombarding the opposition with quotations culled from Darwin's *Descent of Man* (I had once been caned by Mr Little for reading this under the desk when I should have been immersed in the class lesson). He organised a school swimming-gala at Broughton Baths, a thing which had never been done before. He and Mr Rushworth acted as judges. They both wore swimming trunks and everybody commented on Mr Rushworth being so skinny. Still, he was a good swimmer, almost as good as Mr Gale, who went through the water like a torpedo. It was difficult to know for whom to cheer. I liked both of them and I wanted both of them to win. The high spot of the gala, though, was when Miss Pitt appeared in her swimming costume and dived in from the deep end. A tremendous cheer went up: 'Pitt the Tit! Pitt the Tit!' and Dennis Carey nearly fell over the rail of the balcony in his excitement. 'What a lovely pair!' he kept saying, and in such a loud voice that Wanker, who was sitting downstairs, stood up and glared up at us with every muscle in his face twitching.

One day five of us played truant from school and, led by Izzy Schneider, queued up outside the Gaumont cinema in Manchester to see Al Jolson in *The Singing Fool*. Mr Gale let our absence pass without comment. Izzy had already embarked upon his career as a punter and had won fifteen shillings on a short odds winner at Irwell Castle. He stood treat and not only paid for our seats at the cinema but bought us all ice-creams as well. We sat there in that blue and gold rococo temple and sobbed our way through that slushy parody of parental love, and none wept louder than Izzy himself.

About this time, I had become a supporter of Broughton Rangers rugby team and I made a point whenever possible of going to their at-home matches. A gang of us used to crawl through a couple of loose planks in the fence and we saw many fine battles with Widnes, Wigan and St Helens that way. It was that year that I saw my first professional soccer game. Once again, Izzy was my mentor and it was because of him that a big group of us became Manchester City supporters. We went to Maine Road about once a month (it was all we could afford) and generally returned home hoarse from cheering for Alec James, high priest of the game.

School stretches out in front of you, an endless sea of days, horizonless until the end of that penultimate term. Then, suddenly, the horizon becomes visible, in patches at least; then it begins to reveal itself more fully until at last those momentary glimpses of a clump of trees, a tiled roof, a group of bathers, is revealed as a complete but disturbingly vague landscape with figures.

Final term. Jesus! How time creeps up on you. Just a little over three months and I'll be leaving school for good. Good? What's good about it? If it's so good why do I find it so disturbing? Why am I filled with such apprehension? Forget it, don't think about it. There's no point in worrying about it. There's nothing you can do to change it. Just pretend you've got another year in front of you. Enjoy being with Meg and her friends. Enjoy the fact that you are mates with Izzy and the rest of the mob. I bet he's not worried. Or is he? You never know what he's thinking. Come to think of it, you never know what anybody's thinking. Take Dilly Underhill or Dougie Singleton: do *they* lie in bed thinking about what it's going to be like in three months' time? Forget it, live for the moment. What's there to look forward to? The dole? A lousy dead-end job? Errand boy, delivery lad, labourer? That's if you're lucky enough to get a labouring job. Elementary school material, that's you. Elementary job material or, what's more likely, elementary dole material. No point in thinking about it till you have to. It's pointless, just going over the same thing again and again. It impinges upon your consciousness, fills you with unease. Forget it, forget it, forget it!

It's pleasant to lie lounging on the grass with your mates and the girls from Central. Just talking, fooling around, the sun hot between your shoulder blades. Wouldn't it be great if you could stop time, make this last forever . . . it's a good feeling being on the terraces at Main Road shouting your lungs out for City and Alec James with Dave Patterson and Izzy and the rest of the lads.

The only trouble is that you can't help remembering that after the cheering and the joking's finished you've got the long walk home. And Izzy, Dave, Twitcher and Dennis Ryan all go home different ways. Three months! It's no time at all. Twelve weeks and goodbye to all this. Goodbye mates, goodbye girls, goodbye school and out into the big wide world. Doesn't look very wide from here. Des Parsons got a job in the Post Office. Had to pass an exam for it. Harney's dad's getting him a job in the paper-mill, he says. Peg Bateson's got nothing, neither has Dilly or Ryan. But what about me? What am I going to do? Face it. Face it! I'm not much good at anything. Can't go on living off the old lady much longer, and that's what it amounts to: living off her. The bit she earns along with the old man's dole is what feeds me and clothes me but I can't go on forever letting someone else put the food into my mouth. And let's face it, the old man's never going to get another job. Apart from the fact that there aren't any jobs in his line, the poor old sod's really ill, can hardly get a decent breath most of the time. In any case, there's the blacklist. But that doesn't make my problem any easier to solve. Think, think, think, think . . . what's the point? Thinking's not going to get you anywhere. It certainly isn't going to get you a job. My old man's been thinking all his life. Thinking got him on the blacklist, so what's the use? The old lady, though. It's terrible seeing her get up at that time in the morning . . . the crack of dawn. It's before the dawn, it's still night, really. What they call the small hours. Winter and summer, spending her time on her knees cleaning up after a lot of rich bastards. Those miles and miles of dreary offices are worse really, but there's something different about having to get down on your knees and scrub that lot. It's impersonal in a way; bloody hard graft, but there's nobody sitting curled up on a sofa watching you work. That time you went to meet her in that place in Broughton Park . . . the size of that place . . . and the rooms! Carpets and rugs everywhere, must have cost a bundle, and the old lady on her knees polishing the floor of that big posh room with the grand piano in it. Wonder who plays it. Saw Ethel, the cook, there. She came to the door of the kitchen when I was waiting in the passage for maid to tell my mother I was there. She looked different in her cook's uniform but still beautiful, all rosy from the warmth of the kitchen. She'd been baking and her arms were powdered with flour. She said, 'Hello, sonny-boy' and gave me a big smile. Wish I could . . . and this must be the lady my mother works for. She's really very young and marvellous to look at. God, I feel so clumsy. She has an expensive smell. Wearing scent in the afternoon inside her own home. Imagine that! And the old lady gets up from the floor and she seems so old and worn by the side of this elegant young creature. 'This is my son,' she says with pride. Oh, God, why does she have to be so . . . yes Missus, no Missus, three bags full Missus. 'So you're Betsy's son.' A nice voice, she's really trying to be nice to me, I think. She smiled at me as if I was somebody real and not just elementary school material. 'Yes, Missus. 'Oh, Jesus, I shouldn't have called her Missus. She'll think I'm . . . but what should I have called her? Lady? No, never. Then what? She'll think I'm stupid. Well, I am stupid. I'm supposed to be stupid so what does it matter what I call her? I didn't want to come in the first place, it was just that my mother wanted me to . . . No use blaming the old lady. She's only got to give a wrong look and she'll be out on her ear. Imagine If Meg and some of those smart-alec girls from Central were watching. But it's not really something to be ashamed of, is it? It's this young woman – she can't be much more than twenty and yet . . . I wonder how she sees me. A clumsy, awkward, blushing oaf worried about his aitches and the fact that he is wearing one of her husband's old jackets. 'See how well it fits him,' my mother is saying. Oh, God! Please, please let's get out of here. Why am I so ashamed? She does it for me. If it wasn't for me and dad she wouldn't need to go out and clean people's houses. It's for me and dad that she does it. It's so we can eat and pay the rent. And it's for those shilling-a-week piano lessons and the shining black upright piano bought on the never-never, her blazing emblem of survival. I hate the sodding thing. Arthur Caldwell had the right idea when he gutted the old crock Harriet bought at a junk shop and put boot-polish and brushes where the keyboard had been. I'll never be any good at it. I'm hopeless. Practice, practice, practice. That's all they ever say. Doesn't do any good anyway. Even when I learn to play a piece quite well at home, as soon as I sit down by the teacher's side my hands forget it. What's the matter with me? Why am I so scared of everything? The way I blushed when that woman spoke to me! She must have thought I was some kind of half-wit. Walking home with the old lady, it suddenly came over me the way I had acted. I mean . . . Oh, Jesus. What an idiot! What's it going to be like when I've finished at school and have to go out looking for work? How many more Miss Tates will I have to suffer, how many more Shields and left-handed right angles? Still, it's the same for everybody. No use thinking you're any different from anybody else. Well, Ernie Worth was a bit different, maybe, but I expect Dilly and Peg Bateson don't feel all that different. In any case, I've got to find something, some kind of work. The old man left home by the time he was fourteen; and look at Diggy Dow – started earning the week he was fourteen. And look at the way people talk about Les Haughton and Bob Edmundson and they're only a year older than me. Why doesn't the big lump go out and get a job? I heard Mrs Lindsay say that to Mrs MacNamara. That big lazy slummock, letting his mother keep him. I'd be ashamed to let somebody else keep me at his age.

What can I do? I don't know enough about anything to apply for a decent job, even if there were any jobs going. Stan Everard's got an uncle who's going to try and get him a job on a ship. All *my* uncles are in Australia, so there's no hope there. And look at my cousin John. All that stuff about marrying a middle-class girl and now he's working in a butcher's shop in Eccles. Still, it's a job and that's more than I've got in view. So what's going to happen to me? I don't know. I don't know. I don't *bloody well know*! It won't let you rest or enjoy anything any more, not completely anyway. It's always at the back of your mind, nagging away or just waiting to pop out and make you feel miserable. Christ! Is this what I was born for?

Wouldn't it be great if we could all stick together? Izzy, Tolly, me, Duggie Ross, Dennis Ryan, Pete Chandler, Capper, Dave, Dilly and Stan Barlow . . . what about Seghead? He's got a real dirty mouth these days. Not a chance anyway. Izzy's going to be a punter, a gambler, and he won't have much time for any of us once he starts on that lark. Everybody'll go their own way, I expect. We'll probably sign on at the dole at different times. Maybe even at different exchanges. One thing to look forward to is that if I keep on growing like this, my clothes'll fit me. That'll be a real improvement. There's one thing for certain, though. I'm not going to wear that plum-coloured overcoat Mrs Whatsername gave the old lady. Not on your life! The plum-coloured shroud, Izzy called it, and he was right. It's a liberty trying to make anybody wear it. No wonder she gave it away. I could have killed Kathy Livingstone, that big long drink of water, that time she pretended she couldn't see me in it. 'D'you think there's someone in it?' she said, and they all started laughing. Anyway, I refuse to wear it. If my mam's so keen on it, then let her wear it . . . it's like a bloody tent on me. A cherry in a plum-skin is how Stan Barlow put it. That's not bad really, at least not for Stan. Doesn't generally put things in such a neat way. Anyway, I'm not wearing it.

The lads who left school last year and the year before that haven't done so well at finding jobs. Bill Livesey's working at Elkanah Armitage's mill where they're on a three-day week and expecting to be laid off any day. Jimmy Tattersall's just lost his job. He was labouring at Broughton Copper until the American efficiency expert did a hatchet job on the work force. Tolly's brother, Vernon, is in the army. Todd Pyott is on the dole. Dominic Flanagan, Seghead's brother, is filling in holes on a government labour scheme. Jimmy Hobbs, Bert Townsley, Chas Naylor and half-a-dozen others are all on the dole. And Bob Elder, who's working in the Pendleton pit, is expecting to be laid off at the end of the week. Not a single one of them, as far as I know, has any kind of skill. And it looks as if me and my mates are going to be just as unlucky, if not more so. Jesus Christ!

10

Limbo

Ever since you left infant school it has been assumed that you belong with the failures. No one has actually come out and said in so many words that you are a failure but it has been taken for granted that you fall naturally into the group which Miss Tate calls *the scruff*. Is that how Wanker Ellerby thought of us as he faced us on our last afternoon at school? He stood there by the side of Mr Gale's desk looking at us, his face twitching spasmodically. Difficult to know what he was feeling. Disgust? Irritation? Contempt? Or was he overcome with despair? 'You will find', he said, 'that it's a harsh world that you are going into.' I can't remember the rest of his speech. He sounded defeated. He knew, as we all knew, that if any of us were lucky enough to find a job then it would be a dead-end occupation or a dirty job that anyone could do. You had always known it, so that by the time you were fourteen and ready to leave school it was no surprise that there wasn't a great deal to look forward to.

Nevertheless, the day when you turn your back on school for the last time is a landmark in your life. You are excited at the thought of the unknown ahead. And you are scared. Suppose you can't cope? Suppose you can't measure up to what's expected of you? Your schoolmates with whom you have shared five days of every week for the last seven or eight years, are now going their separate ways and you won't be seeing them tomorrow or next week or after the summer holidays. Some of them you are now probably seeing for the last time. Already it is beginning, the feeling of loss, of bereavement, and it will go on and on and on . . . if only you could hold onto this day forever; no, to yesterday or the day before. 'Ta-ra, Joe, Ta-ra, Frank. Ta-ra, Izzy. Ta-ra . . . ta-ra.'

And it's over. This is childhood's end and you are running along the last few streets, eager for the warmth of your home, the familiar haven that has sheltered you from the outside world these fourteen years. Two whole days to get used to your altered state and then the search for a job.

On Monday morning, you are awake before Innes starts his rounds, lying there in the icy-cold bedroom hearing the first clatter of footsteps on the paving stones outside. Who can that be? Needham, perhaps. No, not Needham – he sounds heavier than that. You lie poised between sleeping and waking, vaguely conscious of the sound of a distant locomotive and you are suddenly dredged up from the depths of sleep by Innes' sticks rattling on the glass of Yearsley's window and the knocker-up's rasping abuse of the sleepers. Then sleep becomes impossible. The gathering momentum of morning is now measuring out the minutes and you lie there counting them and anticipating the changing rhythms. First, the solitary footsteps of the first of the employed, the office-cleaners and the odd tram-conductor, followed by the early shift-workers and then the hob-nailed-booted platoons of miners, labourers and engineers, followed by the light infantry of clerks and typists and then, after a half-hour lull, the school bound citizens of that world of which you are no longer part. And you lie there with a feeling of desolation seeping into your bloodstream. You know you must get up and begin your new life, the search for a job, but you delay the awful moment until your bladder forces you to get up and visit the lavatory in the backyard.

The day stretches out ahead of you like an endless desert. This is the day you sign on at the 'broo'. A few more weeks and I'll be eligible to draw 8s 9d a week dole money. Better be up no later than eight o'clock sharp. After you've signed on, the rest of your time's your own. What a laugh! What the hell do you need with time? That kind of thinking's for old men, they're the ones who're always talking about time. For you, and those like you, the days are an empty vista, a landscape without horizon, and time is just a great big yawn.

There is a special kind of shame, a quite unreasonable shame, about being unemployed. After a surprisingly short time you begin to feel unreal, invisible, though your reason tells you that you are all too visible. You try to avoid being seen by your old schoolmates because being unemployed marks you out as a confirmed failure. Miss Tate was right. Wanker was right. Chicken Little was right. You find yourself using the back door more and more until you forget that there is a front door. And there is no Saturday night picture-going, no new clothes and no girls. Girls don't want to be seen going around with lads who don't have a job. Killus is working in an engineering factory in Trafford Park. He's got a racing bike with drop handle-bars and cane wheels. They say he's got a chance of an apprenticeship. Yesterday you saw him coming towards you and you dodged into the entry at the back of Mulgrave Street so you wouldn't have to tell him you're unemployed. He probably knows already. Everybody knows. Sod 'em. And as the days pass you sink deeper and deeper into the morass of loneliness and you would give anything to be able to feel a girl's body close to yours. Oh, sweet suffering Jesus!

Walking through the desolation called Peel Park, from the Lower Broughton end to the top, near the Crescent. The scraggy patches of grass are rimed with frost and park benches glisten as if they have been showered with fine tinsel. Now you walk along cracked concrete paths where, at intervals, prancing, leaping, leaning and crouching plaster-of-Paris dryads and bacchantes pose, their mounds of Venus showing innumerable finger marks, the trade-marks of the lonely and forgotten.

Leaving the park behind, you go through the picket in the canal wall and walk along the cobbled path which skirts the canal with its scum of oil, used condoms and all the discarded flotsam of the factories which line its far bank. Then out from the canal-walk at the bridge and down the street of boarded-up houses which face the railway bank and then left into Albion Street where the shuffling, steaming queue of unemployed are waiting to sign on. The nine-o'clock queue. There will be more queues, right up until five o'clock.

Breath condenses in the cold air and there is an almost continual rattle of coughing. Inside the exchange, the queue divides and subdivides and subdivides again until there are eight lines of men formed behind the eight wire grills at the long counter. One at a time the men and boys move forward and push their unemployment-cards under the wire mesh to be stamped by the clerk. That rubber stamp is all that stands between you and starvation. Once it has been stamped, your day's main task has been completed. You are free. Free! To do what?

The rest of the day stretches endlessly ahead of you. You leave the Labour Exchange and walk briskly back along the road bordering the railway. Then you wonder why you are walking so purposefully. After all, you're not going anywhere in particular. I mean, you don't have any specific destination in mind, do you? Walk slowly, then there won't be so much time to kill. You hear the click of hurrying footsteps from a long way off. Coming up behind you, walking fast. A girl, a woman. Now she's abreast of you. If only. Not even conscious of the fact that you are alive, that you are alive at the same time in the same universe. Then she's past and drawing away from you. Just suppose. Nice legs. Would be nice to . . . Shut out the outside world and try to summon the smiling, wanton girls who live in some remote region of your brain and who taunt you with their eager lips and rosy limbs. Christ! How your loins ache with longing. Once, just once!

Almost without being conscious of walking you have arrived at the smoke-blackened, neo-classical temple which houses the museum and public library. From the steps which lead to the entrance you can look down and see, stretched below, part of the monstrous slum in which you live. You walk through the portico and past the brass-handled doors of seasoned mahogany, for this is one of those monuments erected to the Victorian spirit of aggressive learning. It symbolises the triumphant imperialism of the time when cotton was king, when the mechanical loom, the mule and the spinning jenny were conquering empires. 'Let everything be of the best as befits the greatest empire the world has ever known,' said the city fathers. And the forests of India and Burma gave up their hardwoods; Africa and the Far East contributed metals. The best bricks and slates that money could buy were used and only the best craftsmen were employed.

In the hall, or lobby as we termed it, there was a slightly smaller-than-life-size nymph fashioned out of white alabaster. Her belly and thighs at this time of day showed whiter than the rest of her, having just been scrubbed by a conscientious cleaner. In another two or three hours her pubic area would have grown a mat of finger-marks. Standing to the left of her, on a marble pedestal, was a bust of the late Alderman Tit, modelled to look like the poet Byron. On the steps leading to the museum were more aldermanic busts resembling portraits of Hadrian, Julius Caesar and Pericles. At the base of the steps was a bust of Alderman Tit's wife, modelled to look like Pallas Athene.

The first thing one noticed when entering the library (that is, apart from the simpering face of the nymph and the blind gaze of Alderman Tit) was the smell of disinfectant and furniture polish. Once inside the reading room, that odour was enriched by the smell of old leather, dust, damp and urine. The public section of the library consisted of three rooms: the lending library, the room for newspapers and periodicals, and the reading room where serious students could work undisturbed. The newspaper room was always crowded with men standing at the racks, going through the jobs-vacant columns of the papers or studying the lists of horses running in the day's races. The tables were generally occupied by men reading the trade and technical journals. Like the queues at Albion Street Labour Exchange the room smelt of poverty and failure. In cold weather there was always a huddle of men around the hot-water radiators and occasionally sharp words would be exchanged if someone was thought to be having more than his share of warmth.

At first I used to go there and join the magazine readers in order to while away a few hours. At one o'clock I would go home through the park and after a cup of tea and some toast I would walk the streets, convinced that one day some fabulous adventure would come my way. Or, if it was summer and the weather was fine, I would lie on the grass in the park and dream impossible dreams. Evenings were the most miserable part of the day; they were a kind of limbo situated between day and night. There were no signposts – just a flat, dreary, featureless plain.

From the time I was thirteen I had been drifting away from the street gang and after I left school the break became complete. It wasn't merely that I was lonely; I felt that I had actually suffered the amputation of a limb. In any case, the gang was scattered. Tolly was working in a textile warehouse and was palling around with a bloke from Havelock Street. The rest of the mob had all gone their separate ways. The life of the street had become in some way curiously remote. I was conscious of it all around me but I seemed to be living in a fine gauze cocoon through which everything looked unreal. My parents, too, appeared to exist on a different plane and communication between us was almost non-existent. My mother tried to get through to me. 'What's wrong?' she would say. 'Are you in some kind of trouble?'

'No, I'm all right.'

'Are you sure?'

'Yes, I'm sure. For God's sake, leave me alone.'

'Talk to your mither like that and I'll gie ye the back o' my hand.'

I would mutter an apology and rush to the kitchen sink and hurriedly wash my hands and face and, after plastering my hair down with water, leave the house like someone who had an urgent appointment elsewhere. I would walk briskly to the end of the street looking neither to the right nor to the left for fear of being questioned by a neighbour as to whether or not I had found a job yet.

Only when I turned the gable-end of the street would I slow down. Now what shall I do? Should I turn right or left? Does it matter? Suddenly I found myself hoping desperately that I would encounter somebody that I knew. Anybody. At the same time there was the disinclination to meet any of my old friends. It wasn't just that I was unemployed. I was beginning to think that I was stupid and that I would be unemployed forever. I was particularly determined to avoid any of the girls I had played with as a child. The fact that there were more than three million people in the same boat as me gave me no solace. It was *I* who was lonely and miserable. *I* was the one wearing second-hand clothes that were too big for me, whose ears stuck out like jug handles, who was stupid, clumsy and unemployable. In the face of my personal misery, statistics meant nothing.

I wasn't always successful in avoiding childhood friends and generally when we met my embarrassment disappeared. We would exchange pleasantries, enquire about mutual friends and the girls would smile shyly, conscious of their changed appearance. But I think that all of us were aware that we were becoming strangers and sensed that soon we would have forgotten completely that we had once cheated each other at marbles, stolen each others cigarette-cards, fought off rival gangs, collected bonfire wood together, played doctors and taken part in the same initiation rites. These chance encounters didn't lessen the feelings of loneliness and rejection. If anything, they intensified them.

Signing on at the Labour Exchange and writing applications for jobs took only a fraction of my days. What was left seemed endless. At times I felt I was drowning in tedium and guilt. I had to escape or be destroyed. But how to escape, and to where? To any one of a thousand worlds. How do I get there? Pass through that carbolic-scented domain of the dryad and Alderman Tit and you can exchange this awful grey world for that other more exciting world of books and ideas. Since you have entered this grown-up world where nobody seems to want you or need you, you have come to regard books as your best friends, your only friends. There in the reading room, you anticipate the pleasure of opening one of the books you have ordered, of touching the binding, of turning over the pages and smelling the dry, musty odour of paper and old ink. An unfamiliar world to be explored. Forget the park outside and the streets beyond the park. Forget the landscape which mocks you with mill chimneys, pithead winding gear, cranes and all the signs of men and women working. Forget them – a better world came out of the Frenchman's head. So what shall it be this morning? Papa Gobseck's Paris? The Don of La Mancha's Valencia, or the perpetual titular councillor's Nevski Prospekt? Wonderful journeys, all of them.

And yet I am never free of the disturbing thought that life is passing me by, that I am living in a transparent capsule which isolates me from the tremendously vital and exciting life outside. This feeling of being set apart from the real world is with me constantly. Somewhere, just beyond the edge of vision there is . . . a person, a place, an object, a thing or things . . . which if I could see it, them, him, her, then my whole life would become exciting, vibrant, central to the world of which, at the moment, I am a mere onlooker, an outsider, a bystander. This dimly perceived impression of a world beyond the one of which I am part, hovers on the edge of my last moment of wakefulness and occupies my first moment of waking. Even my sleeping and waking erotic dreams are invaded by it, for even in the midst of orgiastic encounters with bevvies of wanton nymphs I am conscious of the fact that these insubstantial lips and breasts and thighs which promise what they cannot give, stand or lie between me and real flesh-and-blood girls whose beauty renders me breathless.

The reading room is stuffy and my eyes are beginning to prick with tiredness. I leave my books at the counter and go out for a breath of cold air. A watery sun is trying to break through the grey pall of the morning. The hoar-frost on the limestone balustrade of the steps has begun to melt so that it looks like a scrofulitic fuzz. Along the cracked tarmacadam paths, past the plaster-of-Paris dying gladiator and the nose-less water nymph. The paint on the wooden benches has blistered and peeled, giving the wood a slightly hairy appearance. Another work of art: The Three Graces, three plump, naked young simperers, one of whom has lost an arm. A metal rod, looking like a failed prosthetic device, sticks out of the maimed shoulder. And now Diana the Huntress, my favourite among the park's plaster reproductions of Greece and Rome's finest. She wears a very short skirt which draws attention to her very shapely legs. Her breasts, too, are splendid. I am obviously not her sole admirer for both her breasts and thighs are densely maculated by the fingers of countless unknown persons. Oh, sweet Jesus! If only I could . . .

Back to the reading room. How quiet the park is. Nobody around. Less than half-a-mile away, smoke from the mill-stacks, steam from the factories, the clang of metal, the throb and whine of machines, the clunk and chug of shunting-engines at the railway yard . . . what's going to happen to me? Suppose I *never* get a job? Christ. Christ! Fuck the bastards! Back to the reading room. Peel Park to the Boulevard St Germain. Hail Rastignac! Hail Lucien! If only I was Montriveau! Imagine having it off with the Duchesse de Langeais. . . this is my most consistent fantasy, to live naked with a beautiful and insatiable young woman in a library of rare books.

Almost one o'clock. Time to go home and get something to eat. Through the park again. The wintery sun has finally broken through and almost all the frost has melted. Only occasional patches in the shade of rhododendron bushes still show white. Over the bridge, across the black Irwell and past St Andrew's school where the air is shrill with the cries of playing kids. Down through Mulgrave Street, across the square where a noisy game of football is in progress and in through the back door.

My father is sitting by the unlit kitchen fire, reading a newspaper and nursing a cup of tea. He looks up when I enter. 'Any luck?'

'No. You?'

'I'll need more than luck', he says, 'I'll need a bloody miracle.'

My father has changed greatly during the last two or three years. He smiles less and rarely sings. He's beginning to look old. How old is he, for God's sake? Forty-three, forty-four? Is that old? It's the shame of not being able to find a job. It's killing him. I wish I could tell him some of the things I feel. I can't and I don't know why. It's as if there's a wall between us. In the old days, when they were blacklisting him, he still managed to be cheerful – he still sang. There was always somewhere else he could go for a job. But that's not the case any more. It's like this everywhere. Almost all the foundry workers who used to visit us at Hogmanay are now on the dole. I help myself to bread and cheese and pour a cup of tea. In spite of the fact that the two of us are sitting here, the house feels deserted. It's always the same when my mother's out, the place feels abandoned. I can't wait to get out again.

The afternoon stretches out ahead of me, infinite and infinitely boring. Afternoons are hell. They creep by on leaden feet. Fucking sleepwalkers! So what am I going to do? How long before I become part of that great throng of men and women who belong in the world where smoke and steam and clattering metal are born? How long can I go on being lonely, bored and aimless? At the moment there is no ahead, no future, only the afternoon unrolling ahead of me like a road that doesn't go anywhere.

'I think I'll get back to the library and do a bit of reading.'

'You might as well. Knowledge is never wasted.'

Back through the park again. I could walk this route blindfolded. A few more people about. Men, for the most part. Unemployed, whiling away the hours till it's time to go home. The newspaper room's still full. The same young-old men reading the newspapers or sleeping at the leather-topped tables. The attendant in the reading room greets me like an old friend. 'Back again?' she says. 'You'll be living here soon.' I am so overcome with gratitude at being noticed that I blush to the roots of my hair and turn away, embarrassed. I shout insults at myself inside my head. 'Don't be such a . . .' Such a what? I can't think of words to describe my stupidity. Oh well . . . I comb through the index-files, undecided. Should I read for pleasure today or should I pursue knowledge? I decide to split my reading time between *The Foundations of Philosophy* by a Russian author whose name I have forgotten (Bogdanov . . .?) and *The Plays of Eugene O'Neill*. I find the philosophy book fascinates me, though I am irritated at having to refer to a dictionary in order to understand the meaning of some of the words. I take a decision there and then to learn ten words each day from the Webster dictionary, which is the one I happen to be using at that moment . . .

Aard-vark, one of the edentat pple. of L edentare render toothless . .Zool. An order of mammalia characterised by the absence of front teeth. Aba. A new altazimuth Azi . . . an arc of the heavens extending from the Zenith to the horizon which it cuts at right angles; the quadrant of a great circle of the sphere passing through the zenith and nadir . . late ME, cenyth, senith, cinit – OFr cenit (mod Zenith). The point of the sky directly overhead. Nadir, a point in the heavens diametrically opposite to some other point, especially to the sun.

Ten a day! It'll take me a lifetime, two or three lifetimes, to get a vocabulary. On the other hand, is there any reason why I should know about words like azimuth? How can I possibly use it in conversation? I was late for the Labour Exchange this morning – my azimuthal calculations were slightly out owing to the fog which made it impossible to calculate exactly the position of the zenith which, in turn, produced errors in fixing the nadir. *Abacinate.* Now that's more like it. My dad's an iron-moulder, used to work in a foundry where one always runs the risk of abacination. It's got a good ring to it. Abacinate, abacinated, abacination. A slow job, but there's no need to learn them all. Will I ever, for instance, need to use the word *abassi,* the word for a Persian silver coin worth about twelve pence? On the other hand, there's *Abaddon,* the bottomless pit, a perfect name for this bloody place I live in. Abaddon, Abaddon. Three-quarters-of-an-hour spent with the dictionary. Learned something anyway. Knowledge is never wasted. Azimuth, Abaddon.

Desire Under the Elms, The Hairy Ape, and *Dynamo* at one fell swoop. At that first reading, *Dynamo* excited me most. That power-house with its great brooding turbines keeps flashing before my eyes as I walk home. We have electrocuted God! Jesus, I wouldn't mind sending postcards to my friends with that written on them. We have electrocuted God. What friends? I don't know anybody apart from my father and mother and my Auntie Mag and her family. There's the people in the street, of course. But it would look daft sending post-cards to people who live practically next door to you. There's Teddy Hewitson – he's religious, or at least he's a Catholic. Imagine sending one to him and his mother seeing it. She'd go daft. What about the lads I went to school with? I'll bet Izzy Schneider wouldn't mind getting a postcard with *We have electrocuted God* written on it. But I don't know his address, or the addresses of any of my mates. So that takes care of that.

I spend the evening moping around the house. The problem is that if you live in a two-up-and-two-down and share your bedroom with a lodger, there's only one place to mope in and that's the outside lavatory, and that's a bloody chilly place for meditation. In between trying to figure out how to fill this great gap of time I am busily composing sonorous phrases like 'we have electrocuted God'. On the way home from the reading room earlier on, my head was ringing with magnificent combinations of words but I have forgotten them all and the new phrases don't work as they should. The world is drowning/suffocating (yuk!)/choking in . . . what? time? Time is an open sewer, a cesspit, a stinking puddle. The last one's not bad – cuts time down to size. The world is drowning in the sewer of time. Terrible. Sounds like a line from a novel whose hero is called Garth. No, sewers are out. How about 'they have abacinated the future'? Abaddon is a synonym for . . what? What the hell does azimuth mean? Azimuth. Azimuth. Azimuth? We have electrocuted the azimuth and who the hell cares?

What did I think the future would be like? Did I ever have a clear picture of it in my head? You'd start thinking about it and then your mind would shoot off at a tangent. The tangenital mind. The tangent at the end of the azimuth or the azimuth at the end of the tangent. With rod and line up the azimuth. Everything was always so vague, like seeing things through a heavy fog. Then, for a split second, the fog would clear but before you had time to focus your eyes it was swirling round you again. No, it wasn't seeing, it was sensing. Everything was insubstantial but, in a strange way, exciting. In a way, it was like playing rally-o. You raced through the dark streets to find a perfect hiding place. Brokenbrow's back door! No, you're bound to be seen there. The first place he'll look are the back doors. The Farrow's lavatory roof. Quickly! Shin up the wall and climb onto the sloping flagstones of the roof. Don't breathe so hard, someone'll hear you. Lying there in the dark on the cold sandstone roof-slab, smelling the blunt smell of old stone. Raising your head slightly you can see into the Lowrie's kitchen window. Mrs Lowrie is boiling a kettle on the gas-ring. Christ! Someone's coming out of the Farrow's. It's Mr Farrow, he's coming to the lavatory. Your breathing suddenly sounds monstrously loud. Quiet. Breathe through your mouth. I'm getting cramp in my left foot but I daren't move for fear he hears me. God, he's a long time. He pulls the chain, thank God for that! I alter my position on the roof under cover of the noise. Now he's back in the kitchen, but I've still got to lie low. There's been plenty of time for Killus to count to a hundred, and he's a sly bugger. He'll come creeping when he does come. Was that a footstep? The excitement is choking me. I'll have to take some deep breaths.

Excitement! Like thoughts about the future. They were exciting, too, the same mixture of anticipation and dread, of wanting something but not being sure of what that something was. Oh yes, the images in your dreams were clear enough but somehow they became shadowy and then dissipated just as you were on the brink of understanding some terribly important truth. Who is that beautiful girl who lives on the edge of your subconscious? You are walking along in a place where the air smells of phul-nana cashous and there she is, beautiful beyond words, rosy with health, sleek and well-fed. She smiles tenderly as she beckons you. You move towards her, not walking but floating and she takes you by the hand. Why, *why* can't you feel the touch of her hand? 'Wait,' she says, and her voice is so comforting that it brings tears to my eyes. Hand in unfeeling hand, we enter this fantastic house, ascend the wide staircase and enter a lovely warm room with rugs on the floor and the whole place ablaze with sunlight. Her entire body is smiling as we approach the gigantic oval bed with its shimmering, silken sheets and then, miraculously, we are both naked and she is lying on the bed with parted thighs and open arms inviting me to fall on her. And because she knows all there is to know about it, about love-making, about fucking, I am . . . OH JESUS! Even as you are falling into the unknown darkness of her being, you are aware that it is all a dream, that it will *always* be a dream, that nothing like this ever happens, at least not in

Salford and certainly not to an elementary-school reject wearing second-hand clothes and on the dole.

So what about the future? Can this endless succession of empty days be the future? Nadir, abaddon, abacinate, nadir, edentata juvenalis, aardvark, aba, altazimuth, alabaster head of fucking abacinated Alderman Tit. Another day in my useless life frittered away. Fuck off, world.

11

On the Broo

In the spring of 1928, Charlie Harrison became our lodger. My father brought him home from a meeting one night and introduced him to my mother. 'This is Charlie. D'ye think you could find him a bed for a wee while?'

He was a short, neat little man in his late twenties. He had black, curly hair and a heavy stubble of beard which covered most of his face and emphasised his Jewishness. My mother regarded him with obvious suspicion. 'You're no' growing a beard, are ye?' Charlie explained that he was in mourning for his mother and would recommence shaving as soon as the period of mourning was over. His threadbare black overcoat and shiny black trousers must have been part of his mourning attire too, my mother thought, until she discovered they were his only outdoor clothes. A week or so after his arrival, he shaved and was transformed into a personable young man. 'He's no' a bad-looking wee bloke.' Further acquaintance produced a qualitative change in my mother's opinion of him: 'He's a fine-looking wee fella.'

Charlie was a waterproof-worker by trade and a member of the Communist Party. Indeed, he had recently been appointed the branch organiser. The fact that the entire membership of the branch didn't exceed a dozen people didn't prevent him from regarding his new role as an important one and one to be worn with dignity. It was, of course, unpaid. His regimen was strict, based (I suspect) on the one adopted by Lenin during his period of Siberian exile. Every morning, come rain, hail or shine, he was up by seven-thirty. Standing naked in the backyard, he would hose himself down with cold water. This would be followed by a session of Swedish drill and deep-breathing exercises after which he would sit down to his breakfast of brown bread and marmalade. Most mornings he would read for half-an-hour or so, alternating Lenin's *State and Revolution* and Marx's *Paris Commune*. I was greatly impressed with this systematic approach to reading and for a time I considered adopting it. Towards the end of his sojourn with us he was reading Lenin's *Left Wing Communism – an Infantile Disorder* and Engels' *The Peasant War in Germany*.

On signing-on days he would leave the house early and return about midnight or even later. On the days he stayed at home he ate a lunch of cheese-

and-onion sandwiches washed down with a glass of milk and in the evening a cheese-and-onion sandwich and a cup of tea. His abstemiousness grieved my mother and she tried, time after time, to persuade him to partake of a bowl of soup or a plate of stew. He was polite but adamant in his refusals. She complained to my father. 'Is he trying to starve himself to death or something?'

'Not at all,' replied my father. 'It's a matter of principle.'

'Principle, my arse! It's a pity he couldnae get hold o' some o' that Moscow gold the papers are aye talking about and fatten himself up a bit.'

On Sunday mornings, he broke with routine and spent the morning playing gramophone records on his portable machine while he sponged and pressed his shiny blue suit. Since he owned neither a dressing gown nor pyjamas he was driven on these occasions to wear his overcoat and a rather misshapen trilby. To see him standing there wielding my mother's ancient charcoal-burning iron with his hairy legs sticking out from underneath his rusty black coat, beating time to an aria from *I pagliacci* with his left hand, it was easy to imagine that our lodger was really Vladimir Ilyitch or Fedor Dostoevski.

How he loved that hand-cranked portable and his three or four albums of treasured operatic records! On more than one occasion I have seen him interrupt his ironing to wipe tears from his eyes as he shared Punchinello's grief at his rejection by Columbine and, I must confess, I wept with him. His other great love was *Der Ring des Nibelungen,* a work which I found utterly boring though I knew a great deal of it by heart through having to listen to it every Sunday morning for several months. The discs were 78s and overplaying had thinned the walls of the grooves. Some of them were so worn that their shiny black surface had acquired the greyness of unkempt old age. *Die Walkure* in particular, was in an advanced state of decrepitude and both Sieglinde and Siegmund sounded as if they were suffering from violent hiccups. I imitated them for my cousin John and was overheard by Charlie. A few days later he suggested that I make use of my talents by joining a theatre group which some of his friends had organised for the purpose of staging working-class plays and sketches. The group was The Clarion Players and joining it was my first individual political act. Almost all the members were in their twenties or thirties and I couldn't help feeling like a visitor from a distant planet. Nevertheless, I continued to attend the weekly rehearsals and discussions. It was something to do, a break in the dreadful monotony of my existence.

I left school the week after my fourteenth birthday. 2 February 1929. It was a bad period for school-leavers without skills or qualifications and I searched for two long months before finding a job in a wire mill. I was sent there from the Labour Exchange and interviewed by a man wearing a brown overall and an absent-minded expression. After a few perfunctory questions he told me to report for work at eight o'clock the following morning. I was so dazed with the shock of being hired that I forgot to ask what kind of work I would be doing.

Dogsbody, that was my job. The newest – and therefore the lowest – of dogsbodies. The boy who brews the tea, who queues up at the pie-shop for sixteen potato-pies, please, two without gravy. 'Here you! Take this to the foreman of the annealing department.'

'How do I get there?'

'Ask.'

'Collect the day's job-sheets from the manager's office.'

'Take this to the rolling-mill.'

'Take these cores to the labs.'

The noise is terrifying. It smashes against you, pulverises you so that you can't think. 'Which is the way to . . .' Your voice is torn from your throat and silenced immediately. The man waves you on. Don't bother me. 'Which is the . . .' Somewhere between the scream of high-speed copper-strip drawing machines with their whirling drums of gleaming metal and the mind shattering blows of automatic hammers beating out ingots for the diamond-dies.

Into the tinning rooms, where eyes and nose are assaulted by the hot, acrid stink of molten tin. Death Row, they call this place. God, how long can I hold my breath? How do they stand it? And this is almost as bad . . . phosphor-bronze is the name they give that stuff. I'm going to be sick. There's an open door leading to a catwalk that runs right along the edge of the factory. Underneath is the black water of the Irwell with its floating islands of dirty foam. Even *that* seems clean and fresh compared to the stink of the mill. Now into the annealing shed.

If the tinning room is Death Row, what is this? It's worse than the foundry. The heat rushes at you from all directions. The steel plates underneath your feet are shimmering with heat. Hundreds of great steel drums filled with coils of heavy-gauge wire sink to the level of the floor and are heated to just below melting point by thousands of gas jets. Men bathed in sweat and wearing only underpants and wooden sabots spray the drums with hosepipes, creating clouds of hissing steam. In a surprisingly short time I became accustomed to the noise of the wire and strip-drawing departments and to the choking sensation that I always experienced in the tinning room, but the annealing shed never ceased to terrify me.

On the other hand, the cable-housing department, where they wove the sleeves for electric cables, was a place I always looked forward to visiting, with a kind of nervous anticipation. Most of the weavers were young women and all of them were ribald. When they happened to notice me they generally shouted invitations that brought a blush to my cheeks – or they would improvise arguments about the tell-tale bulge in my trousers. 'What's that you're carrying, love? A stick of Blackpool rock, is it?'

'The poor lad doesn't know what it's for,' one of them would say.

Then another voice would come in on cue: 'He hasn't got one.'

'Of course he's got one and it's not been filleted neither.'

I enjoyed these encounters in spite of my embarrassment. My enjoyment came to an end when one day an older woman, with a voice like my Auntie Mag's, declared, 'He'd look good in a bottle.' Three or four girls screamed with laughter and I left in a hurry. I had heard about *bottling* and had no wish to be a candidate.

Bottling was one of those initiation rites practised in factories where the workforce was predominantly women. The victim, usually an adolescent, was captured by a group of girls and forced to insert his penis into the neck of a bottle. Once this had been accomplished, his captors would rouse him sexually to the point where his engorged penis would be trapped in the bottle. I was spared this humiliation by the coming of an American rationalisation expert named Friedman, who set about reorganising the factory with enormous zeal. He was a short, pleasant-faced man with a shock of iron-grey hair, who prowled through the factory like a terrier searching out a bone. He seemed never to look at anyone but you felt that a fly couldn't land on a wall without being spotted by Friedman. In the first three months, he reduced the labour force by some four hundred men. New machines were brought in, new work-practices introduced and the possibility of the sack dangled in front of everyone's nose. A wave of fear, suspicion and alarm spread through the factory like a plague. I was lucky. The most junior of the post-boys in the general office left or was sacked without notice and I was drafted in as a temporary substitute.

I cannot remember exactly when the period of my Grand Erection started. I use the word 'grand' in order to distinguish it from short-term erections. It lasted, I think, the best part of a year, give or take a few days. Perhaps it would be more accurate to call it a long-standing erection, since the word 'grand' possesses, in this context, self-congratulatory overtones. The fact is, I was not proud, at least not in the sense of having a lofty opinion of myself. Only in the physical, tumid sense was I proud. That is an incontrovertible fact and one that caused me a great deal of inconvenience and embarrassment.

At the beginning of my erect period I was already at the wire-works. My working day began at eight o'clock and I rose from my bed at seven, generally dragged out of a wildly erotic dream and still feeling the unpleasantly sticky dampness of my night emission. Downstairs, I fixed the hose on the solitary kitchen tap and fed it through the kitchen window into the yard. That first moment under the freezing cold water was penance for my wet-dreams. At 7.20 a.m. I left the house for my two-mile walk to work. This was, in some ways, the best part of the day. I was free to resume my dreams, and so for six days of every week I walked to work in a cloud of breasts and thighs and sweet-smelling flesh. Occasionally I would descend to earth and note the shape of a passing girl's legs, but on the whole I preferred the compliant beauties of my fantasies.

Once, for a short period of a week or so, I fell painfully in love with a girl in an office that I passed every day. She was a luscious seventeen-or eighteen-year-old with legs like the Diana the Huntress in Peel Park – a peasant-like face with straight golden hair cut in a shingle and a snub nose. She walked with a kind of sexual arrogance that one sees only in young working-class girls. On the Saturday afternoon of that week I was walking through Pendleton to visit a friend when I saw her sitting on a doorstep with a baby on her knee. For a moment I was almost overcome with the strength of my desire for her. I hurried past, blushing furiously and trying awkwardly to arrange my posture so that she wouldn't notice my condition. When I was well past her I began to upbraid myself for having missed an opportunity to talk with her. I could have asked her the time or the way to my friend's house. I could have mentioned that I sometimes saw her going to work. I could have . . . My friend lived just a few houses up the street and in a few minutes we were walking back towards her. My friend shouted a greeting to her when we passed and she flashed him back a warm smile. The baby, he told me, was hers. She had refused to marry the father and her parents had given her a hard time. Things were better now, he said, and she was going strong with an ambulance driver and was probably going to get hitched up. This knowledge had no effect upon my desire for her. God, how terrible it is to be regarded as a child when one has all the desires of an adult!

After the factory proper, I found office work tedious. Only the presence of the typists made it bearable. They were separated from the rest of us by a glass partition. I found them irresistible, while they found me amusing, at least some of them did. I was in the throes of the Grand Erection and I had only to come within three feet of them to become rigid. I was still wearing short pants and my condition showed up clearly. 'What are you carrying in your pocket, sonny?' Miss Taplow would ask, in a voice dripping with innocence. Jennings, who (it was rumoured) was the managing-director's private property, used to follow me around with her eyes, gazing fixedly, without blinking, at my affliction. Miss Kay, a ravishing brunette and head of the typing division, just looked disapproving and called me 'a dirty young devil'. It was a game of knowing looks and words, of sly glances and carefully measured doses of sexual-innuendo. It wasn't meant to go beyond that.

It was different with the diminutive filing clerk, Miss Pratt. She used every muscle of her perfectly formed body as an instrument of provocation. 'She's a prick-teaser,' said Larry, the senior post-boy. He had been laying siege to her virtue for more than a year and he was as far from his objective as the day he began his campaign. She played him like a fisherman landing a salmon and she now played me as well. Her wiles consisted largely of an expert use of breasts and thighs. She was as subtle in their use as a carter with a whip. She had a habit of passing in front of you so close that her buttocks lightly caressed the front of your trousers in the region of the flies. Sometimes she would stand there in front of you, ostensibly busy with something on the desk and then would stand on tiptoe to reach a file above her head. This would be repeated with slight variations until she had brought you almost to the point of orgasm. Then she would move to a different part of the office. She had a whole vocabulary of buttock movements and with them could express interest and disinterest, friendliness, disdain – an entire range of emotions.

Her breast-work, also, was technically sound though a little lacking in subtlety. She would contrive to lean over you when you were seated at a desk and her breast would lightly brush your cheek or rest against the side of your head or come to rest within an inch of your mouth. If you happened to be writing, her breast would magically touch your hand and then your shoulder and if you turned suddenly you would sometimes be rewarded by having a nipple rest for a moment in the hollow of your eye. I lusted after Miss Pratt for three whole months. Larry, even after a year of frustration, still laboured under the illusion that her touching ways were a prelude to more serious encounters.

In the basement of the office building there was a strong-room in which were stored correspondence-files, advice notes and invoices which went back twenty years or more. Occasionally, Miss Pratt or one of the typists would have recourse to one of these old files. They were heavy and the post-boy or junior clerk was usually recruited to lift them down from the shelves. Miss Pratt always chose Larry for this task. On the first occasion he was convinced that she had arranged things so that he could seduce her in privacy. In the strong-room he wasted no time but drew Miss Pratt to him and tried to kiss her. The push she gave him sent him reeling to the opposite side of the room. 'You're being silly,' she said. Larry stood there sulking until she took him by the hand and, with a tender look, whispered, 'Not here. Somebody might come in.' He attempted to argue but she was adamant. He lapsed into sulky silence again, while she proceeded to leaf through box-files in search of a missing advice-note. Larry was confused, for she continued to find opportunities for breast-and-buttock contact. When she told him to hold the ladder firm while she climbed up to retrieve a file on a high shelf, he was aroused beyond endurance and essayed a tentative stroke of her buttocks. She responded by hitting him over the head with a heavy file of old advice-notes and knocking him to the ground. He lay there, dazed, on the dusty floor while she cradled his head against her breast and chastely kissed his forehead. Her skirt was hitched up to her thighs but when he attempted to steal a sly caress of the three inches of skin above her stocking-tops she hit him again.

'A prick-teaser,' Larry said to me, but without rancour. I am now convinced that the sexual games practised in that office were the only way of making the drudgery bearable. Just think of it: Larry, a seventeen-year-old youth, healthy and full of sap, spending eight hours of every day doing work no more exciting or demanding than walking to the post office to buy stamps and register parcels, collecting letters to be mailed out from the various departments, entering them in the post-book, stamping them and doing odd jobs for the senior clerk; and Miss Pratt, a healthy and vibrant young woman destined to make alphabetical arrangements of the records of past sales. The annealing shed was preferable.

I came nearer than Larry to achieving a kind of sexual fulfilment, not with Miss Pratt but with the cheerful, thirty-year-old Miss Taplow from the typing pool. For me, too, the strong-room was the stage. Once inside, Miss Taplow clasped me to her and gave me a smacking kiss. 'Right', she said, 'let's see what it looks like', and set about unbuttoning my flies. In a moment she had taken the cause of my troubles in her hand and was examining it. 'Not bad', she said, 'not bad at all', and fell to caressing it. After a moment in a rather strained voice, she said, 'It would be an awful shame to waste it', and in a single quick movement she had taken off her knickers. 'Put them in your pocket,' she commanded and, still holding me, she opened her legs. As she guided me towards her, my excitement and inexperience combined to thwart her and before I could enter I came in a great rush of scalding semen. She groaned and then snatched the handkerchief from my breast pocket. 'Look what you've done! It's all over my stockings!' She proceeded to wipe the glistening blobs from her stocking and then, ignoring my apologies, took my penis and wiped that too, talking to it as she did so. 'Not so jaunty now, are you, cock? I bet you feel better. What a waste, though.' Taking hold of my hand, she put it between her legs against the hot, wet mouth of her vagina. 'There', she said, 'that's where you're supposed to put it. There, inside. That's it. Go on, go on. Just there.' She was squirming and pressing herself against me and I felt myself beginning to harden again. Suddenly she became tense and pushed me away. 'Quick!' she said, 'there's someone coming.' In a moment she was straightening her skirt and making herself look presentable. I was still fumbling with my flies by the time she had straightened her hair and had touched up her lips. The instant and expert transformation of a sexually ravenous woman into the efficient typist was truly remarkable, so that when, a minute or two later, the office maintenance man put his head round the door, there was nothing to see but two industrious office workers delving among the dusty files of ancient correspondence. 'Don't worry. It'll be better next time,' Taplow promised. That was the only reference she ever made to what had happened between us. Back in the office she was her usual self and at no time did she by as much as a glance show that she remembered our dalliance in the strong-room.

For a short time afterwards the other typists would eye me speculatively when I passed the glass partition but after a time they ignored me. There was no 'next time' as far as Miss Taplow was concerned. Occasionally I would have a brief vision of her standing there with her skirt rucked up around her waist with glistening strings of semen trickling slowly down her thighs and I would remember the urgency in her voice as she urged me on. But it would be gone in a flash to be replaced with the more credible reality of the friendly and somewhat cynical lady of the typing pool. I had forgotten the incident completely until recently . . . indeed, until I sat down to write I have never given a thought to Miss Taplow. On the other hand, Miss Pratt – or rather, her buttocks – is on my mind every time we travel on the A-21 past Pratts Bottom, between Bromley and Sevenoaks.

By the time I had become accustomed to the dull routine of office work, the American efficiency expert had got round to modernising the office and the terror that gripped some of the older clerks was really frightening. The occasional joking and repartee between clerks and typists became a thing of the past. Old clerks were fearful of being sacked because of their age while young

William Miller, Ewan's father.

Jimmie Miller (Ewan MacColl)
at 12 years old.

The boys of Grecian Street School, Salford 1923. Jimmie is sitting in the front row, second from the right.

Coburg Street, Salford, 1959, before demolition in the 1960s.

Ewan MacColl, aged 21.

The Canal, Salford, where
Ewan nearly drowned.

The Red Megaphones, Ewan's Agitprop Group, during a May Day demonstration at Preston in 1932. Ewan is standing second from the left.

Ewan as the Puppetmaster in his own play *Uranium 235* in London 1949.

Part of Theatre Workshop Co. at their first home in Kendal 1945. Ewan is sitting to the right.

Joan Littlewood, Ewan's first wife.

Jean Newlove, Ewan's second wife and mother of his children Hamish and Kirsty.

Theatre Workshop

presents

LANDSCAPE
with
CHIMNEYS

By EWAN MacCOLL

Produced by JOAN LITTLEWOOD

"Landscape With Chimneys" is the story of a street and the people who live in it. There is nothing extraordinary about this street; its prototype could be found in Glasgow, Manchester, Cardiff . . . . anywhere in fact.

—And the people who live in it? Ordinary people; hard-working, patient, persevering; the men and women who's lives pass unrecorded . . . dockers, housewives, engineers, factory hands.

And yet, this compact community of ordinary people is rich in the raw material out of which drama is made. For the street is a world in miniature and by recording a year of its life, its tragedy, its hopes, its humour, its flashes of gaiety, Theatre Workshop offers you a play full of truth and simple humanity.

. . . . IT CAN BE SEEN . . .

Jan. 8—CWMAMAN	Jan. 15—PENTRE	Jan. 22—RHIGOS
Jan. 9—ABERDARE	Jan. 16—RHYMNEY	Jan. 23—COLBREN
Jan. 10—BEDLINOG	Jan. 17—CWM PARC	Jan. 24—RESOLVEN
Jan. 11—TREHERBERT	Jan. 18—PONT Y CYMMER	Jan. 25—GORSEINON
Jan. 12—WATTSTOWN	Jan. 19—BRYN CETHIN	Jan. 26—CWMAVON
Jan. 13—CYMMER PORTH		Jan. 27—YSTRADGYNLAIS

The programme for Ewan's play, *Landscapes with Chimneys* 1951.

Ewan as the Street Singer in *The Threepenny Opera*, Sam Wanamaker's West End production, which opened at The Royal Court in 1956.

Peggy Seeger at 19 years of age in 1954.

The Ramblers, Ewan and Peggy's first group, in 1956-57. *Top row*: Alan Lomax, Bruce Turner, Jim Bray, Brian Daly. *Bottom row*: Peggy, Ewan, Shirley Collins.

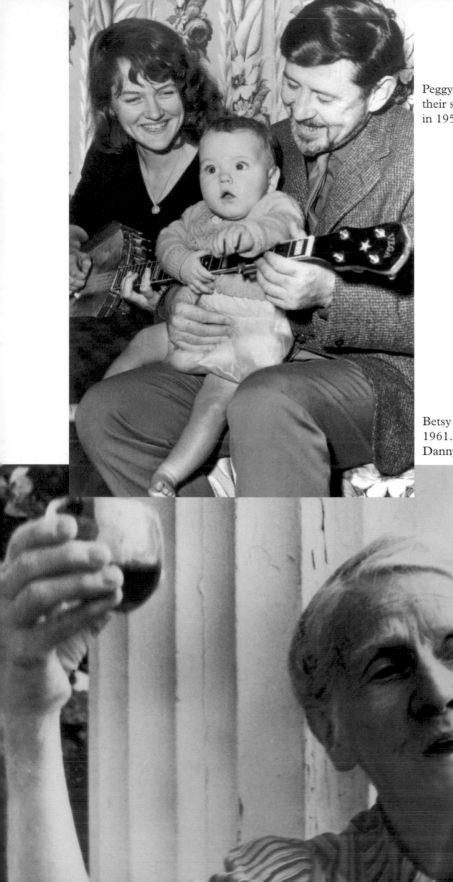

Peggy, Ewan and their son Neill in 1959.

Betsy Miller in 1961. Photo by Danny Seeger.

ones were convinced that lack of seniority would count against them. The fact is that no one felt secure and everyone was suspicious of his or her neighbour. Every time someone was sacked, a sigh of relief went up from those who were left. My turn came in the middle of the rationalisation sweep, a week after my fifteenth birthday.

Back at the Albion Street Labour Exchange, I found that the dole queues had grown much longer during the eleven months that I had been employed. In the first five or six weeks of my enforced freedom I wrote dozens of applications for jobs in response to adverts in the situations-vacant columns of the daily newspapers. On two occasions I was sent after jobs by the clerk at the Labour Exchange. One of them was to a coal merchant who needed a shovel-slinger to fill coal bags. The job had already been filled by the time I arrived. The other was to a large asbestos firm in Rochdale where an office boy was needed. The queue of applicants for this job must have numbered close on a hundred. In the short time that I stood there, another thirty or forty lined up behind me. We stood there and shuffled slowly up the steps and through the entrance to the offices where two young men wielding rubber-stamps put the firm's mark on our chits, proof that we'd actually followed the Labour Exchange's instructions in applying for the job.

As the weeks passed, I began to understand the desperation of men like my father, skilled men whose skills were no longer needed. More and more often I met old neighbourhood friends and schoolmates in the lengthening dole queues and though we tried to re-establish the old camaraderie we felt awkward in each other's company and soon made a point of avoiding each other. I had almost given up hope completely when one of my written applications received an answer. It was from a trade-journal and the advert had called for a 'youth of good appearance to assist editor of new textile journal'. I was interviewed by the editor, a short, slightly balding, chain-smoking man in a crumpled blue pin-stripe suit. He was friendly and went to some pains to put me at my ease. The prospects for the journal, said he, were not very bright. Indeed, he expressed some doubts about the owner's sanity in starting a textile journal at a time when the trade was in such a state of decline. 'Still', he said, 'it's their money and we must do the best we can.' He questioned me about my education, the kind of school I had been to and then we discussed books and writers for quite a long time. Finally he told me I could start work on Monday.

I arrived home in a state of high excitement. When I told my parents the good news they were jubilant. My mother threw her arms around me and wept, overcome with joy and relief; my father was convinced that this was my big chance to embark on a literary career. All those books he had bought for me over the years were now showing signs of bearing fruit.

The preparations for my new career began the next day when my mother, clutching the notebook in which were entered the details of her weekly pay-ments to the clothing club, escorted me to a large clothing warehouse in

Manchester where I was allowed to choose a suit with long trousers. The parson-grey one, she thought was just right. When I demurred, she observed, in one of her penetrating whispers, that she had cleaned offices long enough to know what was worn there. I was stricken and pleaded with her to be quiet. I tried to explain that I was a grown-up, a man of fifteen years and that men don't need to be told what to buy. 'But I'm your *mither,*' she told me. Could I tell her that I was ashamed of the kind of work she did, ashamed of our poverty, our cheap shabby clothes, and – worst of all – ashamed of being ashamed? I chose a blue-grey lightweight tweed which looked smart the first few times I wore it.

I was at the journal's office good and early on Monday morning, resplendent in my new suit, my hair plastered back with water. I was too early, for my new boss hadn't yet arrived and the office door was locked. I waited in the corridor where mahogany, marble and a mosaic floor told of the glory that was Victoria's. Frosted glass doors bore the names of chartered accountants, commissioners for oaths, solicitors, shipping companies, literary agents and distributors of medical appliances.

The editor was half an hour late and full of apologies. 'I forgot to give you a key.' My parents' fantasies about my literary career wouldn't have survived a cursory glance at the office, a small, drab room smelling of tobacco smoke. It was furnished with a battered old desk, two bentwood chairs, a small table and a wooden filing cabinet. An ancient Royal typewriter, which had belonged to the editor's father, completed the sad furnishings. Not quite the kind of establishment I had imagined.

The Textile Trader was a monthly journal and as the fourth issue had recently been distributed there was very little work for me to do. 'I think you'd better familiarise yourself with the kind of stuff we're putting out,' said my boss as he handed me the four back issues. 'By the way, my name's Percy but I prefer to be called Jack.' Then he added, as an afterthought, 'So just call me Bill.' Neither my schooling nor my experience in the office of the wireworks had prepared me for this kind of free-and-easy treatment and my sense of relief and confusion combined to cause me to blush furiously.

I settled down at the table to read through the journals. It was boring stuff but I was prepared to believe that people in the textile business might find it interesting. Percy/Jack/Bill destroyed that illusion. 'Dreadful stuff, isn't it?' I made some non-committal reply, which he ignored and went on, 'I wrote it, so I should know how bad it is. That's something you should understand. One can be a lousy writer and a good editor. I am a good editor but I shouldn't be allowed near a typewriter.' At that moment the door opened and the third member of the staff appeared. Like me, he was new to 'the firm', having been hired the week before to fill the job of rep. He was a young man – just turned eighteen – and large. He seemed to fill the office when he entered. He was what was considered handsome – film-star handsome – in the thirties and yet in spite of his rich, dark brown, curly hair and splendidly aquiline features, there was something oddly unfinished about him, a coarseness. He was *too* big, *too* handsome, and though his raglan-tweed overcoat and fine Threadneedle Street tweed suit fitted him to perfection, they never succeeded in looking like anything but theatrical props. His name was Rex, a fact which provided the editor with some amusement. 'Had a dog once called Rex. Died of the mange. Horribly scabby end, even for a dog.' Rex's job was to canvass subscribers for the journal and he was apparently good at it. He had been educated at the same minor public school as the editor, an experience which (said Percy/Jack/Bill) gave him just the right balance of arrogance and servility necessary to those who sell things.

The editor's hatred of the public-school system amounted to an obsession. A newspaper reference or a mention of public school in a book review was enough to launch him on a half-hour diatribe. Rex, on the other hand, could talk about nothing but his sexual prowess which, if half of his stories were true, must have been phenomenal. He generally dropped in at the office at about four o'clock in the afternoon. Standing with his back to the door he would, if Percy happened to be out, regale me with details of the day's sexual jousting. 'Shagged four today. Three typists and a comptometer-operator.' The actual numbers changed from day to day but there was little variation in the occupations of his conquests. 'Three today. One receptionist and two typists.' Or it could be two filing clerks and one typist or one private secretary, a telephone operator and a typist. The numbers were never less than two. On one occasion he claimed to have had five women in a single day. When I was foolish enough to express some disbelief he came close to my table and thrust his face to within two or three inches of mine.

'Are you calling me a liar?'

'No, I was just . . .'

'Look at that!' I looked and saw that he had undone his flies and taken out his enormous penis which suddenly sprang erect in his hand. 'Have you ever seen a bigger one than that?'

'Never.' I was feeling very uncomfortable.

'How big would you say it is?'

'I've no idea.'

'Get a ruler. Quick!'

Fortunately, there was a knock on the door and the scene ended. On another occasion I walked into the lavatory, which we shared with all the other offices on the first floor, and found him washing his penis in one of the marble basins. It was one of those magnificent Victorian toilets built in the days when Manchester was the hub of the industrial universe: mosaic floor, marble walls, heavy bronze lighting fittings, bevelled mirrors and a line of huge marble wash-basins. Somewhat ostentatious, perhaps, but none the less impressive. Rex stood there in the midst of all this outdated grandeur, soaping his penis with great concentration. I pretended not to notice and crossed over to the line of urinals which looked like upended tombs of Roman emperors. He followed me over, still soaping. 'It pays to be careful,' he observed.

'Careful?'

'You never know who's been there before you,' he said, wiping the soap off with his hand. 'It looks all right though, doesn't it?'

'I suppose so.'

'You don't think it's a bit flushed?'

'You work it too hard.'

'That shouldn't make it red. Plenty of shaggin's good for it. It's exercise.' He began to dab it dry with his handkerchief. 'Every part of the body needs exercise, including your cock. If you don't exercise it, it withers away.' Then he began to describe his day's star turn. 'Manageress of that little restaurant behind Albert Square, the place that looks like an undertaker's. A three-timer, once standing up from the back and twice on the floor. Couldn't get enough. A real madame, pearl necklace, twin set, the lot. Forty if she's a day and fucks like a rabbit. I'm just a bit worried that she may have been packeted.' His occasional use of slang terms – such as 'packeted', a local term used of those who were suffering from venereal disease, wrapped up as they were in his precious public-school accent, always sounded contrived, as if they had been learned from a book. He was a strange, unwholesome individual, libidinous and, I suspect, cruel. He carried with him an aura of repressed violence and morbid sexuality. I never felt at ease with him. Indeed, I couldn't imagine that anyone would find him a congenial companion.

My work at the journal consisted largely of delivering copies of each issue to subscribers who worked in the city. This accounted for two-and-a-half days out of each month. I also addressed wrappers and, once or twice a month, took copy to the printers. On the completion of these simple tasks I sat and read. On the whole, my life was not so very different from when I had been unemployed, spending my time in the reading room of Peel Park library. My employer generally spent his mornings reading the morning paper. The two of us would sit there in companionable silence and occasionally he would read aloud a snippet from *The Times* or *The Manchester Guardian*. The only other sound was the scrape and splutter of a match as he lit another Gold Flake.

The perusal of the morning paper was a ritual. The opening part of it was conducted in silence. Then there would be an interval during which Percy would pay his morning visit to the toilet. Returning, he would sit down, light another cigarette and settle down to reading through the paper again, only this time his reading would be accompanied by exclamations of disgust, snorts, muttered contradictions, barks of satiric laughter and chuckles of approbation. At lunchtime he would leave the office and return just before five o'clock.

I found the afternoons interminable and I soon developed an intense loathing for the small, drab, stuffy cell in which I was confined for eight hours of every day. It's true that I could read but, for some reason or other, I found it difficult to concentrate. Perhaps it was the silence or the loneliness or the feeling of helplessness at being trapped in a blind alley – or maybe it was simply that I was being poisoned by the smell of cigarette smoke. In the reading room at Peel Park you were still conscious of the world outside; there were large windows so that if you looked up from your book you could see trees bending before the wind, or sun, or clouds scurrying across the sky. You were conscious of the thickening dusk, the lights showing in the windows of distant mills. Here there were four walls and a fly-spotted, eighty-watt lamp whose light seemed to wither everything it touched.

I had reached the point of counting the cigarette-burns on Percy's desk when he announced that there was little chance of our journal surviving another issue. I felt overwhelming relief. At the same time I couldn't help but feel a little depressed at the manner in which my literary career had come to an end. We held on for another two weeks, during which Percy's afternoon absences ceased. Now he sat in the office all day reading and muttering as he dropped cigarette-ash over his waistcoat and trousers and discussed the state of the world. Then one Friday afternoon he handed me ten shillings, my week's wages, and told me *The Trader* was finished. He wrote me a glowing testimonial in which he referred to me as his editorial assistant. 'Perhaps it'll help.' He was a nice man, amiable, tolerant and compassionate. I helped him to carry his typewriter out to a waiting taxi, where we shook hands and said goodbye. My career as an 'editorial assistant' had lasted three months and now it was the broo again, the Albion Street queue and, if I was lucky, 9s. 10d. a week dole money.

12

Big City, Big Geordie

By this time, erotic fantasies were no longer my constant companions and I was beginning to escape from the grip of the terrible loneliness which had held me prisoner throughout most of the previous year. I still suffered occasional bouts of despair and I felt frustrated. But not all the time. I was beginning to be conscious of a world outside myself or rather I was ceasing to believe that I was the centre of the universe. I was still lonely, of course, but I felt that I could cope with it. Every Thursday evening I dutifully went along to The Clarion Players meetings and took part in rehearsals of *The Ragged Trousered Philanthropist* and *The Singing Jailbirds*. At first I had been overawed by the other members of the group; they seemed to be so knowledgeable about things and about writers of whom I hadn't heard. Now I wasn't so sure. I was impatient. The rehearsals didn't seem to be leading anywhere. There was too much talk, too many cups of coffee, too many jokes, too many references to people I didn't know. I mentioned my feelings about the group to Charlie Harrison who suggested that I might be interested in attending a meeting of the Young Communist League. A few days later he introduced me to the members of the Manchester branch of the YCL (Young Communist League).[1]

The branch meeting was held in the kitchen of a small house in Openshaw. There were about eight or nine people present, all older than myself by three or four years. This was apparently the entire Manchester membership at the time. After Charlie's initial introduction, no one took any notice of me at all. I tried to look interested in the discussion but it was difficult, as most of it was conducted in what seemed to be a foreign language. I was, however, impressed by the fact that everyone was so fluent (if incomprehensible). Later I became accustomed to the jargon, the use of which was recognised throughout the party as a serious weakness which must be eradicated, part of the disorder known as sectarianism. It was so deeply ingrained that speakers used it even as they were anathematising it.

That first meeting left me feeling confused and a little alienated and it wasn't only because of the unfamiliar words. I had expected something a good deal more exciting, conspiratorial perhaps. What I actually saw was a group of perfectly ordinary young people who, when they weren't using the codified language of left-wing politics, talked about how to sell pamphlets and where to distribute leaflets and how to make meetings more interesting and who would make the tea and prepare the sandwiches for next week's social. Perhaps my feelings of alienation arose out of the fact that, once again, I was the youngest person in the room. When, oh when, am I going to make friends with people of my own age?

In the course of the next three or four weeks I attended further meetings of the YCL and then I formally enrolled as a member. I say *formally* but actually it was anything *but* formal. All that happened was that at the end of a meeting a young woman asked me for my name and address and then handed me a membership card and, *voila!* I had become a cell in the body of the spectre that was haunting Europe. It was a step which was to influence my whole life.

At home things had taken a turn for the worse. For three months my father had been away working in a foundry in Sutton, Surrey. Now it had closed down and he was back in Manchester on the dole. My mother was working an eleven-hour day as a charwoman. Every morning, at half-past-four, she left our house and walked to Manchester where from five o'clock till nine she cleaned offices. Afterwards she travelled by tram to the other side of town and spent the next six hours charring in a private house. She did that five days of every week for a pitiful wage which was scarcely enough to keep us clear of the starvation line. The old days of family singsongs were things of the past, though at the time I wasn't conscious of their passing. I was too preoccupied with the exciting new life that was opening up in front of me. I was still spending a lot of time in the Peel Park reading room and sometimes, for a change, in the temporary quarters of the Manchester Reference Library in Piccadilly. My ten-new-words-a-day programme had now become a habit and I was reading everything I could lay my hands on, including political works like Paul Lafargue's *Right to be Lazy*, *The Communist Manifesto*, Engels' *Socialism, Utopian and Scientific*, Bukharin's *Historical Materialism* and Lenin's *State and Revolution*. I had also discovered Balzac and was beginning to work my way through *The Human Comedy*.

It was about this time that Big Geordie came to live with us. Charlie Harrison had been deposed as the Communist Party District Organiser. He had gone back to his trade as a cutter in a waterproof factory and had moved so as to be nearer his place of employment. I don't know to what extent our new lodger could be said to be 'political'. He seemed to be on first-name terms with everyone and certainly he was welcomed with open arms wherever he turned up. I don't ever remember his taking part in the day-to-day activities of the movement, He never volunteered for jobs like canvassing for *The Worker*, our weekly newspaper, or fly-posting or chalking slogans on walls. At socials, though, he was a tower of strength. These socials were an important feature of YCL activity. Not only did they raise small amounts of cash for an organisation that was chronically in need of money but, more important, they made it possible for YCLers to meet their contemporaries in a relaxed and convivial atmosphere. To be quite truthful, they were not really convivial, not in the early years. Later, when the Party and the YCL had grown to a respectable size, the socials and dances were held in proper assembly-halls, but at this time we were as poor as church mice and had to make do with whatever was cheap and available. Rooms like that on the second floor of the Workers' Arts Club in Liverpool Street were not untypical: a plank floor varnished to make it look like a real dance-floor; a small platform for the 'band'; inadequate lighting, and usually a few paper decorations left over from three Christmases ago. SOCIAL AND DANCE, said the tickets, PRICE: ONE SHILLING. That price gener- ally represented hours of heated discussion. A shilling's too much. Who's going to pay a shilling to come to a crummy joint like the Workers' Arts Club? For a shilling you can dance on a real floor at the Ritz any Thursday afternoon and to a real band. Make it a tanner and you're in business. We need the dough, we're broke, we're on the floor, etc.

The festivities usually began about eight o'clock with a trio or quartet of local amateurs playing last year's dance tunes on a piano, saxophone and drums. Sometimes it would be four brothers playing mandolin, mandola, tenor mandola and guitar. The steppers, or jazzers, as those who could dance were called, would step nonchalantly onto the floor and stand waiting for their part- ners to join them like bullfighters awaiting the bulls. Those who, like me, didn't count dancing among their accomplishments, would approach their partners like semi-paralysed invalids reaching for the nurses who were teaching them to walk. For the next forty-five minutes or an hour the jazzers and the zombies lead their partners – or are led by them – in fox-trots, quick-steps, waltzes, tangos and two-steps trying to follow a band which seems unable to keep time. A break follows during which tea is served from an urn and two of McVitie and Price's best are balanced against the rim of each saucer. There is also sponge cake topped with white, pink and pale blue icing.

Then came the 'turns'. At local run-of-the-mill socials, these followed a rigid pattern: a locally renowned tenor, the friend of a friend's friend, had been per- suaded to come along and now he was going to treat us to a rendering of 'I'll Take You Home Again, Kathleen'. Or perhaps it was a baritone with 'Come into the Garden, Maud', or a contralto with a clutch of Negro spirituals. This was the cultural part of the evening, the imported fare, and was usually fol- lowed by a YCLer standing on a chair and reciting his one and only party piece, a monologue which began thus:

> The tightest man I know was an Irish Eskimo
> Selling pork in Palestine, beneath a blazing sun,
> Trying to straighten out bananas,
> That's a thing he's never done.

This was always greeted with rapturous applause. Then, for another hour, we shuffled and pushed our way, or were pulled, through the haze of face powder and cigarette smoke. For most of us this was the really important part of the evening. In this respect, a YCL dance was no different from any other dance. It was an occasion where unattached young males were intent on capturing unattached young females. There was only an hour of the evening left so you had to move in sharply and try to persuade the girl of your choice to allow you to escort her home. If you failed, then you zoomed in on your second choice. The last half-hour was really panic stations all the way.

The last waltz finished promptly at eleven o'clock and then you were out in the street with a young woman you had met for the first time that evening. However long or short the walk might be there was always time to exchange basic information: name, occupation, place of work. Then came the jockeying for position.

'Are you going steady with anyone?'

'Not really.'

'What does that mean?'

'It means I was, but not any more.'

'What happened?'

'I just got fed up with him.'

'Why?'

'You're too nosy.'

Not real conversation, just ritual; a screen of awkward words behind which your mutual anxieties writhe and twist. How far can I go with her? How far will she expect me to go? She'll think I'm soft if I . . . He'll think I'm too easy if I let him . . . Is she more experienced than me? . . . He's a lot more sure of himself than I am . . . I wonder where there's a good place round here? . . . He's really nice, I think . . . The conversation limps along until she turns and faces you, saying, 'I live near here.'

'Do you have to go in yet?'

'It's late.'

'Stay just a short time, a few minutes.'

'I can't. Really.'

'Please.'

'Five minutes then.'

'Where can we go?'

She takes you by the hand and leads you to a back entry twenty yards back up the road. You enter the tunnel of darkness and she stands with her back against the brick wall and unbuttons her coat. Then your arms are around her and you are kissing her on the mouth. Rapture. Her Woolworth lipstick and cheap perfume are the stuff of which your dreams are made. Kiss, kiss as though your lips are glued together. Breathing her in, rapt. Stillness, just kissing, then slowly, imperceptibly almost, you move your hand towards her breast. After it has rested there for a moment, you take courage and begin to caress her very softly. Then, emboldened, you slide your other hand round to her side and then to her back, searching for the opening of her dress. She resists your fumbling at first but her hunger is as great as yours and soon she gives in.

At this point she is more worried about possible damage to her dress than she is about her ability to deal with your clumsy attempts to explore her person. When she puts an end to your ineffectual groping by unclasping the fastenings to her dress and unhooking her brassiere she is following the dictates of economy rather than passion. It is, however, a gesture which fills you with hope and soon your hand leaves her breast and travels down between her legs. Her resistance is now a little more determined but after a token skirmish she allows your hand to caress her thighs. By now your blood is thundering in your ears and you feel powerful, triumphant, and she doesn't resist when your fingers find a way through the thin stuff of her briefs and begin stroking and probing the sweet, hot entrance to her body. But fingers are not enough, so your other hand tries to undo the buttons of your flies but in a flash her hand grips your wrist with a grasp which refuses to be shaken off. 'Please,' you plead.

'Don't . . . that's enough.' She pulls free of you and starts fastening up her dress. 'Just look at my dress!' She's not really dismayed, just a little irritated. 'I bet my hair's a mess.'

A moment ago she was the Queen of Sheba. Now she is as detached as she was when you first saw her on the dance floor this evening. That passionate moment of intimacy has passed and you are strangers again. But were you ever anything other than strangers? *Intimacy?* Two young animals smelling each other's rumps. Your leave-taking is casual.

'See you around.'

'Ta-ra.'

Good night, sweet lady.

Of course, it isn't always like that. The rules of the encounter change with each couple. The goodnight ceremony can be limited to a chaste kiss or to an orgy of kissing with or without tongue action. It can be kissing without hand movement or with one hand caressing a breast through a blouse or jumper; or the caressing can be raw, that is naked without impediment of blouse, dress or jumper. This was really preliminary skirmishing; the manipulation of the skirt belonged to a more serious kind of engagement. Some girls would allow you to caress their thighs and put your hand against the fabric which covered their pubic area; others would allow your hand inside their drawers and, occasionally, there would be a girl who would step out of her pants, which she would then stuff into your pocket. This was a kind of deluxe version of exploring and it did wonders for your confidence. It didn't necessarily mean that she was prepared to go all the way, but it did suggest that she was an enthusiast and would probably be perfectly happy to fondle you while you fondled her. In my experience it was extremely rare for a young woman to allow herself to be penetrated during a first encounter. Only after a couple had been meeting for several weeks was it regarded as natural for them to aim for the final goal, and then they generally looked for a more convenient place than a back entry, preferably a place where they could lie down. The height of one's partner is of little significance when you are horizontal but standing up against a wall demands considerable adjustment of one's normal stance. Such an engagement is not called 'a knee trembler' without good reason. Goodnight, sweet ladies.

Encounters such as these filled my mind with turmoil. I was swept along in a whirlpool of confused emotions in which desire, frustration, ecstasy, hope and despair rose alternately to the surface. I loved to walk through the dark, empty streets at night or in the early hours of the morning. The perfume of the girl's hair was still in my nostrils and I breathed it in like a dope-addict, feeling it seeping into every crevice of my body, remembering the way her face and shoulders had gleamed in the darkness like mother-of-pearl in a dark pool.

It was at a social and dance that I first saw Big Geordie. His size was the first thing you noticed about him. He really was *big*, well over six feet and broad with it. He wasn't exactly fat but he gave the impression of being rather soft; not plump, just well filled-out. He had pale, very fine skin, lightly freckled and a mop of curly ginger hair. Everyone seemed to know and like him and there wasn't a girl in the room who didn't have a smile for him. He had 'just come doon from Glasgow to see that his auld friends were behavin' themselves'. He was a stylish dancer and I remember feeling rather disgruntled as I stood there watching him sail past with one and then another of the best-looking girls in the room in his arms. When it was time for turns, there were cries of 'Geordie!' and after a little persuasion he stood up and sang Burns' 'Sweet Afton'. He really was very good indeed, a light baritone with an effortless delivery and a style completely lacking in affectation. I was moved and the crowd loved him and gave him their complete attention. For an encore he sang another Burns song, 'Ae Fond Kiss', and once again was received with rapture. Later, during the week, I met him again, this time at a YCL branch meeting and there he told me that he was looking for somewhere to stay. He came home with me that night and charmed my mother into letting him stay with us as a lodger.

When there was work to be had, Big Geordie followed the trade of painter and paperhanger, but at the moment he was studying German and didn't have much time for other activities. As far as I could make out he divided his time almost equally between learning to read and speak German, attending various meetings and in pursuing, and being pursued by, amorous young women. I was desperately keen to be included in this last-mentioned sport but my hints fell on deaf ears. I was, however, encouraged to partner him in his German studies. Geordie gave me a second-hand German-English dictionary which he had picked up for a penny at a stall on Eccles market and every morning after breakfast the two of us would sit down and test each other with words from Geordie's tutor which claimed to be able to teach anyone German in ten easy lessons. Geordie also found me a pen-pal who lived in Saxony and who used to write me long and wonderfully interesting letters about the political situation in Germany. Before long I was regularly receiving, through the post, German pamphlets, songbooks and copies of the *Illustraten Arbeiter Zeitung (AIZ)*, the journal for which, at that time, John Hartfield was creating his photomontages.

Geordie stayed with us for almost two months, a long time for him. He had stayed on, he admitted, for the pleasure of hearing my father sing songs like Burns' 'Mary Morrison', 'Braw Lads o' Galla Water', and Tannahill's 'Are Ye Sleepin', Maggie?'.

When Geordie left, I left with him. We were bound for London, a place which Geordie professed to know well. This wasn't like going for a holiday to Blackpool or Morecambe, this was real adventure. London was foreign parts. My mother took farewell of us as if we were bound for Australia. 'See you take good care of him', she said to Geordie as she hugged me fiercely to her breast, 'and see that he gets plenty to eat.' I slipped my ex-army valise over my shoulders and we turned our faces to the south.

A tramcar took us to Stockport where we thumbed a lift in a lorry bound for Congleton. It was in this Cheshire town that I embarked on my short-lived career as a street-singer. Geordie, an old hand at the game, instructed me. It was really very simple. He would do the actual singing until I got over my initial embarrassment. My job was to knock at the doors and look pitiful. 'And don't knock too loud. It doesnae do to sound aggressive. Not too loud but no' sae soft that ye cannae be heard.'

'It's begging.'

'It's division of labour. I'm selling my labour power and, hopefully, they're going to buy it. So get moving.'

We got moving but by the time we reached the end of the street there was only a couple of coppers in the hat. Geordie shook his head in disgust. 'You don't look right,' he said. 'You're too big. We'll hae to change our approach.' We decided – well, Geordie decided – that we should both sing. We spent ten minutes or so running through the words of 'Huntingtower', a natural duet, and in the next street put it to the test. It worked, and for the next two hours it worked over and over again. Then my voice gave out. We counted our earnings, almost four shillings. With part of our riches we bought fish and chips and then started on the road again.

We weren't the only ones travelling on the thumb. The competition was fierce and we had been walking for more than two hours before we got a lift on an empty truck. It was bound for Evesham, which was off our route, but it was South and we were in no hurry. On the outskirts of Evesham we stopped at a truck-driver's caf' for a bacon sandwich and then set about looking for a place to sleep. 'I think a barn is called for,' says Geordie, and, sure enough, my ever-resourceful mentor found us a barn with a loft where we spent the night. I was desperately tired, but slept only fitfully, disturbed by the scurrying of rats and tortured by fleas.

In the morning we made our way into Evesham and sat in a cafe drinking weak tea and working out ways of extending our repertoire of duets. I was impatient, eager to get to the big city, but Geordie favoured a more leisurely approach. Overnight he had decided that we should travel by easy stages and sing in small country towns. A place like Evesham should be able to support a couple of good street singers; after all it was in similar places that ballad-mongers had sold their wares.

We began our stint in the corner of the busy market place. Our moving rendition of 'Huntingtower' evoked no response whatsoever. No one gave us more than a glance and we began to feel that we were invisible. It was positively eerie. We were on the point of abandoning our efforts when we were given the first indication that the people on the streets of Evesham were not all deaf mutes. It came from a police constable who, I am sure, was affronted by Geordie's stature.

'And what do you think you're doing?'

'We're singing,' said Geordie, mustering all his charm.

'Not here, you're not.'

'We're down on our luck, constable.'

'Bugger off, sharp! We don't want your kind here. Now scarper or I'll book you.'

We scarpered and made our way back to the caf' where we had eaten our bacon sandwich the night before. 'I think we'll forget about country towns and make straight for the Smoke,' said Geordie. A London-bound truck-driver from South Shields gave us a lift. He was a northern patriot and not at all surprised to hear of our Evesham debacle. All of Britain south of Stoke-on-Trent was, to him, one vast graveyard inhabited by the walking dead. When Geordie enquired as to whether Birmingham was included in this judgment, the driver shuddered.

'Birmingham's not so much a place as a state of permanent fucking depression. Arsehole of the fucking world. Zombies! That's what Brummies are, zombies!' It was obviously a favourite and well-rehearsed theme. He went on to discuss the inferiority of the Midlands and the south, disposing with admirable thoroughness of cities, towns, villages, accents, lodgings, food, architecture and women. He was a man of clear-cut opinions. While he was denigrating southern beer and breweries I drifted off into a troubled sleep. We were at Euston Road when Geordie woke me up and our man was just finishing a mopping-up operation on the Metropolitan Police Force.

That night we slept in a Salvation Army hostel in Hammersmith. It wasn't the most auspicious introduction to the nation's capital. The place had the sour smell of institutionalised poverty and I remember thinking that the cold barn near Evesham was preferable. For the second night on the run I slept badly, clutching my boots under the blanket to prevent them being stolen. The next morning we paid for our night's lodging. I was given a mop and bucket and told to swab the floors of the sleeping quarters. Geordie went off with the outdoor gang to saw wood. Then we set off for the West End and the sights of London.

By this time my sense of adventure had given way to resentment and I was hungry and tired. The real truth of the matter is that I wasn't psychologically prepared for London. Its size intimidated me and it seemed so rich and complacent. I found myself agreeing with the sentiments of the South Shields man. It *was* an alien place, arrogant, ostentatious, inhuman. Its people were different from us northerners. They were more sure of themselves, cocky, flighty, mercurial – harder in some ways and yet soft too. The hardness was of the brittle kind that broke easily and the softness somehow contradicted their self-assurance. The man outside that flashy hotel tipping his hat to that high mucky-muck . . . servile bastard. You'd never see a Northerner doing that, no bloody fear. Where the hell was the working class? All these men and women hurrying along Tottenham Court Road and Oxford Street . . . were they class enemies? Was this what the bourgeoisie looked like? My common sense told me this was nonsense, but my regional prejudices were stronger.

I suspect that many northerners react to London in this way, at least at first. It takes time for your feelings of resentment and anger to disappear, to be able to see beyond the facade of the West End with its aura of luxury. Even its historicity can produce feelings of antipathy. How can anyone brought up in the bleak poverty of a northern slum fail to respond with hatred to the callous flamboyance of the miles and miles of expensive shops, the insufferable pomposity of London's buildings, the ripeness, over-ripeness, of the place? When your hatred is compounded with the knowledge that all this wealth is the loot of empire, the swag, amassed by theft carried out on an enormous scale over a long period of time, then it becomes difficult to bear. Perhaps one shouldn't have to bear it – unrequited hate is just as hard to suffer as unrequited love, and a lot more harmful.

That night we got a job washing dishes in a Chinese restaurant in Denmark Street. The proprietor greeted Geordie like a wayward young brother who needed to be taught the value of labour. This was the first time I had actually met anyone born outside the British Isles. Oh, I'd seen Lascars padding through the dock gates in their flat-footed manner or trailing through the Flat Iron market on a Saturday afternoon, but to actually *meet* a foreigner, that was something special. And the food . . .! Now I'd really have something to talk about when I got back to Salford.

We finished work just after midnight, unrolled our sleeping bags and dossed down in a store-room at the rear of the restaurant. We spent the rest of the week there washing up afternoons and evenings, but our being there was only a temporary arrangement and the regular kitchen staff would return from holiday at the end of the week. Where are we going to sleep tonight, Geordie? 'Don't worry', Geordie said, 'I'm working on it.' He was, for at the end of the week we bid goodbye to our Chinese friends and moved to Kensington.

The fierce antipathy which had been my initial response to London had become somewhat tempered by the week in Denmark street, but it flared up stronger than ever in Kensington when I saw our digs, an enormous house in a square of enormous houses. When Geordie pointed to it and said it was to be our home for the next week or so, I thought he was joking. But he wasn't and I panicked as he propelled me up the steps. It was a maid that opened the door to us. 'My God! The Casanova o' the Toonheid,' she said.

'Hello, Mary', says Geordie, 'hae ye been pining for me?'

'You big, bap-faced sumph! And what's this you've brought with you?' Geordie introduced me. I was tongue-tied – and I was tongue-tied for the entire period of my stay there, some eight or nine days. I was overwhelmed by the magnificence of the surroundings. Everything was on such a large scale. The rooms were gargantuan, almost as big as those in the Peel Park museum, and much more grand. Geordie seemed quite at home talking to the maid as she led us to the third-floor guest room. I followed behind, resisting the urge to walk on tiptoe.

Our rooms had a connecting door and as soon as the maid had departed I was in Geordie's room, bombarding him with questions about the owners of the house who were a famous couple who supported left-wing causes. The lady of the house was a Scot who had inherited a fortune and cultivated the arts. Her husband, a Frenchman, was a financial genius who was some kind of high priest in the shadowy world of high finance. Geordie had become acquainted with them through their son, Jean Christophe, whom he had met at a meeting in Hyde Park. They kept open house for their many friends and two or three times a week provided a truly splendid lunch for a dozen or so assorted guests.

Geordie was wildly enthusiastic about these mini-banquets, but as far as I was concerned, the meals were pure torture. Each morning I woke with a feeling of dread at the thought of having to endure another of these terrifying lunches and by the time the lunch-hour arrived I was so sick with nervousness that I couldn't eat. The servant standing by the serving-trolley throughout the meal, the snowy white tablecloth and napkins, the gleaming tureens and salvers, the huge dishes of vegetables, the trays of meat, the gilt-rimmed plates and bowls, the heavy cutlery – all combined to undermine my confidence. God, just imagine being sick in this place! The woman across the table . . . she's saying something . . . is she talking to me? Just look absent-minded, as if you're thinking of something else. Oh, God! That's how it was. I alternated between feeling fearful and feeling stupid and in between I cursed myself for my inadequacy. I was full of groans that only I could hear.

My behaviour was both ignorant and ungrateful. Our hosts were intelligent, tolerant and extremely generous people. They had welcomed us into their home and shown us nothing but kindness. Why, then, did I feel and act like someone awaiting execution? Geordie upbraided me, but finally gave up and announced that he was going to visit an old friend in Reading. I told him I was ready to go back home; he looked relieved and offered to put me on the road. He knew a caf' where northbound lorries stopped for a snack before leaving the Smoke and there he talked a melancholy-looking Welshman into giving me a lift as far as Ludlow. 'You'll easily pick up something there,' he said and handed me eight shillings, half of what remained of our joint earnings.

'There'll be three of us,' said the Welshman as he led me towards his furniture-van. 'Just you and me and Madge.' Madge turned out to be a little fox-terrier bitch. From time to time he tossed gobbets of conversation to her which she acknowledge by raising an eyelid or twitching an ear. For the most part, she slept and what with the heat of the cabin and the singsong rise and fall of the Welshman's voice, I fell asleep too. When I awoke we were going through a town. 'Oxford, boy. This is Oxford.' He didn't speak again until we were through the town, when he asked whether I knew any stories.

'What kind of stories?'

'Something that'll stop me from falling asleep at the wheel.'

'Do you mean dirty stories?'

'I do not. I'm talking about proper stories.'

'I don't know any.'

'Then I'm going to have to pull up and take a nap somewhere.'

I felt he was annoyed with me for having fallen asleep. I tried to think of a story. A story, a story, a story. I must know plenty of stories. 'I know a monologue. It's a bit on the sad side.'

'Carry on. A few tears won't do us any harm.'

I took a deep breath and began 'The Stowaway':

A batch of us boys gathered round Sailor Ned,
As many a fine yarn he had spun,
"You have stowaways often aboard, one said,
And the finding 'em must be such fun . . .

I had heard my father recite this tale of a child's courage in the face of death and now I found myself imitating each of his mannerisms and inflections. It was as well that I did, for the piece is a true tear-jerker and, as a child, I had never been able to listen to it without bursting into sobs. By concentrating on my performance I was able to avoid that indignity. The driver was very impressed. 'You got a real gift there, boy, you know that? A real gift. I tell you, if I could do a recitation like that I wouldn't be wasting my time driving this old van. I'll tell you what I'd be doing: I'd be going round the clubs. There's a good living there, boy, for them that has the talent.'

'What clubs do you mean?'

'The Welfares, boy, the Miners' Welfares. A recitation like that and you'd have 'em drowning in their beers.' He went silent and sat hunched over the wheel, lost in thought. Then he said, 'That mate was a bit of a tyrant, wanting to string that boy from the yard-arm. A real bad bugger, if you ask me.' I suddenly felt very confident, a feeling I hadn't experienced since leaving for London. The Welshman's unstinted praise had soothed my wounded ego and stimulated my memory. Now I wanted to surpass myself. I remembered a Jack London story about a poor and hungry Mexican prizefighter who . . .

I adapted the story as I told it, resetting it in Salford and transforming the Mexican into a Scot. In telling the monologue I had been trammelled by the text I had learned from my father, but now I was using my own words and allowing my imagination to fill out the characters with details borrowed from people I knew. This story was greeted with even more enthusiasm than the previous one. Indeed, it so impressed my driver that he bought me a plateful of ham and eggs at a lorry harbour. I was warmed up now and my head was full of stories. During the next leg of the journey I entertained my new-found admirer with Gogol's tale of Akaky Akakievich's overcoat and a revamped version of a story by de Maupassant about a fat man who hatches a clutch of hen eggs in his armpits. My fat man was based upon Jimmy Tillbrook, the fat philosopher of the Workers' Arts Club.

At the outskirts of Ludlow, we pulled up at a garage and the Welshman told me to wait in the cab while he had a few words with a friend. He came back after a few minutes with the news that a mate of his was taking a load of sheet-metal to Bolton and would drop me off in Salford. He had given his mate an exaggerated account of my story-telling abilities and for the next couple of hours I had to repeat my performance for the new driver. It was about nine o'clock that night that the world-weary *shenachie* and bard, fresh from the fields of poesy and travel, returned to the bosom of his family. From my mother I received a hero's welcome; my father merely smiled and said, 'The wanderer's return'. And that was the end of the first of my travels.

The restlessness which had driven me to London was still there. I still had the feeling that somewhere, just beyond the periphery of my vision, exciting things were happening, wonderful things which could be mine for the taking if only I knew where to look. My daily routine of signing-on and working my way alphabetically through the books in the Peel Park reading room was becoming increasingly burdensome. But how else could I fill my days? The evenings were even worse. I did, of course, have the YCL and the Clarion Players, but they only involved two evenings a week. The fact is that I still hadn't made any new friends since I left school. I was a loner, not by choice but by circumstance. Perhaps, I thought, my cousin John and I might get back to our old close relationship, and I set out with high hopes for Patricroft. It was a fruitless journey. John was working as a butcher's apprentice and spending all his free time training with the Eccles water-polo team. Where shall I go? What shall I do? I could, I suppose, have stayed at home with a book. No, I couldn't. I had spent most of the day reading, and now I needed . . . what did I need? The plain fact of the matter is that I could no longer bear to be by myself.

Leave the house by the back door. No, I'll try the front door for a change. Left or right? What does it matter which way? Just walking the streets in the hope that you'll meet someone you know. If only I knew some girl like May Petrie! Wonder what she's doing? Not a chance. They all roam around in groups, threes and fours, not a chance of meeting one on her own. Not any more. In any case, I wouldn't know what to say. Have you read The *Communist Manifesto*? They'd think I was touched. They've all changed from the girls I once knew into brash young women who are only too eager to scourge you with their mockery.

It was on one of these desolate evening excursions that I stumbled across my old enemy from infant-school days. Yes, it was Horace Evans. He was sitting on his front doorstep greasing a pair of hob-nailed boots and, true to form, he stuck out his foot and tripped me up as I passed. 'How are things?' he asked, after I had finished abusing him. We sat together companionably and exchanged news about old school friends.

'Whose are the boots?' I asked.

'Mine. They're my rambling boots.' Moorland walking, or rambling as it was known in the industrial towns bordering on the Pennines, was a mass sport and tens of thousands of young people – and a few who were not so young – used to leave the Manchester and Sheffield districts each week-end bound for the moors and dales of Derbyshire. My old friend was an old hand at it. He had been going out for ages and had reached the proselytising stage. So the following Sunday saw me staggering up Jacob's Ladder in a pair of ex-army boots which, after an hour's wearing, reduced the skin of my feet to bloody tatters. By the time we had reached the top of the rise I had developed a fierce hatred of Horace Evans, of the makers of my appalling boots, of the retailer who had sold them and of the railway company which had brought us within striking distance of this dreary mass of moorland with its bogs and stony paths.

Shortly afterwards, in a Hayfield tea-house, we shared a table and the cost of a pot of tea with a tall, well-built youth. Like us, he came from Salford and, like me, he was a beginner as far as rambling was concerned. He tagged along with us and by the time we had reached London Road Station we had become friends. Before parting we arranged to meet the following evening. My first day's rambling was scarcely noteworthy, but that encounter in the Hayfield tea-house marked a new phase in my life.

His name was Bob Goodman and he lived about a mile away, in St Mathias' Ward. He had black hair, eyes that were almost black, and a sallow complexion which at first sight suggested that he was liverish. It was misleading for he was in the pink of condition – tall, lean and very quick on his feet. His nose had been broken and flattened in a fight, for he was a boxer who fought at welterweight and whose father had been grooming him for the ring ever since he could remember. In his short career, he had fought eighty-one fights and had lost only four of them.

'You must be good,' I commented.

'I'm scared shitless', he confessed, 'terrified that I'll finish up punch-drunk. That's why I win.'

Since he left school at fourteen, Bob had worked in a small rubber-stamp moulding shop. Not much of a job but better than nothing. The pay was lousy, the prospects nil and the work dead boring, but there were compensations in the actual place of work. It was situated in a ramshackle nest of rooms above Manchester's largest second-hand bookshop – though *shop* is hardly an accurate description. '*Book market*' would be more apt since most of the wares were displayed on roughly constructed shelves which stood in the open air protected from the weather by a tarpaulin awning.

It was among these shelves that Bob spent a good deal of his spare time familiarising himself with the world's great literature. He it was who introduced me to *The Satyricon* of Petronius Arbiter; to James Joyce, Thomas Mann, Alfred Doblin, Sherwood Anderson; and to Hasek's *Good Soldier Schweijk*. I think it is in your adolescent years that books make their greatest impact. We were hungry, eager to explore new worlds and so we fed our friendship with books, absorbing them in dozens. Reading became a kind of game, a competition in the search for new authors and new titles. For example, Bob would produce a novel by Theodore Plivier or Oskar Maria Graf and I would respond with the latest work of Maxim Gorki or Boris Pilniak. We were rarely content to judge a writer on the basis of a single book. No, he had to be swallowed whole. So when Bob discovered Sherwood Anderson's *Storyteller's Story* we pestered the librarian in Peel Park to add *Tar* and *Dark Laughter* to the library's stock.

For the next three years, Bob and I were almost inseparable. Every night when he had finished work he would call for me and we would go off together to YCL meetings – Bob had joined soon after we met – or to Clarion Players rehearsals. He had many talents, but acting was not one of them. In the ring or on a rock face he had a natural elegance, but when he tried to perform even in front of an audience of one or two of his friends, he became dumb with embarrassment. Afterwards, we would walk home discussing the shortcomings of the group and wondering how long it would be before it split apart.

My first impression of the Clarion Players had been of a unified group of individuals, all of whom shared identical views and aims. Actually, there were two groups constantly at loggerheads and their arguments became more rancorous with each rehearsal. One section felt that we should concentrate on 'solid' productions of plays by Toller, Galsworthy and Ibsen. The other was all for getting out on the streets and making our voices heard by 'the masses'. That's for me, I thought, street-theatre! Agitprop! I had been fired by the thought of street-theatre ever since I had begun receiving magazines from my German pen-friend showing pictures of German Blue Blouse troupes in action.

The street-theatre versus curtain-theatre argument dragged on for several weeks, but it was just talk. Nobody did anything. We went on walking our way through scenes and acts which never actually reached the performance stage. We went on drinking our weak coffee and talking about past successes. When a young chemist from the dyestuffs division of ICI joined the group, the talking came to an end.

Joe Davis was a short, bird-like, agile Jew who lived in one of those big mouldering houses at the corner of Camp Street, Lower Broughton.[2] As an actor he was only marginally superior to Bob Goodman. When Bob tried to adopt a different persona he looked manic; when Joe tried, he looked more like himself than ever, more the eternal student, the eternal enquirer, the small boy taking the clock apart to find what made it tick. I never knew anyone who showed such obvious pleasure in acquiring information. He dug, pecked and tugged at knowledge like a bird hunting for worms. To go rambling with him was an education in itself.

Bob and I had become seasoned walkers during the months we had been knocking around together. Every Sunday we were out on the Derbyshire moors, mostly on Kinder or Bleaklow, driving ourselves to cover more and more miles. When Sundays were no longer enough, we took to leaving town on Friday night and returning last thing on Sunday. The old days when I had toiled up Jacob's Ladder like an old man were behind me now. I was as limber, and almost as tough, as Bob and just as fast. We prided ourselves on the way we could lope for hours on end over broken moorland and on the speed with which we could ascend Wild Boar Clough, Middle and Far Black and the Alport. We were fast – but Joe was faster. He could negotiate rocks like a mountain goat, could read a map quicker than anyone I have ever known and could run up the side of Derbyshire stone walls like a cat. He walked with a fast, springy step, only altering his pace to take a short run at a wall or to go leaping down the rocky shoulder of a hill. And all the time he would be talking about rocks and fossils, about Einstein and relativity, about sex and religion, about languages. He had a knack with languages. He knew German and French, more than a smattering of Italian and Russian, and could read Arabic. When we first met him he was teaching himself Gaelic. He loved to sing, too, and knew the words of three or four Gilbert and Sullivan operettas, a truly enormous number of Schubert *lieder* and numerous Kennedy-Frazer-type Hebridean songs. His sense of pitch was less than perfect. Bob Goodman said that Joe's singing gave him a pain in the arse.

Though Joe considered himself to be a Marxist and was in complete agreement with the Communist Party's general line, he never actually joined the party. His reasons for not doing so lay in his personality. He had a wide range of interests and he found it impossible – or perhaps undesirable – to apply himself exclusively to any single one of them. Some of our mutual friends dismissed him as a dilettante. Perhaps he was. On the other hand, I cannot help thinking that our treatment of individuals who should have been our natural allies often lacked foresight. A more flexible approach to those with whom we came in contact might, in the long run, have resulted in a bigger, and possibly better, party. Of course, it is easy to criticise the past from the vantage point of the present. The fact is, we were a tiny group trying desperately to hold back the tide of reaction. At a time when almost the entire western world was singing the praises of Hitler and Mussolini, the communists were almost entirely alone in trying to warn the world of the menace of fascism and the dangers of another world war. Perhaps making speeches at street corners and factory gates, or distributing factory newspapers, handing out leaflets and performing the thousand-and-one daily tasks which are part-and-parcel of party work, seems a hopeless way of bringing about a fundamental change in the structure of society, but it was the only way open to us. We had no money with which to buy newspapers, magazines, films or broadcasting organisations. We were severely limited as to means; indeed, we considered ourselves fortunate in having an old, clapped-out typewriter and a second-hand duplicating machine. We had a vision of the future but of what use is a vision unless there are dedicated people who are prepared to work in order for it to be transformed into a reality? That dedication was measured by the number of badly-duplicated leaflets distributed, by the number of pamphlets sold, the number of meetings addressed, the slogans chalked on walls, the posters carried on parades and demonstrations, the clashes with the police and the fascists. To share in the vision and to avoid the work which would turn the vision into reality was a kind of betrayal, so anything less than complete commitment was unacceptable. Not everyone's cup of tea, perhaps, but we felt that it should have been.

13

Politics, Purience and Fresh Air

My life had suddenly become very full. I had friends whose interests were the same as mine. The YCL and the Clarion Players were now accounting for four or five nights of my week and at weekends there were the moors. It became even more full when, at the beginning of 1931, the division in the Clarion Players widened into a split. There was no dramatic confrontation and no blazing manifestos were issued. All that happened was that at the end of a rehearsal the Ibsenites announced that they were abandoning the group. And that was that. We who were left, the *politicals* as we were sometimes called, set about altering our repertoire and in the course of the next seven or eight months we gave several open-air performances of new sketches and songs. The intentions of the group were good and its politics excellent, but it was short on discipline and rehearsals were just as casual as they had been in the Ibsenite days. The zealots, among whom I was numbered, wanted a tightly-disciplined group on the lines of the German Blue Blouses, though (as was pointed out) most of the Blue Blouse groups were professional, while ours was made up of both employed and unemployed. Some of those with jobs had other evening com-mitments, like attending night school or union branch meetings or whatever, and couldn't afford more evenings for rehearsals than they were already giving. The unemployed, on the other hand . . . why not form an additional group out of the unemployed members, a kind of shock group? The new group was called The Red Megaphones. I, who knew nothing about production, became the producer and general factotum. Later I became the scriptwriter as well.

Initially, it was decided that scripts would be communally written and for several meetings we occupied ourselves sitting round a kitchen table with pencil and paper trying to write a draft of our first sketch. We didn't get anywhere and for a time it looked as if our plans for talking directly to the masses were to be stillborn. In the end we abandoned the idea of a single sketch, opting instead for a program of several parodies of popular songs and an anti-war sketch written by a London agitprop group. This clumsily cobbled show was performed from a coal-cart to several hundred people on May Day, 1931, in Platt Fields, Manchester.

At home the situation was becoming desperate. The blacklist had made it impossible for my father to work at his trade and his asthma, with which he had been able to cope in the past, had now become a chronic condition so that even when he was lucky enough to find a casual labouring job he was rarely able to work at it for more than a few weeks without being incapacitated.

As always, the burden of keeping the family's head above water fell on my mother's shoulders. Her spirit was indomitable and her energy awesome but she was ageing before our eyes, becoming a worn facsimile of herself. My father would comment on it from time to time, hammering on the wall with his fist. 'You're killing yourself, Bet.'

'Well, I'm no' dead yet,' she would say. 'In any case, what else can we do?' What indeed? Unemployment is a kind of creeping paralysis. It takes over the body of a family organ by organ, limb by limb. It gnaws away at your self-respect, renders you unfit for anything but the dole queue. Our family life had been transformed by it; the visits to and from friends, the Hogmanay junketings had given way to a permanent state of siege. Disaster was never more than a few hours away and the only way it could be circumvented was by my mother's unending toil and the sacrifice of her best years. She was forty-five years old at this time, forty-five and already worn out.

I had been on the dole this time for sixteen weeks when I was taken on as an apprentice mechanic at a large garage and repair shop. The foreman there had been a chauffeur for a family for whom my mother had charred. He hired me out of kindness to her and I went to that garage determined to do well.

'And keep your mouth closed,' my mother said. 'Dinnae be like your faither.' I think she must have caught my father's eye when she said that, for she added, 'I didnae mean that the way it sounded, Will. He could dae a lot worse than be like you. But we've got to keep eating.'

I worked hard at the garage, though I soon discovered that I lacked the special kind of affinity with the internal combustion engine which distinguishes the born mechanic. But I was learning, and if I would never be a mechanic of genius I would at least be a competent one. So I worked hard and kept my mouth shut. But the best-laid schemes of mice and apprentice motor-mechanics gang aft agley and a chance encounter made my scheme look like a chewed-up gearbox. The Red Megaphones was performing at a street corner one evening when a junior mechanic from the garage happened to be passing. His name was Laurence Baker and though he was not long out of his apprenticeship he was already looked upon as a brilliant mechanic. He was as intolerant as he was brilliant.

Our sketch was a satirical piece called *Rent, Interest and Profit* and it was a red rag to Laurence's bull. The following morning he confronted me on my arrival at the garage and launched into a hysterical tirade against 'dirty Yids' and 'filthy reds'. He was out of control and rushed off to the manager's office to expose me as a dangerous revolutionary. I was told to report to the manager, where I was cautioned. In actual fact, the manager seemed to be embarrassed by the whole affair and confined his remarks to a warning to keep away from Baker. 'And watch your step' he added as an afterthought. For the rest of the time I worked in the garage, Baker never once spoke directly to me. He muttered derogatory remarks about me to anyone who would listen but no one really took any notice except Tear-arse Johnny, a hulking seventeen-year-old apprentice who had more brawn than brains. The rest just laughed and after a few wisecracks forgot all about my red reputation. Walter Farrow, the shop tinsmith, echoed the manager: 'Better watch out, son. Laurence is a bad bugger to cross. A real bad bugger.' Shortly after this incident I was made Joe Heanan's apprentice.

Heanan, a slightly built mechanic in his late twenties, made it clear at the outset that he wasn't interested in politics. 'No politics and no religion! Give me a nice juicy quim and a big pair of tits and you can keep your politics and stuff 'em where the monkey stuffed the bad nuts.' He wasn't, in any way, selling himself short. I have never met anyone before or since who was so obsessed with sex or who was so ignorant about it. He talked about it all day. Every morning he greeted me with a detailed description of his previous night's labours. He had been married a mere ten months and complained bitterly of the fact that his wife appeared not to enjoy his attentions. 'Every time I slip her a length she cries like a fucking baby.'

'Perhaps she doesn't fancy it every night.'

'She *married* me, didn't she?'

I had recently read a book called *Sex and Society* and was fairly bursting to show off my knowledge, so I hinted that he might be going about things in the wrong way. This wasn't well received.

'I've been up more women than you've had hot dinners!'

With the eagerness of one who has only recently acquired knowledge, I pressed on. 'Have you ever heard of erogenous zones?' Needless to say, he hadn't, so I explained. He tried to conceal the fact that he was enormously impressed not only by my information but by my ability to pronounce words he had never even heard before. At first he refused to accept the idea that his wife – or indeed any *good* woman – would allow a man to 'mess around with her quim'. When I informed him that this was a normal part of lovemaking he was astounded – and suspicious.

'How do you know all this?'

'How do you think?' said I, with a knowing look.

For the next two weeks he pestered me with questions about this or that aspect of lovemaking and I, from the high pinnacle of literary experience, answered him as best I could. Then one morning he arrived looking very pleased with himself.

'You were dead right,' he announced. 'No waterworks last night, lad, not a single fucking tear. At least, not for the first couple of times.'

'For Chrissake, how often do you do it?'

'I used to be able to manage four quick bangs, but that was without any messing about. Y' know, just shootin' your way in and out. Last night, it was as much as I could do to get it up three times. The second time, the old joy prong must have been up her half-an-hour or more. I feel really shagged this morning. Still, you've got to bung it in while you're young. When you get old, your balls grow cold.' Now it was my turn to be impressed.

A few weeks later he was boasting: 'I make her beg for it now.' And from me he was demanding further and further variations in what he now referred to has his 'experiments for quim and cuntry'. But my meagre stock of book-learned facts was now exhausted. He became morose, swore at me a good deal and found fault with everything I did. I told Bob Goodman and he came up with a solution in the form of a recently remaindered sex-manual and a copy of Magnus Hirschfield's book on sexual anomalies. A few hours' perusal of these two fascinating volumes provided me with enough material to play Scheherazade to Heanan's Haroun-el-Rashid.

He was in a seventh heaven of libidinousness, he glowed with concupiscence. Sodomy, coprophilia, fetishism and probably necrophilia were all grist to his mill. Poor Mrs Heanan. At first I found it an amusing game but as the days succeeded each other I began to feel that I was being swallowed up in his dreadful lust. There was something loathsome about the way his pale blue eyes appeared to film over as he savoured some new sexual vision, and if a girl or woman passed the open gates of the garage his entire body became alert. It was worse when a woman happened to come into the garage with her car; then he would embark on a commentary, continuous and lurid, a rapid succession of murmured remarks punctuated with percussive squeals and grunts.

'Look at those legs! I bet there's a beautiful, big, juicy quim up there just waiting to be poked. Ech! God, gimme ten minutes with her and I'd give her a reaming she'd never forget. Uh! Uh! Ram it up! Jesus, what a pair of tits. Whee! You could hang on the fuckers!'

Age made no difference to him. Middle-aged women were as much the subject of his commentaries as the younger ones; he was just a little more insulting. 'There's a real belter. Look at the arse on her. There's a bloody great quim hiding under that lot. Bet you could drive a fucking twelve-wheel Scammel up it. Christ, I bet *she* knows what's what. Wouldn't mind giving *her* a re-bore. Buff it out first then get up with the old joy prong banging away. Uh! Uh! Plenty to hold onto there. Right, here it comes. Splash!'

Heanan's stature in no way matched his appetite. He was small, unprepossessing, with straight, sandy-coloured hair, washed-out, pale blue eyes framed by almost white eyelashes and a mouthful of crooked teeth. There was something rat-like about him and it was difficult to imagine that any woman would feel attracted to him. Like everyone else in the garage, I had come to believe that his sexual prowess was a myth which he had created to make himself interesting.

We were all proved wrong. A young woman who lived in a small terrace which faced the front gate of the garage was in the habit of seeing her husband off to work each morning at about half-past eight. She usually came to the door with an infant in her arms. She was petite, dark and pretty in a quiet sort of way and Heanan lusted after her. I remember him lying under a Model-A Ford and watching her wave to her departing husband. She was wearing a dark blue woollen dressing gown.

'Still hot from the bed,' he said, and then he called a cheerful 'good morning' to her. She look startled and quickly withdrew into the house. 'I'm going to have her,' he said.

'Sure', I said, 'she's mad about you.'

'Just wait. I'll be there within a fortnight and then I'm going to fuck her till she's bowlegged.'

From then on he greeted her each day with a 'good morning' or a 'good afternoon' and a cheerful smile. She responded with a scared look while averting her face. Heanan's big chance came one day when she was standing outside her house looking very forlorn. She had apparently locked herself out and didn't expect her husband back for another two hours. The bedroom window was open, so Heanan brought a ladder from the garage, and in a few moments the door was opened. He had conquered his first pitch. The following day, his customary morning greeting elicited a shy smile and later in the day Heanan took his brew-can over and asked her to fill it with boiling water. He waited on the doorstep while she did so. This became part of a daily routine and then one day he slipped into the house and this, too, became routine. By this time, every mechanic and apprentice in the shop was alert to what was going on and Heanan's campaign was being followed with disbelief and fascination. As for me – well, I had from the beginning reacted uneasily to his salaciousness and found his foul language repulsive, but now my dislike blossomed into loathing which grew more intense with each of his successes. I hated him with every particle of my being and, if the truth be told, I was jealous. I had developed a romantic passion for the young woman myself and I used to torture myself imagining her in the arms of this vile monster. That is how I thought of Heanan: a vile monster, a disgusting body-crab, a pale-skinned, sandy-haired, white-eyelashed parasite that sucked the goodness out of young women.

He had boasted that he would have her in less than a fortnight. He was two days within his limit when he returned from a brewing-up session and, standing in the middle of the shop floor, announced that the young woman was ready for shagging. The entire workforce heard the announcement but it didn't evoke the kind of response one might have expected. 'It's a bloody shame,' said someone. It was the general opinion, though here and there one heard the occasional admiring comment. Harry Burke, the oldest mechanic in the shop and generally one who minded his own business, was angry: 'Yu're a fucking rat-bag, an abortion. They should castrate you.'

'And bollocks to you!' retorted Heanan. Walter Farrow reminded him that the young woman was nursing an infant. 'So I'll get milk in my tea,' was the reply.

'Give her a chance, man.'

'I'll give her more than a chance', said Heanan, 'I'll give her the length of my prick.'

'You're an evil little sod,' said Burke, turning away in disgust.

The following day, Heanan fulfilled his promise and from that time on spent most of his lunch breaks in the house across the road. Relations between Heanan and myself were strained. It was a difficult situation; I was his apprentice, forced to spend most of my working day in his company, forced to listen to his detailed descriptions of his couplings. I spoke to him as little as possible and made no attempt to conceal my hatred of him. A week or so later, the shop was reorganised and Heanan was promoted to foreman of the day shift. I knew my days as an apprentice were numbered.

Harassment began immediately. For days at a time I found myself filing the numbers off old cylinder-blocks, sorting scrap and hosing down old crocks in the yard. All these were tasks that any apprentice might be called on to perform, but not for weeks at a time. Then there was the matter of overtime.

Apprentices were expected to work one late night every week. Suddenly, I was putting in three late nights, often working until nine or ten o'clock. At first I consoled myself with the thought that I would be earning a little extra money. When I learned that apprentices were paid nothing extra for overtime I was beside myself with fury. Now, for the first time, I really understood why my father had been in revolt all his life. That night, when I got home, I wrote out a petition protesting the fact that we were expected to do extra work without pay. My common sense should have told me that it was a waste of effort. Three of the four apprentices were the sons of haulage contractors and were learning the job as preparation for joining dad's firm. They all refused to sign my petition and one of them went straight to Heanan with the news that a dangerous agitator was on the loose. About an hour later Heanan took action.

I was lying half under a car tightening the front brake-rods when he came up and kicked me on the leg. 'Get out!' he shouted, and kicked me again, harder this time. I swivelled round and caught him by the foot. I pulled hard, his knee struck the running board and he fell over backwards. By the time I was out from under the car he was on his feet again calling me every filthy name he could think of. Then he grabbed me by the shoulder and thrust me against the car. Up until that moment I had been in control of myself, but that contemptuous shove unleashed all the hatred that had been building up for weeks and added it to my resentment at being exploited. I hit him, hard. Then I hit him again. I went on hitting him, forcing him back against a workbench. It is significant that no one interfered or came to his assistance. It was only when the manager appeared on the scene that we were separated. By this time, Heanan's face was covered with blood and oil.

'Get your cards at the office,' said the manager to me.

'He started it,' I said.

'Get your cards', he repeated, 'and I'll see that your dole's stopped.'

'Just a minute!' Old Burke came forward, wiping his hands on a greasy rag.

He was not only the oldest mechanic in the shop but in many ways the clever-est. He it was who always got lumbered with difficult jobs, the ones that others rejected as impossible. He was worth his weight in gold to the firm and he knew it. 'Heanan began the whole thing. He kicked him, twice, while he was on his back under that V-8.'

'Is that true?' asked the manager, but Heanan was incapable of replying. 'Better come to my office.' Once there, he was more conciliatory. 'Forget about the dole business. I didn't know the facts. All the same', he went on, 'I can't have you and Heanan working on the same floor, so I'm afraid you'll have to go.'

Financially, the loss of my job didn't make any difference to my family, since my wages at the garage had actually been twopence a week less than the 9s. and 10d. I drew on the dole. It was the loss of *prospects* that was disturbing, particularly to my mother, who had set her heart on my having a trade to fall back on.

'A trade's no' done me a lot of good,' my father observed.

'But you were aye ower concerned wi' the brotherhood of man', said my mother somewhat acidly, 'and he's going the same way.' And indeed I was. Political activity was taking up more and more and more of my time. Politics and the moors.

The days when walking had been a painful chore were behind me. I had reached the stage where I found the steepest ascent an exhilarating experience; even more wonderful was the descent at speed of a steep, sloping shoulder of moorland. The trick was to develop a rhythm of walking and to keep moving, leaping from heather tussock to cushion of sphagnum moss or patch of blae-berry, down through breast-high bracken, taking your way and allowing your feet to do the thinking, miraculously avoiding holes and pitfalls in the jagged fields of tumbled millstone-grit, threading your way via half-submerged boul-ders in the beds of ancient cloughs, only occasionally choosing a loose stone and landing up to the thighs in peat-stained water. The next moment you were off again, feeling your shorts clinging to your buttocks and thighs and hearing the squelch of water in your boots. In five minutes you had forgotten all about it.

Once you became a regular walker and climber in the Derbyshire peak, your body found a rhythm and tempo which allowed you to cover comparatively large distances. It could also, of course, be adapted to suit the North Lancashire and Yorkshire moors, though both of these uplands lacked the High Peak's fur-rowed plateaus of black peat, a congealed sea of shattered breakers. For moun-tain areas where hillsides were steeper, where rivers run faster and deeper, where sandstone gives way to granite and basalt and rocks are correspondingly bigger, it was necessary to develop a different rhythm. This is where the real joy of mountain and moorland walking lies. Your body attunes itself to each new environment, first by registering impressions through your muscles. At least, that is how it feels. Then you begin to look for certain characteristic features like the relationship between certain rock outcrops and the flora around them. You notice where a shelf marks the termination of a bog or where a patch of alpine saxifrage has attached itself to a well-worn but still healthy extrusion of rock. After a time you begin to learn to read the sedges and those emerald green patches where water and plants combine to fool the unwary traveller.

'Give me the mountains and moors in winter' – a walkers' cliché, perhaps, but so true. There is a unique kind of passion to be experienced in battling your way across a high plateau in a silent whitened-out world where the only sound is the crepitation of snow under your boots and where the wind numbs your face and genitals so that you cannot even remember what it was like to have a sense of touch. On the other hand, spring is a fine time to be up there on the heights when the grouse fly from under your feet with hysterical warnings, when mountain larks are everywhere, mounting the bright air and filling it with their ecstatic song. Summer is the midges' time, those hordes of flesh-bandits, victors of countless ambuscades, the lords of bog and stream; but it is also the time when even the sternest mountain can show a benign expression, for then all the minuscular mountain plants are busy flaunting their beauty: the sundews, hung with dewy diamonds; the blue milkwort and the pennywort fringing the peat hags; the water lobelia along the edges of tarns and lochins; heath-dodder and bog-asphodel, early purple orchis; marsh, spotted, fragrant and pyramidal orchis; butterwort, heath-violet, yellow pimpernel, eyebright, biting stonecrop, marsh-helleborine – all synonyms for summer in high places. Yes, summer takes some beating. But then, so does autumn, when rowans stand like burning sentinels at the feet of the bens, when one can lie in the lap of a mountain and slake one's thirst with blaeberries, crowberries, cranberries. Or, if you knew where to look on Robinson's Moss or Swains Greave on Bleaklow, you could find beds of delicious red-and-yellow cloudberries.

Those Sunday forays into the hills of the High Peak and the Derbyshire dales were the high point of our week. For a time we were content to follow the regular routes up Kinder and Bleaklow, but with practice we became more adventurous and chose longer and more difficult routes. What had once been regarded as a hard day's walking was now merely a prelude to a twenty-five or thirty-mile walk across very wild moorland. We were young and, I'm afraid, vain about our capacity to endure hardships and our ability to move fast on the most rugged terrain. We had developed a kind of speedy lope which nothing short of a rock-face could halt.

How wonderful to be in complete command of your body, to know that your hands and feet would obey the dictates of your will and carry you up that high wall of rock, to know that your legs would go on carrying you indefinitely across that sea of black peat with its troughs and heather-topped waves, that no scree was too steep for you, no boulder-strewn shoulder too precarious. And how splendid to be fit enough to welcome the challenge of storm and blizzard, of snow and ice . . . the thrill of seeing familiar terrain transformed into a landscape without recognisable features, where earth and sky have become one and where there is no sound except the dry scampering of ice granules over fields of snow! And that other winter scene, when the world is locked in chains of ice, when every blade of sedge-grass is furred with frost and the peat in the gullies is as hard as pumice, when the water in the cloughs has become ice, when the waterfalls have been caught in mid-flight and the wind has twisted them into weird convolutions, while from the steep rock sides of the deeper cloughs, icicles hang like the tapering trunks of trees.

Twenty miles or so away from Salford and even less from Sheffield! Tens of millions of geological years away! An elemental world of rock and sky, of wind and water, a world of mountains worn down to the bone long before the Alps or the Himalayas were formed. A world without Labour Exchanges, without bosses. A world where curlew, redshank and black-faced sheep were at home, where sparrow hawks, kestrels and rough-legged buzzards quartered the sky in search of hares, voles and adders.

I never tired of those moors.[1] The days of my youth are illuminated by memories of them, of the descent down Shining Clough Moss through pink clouds of pollen raised by our boots from the waist-high heather . . . memories of standing on the edge above Black Ashop Moor and walking into mist as thick as curdled cream and there, advancing towards you, the *Brocken* spectre . . . memories of waking up in a tent on Alport Moor and finding that snow had fallen in the night and almost covered us, of hearing the whirr of wings as red grouse rose under your feet with their cry of 'g-back, g-back!' . . . memories of gruelling long-distance treks like the Clitheroe-Chinley, of crossing the Wessenden Moors at night on the first leg of the Marsden-Edale walk . . .

The more expert we became at walking and climbing, the more we needed the challenge of mountains and rocks higher than the gritstone climbs we were used to, and soon we were spending occasional week-ends in the Lake District climbing Coniston Old Man and Scafell. Our first assault on Scafell is still clear in my mind. We set out on a Friday afternoon and thumbed a lift in a slow truck which dropped us on the road by Thirlmere Reservoir. It was raining heavily and we were soaked to the skin within minutes of starting out. We started walking immediately and took a compass reading for Langdale. It was late in the day, for our truck had been a slow one and we hadn't covered many miles when night began to fall. We pitched Bob's tent in the shelter of a cluster of rocks and settled down, supperless, to wait out the rain. It was a miserable night. The rain fell incessantly and our tent gave scarcely any protection. I think it was made of cheesecloth. Like most of our gear, it was cheap and shoddy. In the early hours of the morning a strong wind blew up and snapped the head-pole of the tent. In silence we put on our sodden boots, rolled up our even more sodden sleeping bags and started on our way again. Halfway down Dunmail Rise the rain stopped and the sun broke through the clouds. Half an hour later the sky was completely clear of clouds and our clothes were beginning to steam. We unrolled our sleeping bags and tent and stretched them out to dry but we were still steaming when we reached Langdale. There, at a farm famous for its half-crown meals, we stuffed ourselves full and set out on the walk up Scafell.

The sun was really hot now, blazing in fact, and not a breath of wind. Not the best kind of a day for walking up a mountain after a sleepless night. Two-thirds of the way up we unrolled our sleeping-bags and tent again and laid them out in the sun to dry while we lay down in a patch of heather to sunbathe. We fell asleep and when we woke up we were both quite sunburned. Though our tent was now dry, our sleeping bags were still more than a little damp, so we decided to make for the Youth Hostel at Boot where we hoped to find drying facilities. We made good time to the top of Scafell, though the straps of our packs chafed against our sunburned shoulders. We kept up a very fast pace during the long descent to Boot. There, finding the Youth Hostel was full, we took the single-gauge railway to Ravenglass and persuaded a fisherman to row us across to the gull sanctuary at Drigg. From a copse of alders there, we cut a stick for a tent-pole and camped that night in the territory of screaming gulls. The following morning we hitched a lift in a GPO van to Wasdale Head, from where we climbed Scafell again, continuing by Great-End to Glaramara and descending by Stake Pass to Ambleside, where we begged a ride from two climbers bound for Kendal. From there we travelled in the back of an empty lorry, bouncing and cursing our sunburn and the driver every inch of the journey to Farnworth. Our money had run out so we walked the rest of the way home.

In the months that followed, we walked and climbed most of the fells of Cumberland and Westmoreland. We also discovered Teesdale and the North Yorkshire Moors and then Tryfan, Crib Goch and Carnedd Llewelyn in North Wales. One Christmas, we hitched up to Glencoe and paid our respects to the Grampians.

The return to Salford after these magical Sundays and weekends was in no way depressing. We were returning to the political struggle refreshed and determined to destroy capitalism. The political battles were, in their own way, just as exhilarating as finding one's way by compass across a moor shrouded in mist, or working out a route on a rock-face. Yes, it was true that there were scores of boring repetitive jobs to be done – addressing envelopes, running off page after page on a duplicating machine, the thousand-and-one things which had to be done if the party was to keep functioning – but these were like the tussocks of bent-grass and the bogs which made crossing Bleaklow difficult. There were the branch meetings, district meetings, conferences, education classes – they were like the bracken-covered braes which led to the high plateaus from which one could see the hazy peaks of the final goal: the end of capitalism and the beginning of a new form of society based upon all mankind's needs, the needs of all men and women, not just the privileged few. This was a vision which was just as exciting as any mountain vista. It sustained and nourished us through the bleak years of unemployment as we listened to the ominous distant thunder of guns.

14

New Comrades

With the growth of political consciousness I became more self-confident and though I still occasionally suffered from feelings of inadequacy I no longer felt haunted by the shame of being unemployed. On the contrary, I now saw myself as part of an historical force which would one day dismantle the shoddy and dilapidated capitalist system and, in its place, create a world where every day would be like the conquest of an unclimbed mountain peak. Romantic? An adolescent fantasy? Perhaps, but only to those who have forgotten how to dream. To a sixteen-year-old brought up in the crumbling brick desert of a Salford slum they were survival dreams.

Sometimes from the vantage point of the Peel Park reading room I would gaze out over the town with its endless streets of identical houses, its rampant church spires and its innumerable factory chimneys pointing accusing fingers at the sky. Even from a distance it looked moribund, a 'place much decayed', and yet I was stirred by it, filled with a disturbing kind of enthusiasm. In that shabby wilderness, with its mean streets and silent cotton-mills looking like abandoned fortresses, in those geometrically arranged warrens and occasional clusters of bug-infested dwellings built in the reign of daft George for 'the better class of artisan', in that wasteland of rotting timbers and rusting iron, of a fouled river and an abandoned canal, a quarter of a million people are born, live and die. It is my Paris. They are my people and if I can learn to master that fucking dictionary they may one day furnish me with the raw material for my own *Human Comedy. Fustian: Middle English. Of language ridiculously lofty in expression. Bombastic. Futhorc, the Runic alphabet.* Very useful, I don't think. *Futile: incapable of producing any result . . . fuzzle, fyke, fylfot, fyrd,* bollocks!

What *is* it I feel for this place? Hatred? Yes, most of the time, but not all the time. Not all the time. What, then? Love? Who's kidding who? *Love?* Fear, perhaps. Do I fear it? Sometimes lying in bed at night I am overcome with the awful fear that I will never escape from this place, that I am trapped and destined to live out my life in this awful rat pit. And yet there are people here who I . . . the fact is, I don't really know what I feel. Of course I hate it, I loathe it, I am scared of being devoured by it; and yet, though I live to be a hundred, it is unlikely that I will ever come to know any place as well as I know this one. That smoke-encrusted brick was among the first things I ever saw. I have absorbed this place through the palms of my hands; the soles of my feet have walked, run, slid, hopped, jumped and skipped along its flagstones and cobbles, through its roads and alleyways, its detours and short cuts, its dumps, cinder-crofts and parks.

My nose is equally familiar with the place. If I were to walk blindfold through this labyrinth of odours my nose would guide me like a well-trained bloodhound. That sweet, cloying smell which seems to register somewhere just behind the bridge of my nose is from the brewery at the bottom end of Liverpool Street. The nauseating, sweet-and-sour smell comes from the Greengate-and-Irwell Rubber Company's factory at Cock Robin Bridge. That dry, coppery stink, which I feel way up at the top of my nose means I'm in the vicinity of the London Electric Wire Company and Smith's. The sulphur used in the furnaces of Hodgkinson's foundry gives Pendleton its special acrid smell. The smell of cow and pig dung from the cattle market on Regent Road is comparatively pleasant. Ordsall smells of cotton waste and over-ripe fruit from the docks on Trafford Road. St Mathias' Ward stinks of advanced decay and in Greengate I try not to breathe too deeply the foetid smell of ancient dirt. And there's the glue factory. Jesus Christ! A whiff of that is enough to make you gag; two whiffs and you shit toads, as the saying goes; three and you're a walking shit-house. They say that British Dyestuffs in Blackley smells worse, but I doubt it.

Down in Blackley stands the Dyestuffs,
Better known as Levenstein's;
Oh, it smells just like a shit-house,
Worse than working down a mine.[1]

But that's in Manchester, doesn't really count. We've got our own troubles here in Salford. There's smells and smells, of course. On the whole, the smells of winter are bearable; half the time you don't even notice them. After all, you've had them in your nostrils since the day you were born. In summertime they are less easy to put up with because then, in addition to the smell of this or that factory or industrial process, there is the stink of sewers and – even worse – the stench that issues from the few houses in the street where the struggle against dirt and squalor has been abandoned. It isn't easy to live in a constant state of siege, with dirt as the enemy. A small number of women spend all their waking hours brushing, scrubbing, dusting and polishing their homes. The majority, however, are content to give the place a good going-over once a week and a lick and a promise the rest of the time. A few give up and live as best they can, despised by their neighbours. Their houses smell bad. In my mother's words, 'they pollute the street'.

In my opinion, the sweet, heavy stink of bedbugs is the most disgusting smell of all. They were regular summer visitors and my mother loathed them to such an extent that she would sometimes vomit when trying to deal with them.

There seemed to be no way of totally eradicating these foul pests. Betsy tried everything. She washed the bed-legs in pennyroyal and oil of peppermint; she stuffed cucumber peel into cracks in the wall and floorboards. She took the bed apart and washed the frame and springs in a strong solution of carbolic or Lysol. When this didn't work, she ran through the entire range of disinfectants and insect-exterminators. She got the sanitary inspectors to come and light sulphur-candles in the bedrooms and for days afterwards they would be uninhabitable. Afterwards we would have a few days' respite from the ravenous bugs – and then they would return. My mother in her frustration and shame blamed 'the lazy English slatterns' that she was forced to live among.

'Mag Watt wasnae English,' my father would observe.

'God, no!' my mother would agree. 'The dirtiest woman in the Northern Union.'

'In any case, it's no' laziness that causes bugs, it's poverty. By God, the rich dinnae ken they're born.'

I found beauty and excitement in many things during the years which opened up the thirties. With political commitment came peace of mind and a wonderful sense of adventure. And time, which I had borne on my shoulders like a heavy weight, was now light as a feather. Apart from Sundays and the occasional weekend spent walking or climbing, I was busy most days from early morning till late at night.

In more ways than one it was a period of discovery. Up until this time Manchester had been a foreign place to me. But now, I was covering several miles of this new territory each day on foot. When Bob Goodman lost his job we spent all our waking time together and we walked everywhere. There were factory papers and copies of the party newspaper to be sold outside Metropolitan-Vickers or Taylor Brothers or Lancashire Dynamo in Trafford Park. So we got up at five in the morning and walked through the empty streets. *The Salford Docker*, a four-page duplicated newspaper, had to be sold to the morning shift at the docks, so we walked.[2] There were factory newspapers to be sold outside Crossley Motors in Openshaw, or at Gorton Tank or at Ward and Goldstone's electrical components factory in Lower Broughton, so we walked there. And having sold, or failed to sell, our wares, we walked back to the party rooms in Great Ducie Street, Ancoats, where we generally made ourselves useful until lunch-time when, if there were no leaflets to be distributed at a factory-gate meeting, we walked to Oldham Street in the city centre and lunched at Yate's Wine Lodge. There, for threepence, we feasted on a miniature brown loaf, a bowl of soup and a mug of tea. Then we would go back again to Cheetham to collect a bundle of leaflets, to Failsworth where they had to be distributed, or to London Road Station where a bundle of pamphlets awaited us.

We walked everywhere and talked about everything: sex, politics, books, music, the nature of the universe and whether Widnes or Broughton Rangers would be the Cup winners that year. We read *The Condition of the Working Class in England in 1834* and Engels' book became our Baedeker to the city. The pin-pointing of Engels' locations added spice to our marathon treks. Crossing the bridge in Ancoats, over the scabrous waters of an old canal bordered by abandoned cotton-mills where broken windows revealed shattered weaving-frames and rusted overhead drive-shafts, we felt a strong kinship with Friedrich. After all, he had lived in Salford, walked the same streets that we walked, looked at the same sights and held similar political views. That gave us a certain proprietary interest and when we discovered an inn in Little Hayfield where he had sometimes stayed with Kitty O'Shea, our partisanship knew no bounds. He was one of evolution's major successes, a judgment pronounced by Bob, paraphrasing my father's customary 'one of evolution's failures'. My father generally employed the phrase to describe scabs, crooked politicians and trade-union leaders who betrayed their members. For us it had a much wider application and included all those who were irrevocably committed to barring the way to social change.

Change of any kind seemed to be a long time coming. As far as I could see, our furious endeavours produced scarcely any results whatsoever. Were we making any headway at all? There was scarcely a minute of the day when we weren't busy compiling, duplicating, typing, writing, printing and distributing factory newspapers, handing out leaflets, selling pamphlets, organising meetings outside factory gates, at street corners, in desolate, shoddy halls. We attended discussions, week-end schools, training classes, education classes, group meetings, branch meetings, district meetings, area meetings, conferences, congresses called by the central committee, the district committee, the secretariat, the political bureau. Three or four of us would leave our beds at half past four in the morning to be outside a factory or a pit when the graveyard shift came off. If we were lucky we might sell a dozen copies of the party newspaper. A dozen newspapers for a labour force of 900 or sometimes 12,000! News that someone had persuaded a workmate to attend a YCL social and dance was greeted as a victory!

It wasn't that we were complacent or self-satisfied, lazy or lacking in initiative. On the contrary, we were forever castigating ourselves for our mistakes, our elitism, our crassness, our lack of real political understanding, our lack of resourcefulness, our inability to grasp basic theoretical concepts, our reluctance to translate theory into practice and, above all, our sectarianism. 'Comrades, we must guard against sectarianism' was a slogan that was endlessly repeated. And we *were* sectarian; how could we possibly avoid being so? We were trying to awaken a population that was still drowsy from its hundred-year-old sleep of imperial greatness, a population suffering fatty degeneration of the brain, obese recipients of a century's imperialist plunder. We were talking about freedom to a people who had held half the world's population in thrall, who were afraid to shout for what was theirs for fear it would disturb the neighbours, who prized respectability above liberty.

We *were* sectarian! Our arguments and political discussions were larded with foreign words and phrases borrowed from Marx and Engels, from Lenin, Stalin, Luxemburg and Liebknecht. We talked about things that nobody else wanted to talk about, said things that nobody wanted to hear. 'Listen . . . listen . . .!' we shouted as we stood on a piece of waste ground and tried to warn our fellow citizens of what was in store for them. It was like trying to fly a kite in a hurricane. The Japanese had invaded Manchuria? Where the hell was Manchuria? What's this stuff about the Scottsboro boys? A railway strike in India? Who cares? Fascism means war? You've got war on the brain.

We were gaining ground, a little at a time. There were new party branches springing up all over the place and the YCL could now boast a dozen branches or more in the Manchester district. To a youth burning with revolutionary zeal, however, the gains seemed microscopic. Our street and factory-gate meetings I found particularly depressing, with rarely more than a dozen in the crowd and the hecklers bombarding the platform with catch-phrases culled from *The Empire News* and *The News of the World*.

I can't remember the exact time that I first saw Alec Armstrong. Probably sometime in the autumn of 1931. It was difficult not to be conscious of him; he was so big and such a perfect specimen of young manhood, well-muscled and with the strength of a young lion. He looked for all the world like one of those tow-haired young proletarian heroes one saw depicted on Soviet posters, the heroic YCLer urging his comrades to fulfill their quota of the Five-Year-Plan. He was good-natured, too; indeed, in all the time I knew him I don't remember him ever losing his temper. By trade he was a slater, generally an unemployed slater. He was also a rambler and climber of some note. Before becoming involved in the political struggle, Alec had been in the habit of going off alone and spending three or four days at a time hiking in the forest of Bowland or the North Yorkshire Moors. He usually slept rough and, whenever possible, lived off the terrain. He caught grouse and pheasant, trapped rabbits and hares and was a past master at guddling for trout.

When less athletic members of the YCL accused him of spending too much time in physical pursuits, he would counter by saying that it was the duty of every revolutionary to be in the pink of physical condition – and *he* certainly was. I have known him to walk through a snowstorm for hours at a time wearing nothing but his climbing boots. It was a test, he said, preparing himself for the revo. I remember one of those tests. It was New Year's Eve, 1932. We had left our gear in a barn in Edale and set out for a quick walk up Kinder Scout. There were half-a-dozen of us, all seasoned walkers and climbers. It had snowed heavily earlier in the week and now the snow was crusted with ice. The night was bitterly cold with a full moon lending the sculpted snow banks, with their icicle-fringed overhangs, a ghostly appearance.

We made good time up the frozen bed of Grindsbrook and crossed Kinder plateau at a steady lope. No one spoke much. It was almost as if we didn't want to disturb that superbly beautiful frozen landscape. At Crowden Head we decided to push on and cross over to Bleaklow, so we descended by Fairbrook, crossed the Snake Road and started up the long climb to the Higher Shelf Stones by Oyster Clough. The snow was much deeper here and the going more difficult. We reached the Shelf Stones just before midnight and stood there in the shelter of those ancient gritstone boulders listening to the church bells of Glossop signalling the birth of 1933. We sang a verse of 'Auld Lang Syne' and then 'The International' and began the descent. At a frozen pool on the Alport, Alec and Bob decided to celebrate the New Year by breaking the ice and having a dip. As Alec dived in, he smashed his collarbone on a concealed spur of rock. We managed to pull him from the pool and helped him to dress. He was in great pain but he walked those seven or eight cruel miles of broken moorland in heavy snow without once giving voice to his anguish.

He spent that night in a hospital bed in Sheffield and most of us envied him, for the barn we were sleeping in managed to be both cold and stuffy. There wasn't much straw in it and the little there was had already been commandeered by a group of Sheffielders who had arrived while we were on Kinder. Four more walkers who had set out from Oldham earlier in the day, intent on prefacing their holiday with the gruelling Marsden-Edale walk, arrived about four in the morning, speechless with fatigue.

This way of spending a Christmas or New Year break was popular with hikers in the North of England and Scotland, for while Christmas had not become the monstrous commercial orgy it is today, it was regarded by many people as an irritating irrelevancy. The hard times contributed to this feeling and there were plenty of smallholders and hard-up villagers who were prepared to offer escape in the form of sleeping accommodation of one kind or another. The particular smallholder in whose barn we were sleeping that night was charging us four-and-sixpence a head for two nights in his barn and a traditional Christmas dinner. Some farmers merely provided hot water and a place to sit down out of the cold and the rain; some provided pots of tea, while others offered shilling teas of bread-and-butter, raspberry tarts and bowls of stewed fruit. Some half-dozen places scattered throughout the moorland and mountainous areas of Britain served the kind of dishes on which legends are fed.

There was the cottage at Ladybower on the Snake Road where they served you with thick rashers of home-cured ham, eggs laid that morning and freshly-baked bread with butter made in a hand-cranked churn. As much as you could eat for 1s 9d. Then there was The George at Woodhead in the Longdendale Valley, where the landlord (known, for some strange reason, as 'Delegrade') would, on occasion, feed his regulars on mutton-pies and roast grouse. And there was a pub on the road between Clitheroe and Slaidburn where you could gorge yourself on hare which had been simmering slowly in a jug of port wine for three or four days. Best of all, there was the farm in Great Langdale, which catered for climbers and serious walkers. The dining-room there was dominated by a large table which could seat fourteen and running the length of three of the walls were trestle-tables laden with a joint of roast beef, a leg of pork, a freshly boiled tongue and a leg of mutton. Another carried the desserts, bowls of stewed apples, pears, plums, gooseberries, blackcurrants, blaeberries, raspberries, custard and cream. On the third table were the breads: scones, oatcakes, jars of jam and honey. You served yourself and ate as much as you could eat for half-a-crown.

Good sleeping accommodation was harder to come by. It had to be cheap and clean and while one occasionally came across places which managed to achieve this combination they were, on the whole, exceptions to the rule. Many of the places were cheap and dirty, some notoriously so. The village of Hayfield, for example, had a very bad reputation among walkers. Its sleeping accommodations were not only unhygienic but, it was rumoured, they were little more than houses of convenience – *knocking shops*, to use the slang of the time.

At Thorpe Cloud, in the valley of the Dove, not far from that delightful spot where Isaac Walton had meditated on the ways of fish and men, there was a place known as The Old Woman's. It was a large, decrepit old cottage where for a shilling you could get a bed, or rather a place in a bed, for you never knew in advance with whom or what you might be sleeping. First come, first served was the rule, a kind of lucky dip. The house was filled with beds, unmade beds with crumpled sheets and pillowcases so ingrained with dirt that they seemed to be spun out of metal. The thought that I might find myself sharing a bed with one or several nubile young women from the potteries was balanced by my feeling of repugnance occasioned by the soiled linen. I slept there but the one time. It had been a day of heavy rain and Bob and I had been unsuccessful in our efforts to find a comfortable barn to sleep in. The Old Woman's was a last resort. The cottage was in darkness when we arrived, but the old woman's ancient spouse let us in and after taking our shillings showed us the room where we were to sleep. There was room in two of the beds, he said, one on the left and the other under the window. 'And no pissing out of the window,' he added. We undressed in the dark, conscious of the sleepers all around us. Bob whispered something.

'What?'

'I said, I'll take the one under the window. Well, here's hoping.' He slipped into bed. The next moment a loud voice was raised in anger.

'What the fuckin' hell . . .!'

'Sshh. . .'

'Keep them fucking feet off me or I'll . . . Jesus Christ, you're like a bleeding corpse!'

'Belt up! We're trying to get some sleep!' A girl's voice. I slipped into bed and tentatively reached out to the body lying next to me.

'What do you want?' Again, the girl's voice.

'I was just trying to find out whether you were a girl or a bloke.'

'Well, now you know.' And then, 'Turn around.'

'Why?'

'Just turn round.' I turned. 'Right, girls,' she whispered and turned towards me. The bed heaved.

'How many are in this bed?'

'There's three of us and you.' She leaned over me to make herself heard and said, 'And let's have no funny business. One wrong move and I'll put your balls in a sling.'

'Look', I said, 'I can't sleep on my left side.'

'Right. Turn over, girls.' The bed heaved again. 'Now, snuggle up,' she said, and she took my arm and pulled it round her so that my hand was resting on her stomach. 'That's nice,' she said drowsily, and fell asleep. So, after a few minutes, did I.

Nearly all the friends of my youth are associated in one way or another with Derbyshire. Bob Goodman, Joe Davis, Tom Fearnley, Bob Ward, Nat Frayman, Alec Armstrong, Martin Bobker. . .but looking back, I realise now that I had two distinct circles of friends at this time. One of them was made up of people like Alec, Myer and the denizens of strange places like Cheetham, Higher Broughton, Gorton and Openshaw. The other was composed of Salfordians like George Pole and Larry Findlay, Alf Armitt, Jimmy Rigby, Ben Durden, George Sumner, Bud Larney and, of course, Bob Goodman. Among the outlanders were Nellie Wallace, Grace Seddon, Bill Benson and . . . so many of them are dead and all, like me, are old. Some gave up the fight a long time ago, some fought on until old age and sickness overcame them.

My Manchester friends – all of them working-class people who lived in houses not so very different from those of my Salford friends – rarely visited the Workers' Arts Club. It was perhaps the unrelieved squalor of Salford's heartland which they found so forbidding – or maybe they were made to feel unwelcome, for there is no doubt that there was a barrier, some antipathy, between the two cities. *Manchester people are stuck-up, standoffish, they think they're posh, fur coat and no drawers,* and so on. *Salford is just a bloody great slum, no city centre, nothing worth looking at, Salford people are dirty.*

One might have expected that politically minded folk would have sloughed off such prejudices, and I am sure that most of them would have been indignant had they been accused of subscribing to such reactionary notions. The fact is, however, that there was little intercourse between the two groups. My Salford mates were more at fault. They tended to regard anyone who lived in Manchester as middle-class, pretty much in the same way as northerners tend to look upon all southerners as middle-class.

I suppose anyone from outside, seeing the Workers' Arts Club for the first time, would find it strange. I remember once Myer Bobker and Bob Ward paid us a visit. I was rehearsing in the cellar with The Red Megaphones when someone shouted from the top of the stairs, 'There's a couple of your posh friends from Manchester here.' Posh friends! Myer, a waterproof worker and Bob an unemployed labourer. Later, upstairs in the bar-room, we stood and listened to the mountainous Jimmy Tillbrook wheezing his way through a peroration on colonisation and Christianity to a small group of admiring disciples. Myer looked on in wonder and delight.

'I think he's got 'em on the ropes', he chuckled, 'he's blinding 'em with science.'

'He's just an old windbag,' George Pole observed. Maybe he was, but it was a civilising wind; it carried no acid rain to wither the listener's brain-cells, no radiation to burn out the speaker's vocal chords. George, a lean, white-faced stripling who lived in the vicinity of the docks, was no mean philosopher himself. At the time, he was leading a small party of us through the labyrinthine passages of Marxism. *Philosophers of the past have explained the world, we have to change the world.* And where did fat Jimmy fit in that concept?

Still, those old men – I thought of them as old – were fascinating to listen to; the things they had seen and done! Some were interesting because of what they were, like Dick France. He was a friend of my father's, an engineer by trade with the most deformed legs I have ever seen. They formed almost a complete circle and made walking difficult. In fact, he rolled from side to side and if you walked with him you had to slow your pace down to a shuffle in order for him to keep up with you. I used to see him in the periodicals room of the public library. They provided him with a box on which to stand so that he could read the newspapers. He read a great deal, mostly technical journals and works dealing with industrial and trade-union affairs. He was a machine-tool maker at Metropolitan-Vickers. He was also an active and militant trade unionist. When the Minority Movement, of which he was a member, was proscribed by the Trades Union Congress (TUC) he lost his job.

The loss of a poorly paid job in paradise was a high price to pay for his opinions, but if he ever thought of abandoning them he never told anyone. Year in, year out, he continued signing on at the broo, meeting my father and the rest of his cronies in the Peel Park reading room, sampling the vicarious pleasures of the engineering journals, distributing leaflets, selling the party newspaper, demonstrating and being kicked in the ribs by a six-foot guardian of the peace. Only rarely did he contribute to the discussion at the party branch meetings but when he did so he always made good sense. For five or six years our paths crossed frequently, then I lost touch with him.

Old Genge wasn't in the party, he was just one of those people whose interests ran parallel to ours. No one could remember ever seeing him without his notebook and pencil and his limp-backed Russian grammar. He was learning Russian and according to Jack Evans (another self-taught student of the language) could read it well but couldn't speak a word of it. He was another silent man, an anarchist, an admirer of Kropotkin. I used to see him on unemployed demonstrations towering over the crowd, shambling along in his unlaced boots, a gentle giant straight out of Hans Andersen.

Jack Evans, on the other hand, looked and behaved as if he had stepped straight out of a novel by Dostoevsky, except that most of Dostoevski's characters come from the middle-class or the aristocracy. Jack's background was solid working-class, though he preferred to describe it as lumpenproletarian and to prove it cited the fact that his elder brother was a policeman. Jack had no trade; he had left school at fourteen and, like me, had worked in several dead-ends before finishing up on the dole. He was five years my senior, but looked forty. He was thin and always looked cold even in the height of summer. 'That laddie's starving,' my mother used to say whenever she saw him. He used to come round to our house to use the piano. He was a self-taught composer and a talented one. He was also a frustrated one. Imagine it: a self-taught working-class youth intent on storming Parnassus not with a song or songs – that would not have been beyond the possibility of achievement. No, Jack's head was filled with symphonies and operas that just had to be written.

He wrote long, formal letters to music-academies, orchestra-leaders, successful composers. Those who bothered to reply confined themselves to mechanical phrases of encouragement or to suggestions that he should regard music as a hobby. Had he possessed personal charm or had any of the social graces, things might have been different for him, but his talent and his tenacity were his only gifts. He finally gave up trying to solicit help and decided on a long-term plan. He would learn Russian and somehow get to the Soviet Union where he was sure he would find the help he needed, tuition in composition and orchestration. Occasionally, he would admit to having set his sights on a few lessons from Prokofiev. So he taught himself Russian, began corresponding with half-a-dozen pen friends in the Soviet Union, immersed himself in Russian literature. Then, one day in 1934, he turned up at the club wearing a floppy beret, the type worn by Wagner. It looked incongruous on him, all the more so since no one had ever seen him wear anything other than the uniform of the dole queue.

A group of us gathered round to find out why he was in fancy dress. He was brief. 'I've got a job.'

'Where?'

'Moscow.'

There was a chorus of disbelief until he took a letter from his pocket and showed it to us. It was in Russian, so he read it to us. Sure enough, it was true; he had landed a job with the State Publishing House in Moscow. A few days later, we saw him off on a train to Liverpool.

15

Agitprop

In the autumn of 1930, my mother went to work as a cleaner at Cunningham's Dance Academy, a momentous event as far as I was concerned since it led to my first introduction to jazz music. The Academy was a thriving concern specialising in ballroom dancing but offering classes in tap, novelty, soft-shoe and various other types of popular dance. Gramophone records provided the musical accompaniment for the classes and a new batch of these were bought every two or three weeks. Those that were found to be unsuitable accompaniment for the fox-trot and two-step were thrown out and my mother would bring them home, a dozen or so at a time – Parlaphone, Regal, Zonophone, HMV and Brunswick labels – offering fabulous riches: Louis Armstrong blowing his marvellous horn, Bessie Smith, Mary Lou Williams, Fats Waller, Pine Top Smith, King Oliver, Jelly Roll Morton and the Red Hot Peppers. There were lyrics, too, where the moon in June was never mentioned:

> Did you hear the story about Minnie the Moocher?
> She was a low-down hoochie koocher . . .

It had been fun listening with my cousin John to those early Layton and Johnstone records and to Morton Downey singing 'Jericho', but these songs had a different feeling to them. 'Stormy Weather', 'I'll Be Glad When You're Dead, You Rascal, You', 'Little Town Gal' . . . I still hear them sometimes, the way they sounded on those old 78s. It's as if a door opens for a moment on a studio where a band is rehearsing. And the smell of a good Havana cigar sometimes evokes memories. The proprietor of the Dance Academy had suffered a heart attack and had been forbidden to smoke, whereupon his wife gave my mother a large box of Romeo y Juliettas and told her to get rid of them. They lay in their box untouched on our kitchen mantelpiece – until I started my next job, this time as a slater's labourer.

Alec Armstrong got me the job. We were on Bleaklow Moor sitting in the shelter of Bleaklow Stones, eating our sandwiches. 'How do you fancy the building trade?' asked Alec suddenly.

'I've never thought about it.'

'It's a good, healthy job. Outdoors, plenty of fresh air. Just the job.' He said there was a good chance that he would be starting on a new job in a couple of weeks. 'About a month's work. Putting a new roof on an engineering factory in Sherborne Street. A doddle. Fancy being my labourer?'

'What would I have to do?'

'Make yourself useful. Hole the slates, carry 'em up the ladder, stack 'em on the roof. Help me fit new laths, nail a few slates. Fetch and carry.'

I didn't know a thing about holing slates, would probably lose my way on a building-site . . . but he dismissed my objections and said I could learn all I needed to know on the way to the Alport. And so as we walked through clouds of heather pollen, he took me through a crash course on the art of slating.

'There's three types of slates used in building. Look at that hare! Imagine being able to move like that. The best are Westmoreland Greens but they're bloody expensive. Only banks and pubs can afford them. The other two types are Portmadocs and Velinellis. They'll be using one or the other on this job. Cloudberries! They're still a bit green. Need another week before they're ripe. Roofing slates are thicker at one end; they're cut like that so that they'll lie flat when they overlap. How about a bit of that chocolate? You punch two holes, one at each side, about a third of the way down from the thin end of the slate. There's a hole-punch that you can learn to use in about thirty seconds flat. And that's it.'

'What do you mean, *that's it?*'

'I mean that's all you need to know. The rest is muscle and common sense.'

'Isn't it dangerous?'

'Dangerous? What's dangerous about it?'

'You said it was four stories.'

'So what? What's so terrible about four stories? You're good on rock and this time you'll have a ladder. You could do it blindfold.' At Alport Castles he indicated one of the spurs and said, 'That's about as high as you'd have to go. Four stories with ladders. A doddle.' He didn't mention the subject again until we had crossed Kinder and were dropping down Nether Tor to Grindsbrook, then he said, 'You'll need a cap if you get the job.'

'What kind of cap?'

'Just an ordinary cap. For the slates. You get a newspaper (any capitalist rag'll do) and you roll it up tight and stuff it inside the rim of the cap. It provides a flat base for the slates to lie on when you're carrying them up the ladder. You can carry twelve or fourteen at a time that way. You get some mad buggers who'll do twenty at a time but they're generally punch-drunk.' So ended the theoretical part of my training as a slater's labourer.

A month passed before I heard from him again. One night he turned up at a rehearsal of The Red Megaphones and stood at the top of the steps holding up his arms like a boxer signalling victory. 'Patience has triumphed!' he shouted. 'Sherborne Street. Half-past-seven tomorrow morning.' The job actually began at eight, but he said I'd need the extra half-hour to get the feel of the job.

I arrived at the site wearing bib-and-brace overalls and my father's cloth cap, well-upholstered with a rolled-up copy of the *Daily Herald*. Alec was already there wearing his climbing boots studded with tricouni nails. The factory was a Victorian brick building, the façade of which was two-thirds the length of the street. It was mid-November. There had been a heavy frost during the night and everything was painful to the touch. After showing me how to use the punching machine, Alec made me practise walking up and down the ladder with a dozen slates on my head. They felt as if they weighed a ton but after several attempts I was able to mount the ladder without dropping my load. 'All you need now', Alec said, 'is to look as if you've been doing it all your life.' So I went on repeating the routine until he pronounced himself satisfied with my performance. He then outlined a small scene he had prepared for me to act out for the boss's benefit.

'When he arrives, I want him to find you finishing holing a pile of slates. Then put a dozen of 'em on your head and bring 'em up the ladder. I'll be waiting for you on the roof and I'll show you how to stack 'em.'

The opening part of the routine went as planned and I actually found enough confidence to whistle a tune as I finished holing the slates. Then I heaved the slates onto my head and jauntily began the ascent of the ladder. It wasn't until I was almost at the top that my confidence suddenly abandoned me. It drained away, leaving me panic-stricken. I tried to remind myself that I was on a ladder and that it was perfectly safe, that I had been on rock faces that were *real* tests of nerve and skill. Nothing helped. I couldn't go on, not another step. I thought of the boss standing underneath. Surely he'd noticed that I had stopped. I heard Alec's voice a few feet above my head. I took a deep breath and climbed the last few rungs quite briskly. Then came the awful moment of stepping off the ladder onto the roof. As I did so, the weight of the slates bore me backwards and for one moment of absolute terror I was poised above the void. I was saved by Alec's arm which shot out, caught me by the shoulder and pulled me onto the roof, where I crouched, trembling. The old roof had been stripped off and four stories below was the foundry with its furnace and overhead gantry. The ladder had been bad, but this was worse. 'I think I'm going to be sick.'

'You'd better not. If you spray the blokes underneath your life won't be worth living.' I could see them a long way below, their faces turned to me. They were shouting something.

'What're they saying?'

'They're calling you the human fly,' said Alec. 'Never mind, a couple of days and you'll be hopping about up here like a bloody sparrow.'

I never became *that* confident but the job was not without its compensations. It was pleasant to be up there on fine mornings when the sun was shining, and Alec was a good man to work with. It wasn't long till I was doing my share of the slate-laying and experiencing the satisfaction of looking back at a stretch of the roof and saying, 'I put that on.' The eleven o'clock break was a good part of the day, too. Alec had brought a Gilwell canteen onto the site and he brewed milky coffee which we drank at our leisure, sitting on the roof. And as we contemplated the busy life of the street below we smoked our Romeo y Juliettas (courtesy of the Cunningham Dance Academy). At lunchtime I would take my place in the queue outside the pie-shop and when we had finished eating out potato-pies and smoked the butt-ends of our cigars we would continue the job again. Before knocking off each day we had to cover the open sections of the roof with huge tarpaulins. If there was a wind blowing this was a hazardous task for not only did you have to wrestle the cumbersome sheets into position, but you were in constant danger of being blown off the roof. We completed the job on Christmas Eve and celebrated by drinking a glass of port wine in Yate's Wine Lodge. The following Tuesday I was back at Albion Street Labour Exchange again, signing on.

When, in 1931, the National Government led by Ramsay MacDonald fired its opening salvos against the living standards of the British working class, the most hard-hit were, naturally, the unemployed. Naturally? Of course. *From he that hath not shall be taken away even that which he hath.* And who has less than the unemployed? Who is more accustomed to suffering the pangs of hunger than the hungry? So now unemployment benefit has been pared down even further and a means test introduced, a humiliating inquisition calculated to squeeze out the last drop of human dignity from every unemployed family in the land. No, it wasn't calculated – our rulers are not like that. They are not conscious of the fact that working people possess human dignity or indeed that they have feelings of any kind. We are engaged in a war, dammit! One attacks the enemy at his weakest point and that point is the three million unemployed and their families. So let's have no more of this human dignity claptrap. And let us hear no more about equality of sacrifice or grinning and bearing it, or how we British can take it. Don't bother trying to conceal your contempt for us and we won't try to conceal our hatred of you.

Our branch of the National Unemployed Workers Movement (NUWM) is calling for a mass demonstration against the new measures on 2 October. For the ten days before that we are out every night advertising the demo. Our publicity methods are cheap and effective. All you need is a good supply of blue-mould, the porous, chalk-like substance which housewives use to brighten up their window sills and doorsteps. It's useful stuff for chalking slogans and announcements on walls. In addition, a rota of public speakers has been drawn up. Their job is to address queues outside Labour Exchanges at various points throughout the day. My stint covers the nine and ten o'clock queues. I'm a poor public speaker and my harangues rarely attract more than a handful of listeners. On the morning of the demo, however, I change my tactics and decide to make my pitch inside the exchange. Almost before I can begin speaking I am seized by a dozen pair of hands, pushed to the counter and lifted on to it. No speech is needed this morning, just the announcement: 'All out against the means test! Assemble at Liverpool Street croft!'

Within seconds the Labour Exchange has emptied and the street outside is filled with the unemployed. We begin moving immediately. A crowd of several hundred are already assembled on the croft and droves of newcomers are arriving every few minutes or so. I feel uplifted, triumphant. At last we are getting somewhere! I am proud of my Albion Street contingent and try to keep them together, but they are moving away and joining friends and acquaintances in the crowd. Stewards wearing improvised armbands are attempting to marshal the surprisingly quiet crowd into four ranks. Others are handing out placards and unfurling banners.

I run into Dick France hobbling along on his misshapen legs. He points to a black banner which has just been unfurled and which dates from some forgotten struggle of the twenties. 'There'll be trouble before the day's out,' he says. 'There's trouble every time that bugger comes out.' There's Old Genge's head above the crowd; I make a bee-line for him, anxious to discover whether he has seen any members of the agitprop group. He points vaguely with his thumb in the direction of the head of the rapidly forming column of unemployed. He scarcely seems aware of the furious activity all around him; his face still wears its customary look of benign abstractedness. Let's hope he sees the cops before they see him. Still searching, I encounter Hughie Graeme, an indomitable Galloway Scot whom I have known since I was a small child and whose early years could match anything in brutality that Dickens ever wrote. His wife is helping him to get into the big drum harness.

The crowd has grown enormous and stragglers are still arriving. I hurry back down the line of restless demonstrators and see two members of the agitprop group. I join them just as an empty coal-cart is pushed onto the croft. Two members of the local NUWM clamber on to it and one of them begins to address the crowd. The half-formed column breaks up and the crowd surges towards the cart. We stand at the back of the crowd and listen to the speaker read out the list of demands to be presented to the town council which is, at this moment, meeting at the Town Hall in Bexley Square. The crowd roars its approval and a sea of hands is raised in support of the resolution. The second speaker isn't allowed to say more than a few words when he is interrupted by Hughie's drum. The crowd is restless; they want to be on the move. In no time at all the column is formed; the first marchers wheel off the croft and proceed up Liverpool Street and along Regent Road.

At first there isn't a great deal of noise, just the regular beat of the drum and the occasional shout. The mood is one of quiet desperation. Along Oldfield Road there are small groups of mounted-police and squads of foot-police waiting in all the side streets. Dick France is not the only one who thinks there is going to be trouble. As soon as we reach the main road, the chanting begins: 'Down with the means-test!' Right down the line the slogan is taken up and repeated. 'Down with the National Starvation Government!' It's extraordinary the way voices travel. A slogan begins way back and a few seconds later a closer group begin chanting the same slogan, and then another group closer still so that the effect is like a blurred action-photo.

'We need a song,' says someone. I hear my name being called and see Ben Durden, the newest member of our YCL group, waving at me from the sidewalk. I slip out of the column for a moment and join him.

'Jimmy Rigby's looking for you,' he says. 'He's about a hundred yards ahead.'

I look back. The line of marchers goes back as far as I can see. 'Jesus! Just look at it. It goes on forever.'

'They say there's 50,000 here. More, some say.'

'Why aren't you marching?' I ask.

'I've been up front. I came to look for you.'

We start hurrying towards the head of the procession. I see my father and Jock Sinclair and wave to them. A little further on, the marchers ahead of us shuffle to a halt while those immediately behind are pushed into us. For a few moments our part of the column becomes a confused and struggling mass of bodies. In those few moments wild rumours are born and hard on their heels comes advice from the head of the column. 'Keep calm! Don't allow yourselves to be provoked.'

We re-form and slowly move off again. 'Down with the means test! Down with the National Starvation Government!' Now I can see the black banner, Dick France's trouble-banner. It's about a hundred yards ahead . . . must be the head of the demo. At the same moment I catch sight of Jimmy Rigby, the fourth member of The Red Megaphones, and hurry towards him. This time there are no rumours, no time for advice about keeping calm. Without warning, mounted-police, wielding riot-sticks, attack us from side streets on both sides of the road. They are followed by foot-police who come at us slashing with their truncheons.

'It's a fucking ambush!' Way back down the column, the marchers are still chanting slogans, not yet aware of what is happening ahead. Here the rhythmic protests have swelled to an angry roar, punctuated by yells, curses, screams and the clatter of galloping horses. In the midst of the melee it is difficult to get a clear picture of what is happening. All around us there is a crush of shouting, bellowing, screaming, angry and bewildered men and women. They are pushing, pulling, trying to avoid the swinging batons of the police and the terrifying hooves of the horses. Some are trying desperately to shove their way out of the ambush, others push forward, intent on reaching the barricades which the police have erected around Bexley Square.

A police-horse looms over us, gigantic, eyes rolling, nostrils flared. The smell of horse-sweat mingles with the smell of our fear. Panic-stricken, we try to escape as its rider leans out of the saddle to give extra impetus to the swing of his club. The blow lands with a dull thud across the shoulders of a skinny man in an old raincoat. I am standing so close to him that the pores in the flesh of his nose look like huge craters and I surprise myself by thinking of Lemuel Gulliver's sojourn among the Brobdignagians and remembering the distaste expressed in the description of the enlarged features of the maids of honour.

The skinny man crumples and sinks to the ground. 'Man down!' A dozen pairs of hands reach for the mounted policeman, but the horse rears up and we cower away.

There's a sudden increase in the noise and then there are voices taking up the cry: 'The deputation! They've arrested the deputation!' There is a great surge of activity as we move forward, carrying the battle to the edge of the barricaded square. Squads of police are dragging arrested marchers across the square towards the waiting riot-wagons. The marchers fight back and the police are busy with boots and truncheons. A great roar of fury goes up from the crowd: 'Down with the Cossacks!' A dozen men leap over the barricades and race towards the battling groups. Two of them are struck down by the mounted-police and the rest surrounded and brought to the ground by squads of foot-police. One of the marchers is bleeding badly from the head and appears to be unconscious. A young cop grabs his arm and starts dragging him along the ground. Until now the marchers have been concerned only to defend themselves, but now the mood changes: a note of fierce hatred, deep and vengeful, is heard as the marchers break *en masse* through the barricades. The square has become a battlefield.

At one point there is a lull in the fighting and, as if by mutual agreement, police and marchers draw away from each other. A riderless horse is picking its way among the crowd and an injured police-sergeant is being helped from the scene by his colleagues. We have suffered more grievously. Several marchers lie bleeding on the road and an injured woman is sitting on the kerb holding her head and weeping. Close by, in the gutter, sits Dick France. I go over to him and help him to his feet. He is bleeding from a gash along his cheekbone. 'Didn't I tell you? Every time that banner's brought out there's a barney like this.'

Alec Armstrong comes by, a wide grin on his face. He is holding a large brass hand-bell, the kind used to summon children back to the schoolroom. He rings it above his head like a town crier. 'Second set in a few minutes!' he declaims, and then goes off crying, 'Anyone for tennis? Anyone for tennis?'

Myer Parkinson approaches, a small boy perched on his shoulders, his wife following behind, pushing a pram with her youngest in it. Two small girls hold on to her skirt. 'Jesus Christ!' says Dick. 'You're off your bloody rocker, Myer.'

'Why's that?'

'Bringing kids to a do like this.'

'They've got to find out about t' police some time. Better now than later.'

'Aren't you feared for 'em?'

'They'll be awreet. They're just babbies, too young to be arrested. Tha's got to be ten years old before they start beating you up.' From anyone else, such irony would sound somewhat heavy-handed, but Myer tempers it with *Lanky* – Lancashire dialect. He talks Lanky and makes the most outrageous remarks sound ingenuous. He is what my father calls a 'rum bugger'. His confrontations with Labour Exchange officials have become legendary and it is said that inspectors at the Board of Guardians go into hiding when they see him approaching with his brood. He catches sight of Hughie Graeme and his wife and begins waving furiously. They come over to us. 'What's happened to the drum?'

'Finished. Kaput!' Hughie bellows cheerfully.

'It's broken,' his wife adds. 'He brought it down on the head of a big fat dick.'

'Jesus Christ!' says Dick. 'I'd have given six months' dole to see that.'

'Just like a bloody circus,' Mrs Graeme says, with a loud laugh.

The lull is over. From behind the town hall, dozens of mounted-police suddenly appear and charge at us, followed by foot-police brandishing their clubs. The first engagement was fierce but the police have tasted blood and are now lashing out at anyone in their path. But we are fighting back and the horses no longer terrify us. Here a mounted cop is pulled from his horse, and there a constable deprived of his baton. But we lack training for this kind of fight – we have no strategy. We fight as individuals, unarmed individuals against a disciplined armed force trained to fight as a squad. Furthermore, we are conscious of the fact that the law of the land is on the side of the police. They can bash us around as much as they like and get away with it. But let one of *us* be caught bashing one of *them* and we will land in the nick as surely as night follows day. We don't need training classes to learn about the police. We have understood their role in society since we were children running about the streets.

How long does this second assault last? Five minutes, fifteen minutes? Half an hour? We are no match for these uniformed bully-boys. We came here to protest against what we consider to be gross injustice. Our intention was to present a petition to our elected representatives. Instead, we are being forced to defend ourselves against an armed and well-fed enemy. The result is a foregone conclusion, but leaves many questions unanswered.

'Stand by, we're on in a minute!' In a theatre, those words would have a special significance. That moment when you stand in the wings awaiting your cue is a magical one: the process of stepping out of your skin and assuming a different persona is completed in that moment though you still have to take one or two steps to enter a new world. Here, on the Liverpool Street gasworks' croft, it isn't like that at all. There is only one world, the world of the grey October sky, the gasometers, the long brick wall and the wan-faced men and women who make up this huge crowd. What other persona is possible – or desirable – in the face of this kind of reality? In any case, there are no wings here, no dark corners where you can make your final preparations, no quiet spot where you can commune with yourself.

'We'll do the 'Billy Boy' thing first and then straight into the Maggie Bondfield sketch.' God! Do we really have to do that awful bloody 'Billy Boy' parody? It seemed funny when I wrote it but now . . . it's terrible. Ridiculous. We really need something absolutely different, rousing. 'Right, Blondie.' We jump onto the cart and begin singing the opening of our anti-means-test duet. Oh God, we've pitched it too high. Bloody hell! I just made it that time. Got to relax or I'll sound like a bloody screeching parrot. Blondie looks quite calm. Smiling away. The crowd like her, you can tell. That was better that time. Four more verses. Christ! More mounted coppers, must be a couple of dozen of 'em. Take no notice. Some of the people at the back have seen 'em. Carry on. Punch line coming up. It gets a roar of applause. Great! Alf and the others are climbing onto the cart. The applause dies away and we begin the Maggie Bondfield sketch. It's funny in parts but full of holes. Needs tightening up. It's going well though, plenty of laughs from the crowd. If only we had a sketch that was *really* suitable for the occasion.

'Trouble,' says Blondie, and the next moment Jimmy Rigby stops in mid-sentence and points. For an endless moment, we stare in disbelief. The horse-police are charging towards us, their riot-sticks held aloft like lances. The panic of the crowd is terrible to behold. They scatter in utter confusion the way ants do when their nest is disturbed. There is some resistance but the terrain is not in our favour. There is no cover, no place to hide. In disarray, we retreat into the side streets, where a small group, mostly young unemployed, reassemble and decide to march to the houses of the councillors who are members of the unemployment tribunal. We start off, a silent group of fifteen or twenty youths. In a surprisingly short time our numbers have increased by more than 200. As we walk we hatch elaborate schemes of revenge and wonder if things will ever be the same again.

The years between 1929 and 1934 were tumultuous ones and I have difficulty in pinpointing this event or that activity. The earlier period has a distinct chronology, thus; I leave school, I sign on at the unemployment exchange, I join the Clarion Players, I am employed at the wire-works, I am erect, I am unemployed again but still erect, I'm employed by *The Textile Trader* (with erection), unemployed again, form Red Megaphones (less erect), become motor-mechanic's apprentice. From then on, everything seems to happen at once. Two or three nights a week I am busy rehearsing and performing agitprop sketches and during the day I am up to the eyes in political work. At weekends I am off rambling in Derbyshire or North Lancashire or the Lake District and I am reading everything I can lay my hands on. I am also active in the Youth Council of the NUWM.

At some point, the relationship between these various activities changes. It is as if I am looking through a kaleidoscope at a particular pattern. I turn the barrel of the kaleidoscope and the pattern changes, though the same components are used to make the new design. Sometimes my memory produces a pattern of rehearsals and performances repeated endlessly; a half-turn of the barrel and the pattern is of meetings and discussions, interminable arguments about the party line, standing under a pre-dawn sky and selling the *DW* outside Metro-Vicks. Another pattern suggests that I spent my entire youth in the Central Library.

I had begun using the Manchester Reference Library in Piccadilly in the period following my stint at *The Textile Trader*. As a repository for the accumulated wisdom of the ages it was unimpressive, having the appearance of a large wooden chicken-house. Still, it was a change of scene and the three-mile journey to it from my home provided me with an illusory sense of achievement. I invented a rigorous timetable for myself. I *have* to be at the library by nine o'clock sharp, so I hurry along Market Street with the army of office-bound wage earners. I mustn't be late, I tell myself, though in point of fact the time of my arrival at the library is of no possible interest to anyone except myself. Still, the routine is important, so at one o'clock I'll knock off for lunch like everyone else and at five I'll hand in my books to the desk and join the homeward-bound army of clerks, typists, secretaries, commissionaires, stock-keepers and warehousemen.

The new Central Library which replaced the chicken-house was an imposing circular structure with an enormous reading room, a small theatre and carrels where serious students could carry on their research without interruption. The portico of this magnificent edifice quickly became a popular rendezvous and 'meet you at the Ref' became a familiar phrase on the lips of students, lovers and unemployed youths. I was there on the opening day and on many days thereafter, the Ref played an important part in my life for I made many new friends there.

The old library in Piccadilly had been patronised, it seemed to me, mostly by old men. The new one, on the other hand, became popular immediately with people of my own age. There were maybe half a dozen of us who met there regularly. We shared the same table and drifted into the kind of companionable relationship whose boundaries are defined by small rituals. There was, for instance, the 'register' or leave-taking ritual which consisted of inserting the details of your whereabouts in volume nineteen of *The Parliamentary Rolls*. And there was the mid-morning break when we would assemble on the steps of the portico and declare our financial state. If our combined resources were sufficient to pay for coffee we would adjourn to the Kardomah in Mosley Street; or if they wouldn't quite stretch to that we would settle for a cup of tea at the Oxford Street Lyons.

Even the cafés kindled my enthusiasm, for prior to this my experience of the joys of eating out had been limited to the lorry-drivers' caf's and the Chinese restaurant where I had washed dishes. These Manchester cafés were different, more like the ones mentioned in Balzac and de Maupassant. Perhaps it was us which made them so, or the marvellous characters you saw there, old men from Aleppo and Baghdad, Sephardic Jewish businessmen playing backgammon and dominoes. Surely that's Papa Gobseck! And isn't that old Pons?

I peopled my world with characters from Gogol, Dostoevski and *The Human Comedy*. In my immediate circle of library acquaintances there was a Bixiou, a Rastignac, a Blondet and a couple of interlopers from Gogol. My Rastignac (I call him mine since I was closer to him than to any of the others in this new circle of friends) was a Jewish law student. Unlike the rest of us who paid scant attention to our appearance, he was always smartly (though soberly) dressed in a suit with collar and tie. *Correctly dressed* is the proper term. I think; in fact, everything about him was correct, from his highly polished shoes to his well-cut hair and beautifully laundered shirt-cuffs. His speech was precise, his manner decisive to the point of brusqueness. A mutual friend apopthegmatised him as 'never leaving the courtroom'. I liked him and I think he liked me. It was a clear case of the attraction of opposites. He was given to delivering encomiums on poets and novelists of whose work he approved. He admired Eliot's *Waste Land* and could, and did, recite it by heart. Joyce, too, had gained his approval and he could quote lengthy passages from *Ulysses*. But it was Proust who enjoyed his highest esteem and in Lyons tea-house he would sometimes read aloud lengthy passages from *Swann's Way* or *The Cities of the Plain* clearly articulating every word like a barrister addressing a jury and generally rising to his feet as he approached the end of a paragraph. These carefully calculated histrionic excursions were, in their own way, minor masterpieces of oratory and in me they found an enthusiastic listener.

There were girls, too, students and friends of my friends. I was impressed by the ease with which they drifted in and out of our endless conversations about the state of the world and by the frankness with which they discussed sex. For sex then, as now (and, I suspect, as always) was a staple of conversational diet. We paraded our knowledge of sexual matters like conjurers showing off their skills. The fact that, for most of us, the knowledge was theoretical rather than practical made no difference; indeed, it added an extra dimension to our performance. It gave us a brave new terminology through which we could express our innermost thoughts, and frequent references to Freud served to legitimise the most outrageous statements. The girls took it all in their stride, sometimes leading the conversation but more often providing us with a sympathetic audience. (Did we ever sit and listen while *they* talked?) These conversations, discussions and debates took place in cafes or on the steps of the library.

Inside the main hall we would settle down to our reading again and one by one my friends would gather up their books and leave for a lecture at the university. Finally, I too, would leave and make my way to Shudehill and pick up Bob Goodman as he left work. And so I would pass from this little daytime world of students and fascinating conversation to the evening world of The Red Megaphones, the YCL and political activity.

We tried to keep our Tuesday evenings free, for (with the exception of the summer months) Tuesday was the day the Hallé performed and whenever we could raise the eightpence needed for a student's ticket, Bob and I could be found queuing outside the Free Trade hall with my library friends and a couple of hundred others. The eightpenny tickets were originally a concession to pensioners but had been extended to include students and unemployed. Eightpenny ticket holders stood at the back of the hall underneath the balcony. We were contemptuous of the seat-holders, particularly of those in the front rows wearing monkey-suits. They were Philistines who only came to the Hallé because it was 'the done thing'. We, on the other hand, *really* appreciated the music and understood it. Well, it wasn't reasonable to suppose that Bach, Mozart and Beethoven would have felt at home with the kind of toffee-nosed *schlemiels* who occupied the front rows. They would have preferred *us*, naturally. It was uncomfortable, stuffy and often stiflingly hot but what a glorious experience it was to be lifted up on that great wave of sound and transported to Olympian heights by Beethoven or Brahms.

It was Rastignac who was responsible for my first encounter with classical music. In the Kardomah one morning he announced that George Szell would be conducting the Brahms Fourth at the next Hallé concert. When he learned that I had never heard any classical music he was horrified. 'But you *must* have heard of George Szell!' When I told him I hadn't, he was aghast. 'He's never heard of George Szell,' he whispered, his hand at his forehead in a gesture of tragic disbelief. Then, rising to his feet, he addressed the domino and backgammon players in the ringing tones of a prosecuting council producing the final and most damning item of evidence against a prisoner accused of murder. 'He's never heard of George Szell! George Szell, the world's greatest interpreter of Brahms!' He then launched into the opening bars of the Fourth Symphony and began to conduct an imaginary orchestra. The manageress of the Kardomah was not amused and threatened to have us barred from the premises. The following week I went and heard the Brahms conducted by George Szell and was completely won over, by both of them.

I became an addict and, in turn, introduced Bob to Brahms. He, too, became addicted. In the period which followed we enjoyed great conductors like Bruno Walter and Toscanini. We heard soloists like Szigetti, Edwin Fisher, Schnabel and Pablo Casals. In addition to greats like Bach, Mozart, Beethoven and Brahms, we also heard works by Bartok, Honegger, Schoenberg, Prokofiev, Hindemith and Stravinsky.

After the concerts, a group of us would congregate at the Imp (Imperial), an all-night café situated under the railway bridge on Oxford Street. There we would discuss the performance – or, to be more precise, Rastignac and Bill R. would discuss the performance while the rest of us would listen and take sides.

The flytings between these two music lovers which followed every performance of a work by Sibelius were models of controlled invective, works of art in themselves. Rastignac usually began his offensive by asking deceptively reasonable questions and then supplying the answers to them. 'There's no point in bringing out the heavy artillery when a feint will do as well,' he was fond of saying. Then the frontal assault would begin and, eyes gleaming with a kind of ferocious enjoyment, he would proceed, point by point, to demolish his opponent. Salvo after salvo would be fired at the hapless composer and at all who had taken part in the performance. And when the bodies of Sibelius and the members of the orchestra lay bleeding on the ground, he would trample on the corpses and then hack them into small pieces.

Throughout this extraordinary tirade Bill R. would be pulling down the frayed cuffs of his jacket in order to conceal the frayed cuffs of his shirt-sleeves, straightening his tie or rolling and unrolling his tobacco-pouch, smoothing the tablecloth in front of him or just gazing up at the ceiling. There would be a momentary silence at the end of the tirade. Then, like an understanding school-teacher addressing a dull pupil, he would say, 'What was it that you found so difficult?' Or, 'You mustn't be upset because you didn't understand it.'

'There was nothing to understand!' Rastignac would shout, pounding the table with his fist. And so it would go on, insult following insult until, inevitably, the conversation moved on to politics or sex. But Bill R. would not allow that. He was adroit at bringing a conversation back on course. He could talk entertainingly upon a host of subjects but music was his special hobby. He knew countless anecdotes about composers and musicians. He could chart in detail the progress of Schuman's madness; he knew what Brahms said to Dame Ethel Smythe, what Beethoven wrote to Bettina von Arnheim about Goethe and whether Schubert's syphilis was contracted or inherited.

I'm afraid we didn't cherish him as we ought to have done. He was a fine example of the English eccentric. He came into our orbit in the spring of 1932 and was constantly on the scene until the middle of 1934. He was one of those strange individuals who, like prehistoric fishes, rise from the deep and are seen frequently for a short time and then vanish as if they have never been.

16

Theatre of Action

The 1930s was my period of exploration and discovery. Politics, theatre, love, friendship, mountains, classical music, jazz . . . the moors and mountains transformed me physically, strengthened my muscles, toughened me so that I was able to cover great distances and gave me the feeling that mine was the first foot ever to trample there. How wonderful to know that my body would be able to cope with any demands that I might make on it, that it would go on functioning in extremes of cold and heat, covering mile after mile and ridge upon stony ridge of moor and mountain. *Blow winds and crack your cheeks* . . . yes, to battle the wind and rain in a wild storm on Grib-Goch or Featherbed Moss was to share a moment of time with Lear on his blasted heath.

And politics and theatre toughened my mind, taught me to discipline my ideas. Indeed, a completely hitherto unused part of my brain became activated for the first time. Throughout my childhood I had been absorbing impressions, collecting and storing memories of people and events. Now I was beginning to interpret those events and to correlate them with each other and with everything I had read and observed.

My feelings, too, were developing, not changing but extending themselves and constantly developing new facets. They were being fed by the *G-minor Toccata and Fugue and the Hammerklavier,* by Mozart, Brahms and Bartok, by innumerable poets and novelists, by Louis Armstrong and Bessie Smith, and of course by my new friends and acquaintances.

This kind of categorisation doesn't really help to create a clear picture of the period. Feelings, thought-processes and physical awareness were part and parcel of each other, inter-dependent elements in a single chain reaction. This is probably why I find it so difficult to write about the 1930s. The early 1920s present no difficulties, as my world was small, inhabited by the small circle of my parents (and stories of *their* parents), their friends and a few neighbours. The second half of the 1920s, too, is easily recalled, even though my world had grown a little and now included school and street. The decades between 1940s and 1970s present themselves as connected episodes; their built-in chronology gives them a certain kind of symmetry and each is revealed as a chain of events and ideas in which the pursuit of creative objectives and the making and breaking of relationships show up as a fairly consistent pattern. They can be envisaged as broad bands of primary colours shading into one another and maculated here and there with black and brown blotches and striations.

The 1930s, on the other hand, is a kaleidoscope of countless coloured shapes continuously changing their relationship to one another . . . politics, theatre, ideas, theories, love, friendship, rambling, climbing . . . theatre, love, politics, climbing. Theories, friendship, rambling, poetry, music . . . ideas, music, climbing, politics, friendship, theatre, rambling . . . Dunbar, Chaucer, politics, rambling, ideas, theories, music, Engels, friendship . . . Great Gable, Lenin, Luxemburg, theatre, ideas, love, climbing, Joyce, Shining Clough, down with the National Starvation Government . . . Politics was the binding force, the cement which bound everything together, but theatre – for the next twenty years – was to be the medium.

The break with the Clarion Players had been carried out with revolutionary fervour. 'We must take the theatre onto the streets', we said, 'we must take theatre to the masses.' Unfortunately, our technical expertise didn't match our zeal. None of us had ever seen an agitprop group in action, none of us knew the first thing about producing a play or a sketch. So how should we go about the task of forging ourselves into a weapon for the class struggle? Well, first of all, we must have a producer and since no one else wanted the job it fell to me by default. The blind leading the blind.

I was determined from the beginning that rehearsals should not be the casual affairs that they had been in the Clarion Theatre days. There would be no coffee breaks, no larking about, no chit-chat. Rehearsals would be serious working sessions and would take place three evenings a week in the cellar of the Workers' Arts Club. Our first production was a sketch called *Rent, Interest and Profit,* and since it involved a fair amount of mass declamation we spent a lot of our rehearsal-time drilling ourselves line by line and phrase by phrase until we reached a degree of proficiency. We also spent quite a lot of time with our backs to the cellar wall shouting at the top of our voices in an attempt to make our voices more powerful. I remember how we would mount the stairs into the living world afterwards like characters in a story by Edgar Allan Poe. Script-writing sessions were, in their way, just as miserable, though in physical terms they were an improvement on the cellar. They were generally held in the back kitchen of my home where there was both light and a fire. There we would sit, the entire group, re-named The Script Writing Committee for the occasion, and search in vain for inspiration. None of us had ever written anything. Well, I had written a couple of small things for the school magazine and a lengthy satirical poem in the style of Walt Whitman. Other than that, our joint experience of creative writing consisted of writing the odd school composition on 'A Day at Blackpool' or 'the Adventures of a Penny'. So we sat there gazing at the ceiling or examining the pattern on the linoleum and after two or three hours we would have four lines of dialogue and ten pages of assorted doodling.

It wasn't that we lacked ideas; on the contrary, we were bursting with them. What we really lacked was the skill and knowledge which would have enabled us to weld our ideas into a coherent form. We were young, full of revolutionary ideals. We wanted to change the world and we wanted the change to come quickly. We were searching for words which would rouse our audience to immediate action, words that would burn like fire and set our slum ablaze. So we sat over our cups of tea and thought and talked and thought again. How well I remember the frustration of those sessions, of being torn in several different directions. I wanted to be doing something important *now*, not tomorrow or next week or next year, but now, this minute! I wanted to be out seeing the world, taking part in the kind of action that would help my transformation into Balzac. I wanted so many things, but most of all I wanted a theatre group that was skilled and talented and infinitely adaptable. Instead, we were a bumbling, unskilled band of amateurs who could scarcely put one foot in front of the other. I was very conscious of our imperfections and often despaired of ever achieving even the most modest proficiency.

Another thing I found very disturbing was the feeling that momentous events were taking place outside in the streets and that we were missing them. There we were, stuck in that miserable cellar declaiming our lines like children chanting a multiplication table while outside the world was in ferment. But was it? You'd come up from the cellar and walk into Liverpool Street and you'd see that everything was as before: the same blackened landscape of tumbledown shops and houses, the cinder-croft and the giant bulk of the gasometers, the little girls intent on their skipping-game and defeated men and women going about their business. So back to the cellar, where we hoped to give shape and substance to our dreams.

It was a period of intense activity, though in terms of actual time it only covered about two and a half years. We did improve during that time, of course, though we never achieved the standard we were aiming for. Most of the sketches we performed were products of the Workers Theatre Movement script-writing section. They were clever, politically sound and occasionally witty but by the time we had rehearsed and performed half-a-dozen of them we began to feel that we were repeating ourselves. Two or three members of the group opted out. All of us were dissatisfied with our sketches which, increasingly, felt drab and full of holes. We discussed them at great length. They were too static and relied too much on mass declamation and static groupings of the actors. They gave the impression of having all been written to a basic formula. They were built around a series of slogans – good slogans, but . . . well, we had begun to doubt the efficacy of slogans shouted at the top of the human voice at a small audience of shoppers or mill-girls.

It wasn't that we objected to the didactic nature of our sketches; it was merely that we wanted the didacticism to be tempered with drama. So when, on the heels of an International Workers Theatre Olympiad, a statement was issued by the central committee of the International Union of Revolutionary

Theatres recommending a return to traditional theatre forms, we embraced it enthusiastically in spite of the fact that our knowledge of traditional theatre forms was minimal. In actual fact, we had no intention of abandoning anything we had learned during our apprenticeship in agitprop theatre. What we were envisaging was an extension of agitprop, a form which would lend itself to performance in any kind of conditions. We wanted our agitprop to be both explosive and subtle, fierce and compassionate, abrasive and, at the same time, sleek as an otter.

The agitprop sketches in our repertoire made no demands on us as actors and this was the real cause of our dissatisfaction. We were clumsy, didn't know how to move properly and knew nothing about developing our voices. None of us wished to return to the kind of activities that had taken up our time in the Clarion Players and since none of us had ever worked in the legitimate theatre we had no nostalgic yearnings for the smell of grease-paint. And we weren't hankering after naturalism and dreaming of elaborate sets and costumes. The fluidity of agitprop with its total disregard for the Aristotelian unities of time and space seemed to us to be the perfect type of contemporary theatre. The fact that we had merely exploited a very limited part of its potential did not alter this fact. What we now wished to do was to explore the agitprop form, determine how far it could be extended and discover whether it could accommodate, or be fused with, other forms. This meant creating a new repertory or adapting part of the old one. It also meant that we had to temporarily abandon the streets as our main performance area. Most important of all, perhaps, was the change of function, whereas previously we had performed sketches which were in line with specific political issues and campaigns (exhorting our audiences to join with us in smashing the National Starvation Government, to demand the release of the Meerut prisoners, to support the cotton operatives' strike against the eight-loom system), we would now be dealing with the ways in which individual men and women responded to the constantly changing pattern of social and political change.

During the next two or three months, the group continued to meet three evenings a week. We continued to talk, endlessly. We discussed possible productions, argued, tried to write scripts and, in between meetings, spent days in the library reading plays, poems and indeed anything that we thought might adapt for the stage. Our final choice was a poem by the Italo-American poet Arturo Giovanetti. 'The Walker' describes the night-thoughts of a condemned prisoner and my intention was to interpolate passages from Vanzetti's last testament into the body of the poem. These would be spoken *sotto voce* by a small chorus while a solitary figure paced the cell and spoke the lines of the poem. At the end of the poem the soft-edged spot in which the scene had been played would slowly fade as the prisoner, speaking directly to the audience, said: 'Nicola Sacco and Bartolomeo Vanzetti, executed 23 August 1927.' Stillness and silence in the pauses between the lines of the poem would be used as a dramatic element. It was, of course, a reaction against the noisy sketches we had been performing on the streets. For some reason, which I have forgotten, we didn't complete the production. A similar fate befell our next venture, an adaptation of Mike Gold's dramatic poem 'Strange Funeral at Braddock'. This was to be a slightly more ambitious production than 'The Walker', for we intended to use percussion (those imaginery drums beat through my sleeping and waking dreams for weeks – I felt like Emperor Jones). 'We are going to perform this as a processional', I informed my friends, 'as a kind of dance-drama with three soloists reading different sections of the poem and the rest of you executing a slow dance.' Everyone was impressed.

They were less impressed when we came to rehearse the dance-mime. What in the name of God is a dance-mime? It was a demoralising experience. We had been conscious of our shortcomings from the beginning but we fondly imagined that with hard work we would overcome all our weaknesses. But this wasn't a weakness; this was a nothing, a complete void. You can't improve on nothing. Oh, we tried – how we tried! The results were bathetic. A couple of members of the group began to talk of leaving and there was a general feeling that we had acted prematurely in abandoning The Red Megaphones. We had abandoned that name when we left the streets. We now called ourselves Theatre of Action.

Disheartened, we continued to search for the perfect sketch until one evening a young woman appeared on the scene and banished our despair. It wasn't merely that she looked good enough to eat or that her eyes seemed to promise to fulfil every dream one had ever had or that . . .

She had the kind of smouldering beauty that you associate with sunlit beaches fringed with coconut palms and, to us, it seemed absolutely incongruous that such a beauty should work as a primary-school teacher. We loved her on sight and when we learned that she had done training in a Margaret Morris dance studio we worshipped her. I didn't know whether she was a good teacher or not, but I do know that all of us hung on her every word and competed desperately for her good opinion.

The particular kind of movement she taught wasn't quite what I had had in mind, though it was valuable and without it we would have continued to be hampered by our physical inhibitions. All the same, I couldn't help feeling unnerved at the sight of Alec Armstrong throwing an imaginary ball to a disgusted Alf Armitage. Alec was deeply smitten by our young 'movement lady' and worked hard at getting into her good graces. Unfortunately, the ceiling of the rehearsal room was rather low and Alec's attempts at fawn-like leaps resulted in some sharp collisions.

In the second or third week of our classes, our group love affair received an unpleasant jolt when our idol's young man appeared on the scene. We hated him on sight and he probably hated us, a motley group of healthy young people, mostly young men obviously enjoying the presence of such a teacher. I recall that the classes were conducted in an atmosphere vibrant with repressed sexuality. That first visit must have sounded the alarm in his head for from that time on he turned up at every one of her classes and for the entire evening stood against the wall regarding us with unconcealed hostility. We held him personally responsible for the fact that May left us at the end of two months. Our sense of loss was indescribable.

Almost four months had elapsed since we had transformed The Red Megaphones into Theatre of Action and so far we had not produced anything at all. 'The Theatre of Inaction' was what some of our critics were beginning to call us, while others accused us of wanting to 'dance our way through the revolution'. In spite of everything, however, we had recruited half a dozen new members and had escaped from our dreary cellar into a rehearsal room, above ground, in central Manchester. Then, out of the blue, we received a script of a short American play called *Newsboy*.[1] It was the perfect vehicle for our group and rehearsals went well from the beginning in spite of my inadequacies as a producer. Prior to this, my production experience had been limited to short agitprop sketches in which action was minimal. *Newsboy* involved a great deal of action and presented me with problems which I had never had to solve before. I learned, but slowly.

The work was speeded up when we recruited a young actress who had recently come up from London the join the Rusholme Repertory Theatre company. She joined us halfway through rehearsing *Newsboy* and even though she was only free to work with us on Sundays, her influence on the group, and on me, was enormous.

Her name was Joan Littlewood, and I had met her briefly at the BBC studios in Manchester where we were both taking part in a documentary feature on the building of the Mersey Tunnel. The rehearsal of *Tunnel* was in progress when I arrived at the studio and Archie Harding, the programme director, called me into the studio where I heard, coming through the loudspeakers, the most beautiful and compelling voice I had ever encountered. 'You must meet her,' said Harding. 'I think you two have a lot in common.' Later, during the tea-break, we exchanged platitudes in the canteen and I walked back to Salford that night with my head full of the echoes of that extraordinary voice.

It was several weeks before we met again and I was finally driven to paying a half-crown to sit through a totally forgettable play in which Joan had a walk-on as a cockney maid servant. Afterwards, I hung around the stage door and met her as she came out. I walked with her back to her digs and there, for the next eight hours, we talked, told each other the story of our lives and discussed what we called *real* theatre. Our views, we found, coincided at almost every point. We were drunk with ideas, lightheaded with talk and lack of sleep and each of us jubilant at having discovered an ally. The morning was well advanced when Joan crept with me to the front door and I went off to the Labour Exchange. We continued our talking marathon right through the next two or three nights.

Joan had few illusions left about the theatre by the time she left RADA and her search for a job in London and Paris had whittled the number down still further. The few that remained were finally banished by her experiences in 'rep' and with each week that passed she was finding her job more irksome. One or two interesting roles might have helped her to bear the tedium of dull productions of duller plays. At that time, Joan had all the makings of a superb actress. It wasn't merely that she had a voice which could charm birds out of trees; it was the sense of truth which informed everything she did. She invested even the smallest walk-on with the deep, shining passion of real art, so that one felt impelled to watch the maid collecting teacups and loading them onto a tray when one should have been watching the mistress stabbing her lover.

So why wasn't she given the roles which would have made use of her great talent? Why was she overlooked when the plums were being shared out? There were many reasons. For one thing, she didn't look the way actresses were supposed to look. The theatre of the thirties demanded a dreary uniformity as far as physical appearance was concerned. Perhaps more important, Joan made no attempt to conceal her opinions about the level of production and acting in the company. She could be dangerously and woundingly outspoken. That deep, velvety voice could be wonderfully soothing one moment and the next could be dismissing you as a 'lousy piss-kitchen', one of her favourite epithets. Then again, who wants to take the risk of being outshone by a person of superior talent, particularly when that person is a newcomer to the scene, a beginner just out of drama school, a chit of a girl with no respect for authority, who doesn't own a decent wardrobe, who has never had a decent hair-do since the day she was born, who doesn't read the 'crits' and who doesn't bother to disguise the fact that she thinks you're all imposters, 'dry chancres on the arse of a great art form'? She treated the producer and the leading man in the company with undisguised contempt and, naturally, they hated her for it right royally. She continued to work at the rep for several months longer but finally, after a blazing row with the producer, left and joined Theatre of Action as co-producer. A week later we were married.

From the very beginning of our work together, we had confidence in our ability to create a theatre which would be more dynamic, truthful and adventurous than anything the bourgeois theatre could produce. Furthermore – and we were adamant on this point – it would be a lot more efficient. By this time, rehearsals were occupying three or four evenings a week and a good many Sundays as well. During the week, we spent most days in the reference library reading plays, essays, criticism, technical works on lighting, stage-design and on anything that had any bearing whatsoever on the theatre.

It was an exciting period. We were full of ideas and had inexhaustible stores of energy. We drew up elaborate work schedules for ourselves, planned theatres with mobile stages and epic productions of plays dealing with the Paris Commune and the Peasant Revolt of 1381. We would discuss an idea and develop it until it cried out to be written down as a play. Then we would begin to write it with great enthusiasm and, ten pages on, we'd abandon it for a better idea. This, too, would eventually be abandoned for a still better idea, and so it would go on, draft after draft, new concept after new concept.

In addition, we were busy learning and rehearsing several long poems which with *Newsboy* would add up to a full evening's performance. The most interesting of these pieces was 'The Red Front', Louis Aragon's surrealistic poem about the Russian revolution. There was also a rousing declamation by an American symbolist poet – 'The Fire Sermon' – and (by way of startling contrast) a shortened version of Shelley's 'Mask of Anarchy'. What kind of impact could that have made on our audience of cotton-weavers, unemployed and workers from the Walls' sausage factory? Looking back down the years, I cannot help thinking what an odd picture Joan and I must have presented: two slightly-built teenage innocents standing shoulder to shoulder on the small stage of the Hyde Socialist Sunday School, passionately declaiming works by a French surrealist, an American symbolist and a 19th-century English romantic poet. I can remember how good it felt to be standing there in the raw light of Alf's home-made spotlight uttering the beautiful words. We were twin Lears hurling defiance at the storm, only our storm was capitalism in decay with its wars and rumours of war, unemployment, fascism and the ruthless exploitation of working people.

The relative merits of agitprop and conventional theatre were still being debated by the Workers Theatre groups throughout the country and finally the Workers Theatre Movement (WTM) central committee called a national conference in London to debate the issue. Joan and I were elected to represent Theatre of Action.

I had visited London only once before, on my short busking excursion. I had felt completely out of my depth on that occasion and this time I was no more comfortable. I loathed the place. Like many northerners, I approached it with deep suspicion and many preconceived notions. But then, Londoners, quite the most parochial people in the British Isles, had their own mythological concept of the north. For them, the north stretched from Watford to John o'Groats and consisted of a series of gigantic factories covering the entire land. Or it was *the country'* – an enormous wilderness with occasional rustic villages which had survived but not abandoned the Middle Ages. The people inhabiting the factories were a wild barbarian horde who communicated with grunts and snarls; the villagers were slow-moving, slow-thinking, slow-talking comics who played the banjolele. Now I was visiting this alien place with Joan, who had been born and brought up there and who hated it even more than I did. Our hostility, exacerbated by a sleepless night in an overheated railway carriage, didn't create the right frame of mind for arriving at a balanced view of the world.

The conference opened with a statement by the delegates who had attended the Moscow Olympiad of Workers Theatres. Everyone had been enormously impressed by the expertise and professionalism of the German, Russian and Czech participants and all were conscious of the tremendous gap between their groups and ours. We would have to work harder. Yes, but at doing what? By writing better agitprop sketches, by dealing with specific issues instead of trying to make each sketch into a dramatised version of a Communist pamphlet on the rise of capitalism, by giving the sketches more immediacy, by using songs and music, by borrowing from the technique of the circus, the music-hall, the pierrot show. Thus ran the argument of the pro-agitprop faction.

The majority of those at the conference disagreed, saying that the agitprop form was limited, constricting. Its didacticism alienated audiences, it was too foreign, it ignored our own British theatre traditions. Now whatever substance there was in the other arguments, this last objection was puerile. It implied that our theatrical history began with Marlowe; it conveniently forgot to mention the country rituals, the mumming plays, mysteries and moralities from which our classical theatre had evolved. Almost all the sketches in the agitprop repertoire could accurately be described as morality plays, not only in terms of their content but because of their form.

The voice of the majority retaliated: surely it cannot be denied that agitprop has led us into the cul-de-sac of sectarianism. It has divorced us from the mainstream of theatre as practised by thousands of amateur dramatic societies throughout Britain. This, it was emphasized, was an important political error and one that we should endeavour to correct forthwith by turning our backs on agitprop and dedicating ourselves to working inside the disciplines of the formal theatre.

We were appalled by the amount of support these arguments received. Unprepared for this line of attack, we voiced our opposition rather incoherently and described at some length how we had attempted to extend the boundaries of the agitprop form in our production of *Newsboy*. We were tired and angry and felt, probably mistakenly, that we were surrounded by enemies. We didn't put our case very well.

Later, in the evening, we sat through a show staged by the combined London WTM groups. There were several interesting musical items, including a set of Brecht/Eisler songs performed by a small choir and a four-piece orchestra. This was far in advance of anything we had ever done and I remember feeling thrilled by the performance. It was, however, merely a curtain raiser for the important part of the entertainment, the production of a shortish, three-act play. I have forgotten its title, but it was the showpiece of the reformed WTM calculated to demonstrate the superiority of the curtain-theatre approach.

It confirmed our worst fears. The crude energy, the burning enthusiasm and spirit of defiance, the bold challenge and denunciation of the enemy, the raw satire which were the hallmarks of agitprop had gone, had been supplanted by the kind of bloodless acting which the West End theatre had made fashionable.

We sat there plunged in gloom while the play limped through its three dreary acts. Someone had, in the fashionable cant of the Eighties, 'got it all together'. It was all there: the clipped speech, the dramatic pauses, the costumes, the splendidly predictable settings, the tycoon's office, the board-room, the moonlit terrace of the tycoon's country house, the cocktail-shaker and the cigarettes by Abdullah. We had returned to the mainstream of amateur British theatre with a vengeance. The conference had dismayed us, the play sickened us and we resolved that night to cut our ties with London and go it alone. We left London the following day like two people fleeing from the plague.

Our production of *Newsboy* brought us several new recruits and *John Bullion*, a surrealist-cum-constructivist anti-war sketch, won several more.[2] It was *Waiting for Lefty*, however, which really swelled our numbers.[3] After that production, there was a steady stream of applicants and almost overnight the composition of Theatre of Action had changed. Up until this time we had all been actors or would-be actors in the theatre. All of us were working-class and almost all of us were under twenty years of age. But now that was all changed; the new membership was roughly equal between young workers and middle-class intellectuals, students, teachers, artists and lawyers, and while most of the newcomers were fairly young, several of them were in their early thirties.

The influx of new members was not entirely an unmixed blessing. We had been functioning in a rather anarchic fashion and no one had questioned the way the group was run. Now, however, an increasingly large and vocal faction began to question our right to take decisions concerning the choice and repertoire and casting. A smaller, but no less vocal, faction began to question our entire concept of theatre. This faction, spearheaded by a university lecturer and his wife, felt that our efforts to win a working-class audience were misguided and a waste of time and energy. The working class didn't patronise the theatre at all and therefore efforts would be better directed at winning over the existing theatre audience. This we could easily accomplish by adopting the kind of policy that was being followed by the London Group Theatre.

Neither Joan nor I was upset by this kind of criticism. We certainly didn't give it much attention. After all, it came from new members of the group, most of whom didn't know much about the theatre. They'll learn in time, we said, that you can't produce a play with a committee. Then one day we were told that an extraordinary meeting of the party fraction had been convened by the district committee of the party.

There were several dozen people at the meeting in addition to Joan, myself and the party district organiser. I was astonished to find so many party members among the new recruits and said so, but my remark evoked no comment. The meeting was held in our rehearsal room, which in some odd way had suddenly begun to look like a courtroom. The people, most of whom I knew, seemed like hostile witnesses; some of them I had regarded as friends, and now here they were gathered to accuse us. Even The Red Megaphones contingent were subdued. They looked like I felt: apprehensive, cowed. I can still remember feeling sick with nervousness and, unaccountably, guilty. But guilty of what?

The district organiser opened the proceedings with a short statement about the state of the nation, the international situation and the history of the Bolshevik revolution. As a tailpiece he admitted to knowing little or nothing about the theatre. This was no less than the truth. Before becoming a party organiser he had worked down the pit in South Wales. At a meeting to discuss trade-union affairs he would have been in his element; here he was completely out of his depth.

Joan and I had prepared a statement, rather earnest in tone I seem to remember, a powerful manifesto larded with quotations from Marx, Engels, Lenin, Myerhold and Pudovkin. We might have saved our breath. Everything we said added fuel to our opponents' arguments. We were prima donnas; we were full of undigested theories; we were opportunists using Marx and Lenin to bolster up our swollen self-esteem; we were individualists, anarchists, nihilists; we cared nothing for the working-class struggle and were completely lacking in understanding of party discipline.

As the discussion developed the criticism became more severe and our alleged weaknesses were transformed into serious crimes. It was as if our critics were competing with one another to see who could produce the most formidable collection of accusations. We sat there, crushed under the weight of our infamy – crushed and frightened. I remember thinking, 'this is how the fox must feel when it finally turns and confronts the howling pack of hounds.' There is an accumulative component in all accusations; no simple accusation remains simple and the accuser gets carried away on a tide of indignation. Our detractors were, at first, not personally antagonistic to us. They merely held views about the theatre which were different from ours. It was when they began to vocalise these differences that they became personally hostile.

The degree of personal hatred which began to develop quite early on in the discussion was quite alarming. Individuals with whom I had never exchanged a word were suddenly seething with resentment and seemed bent on destroying us. Even more distressing was the virulence of the attacks made on us by those whom we had regarded as friends or at least as kindred spirits. One or two of these were people I had known for several years but most of them were recent converts to the party, middle-class intellectuals who until this moment had given the impression of being reasonable human beings. Now they were taking part in an exercise the object of which appeared to be to show that they had learned the party terminology and knew how to apply it.

The council for the prosecution was our university lecturer and his wife. Before becoming a university wife she had worked in a northern repertory company and was regarded by the rest of the dissidents as an authority on theatre. Her husband was an authority by marriage. Between them they had drawn up a lengthy and detailed denunciation of our characters, talents and politics. It was a well-crafted document, somewhat reminiscent of the style of Edmund Burke, lofty and sincere but studded here and there with tidbits of party jargon to give it the common touch. They offered to take over the leadership of the group if they were invited to do so. They were not invited and their interest in revolutionary theatre soon waned. Their flirtation with the Communist Party lasted a few weeks longer and then the lecturer got promoted. That marked the end of their association with the Left. Well, one could scarcely expect them to endanger their career, could one? Some twenty-five years later, Mrs Lecturer became a fairly successful West End actress. Mr Lecturer . . . well, who knows what happened to him? If he isn't dead then he is undoubtedly intent on undermining a colleague somewhere in the hope of getting his job. I am grateful to him. Like many ill-educated working-class people I tended to regard anyone connected with a university as a superior member of the human race or at least as a person of superior intelligence. Our lecturer cured me of that childish nation.

The discussion ended with a motion being proposed and seconded to the effect that a recommendation should be forwarded to the District Party Committee calling for our expulsion. Twelve voted in favour of the resolution and twelve were against it. The chairman cast his deciding vote in our favour.

Although we tried to put a good face on things we were truly desolated by the whole affair. I was particularly affected for I had worked for several years, ever since I had left school, to make a workers' theatre a reality. I fondly imagined that the creation of a successful workers' theatre would be greeted with loud hurrahs by the party. The realisation that such was not the case was like a kick in the stomach. Equally difficult to swallow was the knowledge that our labours had been instrumental in rousing fierce hatred among those we called our comrades. Depressed and angry, we discussed leaving the theatre and finding some other occupation. What kind of occupation? Such talents as we possessed were centred exclusively on the theatre. That was certainly true as far as I was concerned. Joan's position was different. She had won her scholarship to RADA and had also received a scholarship to the Slade School of Art. When I met her she was undecided whether to opt for a career as an actress or as a painter.

We were still debating our future when we received, out of the blue, a letter from Moscow inviting us to become students at the Moscow School of Cinema and Theatre. A covering note from Andre van Gysegham explained that a visa would be forthcoming in a few days. All we had to do was call at the Soviet Embassy and be on our way. Here was our chance to show our true worth, to vindicate ourselves. We would go to Moscow and train under teachers like Myerhold, Pudovkin, Vahktangov, Stanislavsky and Eisenstein and after two or three years we would return triumphantly and confound our critics with productions so brilliant that they would be silenced forever.

Our friends, those who had voted against our expulsion from the party along with Alf Armitage and others who had been active since the days of The Red Megaphones, organised a small get-together (a wake, Alf called it) where we discussed future plans. We promised that we would be back in two or three years time to show those bastards what a real revolutionary theatre was like. Oh dear, what innocence!

The following Sunday, our belongings packed into a Bergan rucksack, we took the cheap excursion to London. Our friends in Theatre of Action collected £12 as a parting gift, Farewell Manchester. USSR, we're on our way!

17

Living in London and Dreaming in Moscow

Act 2, Scene 2:   Fashionable London residential frontage. Iron gate, closed, bored policeman on duty. Light and sound to suggest workday winter London. Enter scruffy couple from down-stage left obviously cowed by the splendid setting.

What hadn't occurred to us was that we might encounter visa difficulties. After all, we had our official invitation on official notepaper. What possible difficulties could there be? To begin with, we couldn't even get to the embassy door to ring the bell. At our first attempt we were stopped by a bored-looking policeman who obviously thought we were suspicious characters. I must confess that even at the time I felt we were wearing the wrong costumes for such a splendid setting. In Salford, at the Albion Street Labour Exchange, we would have faded nicely into the background, but in Kensington we were decidedly noticeable. The copper obviously thought so too. 'Off you go,' he said, gazing over our heads as he edged us towards the kerb. We withdrew to the other side of the road to plan our next move.

After ten or fifteen minutes we tried again. This time we advanced holding the letter in full view and trying to look like people engaged on an important mission. The policeman watched our advance with a combination of indifference and hostility but condescended to look at the letter.

'What's this?' he said. We explained that it was a letter. To us. 'I can't read this,' said he.

'It's in Russian,' said Joan in her most patrician accent, going on to explain that it was an invitation to us to become students in Moscow. The rich, high-class voice issuing from the scruffy young woman confused him. With me, he knew exactly where he was and how to behave. My accent was that of the barbarians of the north, the place where hunger-marchers came from. The young woman, on the other hand – she didn't look like a toff but . . . from the way she spoke . . . well, you never knew. His tone became a shade less aggressive.

'Can you read Russian?' We confessed that we could not. 'Then how do you know what it says?'

'We have a covering letter,' we said, and produced van Gysegham's note. He examined it and returned it to us.

'How do I know you didn't write it yourself?'

This bizarre conversation continued for several more minutes and then, without warning, he turned his back on us and sauntered away. 'Quick, before he changes his mind,' said Joan and we rushed to the door of the embassy. No reply. We tried again and waited and there was still no reply. After fifteen minutes we gave up.

When we tried again on the following day, the door opened after the second ring. The official who ushered us into the bare and sombre waiting room was unimpressed by our appearance. He examined our letter with a monumental lack of interest and then without a word disappeared through a green baize-covered door. A few minutes passed, then another more exalted official entered and after examining us briefly from across the room, withdrew. Eventually, a third official emerged and actually addressed us. Holding up our letter, he said, 'Is this yours?' We nodded, whereupon he too retired from the scene. After half-an-hour or so the first official returned and said that we should call back tomorrow.

'The letter . . .' we began.

'We shall keep it.'

The following day we were given visa application forms which we filled in on the spot. 'And now', said yet another official, 'you must wait.'

'How long?'

The official shrugged his shoulders. 'Two weeks, a month, two months maybe.'

We left the embassy in a mood of black despair. The weather had turned bitterly cold and we were hungry and had no money. How could we possibly hold out for two months, or two weeks for that matter? But we did. We were staying with Joan's grandparents in Stockwell and we walked everywhere . . . to the embassy in Kensington, to the National Gallery, the Tate Gallery, the Wallace Collection, the British Museum, the Geological Museum. For Joan it was familiar territory but for me it was all new and overwhelming. Perhaps I wouldn't have felt so overwhelmed if I had been less cold and hungry, or if I hadn't felt that I was breathing stale air all the time. So we sat in the National Gallery and gazed at Leonardo's *Madonna of the Rocks* or Piero della Francesca's *Nativity* and I dozed off while Joan rhapsodised about this or that aspect of the artist's work.

But museums and art galleries, let them be ever so full of masterpieces, cannot fully alleviate enforced inactivity. We were nineteen years old and bursting with ideas. We were impatient and time, precious time, was passing. London, for us, was merely an overnight stop on the way to Moscow. Where, *where* were our visas? Our daily visits to the embassy had degenerated into a hopeless ritual. We would ring the bell twice and after a brief interval the door would open slightly to reveal a face or part of a face . . . a single, sorrowful eye would contemplate us and we would ask 'Any news today?' The head would shake slowly and the door would close. Another twenty-four hour wait. When someone wise in the ways of embassies and officials warned us that we might have to wait for months, our spirits reached rock-bottom.

Our misery drove us into an Express Dairy tea-room where we spent fourpence on two cups of tea, a rare extravagance since we had eschewed all luxuries since our arrival in London. Our £12 had dwindled to as many shillings. The tea was a measure of our desperation. We sat there warming our hands on the thick white china and discussed our problems, among which the necessity of finding somewhere to live ranked high. The grandparents' apartment was really too small to accommodate us any longer.

'I fancy Cheyne Walk,' said Joan. 'I've always wanted to live there.' Since I had never heard of Cheyne Walk the idea of living there didn't strike me as being in any way preposterous. I must confess that I had second thoughts when I saw those splendid houses overlooking the Chelsea embankment. Joan's plan for finding lodgings in one of them was simplicity itself. We would canvass from door to door and ask the occupiers whether they had any rooms to let. I doubted very much whether high-toned residences like these would be in the business of letting digs; and even if, by some miracle, we did succeed in finding a room, how were we going to afford it? Had Cheyne Walk been in Salford I would never have even gone near it, but this was Joan's home-territory. So here goes.

I was relieved when the first doorbell we rang produced no response. The second was answered by a maid who stared haughtily at us and asked whether we hadn't read the notice saying NO HAWKERS. The third was opened by an over-made-up and incredibly haggard woman who, after glaring at us for what seemed an inordinate length of time, said, 'Yes?'

'We're looking for a furnished room,' said Joan.

'You're looking for a what? Speak up!' Once again, Joan explained our need. 'You mean you want to *live* here?'

'If you have a spare room.'

'But why *here?*'

'We need somewhere quiet so we can write.'

'You're from the north' said the woman and then, in a dramatic voice, cried, 'thank you. *Thank* you. *THANK* you!' Then she stretched arms above her head and said, 'God never made a woman without protection.' In a normal voice, she invited us into the house. As she hobbled before us on enormously high heels, she kept saying, 'God sent you. God takes care of his own.'

The walls of the hallway appeared to be entirely covered with small paintings and miniatures in gilt frames. One of them was askew and she paused to set it right, abandoning God for a moment for 'people who just don't care'. Then turning suddenly and thrusting her face close to mine, she hissed: 'Do you know about films?' I said that I did. 'Oh, isn't that marvellous! It's a miracle, no less, a miracle,' and she ushered us into as room filled with antique furniture and enormous paintings. 'Do you find it cold? I just can't keep warm,' she said. To us the room felt like a hothouse. 'It's my son,' she said. 'I can't begin to tell you. I'm quite terrified of him. Charming when he wants to be. But he's so naughty. He brings those awful creatures off the street and has them take all their clothes off in front of me. Terrifying! Quite terrifying! But I just close my eyes and say 'God never made a woman without protection.' Then he takes them upstairs. Disgusting creatures. You wouldn't believe. And the language! These', she said, indicating enormous battle-grey oil-paintings, 'are all Algy's. Do you like them? Horrid things, in my opinion, but everyone says he's awfully clever. I suppose *you* are awfully clever. *Are* you awfully clever? Everyone seems so clever these days. I do wish *I* was clever. Just look at my poor, dear Chelsea china. That horrid boy!' Every available surface in the room was filled with porcelain figurines of milkmaids, crinolined ladies, girls on swings, courting lovers, flower-sellers, ballet-dancers, girls with lambs, girls with skipping ropes and young men helping young women over stiles. 'The last time he was here he broke all those poor darlings on the shelf. Oh, how I cried. That's why God sent you. Protection! The next time he comes, you'll be able to protect me. And you can turn my book into a film scenario. In it, I want everyone to be born grown-up. No horrid sex. Don't you think sex is a nasty, horrid thing? In the first chapter, I have all the men and women of the world facing each other in long lines. And they come towards each other like this and then they drift away again.'

She tottered backwards and forwards on her high-heels with arms out-stretched and then . . . dreamily . . . 'backwards and forwards, just touching hands. But you've not read my book. Philip had it published for me. He was so sweet. Oh, I loved that man! He was so distinguished and so terribly, *terribly* clever. But then for weeks I didn't see him and I was so unhappy. I just couldn't begin to tell you how unhappy I was. Then it all came to a head one day when I met Nancy Astor at a garden-party and she said, 'It's no use, darling. You'll never be able to hold him, and neither will I. He prefers boys.' I was devastated, absolutely *devastated*. My hair fell out and my poor nails, just look at them. Aren't they frightful? That was the end of Philip as far as I was concerned and it was almost the end of me. That's why I don't want any sex in my film, just the touching of hands.'

In the course of the next few weeks we were treated daily to fresh instal-ments of the Philip-Nancy-Poor Me saga, inter-cut with absurd stories of Algy, Bobby, Basil, Clarissa, Megs, Stella and dear, *dear* Yegor. During this time we were occupying (rent-free) her basement flat in exchange for which we had undertaken to transform her hand-touching vision into a film scenario.

It was, on the face of it, an almost impossible task. The book had no char-acters, just pop-up, cut-out figures thinking sweet thoughts and free of nasty dreams about the real world. It was bereft of all ideas other than 'God never made a woman without protection' and its only action consisted of one half of the human race touching hands with the other half. Not the stuff out of which great epics are wrought. But we undertook the work light-heartedly. After all, it gave us a roof over our heads; and we would be learning something new, for learning-by-doing had become a way of life for us. The fact that we knew nothing whatsoever about writing film scenarios was a little daunting, but what the hell! We had read Pudovkin on *Film Technique* and there would, undoubtedly be books in the local library which would tell us how to go about the job. There were – and soon we were knocking out three or four pages of script each day.

Our ideas leaned towards the spectacular. We were chock full of ideas and as page followed page, our landlady's novel became an epic to end all epics. It combined *The Revelation of St John* with *War and Peace*, flavoured with gobbets of Marlowe's *Tamburlaine* and scenes from *Guzman de Alfarache* (we had just read Mateo Aleman's brilliant picaresque novel in Mabbe's translation). We also borrowed ideas and shots freely from *The Battleship Potemkin*, *Birth of a Nation*, *Storm over Asia*, *October*, *The End of St Petersburg*, *Quo Vadis*, *Ben Hur*, *The Cabinet of Doctor Caligari*, *Broadway Melody (1929)*, *Cimmaron*, *Zero de Conduite*, *The Gold Rush* and Walter Ruttmann's *Berlin*.

Our labours on the scenario occupied our mornings. Our afternoons were taken up with visits to the Soviet Embassy and long walks through London. Our evenings were spent running a training-class for would-be theatre workers. Organising theatre groups had become an important activity with us. Our new group consisted of six or seven young workers most of whom lived in the Battersea area. Unlike our previous groups, this wasn't formed with the intention of mounting productions; it was purely and simply a training-group, a learning unit. It was also a kind of stocktaking exercise which forced us to marshal our ideas about acting and production, ideas which until then we had only talked about.

Our nightly meetings and classes were held in our basement flat and as our landlady had forbidden us to have visitors our gatherings had to be clandestine. *Sotto voce* rehearsals and discussions are difficult, and matters were not improved by the fact that the toilet could only be flushed at specified intervals to avoid rousing the landlady's suspicions.

We managed fairly well – until Christmas Eve. Upstairs, a very noisy party was in progress while in the basement our group was attempting to be festive on half-a-dozen bottles of beer. It was a bitterly cold night and as usual our basement was unheated, with the result that most of us were wearing our outdoor clothes. A visitor might have been excused for mistaking us for a band of Arctic explorers still unthawed after an unsuccessful attempt to traverse the Northeast Passage in a single season without wintering. A visitor did, in actual fact, discover us at our rather mournful junketing. He opened the door which connected our basement room to the outside passage and stood there staring owlishly at us through the enormously thick lenses of his glasses.

He was immensely tall, stoop-shouldered, a long man with a long, melancholy face topped with lank, faded, blond hair. He stood there looking as though he had forgotten something, sucking on a cigarette the way an infant sucks on a rubber dummy. Then he cleared his throat as if he was preparing to make an announcement but then he changed his mind and shambled back upstairs. (This, we learned later, was 'dear, *dear* Yegor', a journalist specialising in foreign affairs and an inveterate tippler whose favourite beverage was the kind of eau-de-Cologne that could be purchased at Woolworth's for sixpence a pint.) Ascending from the nether regions, he announced to the assembled upstairs revellers that a band of anarchists had infiltrated the basement and were, at this moment, plotting the downfall of the state. Yegor was, of course, being facetious, but our landlady lacked a sense of humour and was immediately on her feet, ready to defend her home and England. Down the stairs she wobbled, wearing a crimson dress hung with sundry loops of pearls and looking like an illustration from *Masque of the Red Death*.

'Who are these people? Who are they?' she cried, and without giving anyone any time to reply went on, 'Get them out! Get them out at once!' She stood there glaring at our friends as they filed past her muttering their goodnights and an occasional shamefaced 'Merry Christmas'. Then she called Yegor, and down stumbled dear, dear Yegor. 'Bolt the door!' she commanded, whereupon Yegor bolted the door and fell up the stairs again. Our landlady followed after him without so much as a look in our direction, So much for good will *that* Christmas.

We should have felt humiliated but we didn't. Naturally, we felt embarrassed for our landlady but it was in character, really. After all, rich people have never been noted for compassionate behaviour to those whom they regarded as their social inferiors, nor is generosity one of their strong points. You don't get rich by being generous and, as my mother was fond of saying, 'What can you expect off a pig but a grunt?' The following morning, our landlady gave us orders to quit her basement. She would give us ten pounds to finish her scenario but we must finish it elsewhere. We packed our rucksack and returned to Stockwell.

A couple of days later, a pimply youth called Fergus offered to put us up in his mother's flat in Wandsworth. His mother, a plump, amiable eccentric, doted upon her son and could deny him nothing. Yes, we were welcome to share her flat, and she showed us into an enormous room, bare except for some wooden forms arranged round the walls and a small altar on which stood a cross made of ash wood with the bark still on it, and a silver goblet half-filled with hen's blood. Overlooking the defeated winter landscape of Wandsworth Common were five large windows, framed in purple and gold draperies, the kind of vestments that often grace the windows of old-fashioned undertakers' establishments.

'You can sleep here', she said, 'it's my meeting room.' Mrs Massey was a druid and spent her weekends and (in the summertime) her evenings as well speaking from a small, portable rostrum about the advantages of the old religion. It was slow work, she said, but she was a cheerful lady, a born optimist and if her co-religionists were anything like her, druidism deserves to prosper.

That room, with its funerary drapes, became horribly familiar to us in the next few weeks. During the daytime the room was kept clear for meetings which never seemed to take place and at night four of the wooden forms were brought together to provide a base for a mattress. It was cold and cheerless, but we comforted ourselves with the thought that it was only going to be for a few days, a couple of weeks at the most and then we would be off to the Soviet Union. Or would we? We were beginning to have doubts. Every two or three days we wrote to our contact in Moscow but heard nothing in return, just a resounding silence. Well, be patient. In any case, there was work to be done here in London. What a great, big wilderness it was! And it was no use getting depressed.

But there was plenty to be depressed about, and no mistake. For one thing we had no money and we weren't eligible for the dole. We were hungry all the time. The bread and tea which was the chief part of our diet didn't sustain us or keep out the cold and the members of our acting class were almost as poor as we so we couldn't ask for any handouts. The one member of our group who might have helped us was an old friend of Joan's, a Swedish painter named Sonya who lived with her wealthy parents in Richmond. She was a warm-hearted but completely impractical young woman who had never been hungry and couldn't imagine what it was like to be hungry. When we hinted that we were finding the going rough she rushed off home and returned later with a bottle of expensive claret – the most expensive in her father's cellar, she added. Later that night, in our island bed in the middle of the druid's meeting room, we laughed ourselves into hysterics as we drank the precious wine.

In addition to being penniless, hungry and cold, there was the problem of finding premises for our training classes, for our group – our embryo theatre school – would cease to exist if we didn't find somewhere soon. Then someone suggested setting up a communal house. At first no one was keen on the idea but gradually we warmed to it and after two or three days of discussion and argument we arrived at a state of euphoria in which the communal house had become a symbol for the promised land.

Before the symbol could become concrete reality, we needed money – not a large sum, but enough to pay a month's rent in advance. That would allow us breathing space to find or earn enough to pay the following month's rent. The epic! The scenario! That'll bring in ten pounds! So Joan and I launched into the final assault, and within a week we had it finished. When Joan made a fine copy in her distinctive microscopic handwriting, we raced to Cheyne Walk and handed it to Poor Me, who handed over £5.

'What's this? You agreed to pay us £10.'

'£5 now and £5 after the reading.'

'Reading?'

'It's all arranged. Algy's been an absolute dear. He's got this simply marvellous studio, an *enormous* place. Lots of terribly important people have promised to turn up. Thursday evening. So *do* try and make yourselves look presentable.'

Come Thursday evening at half-past-seven we presented ourselves at Cheyne Walk and were duly picked up by Algy, our ex-landlady's ex-husband. We went on to pick up two more ex-wives and ended up in Algy's studio in St John's Wood. It really *was* simply enormous, a great barn of a place with battleship-grey walls and ceiling, a battleship-grey grand piano and a sofa upholstered in battleship-grey velvet. The effect was sombre and the presence of a huge canvas depicting Vauxhall Bridge dimly perceived through a fog did nothing to alleviate the gloom.

There were a fifteen or twenty people there, a large proportion of whom appeared to be yet more women who had been married to Algy at various times. There were men as well, who (like Algy) merged into the battleship-grey background as Joan launched into the reading of the script. It was a brilliant performance, a kind of oral legerdemain in which the ear usurped the function of the mind. No one present could have resisted that beguiling voice weaving melodies around the nonsense we had created. It was a huge success and our audience gathered around cooing and congratulating us and our landlady on this *tour de force*. We left with our five pounds, our faces aching from having to suppress our laughter.

During the depression years, rented accommodation was easy to find and (providing you could afford the rent) choice was almost unlimited. We found our ideal premises within an hour or two of beginning the search. It was a large Edwardian house overlooking the west side of Clapham Common, a truly magnificent residence, well-built and perfectly maintained. It had eight bedrooms, two bathrooms, dining room and kitchen, laundry room and three reception rooms, each one of which was larger than the druid's hall. A high brick wall surrounded the spacious garden at the end of which was a large studio with its own kitchen and bathroom. The rent was £3 a week, payable a month in advance. We paid and moved in.

Since our possessions consisted of the clothes we stood up in, we had no removal expenses. We also had no bed to lie in, no chairs to sit on, no table to eat off, so we bought these necessary items on the *never-never*, as the hire-purchase system was called, and prepared to live the good life. Our Battersea friends transported their few possessions on a handcart. It was snowing heavily and we must have looked like peasant refugees fleeing before an invading army as we pushed the handcart up Lavender Hill.

We had found a coal bunker with a few pieces of coal in it and with a fire blazing in the grate of the largest reception room the place looked cheerful and welcoming. Our friends, some of whom had not seen the house until this moment, were loud in their praises. None of us had ever lived in conditions where there was so much space, room to breathe, privacy. And two bathrooms! Three, if you counted the studio as well. Then someone noticed there was no stove or cooking facilities. Our enthusiasm was tempered, but only slightly. We'll get a primus-stove for the time being until we can afford a proper gas

stove. In any case, there's the central heating – that should keep us warm. But
. . . we'll need coal for the boiler. A hot debate developed about whether we
could afford such luxuries. No, we could not. It was agreed that a single half-
hundredweight bag of coal should be bought in order to take the chill off the
house. This was done and for three or four days the house was wonderfully
warm. Then the coal ran out and the radiators cooled and the rooms took on
their permanent chill again.

We tried to ignore it, but you could feel your resolution ebbing away as the
cold ate deeper and deeper into your bones. Had we been able to eat properly
we might have withstood the cold but living as we were on cups of tea and the
odd slice of bread we were vulnerable to every little draught. Joan and I had
almost forgotten what a hot meal was like. We would comfort ourselves by
comparing our lot with that of Thomas Otway, who had been so hungry that
he had choked to death on a bread roll that had fallen in the gutter, or thinking
of William Blake going through the rigmarole of sitting down to an imaginary
meal. What really sustained us was our shining vision of a theatre which would
take its place along with the theatre of Aeschylus and Sophocles, Shakespeare
and Ben Jonson and all those others who had held up a flawless mirror to the
times they lived in.

By this time our visits to the Soviet embassy had ceased altogether. Moscow
was a dream that wasn't going to happen. So we had to succeed in London or
go under. Our training classes had now become all-important. But the classes
were not going well. They were just limping along and we were discovering
great gaps in our knowledge. Our ideas about the kind of theatre we wanted
were constantly becoming more concrete and more detailed but we were discovering that before any of them could be fully realised we needed to know a
great deal more about the various types of vocal training and about the teaching of movement. Joan was stubbornly opposed to the kind of elocution she
had encountered at RADA, but neither of us knew of any alternative methods.
Likewise, the job of teaching people how to handle their bodies on the stage
was totally beyond us. Yet we knew that our concept of theatre would be stillborn without such training. Our experiences with *Newsboy* and *Draw the Fires*
had made this clear to us.[1] Finally, we decided that all the problems of training
would become clear as they surfaced in the course of actual productions. By
solving them one by one we would build up a composite picture which would
ultimately enable us to formulate a complete programme of training.

In the meantime the enthusiasm of our small group was waning fast and we
had to admit that our experiment had failed. We owed three weeks arrears of
rent. At a sad meeting, we formally announced the end of the venture. Joan
and I were now at the end of our tether. Moscow had fallen through. Our training school had collapsed. We felt defeated, demoralised. Our deliverance was
like the final moments of a Western when the beleaguered covered-wagons are
rescued from the Indians by the U.S. Cavalry. Our salvation came in the form
of a letter from the Manchester branch of the Peace Pledge Union, inviting us

to produce Hans Schlumberg's *Miracle at Verdun* and offering us a small fee. This was to be the first money I had ever earned in the theatre.

The following day we were headed north again. Our stay in London had been miserable. We had gone there determined never to return to the north except as conquerors. We had looked forward to spending two or three years in close discussion (in fluent Russian, of course) with our friends Myherhold and Vahktangov and then returning accompanied by Eisenstein or Pudovkin, with whom we were to produce a film dealing with Engels' life in Manchester . . . maybe if we hadn't been so cold and hungry most of the time it might have worked out better. Or if we had liked London . . . but both of us hated it. I felt lost in it, depersonalised. And yet, at the time, anything was better than having to return north with our tails between our legs . . . the scorn with which we would be greeted by those whom we had come to regard as our enemies . . . no, we said. Never!

Yet once we were seated in the Manchester-bound train, we were in a buoyant mood and supremely confident about our future. For one thing, we were no longer cold. My father's eldest brother, Jock, had died of a heart attack in his butcher's shop in Glasgow and left £200 to my father, who sent half of it to Joan and me with the injunction that we get ourselves some clothes. So here we were, decked out in our finery: new shoes for both of us; skirt, blouse and a handsome new coat for Joan; and for me, a new suit, the first one I'd ever had that hadn't been bought from a clothing club.

The sun was shining when we walked out of London Road Station and made our way across Piccadilly. Did we imagine the feeling of celebration in the air? We welcomed ourselves back over a cup of coffee at the Mosley Street Kardomah and then, conscious of being much travelled sophisticates, we made our way to the Friends Meeting House where the office of the Peace Pledge Union was located.

When we left the building a half-hour later, we were in a high state of jubilation. The young woman who had greeted us there had informed us that we could draw upon a more or less unlimited supply of helpers. The entire place was a hive of cheerful activity and we had been introduced to young people who were duplicating scripts, designing posters and drafting leaflets. We were shown our rehearsal facilities: three large rooms redolent of wood and furniture polish, centrally heated rooms with parquet floors and conveniently adjacent toilet facilities. A far cry from the cellar of the Workers' Arts Club and the tumbledown studio in Grosvenor Street. As if all this wasn't enough, the efficient young woman who had organised it presented us with a long list of names of those eager to take part in the production as actors, technicians or simply as dogsbodies.

'When would you like to start auditioning?' she asked. Auditioning? It was a completely novel idea. In The Red Megaphones a group of politically-minded teenagers had drifted together in order to present dramatic political sketches. In Theatre of Action we had absorbed into the company almost anyone who happened to be at hand. And now we were to have a choice of actors and actresses!

Miracle at Verdun was not one of our most inspired productions, but it did provide us with a platform from which to proclaim our ideas about theatre.[2] It put us in contact with audiences who had probably never even heard of our previous theatre work and it provided us with a nucleus of people who were willing to work with us. Some of these new recruits left after a few weeks. Others, including a small group of artists, stayed with us for the next five years. Two of them were employed as teachers at Manchester's art school, some were students and one or two earned a precarious living by painting or sculpting. Through them we had access to the services of layout and silk-screen artists and workers in most aspects of graphics. The results were not only apparent in our improved stage sets but in the impressive handbills and posters which advertised our productions.

By the time 1936 was a few weeks old, Theatre Union was flourishing. Most of our old Theatre of Action people were with us again and what with the new recruits, the artists' group and the very professional technicians group, we really felt capable of tackling the most ambitious shows. For years I had lived with failure. I had struggled, almost blindly, to create a theatre. Now I lived in a state of almost permanent euphoria. Joan and I passed our days in a fury of activity. We made plans, read everything we could lay our hands on, talked incessantly about theatre to anyone who would listen. Furthermore, we had found a way to earn a living – not a particularly satisfactory living as far as money was concerned, but an absorbing and creative one.

18

Megaphones to Microphones[1]

I had started doing occasional radio work in 1933 when I had been approached by Archie Harding, the North Regional Programme Director, to read some verses in a feature programme about May Day in England. 'We need a working-class voice,' Harding explained. I was it. For several years afterwards I was the 'working-class voice', the 'rough voice', 'sailor's voice', 'navvy's voice', 'tramp's voice', and sometimes '2nd Narrator (northern voice)'.

Harding, the grey eminence of creative broadcasting had, almost single-handed, created the form of radio-documentary known as the feature programme. On leaving Oxford, he had gone straight into radio, convinced that this new medium held the key to a new important art form in which the spoken word would really come into its own. He maintained that radio was a tool for poets; with it one could manipulate words in the way that John Hartfield manipulated visual images to create his photomontages.

After a brief studio apprenticeship, he became part of an experimental unit at Broadcasting House, and there produced his radio adaptation of John Reed's *Ten Days That Shook the World*, a work which, though never actually broadcast, was said to be a near-masterpiece. Harding was unusually modest about it and said that his role as adapter had been a simple one. His next major work, a superbly documented account of a rising by Asturian miners – *Crisis in Spain* – was indeed brilliant. I can still recall the feeling of tremendous excitement that I experienced when I listened to it for the first time. It had the sweep and intellectual passion of Eisenstein at his best, combined with the kind of inexorable unfolding of events which one encounters in the great ballads.

With the production of *Crisis*, Harding left the comparatively obscure world of experimental broadcasting for the limelight of public broadcasting. He had become a force to be reckoned with. From now on, he was told, the writing and production of documentary programmes was to be his sole activity. 'Choose your own subjects, old boy.' Any misgivings as to the subject matter of *Crisis in Spain* were quickly shrugged off. Harding was a very bright young man. Just up from Oxford. Got to give him his head for a while. A certain degree of rebelliousness is inevitable in the young. He'll grow out of it. Give him a few responsibilities and he'll knuckle under. You'll see, he'll turn out to be a very useful chap in the Corporation.

So this white-headed boy, this establishment nominee was given the go-ahead to produce more brilliant programmes. And he did, a whole fistful of them, and they *were* outstanding, and each one was more politically pointed than the one before. The 'hcid yins' became more disturbed and began to ask each other whether young Harding was *ever* going to toe the line. Their support was finally withdrawn after the production of his *Portrait of Warsaw,* a much-publicised New Year's Eve broadcast of a programme which juxtaposed Chopin's romantic Poland against the realities of the Pilsudski regime. It brought the Polish Ambassador to Broadcasting House the next morning demanding an apology. As a result, Harding was exiled to the North Region and promoted to a position where he would neither write nor produce scripts. He settled down there to the task of cultivating a circle of young writers and . . . no, not actors but readers. He despised actors and was never able to convince himself that they possessed even the most rudimentary intelligence.

He drank a good deal and smoked incessantly. Rumour had it that he was something of a lecher who treated women brutally. True or not, he certainly treated actresses with unconcealed contempt. On more than one occasion I have seen him reduce an actress to hysterics. He surrounded himself with sycophantic smart young men and women, provincial suburban jet setters who organised parties for him and, it was said, provided him with bedmates. He appeared to find his circle of friends monumentally boring but, at the same time, necessary.

He was pathetically eager to meet working people and once, at his invitation, I brought four members of The Red Megaphones to meet him at the studio. It was a fruitless meeting; he was tongue-tied in their presence, in some odd way overpowered by them, though very little was said. I remember thinking at the time that he looked like a small, defenceless boy in a group of adults.

To me he showed great kindness and when he learned that I was intent on becoming a writer he gave me a key to his flat and told me to use the place while he was at the studio. He occasionally spoke at length to me about his ideas, his concept of radio. I drank it all in eagerly but could think of nothing to say myself. I was as tongue-tied in his company as he was in the presence of my friends. I felt awkward and found it difficult to rid myself of the feeling that he was my boss and I was in my traditional role of unskilled labourer. I am sure he didn't think that way at all. I think I was suffering from culture shock. We were from different worlds. He was a southerner, I was from the north. He was rich – at least I thought he was – and I was dirt-poor. He was at home in this environment, I was an interloper. He was a graduate of Oxford University and could express himself fluently; I was an elementary-school product and though I knew a lot of words (thanks to the Pears, Webster and Peel Park public library) I wasn't sure whether I was pronouncing them correctly, so I tended to stumble and stutter a great deal and blush with embarrassment. His size, too, may have contributed to my insecurity in his presence. He was one of those large, well-fed men who assume a slight stoop when they walk and who seem to take it for granted that lesser beings will stand aside for them to pass. His manner of speaking, too, was distinctly off-putting. I have always disliked that affected Oxford drawl with its casual superciliousness. It is so ugly. Harding's version of it with its barely concealed note of derision was particularly objectionable.

Once, at a party, he spoke slightingly of me, referring to me as 'a boy from the slums'. On hearing about it, I went straight to the great man's office and confronted him. He didn't deny it, but assumed the arrogant pose which generally preceded one of his calculated insults. I beat him to it, however, by calling him a 'big, soft shit', a phrase which, though lacking in elegance, is not without force. It seemed to discompose him utterly. When I threatened to beat the same out of him he didn't stop to find out whether I was in earnest or not, but leapt with a bound from his chair and hurled himself out of his office, a large and rather flabby Orestes pursued by a single fury. He took refuge in a cubicle of the gent's lavatory. I hammered on the door and after a few moments he gathered his wits together and responded by paraphrasing a line from *Coriolanus:* 'No good, sir, I will not out of doors', delivered in that ridiculous drawl.

From that time on, he ignored me. I was an un-person, though oddly enough I continued to be offered work as 'rough voice', 'third robber', etc. I heard that the incident, suitably edited and embellished, was reenacted at scores of parties during the next few months. It was childish of me to resent being called the boy from the slums; that, after all, is what I was. Nevertheless, I did resent it. Had the remark been made by any of the lightweight wits who competed endlessly for the position of court-jester, I would have ignored it. But Harding was someone I admired; he had a passionate belief in radio and had actually created a new art form, the radio feature. He loved words and understood their power and he had a vision of a radio art form which could assist the forward march of mankind. He was a big man who occasionally made himself small by making cruel remarks. I learned a great deal from Archie Harding, and through my work with him I built up a gallery of rough voices and mastered several dialects and accents. Later, I graduated to becoming a narrator and poetry reader.

It was John Pudney who gave me my first real chance as a scriptwriter. Pudney, a producer on loan from the London headquarters of the BBC, arrived in Manchester with a considerable reputation as a feature-producer. It was a reputation well earned, for he was far and away the most talented producer I ever worked with in radio. He was a poet of some standing and was able to attract artists of the calibre of Auden and Britten to work with him.

He had a nice sense of irony and an engaging schoolboyish sense of humour. *The Mafia* (his name for the BBC administrative staff) he regarded as natural enemies. The London cashier's department, which was always in arrears with his salary cheque, was a particular target for his hatred. He engaged in a one-man guerilla war against it and bombarded the chief cashier with chamber pots which he bought for a few coppers in junk shops. They were of all types and vintages, made of porcelain, earthenware, stoneware, enamel, and even

aluminium. There were chaste white porcelain ones with gilt rims, a magnificent bone china model with fluted sides and scalloped rims; there were pink
ones decorated with forget-me-nots, pale blue ones with peonies, brown ones
with mottos in black Gothic script, art-nouveau models, baroque models with
bunches of gilded grapes and roseate nymphs scattering rose petals and rococo
ones with flat planes joined together, sporting elaborate scrolls and ornamental
bows. The word must have spread that a mad collector was on the rampage
for the going price for these unfashionable items of bedroom crockery suddenly soared sky-high, with the result that Pudney was forced to abandon his
search for them. He turned his attention to junk pianos. In Huddersfield, he
discovered a junk shop which had a dozen ancient uprights mouldering away in
a back room. He bought four of them and had them sent (cash on delivery) at
weekly intervals to the poor cashier at Broadcasting House. After delivering the
coup de grace (a small lorry-load of stinking fish bought cheap in South Shields
and dumped on the front garden of his victim) he abandoned his campaign,
which had hardly interrupted his official commitment to the BBC at all.

For all his practical jokes and personal vendettas, Pudney was a serious radio
man. His radio career had taken him through the drama department where he
had written and produced several delightfully ironic fantasies, the most notable
of which – *Uncle Arthur* – had been praised by T.S. Eliot and published by him
in *The Criterion*. And now here he was in Features, BBC's most prestigious
department, the holy ground where the most sacred of cows was nurtured.

Pudney's first decisive move as a feature-producer was to banish the narrator, that device which Harding and his disciples had elevated to the point
where it had become a kind of liturgical necessity. Actors who were hired to
read narration were regarded as an elite; they were, as Harding put it, 'the soloists in the choir'. They were chosen because of their 'beautiful voices' and for
being able to take direction. To me, the entire panel of narrators used by the
BBC during this period sounded so alike that I was unable to distinguish them
from one another. That they could take direction was indisputable and I have
known Harding work for an entire rehearsal period on three or four inflections.
No cadences had a dying fall if Archie had anything to do with it. No, indeed.
Words had an importance above and beyond their meaning and each sentence
had to be as carefully engineered as a cantilever bridge.

At times, the narration cult reached absurd proportions, as in D.G. Bridson's
programme dealing with the building of the Mersey Tunnel. Both Harding
and Bridson were enamoured of the catalogue theory which held that a list of
objects – any kind of objects – could produce an emotional response in those
who read it or heard it read. After all, if words had significance beyond their
meaning, then any word could be made to yield emotional sustenance. With
good direction, a well-trained narrator should be able to deliver compelling
readings from the telephone directory and, according to Bridson, there was no
reason whatsoever why an undertaker's list of funerary supplies should be any
less moving than Dunbar's *Lament for the Makars*.

In *Tunnel,* narration and catalogue theory were combined to produce a programme of stupefying dullness. For the best part of an hour, four *beautiful* voices competed with each other in reading lists of statistics about the number of inches dug in number of man-hours, days, weeks, months; the type of rock to be cut through; the number of drills used, the shovels, mechanical grabs, bull-dozers, dump trucks, wheelbarrows, cranes; the amount of steel, iron, copper, zinc, lead, brass, aluminium; the various types of cement and its constituent parts; the number of nails, screws, tacks, bolts; the total and individual weights of all these things in grams, ounces, pounds, stones, hundred-weights, tons; and their single and combined lengths, widths and thicknesses in inches, feet, yards, poles, acres, furlongs and miles.

In this mountain of facts, this vast ocean of measurements, this veritable universe of grades, standards, degrees, norms and criteria, this galaxy of brackets, bars, stanchions, stays, supports, props, bays and buttresses, the tunnellers had been forgotten. It was as if Sisyphus had written the story of the Tarpein Rock. *'Dreary Paleozoic lump! Silurian? Ordovician? Still, lots of graptolites. Good example of Orthograptus. And that Haematomma ventosum adds a lovely bit of colour.'* Is it any wonder that Prometheus wasn't even noticed?

Now here was this upstart from the south, this effete poet who looked like a prosperous farmer up for a day in town, intent on riding roughshod over the well-kept pastures of the featureochracy. No lengthy passages of beautifully crafted narration for Pudney, no dessicated prose that could be bent and angled by cunning inflections. No soloists and no choir. Instead there were the Caption Voices reading adverts about forgotten cures for warts, bunions, consumptions and the falling sickness; brisk statements culled from newspapers, official documents, government reports and royal circulars. In place of the undesignated voices, the rough, smooth, less smooth, official, angry and fluent voices of the classic feature programme, he introduced the characterised voice, almost always accented or in dialect. Not the italicised dialect of a Bridson script, where it was used as an interesting exhibit; now it was a counter to the harsh officialese of the Caption Voices.

Pudney's approach to radio-documentary was not aimed at subverting the classic feature but at humanising it. Harding's early programmes were not only stylistically brilliant and innovative, they were also passionate, political statements, vibrant with anger and impatience. Form and content existed in pet feet balance. In his Manchester period the scripts which he inspired others to write lacked the earlier political conviction and, consequently, the passion too was absent; the form had become all-important, and while this may have interested those who put the scripts together, it more often than not resulted in pomposity and a sententiousness which must have repelled many listeners. Pudney, on the other hand, was able to invest the dullest subject with humour and irony and one was never allowed to lose sight of the fact that a human intelligence was at work in even the most grandiose project.

In the same way that I had drifted into radio acting, so I drifted into script-writing and occasionally into working as a temporary producer of features. On two or three occasions I was even brought in to assist the junior programme engineer operating the 'grams' on which pre-recorded field material and effects were played. All these varied activities would, no doubt, have stood me in good stead had I been interested in pursuing a career in radio; but as far as I was concerned they were merely a means to an end, a necessary, and at times tiresome, detour on the journey to a revolutionary theatre. This is not to say that I found the work itself tiresome or uninteresting. On the contrary, I was frequently fascinated by it, particularly during the first year.

The BBC both attracted and repelled me. The place itself was so different from all the other places I had known, not like a place of work at all. Those who worked there were quite unlike any workers I had ever encountered. Even the ladies who served in the canteen seemed different. There was something rarefied about the place, something unreal. Once inside those Piccadilly studios, the world outside ceased to exist. The distance between them and the Albion Street Labour Exchange was astronomical. It was almost impossible to imagine that the two places existed on the same planet. Mass unemployment, strikes, hunger marches, the mutiny at Invergordon, the Reichstag fire trial – all that belonged to another world.

It is very different now, but at that time the BBC was not unlike a gentleman's club where everyone had been to the same prep school and learned the same communication rituals. It was a world where the human voice had been tamed and moulded so that it blended perfectly with the leather upholstery of the studio couches and the discreetly patterned cheviot of the men's suits. And compare the BBC secretarial staff with the office staff at the wire-works: there they had been employees like me, but here they seemed to be part owners of the place. It is, of course, possible that the working staff (as opposed to the decorative staff) toiled in some remote part of the building and never saw the light of day.

My picture of the staff is of two distinct groups of women. One of them consists of ladies of mature age with names like Marge and Doris. They wore a great deal of make-up and sported numerous ropes of pearls and their girdles tended to make them bend forward slightly when they walked. The other group was made up mostly of alluring young women, the 'well-fed' girls of my cousin John's fantasies. They moved through the corridors in a cloud of perfume, high-heels clicking, pert buttocks straining against skin-tight skirts, and nicely packaged breasts jiggling under pastel-shaded twin-sets. 'Decorative and quite useless,' said Archie Harding. They had been hired, he said, because 'they have fathers who have shares in the Regional Director.' He grumbled frequently about their incompetence and warned everyone that they were 'breeders on the lookout for a suitable consort'. Pudney's comment on them was phrased less politely. 'They can't type and they won't fuck.' Falling somewhere between the two groups was The Lady with the Flowers. That was how I always thought of her. The Lady with the Flowers. The only time she ever appeared in the studios was when she came to change the flowers. She really was a very superior young woman, always serene and beautiful beyond belief. She worked upstairs in some privileged capacity, assistant to the NRD or some such thing. I heard that her name was Marion, but no one ever addressed her as anything but Miss Pusey. What an absurd name for a goddess. Aphrodite would have been more appropriate, or The Lady with the Flowers.

Then there were the actors, the speakers, the voices. They, too, fall into two groups. There were the locals, the *regulars* as they called themselves. They were the larger of the two groups. They were mostly amateurs recruited from well-respected amateur northern groups such as the Unnamed Society, the Bolton Little Theatre, the Rochdale Curtain Theatre and the Huddersfield Thespians. They worked as accountants, solicitors' clerks and insurance men. Some owned their own small businesses. The women were retired repertory actresses, wives of businessmen, failed mistresses. The men gossiped (when they weren't reading their lines or solving *The Manchester Guardian* crossword-puzzle). The women knitted.

The smaller of the two groups were actors or actresses who had been brought specially from London to speak a part considered to be beyond the skill of a local. There were rarely more than two such foreigners in a programme. A local who was on first-name terms with an import was reckoned to have scored heavily in the one-upmanship stakes. At the same time, it was generally agreed that all imports were stuck-up bastards who were taking the lines, if not the bread, out of the mouths of decent northern chaps.

I, too, was an interloper in spite of the fact that I was a northerner. The regulars were solidly middle-class and, in the final analysis, had more in common with middle-class southerners than with working-class northerners. I was not only a working-class youth, I was a working-class *communist* youth and they found that difficult to stomach. In addition, my Salford accent disturbed them. Their own speech was either a genteel mixture of Manchester and occasional southern vowels or a bluff, business-like, mid-English larded with phrases of stage-Lancashire.

It was a precarious way of earning a living, for jobs were few and far between. Sometimes a month or six weeks would go by with neither Joan nor I being offered any work and then one – or both – of us would be offered parts in two or three scripts in as many days. Between us we earned enough to survive on. Our needs were very modest and we owned little. We had the clothes we stood up in and a change of underclothes. We owned a bed and two chairs and a few books. Since we earned only a pittance, we didn't pay taxes. We had scarcely any travelling expenses, for we walked everywhere, and when we needed to study there was the reading room of the Central Library. In retrospect, ours was an enviable existence.

Did we ever sleep? Were there times when the days dragged and the nights seemed endless? I see us moving through those years like characters in a speeded-up film. Did you see the . . . there, now it's gone. Meetings, arguments, discussions, rows, eruptions, reconciliations. Ideas form and burst and shoot like fireworks, like rockets or brilliant Roman candles. Whooooosh! We are the express train October across the universe. We are intoxicated with ideas, with words, with each other, with the world, with the theatre. THEATRE! A theatre which will encapsulate the great soaring universe of Aeschylus and Sophocles, the mocking, laughter-filled firmament of Aristophanes and Jonson, the whirling galaxies of Shakespeare and those who shared their drunken dreams in the stews and taverns of 16th- and 17th-century London.

Rehearsals. Try this out, try that, imagine a stage as big as a football field, as big as a twenty-five acre field, as big as . . . think of an endless place with fields, deserts, mountains, oceans with the sun for a spotlight. Training classes. Let us take the most minute particles of speech, the constituents of vocal activity and of muscles so toned, so tempered that they will respond to even the faintest echo of a memory of an emotion. Names: Myerhold, Vakhtangov, Okhlopkov, Brecht, Piscator, Moliere, Lope de Vega . . . we toss them into the air like gold and silver balls, fascinated by their glitter. Only twenty-four hours in the day, worse luck! Twenty-four hours and so much to be done. But oh, the excitement of doing it! A carrel in the reference library, a private room, no less. And books by the dozen, by the hundred, old books smelling of dust and age. New books smelling of printer's ink and the sharp smell of glossy book-jackets. Look at the date on this one – twenty-three years since it was last taken off the shelves. Before we were born. Dead old Diderot, down old mole! Dried up in this old book. Ideas, phrases encompassing an almost unbearable degree of excitement. Concepts, theories, methodologies, systems. Our friends, yes, and our enemies too, appear, in retrospect, to be somewhat larger than life, more passionately involved in living, more persuasive, more good-natured or more malevolent, more droll, more talented, more wise, more exciting in every way. The present reduces my size or makes *them* larger till I am like Lemuel Gulliver among the Brobdignagians. And all this against the background of another world war in the making. Nonsense, you communists have got war on the brain. Just scaremongers! And yet, and yet . . . Japan has invaded Manchuria. Hitler has planted his crooked cross over Germany and with the Anschluss and the Saar plebiscite, the Nazi plague begins to spread over Germany's borders. The Italians invade Abyssinia, Japan moves into mainland China and now Franco and his fascists have unleashed civil war in Spain. The world is breaking up like sheet-ice in the spring and here are we trying to create a theatre of *ideas* . . .

The first five years of the 1930s was, for me, a period of unremitting struggle in the field of day-to-day politics and political theatre. The Clarion Players, the WTM, The Red Megaphones and Theatre of Action had been stages in the struggle. We had started out as a small, weak group with a great deal of enthusiasm and little skill. Each stage revealed more clearly the immense distance between our objective and our achievements. The more we learned, the more there was to learn. It wasn't enough merely to know what we had done; we had to know what had been done by those who had gone before . . . and those before *them*. It was a paradoxical situation. We were intent on building a forward-looking theatre but were being forced to look back constantly at the Elizabethan and Jacobean theatre, at the classical theatre of Greece, at the theatre of Lope de Vega and Tirso de Molino, Moliere, the *commedia dell'arte*, Brecht, the expressionists, the Russians.

During the second half of the decade, we continued to pursue these studies, simultaneously adding to our practical knowledge by spending more and more time on actual productions. To build a workers' theatre was still our aim and one which demanded every particle of our energy and devotion. As far as I was concerned it was a political task and an important one at that. It involved finding new forms and techniques capable of dealing with the times we lived in and it meant being prepared to salvage all that was best in the theatre of the past. 'The bourgeoisie', wrote Engels, 'have raised monuments to the classics. If they'd have read them, they'd have burned them'. Well, now they were burning them and our task was to save from the flames as many of them as possible so that when capitalism was finally destroyed the legacy of all that was best in the past would still be intact.

We had tried to share our vision and our fears but with little success. *Listen,* we said, as we handed out leaflets at factory gates or stood on a piece of waste-ground and tried to warn our fellow citizens about what was in store for them. It was like trying to fly a kite in a hurricane. Oh yes, the unemployed would listen to us suggesting ways of fighting back against the means-test, but when we tried to warn them about the killing times ahead our voices were drowned out by the daily barrage of propaganda poured out by newspapers and radio.

We live in a democracy but the rulers have a monopoly of the ways of influencing people's minds. So who read the pamphlets we produced in 1929 about the Japanese invasion of Manchuria? Who even bothered to refute us when we described it as a preliminary stage in a planned programme of imperialist aggression? We mounted campaigns against Hitler and the Nazis. Fascism, we said, leads inevitably to war. The media didn't agree.

One or two of the newspapers of the period regarded Hitler as a comic figure, while the more solidly right-wing ones saw him as a strong man who would put Germany's house in order and who, in the process, would give the Bolsheviks their comeuppance. When we produced photographs and case histories of concentration-camp victims we were either ignored or dismissed as scaremongers. Indeed, while communists, trade-union leaders, left-wing intellectuals and Jews were being butchered in Belsen and Oranienburg, eulogies of Hitler were being delivered in the Mother of Parliaments. There were some who suggested that we needed a Hitler of our own and there is no reason to suppose that a little encouragement would not have produced plenty of applicants for the job, while Fleet Street would no doubt have supplied him with a whole army of Himmlers.

Our constant cry, that fascism must be stopped before it led to another world war, was met with deafening silence. 'Herr Hitler will soon conform to the mould created by his predecessors,' was the considered view of the more conservative press. We were still warning people about the dangers of war when Mussolini's troops invaded Abyssinia in October 1935. The Baldwin government made a feeble protest. The League of Nations condemned the aggression and imposed limited sanctions against Italy, sanctions which were largely disregarded by most members of the League, while Hitler made no secret of the fact that he considered aggression the better part of statesmanship. The BBC announcement on 5 May 1936, reporting the fall of Addis Ababa and the virtual end of the Abyssinian war was an occasion for some satisfaction on the part of our establishment.

It wasn't long before another war had erupted, this time in Spain. Surely, we thought, now the government *must* take action. It did – against the forces of the legally elected government. Overnight, Franco and his army of North African Muslims became the saviours of Christianity. Sir Henry Page Croft laid it clearly on the line: 'I recognise General Franco to be a gallant Christian gentleman.' Lord Redesdale, always a great admirer of the fascist way of life – and death – stated: 'General Franco is leading a crusade for all that we in England hold dear.' Tory MP Mr. Lennox Boyd argued, 'I cannot understand the argument that it is in our interest to stop Franco winning.' Some of the newspapers (and the BBC at first) adopted the stance of neutral observers, but that was quickly abandoned when it began to look as if the republican forces might win. Soon the entire media was referring to Franco's army of mercenaries as 'loyalists' and few of them bothered to conceal their satisfaction at the news of Franco's massacres in Badajos, Pamplona, Granada, Seville and Guernica. The campaign of lies and vilification directed at the republican forces and their leaders was not unlike the campaign waged against the miners and their leaders in the strike of 1984–85.

And through the turbulent years, our vision of a theatre remained undimmed. We now had numerous allies and felt capable of undertaking the most ambitious productions: *Fuente Ovejuna* by Lope de Vega; *The Good Soldier Schweijk;* the *Lysistrata* of Aristophanes; and *Last Edition*, a living newspaper dealing with political events from 1930 to 1939. All these productions made enormous demands on what was essentially an amateur company. Not that there was anything amateur about our way of working. We had reacted violently against the casual behaviour of the repertory theatre actors we had worked with during Ernst Toller's production of *Draw the Fires*. Rehearsals were now held on five evenings every week and most people were expected to be available for weekend calls. There were few nights off. By 1939, we were beginning to discuss the possibility of abandoning our amateur status and setting up a full-time professional theatre company.

Part Two
(1945–1989)

19

Theatre Workshop

The war didn't put an end to our plans, it merely postponed them, and shortly after VE Day a handful of us met to put those plans into operation. In the new group, Theatre Workshop, there were only six of us who had been in Theatre Union and there was no one but myself from the days of The Red Megaphones. Joan had joined in the early days of the Theatre of Action; Rosalie Williams had been a student when she joined Theatre Union for the production of *Fuente Ovejuna;* Howard Goorney had come in during *The Good Soldier Schweijk,* as had Bunny Bowen who had left his job in a steel foundry to join us; Gerry Raffles had joined us while still a schoolboy during the production of *Lysistrata.* Four, or possibly five, new recruits would be joining us as soon as we were ready to go into production.[1]

There was little money, a pittance really, but enough to keep a small group of us for a month or maybe a little longer. We weren't unduly worried about finances. After all, the war in Europe was over, it was springtime – and hadn't we been promised a subsidy by the education authorities in Westmoreland? Premises as well – a beautiful old theatre which had been serving as a sweets warehouse and was now about to be restored. Promised? Actually *promised?* Well, nothing in writing, of course, but yes, we *had* been invited . . . hadn't we? Well, never mind, we've waited five years. Surely a little longer . . . So a week passed while we waited patiently with our goods and chattels packed and ready. And another week, and another. A month went by, and by this time tempers were getting frayed; enthusiasm, which had survived five years of war was beginning to turn sour. Our 'friend' who was arranging the subsidy and the premises was now 'that bastard in Westmorland'. Tentatively at first, and then rather desperately, we started to discuss the pros and cons of possible alternative bases. But our hopes had been fixed on Kendal and we were in no mood for alternatives. Backing or no backing, Kendal was to be our base.

It was early summer when we arrived in the little Westmorland town and set up our headquarters in a room above the Conservative Club. There were nine of us now. The new recruits included Pearl Turner, a blonde Botticelli Venus who had been working as a land-girl in Sussex and possessed a clear, unaffected soprano voice which made her a natural choice for one of the narrators in the ballad-opera on which we were about to embark. There was also Ruth Brandes, a handsome young woman with an accent so obviously ruling-class that Kendal shopkeepers, on hearing it, practically touched their forelocks and genuflected. She had a wonderful flair for designing and making costumes, masks and props of all kinds. Before joining us she had been a junior programme engineer at the BBC, as had David Scase, who joined us to do the sound and who proved to possess hidden talents as an actor and eventually was able to do any job in the theatre from rigging and de-rigging a stage to acting a major role. Finally, there was Kristin Lind, our Swede who looked like everyone's idea of a smouldering Spanish beauty. She joined the group as an actress and played leading roles with the company throughout our entire touring period. A short-term member of the group was a young scientist who was working for ICI, H. Verity Smith, or 'Smithy'. He visited us soon after we arrived in Kendal in order to advise us on the most efficient way of building the specialised lighting unit we needed. It took a little longer than he had anticipated, so he persuaded his employers to give him leave of absence and stayed with us for several months.

Bill Davidson, another member of the group with a scientific background, had 'dropped in' to see Kerstin, an old friend, and had fallen victim to the theatre's fatal attraction. The theatre's attraction? But there wasn't a theatre, there weren't even any rehearsals yet. A rather dingy upstairs room in a small town's Conservative Club cannot, in itself, exert any attraction, nor can a motley collection of young people making strange noises at each other or working their laborious way through inexpertly executed dancing exercises. The fascination, I suspect, lay in the atmosphere of continuous excitement and relish which invested the meanest task with significance. The idea, the dream, the vision of a new kind of theatre, or rather of a theatre which saw itself as the heir to all the great theatres of the past, was so palpable that you felt you could use it as a hammer, a drill, a chisel, a knife with a blade for every occasion. I had dreamed of living and working like this ever since I had learned to articulate my desires.

So when Bill Davidson, bound for a climbing holiday in Skye, decided to pay us a visit, he found us in the throes of trying to build a lightweight revolving stage for a production of our adaptation of Moliere's *Flying Doctor*. The revolve had to be sturdy enough to support a functional door and window and its acting area sufficiently firm for four or five actors to cavort upon it without its creaking or obscuring the actor's lines. It must, moreover, be a structure which could be assembled and disassembled in a matter of four or five minutes. Bill found the problem intriguing and set about solving it. He didn't get to Skye. He stayed with us for the next three years and played an important part in the early history of Theatre Workshop.

Serious work began the day after we arrived in Kendal. The working day began at nine o'clock and for the first week or two we concentrated on training and building lighting and sound equipment. The training sessions occupied most of the mornings, starting with an hour's movement session followed by voice production. We would spend the rest of the morning on acting exercises culled from Stanislavski's *An Actor Prepares*. After lunch, which we generally ate at the local British Restaurant, there would be lectures, discussions and more exercises.

We were in the British Restaurant eating a stodgy meal of steak-and-kidney pie when we first read about the bombing of Hiroshima. We were too engrossed in our theatre talk to give it full attention. It wasn't until later in the day that we began to realise the full significance of the event. A few days later the Smythe report was published and, after reading it, Smithy and Bill Davidson suggested that I should make it the basis of a documentary play. I knew nothing about physics or, indeed, about science in general. I had some vague notion about the air being made up of oxygen and nitrogen and that litmus-paper could be made to change colour by exposing it to . . . to what? And *I* should write a play about Hiroshima?!

They insisted. They would tutor me. They would guide me stage by stage through the entire history of atomic science. And they did. They provided me with books, they talked and lectured me by the hour and explained new and difficult concepts. Most important of all, they fired me with their enthusiasm and when that enthusiasm reached fever pitch I sat down and wrote *Uranium 235,* a documentary on the history of atomic science from Democritus to Einstein.[2]

After a couple of weeks our all-day-and-every-day training programme gave way to one which combined training with rehearsals. During this period all our doubts and worries about the future were put aside. We were living in a fury of excitement and optimism. This is not to say that there were no problems. There were countless problems but we felt capable of solving them. The outstanding problem at that moment was to weld this motley assembly of ill-assorted individuals into a compact group of creative artists each of whom would be capable of realising his or her full potential when called upon to do so and who would, at the same time, complement every other member of the group. A tall order. But we were bursting with energy and our confidence was unbounded. And look at the way rehearsals were going! Joan hadn't done any directing since 1939 but inactivity had in no way diminished any of her skills. She still had an inexhaustible store of patience and the ability to coax performances out of actors which were far in excess of their normal level of achievement. She also had the painter's eye, an instinct for colour and composition. These qualities she had always possessed in abundance but now they were being manipulated with a much surer touch and by the time opening night arrived *The Flying Doctor* and *Johnny Noble* were in very good shape indeed.[3]

For us it was an historic occasion. For the Kendal audience it was . . . well, bewildering. *Johnny Noble* had been billed as A BALLAD-OPERA and the audience was apparently expecting something like *The Maid of the Mountains* or *The Merry Widow*. Instead they saw barefoot actors singing a *cappella* about things like fascism, war and unemployment. And where were the sets, the apple-blossom, the stile where lovers sing duets? They were no less confused by *The Flying Doctor,* a *commedia dell 'arte* type production in which a company of bawdy grotesques played havoc with a respectable audience's sense of decorum.

We played those three nights at the St George's Theatre, Kendal, to half-empty houses made up almost entirely of middle-class people. 'Never mind', we consoled ourselves, 'it'll be different when we get out on tour.'

Our first tour was to be a local one, of places within a fifty-mile radius of Kendal. At that time we were convinced that we could win a place in the hearts and minds of the local population. The months that followed were to disabuse us of that notion. Several of the venues chosen for the tour were villages which would have found it difficult to yield enough audience to fill the hall for a single night let alone for the week we had been booked to play there. Moreover, most of the places lacked basic stage facilities and some even lacked stages altogether. We were disappointed but we still managed to joke about it. After all, we were just running the show in. There was plenty of time.

The names of those places are like scars on the memory: Staveley, Windermere, Kirkby Stephen, Keswick, Grange-over-Sands . . . the Victoria Hall, Grange-over-Sands, where we had been booked to play for six nights with two matinees thrown in for good measure! This was a not-so-popular resort in the off-season (did it have an on season?). I recall having to suppress an almost irresistible desire to laugh hysterically at first sight of that faded Edwardian auditorium where we hoped to revolutionise the British theatre. On most nights of our short (but not short enough) run, the actors outnumbered the audience. In *Johnny Noble* I had to make an entrance from the back of the hall and I remember so clearly the feeling of embarrassment which overcame me every night at the thought of disturbing the slumbers of those nice old ladies who had been lured out of their boarding-houses at the thought of being cheered by a performance of *Merrie England* or *The Bohemian Girl.*

And yet we weren't daunted in any way. I think we had all seen too many Hollywood backstage-theatre films in which the gallant hoofers/songsters are rescued at the last moment from penury and eviction. Cut to long-shot of theatre interior where a well-dressed audience are on their feet applauding the gallant – and now successful – hoofers/songsters. I still find it difficult to understand how we managed to delude ourselves so completely. Surely we hadn't scraped and struggled all this long time merely to be accepted by the establishment we despised! We were committed to the task of building a workers' theatre, so why bother about being 'discovered'? In any case, who was going to discover a small, unknown company playing in a village school-hall in Kirkby Stephen? I don't think any of us asked these questions at the time. We were too busy travelling, rigging and de-rigging stages, playing to empty houses and planning the next production.

Yes, in spite of the fact that we had failed to make any real impact and were almost penniless, we were actually preparing to embark on another production.

And what a production! Ever since the publication of *The Lament on the Death of a Bullfighter* in the late thirties, Joan and I had been enamoured of Garcia Lorca, and now were were going to produce his exquisite short surrealistic play *The Love of Don Perlimplin for Belisa in Her Garden*. It would be hard to imagine anything less calculated to restore the fortunes of a failing theatre than this delicate miniature by a poet whose dramatic works were scarcely known to British theatre audiences. It was a play of ambiguities; ostensibly, it dealt with sexual impotence, an old man's fantasies about his young wife and his eventual suicide. In the intellectual climate of the late 1940s the theme was considered to be somewhat shocking and it was made more so by the barely concealed parody of the Catholic mass embodied in the play's structure.

For us, *Don Perlimplin* was an affirmation of our belief in the Art of Theatre – not the profession of theatre but the Art with a capital *A*. 'We have not weakened in our determination to create a thing of power and beauty,' that is what we were saying. It was also a gesture of defiance – we were cocking a snoot at those miserable little halls where there wasn't even a mirror or a wash-basin, at those dreary theatrical digs in Workington and Dewsbury, at the empty seats and the smug culture-vultures' inevitable prologue and epitaph: 'You should have been here last week', or next week or the week after. Never this week. *Don Perlimplin,* 'an erotic alleluya in five scenes' Lorca had called it. It was our way of saying farewell to Salford and Stockwell and the shabby streets in which we had grown up, farewell to austerity and the long grey years of war.

We were playing in Penrith when we held our first reading of *Perlimplin*. We continued to read and discuss it during the next two weeks, constantly discovering new things in it. Back in Kendal we were joined by a young man who had actually stage-managed Lorca's production of *Don Perlimplin* with La Barraca, the Madrid University drama group, in the 1930s. His name was Louis Meana and he was now lecturing in Spanish at Sheffield University. In a series of seminars which continued right up until the dress rehearsal, he opened up the play for us and helped us to reveal the many hidden clues embedded in it.

Only six members of the company actually had acting parts, though the entire company was in the grip of *Perlimplin* fever. The result was a production of extraordinary beauty. Joan had really surpassed herself and so had Ruth Brandes, by creating costumes which would not have been out of place on a Velasquez canvas. And the curtains! Two new set of velvets, one of magnificent cherry red and the other a rich green. How we loved them! For three months we had been working in black drapes and now we were spending our evenings in a cocoon of ravishing hues.

The first night should have been a triumph. Everything was working beautifully, no gaffs, no hitches, no missed cues, no dud lights, no wrong music entrances. And our new, specially engineered semi-circular curtain rails were working like a charm. This is *it,* we told each other. How could anyone fail to fall under the spell of this magical production? Well, the Kendal audience managed it. The curtain went down on a smattering of applause and the audience trooped out avoiding the eyes of those members of the company who had been helping out with front-of-house jobs.

It wasn't unusual, of course, for actors to feel deflated after a first night or, indeed, after any performance which has involved a great expenditure of emotional energy. On such occasions a convivial drink helps, or perhaps a little love-making. Neither of these pleasures was available as none of us could afford to drink and the men and women of the company were in separate digs. In any case, this wasn't the usual post-first night blues. It was at this moment that I first fully realised the enormity of the task we had undertaken. Up until now I had been sustained by a naive notion that excellence was a key which would unlock all doors. Now I saw that this was not the case. Here we had a superbly written short play, a radiant dramatic piece, well acted with moments of real brilliance, magnificently directed and the entire thing a delight to the eyes and ears. Wasn't it? Apparently not.

The following morning showed us how far off the mark we had been in estimating the Kendal audience's capacity to accept new things. Suddenly we had become pariahs, untouchables, moral lepers. People with whom we had become friendly during the last few months now crossed over to the other side of the street when they saw us approaching. Shopkeepers abandoned their professional amiability and served us in silence. Even Ruth, whose impressive upper-class manner and accent was calculated to bring out the lurking servility in the most aggressive northern tradesman, was served with barely concealed disapproval. When Howard Goorney, who had played the role of Perlimplin, turned up at a rehearsal saying that the town was ripe for a lynching, nobody laughed.

During the two or three seasons that *Perlimplin* was in our repertoire, we played it regularly in halls throughout Cumberland, Westmorland, Lancashire, Yorkshire and in Edinburgh and Glasgow. Later we revived it and played it at the Kings Theatre, Hammersmith, and though it never met with the kind of response we felt it deserved, neither did it evoke the kind of hostility that greeted it in Kendal.

What was it about *Don Perlimplin* that made the worthy burgers and burgesses react so violently? What raw nerve did it touch? Were they really shocked at the thought of an impotent old man having sexual fantasies about a young woman's body? Was it, perhaps, Belisa's frank avowal of innocent lust that outraged them? Or was it merely that any public declaration of sexual passion or any mention of sexual deprivation made them nervous? Whatever the reason, it was obvious that our days in Kendal were numbered. So when the company left at the end of the month for another season of touring it was with great relief that we said goodbye to Kendal for the last time.

By now we were beginning to feel like a company. We had been together for some six months and the daily training sessions, the long period of rehearsal, the way we all lived virtually (if not virtuously) in each other's pockets and, of course, the wear-and-tear of touring, had welded us into a closely-knit group.

We had worked hard during those six months and had encountered obstacles and disappointments, but I doubt whether any of us had felt despair. As was to be expected, there were mutual antipathies in the group, but these concerned personal issues unconnected with work or the way work was being done. Wages, which had been the bare minimum at the start, were now reduced to a ridiculously small sum, scarcely enough to pay for lodgings.

The touring policy was what it had been from the start: stands of two to five nights in drill halls, community halls, university general-purpose halls; little theatres and big theatres in the final stages of decay; big, cold empty barns smelling of dust and urine; dressing rooms with broken chairs, disembowelled sofas and sinks in which rust had gouged channels through the blotched porcelain. Wartime economy measures still prevailed and most of these dreadful mausolea were unheated. It was hardly surprising if audiences stayed away – and stay away they did, in great numbers. This is not to say that *nobody* turned up except us – there were always a few hardy souls and sometimes (particularly in little theatres like the Newcastle People's Theatre) we played to full houses, that is to 200 or 300 people. In others, like the Community Theatre, Blackburn, we faced an audience of two-dozen hardy Lancashire folk most of whom had had the foresight to come equipped with hot-water bottles.

Cold was a real problem for us. We were ill-fed, ill-clothed and overworked. That third tour seemed to go on forever and the winter seemed endless too. Stations of the cross: a seaside boarding-house in Whitley Bay in February, where we were so cold that we made a fire of the plastic ashtrays in an effort to warm ourselves; Blyth, where we played *Don Perlimplin* with snow falling onto the stage through a hole in the roof of the Miners Hall; and Liverpool, the David Lewis Theatre, with fog drifting onto the stage and the cold lying in wait in the wings, ready to grasp you in its clammy embrace. Oh Jesus, can the grave be any colder than a cold empty theatre?

Although our optimism was boundless, the last few months of 1946 dealt some hard blows to our illusions and by the beginning of 1947 we began to realise that we were engaged in a war of attrition with a machine that wasn't even aware of our existence. If our ideas were to survive . . . survive, survival. That was the issue now: survival. And we had to be prepared to fight tooth and nail. So we packed and unpacked our gear, rigged and de-rigged stages, and we waited for slow trains on bleak railway platforms in Liverpool, Dewsbury, Newcastle-upon-Tyne, Bury, Whitehaven, Blyth. And sometime in the middle of all this coming and going, Joan and I found time to get divorced.

At Middlesborough a miracle occurs, a real 100-per-cent miracle. It is performed by a woman who is mopping a large area of floor in St John's Hall where we are to play that night. She silently continues to mop as we unload and proceed to rig the stage. We identify with her as one of the world's toilers and call her 'luv' and 'ducks'. Only when we ask her the way to the nearest chip-shop does she appear flustered. Chippies are apparently outside her experience.

She is waiting for us when we finish the rig. Transport, she tells us, is laid on and waiting. Have we heard correctly? Not the words, but the accent. It's pure Ruth, but even more so, a Girton-trained Mrs Mopp! You learn something new every day. And yes, transport *has* been laid on. It is a dark night and we are tired from our labours, so we pile into the three waiting cars. We are so tired that it takes several minutes for us to notice that we are travelling in a Rolls-Royce. Then someone else points out that we are being driven by a uniformed chauffeur. The mystery deepens as we are eventually halted by a pair of enormous ornamental iron gates which gradually open for us. We sail through them, bowing to our imaginary subjects. The headlights show a road running through fields bordered by trees. We make jokes about being capitalists but most of us are overawed. We round a bend and there is the house. 'Jesus, we've fallen on our feet.' We alight as the two other cars draw up behind us. We follow Mrs Mopp up the stone steps. 'What the hell are we doing here?' someone murmurs. After a hot meal, served in the kitchen (which is about the size of most of the halls we have been playing in) we are shown to our rooms.

I am almost asleep when there is a tapping at the door and Howard sidles into the room. 'Tell me I'm not dreaming.'

'Why? What's happened?'

'This', says he, with a gesture which includes the entire universe, 'all this. I don't believe it. And that woman, the charlady . . . who is she?'

'I dunno. Does it matter?'

'No, but it's strange. It's not on. One night we're in a place smelling like an old chip-shop and the next were in this place. Just look at it! You should see my bedroom. It's three times the size of this. Incredible!'

'This was Dean Swift's room. That bookcase is full of his books.'

The following morning we are fed and shown round the establishment by the Colonel and his Lady. In the course of the inspection we are told, quite casually, that we can stay here if we like, for as long as we like. If we like! A large, restoration mansion surrounded by lush parklands; a private wing with its own bedrooms, kitchens, refectory, laundry, workrooms and a rehearsal room situated above Georgian stables which look as if they had been designed as a film set for *Romeo and Juliet*. For six months we have been without a home, without a place to store our gear or rehearse the next production, not even a cubbyhole to which correspondence could be addressed. Now from the ridiculous to the sublime.

Two days later, with a home to return to, we take to the road again feeling completely rejuvenated. The full-length *Uranium* is running smoothly, though scenes are constantly being rewritten and new scenes added. Increasingly, actors and actresses from the outside world drop in on us and after seeing a performance they appear backstage to sing our praises. 'Marvellous. An absolutely superb piece of theatre. Never seen anything like it. Tremendous.' Then they add, 'Miles above the audience' head, of course. Should be in London.'

Were they right? Was *Uranium* such a difficult play? Was the style too foreign?

Was it really above the head of working-class 'provincials'? We were about to be given the chance of finding out. Scarcely a fortnight after we had moved into our new premises at Ormesby Hall, we opened for a week at Butlin's Holiday Camp at Filey, on the Yorkshire coast. We joked a lot among ourselves about the place, pretending that we were prisoners and the redcoats were screws. 'Buchenwald in gay colours,' said Howard. For all that, we were nervous about the whole thing. It is one thing to pontificate about the dramatic appeal of our kind of theatre but it is a completely different thing to face an audience which is more attuned to cabaret, bingo and other forms of popular entertainment. A new ballroom, advertised as 'the biggest in Europe', was scheduled to open at the same time as our second performance. We would also be competing with an all-in-wrestling show.

Our 'theatre' was a huge tent, which was a bonus as far as we were concerned as the more we could escape from the formal theatre set-up the happier we were. We opened at three in the afternoon to a packed house of mums and dads and their children, as typical an audience of northern working men and women as you could find. They treated the play as they would have treated an exciting game of football. They cheered, groaned, shouted their approval, and when one of the actors tried to make a planned interruption from the auditorium they howled him down. After the second performance the wrestling show had to be closed down through lack of spectators and each of our performances was greeted with the same kind of enthusiasm. Even the wrestlers came to see the show.

It was a triumph and a complete vindication of everything we had said about the theatre. A working-class audience could be won for a theatre which concerned itself with the social and political problems of our time; furthermore, such an audience would accept any kind of experiment provided that what was being said continued to ring out loud and clear. In actual fact, what was regarded as wildly experimental by theatre buffs and representatives of the theatre establishment was accepted by our Butlin's audience as a perfectly sensible way of doing things. They were the radio and film generation. It is unlikely that more than a handful of them had ever been in a theatre before, so why should they miss the French windows, the Tudor fireplace and the furnishings by Waring and Gillow?

'Ah, that wonderful bare stage!' enthused our theatre friends. But it wasn't bare to our audience. We had credited them with having imaginations as vivid as our own and if there were moments when they regretted the absence of 'real' sets and stage furniture, there were other things to stimulate the imagination, such as the amplified sound of machines, passing cars, railway trains, explosions, whispering voices, announcements of news items – things all calculated to thrust our stage into the world beyond the theatre. Following a performance of *Johnny Noble* on a *bare* stage in Glasgow, a hundred or so schoolchildren were asked to write an essay on what they had seen. Almost without exception, they described, in great detail, the streets in which they themselves lived. A similar response was made by children in South Wales and County Durham.

The reaction of that Butlin's holiday camp audience was reassuring and company morale was high. Suddenly the future looked rosy again. Now we really were on the verge of breaking through. Through to where? The West End? No, to an audience, the kind of audience about whom we had talked and fantasised ever since we had first embarked on this mad adventure. An audience, that was all we craved. Give us such an audience and all our needs would be satisfied.

We finished the tour and returned to our estate at Ormesby to replenish our energy and prepare for the next touring stint, which was to begin in mid-September. In the meantime, there was a great deal of work to be done and somehow money had to be raised. Our success at Butlin's and the fact that the national press was beginning to note our existence didn't mean that life had become any easier. We were still in our customary state of near-bankruptcy and when we weren't writing passionate appeals for help to the Arts Council we were cudgelling our brains for schemes which would earn us money to mount a new production or, at least, buy a new 500-watt spotlight. The Arts Council was either deaf or establishment-plus. The latter, I suspect. Over the years, no rich heiress was ever courted so assiduously as we courted the Arts Council. We fawned, we beseeched, we petitioned, we pleaded, we crawled on our knees, not for thousands of pounds but for a few hundred to tide us over until things got better. And the individual to whom you are making the appeal suddenly gets that slightly preoccupied look, that sudden glazing of the eyes which can be interpreted as a desire to be some place other than the place he is in at the moment. But Geoffrey or Tony or Robin or Michael (or whatever the name of the official person happens to be) is always polite and nearly always charming, so he allows you to come to the end of the sentence before telling you, with a sigh, that there's no money. 'The kitty, old chap, is absolutely empty.'

'But what about the opera companies and the ballets and the subsidised shows in the West End?'

'Ah well. They are rather different.'

'In what way?'

'If the decision was just up to me, I would willingly give you what you need. But I'm not really empowered to . . . I'm really just a kind of glorified messenger boy, old chap, a tool in the hands of the higher-ups and I'm terribly sorry but I must rush off. I'm twenty minutes late for an appointment with Larry.' So back to Ormesby, seething with anger.

In the days when touring had been part of our collective fantasy, we had envisaged the periods between tours as long stretches of time given over to intensive training and rehearsals. I had vaguely imagined that we would function as a kind of revolutionary collective crossed with a mediaeval-type university where artists and philosophers would cross-pollinate each other's views on the nature of things. Ormesby wasn't quite like that, though we did manage to train fairly consistently for three or four hours each day. We also organised a couple of weekend schools and a fortnight's summer school, all of which were highly successful. When I wasn't rehearsing or taking acting classes, I spent my time working on a very free adaptation of Aristophanes' *Lysistrata*. In between these various activities, we made forays down to Manchester and London for movement and voice training.

Our voice teacher, Nelson Illingworth, had heard reports of our work from friends and became interested enough to travel to Liverpool where we were performing. He liked what he saw and offered to give us free tuition in voice production. We leapt at the offer. We had heard glowing reports about him ever since he had set up his Thames-side studio in the thirties.

He was a strange-looking man, immensely tall and cadaverous. His naturally melancholy expression was given extra emphasis by the myriad of tiny wrinkles which made the skin of his face look like the cracked mud-bed of a dried-up river. When he took off his shirt to show us the muscles of his diaphragm, one saw that the wrinkles extended down to his navel, making him look like a shell-less tortoise. He lived in a house on the river at Staines and when he wasn't teaching voice or talking about voice, he lay in a coffin and read Sir Thomas Browne on *Urn Burial*. As a voice teacher, he had no rivals.

Our movement teacher, too, was in my opinion the best that could be found anywhere. His name was Rudolph Laban and I had been hearing about his theories ever since the early thirties. In Europe they called him 'the dance prophet'. He had blazed across the firmament of the dance world like a comet bringing light where there had been darkness. A refugee from Nazi Germany, he had settled in Manchester where two of his ex-students had opened a dance studio. When we were invited to take part in an open day's movement-training session, we could scarcely believe our good fortune. Ever since *Newsboy*, we had been conscious of a crippling need for movement training and we talked longingly of a theatre where the actors could handle their bodies like trained dancers or athletes; and now we were going to meet *the man* who could make it all possible. We went to the session and Laban, after a brief conversation, promised to come and see us perform the following week at Bolton. As a result of that visit, he undertook to train us whenever we were free and in the area. It was a magnificent offer, so during the summer break we made our way down to Manchester where Laban and his personal assistant, Jean Newlove, introduced us to a new world of movement. When we returned to Ormesby, it was with the understanding that Jean would visit us once a week and continue to train us. She turned out to be a magnificent teacher, serious but good-natured, full of ideas and quick to recognise the unique character of Theatre Workshop. Under her tutelage, the dormant capabilities of the actors in the group underwent a complete transformation and it wasn't long before our part time tutor fell under the spell of the theatre and joined us. And it wasn't long before I fell under the spell of our dance teacher and married her.

In many ways, we were living a very privileged existence. We were doing work which satisfied us, we had instructors who were leaders in their chosen fields and we were living in a beautiful place in beautiful surroundings. Yes, we lacked money and our diet was a little monotonous, but that was a small price to pay for the privilege of living in Utopia. Well, not exactly Utopia, since that place is incomplete without perfect inhabitants and we were far from perfect. We were young, industrious, confident in our own ability to overcome most obstacles, tenacious, single-minded, capable of sacrifice. We were also rather stiff-necked, intolerant of those whose ideas on theatre ran counter to our own. And we were impetuous, lusty, ever ready for sexual encounters. The tensions and cross-currents that one finds in any group of people who are forced by circumstances to spend almost all their waking hours in each other's company tends to blur the image of Utopia. There were moments when we became exasperated with each other, when sheer physical exhaustion made us quarrelsome, when all other feelings were swallowed up in a great wave of resentment and irritation. And then there were the mutual antipathies around which everyone had to tread very carefully and which would occasionally erupt in sudden bursts of angry abuse.

For a surprisingly long time there were no disagreements on matters of theatre policy and no one seemed to have any doubts whatsoever about our theatrical base. Perhaps organised discussion might have revealed such doubts but at the time all our discussions centred upon productions in progress and on attempts to work out a plan for survival. When you are faced with the urgent task of raising eighty or ninety pounds to buy materials for new costumes or the thirty-five pounds needed for spotlight bulbs, the discussion of ultimate aims and objectives seems irrelevant. And yet, subsequent developments have, in my opinion, shown that our failure to initiate such discussion was, to a large extent, responsible for the ultimate failure (or for what *I* regard as failure) of Theatre Workshop. Success is surely determined by how close you come to achieving aims which you have set yourself. If the objectives are not clearly defined, then there can be no success.

We had defined certain of our aims in the pre-war period of Theatre Union and some of us who went back that far assumed that those aims had not changed. We still believed in the necessity and the possibility of creating a popular theatre with a broad working-class base. In order to achieve this objective it was necessary, as a first stage, to build a company of actors who would train together and whose training would encompass singing and dancing as well as acting. Such a theatre would take all that was best from the theatres of the past and at the same time would create a new repertoire incorporating all the new theatrical forms which were expected to evolve in the course of our work. An ambitious programme!

Well, were we not in the process of achieving it? Our actors could already move better than most actors in the commercial theatre and Laban and Newlove would soon have us dancing and expressing the most subtle shades of feelings with our bodies. And surely the new plays in our repertoire were fulfilling part of our programme. The working-class base was much harder to achieve but our Butlin's experience had proved that it could be done. Workers would respond to our kind of theatre providing that we could find ways of persuading them to come in and see us in the first place.

I think that only five or six of us had a clear notion of the company's ultimate objective and of that number maybe half were philosophically equipped to meet whatever contingencies might arise. Almost everyone was imbued with a genuine desire to work in and for a better theatre and though not everyone shared the same Marxist vision there was enough good will around to make its realisation a feasible proposition. Good will, of course, is not an adequate substitute for political understanding. And so, almost imperceptibly, the objectives changed. There was less and less talk of a revolutionary theatre and more and more talk of being discovered and transported on a magic carpet to the never-never land of board-treading, greasepaint-smelling success.

During the next three years we continued to pursue the chimera of the 'break-through', the quest for the discoverer. 'Who's out front tonight?' became a regular dressing-room quip and rumours of influential visitors were an important feature of every performance. There was no limit to the number of important, and very important, and very, very, very important people who were coming to see us in Bury, Bolton, Dewsbury, Gateshead, Blyth, Leeds, Workington, Grange-over-Sands, Windermere and Darlington. All kinds of big shots, Binky's emissaries, West End managers with contracts in their pockets, provincial theatre owners with leases in their pigskin briefcases, Hollywood talent-scouts with dollars and Arts Councillors with subsidies. Ghosts that never materialised.

Touring was getting harder; or perhaps we were getting less able to cope. In addition to *Johnny Noble* and *The Flying Doctor, Don Perlimplin* and *Uranium 235,* our repertoire now included *The Proposal* by Chekhov, *Operation Olive Branch* (my free adaptation of *The Lysistrata*), *The Other Animals* (my most ambitious work to date) and *The Gentle People,* by Irwin Shaw.

Our touring venues were changing, too. We were still playing at the Masonic Hall in Kirkby Stephen and the Victoria Hall in Grange-over-Sands but these and similar venues now alternated with small or decayed theatres and pier pavilions. Audiences were still thin, though there were occasional successes at places like the Library Theatre, Manchester, and short seasons playing at Edinburgh during the festival. We were not part of the official festival, of course, but we were officially part of the unofficial People's Festival, a phenomenon which in later years evolved (or devolved) into The Fringe.

There were also rather grand tours of Western Germany, Czechoslovakia and Sweden. These were not only good for the company finances but they gave much-needed sustenance to our battered ego. The Swedish tours, in particular, were immensely rewarding, for not only were we playing to packed houses in superbly equipped theatres but we were meeting writers, painters and actors who treated us as serious artists. It was an unfamiliar experience. Back home, the praise of our actor friends was generally mixed with condescension and pity while professional reviewers tended to be suspicious of anyone daring to voice unpopular ideas, or indeed any ideas at all. The Swedish critics, on the other hand, were prepared to welcome new ideas and if they didn't always agree with them they were prepared to deal with them with understanding.

It was always with a deep sense of letdown that we returned to touring in Britain. We missed the splendid facilities of the continental theatres, the cleanliness, the dressing rooms with hot water and adequately lit mirrors where you could make up without going blind, the stages where you weren't in danger of freezing in winter and suffocating in summer. Back home in the land of Shakespeare and Ben Jonson we were used to theatres where the mirrors were so fly-specked that anyone looking into them appeared to have contracted smallpox. And there were the halls where the caretaker followed your every move during the rig to see that you didn't drive any screws into his precious platform. And there were the places where there were no dressing rooms at all and no mirrors, no washbasins and where the toilet wouldn't flush . . . the moribund theatres where the stage smelled of urine and the dressing rooms of mice and the streets around smelled of poverty and defeat.

Worse than any of these things were the hiatuses caused by a tour being discontinued for lack of money or because a little-theatre manager couldn't be persuaded to let his crumbling ruin to an outfit with no reputation. 'But we have a reputation. We've just come back from Czechoslovakia and Sweden.'

'That doesn't cut any ice around here. Now if you'd done well at Doncaster . . .'

At such times we would all make our way as best we could to Manchester or Glasgow, each of which, in turn, became our base after we left Ormesby. These were desperate times. We had no money and little prospect of earning any. No one, however, suggested disbanding the theatre. We were still determined to go on, though from time to time we would question our touring policy. It wasn't touring as such that was being criticised but the kind of touring we were doing, or rather the kind of venues provided by the tours. Out-of-season bookings at the Grand Theatre, Llandudno, The White Rock Pavilion, Hastings, and Alexandra Gardens, Weymouth, couldn't be expected to yield the same kind of success as Butlin's or Stockholm and Prague. In point of fact, they were disastrous and it was after such a tour in March 1950 that the company decided to temporarily disband itself, for it was now obvious to everyone that it was no longer possible to continue with this kind of touring. From now on, we would avoid bookings in dilapidated theatres and play in more modest places situated in the heart of working-class communities. Moreover, we would limit ourselves to one-night stands.

The interregnum lasted for four months, almost up until the birth of my son Hamish. This event seems to have banished all other activities at that time from my memory. I know that I wrote a political thriller called *The Travellers* but I cannot remember any of the circumstances involved in writing it. And it was probably around this time that Hugh MacDiarmid and I discussed the possibility of collaborating on a Scots play about Macbeth.

20

On the Road

When the company reassembled in Manchester we immediately began rehearsing *Uranium 235* for a one-night stand tour of South Wales. It was an ideal play for such a tour as it called for neither solid settings nor elaborate costumes. We had devised a fairly flexible curtain-rig and, since we carried our own switchboard and lighting units, we felt ready for any contingencies. We needed to be, for this was all to be very different from the kind of touring to which we had become accustomed.

We had acquired an old ex-GPO service-truck and equipped it with the shell of a jettisoned furniture-removal van. It was to carry our switchboards, lighting paraphernalia, curtains and costume-skips and us, the company. It was cold, draughty, crowded and uncomfortable, but it carried us and rarely broke down more than two or three times a day. On our previous tours we generally had a whole day to spend on the rig and lighting rehearsal, sometimes we even had the assistance (albeit reluctant) of resident stage-hands. But that was in the past. Now we were playing in halls which hadn't been built to accommodate theatrical performances. They lacked height and adequate wing space and some of them, like the Methodist chapels, didn't even possess a stage. It took ingenuity and brute strength to overcome many of the problems.

The majority of the halls were Miners' Welfare Clubs situated up two or three flights of stairs, up which our effects had to be manhandled before the day's work could begin. Everyone had their particular tasks and the work of the riggers would sometimes continue to within an hour of the opening of the show and then they would change their costumes and become actors. And when did we eat? Whenever we could and whatever we could find: hot pies consumed up ladders, seated on skips, grabbed between changing from one costume to another . . .

'Stand by, beginners!' Forget the rig, the dirt, the cold; they are all irrelevant. There is only one problem now and that is to make your body and mind remember all those crystallised moments of truth you discovered at rehearsal, to portray the inner life of a human spirit, to live the role or roles. Difficult enough if you are actually on the stage, but if your role is that of a narrator standing in front of the proscenium arch in a harsh spotlight, then it is virtually impossible. Oh, Christ! How many are in the house? Standing there you can see every empty seat. Your narration is supposed to add a heroic element to the show, but how the hell do you convey heroic sentiments to a multitude of fifteen people? Why do we do it? *Why* in the name of God aren't we sitting in a cinema or a pub with friends who work at sensible jobs?

And Joan would be out front with her notebook recording missed cues, late entrances, gabbled lines, over-acting, falseness and dullness. When the curtain came down and the audience had departed she would read her notes to us as we changed out of our costumes. A missed cue or a late entrance earned you a slap on the wrist, so to speak; falseness, particularly when it had been carried over from a previous performance, earned you a tongue-lashing which left you shaking.

Then the de-rig would begin. Costumes had to be checked, folded and packed into their appropriate skips, curtains taken down, shaken, folded and packed away. There were spots and floods to be de-bulbed and crated, lighting cable to be coiled and tied. Then, when all this has been done to the satisfaction of the stage-manager, we manhandle it down the stairs and into the truck. There is no singing, no excited conversation. We pile into the truck and huddle down among the boxes and crates as the worn-out vehicle wheezes its way through the midnight streets of Rhymney, Bargoed, Treherbert or Tonypandy, taking us to our digs and, hopefully, a bowl of soup or stew or sausage-and-mash. Fleur-de-Lis, Ystrad-Mynach, Brithdir, Deri, Aberdare, Cwmamman, Wattstown. Sixteen one-night stands in sixteen days. Sixteen loadings and unloadings. Sixteen rigs and de-rigs and sixteen attempts to act with truth and skill and passion in the face of exhaustion.

And did audiences match our expectations? After all, we were now working in the kind of solidly working-class environment some of us had longed for. But people didn't come. In one or two places we had full houses, but for the most part we were still playing to half-empty halls in which women and children outnumbered men by five or six to one. When we asked the reason for this, we were informed that in the valleys theatre-going was not regarded as a manly pastime. So men sent their wives and children along while they themselves spent the evening in the club, the Miners' Welfare. Even when our performances were actually taking place inside the club premises they tended to avoid us. Those who did come were very enthusiastic indeed about the shows. One particular performance sticks in my mind. It was in the chapel at Treherbert, a smallish hall but full, and we had given a good performance. Even Joan was satisfied. Our curtain call was greeted with a light smattering of applause and then, in silence, the audience trooped out into the night. We were puzzled. We knew the show had been good. What had offended them? Then there came a rather tentative knock on the changing room door. When we opened it, we found the entire audience gathered outside. One of them stepped forward and thanked us, upon which the rest of them broke into enthusiastic applause. Dazed, we asked why there had been so little applause *inside* the hall. 'It wouldn't have been right. Your drama, it was like a sermon. And you don't applaud a sermon.'

The tour finished on 15 December 1950, and now we had a clear month to rehearse a new show for our second South Wales tour, due to begin on 8 January in Cwmamman. We needed another show which could be played in black drapes, so I sat down and wrote *Landscape With Chimneys,* a loosely constructed episodic play with songs. We rehearsed it over Christmas and New Year and were back in South Wales in time for the tour.

It was a miserable trip. The roads were icy and by mid-afternoon, those of us cowering in the back of the van among the skips and crates had been reduced to a frozen, numbed silence. Then fog descended and after crawling for an hour or more, our truck shuddered to a halt and refused to start again. We were too cold, too demoralised, to complain or even swear. 'Everybody assemble in Cwmamman tomorrow. Half past nine.' We split up and hitched to Shrewsbury, the nearest town. It wasn't easy getting lifts that night. The verges on both sides of the road were filled with trucks and cars which had skidded off the road and those that were still moving weren't inclined to stop for a bunch of benighted pedestrians.

Shrewsbury wasn't welcoming. We searched for almost an hour before we found a place where we could get a hot cup of tea without buying a meal. It was a small private hotel kept by a Dublin woman who took pity on the five frozen refugees who stood at her door. She told us to wait in the lounge. 'You'll find some queer birds in there', she said, 'but it's warm.' It was. The *queer birds* seemed at first to be quite ordinary people, middle-aged men and women, with the women outnumbering the men by three-to-one. There was lots of tweed, gay woollen jumpers and cardigans, costume jewellery, rings, necklaces, chokers, ear-rings, flamboyant bracelets and perfume. The air was heavy with perfume. In most hotel lounges, private or otherwise, silence appears to be the rule. This lot, however, were very animated and didn't stop talking for a moment during all the time we were there. Our benefactress didn't only serve us with tea and toast but arranged a lift for us with a truck-driver who was bound for South Wales. Before we left, we asked her about the people in the lounge.

'They're ghouls,' said she. 'They travel from all over the country to towns where there's going to be a hanging and they find out where the hangman'll be staying and they book in there so as to be near him. A poor soul's going to be hanged here tomorrow. That's why they're here. Did you every hear of such a sick thing?'

Our lift was in an empty five-ton truck. The fog had cleared and it was freezing hard once again. We lay on the metal floor under a tarpaulin and bounced our way to Cwmamman. It was a wild ride, but we were too cold to care, too tired.

If the first tour had been hard, the second was brutal. Winter had suddenly swooped down on the valleys bringing ice and snow and east winds which hurled themselves at you like mad dogs. It was painful to handle the steel frames of the switchboards and we crouched in the back of our repair truck as if to present as little surface as possible to the cold. We were determined that people should know about us, so we sold tickets from door-to-door like pedlars selling bootlaces. We made our way into pithead canteens and talked with miners as they came off their shifts. We tried to sell tickets to chip-shop customers, to drinkers in pubs and to miners in the Welfares. Just how effective these tactics were is difficult to say. Audiences were certainly larger than on the previous tour. On average I would guess that the halls we played in were about two-thirds full, or possibly a little more than that, and there were many more men than on the first tour.

The weather, the inadequate diet, insufficient sleep and the massive expend-iture of energy, were beginning to leave their mark on the company and before we were halfway through the tour, three members of the group were suffering from bronchitis. Influenza seemed to have found a permanent home among us. Then we met David Thomas. There were many in South Wales who regarded Doc Thomas, as he was known throughout the coalfield, as a doctor of genius. He loved the practice of medicine with a consuming passion that was almost equal to his love of the people of the valley. He was indefatigable in his battle with disease and sickness and eloquent in his defense of the people he served. A dozen times a day we saw him racing along the valleys in his Land Rover like some mediaeval knight racing to do battle with the giant or dragon threatening his patients.

The first time we met him was on the road to Hirwaun. Our truck had refused yet another incline and we were pushing it and cursing at every step we took. He stopped the Land Rover behind us and gave us the benefit of his broad shoulders. He was a short, solidly built man – rock-like is the adjective which springs to mind – and he had a rather hoarse voice. At the top of the hill we introduced ourselves and that night he came to the show, staying afterwards to watch us de-rig. He had a doctor's eye and he took me aside: 'How long do you think you can all go on like this?'

The following day he turned up during the rig and examined the three or four sick members of the company. He returned again just before the perform-ance and administered antibiotics to the sick and massive injections of vitamin B-1 to the rest of the company. Thereafter, for the rest of the tour, he was there every night with his medicines and vitamins, our sword and buckler against exhaustion, cold, hunger and overwork.

Once, on the occasion of a night off, he took me with him on his rounds. We visited an old miner who was dying of cancer. Old? He was in his early forties. His family had brought his bed downstairs where it was warmer and he lay there waiting for his long shift to end. There was a dim light in the room and Doc Thomas turned it up for a moment and I saw it, the exfoliating cancer growing out of the man's neck like a monstrous red-cabbage. Pain sliced through me from my chest to my testicles and for a moment I thought I was about to faint.

The man was in terrible pain but he was articulate and patient. Doc Thomas ministered to him, giving him the most intimate and personal care, talking to him as to a brother-in-arms. Outside, in the street, I asked David whether there was no way of alleviating the man's agony. 'I could give him drugs', he said, 'and he would feel nothing. But he has refused them. He wants his family to remember him as a man rather than as a vegetable. That's all he's got left to give them – his courage.' That man has stayed with me down through the years. I would even say he has given me courage.

Those two long tours of the Welsh valleys were hard work but they won us a loyal audience, and when we returned for a third tour later in the year we had full houses almost everywhere. In the Durham and Scottish coalfields we had similar experiences. Unfortunately, the increase in the number of people who came to see us made little difference to the company finances. We lived on the brink of disaster. There was still no possibility of paying anyone a decent wage, no money to mount fresh productions, no money for publicity and, as far as we could see, there was no way that things were going to change. It was an automatic ritual to apply to the Arts Council for help, and the refusals were equally automatic. We were like beggars who continue to ask for alms in an empty street.

A tour of Norway and Sweden was a tremendous *succes d'estime* and it gave us all a month of good feeding and comfortable digs, but afterwards we resumed our penurious existence. Oh, there were (from time to time) triumphs in Britain too, like the People's Festival performances in Edinburgh when audiences found their way to us in spite of the lack of publicity and cheered themselves hoarse at the end of *Johnny Noble, Uranium 235, The Flying Doctor, The Other Animals* and *The Travellers*.[1] There were other successes, too, but they were sporadic occurrences and their alleviating effect on our conditions was only temporary. Our work and our lives, at this stage, lacked continuity. Only the one-night stands of the coalfields had any continuity, but the wear-and-tear on the members of the company was such that it would have been impossible to continue such work for more than a few weeks at a time. Furthermore, such tours made training impossible; almost every minute of the working day was taken up with travelling, rigging, performing and de-rigging. And yet without training, how could we improve, how could we fulfil our aims?

Short runs of two or three weeks at the Library Theatre, Manchester, or St Andrews Hall, Glasgow, were the kind of bookings which left us time for training, but they were few and far between and they were generally followed by blank periods during which we would, in desperation, mount shortened adaptations of *Twelfth Night, As You Like It* and *Henry IV* for schools presentations in Glasgow, County Durham and Manchester. In between we rehearsed whichever show, currently in the repertoire, needed refurbishing.

It was while we were rehearsing *Uranium* in Manchester that we came nearest to being actually discovered. Sam Wanamaker, an American actor who had fallen foul of McCarthy's witch-hunters and who had since been working in Britain, was on tour in an Odets play, *The Big Knife*. He dropped in on our rehearsal and left in a state of high excitement. He returned the next day and brought Michael Redgrave with him. The rehearsal was in progress when they arrived and they sat huddled in their overcoats for the next two hours trying to ignore the cold and the damp running down the walls. Like almost all our rehearsal rooms, it was a cheerless, miserable place with the kind of lighting that gave you the feeling that fog had crept under the door and was slowly filling the room. A stage area had been chalked out on the floor and we were wearing our ordinary working clothes (our only clothes, for most of us). None of these things appeared to worry our visitors. They sat there for the entire rehearsal without once uttering a word, their whole attention centred on that chalked-out space.

At the end of the rehearsal, they talked. Sam was wildly enthusiastic and said it was the best goddamned show he'd seen since the Federal Theatre's production of Mark Blitzstein's *The Cradle Will Rock*. It was imperative that we appear in London. They went on to promise that they would personally see to it that we got a London showing. Obviously we enjoyed the praise; everyone likes to be praised for work well done. But as for a London showing . . . we'd heard it all before, many many times. Enthusiasm, hyperbole, excessive eulogies: these were all part of the actor's stock-in-trade, were they not? But they were just words and must not in any circumstance be used as evidence. The pursuit of a career left an actor with little time or energy to indulge in more than gestures.

But in less than two months we found ourselves playing under their sponsorship at the Embassy Theatre in Swiss Cottage. Wanamaker and Redgrave had worked well on our behalf in getting maximum press publicity and, in order that our London run should not go unnoticed by our peers, they had arranged for a Saturday morning performance for the profession. It was a memorable occasion, with actors, actresses and directors from almost every theatre in London, and if there is a better audience than one composed of one's colleagues then it has escaped my notice.

The three-week run at the Embassy theatre was immensely successful and from there we transferred to the Comedy theatre in the West End. That was less successful; it was the month of June, a comparatively quiet time for theatre, and, except for weekends, the house was rarely sold out. We closed after two or three weeks and went straight into rehearsal of *The Travellers*, which was to be our offering at the Edinburgh Festival that year.

Like all our previous productions for the People's Festival, *The Travellers* received a great deal of praise from the press and the BBC Festival Round-up programme hailed it as the most exciting production of the entire festival. Audiences were enthusiastic and most performances were sold out. Unfortunately, the hall was too small to make any substantial difference to our financial position and the festival ended with us, as usual, wondering where the next meal was coming from. We held on in Edinburgh for another fortnight and at short notice put on a double feature show of *Johnny Noble* and *The Flying*

Doctor at the hall where we had been playing *The Travellers*. A week later we were in Glasgow trying to stave off collapse with a schools tour of *Twelfth Night*. By early November the position had become desperate. We were once again penniless and homeless.

Apart from those early few weeks in Kendal, ours had been a truly hand-to-mouth existence. Even when we played to full houses all the way we still hadn't earned enough to pay the company a living wage. The plain fact of the matter is that touring *cannot* be made profitable. Even if your actors and technicians work for next-to-nothing, as ours did; even if the cost of maintaining equipment is kept at the bare minimum, as ours was; even if settings, costumes and furniture are kept as simple as possible, as ours were; even then you cannot make enough to meet all your overheads. Not with twelve to fifteen people to feed and accommodate, not with a theatre whose policy includes a permanent training programme for its actors. No, touring only becomes feasible when it is heavily subsidised and that is only part of the solution.

And yet touring is important. It should be a necessary part of any actor's life. Those who work in the theatre tend to be cut off from the rest of society and, as is sometimes said of grocers and butchers, 'they live in the shop'. Actors often 'live' in the theatre; that is, their talk is shop-talk, their circle of acquaintances is limited to people in their own profession. They read the newspapers, of course, and (if they're not working) watch television. As a result they know something of what goes on in Bangladesh and Brazil, but know nothing about the way life is lived in Ammanford, Alloa or Hackney. Perhaps this is one of the reasons why so much of the acting one sees in the theatre today is dull and unconvincing. I have never known an actor or actress yet who wouldn't benefit from a spell in a coal town or a season in Gateshead, Salford or Easterhouse.

Furthermore, there are millions of people up and down the land whose only chance of seeing live theatre is when a touring company visits their locality. There is really no excuse for depriving the people who create the nation's wealth of all that is best in our theatre. A little goodwill is all that is necessary and, of course, a belief that money would be better spent enriching people's minds than on perfecting ways of blowing their brains out. It is a measure of the malaise affecting our society that such notions are regarded as, at best, naive or, at worst, sinister.

By the beginning of 1952 we had reached the end of our tether. Our *Twelfth Night* tour was over and no further bookings had been arranged. We made our way down to Manchester where many of us had friends or relatives. There we assembled for a crisis meeting where we were told what we already knew: that we were broke, homeless, and that touring was a dead loss. Similar crisis discussions had featured fairly regularly in our irregular existence. They followed a set pattern. A statement would be made about our losses, our appalling financial state and the hopelessness of our position. Then we would continue to function as before.

This time was different. I don't think that anyone was in any doubt about the seriousness of our position. It was plain that we had reached the point where we would either have to disband or find another way of working. I think it had been slowly borne in upon us, ever since those disastrous tours of Cumberland and Westmorland, that our aims could not be achieved by touring, at least not unless we were subsidised. We had made countless appeals to a deaf Arts Council; we had approached trade unions and government agencies, convinced that someone somewhere would consider us worthy of assistance. And we had gone on working, postponing the inevitable decision.

Now it could no longer be postponed. We had to put down roots. We needed a base, a building, an old warehouse preferably, where we could perform and train and around which we could build an audience. But where should this base be located? For two years or more, the question of *where* had been the subject of numerous unresolved debates. Glasgow, Manchester, Tonypandy, all had their advocates. London, too, was mentioned, rather tentatively at first but with increasing emphasis as the time of decision approached.

My particular choice was Glasgow or somewhere in the vicinity of Glasgow. We already had something of a following there, enough to build on anyway, and we liked the Glasgow audiences; they were lively, articulate and seemed to be in sympathy with what we were doing. Then again, Scotland was in the throes of a cultural renaissance; it was an exciting place to be in, and the poets, novelists, painters, composers and dramatists that we met greeted us with open arms. There was another, more personal reason: I wanted to write in Scots and for that I needed a Scots audience. I had written a scene in Scots in *Operation Olive Branch* and had introduced a Scots-speaking character into *The Other Animals,* and to my astonishment I discovered that I could write more easily in Scots than in English.

I canvassed the opinions of a number of my friends, including Hugh MacDiarmid, Sydney Goodsir Smith and Hamish Henderson, on the subject of a Glasgow base for Theatre Workshop. All of them were enthusiastic and later in the year Hamish wrote to both Joan and myself suggesting East Kilbride as a possible location. I wrote asking him to find out whether we could expect any immediate support from the municipal authorities there. Unfortunately, Hamish had gone off to do some work in Italy and by the time he returned, East Kilbride was no longer on our agenda.

The arguments and discussions in the group at this time were not conducted without rancour, and there were rivalries and personal antipathies which tended to exacerbate genuine differences of opinion while at the same time glossing over fundamental issues. We still talked about a theatre which would be sufficiently flexible to reflect the rapidly changing 20th-century scene and which would concern itself with the struggles and problems confronting the working class, a theatre not afraid of the sound of its own voice. How can we possibly achieve this without settling in London and winning the good opinion of the drama critics? This was the voice of sweet reason. When it was pointed out that such a course would distort the ideological basis of the theatre, it was argued that there was no reason why critics and a working-class audience shouldn't co-exist peacefully. Another voice in the debate suggested that only after the theatre had become successful could it afford the luxury of a working-class audience. And in any case, what do plays like *The Flying Doctor, Don Perlimplin* and *Operation Olive Branch* mean to the working class? We quoted Marx at them:

> The ability to get at the basis of reality and skill in portraying its basic content made great artists of the past the outstanding critics of their time; it made realism an objectively democratic force.

I was opposed from the beginning to establishing our base in London. Our best audiences had been in industrial areas like South Wales and the northern coalfields, in cities like Manchester and Glasgow, places with working-class traditions. We were familiar with such places and with the people who lived and worked in them. We had spent seven gruelling years hammering on the doors of these places and now, when they were opening to us, we were contemplating turning our backs on them. For what? To work in a place where we were practically unknown, and all so that we could be written up by the drama critics! Hadn't we proved that an audience could be won without the help of the critics? In any case, why should critics who regularly hand out bouquets to the most meretricious trash, who heap lavish praise on mediocrities, suddenly turn about and embrace our concept of theatre?

At first Joan, too, was opposed to the London-base solution, but was later won over to the move. At that final crisis meeting in Manchester, it was decided that we should apply for the lease of the Stratford Theatre Royal in London E15. From that time on, my involvement in the work of the theatre was limited to taking part in occasional productions of those shows which had formed part of our touring repertoire. In the autumn of 1954, I made a new adaptation of Jaroslav Hasek's *Good Soldier Schweijk*. In 1956 I wrote *So Long at the Fair,* which was never played in England but played extensively in Germany. After that I ceased to play any part in the fortunes of the theatre.

Was it worth it, to give twenty years of one's life to the pursuit of an idea? Of course it was. All of us who worked in Theatre Workshop in those early days benefited from the experience in one way or another. We did not, however, make any lasting impression on the English theatre as a whole. For a short time I believed that we had, but twenty years of theatre-going has since disabused me of any such notion. With a few exceptions, the acting is just as mediocre as ever it was, the productions just as puerile – gimmicky, pretentious and puerile. Other nations have produced a theatre of cruelty, a theatre of the absurd. We have produced as theatre of dullness. And what is more, we are proud of our dullness.

21

Enter Alan Lomax

My break with the theatre was not a sudden event but a gradual process. After the move to Stratford East, I continued for several months playing roles in revivals of plays which I had written for the company during its touring days. But the theatre had changed and throughout the next few months it was to change even more. Almost from the moment we occupied the Theatre Royal my relationship to the rest of the company was subtly altered. More and more I felt like a stranger, and an unwelcome stranger at that. It was an uncomfortable state of affairs and when I finally turned my back on Theatre Workshop for the last time I felt few regrets. Of the original company only Joan, Gerry Raffles and Howard Goorney remained. The rest – Bill Davidson, Rosalie Williams, David Scase, Pearl Turner, Ruth Brandes, Kristin Lind, Nick Whitfield, Phyllis Gladwyn and Dennis Ford – had all gone their separate ways, and with them had gone much of the passion and intellectual excitement which had made those early years so memorable.

The move to London and the changing nature of the company weren't my only reasons for leaving the theatre. During my twenty-five years' apprenticeship, I had written innumerable ephemeral pieces, sketches, songs, interludes and documentary scripts.[1] Three of them – *Johnny Noble, Landscape with Chimneys* and *Uranium 235* – had been experiments in theatrical form. The others were what I call *genre* experiments. In the first of them, *Blitz Song,* I had placed a love-triangle in the framework of a plot which parallelled the *Agamemnon* of Aeschylus and had set it against a 1940s air-raid. The heightened prose which I adopted in order to elevate a sordid domestic intrigue into a major tragedy made the play seem overblown and melodramatic. My second full-length effort was an attempt to write a play on Jonsonian lines. I called it *Hell is What You Make It,* a comedy inspired by *The Devil is an Ass.* The plot worked well enough though the characterisation was poor and the dialogue mediocre. Ben Jonson's influence was still fairly obvious in my next play, *Rogues' Gallery,* a comedy in which I experimented with slang. It had its moments but I still didn't come any nearer to solving the question of the kind of language best suited to my needs. It was in *Operation Olive Branch,* my rather free reworking of the *Lysistrata,* that

I began to feel that I was making progress, particularly in the dialogue of the inter-cut soldiers' scenes. *The Other Animals* was a verse drama and my most ambitious play. I followed it immediately with a political thriller, *The Travellers* and eighteen months later with *So Long at the Fair*.

In all these works, with the exception of *Hell is What You Make It*, I had attempted to evolve a dramatic utterance which would crystallise, or at least reflect, a certain kind of working-class speech. In each of them there are moments when the language takes off, comes alive, but they are only moments and I was always aware that I was far from having solved the problem I had set myself.

My growing disenchantment with the theatre I had helped to build and my dissatisfaction with my work as a writer coincided with the arrival on the scene of Alan Lomax, an event which was to produce a major upheaval in my life.

Lomax is famous for . . . but really, to try and pigeon-hole Alan by pinning a title on him is like saying that Laocoön was troubled with worms. Lomax is a folklorist, collector, cultural anthropologist, an innovator and explorer of virtually unknown territories and a seminal force in the realm of ideas. All these attributes, qualities, qualifications or what have you, when added to his compulsion to share with you everything he knows, plus his love for those who make the people's music, add up to a unique human being.[2]

My first meeting with him took place at the BBC. I had turned up there after a brief telephone conversation with a stranger who spoke in the accents of an America which had not yet found its way into the world of television. I can still remember the feeling of urgency and excitement conveyed by that voice.

'Ewan?'

'Speaking.'

'How are you?'

'I'm fine. Who's that?'

'Listen, Ewan, my name's Alan Lomax and I've got to have you record for me.'

'Record what?'

'Some of those beautiful songs they tell me you've got.'

'When?'

'How about right now?'

And so, an hour later, I was being whisked away from the reception desk at Broadcasting House by an enormous Texan. In point of fact, the hugeness is an illusion. He is big but not gigantic. The illusion of size is the result of his expansiveness and of the warmth he generates. At times he gives the impression that he is expanding in front of your eyes as he gorges himself on ideas, concepts, systems and philosophies. Everything in his world is big. Words like *English, French, Italian, American* don't come readily to his tongue. He sees human beings in anthropological categories, as groups and sub-groups, as representatives of this or that culture or sub-culture, this or that linguistic area. His one conversational lack is small talk.

Almost before we have finished introducing ourselves he has launched into an enthusiastic encomium on the singing styles of Ireland from whence he has just arrived. I follow him into the lift, floating on a flood of talk. By the time we reach the seventh floor I have been completely enveloped by this extraordinary person. It is late and apart from ourselves the place is deserted. The empty studios are full of the atmosphere of mystery and menace which often seems to lurk in abandoned work places.

For an hour or so I sit there alone in a little pool of light surrounded by darkness, singing into the small metal tube which will allow my voice to be captured on quarter-inch magnetic tape. Afterwards we make our way along deserted corridors to the lift. During the descent Lomax is silent, almost asleep; the exuberance, the almost profligate expenditure of energy, has given way to a leaden immobility. His face has changed too; it is no longer that of a vital young man but that of an old North American Indian.

We meet again a fortnight later in Tow Law, a small pit village in County Durham where Theatre Workshop has based itself for a short tour of the Durham coalfield. We are in the midst of the rig when Alan turns up intent on recording more songs from me. It just isn't possible, there is too much work to be done. So he produces a guitar and starts to sing. For a couple of hours he serenades us with songs recorded in the coal towns of West Virginia and Kentucky, with chants and hollers learned in the prison camps of Texas and Florida, with blues from Mississippi and Tennessee, with lowdown ballads from Louisiana. I had heard snatches of this kind of music on record and, very occasionally, on radio programmes, but this was different. The man singing these songs had actually heard them sung in coal camps, had actually listened to convicts singing them on prison farms. It was an education and an entertainment which I doubt any of us, rigging the stage that night, will ever forget.

In the course of the next year or so I spent more and more time listening to Alan's enormous collection of tapes, to songs from the Americas, Africa, India, Italy, Spain and Britain, arguing, discussing, learning and trying to acquire Alan's world-view of this extraordinary corpus of songs and stories. I was also meeting a lot of people who had no connection with the theatre, people like Seumus Ennis, a collector of Irish songs and an uillean piper of genius; Peter Kennedy of the English Folk Dance and Song Society, an indefatigable collector of English folk-songs; Gilbert Rouget of the Musée de l'Homme, a musicologist and collector specialising in African music; and I renewed my acquaintance with Hamish Henderson, poet and folklorist, whom I had first met in 1948 through my friend, Hugh MacDiarmid. Hamish, in addition to possessing a profound knowledge of Scots literature (in particular, vernacular literature), had at this time recorded a number of fine traditional singers in Aberdeenshire and Banffshire. Later he was to put his considerable scholarly talents at the service of the School of Scottish Studies.

Oddly enough, however, I had not yet met A.L. Lloyd. This was strange, since our interests and beliefs coincided at numerous at various points. Both of us had written BBC feature programmes dealing with various aspects of working-class life, had moved occasionally in the same circles and were members of the same political party. Furthermore, both of us were interested in folk music and both of us could actually sing the songs. Alan thought it extraordinary that the two of us had not met. Only among the British were such non-meetings possible, said he. It was part of our oddness, an example of our awful insularity, the 'self-defeating cult of each man being his own island'. So Alan did what neither of us had ever thought of doing: he arranged for us to meet.

We met in Stratford East outside the Theatre Royal where I had been taking part in a Theatre Workshop production. It was a balmy summer evening and we stood there for an hour or more talking and singing snatches of songs at each other until we were moved on by a policeman. At this time Bert Lloyd was heavily involved in the compilation of his book of coal-miners' songs, *Come All Ye Bold Miners,* and we didn't meet again for several weeks.

In the meantime, Alan had become deeply preoccupied with the idea of a British folk-song revival. He had been fascinated by the *waulking* songs he had recorded on the Hebridean island of Barra and argued that they could eventually provide us with a musical form as popular as the blues or the corridas of Mexico. His enthusiasm was infectious and I began to see in my mind's eye an invading army of singers and fiddle-players, of troupes of dancers, actors and storytellers. 'And why not?' said Alan. 'Take the ballads, for instance. Imagine the kind of magnificent theatre they'd make.' And we're off in pursuit of another exciting vision.

Alan has amazing energy. Everything is done at breakneck speed. No sooner is a task completed than he is hurrying to begin the next one. In fact, he rarely has less than four or five projects on the boil at the same time. At the moment there is the Columbia record series, *The Primitive Music of the World's Peoples* and a further record project is in the pipeline. There are the proofs of a collection of children's folk-songs to be corrected and the final organisation of yet another book is in progress. Then there is a series of three feature programmes which the BBC has commissioned and an African musicologist has just turned up with an armful of tapes which he insists on playing right away. That letter from the guy who has been collecting ritual songs in the Kamchatka must be answered immediately. Then there is the telephone. Through every one of Alan's frantic activities there is the telephone. Conversations take place over and around greetings and salutations to friends in Mexico, Sydney, Washington, Marseilles, Rome, Accra. Through all these conversations and telephone calls is interwoven the open-ended discussion on how a theoretical British folk-music revival can become a reality.

Among other things, the Trade Unions must be made aware of their cultural responsibilities. They must be involved in providing a base for the vibrant sub-culture that is about to be resurrected. So every Friday evening for several weeks in succession, we make our way along Euston Road to the headquarters of the National Union of Railwaymen where the executive committee holds its meetings. After union matters have been dealt with, Alan talks for a few minutes about the songs and stories which have been created around the building of the American railroads. Very much the timid apprentice, I follow with a few words about the three or four railway songs recently collected here in Britain. Both of us make history by singing, an activity previously unknown at executive meetings. There is plenty of interest and a couple of union members oblige with songs of their own. Afterwards we describe in some detail the kind of archive we would like the union to set up. They are sympathetic but not very hopeful. There is nothing in the union's constitution which would sanction the expenditure of union funds on such a project. 'Couldn't the constitution be amended or the rules altered? How about inserting a clause making it possible for . . .' Tolerant smiles greet our naivety. 'Things are not that simple, brother.'

Our timing was wrong. We were too early by five or six years. After all, we represented no one but ourselves. Later, we would have had several thousand folk clubs behind us with several hundred thousand members who would have made all the difference. The fact that we didn't have such backing (or indeed any backing all) didn't prevent us from continuing our campaign to win the Trade Unions. For almost six months Bert and I sang at trade-union branch meetings and at trades-councils. One of our favourite venues was a west London branch of the Amalgamated Engineers Union. The branch secretary, Wal Hannington, had been a national leader of the unemployed in the thirties and didn't need convincing about the power of song. He himself wrote satirical songs, rich in workshop humour, about the problems confronting engineering workers. And he not only wrote them, but performed them at branch meetings where they were greeted with considerable enthusiasm.

The early years of the British folk-song revival can be likened to that stage of the weaving process at which the warp is manufactured. This warp consists of twisted threads lying parallel to, but separate from, each other. They need to be crossed with the threads of the weft to form a whole cloth. In folk revival terms, the threads of the warp were the varied activities of a small group of individuals. The weft was popular participation, and that was still in short supply.

The late 1940s and 1950s saw an increasing number of threads being added to the warp. There was the publication of song collections like *Folk Song: USA, Scotland Sings, Come All Ye Bold Miners* and *Ballads of World War Two*. There was the theatre workshop production of the ballad-opera *Johnny Noble* and the release of half-a-dozen industrial folk-song discs (78s) by the Workers Music Association. There were BBC broadcasts of feature programmes such as Lomax's *I Heard Scotland Sing* and drama and music programmes like *The Birth of the Lad* (Lloyd), *As I Roved Out* (Kennedy) and *Ballads and Blues* (MacColl). The annual *ceilidhs* organised by Hamish Henderson for the people's festival in Edinburgh were important, as was the plugging of the songs of Woody Guthrie and Leadbelly by the jazzman Ken Colyer.

These were all significant activities, but they didn't add up to a revival, not yet. A revival needs a mass base and must involve more than the activities of a few specialists. The publication of song collections, the broadcasting of radio features and the touring of theatrical productions are all tasks which can be carried out by comparatively small groups of individuals. Even popular *ceilidhs* and jazz concerts rarely call for more than a handful of performers and their audiences generally regard themselves as *cognoscenti*.

Indirectly, it was Colyer's jazz group which broke the mould of exclusiveness. Colyer, a fanatical admirer of the American folk poet Woody Guthrie, instituted a half-hour spot in his weekly band sessions during which the songs of Guthrie and Leadbelly were performed by a vocalist backed by guitar, tea-chest bass, washboard and, occasionally, clarinet. It was this group which gave rise to the spectacular *skiffle* movement.

Skiffle groups began to crop up all over the London district of Soho and soon the entire country had gone skiffle mad. Most of the Soho groups performed in cellars or in the upstairs rooms of pubs. Guitars, tea-chest basses and washboards were the most common form of instrumentation, though banjos, mandolins, harmonicas and kazoos were not uncommon. The guitar was, of course, the primary skiffle instrument and the symbol of this new craze. One saw them everywhere from Land's End to John o' Groats, carried raw, that is, without a case, for a skiffler who carried his guitar in a case was as unauthentic as a cow-hand in white tie and tails.

And with the guitar went the frayed and faded blue-jeans with the washed-out horizontal stripes which proclaimed you a fugitive from a chain-gang. The more extreme cultivators of the American image sent to the U.S. for those little sacks of Bull Durham tobacco and learned to roll their own with one hand as they gazed over the endless prairies of Doncaster, Hanky Park and the Toonheid. And everywhere, in every dialect of English, Scots and Welsh you heard 'The Rock Island Line', 'The Midnight Special' and 'The House of the Rising Sun'.

At the time, those with pretensions to cultivated taste were inclined to dismiss the skiffle phenomenon as a temporary teen-age misfortune like acne. Professional musicians referred to skifflers as 'three-chord strummers'; to music critics they were musicians *manqué;* to the importers and manufacturers of cheap guitars they were natives who had just acquired colonial status and were willing to exchange gold for glass beads. Few recognised it for what it was: a unique and extraordinary awakening, the first salvo in what some have called 'the youth revolution' and others 'the fake revolt'.

The skiffle generation had been born in the stormy years just before the Second World War. Throughout their childhood and early youth the media had force-fed them on 'Down Mexico Way', 'Roll Out the Barrel' and the half-dozen depressingly similar tunes churned out by the BBC's musical conveyor-belt. Now they were rejecting that fodder – at least temporarily – and discovering songs which dealt with the kind of reality they could comprehend. Their heroes, too, had changed. Not for them the smooth-voiced crooners of their parents; for their models they had chosen two of respectable society's misfits: an Oklahoma dustbowl refugee called Woody Guthrie and Huddie Ledbetter, a paroled convict from Louisiana.

The führers of Tin Pan Alley were stricken. What was happening was beyond their comprehension. They had always claimed to know which songs would 'go' and which would not. They were the experts on public taste, they knew what the public wanted. And the public, their public, was giving them the finger. This was *lèse-majesté* at its most offensive, they were hurt, indignant, angry, bitter. They appeared on television looking like politicians who had been rejected by the electorate; they gave interviews to the press which read like obituaries and, after a year of indecision, they bought out the skiffle movement, cosmetised it, compromised some of its leading performers and settled down once again to telling the people what the public wants. Within months the skiffle craze was over and its thousands of participants in disarray. Some of them drifted into the ranks of the folk movement while others, the majority, formed themselves into the kind of ensembles which were later to be known as rock groups.

While all this was happening, my personal life was undergoing some radical changes. Three of my plays had been translated into German, another was playing in Poland and I was beginning to be regarded by theatrical agents as a 'property worth keeping an eye on' – not a valuable property yet, but one which might become valuable in the course of time. I was no longer interested; my obsession with the theatre was over. I still took part in occasional Theatre Workshop productions, but more of my time was spent running all over London singing, sometimes solo and sometimes with Bert Lloyd, at small concerts, political meetings and festivals. The little money I earned writing radio scripts and reading documentary film commentaries just about kept us alive. Then an unexpected royalty from a German publisher made it possible for Jean and me to rent a flat in London.

It was a strenuous period but an exciting one. I was exhilarated by all the new things I was doing and experiencing. The limited success of *Uranium 235* had brought my name to the notice of a fairly large circle of professional people with the result that I was showered with invitations to dinners, parties, embassy functions, private viewings, week-ends in the country, propositions from agents and offers of commissions to write this or that script. Looking back, I am astonished at my casual acceptance of many of these commissions and of the ease with which they were fulfilled. It was one such script, or rather a series of scripts, which provided the impetus needed to launch the folk revival.

The series – *Ballads and Blues* – consisted of six half-hour programmes each dealing with a different theme such as war and peace, love, the sea, railways, work, the city. Each of the programmes featured seven or eight British and American songs about these subjects, sung by American singers Big Bill Broonzy, Jean Ritchie, Ma Rainey and Alan Lomax. Bert Lloyd, Isla Cameron and Ewan MacColl sang the British songs. Humphrey Lyttelton's band was there to provide instrumental colour. The main objective of the series was to demonstrate that Britain possessed a body of songs that were just as vigorous, as tough and as down-to-earth as anything that could be found in the United States. Against American songs like 'Frankie and Johnny' and chain-gang chants like 'Another Man Done Gone' we juxtaposed traditional murder ballads and treadmill songs. In the subject of love, we more than held our own and if we were a little short on railway songs we won hands down when it came to sea shanties and forebitters. The programmes were a huge success and were transferred from the Home Service to the Light Programme in a run of Saturday night repeats.

Encouraged by their reception, we staged three Sunday afternoon benefit concerts for Theatre Workshop at the Theatre Royal and these, too, were enormously successful. Following hard on the heels of the Stratford concerts, a newly formed concert agency offered Lloyd and myself a short tour of the main Scottish cities. They were prepared to promote a national tour if the Scottish series was successful. The new agency had plenty of faith but little money and though the tour paid for itself there was little profit. Smaller venues might have made all the difference, but halls like St Andrews in Glasgow, the Usher Hall in Edinburgh and the cavernous Caird Hall in Dundee were altogether too overpowering for the kind of music we were presenting. We had been joined by Isla Cameron, Alf Edwards (wizard of the English concertina) and Fitzroy Coleman, a calypsonian. We were not an ensemble as such but a small group of soloists who were not prepared to make more than a few concessions in terms of vocal style or in repertory. If our audiences could be numbered in hundreds rather than in thousands, it was not surprising.

Glasgow was the most successful point of the tour, for not only did we attract a substantial audience to St Andrews Hall, but on the following day we played to several hundred teen-age schoolchildren. From that gathering many of the early leading performers in the Scottish revival were later to emerge.

I began to write songs again.[3] From childhood I had possessed an aptitude for writing song lyrics. As a very small child I used to make up additional verses for songs that I liked, and later I made up tunes as well. In the early days of The Red Megaphones I had written dozens of song-squibs, mostly satiric pieces written around specific political issues. Some of them weren't *written* at all, but were conceived and sung straight from the head without recourse to the intermediate stage of writing. I didn't regard this facility as anything particularly noteworthy or important. It was something I did as naturally as talking.

In Theatre Union I had cobbled songs for *Fuente Ovejuna, The Good Soldier Schweijk and Last Edition.* In Theatre Workshop I had written melodies to fit the words of Lorca's songs in *Don Perlimplin,* for our stillborn production of *The Blood Wedding,* for *Johnny Noble, Uranium 235, Operation Olive Branch* and *The Other Animals.* All of these songs (with the exception of those in *Johnny Noble*) were minor elements in the plays for which they had been written. I made them up in my head, repeated them until I had memorised them and then taught them to the actor whose job it was to sing them in the play. I didn't write them down because I didn't know how to write music. I still don't. Only for the songs in *The Blood Wedding* did I depart from my customary way of working. We were playing at the Pavilion, Felixstowe, and I discovered that the piano in the orchestra pit had been left unlocked. I sat at it for a whole day and made up Spanish-sounding melodies for Lorca's tragedy. That was the first time I ever felt that I was a *real* songwriter. The feeling soon passed and I returned to my role as actor-cum-scriptwriter, as one who could be called upon to cobble a tune in between rehearsals. It didn't bother me at all that my songs were expendable, ephemeral pieces that could be dropped without trace from a production. Only 'Dirty Old Town', which had been written to cover a set-change in *Landscape with Chimneys,* could be regarded as a song in its own right.

But now my attitude to songwriting changed. I began to look upon it as an activity just as important as writing plays or novels or painting pictures and one which could, and must, play a vital role in the folk revival we were trying to bring about. Unlike my earlier pieces, the new songs must pay homage to the old ones by accepting some of the old disciplines. They should, for example, eschew high-flown turns of phrase, bookish language. They should use adjectives sparingly and strive for simplicity of expression.

In my earliest songs of this period I tried, not always successfully, to follow these precepts. I was encouraged by the example of Guthrie but my main influence, at the beginning, stemmed from the handful of Irish street ballads I had heard Seumus Ennis sing, songs like 'Boston City' and 'The Limerick Rake'. My Irish phase was short-lived. I had recently become acquainted with English country songs through Bert's singing and through field-recordings made by Alan and it was these that provided models for my next group of songs, which included 'The Dove', 'The Trafford Road Ballad' (written for my son, Hamish), 'Cannily, Cannily', 'Ballad of the Carpenter' and 'Go Down, You Murderers'.

The last-mentioned, a ballad dealing with a sensational murder case and a gross miscarriage of justice, was the most widely circulated of the new songs in the folk idiom. The conscience of the public had been aroused by the case of Timothy John Evans and consequently the song was considered to be newsworthy by television companies. It was featured in news programmes and documentaries a dozen times or more before one of the companies developed cold feet and insisted that we cut a vital stanza from the text. We refused and there followed a series of ridiculous conferences of programme planners, lawyers, station heads and hired men with suits and anguished faces.

In my youth I had once read with fascination an enormous tome dealing with the history of epidemics. Sandwiched between chapters about bubonic plague, cholera and exanthematic typhus, were descriptions of 17th-century epidemics of madness. I had been left wondering how madness could be so infectious. Now I knew. Those meetings of distraught broadcasting officials made everything clear and since that time I have never had any difficulty in believing that many of those who plan the nation's entertainment are feeble-minded.

This, of course, did not prevent us from spending a good deal of time working in what today is known as the *media*. Both Bert and I, quite independently, were writing scripts dealing with various aspects of folk-song for the BBC Home Service and the Third Programme. Alan, much more perceptive than either of us about the future of television, presented three one-hour programmes on the BBC in which singers and instrumentalists from all over the British Isles demonstrated the magnificent riches of our traditional music and song. The programmes were produced by David Attenborough and though they delighted the hearts of the small band of folk enthusiasts who witnessed them, they were not popular with the general public.

Nothing daunted, Alan switched his efforts to Granada Television and persuaded them to film a series of fourteen one-hour programmes which would present folk-music in a popular form. The title of the series was *The Ramblers*. Alan planned to have a small resident group which would be supplemented from time to time by Bert, Fitzroy Coleman, Alf Edwards, Bruce Turner, Seumus Ennis, Michael Gorman and others. Our search for the perfect group took us to West Indian clubs, where calypsonians and singers of *mentas* competed with each other for audience approval; to a converted warehouse behind Goodge Street where Haitian drummers with filed teeth made wild music; to the Abelabe Club in Brewer Street where nose-flute players and performers on thumb pianos were the norm. It was in the Abelabe that we recruited an African harpist and, with difficulty, eluded a man who claimed to be able to whistle through his ears.

Our numbers were now almost complete. Almost. 'What we're short of', said Alan, 'is a five-string-banjo player.' Since the five-string-banjo was an instrument virtually unknown in Britain at the time, the chances of finding such a musician seemed unlikely. 'There's one on the way,' continued Alan.

'What's his name?'

'It's not a he, it's a she. Peggy Seeger. She's the best, the very best!' and he closed his eyes and gave the sudden sharp twist of his head which is his way of signalling endorsement of a special talent. She was coming over from Denmark, where she was travelling, to play banjo and act a small part in *Dark of the Moon*. When someone commented on the coincidence of our banjo player turning up at just the right moment, Alan confessed that he had given the BBC a nudge in Peggy's direction and had even phoned her father in California to discover her whereabouts in Europe. I first met her in Alan's basement flat in Chelsea.

She was much younger than I had expected, a girl straight out of her teens, tallish, fresh-faced and blue-eyed. Even though she had just arrived after a thirty-hour train journey, she was a complete picture. She wore a great deal of make-up and her hair was piled modishly on the top of her head; she sported very high heels and an ensemble that would have graced a fashionable young lady headed for a tea-date at Grosvenor House. I felt shabby and out-of-place.

Then she picked up her banjo and began to play. She stomped with her high heels on the floor as she launched into 'The House Carpenter'. This was as far away from the metallic plinkety-plonk of the average tenor banjo as the cor anglais is from the kazoo. When her voice joined in with the rippling banjo lick, my senses were utterly ravished.

The following day, a completely different Peggy turned up for rehearsal, unkempt, a little grubby, in old blue-jeans and a shirt much in need of washing. It appeared that upon her arrival, Alan's girlfriend, a model by profession, had been so horrified at her appearance that she stripped Peggy down, put her in the shower and began building, from the bottom up so to speak, the vision I had seen the day before. The true Peggy was now back in her customary uniform of jeans, sneakers and blouse. Five years later such garb would become the obligatory apparel for almost everyone under thirty but on that day in March 1956 it was a decidedly exotic costume.

She possessed a wholesomeness which I found immensely attractive. Then there was her musicianship, at which I marvelled, for she was not only skilled on the banjo but proficient on the guitar, Appalachian dulcimer, autoharp and piano. She could also, when called upon, provide an adequate accompaniment on the mandolin. She will argue that there are many banjo players more skilled than she and, in terms of technical expertise, she may be right. But technique is only part of musicianship. There are other qualities which are necessary if a performer is to be anything more than an able technician. Love, not merely of the instrument but of music itself, is equally important, as is an understanding of the specific disciplines which have been operative at the time of the original creation of the musical work. It is such love and understanding which makes Peggy's accompaniments so outstanding.

Within six weeks Peggy and I had become close friends and during the next six months we worked together on a series of projects which, in addition to the twelve episodes of *The Ramblers* television programmes, included recording several discs which I had undertaken to cut for Riverside and Prestige, two American companies. I had made my first recordings in 1950 when, under the auspices of the English Folk Dance and Song Society, I had recorded two 78s for HMV. The songs I recorded on that occasion were 'Eppie Morrie', 'Sir Patrick Spens', 'Lord Randal' and 'Van Dieman's Land'. It was my first experience of recording a disc and I found it unnerving. It was lonely sitting in the centre of that enormous studio with only the microphone for company. I didn't know anyone in the place and nobody had spoken to me except to tell me where to sit. The technicians, looking like hospital orderlies in their white coats, did nothing to reduce the tension and formality of the occasion. When they discovered that none of my four songs were short enough to fit onto the two-and-a-half minute side of a disc their silent disapproval so undermined my self-confidence that on the second take I actually sang the songs at almost twice their normal speed in an effort to bring them down to the required time.

Enter Alan Lomax

In the following year I cut several more discs, some of which were recorded with Bert in the kitchen of my Croydon flat, with Hamish, aged five, then six, acting as recording engineer. He also recorded our next project, a five-album set of Child's *Popular Ballads of England and Scotland*. I can still hear that small commanding voice shouting 'Three-two-one, go!', can still picture the lovely curly head poised intently as he turns the cumbersome dials on the elephantine old Ferrograph.

This was the recording set-up which now welcomed Peggy, scarcely more experienced than I at recording. There was Bert, Isla Cameron, John Cole (harmonica), Ralph Rinzler (USA singer/musician) and many others at those early recordings. One microphone, and Hamish, now a veteran at aged seven.

1956 – I find it impossible to remember the actual sequence of events during that time, it was so chaotic. For me, it was a period of great change, of excitement and discovery in my work, of happiness, despair and uncertainty in my personal life. As far as work was concerned I had been incredibly fortunate. Here I was, entering a new field of activity and, just at the right moment, I had been able to join forces with a talented young woman whose musical abilities and experience of this new world were far in excess of my own, although Peggy would say that they complemented mine. While I had been sitting in the back of a converted Post Office truck dreaming great dreams of a worker's theatre, Peggy had been growing up in Washington, DC, in a house where many of her relatives and friends were experts in – or at least conversant with folk music. Peggy was heir to a knowledge and an expertise which she carried in her head as easily as she carried her musical instruments in her hands or on her back. Furthermore, she had brought a new American dimension to the burgeoning British revival. Our concept of American folk-song had been bounded on the one hand by blues, work songs and hollers and on the other by the songs of Woody Guthrie. Peggy brought the classical folk-song repertoire: American-style traditional ballads, love songs, murder ballads, banjo songs and children's ditties.

I found working with her an educational and stimulating experience and I was anxious that it should continue. What I hadn't bargained for was falling in love with her. Poets down the ages have written about the grandeur, the sublimity, the beauty and the ecstasy of love, but few (if any) have written about its inconvenience. I was forty, married and with a young son. I was newly embarked on the exploration of a new world of ideas and had only the sketchiest plans for earning a living. And I was in love with a girl half my age.

Neither of us ignored our feelings. The fact that we were both involved in the same kind of work and tended to mix in the same circle of friends meant that we were constantly in each other's company. I seemed to be living in a world where frustration, exhilaration and guilt were my constant companions. At the same time, I found it impossible to make any kind of move to end my suffering.

Peggy, equally unable to cope with our dilemma, returned to the United States. This drastic 'solution' to our problem left me even more wretched than

I had been before and things didn't improve with the passing of time. Together we had planned a number of recording projects, all of which still needed a good deal of work. It wasn't only a matter of accompaniment – we had been trying to arrive at a rationale of performance. What, for example, was the proper pace for a particular song, what kind of vocal approach should be used, which was the most interesting key (for C-sharp *does* sound different from C or D), was the song better accompanied or unaccompanied, and so on. How much did a particular type of accompaniment alter the phrasing of a song, did the banjo or the guitar dilute the national idiom of a Scots ballad? At the time neither of us were absolutely sure about any of these things and we made some recordings that show great lack of perspective and judgment; but our partnership was so new and wonderful that objectivity was often lost in the delights of being together. But in all these arguments and discussions, the technical knowledge which Peggy had derived from her formal music education was invaluable. Her absence as a collaborator, added to my love-sick misery, rendered me incapable of continuing with the projects.

Furthermore, many of my erstwhile friends were hostile to the work in which I was now engaged. Over the years I had struck up friendships with painters and writers among whom were several Scots poets. Within months of my leaving the theatre to work in the field of folk-song, the attitude of most of them had become noticeably cooler. A dear friend, Christopher Grieve (by pen-name of Hugh MacDiarmid), in the course of an expostulatory letter, said that in his opinion ('and in the opinion of many of your well-wishers up here') I was wasting my talent on what was essentially trivial material. It was a warm, friendly letter and I was touched at the thought of how concerned he must have been to write it, for I never knew anyone less inclined to interfere in other people's affairs than Grieve. I sat down to answer it but after wrestling with my ideas for an hour or two, I gave up. If a poet of MacDiarmid's stature, a man whose talent I admired wholeheartedly, had not discovered anything of value in the vast corpus of songs and folk-tales which had been collected in Scotland, then how could I hope to change his mind by writing a letter?

Later I spent several days with him in Bulgaria. We were guests of the Union of Writers and a good deal of our time was spent travelling, during which time we argued endlessly about the merits – and demerits – of folk-song. Theoretically, he was prepared (reluctantly) to accept that ordinary men and women might (just *might*) have created a huge body of splendid songs, particularly if they were Scots. And yes, there were fine things in the ballads, in 'Hughie the Graeme' and 'Patrick Spens', but they were scarcely in the same class as Rilke, Dunbar or Paul Valery. The pen, it would seem, is not only mightier than the sword but the superior of every other form of expression. This is a not uncommon point of view. The science of folklore, as opposed to the folklore itself, is perfectly respectable; it is the *practice* of it which is regarded as odd. Go through the entire lexicon of the arts and you will find no word, or combination of words, which has such a pejorative ring to it as 'folksinger'.

Enter Alan Lomax

Tell a person that you are a folklorist and that person will almost certainly respect you, in spite of the fact that he or she hasn't the foggiest notion of what a folklorist is or does. Tell them that you teach a course in folklore at a university and they will be impressed. Tell them that you are writing a book on this or that aspect of folklore and they will regard you as an intellectual. Tell them that you are a folksinger and they will look embarrassed and hastily change the subject. You can tell a person that you are an opera-singer and, even if they loathe opera above all other things, you will not have forfeited their respect. Tell them you sing madrigals and it will automatically register that you are a person of some refinement. Tell them you sing baritone in a male-voice choir and they will tell their friends that you have a fine voice. Say that you 'do the vocals' in a rock band (even if that actually means you are singing *da-da-dit-dit* in the far background) and they'll envy you for all the money they think you're making. But tell them that you sing folk-songs and they regard you as feeble-minded.

Music, like every other man-made thing, has functions and associations which go beyond intrinsic merit. It has status values, prestige ratings. Generally speaking, the more incomprehensible a piece of music is to the general public, the higher its status. Serial music for strings has an extremely high status, as does all atonal music. All Western European classical music rates high on the prestige scale. All opera does likewise, though, naturally, grand opera ranks higher than operetta.

It should be noted that popularity has nothing to do with status; indeed, the less popular a piece of classical music is, the more likely it is to have a high prestige rating. An obfuscatory cloud compounded equally of pride, prejudice and plain bloody ignorance surrounds all music criticism and discussion. It is, for example, tacitly accepted that classical music is superior to all other kinds of music and by *classical* we really mean *Western European* classical. Some years ago I was serving on a panel of judges for the musical events at an international festival. The categorisation of the classes or types of music was in progress when I arrived. To my astonishment, I discovered that Indian, Chinese, Japanese, Thai and Korean music of the classical tradition had all been lumped together as folk-music. On what criteria are such judgments based? And where is the evidence which makes one assume that a string-quartet is superior to a slip-jig performed by two fiddles, a flute and uillean pipes? In what way is it superior? In the terms of its complexity? Are complexity and beauty really synonymous? Is a computer more beautiful than an Eskimo soapstone carving of a seal, or than that gigantic Pharaonic arm in the Egyptian gallery of the British Museum?

Perhaps the difference lies in the fact that our classical musicians read the music off the page, and are therefore skilled. Perhaps I had felt similar insecurity, if sitting down at a piano to *compose* a tune made me feel like a *real* song-writer. Or perhaps the difference lies in what is being said. But what exactly is being said by either the quartet or the slip-jig? Does anyone know? The composer may have given us a hint in the title of the work but that is all we have to go on. There is certainly no argument being developed, in spite of what those elaborate programme-notes on the disc sleeves tell us. But surely there are the emotions . . . ah, the emotions! Of course. But does classical music express the emotions any better than folk-music? I am passionately fond of Bartok's *Concerto for Orchestra* and I have been moved to tears by Vivaldi's *Concerto for cello, strings and continuo in E-minor.* I am partial to Bach's organ preludes and every morning I do forty-five minutes yoga exercises to, among other things, Mozart's *Serenades and Divertimenti.* I enjoy them all but I don't see them as a more worthy music than, say, an Azerbaijan bard's ecstatic singing, or the high lonesome sound of Texas Gladden's 'House Carpenter' or that gut-shaking rendition of 'Rosie' collected by Alan Lomax from black convicts in the Parchman State Farm in Mississippi.

When it comes to dealing with the real world, the world in which people live, work, love and die, the traditional song-makers and singers are, in my opinion, far superior to their classical counterparts. This is not to say that folk-song doesn't have its *longueurs.* Of course it does; but I would venture to say it has fewer than the classical repertoire. Its texts, even when they are in decline, are a good deal more interesting. Their protagonists, unlike those in most classical songs, are recognisable human beings. Their names have not been chosen from a dictionary of classical mythology – there are no Chlorises or Phillidases, no Corinnes, Hectors, Ganymedes or Leanders in the folk-songs – just Maggies and Annies and Jeans, Willies, Jimmies and Hughs.

In classical love songs, the lovers exist only to love and be loved or, alternatively, to love in vain. They inhabit an abstract landscape, as do lovers in contemporary rock songs, and the season is always summer. In traditional songs, love flourishes throughout the year; a young woman encounters her love 'early, early in the spring', 'on a cold winter's morning' or 'during the falling of the leaf'. And the weather makes no difference to the lovers' ardour:

> The nicht it is baith cauld and weet,
> The morn it will be snaw and sleet,
> My shoon are frozen to my feet,
> Wi' standin' here my lane, jo.'

The lover in traditional songs is not merely a lover; he is also a shepherd, or a coal-miner, a weaver, a soldier, sailor, tinker or tailor and his inamorata is a shepherdess, a weaver, a bleacher lassie, a farmer's daughter who can spin and weave and help with the harvest:

> She can milk baith cows and yows,
> For the work she has the will, O.
> She'll work in the barn, she'll winnow your corn,
> She'll gang to the byre and mill, O;
> In time o' need, she'll saddle your steed
> And draw your boots hersel', O.

Ewan at The 'Ballads and Blues club' at The Princess Louise in London, 1957-58 (*top*); with his early singing partner, Bert Lloyd (*middle*); with Fitzroy Coleman. Photo by Colin Dunn (*bottom*).

The Radio Ballads. During the making of *Singing the Fishing* at South Shields, 1961 (*top*); Charles Parker on board the Honeydew recording a fisherman (*middle*); Ewan interviewing a fisherman (*bottom*).

Ewan and Peggy on tour in Toronto in 1960 (*top*); at Newport Folk Festival in 1960 (*middle*); playing in Havana, Cuba, in 1968 (*bottom*).

Hamish MacColl,
Ewan and Jean's son.

Ewan, Peggy, Neill and
Calum at The Singer's
Club, London, in 1980.

Neill MacColl on a session for the album, 'Two', with Kathryn Williams in 2008.
Calum MacColl in the studio.

The extremely talented
singer and songwriter
Kirsty MacColl, who
died in an accident on
December 18 2001;
with her father Ewan;
with her godmother,
Joan Littlewood and her
mother Jean.

Kitty MacColl in 2007. Photo by Alan Boyd.
Peggy Seeger in 2005. Photo by Martin Rosenbaum.

Ewan with folklorist and catalyst Alan Lomax in 1988.

Ewan accepting his first honorary degree at Exeter University in July 1986.

All the facts which are necessary to the plot – the weather, the season, the time of day or night, the occupations of the lovers and their social status (rich or poor) – are given in the first two quatrains of many traditional love songs. In the third stanza, the loved one's appearance may be described and the lover declares his feelings. It is also likely that he will invite the young woman to elope with him or lie with him. The offer is either refused or accepted by the fourth stanza. If it is refused, then the young man goes off to try his luck elsewhere. That is stanza five. If the invitation is accepted, then stanza six deals with the young woman's pregnancy and the birth of her baby, usually a son. In stanza seven, more often than not, the lover has departed leaving the young woman to lament her unkind fate and to warn other young women against the inconstancy of young men.

It is this cause-and-effect element in the plots of traditional love songs which contribute to their great strength. It can be argued that such cut-and-dried plots are extremely trite, commonplace. Subject the plots of the love songs of Schubert, Hugo Wolff, Scriabin or any of the English madrigalists and you will find plots which are equally trite and a lot less plausible. Then, again, a commonplace series of events often becomes less commonplace in the telling. The story of Cinderella and her two cruel step-sisters is an ideal pantomime plot and like all pantomime plots it is simple. But when Cinderella is transformed into Cordelia and the two ugly sisters become Regan and Goneril, the simplicity of the plot is forgotten. In the same way, the most commonplace situations dealt with in folk-songs are transformed into universal experiences. As for the melodies – well, our traditional songs are the results of a melodic tradition which goes back a long way. They reflect the skills, the subtleties and wit of all the nameless song-makers who down the years have created and adapted and fashioned new tunes out of old ones. The fact that they weren't working in an harmonic tradition doesn't appear to have limited their inventiveness; on the contrary, it seems to have spurred them on to create a body of unique melodies, strong in character, varied in structure and rich in beauty.

When I argued thus with my disapproving literary friends, they listened with barely concealed impatience. Their minds were made up. I was wasting my talents on a worthless trifle. The singing of folk-songs, notwithstanding all that I had said, was not a fit pursuit for a thinking individual. Later, when guitars became almost as common as jeans and the singing of folk-songs had become a fashionable pastime, they relented a little – at least some of them did – but when the folk-song vogue had passed they reverted to their original hostile position. This kind of hostility is extremely widespread. It's as if people feel threatened by the very idea of folk-song. I have friends who have no time for any kind of music but are prepared to live and let live; except when it comes to folk-music, and then they become aggressive.

MacDiarmid who, in the course of his work, made occasional admiring references to Schoenberg and Hindemith, confessed to me that he never listened to music if he could avoid it. He did, however, concede that the composition of *serious* music was a perfectly legitimate exercise for an intelligent human being. Folk-music, on the other hand, was a puerile waste of time. 'And look at the kind of folk you see doing it! Completely unimportant people. Nonentities! Useless, absolutely useless!'

The revival was already well established when he made that remark to me and there was, perhaps, some justification for it. The revival was booming and, like all sudden fashions, it had attracted more than its share of misfits and poseurs along with the genuinely interested and talented new singers and musicians. The widespread myth that the singing of folk-songs required no special skills made it a simple matter for mediocre performers to gain a foothold in the rapidly expanding club movement, and a breed of mid-Atlantic cowboys suddenly appeared on the scene. 'Skifflers gone to seed,' as some wag put it. MacDiarmid had apparently encountered several such specimens in his social round and had reached the conclusion that the entire folk movement was composed of morons and people 'on the make'. It was a harsh judgment. When I taxed him with being prejudiced he admitted that the literary profession, too, had its share of untalented and dishonest writers. So, indeed, did all the other arts.

So why had he chosen to single out the folk revival as a special target for his venom? Because of the Kailyard, the 19th century parochialism which had poisoned Scots literature and condemned it to a debilitated existence in the cabbage-patch. MacDiarmid had rescued it and, with the help of a talented band of devotees, restored it to its proper role. And now it was being threatened again by vandals calling themselves folk-singers, by a movement which had within it seeds which, if allowed to germinate, would produce such a crop of weeds that the kaleyard would triumph again. MacDiarmid's fears were not entirely unfounded.

22

Into the Folk Revival

One of the most interesting developments of the folk revival was the growth of the club movement. It had begun in London with the opening of the Ballads and Blues Club at the Princess Louise, a pub in High Holborn. The year was 1954 and the skiffle movement was at the beginning of its decline.[1] The Ballads and Blues Club was an immediate success. Every Sunday evening, the large upstairs room of the pub would fill with young people, many of whom carried guitars. They would seat themselves on the large, semi-circular front row and spend a communal twenty minutes tuning up before the show proper began. Fitzroy Coleman, the club's popular resident guitarist, would shout out the chords as he played and the participants in the front row would search feverishly along the strings in a desperate effort to keep up with him. Six bars of A-ninth, two-and-a-half bars of diminished-on-D, one bar E-seventh . . . Fitzroy's cheerful easy skill juxtaposed against the painful concentration of the army of front-row strummers.

Resident performers in the club included Bert, Seamus Ennis, Fitzroy, Peggy (after 1956) and myself. Between us, we could handle a sizeable swatch of songs and ballads from North America, Australia, England, Ireland, Scotland and the West Indies. While the greater part of our programmes consisted of the kind of songs which even the most strict traditionalists would class as folk material, i.e., country songs, versions of the English and Scots popular ballads, sea shanties and forebitters, we were also attempting to extend the national repertory by introducing children's street songs, industrial songs and ballads, epigrammatic squibs, popular parodies, broadside ballads and new songs written in the folk idiom.

Within twelve months of Ballads and Blues' being formed, folksong clubs began to spring up throughout the London area and in places as far afield as Manchester, Bradford, Liverpool and Glasgow. Most of them lacked our resources and, as one would expect, there was a certain degree of unevenness as far as repertory was concerned. To some extent, the repertory of a club represented the taste and skills of particular performers. Almost all club audiences liked to sing shanties and there were generally one or two singers in each locality who fancied themselves as shantymen. A club might achieve local fame through its audience's lusty singing of choruses; another might rely on a young woman who had once been in a girls' choir and had a *nice* voice, or on a young man who could play the guitar and produce an acceptable version of an American accent. Then there were the duos, trios and quartets performing jazzed-up versions of songs they had heard on radio broadcasts or from records of Pete Seeger and the Weavers played over and over again until the grooves of the discs were so worn down that the voices sounded like the cries of agitated ghosts.

For many of the clubs in the early days, the largest single source of repertoire was Ballads and Blues, where it was the practice to distribute duplicated song-sheets to the audience at the beginning of each session. The speed with which songs sung at the Princess Louise winged their way over the country was truly amazing. One could hear Bert Lloyd sing 'The Fowler' or 'The Captain's Apprentice' on a Sunday night at Ballads and Blues and, a week or two later, hear it repeated in a club in Sheffield, Newcastle or Wolverhampton. Only Scotland differed from the general pattern. There, the repertory fell into three distinct categories: there were the traditional songs popularised by Hamish Henderson's *ceilidhs;* there was a category made up almost entirely of the songs of Woody Guthrie for, oddly enough, the skiffle repertoire persisted in Scotland long after it had been abandoned elsewhere; the third, and in some ways the most interesting, group was made up of songs celebrating the lifting of the Scone Stone. Scotland's 'stone of destiny' had been carried off to England in the summer of 1296 by Edward I and had regularly played its part in the coronation of English sovereigns. At Christmas, 1950, the stone was lifted from Westminster Abbey by Scots nationalists, an event which gave rise to dozens of splendid songs by Thurso Berwick (Maurice Blythman) and others. Many of these pieces achieved wide and instant popularity.

Folk club evenings tended to follow a pattern. The Ballads and Blues format was not untypical. The resident performers, generally two or three in number, sat on the stage and traded songs. Sporadically, the platform would be thrown open to anyone who wished to perform. A surprising number of these floor singers chose to sing Russian, French, Greek and Israeli songs. Peggy, having spent some of her college years song-leading at the International House in Cambridge, Massachusetts, had a sizeable repertoire of songs in French, Russian, Spanish and Italian. I myself was no slouch at 'Sixteen Tons' and 'Sam Bass'. As the months went by, we found that we tired of singing songs in a language we didn't speak fluently or, sometimes, didn't understand at all; or if the songs were from an alien culture or lifestyle, they began to lose their conviction. We felt no real sense of identity with them. Other performers from other clubs were exhibiting the same malaise. Furthermore, Peggy found it difficult to keep a straight face when she heard cockneys and Liverpudlians singing Leadbelly and Guthrie songs, pieces which she had drunk in with mother's milk. She felt that the songs didn't ring true and then it occurred to us that perhaps our own repertoire of foreign songs might not ring true to natives of the countries whence those songs came. A polemic began. It wasn't that we were hostile to so-called 'foreign' songs. On the contrary, we were eager to attract foreign performers to the club. Our problem was English, Scots, Welsh, Irish and American performers singing songs whose idiom, whose language, they did not understand, hence mishandling the songs.

We were also intent on proving that we had an indigenous folk-music that was as muscular, as varied and as beautiful as any music anywhere in the world. We felt it was necessary to explore our own music first, to distance ourselves from skiffle with its legions of quasi-Americans. The folk club should be a place where our native music should have pride of place and where the folk music of other nations would be treated with dignity and respect. So the resident singers of Ballads and Blues decided on a policy: that from now on residents, guest singers and those who sang from the floor should limit themselves to songs which were in a language the singer spoke or understood. We became what began to be known as a *policy* club. It was an unpopular decision and for weeks after it was made our audience was reduced to a handful of devotees.

This was the first real point of dissent in the folk revival and one still occasionally hears faint echoes of it some thirty years later. It was fed with rumours, the most persistent of which was that foreign language songs were banned at Ballads and Blues. This rumour circulated at the same time that the club had two resident North American singers and at various times featured Indian, Italian, Spanish, Portuguese, Swedish, French, Venezuelan and Chilean performers. It took us several months to build up the audience again. They returned, and they stayed. Thirty years later some of them are still with us at the Singers Club.

There was murmuring heard in the other clubs about dictatorship and censors ('Bert Lloyd and Ewan MacColl are telling us what to sing', etc.), but it gradually disappeared and one by one clubs began to follow our example. By the early 1970s it was estimated that there were upwards of two-and-a-half-thousand folk clubs in Britain and that a large majority of them tended to concentrate on English, Irish and Scots traditional music, or at least on what they regarded as traditional music.

They were good days, those early days and late nights of the Ballads and Blues. I can recall them well: the young faces of boys and girls who had spent their childhood and youth in the war years. But now the blackouts, the daily war-bulletins, the air raids and most of the major discomforts of the war were things of the past. There was a new world to be discovered and this was part of it. I would guess that most of this new audience were in their late teens. Certainly few of them were over twenty-five and some hadn't even left school.

Most of us who helped pioneer the revival were, I believe, astonished by the ease with which objectives were accomplished. Visitors to the clubs were surprised too by the vigour and beauty of the songs, by the fact that we, the English, Irish and Scots, had produced such an enormous body of songs dealing with the lives of people like themselves. It was a revelation for most of them and it seemed as though their appetite for these songs would never be satisfied. It wasn't only the songs – there were the musical instruments like the uillean pipes, for example, which many were hearing for the first time. And they were being introduced to them by one who was a prince among pipers.

To hear Seumus Ennis, in his prime, play the pipes was to be transported to a magical realm where earth, sky, sea and land had been transmuted into the laughter, the rippling joy, the anguish and leaping exultation of the pipes. It wasn't only through your ears that you were conscious of the moment of wonder; your eyes, too, would record the signal as the colour drained from Seumus' face so that it took on the appearance of a death-mask. There was something uncanny about the change; it gave a quality of immediacy to those tales of fairy pipers who lure men and women into places where time has ceased to exist and where dreams are pursued through enchanted landscapes.

As a singer, Seumus was not in the top class, though he had his moments. His song repertoire was extensive and he was a storyteller of no small merit. In some ways, he looked odd sharing the platform of Ballads and Blues with left-wingers like Bert and myself. He was a black Catholic, a stone-age reactionary who felt that he was imperilling his immortal soul every time he appeared with us. Indeed, it was widely rumoured that he regularly confessed his association with us and lit candles for us in the hope that we would be guided towards the light. It was his dilemma that his love of music drove him into the company of those who were damned. Apart from music, he had little in common with any of us, except Bert, with whom he shared a similar taste in dress. At a time when jeans, sweatshirts and pullovers had become universal items of clothing, neither Bert nor Seumus ever appeared in public wearing anything other than three-piece suits and collar-and-tie. Seumus once told me that he had worked as a truck-driver, but I found that hard to imagine. There was a certain elegance about him; he moved gracefully and had a lean and hungry look, like a stage-dancer between tours.

Bert, on the other hand, was rather short in stature and somewhat plump. He radiated amiability and good humour, a walking toby jug. I never saw him look really angry; affronted, scandalised, shocked, disapproving, even peevish, yes, but never downright angry. He reminded me of one of those kindly uncles in Dickens who saves the orphan from a life of misery, though sometimes when he was introducing a song he would assume the persona of an amiable auction-eer taking bids for an undisputed masterpiece I once heard a young woman describe him as 'straight out of Trollope', and, indeed, he would not have looked out of place taking tea with the Dean of the Chapter. Words like *amiable* and *agreeable* figured largely in his conversation.

His appearance was belied by the man himself and by the kind of life he had led. As a young man he had worked on a citrus farm in the Cape province of South Africa and later as a sheep-herder in Australia. For a short time he had done a stint in South Georgia on a whaling ship and had then followed the occupation of journalism. This latter profession had taken him to South America on several occasions and to other parts of world. He wrote well and fluently. On the subject of folk-music and folk-song he was a mine of information, and his knowledge wasn't merely theoretical but practical as well, for he was highly regarded as a singer. His light, rather high, tenor voice had a tendency to waver, though he rarely went completely off pitch. He sang English traditional songs and Australian sheep-shearer ballads with a great deal of skill and authority. His repertoire was extensive and included good examples of almost all the categories of English country songs as well as sea shanties and forebitters. He was at his best, in my opinion, when he sang Australian songs and short English songs like 'The Cruel Ship's Captain' and the ballad 'Lucy Wan'. With the longer traditional ballads he was not entirely comfortable and in the latter part of his career dropped most of those he knew from his repertoire. His attitude to them was ambivalent; on numerous occasions he referred to them as 'boring old songs', or as disagreeable. This didn't prevent him from adding to his repertoire 'Tam Lin' and 'The Twa Magicians', both of which he Englished from Scots versions with a great deal of skill.

These 'borrowings' from Irish, Scots, North American and even Balkan folk-songs evoked a growing chorus of criticism among folklorists over the years and accusations of forgery were murmured with increasing frequency. Forgery! In a sense, all folk-songs are forgeries. There is, as far as we know, no Ur 'Barbara Allen' or Ur 'Lord Randal'. All that we possess is a body of texts and tunes in a state of constant change, of evolution and devolution. There must obviously have been an original set of words and an original melody for every one of these songs but, in the course of time, texts were altered sometimes for the better, sometimes for the worse. They pass through the mouths of singers who drop a word here because it seems superfluous and a word there because it doesn't lie easily in the mouth. A singer substitutes a cadence for one he or she has inherited or, possibly, ornaments a line so lavishly that its original shape is permanently changed. Another singer may jettison the entire tune and make up a new one which is more pleasing. Harry Cox, surely one of the most extensively recorded of English country singers, told us an interesting story. We asked him if he had ever learned songs from print, and he answered in the negative. Then he sang his version of 'Van Dieman's Land' and we noticed that when he sang the words 'Warwick gaol' he pronounced the central w and made gaol rhyme with mole. We asked the reason for this and he explained that he had learned the text from a penny songsheet which his mother had bought from Norwich market. To him, this was not 'learned from print', as books were print and songsheets were not. We asked him where he got the tune. 'It didn't have a tune on the sheet', he explained, 'so I made one up. I'd have made the words up, too, if I could ha' spelt.'

This kind of thing has always gone on. It is because of the inventiveness and creativeness of singers that we have such an enormous body of fine traditional songs and ballads. Great traditional singers are rarely content merely to copy their teachers or models. While they are learning, yes, then they copy. But when they have served their apprenticeship they are themselves driven to create inside the boundaries or disciplines of what we call the tradition.

Bert's adaptations and 'borrowings' (and this applied to myself as well) from foreign repertories was in the spirit of those other borrowings, when songs and tunes brought by Irish farm labourers to the East Anglian potato fields infiltrated the local repertoire and, in the course of time, became indistinguishable from it. To the task of cobbling Irish or Scots patches onto an English song or strengthening a run-down text by re-writing a line or even a complete stanza, Bert brought both skill and taste.

Why, then, did he not take that final step into the realm of song-writing? His literary skills and his profound knowledge of traditional song should have equipped him to write songs. He made beautiful and sensitive translations of Lorca's masterpiece 'Llanto por la muerte de Ignacio Sanches Mejias' and *Bodas de Sangre,* and yet he himself wrote no poems, no plays. He fervently admired the works of E. M. Forster and Alejo Carpentier, but never tried his hand at a novel. Once, when he was engaged in writing a technical brochure for Shell, he told me, with a craftsman's pride, that he could write about anything. And that was no more than the truth. He could write *about* songs, *about* poems, *about* novels but he lacked the special talent which is needed to actually write them. It was in the field of scholarship that he felt most at home. He once told me that he looked forward to his old age when he would be able to sit with his books doing the thing he loved best without interruptions from the outside world. It was the saddest thing I ever heard him say.

As far as I was concerned, the *swinging sixties* began in the early 1950s. I was meeting people, making friends (and enemies), arguing, discussing, planning future works. For a year or more, MacDiarmid and I had been planning to collaborate on a play dealing with MacBeth and written in Scots. I kept finding reasons for postponing the project. The real reason was that I was loath to cut myself off from all the exciting things I was doing. What exciting things? I really don't know. At the time I was in a state of constant activity. I was writing songs by the dozen. Scarcely a day passed without a new batch being turned out. I would start writing on the tube at Oxford Circus and finish the song before I reached Stratford East. I wrote while travelling on the tops of buses, while walking along the street, while sitting in the dentist's waiting room. I was performing at political meetings, attending conferences, trying to earn a living by writing radio scripts or reading commentaries for documentary films. It all sounds very dull now, but at the time I found it stimulating. All these activities involved meeting people, writers, composers, directors, technicians; a dubbing session might be followed by a protracted lunch with Benjamin Britten or Olivia Manning; more often than not, it would be a noisy discussion in The Stag or The Bedford Arms with Dylan Thomas or Brendan Behan.

Into the Folk Revival

The revival of interest in folk-music was not a new phenomenon. What *was* new was the nature and size of the audience. Previous folksong revivals, both here in Britain and abroad, had been almost exclusively middle-class affairs. In North America, and in most parts of Europe too, it was students who provided the audience for folk musicians and singers. But by the mid-sixties, the British folk movement was growing at an astounding rate. There were clubs everywhere; they seemed to proliferate in the night like mushrooms and they often disappeared as quickly. By the end of 1968, Peggy and I had sung in 482 clubs in Great Britain and it was our impression that the bulk of our audience was working-class. The Ballads and Blues club, re-organised in 1960 under the name of The Singers Club, had a membership exceeding 4,000 in 1967. A questionnaire circulated among the members over a three-month period showed that 67% were manual workers under twenty-four years of age. Less than 5% were students and a surprisingly large number of them had started out as Beatles fans.

This was the type of audience that Theatre Workshop had tried to attract. And now here they were, young, eager, denim-clad, ready for anything we could give them in the way of songs and information about the songs. Where were they hiding when we were stumping the country with *Johnny Noble* and *Uranium 235?* Yes, we had eventually won a working-class audience in South Wales and County Durham but it had taken us seven years and even so a full house was still a rare phenomenon. The clubs, on the other hand, were packed to suffocation with young men and women, 'all with shining faces', as the Newcastle anthem would have it.

On one occasion we were booked to sing at an Easter Monday afternoon concert in Southampton. The local city council had, over the years, established a tradition of municipal folk concerts where the audience came dressed in their best to greet the spring. Just before we were due to sing, we were approached by a scruffy young couple in jeans who expressed surprise to find us singing in such surroundings. They went on to point out that we were wasting our time singing to such a petty bourgeois group of people. 'You should be singing to the working class.' We suggested that workers might be lurking in this audience. The young man commented that they were too well dressed for workers. The girl added contemptuously, 'There are no workers in Southampton, no bloody working class at all!' She was Scots and a high-class accent was lurking defensively behind her assumed Glasgoese. There wasn't time to develop the argument as the master of ceremonies was introducing us.

We sat there on the stage facing our petty bourgeois audience and began by asking them what they did for a living. We went right along the front row. A man on the end seat told us he was a plasterer; he was there with his wife. Next to them sat a docker and his wife and child. An apprentice boiler-maker and his girl-friend who worked as a nurse were next and then a factory store-keeper. Across the aisle from him was an unemployed core-maker, a typist, a filing clerk, an unemployed railwayman and his wife, who worked as a cook at a comprehensive school, a merchant seaman and a shop assistant. And so it went on. We turned to our two young critics. 'And what do you do for a living?' The young man answered, 'We're students. We're both at Cambridge.' He had the grace to blush.

Clubs varied enormously, and still do. Some were well organised with officers chosen at annual general meetings others limped along from week to week never quite sure whether or not they were doing the right thing. There were clubs where the resident performers competed with each other for platform time, clubs where one or two lone residents kept things going. And there were clubs which, in some miraculous way, managed to survive without any resident performers at all. Some of the clubs counted their members in thousands, some in hundreds and some found it difficult to muster more than two or three dozen.

Club premises are mostly located in public houses or, in the case of Scotland, in small hotels. There are large, comfortable club rooms and small, uncomfortable ones; rooms without soft furnishings where your voice rings out loud and clear; and carpeted rooms with heavy curtains where it's like singing into a wad of cotton wool. There are rooms with platforms, without platforms, well-lit rooms and murky rooms, rooms where the audience sit at small tables and rooms where the chairs are arranged concert fashion. There was one room in the Midlands where the entire audience, except for the front row (who crouched on a low plank set on cinder-blocks), stood for the whole performance. There were pubs where the landlord or landlady was friendly and obliging and places where the proprietor made it quite clear that he was decidedly suspicious of the people who were using the pub room for such dubious entertainment.

Until recently, there was one thing which all club rooms had in common, and that was the almost impenetrable pall of cigarette smoke that shrouded singer and audience. Audiences might agree or disagree on the need for tables to sit at, on whether to provide a raised plinth for the performers, on whether microphones were or were not needed, whether accompanied or unaccompanied singing was the most traditional; whether this or that shanty should be sung slow or fast, whether 'Off to Sea Once More' should or should not have a refrain, whether the guitar was an apt accompaniment for English country songs, etc, etc, . . . but cigarette smoke: that was an absolutely vital feature of any folk club. It was part of the mystique of an entire genre of musical performances, of jazz, of blues, and now folk. This vital ingredient is less necessary now that cigarette smokers are on the defensive, but there are those connoisseurs who would say a folk club is not a folk club without smoke.

Drabness of location was also part of the fascination. The particular brand of drabness common to most folk clubs was compounded of the stale smell of beer, old cigarette smoke and air which had been used too often. And it had its visual form, too, its odd assortment of wooden chairs, inadequate light-bulbs backed, occasionally, by a malfunctioning spotlight of low wattage and fly-spotted framed photographs of dead-and-gone functionaries of the Oddfellows or the Royal and Ancient Order of the Buffaloes. All this enclosed in a room which, more often than not, felt like an attic partly stripped of its lumber.

All these qualifications, plus a complete lack of ventilation, made a room into a perfect venue for a folk club. Well, not absolutely perfect; for that there would have to be a functioning bar actually in the club room. There are such places. We have sung in them, not often and never willingly. To sing above the clank and rattle of a cash register is a daunting experience. A bell pinging and a drawer clattering open at the end of every stanza of 'Tam Lin' or 'Gil Morice' tends to discourage concentration. Manual expertise can be equally distracting. We have dreadful memories of a bar-lady at a South Shields club who insisted on counting the take on the counter of the bar every time an unaccompanied song came up, or rather every time an unaccompanied song was attempted, for that woman made a mockery of the term 'unaccompanied'.

Traffic noise can also be a serious problem. Pubs are frequently located on busy thoroughfares so that one is faced with having to battle with a constant rumble in the background. The Singers Club met for years in the Union Tavern, at the corner of Kings Cross Road and Lloyd Baker Street, an intersection where the traffic lights are just outside the window. Buses and lines of cars would come to a halt and wait for the lights, often impatiently. Every forty seconds or so, there would be a massive movement of traffic, grinding of gears and hooting of horns. The club was there for eight years.

The Southampton Fo'c's'le club used to meet at such a place. It was so noisy that all the windows had to be kept shut. It was invariably packed and after a half-an-hour there was no oxygen left. Peggy was singing at the time and I remember watching with fascination a man in the front row trying to light a match for his cigarette. The match kept going out of its own accord. There was not even enough oxygen for that tiny flame. Yet no one suggested opening a window. If you had to choose between breathing and hearing, well . . . you came to a folk club to hear the music.

I think, however, if I had to choose between the juke-boxes, cash registers, pin-tables and traffic on the one hand and the average pub acoustic on the other, I would choose the former. You can ignore the juke-box, to some extent. If you are singing unaccompanied you can get in tune with it. But the average pub room, particularly those with soft furnishings, is death to the folksinger. You get no come-back at all and your quiet songs just disappear into thick air. By the time you've sung for an hour you are completely exhausted.

These are just a few of the problems encountered by folk-club performers, and I haven't even mentioned the problems of digs, food or transport. Most singers manage to cope in one way or another, though there are many reports of memory lapses and temporary blackouts. The repertoire of some club singers may number several hundred songs and ballads or may be limited to a couple of dozen items. Unlike the actor, who may undergo a memory lapse, the singer cannot fall back on the whispered cue of a prompter, unless he works regularly with a partner. The entire repertoire must be carried in the head and must be ready for use in spite of juke-bases, trucks changing gear and all the other noises calculated to make a singer's life unbearable. And yet . . . all right, so you dry up in the middle of a line. What do you do? Well, it obviously depends on the kind of song you are singing. If it is a slow, unmeasured song, the problem is not a difficult one. Providing you are familiar with the plot and are, so to speak, steeped in the idiom, then it is comparatively simple to improvise lines and even to provide rhymes if they are called for. If you're singing a rhythmical ballad which moves at a brisk tempo, then the problem is more difficult, for not only will you be called on to improvise lines which carry on the story but they must be in the same meter as the rest of the ballad. Keen ballad singers would do well to prepare for such an eventuality. Peggy and I used to purposefully 'forget' parts of a ballad text and improvise parallel stanzas. Ballad buffs in the audience who know our joint repertoires often comment on this or that new version, sometimes enthusiastically.

I have always been amazed at the fortitude of folk club audiences, at the way they will sit for two or three hours on uncomfortable chairs, or stand pressed against each other without moving for an entire evening, apparently managing to survive without breathing. In the early days of Ballads and Blues, we tried to make life a little easier for them by moving to a comfortable hotel in Bloomsbury. The room was spacious and well cared-for. It could accommodate over 300 people. There were easy chairs, low coffee tables for your drinks and an acoustic which made singing a pleasure. Almost 400 people turned up for the opening night there. The following week there were little over 100 and about half that number the week after that. The audience was unhappy with so much space. When the number dwindled to several dozen we moved to a wretched L-shaped pub room which was reached by a rickety flight of stairs covered with tattered linoleum. It was a miserable hovel and it was packed to suffocation every club night.

Not all club rooms are, of course, like those I have described. Some were worse, much worse. There was a club in the Yorkshire woollen belt which was held in the foyer of a bowling alley, where the customers had to cross in front of the singer in order to reach the toilets and where the crash of demolished nine-pins rendered part of every song inaudible. And there was the Tyneside club where the performer sat on a small platform surrounded on three sides by pin-tables and competed with the manic buzz of electric bells ringing up astronomical scores for their zombie-like manipulators. There is a wonderful club in Leigh-on-Sea where commuter-trains come through every half-hour or so. There was a club in Edinburgh where express trains roared by every few minutes and where the audience had learned to lip-read. It was a wooden building in an advanced stage of decrepitude and it shook continuously like an old man sick of the palsy. Several club premises were in the crypts of churches, in town halls, committee rooms, cricket pavilions, converted stables. There was one such rustic location in High Wycombe, where the audience snuggled down in the straw and the singers sat on the threshing floor. It was literally a one-man show that night, for Peggy gets such catastrophic hay fever that her eyes and nose stream. That night she had sneezing fits and totally lost her voice.

By the end of the 1960s, the folk boom had created a situation where there were more clubs than there were resident performers and club organisers were competing with each other for the services of so-called 'stars'. A star was anyone who had been on the folk club touring circuit for more than a year. It was a microcosm of Britain's immediate post-war predicament: too many jobs for too few people. The slack was taken up by a horde of new soloists and groups eager for the fame and fortune awaiting the stars. It is a fact beyond dispute that at this period anyone who could carry a tune and had a repertoire of a dozen songs could earn enough to live on. It wouldn't be a fortune by any means but it would be enough to keep the wolf from the door. It was not enough, however, to keep the wolf of decay from the revival's door.

I am not suggesting that all the singers who came into the club scene during the folk boom were without talent. Many of them were (and are); and an even larger number were (and are) incurably mediocre. By the sheer law of averages a small number of them were good or potentially good. The same is probably true of every profession. Not all painters are Leonardos or Piero della Francescas or Picassos and there are more bad actors than good ones. But among singers making their living in the folk revival, the disparity between the good and the bad is enormous and this, in my opinion, is largely due to the mistaken belief that folk-singing requires no special skill.

'Anyone can do it. After all, everyone, or almost anyone, can sing.'
'Can everyone sing grand opera or *lieder?*'
'That's different.'
'In what way is it different?'
'They're completely different.'
'Surely not completely. They each employ lyrics and notes strung together to make melodies.'
'They use different idioms.'
'But isn't *lieder* a different idiom from grand opera?'
'Well, yes . . . but folk-singing is more natural, less artificial.'
'Walking and talking are both natural, so are running and jumping and swimming but not everyone who walks, talks, runs, jumps or swims would describe themselves as walkers, runners, jumpers or swimmers and they would not charge a fee in order that the public could watch them running, jumping or swimming. Would they?'
'Well, no . . . but folk-singing *is* rather different.'

If I have presented a picture of the average folk club as having no redeeming features, then I must set the picture to rights. All that I have written is true but it is also true that the folk club can be a magical place in which to sing. Unlike theatre and cinema audiences, the folk club crowd generally constitutes a kind of instant community rather than a collection of strangers. There is a relaxed informality; everybody is on a first-name basis and if, occasionally, there is the merest breath of 'showbiz' it is either considered out of place or it is so low-key as to be almost invisible. Where else can you hear people singing songs made up by farm-labourers, sailors, weavers, coal-miners and others, 100 or 500 years ago? Where else can you go and hear a song made up yesterday about an incident reported earlier on the media? At which other kind of entertainment does the person sitting next to you suddenly get up and sing a song? Where else would you, yourself, get up and sing to a hundred or 200 strangers? I cannot count the number of times a floor-singer at the Singers Club has turned to me after singing and said, 'I never thought I could bring myself to do that.'

A few weeks ago, a young woman with whom we were slightly acquainted came to the club. The publican had double-booked the room we normally use and we were relegated to an upstairs room without chairs. Everyone sat on the floor without complaining. Our acquaintance, who had never been in a folk club before, looked absolutely bewildered. Who were all these people? I was in the middle of a long Scots ballad when she arrived and that must have added to her dismay. Eighty people, including weirdly accoutred punks, sitting in complete silence following every word of a complicated story in heavy Scots! When the ballad was followed by a new song satirising the Prime Minister and her cabinet, her confusion turned to panic. She still looked dazed when she left the club two and a half hours later.

The informality of the folk club is, in some ways, its most attractive feature. It has been described as part seminar, part prayer meeting and part beer festival. There is rarely a stage and sometimes not even a raised platform. Most clubs have no special lighting effects and there are no stage-sets, just chairs for the performers. Singers wear no stage makeup and, with the exception of one or two oddballs, no special costumes. Unlike actors, they make no special effort to project themselves. While doing their stint they appear to be just as relaxed as when they were standing at the bar ordering a drink and, for the most part, they seem to be content to be themselves. During the interval they mingle with the audience, take requests, renew old friendships and make new ones.

There are exceptions of course: young men playing at being daredevils with a wicked past or wee hard men just two or three steps ahead of the busies; young women being a Margaret Gautier or Moll Flanders or Cathleen Ni Houlihan costumed by Aubrey Beardsley; rustics of both sexes, and those who associate sartorial negligence with folk authenticity. But these are atavisms, or perhap survivals, from the early days of the folk boom. There are, these days, fewer trios and quartets made up of university drop-outs disguised as roaring boys bashing away on guitars, fiddles, crumhorns, mandolins, zithers, bouzoukis, uilleann pipes, five-string banjos, concertinas, piano-accordions, flutes, hurdy-gurdies and jaw-harps and making use of every spare minute to add to their legends of being men of gigantic thirst and insatiable sexual appetite. These days they tend to confine such performances to the European club-and-folk-music-concert scene. German audiences, in particular, seem to be partial to the more bizarre aspects of Celtic romanticism. Back home, the fashion is for a more laid-back or cool approach. Musicians, for instance, adopt the craftsman's image and no longer consider it obligatory to have a lighted cigarette burning away on some convenient part of their instrument.

Unlike actors, performers in the folk clubs do not appear to regard themselves as members of a professional elite and there is none of the mystique which tends to surround the members of a craft-guild. The majority of actors, be they new recruits to the profession or its most exalted stars, be they good or bad at the job, are liable to show a proprietary attitude to everything connected with 'the business'. Folk club performers have no such attitude, or if they have they manage to conceal it. Indeed, as far as I can judge, the greater number of those who earn their living in the clubs would seem to have no interest whatsoever in each others' performance. This I find strange, particularly as all of us share a common repertoire of traditional songs. Actors who are 'free' or 'resting' will often go to a great deal of trouble to see a new production of *Hamlet* or a new Lady MacBeth, to see how X is tackling Lear or Malvolio, how Y is approaching Mother Courage, Cleopatra or Vittoria Corombona. They go to be moved and to learn, to see what to avoid and what to assimilate. They go to be stimulated, to compete, to pass judgment, to take in as one takes in food.

It is more difficult for the folk club performer. The successful singers and instrumentalists earn their bread-and-butter by being on the road in a series of one-night stands. Monday Nottingham, Tuesday Lincoln, Wednesday Sutton-Coldfield, Thursday South Shields, Friday York, Saturday Glasgow, Sunday Aberdeen. And this is the kind of schedule for weeks on end. But there are surely times between tours, blank periods in the schedule when performers have the time to see the performances of colleagues, should they desire to do so. They apparently desire no such thing. Odd. Distinctly odd.

The strangest group of individuals associated with the folk movement are not really part of the revival at all, on the contrary they would be insulted if one were to refer to them as revivalists. They are older than most people in the revival (they have always been older) and are 'a better class of person'. They have been in The Society a long time and knew Douglas and Maude and R. V. W.[2] Ah, the good old days before the floodgates opened and allowed the riff-raff to come in. It's not that they object, *really* object, to the folk; but who would have thought that the folk and this motley crew were one and the same! How they regret the days when the folk was represented by a charming old fellow from Chipping-Camden, who stood there with his cap in his hand and answered their questions, or by a nervous old lady who had at one time 'done' for the vicar and now, in a tremulous voice addressed them as 'sir' and 'madam' (not quite sure which was which).

Their intentions had, no doubt, been good but their class prejudices had got in the way. They approved of folk-songs but disapproved of the folk. For a short time they were in a position to turn their backs on the folk-life museum in which their ossified spirits had lain for so long. They had merely to step forward and alter their pace in order to join with life itself. The challenge went unheeded. Instead they huddled together and formed a barrier between *The House* and the vandals who would have dragged the *English Folk Dance and Song Society* into the real world.[3]

To become involved with folk-music is like falling in love. It goes in stages. First there is the period which follows the first impact of the music when you attend as many clubs in a week as you can afford. You are determined to repeat the experience of that initial extraordinary revelation. So you look and listen widely, indiscriminately, for several weeks or maybe more. Then you reach the point when you decide that a certain type of song or a particular singing style is what you are most interested in, so you search for a club where that type of song and that type of singer may be heard. (Or, if you can manage it, you follow one singer from club to club when they are on a local tour, as a group of Glaswegians used to do with us. Every time we were in their area, there they were, five or six of them, planted stolidly in the front row, waiting to hear new songs and wanting to hear the old ones. They were a splendid challenge.) You make friends at your regular clubs with people who seem to be well informed about the music. Someone lends you a book and you start reading about the songs, their genesis, their hidden meanings, their folklore, their history. You listen to all the records you can get your hands on.

If you are lucky you may survive this stage of your voyage of discovery with all your senses unimpaired; indeed, increased knowledge may have honed them to a fine edge. On the other hand, this new-found world of cunningly concealed clues and fascinating symbols often proves to be a *Tir-na-nOc,* the land of everlasting youth, which makes it impossible for voyageurs there to ever re-enter the real world again. I have known several people who were beguiled into believing that antiquarianism and scholarship were one and the same thing. It is sad to observe vibrant enthusiasm transformed into dull, nit-picking pedantry. The delight and concentration which the songs once evoked appears to have deserted them. They no longer listen to songs at all; instead they collect 'versions' and associated trivia. Their conversation is limited to who recorded what from whom. Wars and rumours of wars, earthquakes, volcanic eruptions, floods, draughts, hurricanes, typhoons and political cataclysms are trivialities compared to the news that so-and-so has just recorded a three-line fragment of 'Robin Hood and the Tanner' from a retired mortuary attendant in Stow-on-the-Wold.

The interval during a performance is supposed to allow the artist some relaxation but since most folk clubs meet in pubs there is nowhere to retire to. You must stay with the audience, many of whom have questions to ask or comments to make. And there is always, in every audience, at least one bore who makes a bee-line for you the moment the interval begins.

They bear down on you and you have to be very alert indeed if there is someone else you would rather talk to. They come in all shapes and sizes. The ones I dislike and fear most are the eyeball merchants who bring their faces within an inch or two of yours and give you the full flavour of their garlic-laden, tobacco-poisoned breath. I am pursued by a regular tormenter in London who keeps his foul-smelling pipe in his mouth and brings his face so close to mine that he has several times managed to scorch one of my ear lobes. He assaults me with a rapid-fire recitative accompanied by his gurgling and sputtering smoking machine. In moments of excitement (and excitement comes naturally to him) he takes his pipe out of his mouth and showers me with a fine spray of nicotine-flavoured spittle. Sometimes he suggests subjects for songs that I might write. He would write them himself but lacks the time.

Then there's the young man in Chicago who is convinced that he's related to Peggy. He doesn't know just how they are related but he's sure that they are. He writes long, rambling letters and turns up the concert full of love and affection for all his self-extended family. There is the Japanese gentleman in San Francisco who accuses me of having changed my interpretation of 'Lamkin'. 'You sang it different in 1959.' There's the man in Adelaide who comes back three or four times during the interval to ask me to sing 'Let Me in this Ae Nieht'. And the man-and-wife team who seem to be on permanent holiday and who turn up at clubs and concerts all over the country bringing greetings from Charles and Bob and Sandra in Redditch. We tell them we don't know anybody in Redditch. They laugh loudly and long and carry on as if we hadn't said anything. 'Sandra's had her baby, a gorgeous little boy. I suspect you'll be seeing him soon.'

For us, the routine of a club evening scarcely varies at all from club to club and from year to year. Round about eight o'clock the club organiser stands up and welcomes the audience and introduces one of the club's residents who comes forward and sings two or three songs. These are sometimes accompanied by a guitar or concertina or are sung unaccompanied. A few more club residents may follow in quick or slow succession and then the guest of the evening is introduced. You're on. You have half an hour or, if you prefer, an hour to sing songs of your choice, tell stories, play instrumentals or whatever. At the end of your first spot there will be an interval, after which the entire procedure will be repeated.

The balance of your programme is important but how you achieve that balance is a matter for you, the singer, to decide. If you choose to plan purely in terms of a performance tempo then programming is a simple matter of juxtaposing up-tempo songs against slow and unmeasured ones. If that seems a little too mechanical, then ringing the changes between triple and duple/quadruple time songs will provide more subtly contrived contrasts. You can, of course, programme on the basis of subject matter: a light-hearted song followed by a tragic balled, a rural song contrasted with an industrial or urban one. Some singers prefer a programme to be a kind of sampler of the different categories of traditional song, such as long narrative pieces, love songs, sailors' songs, harvest songs, ritual songs, and so on.

For Peggy and myself, who both have large repertoires and can draw upon sections of the traditions of Scotland, England and the United States, the problem is not so much a question of variety but of what to include and what to leave out of a programme. Since we sing both folk-songs and contemporary songs in the folk idiom, our first concern is to make a proper balance between the old and the new. This generally works out at about sixty per cent traditional and forty per cent contemporary. We both enjoy singing the traditional ballads, perhaps more than any other type of song, so we rarely programme without including at least two ballads in a performance, and occasionally as many as four or five. On the rare occasions when we have not included one we have both been conscious of a lack of substance in the evening. The ballads provide the programme with an anchor; without them the evening is like a ship drifting on the tide.

Apart from deciding how many ballads we feel like singing and which contemporary songs we will include, we don't plan our programme in advance, preferring to rely on our mood at the moment of choice. Well, it isn't quite that simple. For the last thirty years we have kept records of every programme we have ever given. As a result we can, in a matter of minutes, check on which songs we have sung in any given place and can plan accordingly. For example: we are booked to sing in Newcastle-on-Tyne. We know there will be a small body of the same people there as were there at the previous performance and the one before that. So I make up a categorised list excluding those items which I have sung in Newcastle previously. (Peggy does this too but also makes a note of the songs sung there before.) My list will comprise forty or fifty titles from among which I will choose twelve or thirteen. The choice is made on the platform, it will be an on-the-spot decision.

We follow the same procedure when planning for the concert platform, though it isn't really quite so necessary to avoid songs we've sung there before. The temporary rejection of certain songs is as much in our interest as in the audience's. A song can suffer from over-singing in the same way that a field can suffer from over-planting. The field benefits from lying fallow for a period; so does a song, any song. A singer who values his or her reputation will do well to remember that any staleness creeping into a performance will be noted and commented on. Each time you appear at a club you are being tested, measured against the best in your field or against one of your previous performances. Club audiences number in their ranks some of the most well-informed individuals (in folk matters) that one could meet anywhere in Britain today.

Appreciation from members of the audience is gratifying and, at times, moving; I suppose this is one of the reasons why singers, actors, acrobats and other public performers are prepared to accept the insecurity, disappointments and frustrations of their professions. It is not the only reason, however, or even the main one. More important, I suspect, are those moments of metamorphosis when you catch a momentary glimpse of yourself in the cave, the primordial teller of tales.

Maybe that's why I find traditional ballads so satisfying to sing. They provide you with an opportunity to slip out of your everyday skin. When it happens successfully, you forget all about the hours of rehearsal, the research and analysis; the song takes you over, projects you into a timeless world where Willie drowns and goes on drowning forever in the deepest hole in Clyde's water; where Eppie Morrie, naked and beautiful, fights valiantly through an endless night; where engorged crows and ravens hop forever on the body of a young man dead in a ditch. Extraordinary moments, these, when everybody in the room seems to be using the same pair of lungs, taking long, deep breaths, but quietly so as not to disturb the overall silence, a silence in which the only sound is the subdued clatter of horses' hooves clattering through Kelso's darkened streets or the echoes of the screams of the Forbes' children burning in the flames of Towie Castle. And you burn with them, lament with their mother, and share Edom o' Gordon's remorse; and, most wonderful of all, your mind touches the mind of the ballad's creator. For a moment you are a multiple personality, with all facets functioning simultaneously.

And then the story is finished, the song is ended and you emerge from that strange world feeling a little dazed as the corporate imagination begins to fragment into its individual components. This doesn't happen immediately; there is a brief moment of stillness followed by applause, which breaks upon your own inner world like a wave of cold water. You have experienced one of those magical moments when the audience, the song and the singer become a single entity. There are, of course, times when this fusion does not take place. Three or four stanzas into the song you become conscious of having pitched it too high, not high enough to be unpleasant but enough to impose a strain on your voice so that you are no longer free to give all your attention to the story. Alternatively, in order to avoid pitching too high, you overcompensate and pitch too low, with the result that the ballad loses its emotional intensity and becomes slack and flabby. Perhaps it is the pace that is making you feel uneasy. You've started it too fast or too slow or the rhythm doesn't seem quite right. Why do the words feel heavy in my mouth? Am I hitting them too hard, using the wrong effort? Or perhaps I don't really like singing this ballad right now and shouldn't have started it in the first place.

I am sure that ballad scholarship would be greatly improved if the students underwent an apprenticeship during which they had to learn the art of ballad singing.

It is difficult, if not impossible, to make a completely objective assessment of your own performance; there are too many factors involved. Your state of mind and physical condition before and during the performance are obviously going to affect your singing, and not merely the way you sing but your judgment of the quality of your singing. I have frequently finished a performance feeling utterly depressed. This song was pitched too high and that one too low. I forgot two key stanzas of 'Clerk Colvil' and 'Thomas Rymer' was a debacle. How can I survive the shame? Then enthusiastic listeners congratulate me on my performance. I used to feel mortified by such praise. Was it possible that all my efforts to interpret these songs with skill, truth and imagination counted for nothing? Or were they just being compassionate? No, they really mean it. Of course, they could be right. Maybe I wasn't as bad as all that. After all, there's no rule which says that 'The Bird in the Bush' has to be sung in my top range. Perhaps it works just as well in a lower range and perhaps no one noticed that I forgot two stanzas. Perhaps my feeling about the performance is coloured by the fact that I've been a bit under the weather all week.

But I still find it difficult to conceal my chagrin when someone congratulates me on my performance and in the next breath lavishes praise on a singer whom I regard as a bare-arser and the last word in Mickey Mouserie. These are performers who will do anything to gain a laugh, who (when all else fails) drop their pants. I think it was Seumus Ennis who first took the name of Disney's creation and used it as an abusive epithet. Now it is widely used by traditional singers and musicians to describe performances which are showy, meretricious, plasticised and exploitative. It is not a comment on skill or competence but on a performer's attitude to the music he or she is performing. A fiddler or a piper with great technical skill can still be a Mickey Mouse performer, as can a singer with a fine voice and perfect pitch. Singing groups and musical ensembles are particularly prone to MM-ism. Perhaps it is the prevalence of so many rhythmical pieces which leads to all that foot-stamping, hand-clapping and there-you-are-me-fine-girlisms. So much fake heartiness and phony excitement tends to produce a feeling of hysteria rather than enjoyment. Perhaps the performers have been influenced by television rock-concerts where yelps, screams, grimaces, twitches and chicken-like movements of the head are as much part of the ritual as the theatrical costumes and extravagant lighting effects.

With the growth of the revival in Britain there began a corresponding revival, of sorts, throughout Europe. The strength and interest of that revival varied from country to country but nowhere did it match the British scene either in its scope or in its working-class base. It did, however, result in an expanded wage-earning area for British and American folk performers. Indeed, there were some who earned their living entirely by touring Western Germany, the Low Countries and Denmark. Unkind critics have suggested that these expatriates were performers who were incapable of winning an audience in their native land. That may or may not be true but it is certainly true that few, if any, performers can maintain the integrity of the traditional material if constantly called upon to sing songs in a language foreign to that spoken by the audience. Consequently, the performance emphasis is transferred from the song to a complicated or showy instrumental accompaniment, or to the effort to become 'a character'.

It is no accident that so many English, Irish and Scots singers who tour Europe regularly adopt the blues repertoire, for not only are the texts and themes dealt with easily understood but they come with their own ready-made aura, the romantic, raffish, devil-may-care, somewhat seedy aura of the barrel-house and bordello. And so the perfectly respectable clerk from Glasgow or the ex-schoolteacher from Ashby-de-la-Zouche can adopt the persona of Big Bill or Cat-Iron or Lonnie Johnson without going to the trouble of being born black.

Personally, I find it daunting singing for an audience whose main language is not English. You are tempted to sing your simplest material, to settle for atmos-phere, or to sing more accompanied songs. You are tempted to cut even short pieces to the bone. Ballads seem impossible. The oblique references in the contemporary political songs seem all of a sudden to be irrelevant to the place and time of singing the song. Even as you sing it all seems a bit like Liberace's three-minute version of Tchaikovsky's first piano concerto. So many of the songs have been codified by the passage of time, by colloquialisms, slang and dialect. Love and erotic songs are often based on elaborate sexual metaphors one's understanding of which depends upon one's familiarity with a specific idiom. And who has not groaned inwardly at the thought of cheerfully embark-ing on one of those humorous pieces which need laughter to make them work, for the sense of what is funny differs widely from country to country. Even when the words are only of secondary importance, the tendency is to exagger-ate more obviously brilliant parts of the melody, to hit the rhythm with more force than usual, to speed up the tempo. This is equally true of instrumentalists performing their native traditional music to a foreign audience. The language barrier can make Mickey Mousers of us all.

Singers and players in the folk revival have, for the most part, resisted the impulse to costume their performances, to dress up in the guise of farm-labourers, 18th-century highwaymen or 19th-century sailors. There have been a few outbreaks of odd headgear: a Northeast singer one arrived at a London club wearing a pit-helmet; an East Anglian used to appear regularly got up to look like Dante Gabriel Rossetti's mistress wearing Gordon Craig's floppy velour. During the sixties there was a brief period when some of the more recherche Mickey Mousers performed with their shirts open to the navel so as to show off their shiny medallions and fake mediaeval crucifixes.

But as far as dress generally is concerned, folk performers have cleaved to the sober uniform of jeans and tank-tops. Faded or patched, they were equally *de rigueuer*. To appear on a folk platform in the sixties and seventies wearing anything but jeans (if you were a man) was regarded as definitely odd. My habit of turning up to sing dressed in my best pair of navy-blue trousers, clean shirt and woollen cardigan branded me as an eccentric. The jeans-clad image of the British folksinger was so widespread that when we were touring Western Germany in 1975, the newspapers gave more space to our unusual dress than they did to our performance.

If jeans were the uniform of the revival then hair was its banner. In the earli-est days both audience and singer were clean-shaven. At the Ballads and Blues club I was the only bearded member for quite a long time. Then hair arrived. It grew longer and longer, both on men and women, until it became difficult to distinguish one sex from the other. Then came the beards, proliferating and luxuriating in an incredible way. There were times when one had the impression of singing into an impenetrable hedge of hair, a veritable Birnam Wood of whiskers. I was often reminded of those old Hollywood films where the white hunter and his blonde companion stagger bravely through dense jungle where hostile eyes peer through every bush. And, like Caliban, I sometimes heard voices in the air or – more accurately – from a hairy bundle which on closer examination usually turned out to be an old friend. Even when the heads began to sport less hair, the beards kept on growing. Indeed, it is only lately that the tide of facial hair has begun to recede. There are still plenty of beards: close-cut beards, three-quarter beards, trimmed half-beards, straggly Ho Chi Minh beards, dashing arrogant, roistering, philosophical, insinuating beards, Sir Philip Sydney beards, Lincolnesque shovel-beards and turn-of-the-century imperials. But the heroic, Marx-like, Jovian growths of yesteryear have become an endangered species.

In 1964, an established Tyneside singer resident in London said, in the course of an interview, that Lloyd and MacColl should share the benefits of their enormous experience with all those newcomers on the scene who were anxious to improve themselves. After reading the article, I phoned Bert and suggested that it might be a good idea to start a discussion group. He was distinctly cool and refused to be involved. Peggy and I mentioned it to two or three friends and almost before we had realised what was happening we found ourselves taking part in a discussion on the problems of the revival with several dozen young singers.

We had, previous to this, tutored several other singers singly. Our original intention in taking on the group was to describe some of our own experiences and to give warnings of the dangers and pitfalls which confront those who make singing folk-songs a full-time job. It didn't work out like that. Within a short time we found ourselves devoting one or two evenings each week to a group whose numbers fluctuated between twelve and twenty-five. It was a mutual-aid group where everyone gave a hand in solving each other's problems. For instance, at a number of meetings, a singer would sing a song with which she or he was having trouble with, or present a performance of a number of songs meant to represent a 'spot' at a folk club. Afterwards, the group would discuss and analyse what they had heard.

The objective of these sessions was to improve a singer's performance by seeking out the weak spots and then working to eliminate them. Since new problems were constantly arising, new techniques of dealing with them had to be developed and old techniques had to be adapted. We introduced the kind of voice exercises that had been taught in Theatre Workshop by Nelson Illingworth. We invented exercises based on Laban's effort-scales and we had exercises for relaxation and to improve articulation and the sense of pitch. These formed the basis of our purely physical work.

To extend the range and improve the quality of your voice is a comparatively simple matter. To reach an understanding of what is meant when the term 'traditional style' is used is more difficult. For weeks on end we listened to tape and disc recordings of traditional singers from every corner of the globe and entire sessions were spent on trying to imitate Phil Tanner, that wonderful old singer from the Gower peninsula, or Joseph Taylor, the Lincolnshire singer recorded by Percy Grainger in the early part of this century. Joe Heaney, Maggie McDonach of Feenish Island, Mrs Elisabeth Cronin of Cork, Robert Cinnamond of Tyrone and many others became the subject of our studies. We even branched out into imitating Balkan, Italian and Spanish singers. Learning to mimic an accent or to copy an ornament is not so difficult; the real difficulty lies in trying to imitate the tonal qualities of a voice. We worked hard and sometimes we succeeded in producing fairly accurate copies. We failed just as frequently, though the time spent in making the attempt was never wasted, for we learned a great deal about our own voices and how they worked.

For that was the object of the exercise: to make the voice supple, able to do what you wanted it to do. The object was not to end up singing like McDonach, Heaney, or Cronin. It was to develop the muscle of the voice and then move on to your own particular style. This had to be done, as all of the singers in the group had been brought up with pop and classical style music and they had no idea how the voice should – or could – be used in folk-singing. Violinists who want to become fiddlers have to do the same thing. The bowing is different, the way of holding the fiddle, the impulse given, and so on.

There were also sessions which dealt with researching songs, comparing different versions, compiling histories. There were sessions in which the singer's relationship with the audience was discussed or the building of a repertoire, the nature of folk accompaniment, microphone technique and collecting in the field. All these activities were in progress during the same time that a performance critique was being formulated. In the course of discussions on interpretation an interesting innovation was adopted, the introduction of Stanislavski's acting method, or part of that method, as part of the preliminary work on a song.

Stanislavski called this aspect of his technique 'the application of the idea of *if* to a role'. For a singer of folksongs the technique is used thus: We will suppose that you have a song in your repertoire which is no longer working as it should. We will use 'The Bonnie Earl of Murray' for our example. Now, at the outset you are provided with certain given circumstances. There is first of all, the text.

In addition to the text, you have a tune. You consult the note to the ballad in Professor Child's *English and Scots Popular Ballads,* where you learn that in February 1592, James Stewart, the Earl of Murray, died at the hand of the Earl of Huntly, who had the king's commission to arrest and bring Murray to trial for his part in the Earl of Bothwell's treasonable plot. You learn also that Murray was 'a comely personage, of great stature, and strong of body like a hemp'. Taken at their face value these few given circumstances might well justify the singer interpreting the ballad simply as a lament. Indeed the second stanza would seem to confirm such a reading beyond all doubt.

But on the other hand, the 'I' of the ballad is the king who had given the order for Murray's arrest. Furthermore, he had chosen Murray's most bitter enemy to carry out the arrest. Is it reasonable to suppose that the ballad is a mere expression of royal remorse? Or is something different being said, or at least inferred? Murray was a powerful political opponent with the kind of popular appeal which might have made him a successful usurper of the crown. This is stated unequivocally in the final stanza: 'and the bonnie Earl o' Murray he micht hae been a king'. The previous stanza says that the bonnie Earl was the queen's love. It is unlikely that this would have endeared him to the king. This reading of the text will obviously result in a performance in which the pathos of the lament – if a lament it is – is toned down. The singer is not required to make an emotional leap into the dark. He or she merely has to answer a question based on a series of assumptions which have arisen out of a close reading of the text and a little historical research.

If you were a Protestant ruler in 1592, threatened by Catholic conspirators, one of whom was said to be the beloved of your queen, and if you instructed that man's most bitter enemy to arrest him and at the same time whispered that you wouldn't mourn unduly if he were dead, how would you greet the news of his death? And how would you sing a ballad dealing with all these facts? Triumphantly, with sorrow, satisfaction, mockingly, regretfully? Perhaps with a nice blend of sorrow, satisfaction and irony with a touch of triumph in the final stanza. An honest answer to an honest question.

Suppose we change one of the circumstances and decide that the singer is not deputising for the king. Who is he, then? An enemy of the king, perhaps a supporter of the Catholic faction. So the question must now be posed differently. *If* (the application of the idea of *if* to a role) Scottish Catholicism's favourite son had been murdered and the man who commissioned the murder was publicly shedding crocodile tears, how would you, an observer, sing about the events being described in the ballad? A different question, demanding a different answer. There would certainly be no note of triumph or satisfaction. Sorrow, yes, anger and hatred or contempt for the murderer and he who inspired the murder.

Another set of ideas: suppose the maker of the ballad was opposed to the parties of both the king *and* Murray? How then would you pose the question? It would be necessary to re-interpret that part of the text which deals with the courtly pastimes of Murray. John Knox had castigated tennis, or playing at the ba', as an effeminate, foreign importation, and the ring and the glove as empty pursuits of a decadent Catholic aristocracy. If, then you were one of Knox's ardent young followers with a liking for the old songs, how would you go about singing a ballad which contained all the above information? You could go on ringing the changes on the given circumstances for quite a long time and each change would result in a different interpretation of the ballad.

Into the Folk Revival

The Critics Group[4], as we called ourselves, spent much of its time in this kind of work and, in addition, began to explore the possibilities of developing folk-theatre. Our first excursion along this rarely travelled road was a production of an up-dated version of the mumming play *St George and the Dragon*. We toured around the clubs for over a year with this highly successful play, in which the our George (a butcher by trade) was played as a ton-up kid, complete with motorcycle clobber and helmet. Then the group decided to embark on something more ambitious. After some discussion we decided that our first major theatrical venture should be a political review of the year's news, twelve or more dramatic episodes loosely organised into a simple framework based on ideas suggested by the ancient Festival of Fools[5], the annual Saturnalia of antiquity, when slaves were permitted to ridicule their masters and unruly youths poured scorn on the princes of the church, with the permission of the church.

The daily task of gathering cuttings from half a dozen newspapers and as many journals and magazines was one to which everyone in the group lent themselves. The organisation of the various activities involved in such a large undertaking was Peggy's responsibility. Mine was to write the script, compose most of the songs and act as the producer. Our 'theatre' was a room in The New Merlin's Cave, a pub in Margery Street off Kings Cross Road. It was a large room with a small but serviceable stage. We built two additional platforms so that we had three acting areas.

It was an ambitious enterprise for a company of amateur actors whose experience up to now consisted of playing in a simple mumming play where rough clowning and slapstick humour were enough to sustain the very simple story. The occasional flashes of brilliance, the camaraderie and the sheer vitality of the actors managed to keep the ideas afloat. The first *Festival of Fools* was a very amateur show. The following year it was infinitely less so, and by 1968 the Critics Group production of the annual *Festival of Fools* had become an event of considerable merit. The dedication of the group members was incredible; they were all holding down nine-to-five jobs. Their daily schedule doesn't bear thinking about. We all managed on five or six hours of sleep a night and full-time energy-consuming activity from seven in the morning till midnight every day seven days a week.

By 1970, we were on the brink of becoming a professional touring company. Unfortunately, internal dissension split the company and at the end of a twenty-eight night's run, the Critics Group ceased to exist. It had survived for six years and had produced several skilled folksingers. It had roped dozens of members of The Singers Club audience into productions of the yearly event. It had pioneered the way in folk- and pub-theatre. Its members had initiated or taken part in training programmes in a dozen provincial centres, had written songs against the Vietnam war and apartheid, about racism, fascism and the attacks on organised labour. For Peggy and myself, it was an intense period of learning, it was that old excitement again, that pushing back of the frontiers of knowledge and self-awareness. And yet that period, that work, that effort, those productions, passed without comment on the part of the handful of newspaper columnists who wrote about folk matters; nor was it mentioned in the folk mags and fanzines which at the time were as numerous as spots an the chest of a child stricken with measles.

Almost from the first week of its birth, The Critics Group had been a target for suspicion and abuse. The suspicion fed on itself and created its own myths which, in turn, exacerbated the situation and produced even more abuse. The name *Critics Group* was seized upon by rabid myth-makers and held up as proof of our arrogance. 'What right have they to criticise us?' was the cry. In actual fact, we were criticising *ourselves*. I think it was the idea of a folksinger having to train like an athlete or a carpenter which stuck in the craw of most of our critics. 'Did Harry Cox or Sam Larner or Jeannie Robertson – or any field singer – have to train?' There were, of course, several answers to that. Joe Heaney, for example, *did* train, *did* plan his decorations, the use of this tone here and that tone there. We have recordings of Paddy Tunney talking about how he decorates, how he approaches a song, who his models were when he was learning. Then there was the fact that the traditional singer had been a neighbour among neighbours who know his repertoire almost as well as he did. Furthermore, field-singers were not expected to sing twelve or fourteen songs in a row three or four times a week in front of strange audiences. The job of the revival singer is very different from that of a traditional singer. Nonetheless, it is still a common myth that all folksingers are really amateurs. We were in Bletchley one night at a club and a member of the audience happened to be present when we were being paid. He was astonished. 'You get *paid* for this?' he said. 'You shouldn't. You were just doing something you enjoy doing.' A compliment, perhaps, but also indicative of a commonly held opinion as to the professional status of folksingers.

Even now, nearly twenty years after the dissolution of the Critics Group, myths are being created about it. Recently, in what purported to be a serious if somewhat shrill exposé of the folk revival, the Critics Group was described as an organisation which met *in secret*. The author had in his possession a tape-recording which apparently had been *smuggled out* of one of these clandestine sessions. In view of the fact that a great number of the meetings were recorded and access to the recordings is simply a matter of obtaining permission from the National Sound Archives or The Charles Parker Archive in Birmingham, no great skill was required to 'smuggle them out'.

Should one, on encountering myths of this sort, rush to one's typewriter or word-processor and dash off a repudiation? Perhaps; but I have had neither the time nor the inclination. Apart from the fact that you could easily spend most of your working hours dealing with misinformation, there is something rather endearing about the idea of a group of conspirators plotting to re-establish a group of songs which are the nation's rightful heritage. Less endearing is the myth of 'Charles Parker's radio-ballads'.[6]

23

Radio Ballads[1]

I met Charles Parker for the first time in the mid 1950s. I was recording a talk on experimental theatre for the North American Service of the BBC and Charles was the producer. He complained of being over-worked and said he was longing to get his teeth into something worthwhile. When I next met him he had become a features producer for the Midland Region and was working on a Christmas programme which Alan Lomax had written and in which I was to take part.

Charles and Alan were an impossible mixture. Temperamentally, they were complete opposites. Alan – volatile, expansive, warm, outgoing, a man of the south. Charles – withdrawn, inhibited, on guard, mindful of his dignity – the northern man. In outlook, too, they were poles apart. Alan was a Marxist, a left-wing intellectual, a man whose mind was constantly at work correlating social, anthropological and political ideas, an enquiring man, intolerant of all kinds of intolerance. Charles was a true-blue conservative with an occasional tendency to glow pink. He was a practising Christian, a churchman active in parish affairs. He loved ritual of all kinds and accepted the hierarchical structure of society as a natural phenomenon.

At a rehearsal of the Christmas feature, Lomax sat in the studio and observed Charles with astonishment. Later in the canteen during a coffee break he said, 'I have the feeling that somebody's trying to put one over on me. I don't believe he's real.' Shortly afterwards, he made an excuse to leave the studio and didn't reappear until the transmission. And that was surely a measure of his discomfiture. It was one of the very few times I ever knew him to leave a studio while a production was in progress.

In the autumn of 1957, Charles asked whether I was interested in writing a script for him. Peggy was travelling in China and Poland and though we wrote regularly we seemed very far apart. So yes, I was interested, and Charles gave me an outline of the following story. John Axon, a steam-locomotive driver from Edgely, near Stockport, had recently been posthumously awarded the George Cross for an act of heroism. Just before the downhill run into Dove Holes, the steam-brake pipe on Axon's locomotive had severed. The train was moving rather slowly uphill and Axon could easily have jumped clear. Instead, he chose to hang spread-eagled on the outside of his cab in order to warn men in signal-boxes along the route. His decision cost him his life.

We travelled across country to Edgely in Charles' ancient Morris Minor and discussed the form the programme should take. Charles favoured something on the lines of *Lonesome Train,* Earl Robinson's cantata on the death of President Lincoln. He had heard it while working in the United States for the BBC and it had made a profound impression on him. Indeed, *Lonesome Train* and *John Brown's Body,* Stephen Vincent Benet's verse narrative on the American Civil War, were initially responsible for Charles' interest in folk-song. It was the vernacular elements in both these works that attracted him; they reminded him of the songs he had heard at concerts in the officers' mess in Alexandria, songs like 'Cindy', 'Frankie and Johnny' and 'The Blue-Tailed Fly'.

When we began working on *The Ballad of John Axon,* we didn't intend to depart from the pattern of the normal radio feature programme. We would record Axon's widow and some of the men with whom he had worked and then, using the recordings as a guide, I would write a dramatic reconstruction of the events which would eventually be performed by actors and musicians.

It didn't work out like that. Charles' budget allowed for a total of four or five days' recording in the field but in real terms the time spent in the area was nearly fourteen days spread over a period of a month. We finally returned to base with over forty hours of recorded actuality.

Now it was up to me to listen to that enormous mass of recorded speech and write a script based upon it. I played through those tapes for several hours a day for a fortnight, running some of the more striking statements over and over again. Their impact was tremendous; the flat, deliberate northern voices evoking the past, paying laconic tribute to a dead comrade and encapsulating a lifetime's experience in a simile: 'When you work in steam, railways go through the back of your spine like Blackpool goes through rock'. (What a powerful simile that is: who, as a child, has not held one of those sticky pink and white rods of boiled toffee and licked and licked and licked and seen the glowing red letters of the name of a seaside resort, visible to the very last lick?)

As I listened it became obvious that on these tapes we had captured a remarkable picture of a way of life, a picture in words charged with the special kind of vitality and excitement which derives from involvement in a work-process. The problem was how to use it. Could I rewrite it without falsifying it? The more I listened the more I became convinced that neither the standard format of the radio feature nor the elegiac framework of *Lonesome Train* could accommodate the wild stuff we had recorded. It wasn't merely that the recorded speech had the true ring of spontaneity; there was something else – the excitement of an experience re-lived and communicated directly without dilution of additives, living speech unglossed by author's pen or actor's voice.

The planning of the script of *John Axon* was a simple matter. Axon's last journey from the Edgely loco-shed to the station at Chapel-en-le-Frith in

Derbyshire provided the perfect framework for a programme into which I could slot blocks of recorded speech for I was convinced after listening to the first play-back that the Axon story would have to be told by the railwaymen themselves and not by actors imitating railwaymen. As for the songs . . . ah yes, the songs! Something like *Lonesome Train,* Charles had said. Not with the kind of actuality we had recorded! Those soft Cheshire and southeast Lancashire accents would have sounded incongruous in an Earl Robinson setting. The American railroad song tradition could surely provide more appropriate models.

I wrote the music for *John Axon* in ten days, conceiving each song as an extension of a specific piece of actuality, as a comment on that actuality, or as a simple frame for a collection of actuality pieces. Some of the lyrics were written to traditional tunes, others were based on melodic motifs common to the English, North American or West Indian folk-music traditions. One entire sequence used ideas borrowed from traditional jazz. The main weakness as far as the music was concerned was that it was rhythmically and harmonically orientated towards the American tradition rather than to the British, a point on which none of the critics commented until some eight years after the original transmission.

The songs completed, I proceeded to assemble a tape in which songs and actuality were brought together for the first time. I can still remember the feeling of excited anticipation when I pressed the playback switch on my Ferrograph. The excitement quickly gave way to dismay. The programme in my head and the one on the tape were so far apart that I almost abandoned the project there and then. Fortunately, at this point Peggy returned from her travels. When she listened to my rough assembly (it was very rough indeed) she was impressed by the vigour of the form and immediately set about writing accompaniments to the songs and incidental music tailored to the actuality. My crude and halting sequences were transformed into the smoothly flowing episodes of my imagination. When the time came for us to show Charles the result of our labours we had created a fairly complete script, lacking only the timings for the improvised sequences.

Charles received the script with a distinct lack of enthusiasm. It was a long way from *Lonesome Train.* Perhaps it would have been more acceptable had we transcribed the actuality in full but we didn't. Instead, we gave cue numbers which matched the actuality excerpts. These with the song lyrics and musical tag references only added up to nine foolscap pages, a meagre offering compared with the thirty or forty pages of the average hour-long feature programme. And he doubted whether he could get away with using raw actuality; moreover, some of our proposed actuality excerpts were so short that there wouldn't be time for them to register on the listener's ear. Peggy started on the musical scores and Charles, still a little dubious about the nature of the speech, began the tape editing.

The method of tape assembly and its use had become current BBC practice. Our team of singers and instrumentalists rehearsed and recorded, over a period of two or three days, all the songs and instrumental music for the programme. In normal circumstances, Charles would have spent two or three days marrying the songs and music to the actuality. In the case of *John Axon,* this particular part of the production was made impossibly difficult through a malfunction of the studio recording machines, with the result that all the studio-recorded material (much of it meant to mirror or interlock with actuality) was running at a different speed from that recorded in the field. In one instance, two takes of a piece of music, which had to be edited, had been recorded on two different studio machines, which ran at different speeds. It was a nightmare, but Charles met the situation head-on and locked himself in the studio control-room and accomplished miracles with innumerable scraps of tape ranging in length from pieces yards long to shreds and slivers of microscopic size. If, after correction, the musical pitches were not as firm as they might have been, they were not so infirm as to be unbearable. It must be stressed that at this time we were recording on quarter-inch single-track tape; multi-track recording facilities were still far in the future.

Charles' reservations about the form we had presented him with had disappeared completely by the time we finished working on the programme. Indeed, he had become an enthusiastic advocate of the form, which we called the *radio-ballad.* It was, I think, in that small editing cubicle at Maida Vale that he first discovered in himself an extraordinary talent for manipulating tape. In these days of multi-track recording, the scissors-and-razorblade type of editor is a thing of the past. In the late fifties, it was the only way and Charles had, in the space of a few days, become a master editor.

In view of his magnificent contribution to the programme, I suggested that the credits for *John Axon* be shared out equally between Charles, Peggy and myself, an unusual arrangement. Peggy rejected this division as she hadn't been involved in the project from the beginning and Charles felt that three names might present billing difficulties. So it was decided to attribute *The Ballad of John Axon* to Ewan MacColl and Charles Parker with musical arrangements by Peggy Seeger. Had this particular billing been confined to *John Axon* it wouldn't have been unreasonable but unfortunately it was used for each of the subsequent radio-ballads. It was grossly unfair, as Peggy's role in the creation of the radio-ballad form was a major one. I wonder whether we'd have had any billing problems had our musical director been a man.

When *John Axon* was finally broadcast it received the kind of publicity that is usually accorded to a controversial play or to a novel banned by the censor. The radio critic of *The Sunday Times* wrote: 'As remarkable a piece of radio as I have ever listened to.' *The Observer*'s reviewer was equally enthusiastic: 'Last week a technique and a subject got married and nothing in radio kaleidoscopy, or whatever you like to call it, will ever be the same again.' 'Even *The New Statesman,* generally cautious in handing out praise, was congratulatory in a piece signed by Tom Driberg: 'Flecker's dream of being read by a poet living' a thousand years hence is unlikely to be realised, but a generation from now, listeners will surely still be moved by the recording of *The Ballad of John Axon.*'

Radio Ballads

This was praise indeed, and the BBC put its own seal of approval on the work by choosing it as the British entry for the 1958 Prix d' Italia. Those of us who had been most closely involved with the programme were far from satisfied and were aware of its many defects. The story of Axon's death was, in itself, highly dramatic; it possessed a built-in chronology and a natural dramatic climax. Who could fail with such a story? Naturally it fitted into the ballad form, said the wiseacres. You just happen to have hit on a story which falls pat into the 'Casey Jones'-'Wreck of the Old 97' formula. Poets and composers who, prior to this time, had viewed the folk revival with barely concealed contempt, were now prepared to concede that it wasn't entirely lacking in artistic potential. The poet Louis MacNeice commented: 'So you have proved that the ballad can be a valid form of expression for the 20th century and for the mass media. But only when applied to a simple black-and-white situation.' It was with statements like this ringing in our ears that we embarked upon a radio-ballad which was to deal with the building of Britain's first modern motorway, the M1.

Of the 19,000 men employed on this project, more than half were Irish, descendants of the men who had built Britain's canal and railway systems. There were tradesmen of all kinds: engineers, scaffolders, bridge-builders, bricklayers, carpenters, asphalters, pavers, cement-mill operators, pick-and-shovel slingers, ditch-diggers, concreting gangs, tea-nippers and the rest. There they were with their bulldozers, Euclids and dumpers, their caterpillar-tractors, steam-cranes and automatic shovels, their picks, rock-drills and nine-pound hammers, stretched across the first fifty miles of the projected route in a line roughly parallel with that other road which had once served the cohorts of Persian archers, Gallic swordsmen, Scythian spear-throwers and Iberian cavalry who made up Caesar's legions. In addition to the motley army of Irish, Scots, Welsh, Indian, Pakistani, Greek, Polish and English labourers, there were designers, geologists, soil-chemists, archaeologists, planners, statisticians, contractors and sub-contractors.

The building of the M1 provided us with a marvellous subject for a radio-ballad, one that could surely have proved that the techniques of folk creation were capable of dealing with the 20th century in whatever guise it appeared. Had we approached the subject with the daring and zest which it demanded, we might well have created one of the great radio programmes of all time. As it was, we fumbled the opportunity and produced a work that was an unhappy blend of radio-ballad and radio-feature.

It was not until after we had signed the contracts for *Song of a Road* that Charles informed us that the head of his department in Birmingham felt that a less subjective approach than that used in *John Axon* might be more appropriate for the new project. Charles tended to agree. The euphoria which had borne him along during the final days of the first radio-ballad had receded and left him feeling unsure of himself and of the radio-ballad form. Perhaps, he suggested, the subject matter called for a treatment more akin to the classic feature programme. After all, the M1 was a national affair, unlike the Axon tragedy which had been concerned with an individual and the small circle of his friends and colleagues. It was right and proper that a single act of heroism should be given the kind of emotional treatment we had given the Axon programme but now a more restrained approach was needed. Perhaps if we married the radio-ballad form with the formal feature programme we might just hit the right note . . . and, in order to achieve the perfect balance, this time we must allow the management to be heard as well as the workers. The result was a thoroughly confusing – and at times boring – programme.

When *Song of a Road* was finally broadcast, *The Sunday Observer* radio-critic described it as 'a near-triumph by *John Axon* standards and an absolute marvel by any other'. Peggy and I considered it a debacle with a few bright spots, but it taught us a very valuable lesson about the precise nature of the relationship of speech to class and to traditional songs.

In the course of playing back the road builders' actuality we had observed that there were basic differences in the way in which words were used by the manual workers on the one hand and by the planners and white-collar staff on the other. The latter, though educated and 'articulate', were tedious to listen to. We found that our concentration would begin to dissipate after a few minutes. To our 'uneducated' speakers, however, we could listen for long periods without any decline in concentration. This was odd, since the soil-chemists, designers, planners and surveyors were presumably getting more job-satisfaction from what they were doing than, say, the navvies, dump-truck operators and joiners turning out mile after mile of rough shuttering. We tried out a listening test on friends, on BBC typists, canteen-workers and messenger boys. The result was the same. They could remember whole passages of the West Country man talking about the beds in the hostels but couldn't remember the sequence of this or that technique or the components of cement.

We made a rough analysis of the speech in a number of tapes chosen at random and came up with some interesting facts. The managerial contributors tended to use an extremely small area of the vocal-effort spectrum. Irrespective of the subject under discussion, they scarcely ever varied the tempo of delivery. Almost all of them made constant use of the impersonal pronoun. *One* was consistent in *one's* use of tenses and *one* rarely changed direction inside a sentence or phrase; verbs were given more vocal weight than nouns and similes and metaphors were almost totally eschewed. They spoke *at* you rather than *with* you. The total result was a reasoned, impassive, uninvolved stream of sound. And it was dull.

The labourers, on the other hand, used similes and metaphors with obvious enjoyment. They changed tense frequently (this happens a great deal in folk-song) when they wanted to emphasise a point or to sharpen an argument. They made use of extended analogies and emphasised verbs in such a way as to give every sentence an effort-peak. Almost all of them used the first-person singular and the present-historical with equal effect. Their spectrum of vocal efforts was, on the whole, much larger than that of the managerial group.. The workers were speaking for dramatic effect and watching the result, not just giving information.

The selection of actuality is a task which requires a great deal of patience. You play the tapes over and over again in the hope that some profound statement which you have overlooked the first time round will suddenly reveal itself. The typed transcript is a useful guide to subject matter but it is limited. Your choice must be based on additional factors such as speed of utterance, rhythm, pitch and timbre of voice and the speaker's effort-pattern. By the tenth time you have listened to a forty-five-second passage of actuality you begin to feel that the words originated in your own mind and took form in *your* mouth with breath taken from *your* lungs. You have become familiar with every vowel and consonant, with every hesitant pause, every inflection, and – most important of all – you have discovered whether there is anything to be found beyond the words.

We incorporated our findings in a memo which we sent to Charles and in the course of the next three weeks the three of us met several times to discuss future plans. These discussions produced guidelines which were to prove useful in the creation of each of the subsequent radio-ballads. Among other things, it was agreed that the selection of actuality should, from now on, be left to Peggy and me and that selected actuality excerpts with possible alternatives should be sent to Charles as soon as an episode of the script was completed. Finally, we decided that the radio-ballads should not be primarily concerned with work-processes but with people's attitudes and responses to those processes; in other words, not with things but with the way people related to things and the way in which those relationships were expressed in words. The idea of fairness to both sides was never mentioned again.

Our third radio-ballad, *Singing the Fishing,* dealt with the herring-fishing industry and, unlike its predecessors, it went without a hitch from the beginning. By this time Peggy and I were living together and she was nursing our new son, Neill.

In accordance with our decision to let the actuality mould the shape of the programme, we embarked on the field recording for *Singing the Fishing* without any preconceived notions as to what the finished product would be like. The areas chosen for field-work were East Anglia (the traditional but decayed centre of the herring-fishing) and northeast Scotland (Fraserburgh, Aberdeenshire and Banffshire), the centre of the new post-war industry.

In East Anglia we hit pay-dirt immediately when, through Philip Donnellan (a BBC television director) we were introduced to Sam Larner, an octogenarian ex-herring-fisherman from Winteron, Norfolk.[2] What a wonderful person he was! Short, compact, grizzled, wall-eyed and slightly deaf but still full of the wonder of life. His one good eye still sparkled at the sight of a pretty girl. We brought him to London to sing at the Ballads and Blues and for several hours he sat and sang and talked to the several hundred young people who hung on his every word and gesture as though he had been Ulysses newly returned from Troy to Ithaca. He never forgot it. 'They liked them old songs, they did. Yes, they did, they liked 'em. All them pretty young girls sitting down there on the front row with their short skirts. Yes, real short, they were. They was bootiful, real bootiful.'

Larner had first gone to sea in 1892 on board a sailing-lugger and, in the course of his working life, had seen the sailing fleet give way to steam-drifters. He had lived through the industry's golden age when Great Yarmouth had reckoned up the annual catch by the million barrels. Furthermore, he could sing and he knew dozens of country songs, traditional ballads, local legends and mnemonic rhymes for navigation. In the course of recording him we set up a pattern which subsequently became our regular recording procedure.

In the first few days we dealt with the broad outlines of his life and work. We then played back the recordings and noted carefully which type of question and method of questioning elicited the best response. We listed lacunae in the narrative, made preliminary sketches for songs related to his speech rhythms and broke down the chronology of the narrative into manageable sections. Then there followed a fortnight's intensive recording period, during which specific areas of Sam's life were dealt with in some detail. For three or four days, for example, we listened to him recalling the days of his early childhood. We probed and constantly changed the perspective of our questions until his emotion-memory was in full flight and he began to re-live and re-feel the experiences and emotions of three-quarters-of-a-century earlier.

There were times when the force of memory was so strong in the old man that he would forget we were present and re-enact conversations with friends and neighbours dead these fifty years. The period of his adolescence and early manhood were dealt with in a similar way and in each successive recording session his eagerness to reveal the meaning of his life became more apparent. At the same time, the more deeply he entered into his past, the more rich and varied became his verbal imagery. Similes, metaphors, proverbs, biblical quotations, weather rhymes, bawdy aphorisms, all combined to make his speech as active as his life had been.

We noticed also that as time wore on, he ceased to censor his memories. Work, hunger, sexual appetite, pain and joy were all recalled with equal frankness. 'I been a wicked man in my time,' he said, with obvious relish. 'Ain't that right, Dorcas?' (this to his wife who was sitting by the fire, opposite him).

'You have, Sam, you have,' agrees Dorcas philosophically.

'Yes', says Sam, his one good eye alight with concupiscent memories, 'I done some wicked things.'

'You been a wicked bugger, Sam,' comments Dorcas again, and Sam shakes and wheezes with delight.

'See? She knows what I mean. Don't you, my old dear?' Then, with passionate intensity, he says, 'And I loved it. Yes, I loved it! And now that I'm too old for it I don't care whether I live nor die. No, I don't, truly I don't!'

Sam, Sam – survivor of hard days and rough nights, of big seas and small boats, of storms and the dole!

After this phase of the recording programme, Peggy and I spent several days transcribing the material and making a rough selection of the passages most relevant to our purpose. By this time the rough shape of our programme had begun to emerge. Sam Larner had inadvertently revealed, through the three main periods of his life, the three main sections of our radio-ballad: the periods of sail, steam and diesel. We decided to base the first part of the programme on Sam's life. Some of the songs were already beginning to take shape from the actuality and I was by this time so attuned to the rhythm of his utterance and so familiar with his breathing patterns that I could imagine how the songs and actuality would dovetail and complement each other.

The quality of the actuality was remarkable. One could have chosen at random enough fine passages to have furnished a dozen radio programmes. But we had got the taste for Sam's conversation and wanted more; or perhaps it was just that we were reluctant to abandon our Winterton oasis for the outside world. Just two more days, we said, two more days' recording during which we would persuade him to talk about his fundamental concepts, his philosophy of life.

It was an ambitious undertaking. We virtually asked that he should sum up his eighty years' experience of living, define his relationship to the community in which he lived, comment on the changes which had taken place in that community, define his attitude to politics, religion, work, to the songs he sang, to old age and death.

His vision of death was akin to that of Langland in *Piers Plowman* and to the tellers of folk-tales. Death was a cunning adversary perpetually engaged in a series of all-in wrestling bouts with human challengers. Naturally, death won all but one of the contests, though he could be tricked and vanquished by a man of wit and determination. 'It won't be the first time he come for me and it won't be the first time I cheated him! That time he come for me in the North Sea, when he come in the storm, when all the young chaps were cryin' and prayin' down below. I done him then.' Returning to the theme, he said, 'Soon I'll be pushin' up the daisies. Ain't got long now, but when he come for me I'll look him in the eye. I ain't got nothing to be ashamed of.'

The total time spent in recording Sam Larner covered two-and-a-half weeks and, after excising repetitions, introductions, interruptions, the sound of our own voices and the endless clatter of tea being made, poured, sugared and passed around, we were left with almost thirty hours of magnificent talk and three hours of songs, ballads, stories and miscellaneous rhymes. A wonderful haul! Too wonderful, perhaps. Where were we going to find actuality that could match it dealing with the days of steam and diesel-driven drifters? Sam Larners don't grow on trees, or so we thought.

It had been fine spring weather all the time we had been recording in Winterton, warm enough for us to lie sunbathing on the deserted beach between recording sessions. But now the weather had broken, winter had come again and it was raining heavily when we set off for the docks in Great Yarmouth. 'How do you set about getting people to record for you?' is a question often asked. How indeed. Generally you have a lead on someone who can furnish you with names or at least with a friend who knows a chap who's father knows, etc, etc. This time, however, we had no lead at all, hence our visit to the docks. It was difficult to believe that this abandoned waterfront had once been the herring-fishing centre of the world. Now there were three or four drifters rusting away in their berths and a few pleasure craft. Charles accosted a harbour official and told him that we were looking for herring-fishermen to record. 'There's no herring here', said the man, 'and no herring-fishermen. It's all finished. Gone.' He went on to tell us how a great fishing port had died. It was very depressing and for a moment it looked as if our programme had hit a brick wall. At the end of his jeremiad, he said, 'You should talk to the chap who was master of that boat over there,' indicating one of the drifters with a FOR SALE sign on it. 'He could tell you all about herring. Name of Balls. Ronnie Balls.'

Once again, we had stumbled on a fine rich lode. Ronnie Balls, retired steam-drifter skipper of Great Yarmouth did for steam what Sam had done for sail, but whereas Larner had used words in the manner of a dramatic poet, Balls' approach was that of a master of the lyric form. To hear the soft East Anglian drawl of this youthful sixty-year-old describing the finer points of a steam drifter was to know tenderness and love in its most pure form, and that is not exaggeration. Ronnie Balls loved steam-drifters with the same kind of consuming passion that lovers in mediaeval romances reserve for their mistresses. 'Ah, the steam-drifter', he said, in a voice that would have won the heart of Tam Lin's elfin queen, 'the loveliest ship for the job that ever was built.'

The *job* was herring fishing and that, too, he loved – physically, spiritually, intellectually.

> There's no feelin' like comin' into harbour with a good catch of fish. Hundred cran! Cor, lovely shot! Get your sample out, let's be sellin' 'em. See? And you . . . you just lean back in the wheelhouse and you look. All I can think of is . . . you know, if you was one of the old hunters in the tribal days. How you've brought home the meat. You share it out. Do what you like with it. I've done my bit.

Until I heard Ronnie Balls' eulogies of the sea and of the indomitable little ships that had ploughed their way from the Outer Minch to the Norwegian Deeps, I had believed that the English tongue had lost its magical powers. This man, in whose voice enthusiasm danced like the rays of the sun on the waves of a smiling sea, proved me wrong. He sat there in the front parlour of his semi-detached and talked, and behind each word there echoed the voice of Deor, court singer of the Heodenings.

In between the two world wars, the herring-fishing industry had declined and Great Yarmouth had declined with it. After the Second World War a new

Radio Ballads

fleet of diesel-driven boats was built, equipped with radar and echo-sounding gear. The centre of the industry moved to the Scottish northeast coast.

So now we made our way northwards to record actuality for the third part of *Singing the Fishing* and set up base in Gardenstown (Gamrie), a small herring-fishing community on the Banffshire coast. There we learned that the fisherfolk were, almost to a man and woman, members of a fundamentalist sect, the Closed Brethren. Social contact between them and the ordinary country folk living adjacent was practically non-existent. Towards us, however, the fisherman and their families appeared friendly enough and in the two or three weeks we were working with them we were accepted into their community in a way that the country people were not.

On board the *Honeydew*, we got our first real glimpse of the herring-fisherman's way of life. She was a trim, diesel-driven drifter that rode the big Atlantic rollers like a cork. She was small, after the manner of drifters, but tough and indomitable like the men who sailed in her. During our time aboard her, Charles and I organised our recording schedule so that there was never a time in the twenty-four-hour cycle when one of us was not on hand with a tape-recorder at the ready. We kept them running while we sat at meals in the galley and in the wheelhouse where a radio-receiving set kept up a continuous chatter of information from every drifter within a fifty-mile radius.

We caught the marvellous burst of excitement as the lookout sighted a shoal: 'Herring on the port bow! Herring! Herring!' We were there to hear the skipper, Frank West, cry out like a man in the throes of religious ecstasy; 'There they are, the silver darlings!' We recorded the rhythmical clacking of the winch as the two-mile-long nets were played out and noted that it would make a fine cross-rhythm against a triple-time song. We waited on the blacked-out deck as the men pulled the herring-filled nets from the sea, hour after hour, until it seemed that the world was a bottomless hole from which the shimmering green fire of herrings would never stop rising. If a red herring was pulled in, one of the fishermen would put it in his mouth, his teeth clamped on the wriggling fish, and keep it there for luck as he continued pulling.

Ten hours of pulling and two miles of fish-filled net drawn from the sea! A good catch, well above average for the time of year. 'You've brought us luck,' says the mate, an amiable giant from Cairnbulg. One by one the weary net-haulers pass on their way to the galley, clapping us on the back, shaking hands with us and thanking us for having brought them luck.

Then it's a race back to Ullapool in Wester Ross, to catch the market while the prices are still high. An hour or two to unload and then back to sea again for more. And it's like this six days of the week, fifty weeks of the year, work calculated to age a man prematurely and to kill off those with without enormous physical stamina. Brute work, and yet the men are not brutalised. They are serious-minded men and when they talk it is of important things like man's relationship with his maker, the price of fish, of work and the bad old days of the Depression, the memory of which haunts all of them. They speak with the

-311-

slow deliberation of seers and prophets. If the East Anglian men's speech evokes occasional echoes of Langland and the maker of that fine old English poem *The Seafarer,* then these northeasterners have the tongue of the ballad-maker.

I am sailing with them through the Northern Minch in a seven-point gale. The *Honeydew* looks and feels like a toy boat lost in a grey wilderness of sea and sky. At one moment she is lifted to the summit of a great peak and the next she's ploughing through a deep trough ridged by banks of white-topped waves. I stand there on the deck, terrified, clinging desperately with one hand to a steel cable, while in the other I hold up a microphone in a vain effort to record the storm. By my side is Louis Cardno, a Huguenot Scot from Cairnbulg who, in order to illustrate a theological point, is howling into my ears a lengthy quotation from Fox's *Book of Martyrs.*

The playback and transcription of the actuality of *Singing the Fishing* took Peggy and me the best part of three weeks. After choosing and timing the actuality for the programme and compiling a tape of alternative pieces, we spent three or four days making a working script, that is we related specific pieces of actuality to slips of paper bearing the titles of songs which hadn't yet been written. These slips represented the first part of the process of transforming the raw material into a musical statement. The slip might carry only a title or a single word such as 'hauling' or 'the catch' or it might be a short memo: 'Here, four-line stanza with short refrain.' Or it could be a suggested shape for a sequence: 'Interpolate actuality between second and third stanzas. Substitute voice shouting command for third stanza's refrain.' It could be a phrase of actuality: 'living gale', or 'that night it blew a living gale'. Or it could be actuality incorporated into a lyric:

> In the stormy seas and the living gales,
> Just to earn your daily bread you're daring . . .

And occasionally, just occasionally, it might be an entire song-text which would only require a little polishing.

The writing of the songs took me about a month, or maybe a little longer. Some of them took only an hour or two, some took days before they fitted comfortably in the mouth. I wrestled with the ideas for 'Shoals of Herring' for over two weeks. Nothing came right. Every time I sat down to write, the economy and simplicity of the form I had chosen would elude me. When, finally, I hit the right note I completed the song in fifteen minutes.

Peggy spent a fortnight making and writing out the musical arrangements and compiling tapes and scores for the musicians. Some of the scores had whole sections left in them for the musicians to improvise (which baffled Alf Edwards, the concertina-wizard, for the first three or four radio-ballads; he afterwards became quite proficient at, as he put it, 'surviving without the dots'); parts of the score were timed down to a half-second to allow the actuality to weave in and out. We then made rough tapes of the songs and played them to Sam and Ronnie and anyone else who was prepared to listen. Occasionally they would criticise a word or a line or a phrase or they would question a piece of information, whereupon I would re-write the offending word or phrase and go on re-writing it until it met with their approval. When I finished writing 'Shoals of Herring' we sang it to Sam Larner on our next trip up. He was delighted that I knew it for, as he declared, 'I known that song all my life.' A later informant, upon hearing a song Peggy made from her words, said, 'I hear myself talking.' A song about fishermen must please fishermen, a song about miners must be convincing to miners, or there is something wrong with it.

The studio work on *The Ballad of John Axon* and *Song of a Road* had consisted of two or three days' intensive work with singers and musicians; during these sessions songs and music transitions would be recorded. The marrying of music, songs and actuality was performed by Charles and his editing staff (for he did not do all the editing himself). The studio technique for *Singing the Fishing* was entirely different. Actuality was pre-edited, timed and assembled in sequence on master tapes with leader tape in between each cue. Sound-effect sequences were built up on additional tapes. Tape-machines for feeding in actuality and sound effects were installed in the performance area of the studio and tape-machine operators became members of the musical ensemble. A Gramophone operator was upstairs in the cubicle, practising dropping the needle on *exactly* the right groove for effects that could not be pre-assembled. This studio layout was Charles' brainchild and by adopting it we found it possible to record complete sequences in one go, sections in which music, songs, actuality and sound-effects dovetailed or flowed into one another. Singers and musicians were no longer working in the dark but could match every nuance of speech, could alter vocal density so as to ride with a speaker's changes of pitch resulting from a rising or lowering of the emotional level. In the same way, pulses and rhythms of speech could be matched exactly by a musical instrument without destroying the guidelines of the musical arrangements. For the tape-machine operators, it meant that actuality feed-ins could be conceived as continuations of a melodic line, that the first heavily-accented word in a passage of speech could be made to coincide with the accented beats in a bar of music, that short passages of actuality could be interpolated between the verses of a song in place of musical tags or that they could be fed between two lines of a stanza and serve as refrains. In short, the tape-machines became another instrument in the orchestra.

Third day of recording. So far everything has gone smoothly. There's a good atmosphere in the studio, though Alf Edwards still complains about having to spend time in Birmingham. 'Surely the barn would have been more suitable' (the barn is the big music studio at Maida Vale). He has trouble sleeping in strange beds. 'Done too much of it, old chap.' Still, he looks spruce enough, always does. Always the perfect gent, Alf. Well-cut suit, a bit on the sober side but not funereal. Discreetly striped shirt and club tie, probably Variety Club. And, the shoes, always beautifully polished. Greying blond hair sleeked back, nails always neatly trimmed. Looks like an old-fashioned banker. When he was slimmer and younger he played the night-clubs. I wonder how old he really is.

'Alf, how old are you?'

'Old enough to have learned never to ask anyone's age before midday.'

Must be in his sixties at least. Knows and is known by almost every musician in the business. Played every kind of gig, 1930s dance bands, music halls, busked on beaches at seaside resorts, pit orchestras, the lot. Was born in a circus, father and mother were musical clowns. 'My mother played a dozen or more instruments; used to play the violin while balancing on her head on a tightrope. First class act. She used to give me sixpence for every new instrument I learned to play. That's how I came to learn the concertina.' He also plays piano, organ, saxophone, clarinet, trombone, drums, the great highland bagpipe and several other instruments. In this morning's session he will be playing the English concertina and the ocarina. Meticulous in everything he does, he is sharpening pencils right now, for he always marks his score. He catches my eye and smiles. 'I hate an untidy score.'

The chair to his left is occupied by Brian Daly who has just finished re-tuning his Gibson. After running through a few skittering *arpeggios* he puts it back in its case and picks up his custom-made Mogford. He is a craftsman and his guitars are his tools. He handles them with the same sureness that a cabinet-maker handles his Swedish steel chisels. He's putting on weight these days in spite of his vegetarian diet and his fingers seem thicker than ever. 'Brian, you're gaining weight.' 'All solid, all solid, mate.' And he gets you to hit him smartly on the stomach. Your hand hurts. He looks as solid and square as the TR-90 which stands three feet away from his left shoulder. I am always amazed at his ability to play so delicately. He's changed a lot in the six or seven years I have known him.

Jim Bray, on the other hand, has scarcely altered at all. He stands slumped over his double bass immersed in a paperback edition of Dostoevski's *Idiot*. Jim is a jazz musician who loves fine literature and Indian cooking. In the dozen years I have known him I have never seen him dressed in any other clothes but the ones he is wearing now, a grey roll-neck pullover and dark trousers of indeterminate hue. When I first met him he owned an enormously long Mercedes open tourer which had once belonged to King Zog of Albania. He sold it because parking it was too expensive. Now he rides a motorbike and relies on taxis and friends with cars to ferry the double bass.

Bruce Turner sits next to him. Jazz musician, plays clarinet and alto sax. I got to know him during the Ballads and Blues radio series, an eccentric but superb musician. We have been working on sequence thirteen for the last hour and a half and Bruce still gives the impression of having just arrived. He misses his entrance cue on every run-through and now looks thoroughly confused. Or is he embarrassed? No, that's not right either; confusion or embarrassment suggest agitation, and Bruce is never agitated. Tentative is a better word.

'You were late again, Bruce,' says Peggy. She is perched on a high stool with the full instrumental score in front of her and the banjo slung over her shoulder. This sequence requires her to play while directing the orchestra. She does this by waving the banjo neck up and down while playing, pointing it to cue the other participants in.

'Oh', says Bruce, 'I thought there was something wrong . . .'

'Bar fourteen on the offbeat.'

'Fourteen.' A long pause while Bruce peers at his score. 'I thought . . . Oh. Sorry, Dad.' Everyone is 'Dad' to Bruce.

'Have you marked it on your script?'

'Oh, yes . . . I see . . . bar fourteen.' He looks at the score as if it were in an uncrackable code. Peggy waits patiently. Alf lends him a pencil. It lies, unused, on the music stand.

But when it comes to a take, the actual recording, Bruce is there. He never fails to produce music of great originality. He is a master of the unexpected phrase, an improviser of genius. We all know this and we all look forward to the takes. Play on, Dad!

The second TR-90 stands next to Bruce. Alan Ward, its operator, is working from a musical score rather than a script. Both of the operators are playing their machines like virtuoso musicians.

In the screened-off area of the studio the chorus is being re-positioned by the studio-engineer and the two Stewart sisters have just arrived from Aberdeen, their first experience of railway travel. They sit there beside the big Bluthner grand with their hands in their laps. They look apprehensive, like patients in a hospital waiting room. Bert Lloyd, Ian Campbell and the other singers are scattered round the studio. Peggy gives her last instructions as Charles' voice blasts through the studio speakers: 'Stand by for a take. This will be take four, purple.' I adjust my position at the centre microphone. Alf's concertina wheezes as it is drawn into the extended position. Bruce wets the mouthpiece of his saxophone. Brian checks the tuning yet again and Peggy raises the neck of the banjo as the voice of God sounds on the huge studio speakers: 'Take four, purple!' The green light flashes.

It took almost a week to record all the sequences. Everything had to work simultaneously and the balance of all the elements had to be just right. It was exhausting work for everyone, sometimes taking as many as fifty or sixty takes of as six- or seven-minute sequence, but it was exhilarating and all of us were conscious of being involved in an act of mutual creation. Our original script had scarcely undergone any alteration. Of the actuality we had chosen, only one small passage had been rejected in the assembly. When the sequences were roughly joined together on the last day of recording, their total time was only one minute and fifty-two seconds longer than the final broadcast version. Even more exciting, the singers, musicians, technicians and producer could sit and listen to a rough-cut version of the whole thing before breaking camp and going home.

I have dealt at some length with *Singing the Fishing* mainly because in the course of working on it we developed a routine which was followed in all subsequent radio-ballads. Unfortunately, the allocation of credits in the billing of radio-ballads had also become a routine matter. Peggy and I had presented Charles with a completely detailed script in the preparation of which Charles' role had been confined to recording actuality. Peggy had taken part in every stage of the work, had collected in the field, transcribed tapes, joined with me in choosing and timing actuality sequences, had helped decide which passages of actuality needed a musical commentary, suggested subjects for songs, arranged the music and directed its performance. It was grossly unfair that she should be credited with only the arrangements. We raised the matter with Charles but were told that a copy of the tape, complete with credits, had already been submitted to the Italia Prize judges. To raise the question of credits at this point might do more harm than good. At the time it seemed to be a reasonable explanation so we let the matter rest.

Peggy was definitely denied recognition as part creator of the radio-ballads. Was it mere folly or was I just another male chauvinist? I hope not, although it could have been that automatic attitude to women that also made Peggy and I call our joint company Ewan MacColl, Ltd. Male chauvinism has many faces, some of which are sanctioned by women and many of which are automatic to men. But ignoring the apportioning of credit had been the pattern of my work up till that time. Throughout most of my life I had worked on projects where group creation was all-important. The *idea* was what mattered and the satisfaction was in the work itself. The name on the wrapper was without significance to me; all that was necessary was that the contents should be a true reflection of our group's labour. Naive? Yes, it was. As a principle it worked well enough in a group made up of individuals who all shared the same philosophical and political beliefs. In a large culture factory like the BBC it was utterly ridiculous. Peggy did not come forward to claim credits and I dropped the matter too easily.

Charles' response to the matter of credits was curious. When I suggested that he should share the billing of *John Axon* as part author he was overcome with embarrassment and protested that he had only done what any other producer would have done. In some respects this was quite true except that what he had done he had done brilliantly. *Song of a Road* was, as I have said, such a butchered work that neither Peggy nor I was particularly keen to have our names associated with it. By the time we had finished *Singing the Fishing,* Charles was taking for granted the right to claim part authorship and when he and I went to Trieste to accept the prize it was Charles who posed for the photographers and gave interviews to the press. From then on, he was an indefatigable press-interviewee. The radio ballads had become the mainstay of his existence, what the North Americans call his *claim to fame.* He ate, slept and dreamed radio-ballads.

In the meantime, Peggy and I were drawing up a balance sheet which would, we hoped, show whether we were any nearer answering the question of whether traditional folk-song was capable of reflecting 20th-century industrial society. *Singing the Fishing* didn't really answer this question since the theme was one which lent itself to traditional-type songs and the fishermen whom we had recorded lived in the kind of communities which, in the past, had created the kind of songs and poetry out of which our folk traditions had been formed. Then again, the mere fact that the sea was involved guaranteed, as it were, the quality of the drama. How could one fail with people like Sam Larner and Ronnie Balls? But, the argument went, 'they are survivals from the past, representatives of a bygone age, individuals drawn from a way of life and work which survives freakishly in a world where individuals are themselves freaks. They spend their lives fighting an elemental force – the sea – and they are themselves elementals.'

This kind of argument was not easily countered; it raised questions which went beyond the validity of the radio-ballad form. It questioned the entire basis of the folk-music revival, not only in Britain but everywhere in the modern world. We had learned many things in the course of being constantly in the company of railwaymen, road-builders and fishermen but all of us needed to learn a great deal more before we could accept or reject such a point of view.

Singing the Fishing had taught us the value of depth-recording, had taught us to recognise the moments when a person would use the kind of language which could transform an individual response into a universal one. It had taught us to recognise the necessity of lying in wait for the moment when the individual ceases to be one who is being interviewed and becomes, instead, one compelled by some inner need to give creative expression to all the things he or she has experienced. It also taught us that in actuality could be found the subject matter for songs, usages, turns of expression, rhythms, pulses, idioms, all the elements out of which songs can be fashioned. A fisherman might, conceivably, accept a third-rate song about farm life as a true expression of the country man's attitude but he would never make the same mistake about a song which dealt falsely with the subject on which he is an authority: fishing and fishermen. Finally, we had learned to trust the actuality and to allow it to shape the entire work.

Armed with these lessons we began work on *The Big Hewer*, a radio-ballad about the miners of the Northumberland, Durham, South Wales and the East Midlands coalfields. For over a year. Peggy and I had worked for the National Coal Board film unit, one of the largest and most productive documentary-film units in Europe. I had written songs and music for *The Mining Review*, a magazine-type film programme which was shown regularly in cinemas throughout the coalfields and our visits to the coalfields had whetted our appetites. We told Charles, 'It's coal-miners or nothing.'

Within the first week in the field we encountered for the first time the legend which gave the programme its title, the Big Hewer, the mythological superman of the British coalfields. In the weeks that followed we encountered him frequently, under a variety of names: Jack Tempest and Bob Temple in

Northumberland; Bob Towers in County Durham; Jackie Torr in Derbyshire; Big Hughie in Scotland and Isaac Lewis in South Wales. It is a sad commentary on the state of British folklore studies that no collector of folk-tales has ever noted this extraordinary legend which is not only widespread but is also a unique example of themes and motifs common to the classic folk-tales of the Indo-European tradition surviving in and adapting to industrial society.

We took our tape-recorders into pit-canteens, pithead baths, into pubs and welfares; we dragged them through the galleries of drift-mines in western Durham and Northumberland, down the deep shafts of east Durham and the hard rock mines of Wales, along the wide, straight roads of East Midland horizon mines where the coal-getters advance like military units, tearing at the coal-face with rotary cutters, shearers and belt-drives ploughs in a twenty-four-hour cycle. We dragged ourselves along impossibly narrow passages into the hellish places where solitary miners lie on their sides and jab with short bladed picks at the eighteen-inch coalface. We sat nursing hot mugs of tea in pithead canteens while miners, still in their pit-dirt, answered our questions; we talked in kitchens with men who hacked words out of their ruined chests, in pubs where men drank their beer out of personalised mugs with quotations of Marx and William Morris engraved on the rims.

At the end of our field-recording stint we had taped between eighty and a hundred reels of mining *crack,* the conversation of men who can make words ring like hammer blows on a face of anthracite; who, when they talk, enrich the bloodstream of the national vocabulary with transfusions of pitmatic – the bold, bitter, ribald, beautiful talk of miners.

Miners' conversations are generally interesting in their subject matter. Work and politics are favourite subjects. This is particularly so in South Wales, where miners often bring to their discussions the poetically-turned phrase and the rhythms of remembered chapel services. I found nothing surprising in their ability to express themselves. After all, I had been brought up among people who talked about important things like politics and revolution and who referred to Burns and Tannahill as if they had been members of the family circle. Furthermore, I had been fairly familiar with miners and their families ever since the days of my childhood. During my Theatre Workshop days in the coalfields of Fifeshire, Lanark. Durham and South Wales, I had become accustomed to the conversational skills of miners.

For Charles, meeting miners was a shattering experience. Up until this time he had managed to hold on to the Panglossian view that everything was alright (or nearly alright) in this best of all possible worlds. The coalfields changed all that. Before we were halfway through the field work he confessed to feeling utterly uneducated in the presence of miners. Prior to this he had maintained a fairly formal relationship with his informants (I dislike that word but there is no adequate substitute for it). During our first days of recording miners, Charles would talk more than the person he was recording. In a way, he was trying to justify his beliefs, his presence. It was Dick Beamish, an articulate and militant union shop steward, who finally silenced Charles in a series of brilliant outbursts. After that, Charles learned to listen.

The Times greeted the broadcast of *The Big Hewer* with a two-column review under the title of 'Poetic documentary with worker heroes'. It described the three radio-ballads thus far made as being 'among the few landmarks of post-war radio' and concluded by saying:

> The total impression left behind is as genuinely heroic as that of the fishing communities in *Riders to the Sea* and *La Terra Trema* and as tragic as that of the Japanese peasants who worshipped the volcano – a god who pours fertility on their lands in the interval before he destroys them.

On the whole, the press was fairly unanimous in regarding *The Big Hewer* as a serious and successful attempt to apply the techniques of folk creation to a contemporary situation. But there was also a general feeling that we had taken the form as far as it could go and there were those who argued that the technique of the radio-ballad could not be used for themes and subjects which lay outside the orbit of the epic, situations where the dramatic conflict was confined to man's struggle with elemental forces. This gave us new problems to solve. And Peggy was pregnant again.

In spite of their enthusiastic reception by the newspaper critics (or perhaps because of it) the radio-ballads were not without their detractors. They were not, it was argued, documentaries in the real sense of the word; they were romantic, backward-looking; they were full of value judgments; they took sides; and whoever heard of navvies and locomotive drivers singing about their work? Really!! Then again, they were enormously expensive to produce (in point of fact they were pitifully under-funded). And just between ourselves, old boy, the DG disapproves strongly of them. (A story going the rounds of the BBC told how the DG, on being informed that a radio-ballad dealing with coal-miners was in the pipeline, responded with 'Oh God, not another working-class epic!') But mum's the word, old boy. It's a nice story. Good for a laugh in the coffee break or between pints in the Stag or the Bedford Arms. And who cares that it contradicts the BBC Director General's earlier pronouncement on *The Ballad of John Axon* as 'the most originally conceived, the most brilliantly executed and the most moving radio programme I've ever heard'.

Among our critics there were some who, while agreeing with the DG's praise, questioned the adaptability of the radio-ballad form. It required, they said, heroic subjects like building a road or battling with the sea, but it couldn't handle psychological issues. Now, Peggy and I always had more than one project on the go and between the last two radio-ballads we had done the songs and music for a documentary film dealing with the problems of people stricken by polio. The film was marred by its very stagy dialogue and would have been immensely improved by the use of recorded actuality. Why not approach the subject again in a radio-ballad? It would, once and for all, determine whether the form was capable of embracing themes and subjects suitable for a small canvas. A radio-ballad dealing with the psychology of pain: that was our original proposition to Charles, although in the course of numerous discussions it was modified into a journey into the minds of two partially and three totally disabled people.

The amount of money available for the programme was much less than our previous budgets and field work had to be reduced to the bare minimum. By limiting the number of informants and confining actuality to five or six topics we succeeded in simplifying the entire operation. Charles recorded all five of them in a single hospital in the course of a fortnight; the transcription, song-writing and arrangements were completed in another couple of weeks. The actual selection of actuality, however, took longer than usual. As early as *Song of a Road* I had suggested using selected passages of actuality in the form of montage sequences which would have something of the feeling of the stream-of-consciousness episodes in Joyce's *Ulysses*. Seeing the film *Last Year in Marienbad,* with its extraordinary montage sequences, strengthened my conviction that this *would* work beautifully in the radio-ballad form.

The idea was to cross-cut from speaker to speaker without resorting to the smooth transitions in time and space which had become one of the hallmarks of the BBC feature programmes. Charles felt it was a rather gimmicky notion, so we made up a composite block composed of some two dozen passages of speech from the five speakers, each passage being a comment, or part of a comment, on the sensation of returning consciousness. The overall effect was overwhelming and Charles immediately began to see how the craft of tape editing could be brought to a fine art. He found the technical challenge exciting, but continued to regard the montages as a surrealistic trick. Nevertheless, he became expert at constructing them and they appeared frequently and with electrifying effect in *The Body Blow.*

The songs in the programme were meant to serve as compass-bearings on the journey from unconsciousness and delirium, through the varying degrees of returning consciousness and pain. There were songs about re-entering society, songs about physical therapy, songs about adjusting to total paralysis. Peggy scored the music for two singers and four instrumentalists. After four days in the studio our chamber-ballad was ready for broadcasting.

Almost without exception the press had greeted the BBC's announcement of a radio-ballad dealing with poliomyelitis with scepticism – some of the pre-broadcast press releases suggested that the project was in bad taste. On the day following the broadcast the critics were just as unanimous in declaring it to be a *tour de force,* which it was not. On one level it was an attempt to extend the vocabulary of the genre in an area of human experience removed from labour; on another more important level it was an attempt to re-establish communication between two groups in our society – the physically disabled and the healthy – alienated from each other by feelings of rejection and resentment on the one hand and by pity and ignorance on the other. On both counts *The Body Blow* scored a limited success. It has since been used in several large hospitals as training for nurses and hospital staff.

Encouraged by this, we embarked on a programme on Britain's teenagers. Friends and well wishers told us, 'You've really bitten off more than you can chew this time. You'll never get them to talk.' This was repeated so often that we began to believe it ourselves. I cannot account for how such a widespread myth had developed. Perhaps those with doubts were basing their opinions on the difficulties they were experiencing with their own adolescent sons and daughters, because from very early on it became obvious that it was not difficult at all to get them to talk. It was as if they had been waiting for someone to listen to them and once started there was no stopping them. Everything poured out: their hopes, anxieties, fears, doubts, bewilderment, dreams, fantasies. This was the post-Hiroshima generation and the bomb loomed large in their conversation. 'It's like a big dustbin-lid covering the sky,' said a seventeen-year-old Salford girl. Her name was Dot Dobby and she worked in a factory, sewing pockets on to cheap aprons. She had total recall and a gentle way of describing things in a voice in which wonder and bewilderment were equally balanced. I have only to close my eyes to hear those quiet, desperate words: 'There's a world in front of you and you've only got a certain space to go. I go to me factory and come back and that's supposed to be my bit of seeing the world. The whole world in front of you, the whole world to see and things that haven't been discovered.' She was fully conscious of her position in the scheme of things but was unreconciled. She was hopeful and despairing and both these emotions informed everything she said. What could be bleaker than her vision of the world? 'Can't see why we're here, really. We only die and wither away. It's all going to end in the end.' And yet the words were said in such a way that one felt she was pleading to be proved wrong.

Her ability to articulate her thoughts and dreams was quite extraordinary. With a few hesitant words she could evoke a city at night or a Salford street on a hot summer's evening. 'People sat at the doorway, women gossiping. I know it's not a beautiful sight but it seemed like home . . . like home, y'know. I know it's only Salford . . . people stood on the doorsteps on the hot summer night, drinking the beer what they'd just got from the corner. It seemed that nice. And you stood there just looking at these people in the evening when the sun's just going down. People stood there and sat there . . . The darkness comes and the people go in their houses and it's something really kind of . . . unspeakable.' Is it nostalgia that gives these words the power to move me so deeply? Or is it the memory of the voice that utters them? It is a young voice carrying echoes of my own childhood's hopes and fears. Even when the utterance is affirmative the voice has a note of uncertainty, as if the speaker is conscious of her vulnerability. 'Going away and seeing beautiful scenes and lakes and the objective of life . . . the way man thinks and creates for himself . . . the future . . . and to think that we're part of it and that only us can do that. Just the beauty of life itself.

Glad that I'm alive and can do these things. Just to be alive and meet people and laugh and be friends with everyone.'

A remarkable young woman. But then we met many remarkable people during the recording of *On the Edge*. How do you meet them? We are often asked that. There is no set way, no regular routine. You use whatever means are at hand to make contact with people who might have important things to say and a unique way of saying them. In the case of Dot Dobby it was fairly straightforward. We happened to be at a folk club in Manchester and mentioned to a friend that we needed half a dozen teenagers to record for us. He passed on the news to a friend who arranged a Saturday morning session at his home in Ordsall. There were five boys and two girls. On this first occasion Dot said relatively little but what she did say was pertinent and had the kind of spontaneity which forces you to listen. The other girl present was mute throughout. The boys all spoke, three of them very well.

We had looked upon this particular session as a kind of audition, an exploratory encounter. All our previous recordings for radio-ballads had been-made on a one-to-one basis and we had come to believe that no other arrangement could produce the kind of actuality we had come to expect. There are some things people do not want to say in company. But for three hours Dot and her friends spoke non-stop about the teenage image presented by the media, about rumbles between mods and rockers, about motor-cycles and ton-up merchants, about pop music, sex, parents and the generation-gap. All of it was interesting, much of it profoundly moving. We arranged a second meeting with Dot, at our house in south London.

This meeting proved that we had stumbled on one of those rare human beings who can give utterance to their most secret thoughts while at the same time re-creating emotions they have experienced. Contrary to our usual practice, Peggy did much of this recording alone with Dot who would just close her eyes and after a few minutes of preliminary questioning, retreat into some private world and then in a stream-of-consciousness fashion recall scenes, moods, conversations and events. We were completely bowled over by her ability to articulate her perceptions of reality and those shadowy areas of feeling which overlap with the unconscious. We heard, a year later, that she was married and already pregnant with her first child.

In Glasgow, a schoolteacher friend arranged for us to meet several of his pupils and it happened again, this time in the form of two personable eighteen-year old students, both named Ann, who could not only talk coherently about the bomb, sexual fantasies and the state of the world in general but did so with considerable wit and humour. Nottingham and Bristol were 'cold' – that is, we had no contacts there, no one to introduce us to likely young people – so we were driven to standing outside school gates and accosting the first half-dozen pupils who came out. They came forth eagerly and a session was arranged. What was truly amazing to us was that half-a-dozen individuals, several of whom didn't even know one another, were prepared to talk so freely and uninhibitedly in each others' presence. As anyone who has ever conducted an interview knows, some skill is required to make their subject being interviewed feel at ease; the interviewer must look and sound casual while concentrating fully and feeding interesting questions into the conversation. With our two randomly chosen groups our intervention was reduced to naming a topic. 'Parents,' we would say and off they would go like greyhounds after the hare until we mentioned another word, then off they would go again. Often, when one person was holding forth on some intensely personal subject, another would burst out, 'I didn't know anyone else felt like that!' indicating that they rarely got down to these depths of communication amongst one another. It had taken a catalyst – us – to start them off.

Peggy and I recorded almost all of the actuality for *On the Edge* as Charles was busy with other programmes at the time. We interviewed them singly and in groups, the sons and daughters of labourers and company directors, of professors and railway porters, miners, filing clerks and factory hands. There were schoolgirls and boys, apprentices, mods and rockers, waged and unwaged; fifty-two of them from Glasgow and Stirling, Newcastle, Washington (County Durham), Salford, Burnley, Leeds, Castleford, Nottingham, Birmingham, Bristol, Reading, Hackney, Poplar, Mile-End, Hampstead, Camberwell, Brixton and the Old Kent Road.

The press loved it. Peter Wilsher of *The Sunday Times* wrote: 'I have sometimes had serious reservations about the way this method tends to swamp the material. With *On the Edge*, their remarkable study of a youngster poised between childhood and growing up, I withdraw these completely. The match was near perfect.' Ian Rogers of *The Guardian* numbered the radio-ballad team among 'the Brechtians of today'. He concluded his critique by returning to the comparison. 'Mr MacColl and Miss Seeger struck that note of sincerity which is necessary to the ballad form by not trying to be too clever musically. Their intoned narrative came close to the intent which Brecht had when he used all those placards.'

On the Edge should have been the brilliant success which the critics said it was. Certainly the actuality was brilliant enough. The fact is, we had been beguiled by its richness. We were glutted with it, had swallowed it whole and still hadn't digested it when we went into production. There were good things in the programme, including a brilliantly effective three-part conversation between spoken voice, clarinet and singer. Many of the songs were uneven, however, and frequently failed to relate totally to the actuality. At best they illustrated the text without amplifying it or contributing an extra dimension to it.

The Fight Game, our seventh radio-ballad, was (as far as the team was concerned) an unqualified success, though its actuality was nowhere near as rich as that of *On the Edge* or *Singing the Fishing*. Its songs, unlike those in the earlier industrial radio-ballads, could not easily be sung out of the context of the programme. Nevertheless, everything worked beautifully and one of the reasons why it did so lay in the ritualised training programme which is part of every prize-fighter's working day. The training of a boxer follows a series of rhythmic patterns: running, shadow-boxing, punching a speedball, skipping, throwing a medicine-ball – all these are actions done to specific rhythms. Our task was to note those rhythms and to incorporate them in songs, musical sequences and actuality blocks. By ringing the changes on a sequence of rhythms we could have a new episode without breaking the links with all the other episodes.

We had chosen professional boxing as a subject to try and escape from the huge canvas of industry and the intensely private world of the sick and the adolescent. We were also tired of problems, people's problems; our original intention was to make a cheerful, light-hearted programme. Instead, we found we had entered a world inhabited by people who regarded the prize-ring as a symbolical representation of the world. Boxers, managers, trainers, sports-commentators all stressed this point over and over again. Furthermore, we discovered that boxers, more than any other group with which we had worked during the six years spent on the radio-ballads, appeared to possess a strong sense of history. Almost without exception they compared themselves with Roman gladiators and their audiences to those who pointed their thumbs down or up, who 'got their kicks from seeing Christians thrown to the lions'. *The Fight Game* was essentially an ironic allegory in which songs and actuality existed in a constantly changing relationship to one another. We did get some cheerful, light-hearted songs dealing with the hierarchy of the boxing world, and it was certainly great fun to record. Peggy added trumpets and trombones, drums (and quite a lot of musical noise) to the usual line-up of folk instruments There was a brassiness about the program that to a certain extent was a break-out from the introspective world of polio and teenage. It is the one radio-ballad which gives both of us great pleasure to listen to over and over, especially that point where the trumpeter played exactly what Peggy had written for him. It was two notes higher than the trumpet could go, but he hit it and split his lip. It *sounded* as if he was splitting his lip and came at just the right point in the actual fight for it to sound painfully authentic.

The final radio-ballad in the series, *The Travelling People,* was a study of gypsies and tinkers.[3] They were perfect subjects for a programme of this type. Apart from any other considerations, the Travellers, along with the profes-sional and semi-professional singers and musicians of the folk revival, are now the chief carriers of the English and Scots folk-song traditions, a fact which made the choice of musical idiom a natural one. Furthermore, as custodians of the classic folk-tales, they number in their ranks storytellers of great skill. It was from these that the programme was to take its pace and overall style. In social terms, too, the subject was a good one. Gypsies and tinkers, for whom the family has always constituted the basic social unit, had continued to survive for some four or five hundred years in a hostile society, the social organisation of which had been determined by modes of production. As foreigners they had been persecuted and discriminated against from the time of their first arrival in Britain and, in spite of it, they had survived as a group. They possessed many skills of which rural society made use from time to time. They were past masters at working with iron and tin; they were excellent horse-copers and animal doctors; they could weave straw mats and make baskets and creels from willow saplings and, at harvest time, they were fast and willing workers. Above all, their labour was cheap. Consequently, when they were needed they were tolerated. When they were not needed they were driven away. This has been, and still is, the enforced life-style of Britain's travelling people. Changes in the social structure have, at times, distorted the pattern but have not altered the essential nature of the problem.

The 20th century, however, has subjected the Travellers to a series of crushing blows, each of which has made the possibilities of survival more difficult. The horse has been usurped by the automobile; mass-produced kitchenware has made the tinker's skill with tin and iron superfluous; the invention and development of plastics has put them out of business as basket-makers; and machines are more and more taking over from human beings in fields and orchards. At the same time, regional, county and borough authorities have introduced legislative acts which have given them control over every inch of potential camping or stopping ground. The Highway Code, The Litter Act, The National Parks Act and numerous other factors have combined to make the lot of the Travellers more and more intolerable.

With *The Travelling People* we had reached the end of the road as far as the BBC was concerned. For one thing, the radio-ballads were expensive to produce – not quite as costly as half an hour's all-in wrestling on TV but expensive by radio standards – and the budgets for radio productions were shrinking fast. Then, again, there were the listener-research figures which showed that disc-jockey programmes of pop-music appealed to audiences many times larger than the audience for the radio-ballads and for a fraction of the cost. Paul Ferris, in the columns of *The Observer,* wrote: 'If this is the best reason anyone could produce for the act of murder . . . it's a miserable one.' Referring to an article which Charles had written for the journal *New Society,* Ferris went on to say, 'as a statement of aims and supported by the evidence of eight pro-grammes, beside which many of radio's attempts to mirror life sound like baby talk, it makes the charge of extravagance seem a very thin and impotent reason for ending radio-balladry.'

Our original thesis had been based on the idea that techniques implicit in certain types of folk-creation could be applied to the mass media in a way which would be mutually beneficial to both media and traditional music. We found that it worked. The theory became the radio-ballads which Francis Newton, in the columns of *The New Statesman,* described as 'the most valuable products of the British folk-music movement'.

Charles continued to talk and give interviews about the radio-ballads and fairly soon the media was beginning to refer to our collective work as 'Charles Parker's radio-ballads'. In November 1972, Gillian Reynolds, in *The Guardian,* published an appreciation of Charles in which she wrote: 'He developed a style of programme called the Radio Ballad.' In the four columns which followed, she referred several times to *John Axon, Singing the Fishing* and *The Big Hewer* without even hinting that anyone other than Charles had been involved with them. Peggy, incensed, wrote to Charles:

> In a radio-ballad script you could take away production, effects, arrangements in many cases, and you would still end up with a programme that had flow, rhythm, artistic integration of speech and music, i.e., you would still have a radio-ballad. This musical and dramatic flow came not from me, not from you (although we augmented it) but from Ewan. He gives ideas right and left and doesn't bother to claim credit for them. So many of the features of the radio-ballads were his and his alone – the subject, the songs, the ideas of montage, use of dialect, dismissal of the narrator, etc . . . and now an article in which all this is invested in you! I know what press people are like – they mix up facts, they mis-spell names, but they don't expunge them once you've mentioned them. I think a public rebuttal of the solo authorship is due . . . overdue! I think you should make some kind of statement now in the interests of intellectual honesty.

A few days later a letter from Charles appeared in the readers' correspondence columns of *The Times* and *The Guardian, whose essence was:*

> If one name is to be associated with what was, in fact, a team operation, that name must be Ewan MacColl. It was my privilege to be able in some measure to provide the production and tape-editing techniques his genius demanded as it was Peggy Seeger's to meet the comparable music demands, and while both she and I can honourably claim co-authorship, the first begetter and continuing inspirer of this work is Ewan MacColl.

To credit Charles with achievements other than his own is to diminish his real worth and detract from his real achievements which, in my opinion, were more significant than the creation of this or that piece of work or the development of this or that new approach to the art of documentary. Charles re-created himself and that is a very great achievement indeed.

The growth of Charles' passion for the recording of actuality, the discovery of Marxism, his first real contact with working-class people and his discovery of the class-struggle all happened within the space of two years. Having made his discoveries, he acted upon them immediately. He threw himself into the struggles of the Travellers and spent as much time as he possibly could, getting to know working people by recording them, questioning them about their lives and their ideas. Had he been content to keep quiet about his recording activities and his newly born political enthusiasms, the higher-ups in the BBC hierarchy would most likely have been prepared to look the other way. But that wasn't Charles' way; he must share his joys and his new-found knowledge. So he talked to anyone who would listen, face-to-face, over the telephone, in the BBC canteen over the meat-and-two-veg, in the corridors of Broadcasting House and in the car park leaning on the roof of his clapped-out Morris.

When his bosses could no longer reconcile themselves to the new Parker image, they sacked him – after twenty-four years' service. He continued to do full-time what he had been doing in his spare time, i.e., working in folk–song activities and helping to build Banner Theatre, a group specialising in the production of political documentaries in which actuality recordings, songs in the folk idiom and acted-out dramatic episodes were combined into an exciting whole. Charles succeeded in imbuing his co-workers in Banner with his belief in the value of recorded speech and, in addition, convincing them that a truly revolutionary theatre must be based on a working-class audience. He felt that this was the most useful contribution he could make. He continued to drive himself like a maniac until the day he died. Not since the early days of Theatre Workshop have I encountered such a sense of dedication.

When Charles died in 1980 the radio-ballads experienced a brief resurrection. They were, of course, referred to as 'Charles Parker's radio-ballads'. Even the BBC's hollow men who had so callously sacked him a few years earlier now described him as 'the brilliant initiator of the radio-ballad technique'. Occasionally there might be a grudging reference to MacColl 'who wrote the songs' but one would have searched in vain for a mention of Peggy.

As a dramatist I am interested in people's motivations, my own included. I have never solicited praise or courted fame. At the same time, I feel uncomfortable when I hear that Tom, Dick or Harry has been credited with something I created. I don't mind when 'anon' claims my work, but we have watched traditional songs – and the royalties accruing from their exploitation – appropriated by pop groups for the last thirty years. It is obviously one of the hazards of collective work, a possible payment for the excitement of watching an idea geminate and produce a chain reaction in a group of people. As a singer, it is unlikely that I will be besieged by hordes of young women clamouring for a few hairs of my beard, and my chair will never go up for sale at Sotheby's. As a folklorist I find it intriguing to be in a position to chart the development of a burgeoning myth. But as a writer, however, I am not amused at seeing myself reduced to a footnote in that myth.

24

Singing and Song Writing

The 1960s and 1970s, as far as the revival was concerned, was a period of enormous growth. The clubs continued to grow both in size and in number, as did the summer folk-song festivals. The confusion was growing, too. As at the beginning of the revival, enthusiasts still found their way to English, Scots or Irish traditional songs via Leadbelly and Guthrie. Others came via radio programmes featuring new singers of old songs and some – a very small number – came because they had heard a recording of some old traditional singer and were intrigued. Some came to find out what the hell it was all about. They were lucky if they succeeded.

In the early days they might have been fortunate and heard a few skilful performers; they might also have heard a number of mediocre ones and a smattering of appalling ones. But the bulk of them would be singing – brilliantly, adequately, poorly or appallingly – traditional songs from these islands. By the late 1960s these performance categories would have been extended to include 19th-century Lancashire dialect poems set to music; mock-Tudor songs about witches and knights succouring almost-ravished maidens. It would include macho performances of thinly-disguised men's changing-room arias from *The Rugby Songbook,* incredibly involved guitar solos transcribed from sitar arrangements of Scots ballads, and funnymen . . .Oh, those awful funnymen cracking their tired old jokes and daring the audience not to laugh. There were, as well, a growing band of young singers who could handle most of the traditional repertoire. Their numbers, however, were small and their influence correspondingly limited.

The earliest manifestations of the revival went unreported by the media. After all, there was nothing particularly noteworthy or newsworthy in a couple of earnest folk-song enthusiasts rushing around London singing two or three songs at a union branch-meeting or in the presentation of a concert of folk carols in a BBC Christmas programme. In the years between 1955–59, however, the tempo began to speed up and the popular press was forced to pay attention. The jazz and popular music press was sympathetic to us from the beginning and, for a short time at any rate, those organs of the popular press, which deigned to notice us, were content to adopt a rather jocular tone. When it looked as if the revival was becoming a force to reckon with, the smile became a snarl. It was time for a take-over.

One of the less respectable Sunday newspapers fired the first salvo by featuring a photograph of several young people standing on the pavement outside the Princess Louise, which at that time housed the Ballads and Blues club. 'ARE YOUR CHILDREN BEING CONNED?' screamed the headline and the column, which followed, went on to expose the revival as a communist plot. A week later one of the quality papers took up the story and then one or two dailies added their two-pennyworth. Now, it is true that both Lloyd and I were members of the Communist Party at the time and regarded ourselves as Marxists who used dialectical materialism as a tool for interpreting the world and its events. But the attack was on. We were laying plots and snares; we were using traditional songs and music to entice people into the Communist Party; we were using the clubs as recruiting stations.

Both of us had been born into the working class, had grown up in a world where unemployment, fascism and war were part of our inheritance. We were keenly aware of how the best remnants of genuine working-class forms of creative expression were being eliminated by the mass media and particularly by Tin Pan Alley and Denmark Street. Our efforts with folk music did not lack ideological purpose. We were intent on resisting that final act of destruction. By exposing people to the incredibly rich repertoire of traditional songs and ballads of farm labourers, seamen, weavers, coal-miners and all those working men and women who had created them, we hoped to arrest the plasticisation of the popular culture. We hoped that these songs would help English, Irish, Scots and Welsh workers to assert their national and class identity. Then, again, it was necessary to preserve this highly specialised treasure of social and political information against the day when the workers came into their own.

These were important considerations but I doubt whether they would, on their own, have provided us with a powerful enough stimulus to launch the revival had we not loved the songs and enjoyed performing them. For, like most people who have discovered something of great beauty, we needed to share our discovery with as many people as possible. It was a conspiracy: we conspired to create a climate in which songs like 'Pleasant and Delightful', 'The Foggy Dew' and 'Barbara Allen' might thrive and flourish. In a way, our opponents were correct in regarding the revival as an aspect of class struggle and, like us, they were fully aware of its political implications. For most people, folk music was – and is – a relic, a survival from the past – a charming survival, perhaps, quaint, amusing, interesting and quite harmless, a music without teeth or claws. Many saw it as a fragile antique, which might disintegrate on contact with the air; it should be taken off the museum shelf only when dusting became necessary. For scholars it was something to be studied, analysed and discussed at annual conferences alongside learned papers on smocking and corn-dollies. It was the creation of *grand old* men and *wonderful old* women whose grandness or wonderfulness didn't prevent them from passing their final days in workhouses. These were The Folk, a classless, amorphous collection of grand, wonderful (and neglected) individuals.

For us, on the other hand, they were exploited members of an exploited class: men and women who had preserved and cherished songs, which were part of our common heritage. The songs were not merely interesting or charming survivals: they had teeth, they were tough and, given any help at all, they would go on surviving and adapting, would thrive and flourish in the modern world. Naturally, there were obstacles to be overcome, not least of which was the popular music industry. Its owners could dictate public taste, could decide which musical fashion might be tried next and which formula should be used where and when, and which performers, which writers and composers could be manipulated most easily, who can be bought and for how much.

The wheelers and dealers had enormous resources. They owned record companies and publishing houses and they had radio and television interests. As far as they were concerned, music was a commodity like soap-powder or cosmetics, only more profitable. It was expendable and each new hit could be abandoned as soon as the sales figures dropped below an agreed minimum. The Tin Pan Alley machine hadn't been programmed to deal with songs about the lives of farmhands, sailors and kitchen maids. Lop off a few verses here and there, change the words a little, smooth out the tune, change the rhythm and then it's just possible that something might be done with a few *numbers*. But really, why bother? There are so many things wrong with them: all those gapped scales, irregular rhythms, dreary stories! Oh dear, forget it! It'd be more trouble than it's worth to try and make them into commercially viable properties. As for songs being able to survive for two or three *centuries* or more . . . are you trying to wipe us out? Expecting the music industry to concern itself with songs of that kind would be like asking a shoe-manufacturer to make everlasting shoes, like asking Ford or Fiat to build cars which would never wear out. Ask, by all means, but . . .

Right from the early days of the revival, Alan Lomax, then Bert and I and then Peggy, had been stressing the fact that our traditional music was not only valuable in itself but could also serve as a model for contemporary popular music. It was, perhaps, this aspect of the revival that gave rise to the conspiracy rumours. When young men and women were seen accompanying their home-made songs and chants on guitars and banjos as they marched from Aldermaston to Trafalgar Square, the media was quick to label them 'skifflers' and 'folkies'; by the late 1950s, even the word *guitar* had acquired a pejorative ring and was rarely mentioned in popular journalism without an accompanying derisory adjective or phrase (folksingers who only know three chords, etc).

The press campaign against the red folkies was soon abandoned and appears to have had no effect whatsoever on the revival. Soon the better class of newspapers began to mention folk music on the arts pages and even glossy magazines like *Vogue* included features on the 'new' and very much with-it musical phenomenon. Indeed, the entire mass media suddenly discovered the revival and during the next three or four years practically every channel of BBC radio carried a folk programme of one kind or another. Some of these were highly specialised features dealing with ritual music, work songs, traditional ballads, broadside ballads, and so on. Others included a weekly series of traditional songs culled from the folk archives. Television, too, both BBC and commercial channels, featured folk music from time to time, though rarely with the same serious approach that radio had shown. Lomax's three programmes for BBC television had been serious attempts to present a balanced folkloristic view of the nation's folk music. They had never been followed up though attempts had been made to adapt the techniques of folk creation to television. Tyne-Tees Television, for example, produced a group of three splendid documentary films in which the narration was sung in traditional ballad style. Grampian Television broadcast a short film dealing with the theme of love in folk-song. ITV went the whole hog and assembled most of the well-known singers and musicians of the revival for the 1962 prestigious. New Year's Eve programme. The BBC scooped the pool by having a daily singing-news-item as part of the six o'clock news. While most of these programmes treated the music with some respect, it is also true to say that the search was on for a more acceptable form of folk music. For 'acceptable' read undisturbing, accompanied, pop orientated, simple, non-controversial, music-to-tap-one's-feet-to, etc.

Meanwhile, more and more folk clubs sprang up, not only in the big cities now, but also in small towns and even in remote villages. Dramatists like John Arden and Arnold Wesker wrote plays in which folk songs were an integral feature; revival singers were courted by charity concert organisers and party-givers in St Johns Wood, Chelsea, Kensington and even (it was rumoured) at the palace itself.

The revival was not without its crises, its polarisations, its quarrels, skir-mishes, attacks, counter-attacks and occasional mobilisations. Many folk-singers, like people everywhere, were outraged by the United States' attack on Vietnam in the summer of 1965 and a group of us met and drew up a manifesto expressing our opposition to the war and calling for support of the North Vietnamese. More than sixty of the leading figures in the revival signed the manifesto and a few weeks later a committee was formed, Folksingers for Vietnam (FFV). Its objectives were simple: to make folksingers throughout Britain available to the organisers of public meetings called to protest against the American presence in Vietnam, to help raise money for medical aid, to draw attention to clandestine British involvement and to assist the Vietnamese people's struggle against U.S. imperialism. The Critics Group members were enthusiastic supporters of the FFV and participated in scores of fund-raising concerts as well as writing a number of fine songs dealing with the social and political implications of the war.

The new-songs-versus-old-songs argument was one of the most disturb-ing aspects of the revival and while it never achieved the status of a national controversy it did a great deal of damage. The aggressors in this running skir-mish were generally found to be in the old songs faction whose stance was not dissimilar to that of a connoisseur of period furniture or a collector of antique coins. But how old must a song be before it becomes acceptable? 50 years? 100, 200 years? I have put this question to dozens of old song enthusiasts and all of them have avoided answering it properly. Some reject *all* songs tainted with the poison of modernity (and modernity includes the entire 20th century). Others confine their antipathy to political songs. But here again there are inconsisten-cies. A club organiser who tells you that 'the audience here doesn't like political songs' is liable to be dismayed when you tell him, or her, that the entire corpus of Jacobite songs has just been put on the blacklist. 'No, no! I didn't mean *that* kind of political song. I meant . . .' The meaning is that songs should have no immediate significance. They should be like empty shells which you pick up on the beach and which rattle around for years in a drawer until one day they finish up with a score of similar mementos in a dustbin or at a jumble sale.

New songs and the clubs are part of the chain of cause-and-effect. The clubs help to create and feed the audience for folk-song. They bring the individuals who make up the audience to a place where their appetite for folk music can be catered for. Among those individuals are some who are inspired to try their hand at making up songs themselves.[1] The results are occasionally spectacular. And the fact that many of the new songs deal with political issues is not really surprising since TV news programmes have made everyone aware of the fact that politics and survival are indivisible.

Peggy and I have always regarded new songs as part of the same continuum that made folk songs. I love the old songs. I am frequently moved by them and sometimes inspired by them to write songs about things which affect me and strike me as important. But I do not treat them as museum pieces or as sacred objects. They are beautiful because they are alive, and they live because they continue to be taken into the throats, mouths and minds of singers. They are tough enough to survive the competition of newcomers. Indeed, they can be made to serve as touchstones against which the modern pieces can be tested and compared.

The self-styled purists and antiquarians have tried to ignore the revival. Its reviewers have attempted to determine its course. I think the first mention of non-American folk-music to appear in the popular press was a short notice by Max Jones in *The Melody Maker* It followed close on the heels of a lengthy article in *Jazz Journal* under the name of Derek Stewart-Baxter. Both items were sympathetic, enthusiastic. But they were one-offs. Thenceforward, news-paper reviews of the folk scene reflected the house-journal, all-pals-together tone of the fanzines. Everything was chummy, first name stuff, the backslap-ping, have-one-for-the-road style of journalism. Until, that is, the advent of rock-music and then the young old gods failed. All those long ballads sung without accompaniment, those country songs plain and unadorned, didn't really belong in the *swinging sixties*. There were new prophets now like Mick

Jagger and Jimmi Hendrix, young Turks in revolt against . . . what? Melody, perhaps? Audibility? Coherence? Shirts with buttons? The old fuddy-duddy traditionalists (as one would-be with-it folkie reviewer put it) should be getting out – or was it *down?* – into the market place with Dylan and the rest of the modern whiz kids of music.

Newcomers to the scene could scarcely be blamed for believing that electric folk, folk-rock and folk-pop were the folk music of the 20th century, for this was the line taken by the press. Meanwhile, those who were content to sing the ballads and songs of tradition without the benefit of rock backing were repeatedly branded as eccentrics or – worse – as reactionaries who were afraid to bring their unimproved music into the big, wide, vibrating, amplified, four-beats-to-the-bar world.

The BBC's search for a more acceptable type of folk music was beginning to bear fruit. Sad to think that some of the most enthusiastic searchers were leading figures in the folk scene. But the days of plenty were ending. The radio-ballads were discontinued, the number of folk-music programmes was drastically reduced and those that did get past the programme-planner's pruning knife were what an inter-departmental memo called 'popular folk-music', that is, music with a beat, music which made no demands on the listener, the kind of folk-music we had all rejected at school, music which avoided subjects like politics, exploitation and normal bawdy sex; music – in short – which was more like pop-music but watered down so it could still be regarded as an alternative. Folk-rock was OK, of course, and any of the foot-stamping, hand-clapping, fine-frenzied groups . . . but the Corporation's ideal purveyor of 'popular folk-music' was a northern group which had once described itself as *mid-Atlantic* and which for a period of two or three years (it seemed an eternity) had set out to prove to television audiences that folk-song could be just as vacuous, dreary and utterly mediocre as the most imbecilic teeny-boppers' pop-music. Yes, and performed with a good deal less expertise.

While the student rebellion of the 1960s and 1970s sputtered out like a fart in a colander, its leaders abandoned their Marxist textbooks in favour of the new and enlarged edition of *Smith and Bradstreet*. As for the much-publicised road to revolt, it led directly to the multi-national, multi-billion-dollar music industry, while that other mystical revolutionary highway petered out in the desert of the CIA and army-sponsored drug culture.

It is a futile occupation to speculate on what might have been or to try and estimate to what degree this or that factor influenced the course of the revival. Looking back, one cannot help but be amazed at the speed with which we achieved our immediate objectives. We had set out to spread the news that Britain possessed a body of songs which in terms of beauty, realism, toughness and variety were the equal of songs anywhere in the world. It had proved to be a ridiculously easy task. We had made our mark in radio within two years; on TV within three years; within five years large-scale concerts of folk music had become a feature of big city entertainment and within ten years we had seen the entire country covered with a network of clubs. It was the most widespread do-it-yourself music-making phenomenon these islands had ever seen.

At the peak of the folk boom there were scores, if not hundreds, of club magazines and newsletters ranging from the literate to the unreadable; printed, cyclostyled, photocopied, written in longhand, stencilled without ink; some came out on a regular basis, others when the spirit moved an organiser or member of a club to put pen to paper. Many of these efforts were of the fanzine genre; others carried articles on popular folklore. From time to time there would be more or less serious essays on how to deal with club finances or on the organisation of festivals, but at no time, as far as I know, did any of them attempt to develop an in-depth discussion on matters of style, for instance, or on the relationship of the new songs to the traditional repertoire, or on the political implications of folk-music. Such discussions would have done much to dispel the mists of mythology that shrouded – and still shroud – many very important issues.

The 1950s and 1960s was a period of rapid development as far as the folk revival was concerned. By the seventies, the revival could boast quite a large number of talented instrumentalists but of only a handful of skilful singers. And by the eighties that number had dwindled still further. Not only were there fewer singers, but audiences were drifting away. The great thrust of the revival seemed to have spent itself. There were still clubs, maybe as many as two to three hundred, located mostly in large towns, but this was a mere fraction of the thousands which had flourished in the late 1960s. Furthermore, there was now just a scattering of really youthful faces at club evenings. Most of the audiences were in the late twenties, mid-thirties, or even older. Sometimes we would recognise mature and careworn versions of boys and girls we had first seen ten or a dozen years earlier. They would turn up with sons and daughters who were almost as old as they themselves had been when we first met them. 'We don't get much time to go to clubs these days, what with the kids and one thing and another . . .'

Between 1980 and 1983 I spent a good deal of time reviewing my repertoire of traditional ballads. Both my father and mother had known a number of these songs, as had my Auntie Mag. They were an important part of my inheritance and when I began singing in public they formed the centrepieces of my repertoire, songs like 'Eppie Morrie', 'Lord Randal' and 'The Dowie Dens of Yarrow'. I sang them without giving them much thought, relying on the physical act of singing to give me the right emotional charge. Sometimes that approach worked, sometimes not. I always felt bad when it failed, ashamed to look anyone in the eye who had witnessed my failure. I experience the same kind of embarrassment when I am forced to watch an actor maltreating a role.

Most folk-song scholars would probably regard such self-consciousness as something completely outside the ken of the genuine (as opposed to revival) folksinger. I think they would be wrong. I have seen a singer, normally a garrulous person, sit in morose silence throughout an entire *ceilidh* because earlier in the evening he had sung with less than his normal skill. I have on more than one occasion heard a singer break off in the middle of a ballad and say, 'Ach, tae hell! I'm no' singin' it richt!' Professor Betrand Bronson, for whose work I have the most profound respect, has, in the course of some remarks on professional singers of folk-song, pointed out that 'genuine folksingers . . . often bring to their singing a high degree of individuality. But this personal contribution is properly involuntary, inescapable and below the level of conscious intention. It is an attribute of the song, as in their singing the song exists.'

I believe it is necessary to make a distinction between those men and women who are regarded by their communities, and by themselves, as singers and those who are song-*carriers,* that is people who can carry a tune and who carry in their heads a repertory of old songs. The singers, naturally, know the songs and regard them as their own, their private property on which they have put a personal stamp in the form of melodic ornaments and cunning rhythmical variations. The choice of a particular ornament or a way of phrasing or, indeed, of a particular pace, is rarely involuntary or below the level of conscious intention. Folk-song and folk singing have their own disciplines but inside those disciplines the singer is free to choose and, if he wishes, free to invent. The proliferation of song and ballad versions is not *all* due to lapses of memory or imperfect hearing. Perhaps more than a few versions are the work of singers who didn't like a tune or who found that this or that stanza didn't lie easy in the mouth. It is a mistake to lump folksingers together as if they were soldiers on parade. Like dancers, composers, dramatists, actors, poets and potters, they display different levels of skill and creativeness. Some are good, some less good and some downright awful. The same goes for degrees of intelligence. It is a kind of reverse snobbery to regard all field singers as infallible custodians of the folk memory. But good, bad or indifferent, few singers I have ever met are content to present the listener with an exact copy of the way their mother, father, uncle, aunt or grandmother sang it.

I had been a song-carrier since early childhood, listening to my father's splendid voice and artistry. But from the time of folk revival, singing and recording had begun in earnest. There were a dozen companies ready to record anything a good singer would put down. We did themed records, records featuring ourselves as singers; we did albums of whaling and industrial songs, love songs, sets of traditional ballads, discs of matching British-American songs, children's pieces.

In the early 1970s, Peggy and I undertook *The Long Harvest,* ten albums of English, Scots and North American versions of ballads in the Child Collection. This was a big project involving research and calling for plenty of physical stamina. Almost all of the ballads sung by me – and large number of those sung by Peggy – were without instrumental accompaniment. It might be imagined that this would simplify the recording process but, on the contrary, it creates more problems than it solves. The presence of instruments can cover a multitude of sins and technical imperfections; it can mask sharp intakes of breath, the over-sibilant s, swallowed vowels, garbled consonants, sloppy cadences. By providing something on which you can lean, it can disguise the occasional hoarseness which creeps up on you in the middle of a stanza, and the mispronounced word. It can totally change the internal rhythms of a line and can often even determine the pitch chosen by the singer.

The microphone is like a searchlight bent on seeking out and exposing every vocal blemish and the unaccompanied voice has no screens, crutches or disguises. I have heard it argued that all this is offset by the fact that it is comparatively easy to retake any given stanza in a ballad since the tape-editor doesn't have to interrupt anything but one voice plus silence. Theoretically that is so – but in practice retakes of sections of a ballad are rarely satisfactory. The problem is one of tension. To some extent the ballad-singer's art lies in the ability to maintain the right degree of tension throughout all the ballad's stanzas and in the pauses between the stanzas. Once the tension is broken it is very difficult, if not impossible, to re-establish it. If, therefore, the singer fumbles any one of the ballad's many stanzas, he might do well to begin again at the beginning.

But, you may ask, if it is so difficult why not use the crutches, the masks, the disguises? Why shouldn't you use instrumental accompaniment? After all, in the United States it is not unusual to find ballad-singers singing versions of these same ballads to the accompaniment of five-string banjos, guitars, auto-harps, harmonicas, Appalachian dulcimers. And the results are very pleasing, even exciting. But the fact is, the versions are different: they have either accommodated themselves already, the tunes and words have shifted around, the instrument has already taken over part of the role of ballad-singer. What we were doing in the revival was adding instruments to highly developed musical pieces that had been unaccompanied for several centuries or longer.

The singing of a ballad is, among other things, an exercise in discipline. The form is deceptively simple. The singer is presented with a narrative poem organised into a series of four-line stanzas with a consistent rhyming pattern. The melody to which these stanzas are joined must facilitate the flow of words without distracting the listener's attention from them. Any changes in tempo, phrasing, dynamics or vocal intensity must be kept to a minimum; indeed, they should be limited to a point where the listener is not conscious of them. How, then, does the singer achieve the effects necessary for the successful rendition of the story? Obviously the clichés and vocal mannerisms of the classical concert vocalist are unacceptable in this context. They must be replaced by the clichés and vocal mannerisms of the folksinger. Histrionics are out; or at least they must appear to be out. So here we have another feature of the ballad-singer's art: the ability to conceal the mechanism of art under the cover of artlessness.

Many of the ballads deal with situations of high drama comparable to those dealt with in *King Lear, Macbeth* and *The Oresteia,* and, like them, contain scenes of great violence. Unlike the plays, the ballads are narrated by a single voice. Furthermore, the ballad can be sung anywhere, from a stage in a large concert hall or theatre, from a pub floor in a folk club, in a farm kitchen or in the back seat of an automobile. Try staging *Lear* or *The Agamemnon* in a Mini-Minor!

So how does the folksinger deal with a work of art comparable to the best in tragic drama while still observing the disciplines implicit in the ballad form? That is the problem and one which calls for a fine sense of balance. It is really a matter of nuance; you have to give full expression to a series of tragic or comic events while at the same time drawing the attention of the listener to the marvellously economical use of language. It is, of course, possible to suggest dramatic change by subtle thickening and attenuation of lines in the text, by making almost imperceptible changes of tempo, by lengthening a pause micro-scopically or by giving that pause added charge by the way that you come off a note or terminate the cadence that proceeds it. All these devices are part of the ballad- singer's technique but, it must be emphasised, they should be used like dangerous drugs: sparingly, in minute proportions. It goes without saying that such subtleties are not to be used arbitrarily but should grow out of particular points of the narrative. Instrumental accompaniment can obscure – even obliterate – them. In our early days together, Peggy and I were not very discriminating about the use of accompaniment and a number of our early attempts at accompanying ballads were disastrous.

When, at the beginning of the 1980s, I began reviewing my ballads, I soon realised that they possessed many features which I had missed the first time round. This was particularly true of the ones I had learned as an adult. Those learned in childhood had been assimilated slowly over a long period of time, had taken root in my imagination and had grown with me. Their stories were intertwined with memories of my mother standing in the fire-lit kitchen and ironing the mountain of washing she took in every week; memories of the smell of freshly-baked bread mingling with freshly-laundered linen, of my father standing at the bar of the Workers' Arts Club singing 'MacGregor's Gathering' or 'The Dowie Dens', of Hogmanay nichts with our house full of exiled Scots and my father mellow with beer and good fellowship sitting by the corner of the table singing while Auntie Mag peers at him with her head cocked on one side like a robin as she greets every development of the ballad narrative with 'Go on, Will', 'That's right, Will', 'That's the truth, Will', and so on. The ballads I had learned in the early days of the revival had been gobbled up too quickly, swallowed before I had savoured their unique taste. I learned too many at a time for recording purposes. Now I was realising what I had missed. So I determined to learn them again, one by one, not just the words and tune and the way the two were joined together but all their secrets . . .

The first step was to map out the terrain so that I would know just how much room there was for manoeuvre. By *terrain* I am referring to what Stanislavski, in *An Actor Prepares*, calls 'the given circumstances' – the text and information contained therein, plus the melody. I began my review with the ballad 'Lamkin', using Child's A-text and a melody from Christie's *Traditional Ballad Airs*. The ballad tells of a stonemason, Lamkin, who builds a castle for the lord who, after refusing to pay the mason for his work, goes abroad. Lamkin, aided by a woman employed by the lady as a wet-nurse, gains entrance to the castle and stabs the lord's son as he lies in his cradle. The cries of the dying infant bring the lady downstairs and she, too, is murdered. The lord returns from abroad to find his wife and son dead and the walls of his apartments daubed with their blood. Lamkin suffers death by hanging and the nurse is burned at the stake.

See the 'ballads section' at http://www.ewanmaccoll.com for the full text of 'Lamkin' (Child 93)[2]

A bloody tale! But how to tell it, or rather how to sing it? I think the answer to this question is to be found in the incremental repetition which is such an important part of the structure of the ballad. Incremental repetition, the name given to the iteration of a phrase or line, a device used frequently in traditional ballads, occurs in twelve of the twenty-seven stanzas of 'Lamkin' and in all of those twelve, direct speech is used. The use of verbatim dialogue not only highlights specific details of the plot and character, but succeeds in changing the tense from the past to the present. Its function is similar to those acted-out scenes which interrupt the narration in a documentary play. Here, the action of the drama is between narrator and actor, between past and present. The first stanza is a pithy narration of facts in the past tense; we are told that Lamkin was a skilful mason who built a castle for Lord Wearie but received no wages for his labour. The three stanzas, which follow, are incrementally repetitious and effectively thrust us into the present by showing us a close-up of Lamkin's state of mind. The 'Pay me!' which peremptorily opens the second stanza suggests that we have entered in the middle of an argument. When it is repeated at the beginning of the third stanza, Lamkin's impatience is obvious and by the fourth stanza he is really angry and doesn't attempt to conceal the fact.

So how, as a singer, do I deal with this emotionally charged situation? The story has a long way to go before it reaches its climax, so I must guard against being too precipitate. After trying several different approaches I settle on a slight increase of pressure on each of the *p*'s which begin stanzas 2, 3 and 4 and by hardening the tone of the final word of each of the second lines. These are small technical points but they give body to the lines and, providing they are used with circumspection, they help to contain Lamkin's fury. The significance of the warning with which Lamkin ends the argument is reinforced by being carried on the second part of the melody. Christie's air is a two-strain one and for the first three stanzas I have confined myself to using the first strain, reserving the second and higher part for the fourth stanza. In stanzas 5, 6 and 7, the narrator takes over again and once more we are in the past. The four stanzas of incremental repetition which follow are tremendous in their power to rouse the imagination. They also slow down the action for a short time and in so doing intensify the feeling of impending catastrophe. The same device is used in the children's story of 'Goldilocks and the Three Bears': 'Who's been eating my porridge?' says Daddy Bear. 'And who's been eating *my* porridge?' says Mammy Bear, etc. In 'Lamkin' the questioner becomes more sinister, more menacing with each stanza: 'Whaur's a' the men o' this hoose?' 'Whau's a' the men?' and so on.

Some of the experts feel that the name *Lamkin* has no special significance beyond the fact that it is an Anglicisation of a Flemish name. It is my opinion that the name is used derisively in the ballad. To build a castle, even a small one, must have taken a considerable amount of time and the mason whose name probably set people bleating and baaing must have been hard put to it to suppress his hatred for those who made him feel diminished. The final insult of non-payment was merely the straw which broke the camel's back. As a singer I find this interpretation helpful.

With the eleventh stanza the stage is set for the bloodletting and again I use the second strain of the tune to end the incremental repetition, leaving an infinitesimal pause before embarking on the next section. These are three narrative stanzas in the past tense, with the actual murder in the middle:

And Lamkin rocked the cradle
And the fause nurse she sang
And frae ilka bore o' the cradle
The red bluid ootsprang.

These are complementary verses in which the naked brutality of the stabbing must be brought out without going over the top. Stanzas 15–17 must convey the lady's increasing concern and the nurse's increasing temper. I do this through an increase in tempo, retarding slightly on the last line of stanza 17.

Stanzas 21 and 22 are, for me, the highest point of the narrative and the few words exchanged by Lamkin and the nurse at this point suggest a pitch of fury not often encountered outside tragic drama, though there is as much despair as hatred in the magnificent stanza 22, which take on the second strain and follow with another very brief pause. When I use the word *pause* in this context I am referring to a momentary hesitation and not a noticeable break in the regular flow of the story. The final five stanzas I regard as a dénouement.

This is not a blueprint for the singing of 'Lamkin' but a rough guide to the way I, Ewan MacColl, sing 'Lamkin'. It is the result of much trial and error. There are undoubtedly sceptical readers who at this moment are finding it all a bit mechanical as I have presented it. But this is only the beginning of the work – the use of emotion memory, application of the idea of *if* and other methods of keeping fresh material which must be performed over and over again, will be brought into play as well. There will also be critics who will rightly observe that not all ballads lend themselves to such a convenient arrangement, but a surprising number of them do. By relying purely and simply on intuition or inspiration to light the way to an effective interpretation one runs the risk of confusing the audience or, worse, boring them. The secret lies in tracing the skeleton through the flesh and tissue of words and melody. The division of a ballad into distinct units of action is a simple enough task and one well worth practicing.

I had trouble with 'Tam Lin' from the beginning. Unaccountably, my performance would start sagging somewhere around the twentieth stanza or, if I surmounted that hurdle, I would find myself grinding to an emotional halt three-quarters of the way through. The simple fact is that in attempting to swallow the ballad in one gulp – and reproduce it in the same way at concerts – I was bringing on an attack of acute indigestion. Had I not found Tam's story so fascinating I would have abandoned the ballad. Instead I devoted time and serious thought to it. For almost a year I confined myself to singing it only when I was alone or during long car journeys. When I started singing it in public again it was with enormous pleasure, pleasure which has not diminished in the quarter of a century since then.

See the 'ballads section' at http://www.ewanmaccoll.com for the full text of 'Tam Lin' (Child 39)[3]

Unlike 'Lamkin', in which the action all takes place in a single location, 'Tam Lin' takes us from castle to greenwood, to castle again, and from castle to greenwood and thence to Miles Cross. Each change of location is signalled by an incrementally repetitious couplet:

Janet has kilted her green kirtle
A little abune her knee . . .

It is a device which is both convenient and satisfying: convenient because it tops and tails each of the ballad's units of action and allows the singer to introduce small variations in tempo at points where changes will not be obvious; satisfying because the repeated phrase possesses a lightness which allows it to come trippingly from the tongue.

In 'Lamkin', incremental repetition is used to create suspense, to build up the sense of impending doom. It does so by slowing down time. When Lamkin asks the questions concerning the whereabouts of the men, women, bairns and lady of the house, I see him standing there in the centre of the flagged floor of the hall he has built, his shadow enormous on the rough stone of the walls and the wickerwork cradle crouched on the edge of the light. The effect is of cold and stillness, as if time had been frozen in a moment of terror. The action is slowed down again in stanzas 15, 16 and 17 so that the effect is of the lady of the house making a very slow descent of the stairs, dreading the discovery of what awaits her in the hall. In 'Tam Lin' the incremental repetition actually has the effect of speeding up the action and adding a sense of urgency to what is happening. In 'Lamkin' time is concerned with past and present. In 'Tam Lin' it is past and future.

'All this rigmarole just to sing a song, a simple 'ballad,' says our inspiration-alist friend. 'Isn't it all a little out of proportion? In any case, how many of the people who listen to you sing know anything about incremental repetition? Do you really imagine that they are aware of changes of tense or differences in the function of time? And even if they were, do you think it would enhance their enjoyment of your rendition? Aren't you in danger of analysing the song out of existence? 'Tam Lin' and 'Lamkin' are a couple of folk-tales set to music, perfectly straightforward stories. Why burden them with all this analytical nonsense?'

Are the songs such fragile things that they can't be taken apart? Of course not. They are remarkably tough. They've had to be in order to survive the passing of the years. And I have never suggested that a knowledge of incremental repetition or a recognition of time and space changes are essential items of knowledge for an audience. But they *are* necessary for the singer. How else can he or she be sure that their interpretation of the ballad doesn't run counter to the author's original intention? Furthermore, storytelling itself is an art. The pauses, the nuances are not just superimposed on a text. They are worked out carefully and if they fail they are re-worked out until they are successful. 'Try', I say to my sceptic, 'and lay down that book of fairy-tales you are reading to your child and tell the story out loud. You'll learn what is *simple* and what isn't.'

25

The Joy of Living

'Do you mind being taped?' he/she, the interviewer, asks.

'Not at all,' says I. She/he knows perfectly well that I don't mind.

Anyway, why should I mind? It's a bit time-consuming and more than a little boring. It wouldn't be so bad if they came up with one or two new questions. God, it's so depressing having to listen to the same questions over and over again. On second thoughts, it is perhaps the answers rather than the questions themselves. Yes, I'm beginning to bore myself. I've tried ringing the changes on the answers but there's a limit to the number of ways you can make a simple statement about this or that aspect of this, that or the other.

> HE/SHE: If you could talk specifically about song-writing . . .When, for instance, did you begin writing songs?

Now there's a tough one. I can see where this is leading. Must head 'em off. Nick in, quick, Nikiforivitch. He/she is heading straight for 'I'm a Rambler' . . .

> ME: *Writing* songs sounds a bit grand. *Making up* songs in my head would be a more accurate description. Or rather not so much actually making up songs as filling in missing lines and verses of songs. I'd be about ten or eleven when I started singing the current pops with my cousin John Logan. Occasionally he'd come along with a verse or two of a song he fancied and I would make up additional verses. Or I'd hear a song and memorise the tune and get a kind of general impression of the lyric and for a day or two I'd be satisfied to go around humming it. Then I'd get fed up with the tune running round and round my head so I'd make up a verse or two to make it more interesting.

Actually, I started doing that kind of thing much earlier. I vaguely remember adapting short pieces form my parents' repertoire and singing them to the dust-bin-recess choristers. I'd be seven or eight years old at the time. And even earlier than that, I remember making up a song when I was in hospital with diphtheria. I would have been about five years old. I cannot recall any of the words, though I can remember well enough the ward sister about whom it was written.

ME: It wasn't really until I became politically active, that is when I was fourteen or fifteen that I really began to cobble songs more regularly or more consistently.

HE/SHE: You say *cobble* . . .?

ME: You know, the way a cobbler repairs shoes: cuts a bit of scuffed leather off here and adds a bit there, adds a rubber heel tip to a run-down heel and cuts out a new sole for a bigger job. That's what I was doing – making cast-offs fit for use again. Squibs, two-liners, four-liners, sometimes an eight line stanza for *The Salford Docker*, *The Ward & Goldstone Spark*, *The Crossley Motor*, *The Metro-Vick Worker*, the duplicated four-page factory newspapers which communist activists were producing during the early thirties. And then there were the parodies I was writing for the Red Megaphones and for hunger marches:

> Forward, unemployed! Forward, unemployed!
> Led by the NUWM, we fight against the cuts again,
> From fighting Birkenhead, we've learned our lesson well,
> We'll send the national Government and the means-test all to
> hell.

I probably wrote scores of pieces like that in those early days.

SHE/HE: And wasn't it just about that time you wrote 'The Manchester Rambler'? For a mass-trespass over Kinder Scout?

ME: It was written a little time after the trespass. In actual fact, I wrote three songs specially to popularise the idea of the trespass. One of them was to the tune of 'The Road to the Isles'. The only bit I remember went like this:

> By Kinder and by Bleaklow and all through the Goyt
>   we'll go,
> We'll ramble over mountain, moor and fen;
> And we'll fight against the trespass laws for every
>   rambler's rights,
> And trespass over Kinder Scout again.
> For the mass-trespass is the only way there is
> To gain access to mountains once again.

Not exactly a memorable lyric, is it? And indeed, it wasn't remembered. I was still doing the same kind of cobbling in the early days of the Theatre of Action. In Theatre Union I wrote and adapted songs for *Fuente Ovejuna*, *The Good Soldier Schweijk*, *Lysistrata*, *Last Edition* and a short political review, the title of which I cannot recall.

HE/SHE: I get the impression that so far you didn't regard song-writing as an important activity. More like a hobby, perhaps?

ME: Not even that. It was a simple chore to be sandwiched between more important chores. The truth is that I found writing songs as easy an occupation as talking into this microphone. It was *too* easy. I can't recall ever sitting down with a pen in my hand and saying *Now I'm going to write a song.* I made them up in passing, so to speak. Even *Johnny Noble,* my most ambitious musical work up until 1945, was a fairly casual affair. I wrote the entire thing, songs and all, in a couple of days. With the exception of those written for the projected production of *The Blood Wedding,* most of my songs were composed without the aid of a musical instrument. I went on writing songs in this way up until the late fifties.

SHE/HE: Wasn't it a rather cumbersome way of working? I mean, it must have been a somewhat slow business having to memorise each line before you went on to the next one.

ME: I don't know that it was any slower than any other way of working.

HE/SHE: More limiting, perhaps?

ME: Possibly. Of course, a lot of the songs I made at this time were set to existing tunes. That's the beauty of having a big repertoire of songs. You can dip into it whenever you're stuck for a tune or in need of a bit of inspiration. Songs like 'Twenty-One Years' and 'Champion at Keepin' em Rolling' were both written to Irish traditional tunes.

> I am an old timer, I travel the road,
> I sit on my wagon and lumber my load;
> My hotel is the Jungle, a caf's my abode
> And I'm well-known to Blondie and Mary.
> My liquor is diesel-oil laced with strong tea,
> The old Highway Code was my first ABC,
> And I cut my eye-teeth on an old AEC,
> And I'm champion at keepin' 'em rolling.

I'd spent a fair amount of time in transport caf's during my hitch-hiking days and my stint as an apprentice motor-mechanic had made me familiar with long-distance lorry-drivers' talk. I had made up both songs for a BBC feature programme called *Lorry Harbour,* broadcast sometime between 1947 and 1949. During the next three or four years it became a popular piece among truck drivers and by 1960 it had gathered unto itself half a dozen new verses, mostly obscene.

SHE/HE: So that was really before the revival had started. I mean 1947 or even '49 was way before the revival. So you could say its popularity was a simple matter of oral transmission.

ME: Providing you include a radio broadcast as part of the oral transmission. A better example would be 'The Manchester Rambler'. That had achieved widespread popularity long before its first radio broadcast. Not long afterwards, in 1959, I met a young geologist in Canada who claimed to have heard a version of it sung in a logging camp up the Fraser River. He sang me a snatch of it:

> I'm a logger, I'm a logger from old BC way,
> I get all my pleasure by sweating all day . . .

By the time the revival was in full swing I don't think there was a walking club anywhere which didn't have its own particular version of the song.

HE/SHE: When you're writing a song, which comes first, the tune or the words?

ME: Sometimes one, sometimes the other and sometimes both at once. I'm not saying that I suddenly find myself bursting into song with a fully-fledged melody and text but occasionally a line or two which I have read in a newspaper or heard in a TV newscast will pop into my mind fully clothed with a tune. This is particularly true of my political songs. On the other hand I am often prompted to write a song on a particular theme and sometimes thrash around for hours at a time just trying to find the best point of vantage from which to make the approach. There are times, too, when I go for days with a musical phrase repeating itself over and over again in my head. That can be maddening – the same phrase round and round and round . . . I can remember making up an anti-nuclear love song in 1956, called was called 'Come Live With Me and Be My Love'. The title was also the first line of the song and I just couldn't get it out of my head. It just went on and on repeating itself. I'd find myself humming it when I woke up in the morning or when I was sitting at the table having a meal. Round and round it went. Even when I was talking to a friend I would go on humming it under my breath and not merely humming it but humming it faster and faster. It was like being on a treadmill operated by a madman. I don't remember how long it lasted. A couple of weeks, I think.

SHE/HE: Doesn't that happen whenever you write a song? To a lesser extent, of course.

ME: Not at all. There have been times when an idea for a song has flashed into my mind and words and tune have arrived almost simultaneously. In the days when I used to write a fair number of radio scripts I would sometimes find it easier to write a new song to fit into a slot in the script than to spend time searching for a traditional one. Again, if a programme of songs on a particular theme called for a change of mood or pace or mode then I would write a song which would achieve that purpose. In the *Ballads and Blues* series, for example, the programme dealing with railroad songs was rather heavily weighted with hard-driving, rhythmical pieces like 'Midnight Special', '900 Miles', 'The Wreck of the Old 97' and similar favourites. In order to slow the pace down I wrote a lullabye which Isla Cameron sang without accompaniment.

Cannily, cannily, bonnie la'l bairnikie,
Divn't tha cry, my la'l pet;
Wheesht at thy greetin', your daddy is sleepin',
It's no' time to waken him yet.

Seun he'll be gan to the shed for his engine,
Seun he'll be drivin' his train through the night,
Working for pennies for you, my la'l trasure,
So haad thy noise, hinnie, yor daddy sleeps light.

When that art grown tha shalt have tha own engine,
The biggest that ever was seen on the line.

And all o' wor neighbours will point to my Johnny
And knaa he's the king of the North Eastern Line.

Pure magic! The effect, I mean. Isla's clear young woman's voice following on Bill Broonzy's slightly hoarse invocation of the twin gods of rolling stock and freedom.

HE/SHE: That song has the sound and feeling of a traditional one.
ME: Which song?
SHE/HE: The one you've just sung, 'Cannily, Cannily'. I mean, it could easily be mistaken for a folk-song. Were you trying to achieve that effect?
ME: Yes, of course. It was to be sung in a programme about folk songs.
HE/SHE: But it was a new song which you had made up.
ME: It was indeed.
SHE/HE: So how did you happen to . . .?
ME: For the best part of twelve months I had been listening for hours every day to recordings of traditional songs and singers from all over the place. And you must remember that I'd grown up in a household where traditional songs and ballads were part and parcel of our everyday life. Both my parents had sung to me from the time I was very young. I had heard them and their friends singing throughout the first ten or twelve years of my life. I was steeped in this music and now I was steeping myself still further listening to recordings of Harry Cox, Charlie Wills, Maggie McDonach, Bridget Tunney, Elizabeth Cronin, Colm Keane, Michael Gallagher, Ironhead, Blind Willy Johnson, Texas Gladden, Aunt Molly Jackson. Singers, pipers, fiddlers, harmonica players, heroes of my world, along with Marx, Engels, Lenin, Dick France, Karl Leibknecht, John Ball, Rosa Luxemburg, Wat Tyler, Theophile Ferre, Louise Michel, Wee Morris, Ted Ainley, Andrew Hardy, Jock Smilie, Robbo, William Wallace . . .
HE/SHE: And you still didn't, at this time, regard yourself as a songwriter?
ME: No, I didn't.

Strange, that. At different times I've thought of myself as a dramatist, a slater's labourer, tea boy, errand lad, ballad-singer, apprentice motor-mechanic, unemployed . . . but never as a song-writer. I even started to think of myself as a writer when I started work on this book! Perhaps if I sat down every day (or even five days a week) and wrote songs the way one lays slates or fits new brake-linings on an A-model Ford, well, maybe then I'd feel like a song-writer. Writing a song isn't like working on a novel or a play. A novel can occupy its author for months and sometimes years. A play can take weeks or sometimes months to write (unless one happens to be Lope de Vega). But a song can be written in a day, a couple of hours or even less. Occupation? Songwriter. Would anyone write that on their passport? To write a book, almost any kind of a book, demands a routine. So many hours a day, for a period of weeks or months, sitting at a desk or table with as few interruptions as possible. And you have to keep at it. It's work, often hard work, and mostly lonesome work.

SHE/HE: Surely your perception of yourself as a songwriter must have changed after the enormous success of 'The First Time Ever I Saw Your Face'?

ME: I don't think it did. If the success had followed hard on the heels of the song's composition it might have been a different story. I mean, I might have noticed what was happening. But it took more than fifteen years to take off and hit the jackpot. Peggy gave it its first performance at a solo concert in Los Angeles. It was part of an eight-week tour of the USA, for which, at the last moment, the State Department had refused to grant me a visa.

Oh, those dreary dossier people! How do they manage to look both arrogant and fearful simultaneously? For a people who pride themselves on being ruggedly individual, they are incredibly conformist. They look as though they all use the same tailor, the same barber. McCarthy's progeny. Meanwhile, Peggy's slogging it out alone. Winnepeg, Saskatoon, Edmonton, Vancouver, Forest Grove (Oregon), Reed College (Oregon), San Francisco, Sacramento, Oakland, La Jolla, San Diego, Hollywood, Tucson and men with big flags and bigger bellies picketing outside The Temple of Music and Art against the notorious Red Peggy Seeger. Salt Lake City, Minneapolis, Milwaukee, Chicago, Beloit (Wisconsin), Meadville (Pennsylvania), Ohio Wesleyan, Defiance (Ohio), Antioch, Yellow Springs, Pittsburgh, Winnipeg again. Three concerts in Toronto, Madison, Wisconsin, then back to Chicago, Philadelphia, Oberlin, St. Louis, Boston, Detroit. Then home. Hello, stranger.

ME: A miserable separation. Still, it repaid what we'd borrowed to buy a flat and it saved God's own country from a fate worse than death. It also meant that a lot of people heard 'The First Time Ever' sung in the way it was meant to be sung. Twelve months later The Kingston Trio recorded it in a sanitised version – they changed 'The first time ever I lay with you' to 'The first time ever I danced with you'. Several more months passed and it was recorded again, this time in a more apt arrangement by Peter, Paul and Mary. It was slowly catching on and in the months that followed it appeared on albums made by The Brothers Four, The Smothers Brothers, Harry Belafonte, Elvis Presley and others.

HE/SHE: You must have been thrilled.

ME: It made singularly little impression on me. I was scarcely conscious of it. I had lots of other things on my mind, not least of which was the need to earn a living.

SHE/HE: But surely royalties must have been coming in.

ME: Not at this time. A small amount, yes – a pittance, and not enough for luxuries like food. It wasn't until 1971 when Roberta Flack recorded her soul version of the song that I became aware of having written a commercially successful 'hit'. At first I didn't realise just how successful. A friend happened to mention that he'd heard it sung in a pop-music programme on the radio. I was unimpressed and continued to be unimpressed. I was in my mid-fifties and had lived hand-to-mouth

for almost all of my life. The eight years I had spent touring with
Theatre Workshop had convinced me that I was unlikely to encounter
fame and fortune around any corners. I'm not even sure that fame
and fortune figured in any of my dreams.

HE/SHE: But you must have been ambitious . . .?

ME: No, I don't think I was. After all, for more than forty years I had been
engaged in the kind of work I loved. I had survived without making
compromises. The fact that I had made very little money didn't really
worry me. I had never had much money. I had grown up in a household where money was always in short supply, in a district where
security was unknown, where survival was the only ambition. What I
do remember about the early days of the success of 'First Time Ever'
is a curious phone-call. In 1971, an American voice at the other end
introduced itself as belonging to the London representative of an
American magazine.

> 'I'd like to ask you a few questions,' said the voice.
> 'Go ahead,' says I.
> 'How does it feel to have written the Number One Hit in the
> States?'
> I had just started to reply when the voice cut in again, the smooth
> interviewer's manner collapsing before the sudden flood of hate
> and anger. 'How does it feel to be a dirty fucking cocksucking red
> bastard . . .' At this point he became inarticulate with rage and
> began to shriek obscenities. I was shaking when I put the phone
> down. Completely unnerved.

SHE/HE: How extraordinary.

ME: The success of 'The First Time Ever' was a kind of watershed in our
lives. Both Peggy and I were now in a position to spend a lot more
time on political song writing.

HE/SHE: And your way of working . . . did that change? Your approach to song
writing, for example?

ME: That had already changed. The radio-ballads and, in particular,
Singing the Fishing, had added a new dimension to our work.

SHE/HE: You mean through the use of tape-recorded actuality?

ME: Yes, there was that. But my approach to tune making had undergone
a radical change as well. Before the radio-ballads I had, as it were,
pulled the tunes out of thin air, invented them, spun them out of my
. . . I was about to say my subconscious but that's not quite true. They
were the fruits of inspiration and if occasionally one turned out to be
a lemon, well, I could always hope that I'd have better luck next time.
But with a radio-ballad I couldn't afford to leave anything to chance
and it wasn't a matter of writing one or two tunes but a dozen or
more. Furthermore, each of them had to dovetail with actuality and
to be in a recognisable folk idiom.

Techniques of folk creation . . . Bartok's phrase. Is this one of them? I think it is.
Yes. Immersed in traditional songs, ballads, tales. Teeth-chattering mountain

pool, lochan, loch, river, ocean. Problem to make up melody sounding new and familiar at the same time. Try joining those numbered in the clan of Orpheus. Startling and exhilarating feeling of newness, like crawling out of tent pitched on shoulder of Aonach Beag. Spring into summer morning, sun perched on rim of rock and first gulp of mountain air. The feeling to aim for. Oh, it was a fine and a pleasant day. Bob! Alec! Joe! Get up, you lazy sods!

ME: For each of the song sequences I chose a specific model, a song with the kind of melody I thought most suitable for a specific mood. I would then sing the tune into a tape recorder and go on singing it, altering it a little more each time until I either reached a point where I could go no further or I found myself working a rich melodic vein full of tunes waiting to be prised out. The trick was to get them out intact still attached to the fragile link that connected them to the original models. A matter of some delicacy . . . To break the link would mean risking the loss of the inner feeling of the original model, abandoning the spirit of the tune. For 'The Shoals of Herring', I tried out and rejected more than a score of tune models and in the course of a fortnight sang hundreds of first-line variants before I found one that pleased me. After that, it was a matter of seeing whether the rest of the tune soared naturally out of that first line or whether it had to be coaxed into the open. So I'd try moving up the scale a little at a time. See how a minor second above the last note of the first line . . . . hopeless. Try a minor third, as major third, a fourth, and so on. Reverse the process. Try descending. Suppose . . .

Important to try and match that note or notes in this or that piece of actuality, specifically in Sam Larner's voice. Regret, longing, old man's longings. And a kind of serenity, farewell, a fond farewell. 'I loved it!' he said, 'I loved it! Yes, I did!' I'm with you, Sam. My hand, like yours, smells of mortality. Take it, old friend, and together we'll go searching for the shoals of herring. Yes.

ME: And so it would go on. One of the techniques of folk creation, a kind of concertina-ed version of the folk process, taking hours or days or weeks to try and accomplish what normally takes years. When the final version felt as if it had always existed, then you knew you had done something worthwhile.

HE/SHE: And what about the political songs? Did you work on those in the same way?

ME: Only occasionally. It really depended on the kind of political song, on the kind of statement I wished to make and on the effect I was trying to produce. My first efforts in the political song genre were parodies and squibs written in the thirties for factory newspapers and The Red Megaphones. They dealt with domestic issues and frequently lampooned prominent politicians. They were crude but lively pieces, conceived in a hurry and easily forgotten. Nevertheless they were a jumping-off point for a category of political song which I started to develop in the seventies and eighties. They included pieces like

'The Parliamentary Polka', 'Blast Against Blackguards', 'In Praise of Famous Men', 'Dracumag' or 'Thatcheratoo the Vampire', 'Public Unpublic' and 'Legal-Illegal'.[1]

> It's illegal to rip off a payroll,
> It's illegal to hold up a train,
> But it's legal to rip off a million or two
> That comes from the labour that other folk do,
> To plunder the many on behalf of the few
> Is a thing that is perfectly legal.

More than half a century had elapsed between that song and the agit-prop parodies of the thirties. In the meantime I had become familiar with the huge corpus of political broadsides of the 17th and 18th centuries and with the songs of the Jacobite rebellions. The broadsides at their best had some of the same kind of rough, bawdy wit that had made my Auntie Mag's verbal engagements so enjoyable. Yes, they were wordy and often clumsily put together. The club was the favoured weapon and frequently missed its mark but when it *did* connect it could bruise and break bones. The Jacobite songs, on the other hand, are (more often than not) brilliantly crafted works of art. And their scope is enormous. They reflect an entire spectrum of feelings: anger, hatred, contempt, irritation, love, tenderness, melancholy and the sheer pleasure of juggling with words. And tunes – fiddle and pipe tunes to suit all the nuances of feeling so that one is constantly thrilled by the sheer expertise of the songwriter. For sheer insouciance, you'd have to travel a long way to find a song that could match 'Came Ye O'er Frae France?'

> Came ye o'er frae France?
> Came ye down by Lunnon?
> Saw ye Geordie Whelps
> And his bonnie woman?
>
> . . . .
> Many a sword and lance
> Swings at Highland hurdle,
> How they'll skip and dance
> Over the bum o' Geordie!

No frenzied bashing with a club *there* and no rapier either, just a buttoned foil in the hand of a master, darting and feinting and dabbing at will, at the arm, left shoulder, breast, stomach, groin, all palpable hits and a light kick up the backside to see the booby off. Dance tempo. Gie us a tune on the pipes, man! Something to make the blood dance! Gie us 'The Haughs o' Cromdale'.

> The loyal Stewarts, with Montrose,
> So boldly set upon their foes,
> And brought them down with Highland blows
>   Upon the haughs of Cromdale.

Of twenty-thousand Cromwell's men
Five-hundred fled to Aberdeen,
The rest of them lie on the plain
   Upon the haughs of Cromdale.

Ach, they were a wild, drucken lot following a Frenchified ne'er-dae-weel and a puckle o' lairds on the make that had backed the wrang horse. Whoremongers and wastrels, but by God they could write songs. And naebody kent mair aboot the magic o' names.

The laird o' Macintosh is coming,
MacCrabie and MacDonald's coming,
MacKenzie and MacPherson's coming,
A' the wild MacCraws coming.
Little wat ye wha's coming,
Little wat ye wha's coming,
Little wat ye wha's coming,
MacGillavry o' Drumglass is coming.

Ay, they were gallus chiels, gey high-kilted at times, ramsh, gien to quarrelling amang themselves but betimes they wrocht and sang songs that could hae wrung the heart o' a bumbailiff.

This is no' my ain hoose,
I ken by the biggin' o't.
Wi' routh o' kin and routh o' reek,
My daddy's door it wadnae steek;
But bread and cheese were his door-cheek
And girdle-cakes the riggin' o't.

ME: The broadside ballads provided me with models for songs like 'Legal-Illegal' but Jacobite songs like 'This is No' My Ain Hoose' convinced me that political songs need not necessarily be agitational. They could be reflective, tender as a love song; indeed, why not a political love song? A duet, perhaps?

    Let me look into your eyes, love,
    Let me drown, love, in a kiss.
    Kiss away, love, but remember
    We stand on the precipice.

      Love your lips so warm and tender,
      Love the look that's in your eyes.
      Eyes to face the facts of life, love,
      Lips for shouting battle cries.

    Love will help us teach each other,
    Teacher, pupil, both in one,
    Then we'll start a chain-reaction,
    What you know, love, pass it on.

Adding two and two together,
Learning to explain the world,
Pooling all the knowledge gained
And using it to change the world.

The folk-song revival, for many people, represented a reappraisal of music in general and of popular music in particular. As far as I was concerned it also meant reappraising the songs of the working-class struggle. For the most part, in Britain at any rate, songs of 'the movement' had been 19th-century creations, 'mass' songs constituting a kind of revolutionary hymnal. In the Soviet Union and, to an even greater extent in pre-Hitler Germany, attempts had been made to create a repertory of songs more contemporary in feeling. Some of these had been translated into English. A few of us sang them, passionately and, I'm afraid, defiantly. Our defiance was directed at the listeners, our contemporaries, young workers and unemployed youths like ourselves. Whatever did they make of songs like 'The Red Airmen'?

Our engines roaring, roaring to the battle,
High in the air, above the clouds we speed;
Our bombs are ready, our machine-guns rattle,
Against the world's imperialistic greed.

Fly higher and higher and higher,
Our emblem the Soviet star,
And every propeller is roaring 'Red Front!'
Defending the USSR.

The second stanza contains a memorable couplet:
We drop them leaflets while we bomb their bosses,
The first red air-fleet in the world.

Another popular Soviet song of the period (popular with *us,* that is) was 'The Shock Brigade':

We are the workers' vanguard, the shock brigade,
We build the workers' country, we're unafraid;
Constructing heavy industry, wide-spreading electricity,
We've organised ourselves to speed the Five Year Plan.

Five Year Plan of socialist construction,
We compete, we'll complete,
Complete the Five Year Plan in four,
Complete the Five Year Plan in Four.

In the Soviet Union during the heady days of the early 1930s, such a song would probably have had tremendous point, but Saturday morning shoppers in Gorton or Rochdale must have found it bewildering. The half-dozen songs of Eisler and Brecht (translated from the German) were nearer to us in feeling but for some unaccountable reason they failed to arouse much interest in the left-wing movement as a whole. I have a feeling that it may have been the bareness of Brecht's lyrics, the absence of these dear old cliches like 'Comrades, the bugles are sounding, shoulder your arms for the fray', or 'Whirlwinds of danger are raging around us', lines heavy with the diction of 18th- and 19th-century verse. Others were of the opinion that the problem lay in Hans Eisler's melodies, which were, they said, too modern, too deeply rooted in Schoenbergian atonality. When staged as part of a theatrical performance and sung by a trained or disciplined workers' choir, they were very effective indeed, but as mass songs they were non-starters. By *mass* songs I am referring to anthems like 'The International' and 'The Varsavianka', two typical 19th-century revolutionary songs – that is, revolutionary in sentiment but not in diction. I am not suggesting that there isn't a place for them in contemporary working-class struggle. There is, indeed. In certain situations they have no rivals. One might also include 'La Carmagnole' and the lesser known 'Auf, Auf, Zum Kampft'.

> Then forward to the fray, we all are born for struggle,
> Then forward to the fray, for struggle we are prepared,
> Our glorious pledge to Liebknecht we have given,
> We go the way that Luxemburg has dared.
>
> Then stand we man to man, firm as a rock together,
> Then stand we man to man, full many a shock we've met,
> Though morning witnesseth our last endeavour,
> We go the way that Spartakus has set.'

SHE/HE: Are you saying that the mass song as a genre, a category, has no place in the contemporary scene?

ME: I am saying that, with a few exceptions, the mass song written in archaic language has no place. If we are to have mass songs for today they should be written in today's language. Not the bookish language of royal epithalamia but the language of the street, the kitchen and the factory.

HE/SHE: Can one apply that criteria to love songs?

ME: Why not? People in the kitchens, streets and factories fall in love without the aid of Orlando Gibbons or John Donne.

> Come live with me and be my love,
> And we will some new pleasures prove,
> Be my mate, love, it'll be too late, love,
> If the armies begin to move.
> Oh come, my love,
> Walk in the sun while the sun's still shining.
> The sky above
> Is clear of the planes that could end our love.
> Put your hand in mine, love,
> There won't be much time left for loving
> If the storm comes and the strontium rain.

SHE/HE: But surely it's stretching things a little to call it a love song. It's a song against the bomb.

ME: It's a lover's song against the bomb. Love may be blind but not so blind that lovers lose the will to survive. So the song is also a song about survival. I once wrote a song called 'The Vandals', an apocalyptic duet about the bomb. It was completely lacking in any hope or belief in survival and, consequently, alienated anyone who listened to it. After two or three performances we dropped it from our repertoire. This doesn't mean that one shouldn't write and sing songs which deal with the horrifying effects of an atomic war. Peggy has done so, brilliantly, in 'Four-Minute Warning', a song of extraordinary power.[2] She describes, district by district, the effect of an atomic bomb dropped on central London. The sense of horror is built up in seventeen brief stanzas, in which familiar place-names evoke echoes of Hiroshima.

> North, south, east and west, see the heath and the river,
> With Chelsea on one side, Mile-End on the other.
>
> There's a circle around you, six miles to the rim,
> From Acton to Popular, from Finchley to Balham.
>
> Dulwich to Hendon, it's the heart of the nation,
> Not a blade of grass standing, complete devastation.
>
> There's a circle beyond where firestorms roar,
> From Redhill to Hornchurch, from Hemel to Slough.

At the point where the vision becomes almost unbearable, we are made to realise that we have been participating in a waking day-dream.

> Open your eyes, tomorrow comes morning,
> You have been hearing a four-minute warning.

The song lasts exactly four minutes, and there is still hope, time for us to do something about the bomb, about the state of the world. In a way, writing songs is, or should be, an act of optimism since it implies that there will always be people eager to listen to them. I still write songs about all kinds of things, even about the bomb. Well, not exactly about the bomb but about nuclear energy and those govern-ment agencies which are at such pains to convince us that nuclear reactors are safe, clean, economical and the only alternative to a dirty, drab, expensive future. I am afraid that those glossy, three-colour bro-chures which terribly terribly clever whizz-kids design for the nuclear barons bring out the cynic in me.

> If you keep an open mind, examine all the facts you'll find that it is
>   true.
> Mrs Thatcher says so and the clever chaps who run the ETU,
> All the smart, fast-talking smoothies, all the CEGB groovies,
> And the monkeys in the British nuclear zoo.
> They never lie, they're always right,
> Their consciences are crystal-clear, whiter than white,
> They're working for the underdog,
> There's no doubt that nuclear energy means jobs.

If a pressurised reactor blows its top and radioactive clouds are
    looming overhead;
And for fifty miles around the towns and villages are silent, glowing
    red.
There'll be jobs for undertakers, statisticians, coffin-makers
And demographers to estimate the dead.
And there'll be jobs for those who're saved,
Like scraping dead folks off the walls and digging graves,
Or you can work, if factory-trained,
At making plastic bags for our remains.

HE/SHE: Not what I would call optimistic.

ME: Oh, but it is. It takes for granted that everyone is capable of seeing through those pretty pictures of future Chernobyls and those bland reassuring statements about how the spread of leukemia and other cancerous diseases is just a coincidence. Not to worry! Big Daddy will take care of you!

SHE/HE: In what way does that song, or 'Four-Minute Warning' relate to traditional folk-song?

ME: Well, it relates directly to the traditional ballad form.

HE/SHE: But it has no dramatis personae or chronology.

ME: The dramatis personae is the collective *you*, the population of London and contiguous areas. The chronology (or what I prefer to call the *development of time*) is transformed into the development of place. And, as in the traditional ballads, there is no preamble; we are thrust into the action immediately, right in the centre of the city, at the Post Office Tower 'whose crown turns around fully once every hour'. From then on, each stanza extends the circle of destruction. First from Chelsea to Mile-End, then from Acton to Poplar, from Finchley to Balham. Then the ring of chaos widens to take in Redhill and Hornchurch, Hemel and Slough and, wider still, engulfs Weybridge and Harlow. Finally, the fallout drifts over to Banbury, Winchester and beyond Dover. Of all the new songs written during the last few years I don't know of any which is closer in feeling and construction to the traditional ballad than this one.

SHE/HE: And the nuclear song . . .?

ME: 'Nuclear Means Jobs'. Well, there the connection is, to say the least, tenuous, but there is a relationship, nevertheless, through the broadside ballads, that huge corpus of printed songs which Professor Child called a 'mere barbarian dunghill'. I think he was being a little over-critical, for while it is true that many of the broadsides are fashioned out of shoddy stuff, there are same few which are not entirely lacking in merit. Indeed, a surprisingly large number of them have been assimilated into the folk-song repertoire.

HE/SHE: So in a roundabout way, 'Nuclear Means Jobs' may become a folk-song.

ME: *May* is the operative word, though it isn't likely. For one thing it is too wordy and that thirteen- and fourteen-foot third line will, I think, be enough to guarantee its exclusion from the fields of folk poesy. It is, however, one of the best broadside-type political songs that I have written.

Lampoons, most of them – fun to write and even more fun to sing. What a bunch of sitting ducks. Statesmen? I've shit better. Echoes of Bob's flat Salford voice. Statesmen, politicious, meretricious, vicious . . . that's Joe's wordplay, kind of. Carryover from agit-prop satires. 'Wonder Boy' – how did it go?

> Raise a cheer, never fear
> For the safety of the nation while he's here;
> He's the man of action who is
> Known from Wigan Pier to Suez
> And wherever there's confusion he is near.
>
> When Eden bombed that old canal, our hero Mac the Knife,
> Said, I'll stick by you, Tony, and be your pal for life . . .

MacMillan seems, in retrospect, to have been a pillar of probity. And what a man of rectitude old Lizard-Face was; fearful reptilian eyes gazing at nation from the box. Switch the bastard off, but you know he's still there, waiting to strike. Thin lips mumbling paper-thin threats and warnings like rustle of secret documents. What! No songs, no trilled memorials? Too sinister! More than McCarthy? Dulles? Remember Dulles? There's a big man they call Dulles, Known as Batman to his cullies, He could win a competition if they held one just for bullies . . . And Harold: dear, plump, pipe-smoking, reliable Harold. What a fine figure of a raincoat with a man in it! Splendid chap! A born statesman. Just listen to the way he clears his throat before making important pronouncements! Mark of a real statesman.

> They can have their revolution, and yet the time will come
> When, led by L.B.J. and Harold, we shall overcome,
> With Harold's Little Yellow Book we'll strike opponents down
> And Britain will be stronger through the thoughts of Georgie Brown.

SHE/HE: I wonder if people remembered who L.B.J. was? And how many of your audience have ever heard of George Brown?

ME: I doubt whether there's more than a handful. It's one of the penalties of writing political broadsides that they become obsolete as soon as the political situation which gave rise to them passes. And it's even worse when politicians are named. I once wrote a song about Edward Heath. He was Prime Minister at the time. Unfortunately, he lost the job just before I had a chance to sing the damned thing. Even big international issues like the Vietnam War are soon forgotten. Peggy and I must have written a couple of dozen songs or more about that war. We used one of them as a kind of epilogue to every single one of our performances over a period of four or five years.

> Disc of sun in the belching smoke
> Blazing huts where children choke,

Burning flesh and blackened blood,
Charred and blistered like smould'ring wood.

> Oh brother, oh brother, did you weep?
> Oh brother, oh brother, can you sleep?

Wall-eyed moon in the wounded night,
Touching poisoned fields with blight,
Showing a ditch where a dead girl lies
Courted by ants and hungry flies.

> Oh brother, oh brother, did you weep?
> Oh brother, oh brother, can you sleep?

Scream of pain on the morning breeze,
Thunder of bombs in the grove of trees,
Hymn of rubble and powdered stone,
Anguished flesh and splintered bone.

> Oh brother, oh brother, did you weep?
> Oh brother, oh brother, can you sleep?

Programmed war, efficiency team,
Punch cards fed to thinking machines,
Computed death and the murder plan,
Total destruction of Vietnam.

> Oh brother, have you got no shame?
> Oh Jesus! They're killing in my name!

Within a week of the war ending the song had lost its edge. Mind you, it doesn't always happen like that. Occasionally you make up a song about specific issues and discover, twenty years later, that the issues are still as relevant as when the song was written. That can be a bit depressing.

HE/SHE: You've written a lot of songs about Mrs Thatcher.

ME: Well, she's been around a long time and, of course, she's a heaven-sent gift for satirists; that extraordinary elocutionised voice dripping with unctuous concern as it dribbles platitudes into the ears of the voters. Horrifying!

SHE/HE: How many have you written?

ME: Thatcher songs? There's 'The Androids', 'In Praise of Famous Men', 'Get Rid of It!', 'Thatcheratoo the Vampire', 'Second-Rate Chancers' (that's about Thatcher and her cabinet of monstrosities), 'True Love' and 'The Economic Miracle'. My most recent song about her is a piece in the come-all-ye style called 'The Grocer'.[3]

HE/SHE: There seems to be a kind of pattern in the way you write a number of songs on the same theme. Anti-apartheid, for example. The cassette you made for the Anti-Apartheid Movement – there were at least a dozen songs on it.

ME: They weren't all by me. Peggy wrote some of them, Hamish Henderson wrote one. We made our first three A-A songs in April

1960, about a fortnight after the massacre at Sharpeville. All of them are still relevant, unfortunately. 'I Support the Boycott', Peggy's song, was one of those three – a campaign song, still as fresh as new paint.

SHE/HE: And the miners' strike[4] – you did a bunch of songs for that, didn't you?

ME: A labour of love. I suppose this song-cycle habit dates back to the sixties when we were working on the radio-ballads. With each of them we were presented with a subject, a theme around which we had to write a dozen songs or more. Obviously each song had to approach the subject from a different angle, with different perspectives. So, if you're faced with a big subject like anti-apartheid or atomic weapons you use the same approach. Peggy, for instance, has recorded two albums which deal with women and their struggle to be regarded as independent first-class citizens. That's about twenty songs dealing with one subject and I don't doubt she will work the theme again and again.

HE/SHE: Is there anything you *haven't* written about?

ME: Of course. Hunger and famine, the ruthless exploitation of the third world, racism in Britain, drug abuse, the ecology . . . Peggy's already written a couple of songs about the threat to the world itself. I'm way behind. Still, I've not been wasting my time. In the last couple of years I've been developing a more lyrical approach to political songs. 'My Old Man', 'Don't be Surprised', 'Kilroy Was Here', 'Nobody Knew She was There', 'The Tenant Farmer' and 'The Island' are all part of this new vein of ideas.

> The island lay like a leaf upon the sea
> Green island like a leaf new fallen from the tree,
> Green turns to gold and morning breezes gently shake the barley,
> Bending the yellow corn.
> Green turns to gold and morning breezes gently shake the barley,
> Sun in the yellow corn.
>
> They came in their longships from lands beyond the sea,
> They came in their longships and they saw the land was green,
> Wind in the barley, trout and salmon leaping in the rivers,
> Sun in the yellow corn.
> Leaping ashore, they slaughtered those who laboured in the
>   barley,
> Scything them down like corn.

SHE/HE: 'The Joy of Living' . . . that's the most lyrical of your latest songs.[5]

ME: Possibly. It's my testament. It started out as a farewell to the mountains and developed into a passionate embrace of Peggy and my five children.

> Farewell, you Northern hills,
> You mountains all, goodbye.
> Moorland and stony ridges,
> Crags and peaks, goodbye.

The Joy of Living

Glyder Fach, farewell,
Cul Beig, Scafell,
Cloud-bearing Suilven.
Sun-warmed rock and the cold
Of Bleaklow's frozen sea,
The snow and the wind and the rain
Of hills and mountains.
Days in the sun and the tempered wind
And the air like wine,
And you drink and you drink till you're drunk
On the joy of living.

Farewell to you, my love,
My time is almost done;
Lie in my arms once more
Until the darkness comes.
You filled all my days,
Held the night at bay,
Dearest companion.
Years pass by and are gone
With the speed of birds in flight,
Our life like the verse of a song
Heard in the mountains.
Give me your hand then, love, and join
Your voice with mine,
We'll sing of the hurt and the pain
And the joy of living.

Farewell to you, my chicks,
Soon you must fly alone.
Flesh of my flesh, my future life,
Bone of my bone.
May your wings be strong,
May your days be long,
Safe be your journey.
Each of you bears inside of you
The gift of love.
May it bring you light and warmth
And the pleasure of giving.
Eagerly savour each new day
And the taste of its mouth -
Never lose sight of the thrill
And the joy of living.

Take me to some high place
Of heather, rock and ling.
Scatter my dust and ashes,
Feed me to the wind.
So that I will be

Journeyman

Part of all you see,
The air you are breathing.
I'll be part of the curlew's cry
And the soaring hawk,
The blue milkwort
And the sundew hung with diamonds.
I'll be riding the gentle wind
That blows through your hair,
Reminding you how we shared
In the joy of living.

26

Time Steals on and Steals

I that in heill was and glaidness,
Am tryblit now with gret seikness,
And feblit with infirmitie . . .

Ay, and it's a gey lang time between drinks and langer since ye muvit forth
alane upon the Midsummer evenin', neir as midnicht was past. But time steals
on and steals, as the Senecan chyld observed, though I don't remember ever
pausing in the old days to think about the passing of time. The old days! When
exactly *were* the old days? Or rather, when did I begin thinking of them as the
old days? In the seventies? Or was it earlier than that? Sometimes when I get out
of bed in the morning I am reminded of the words which Georg Buchner put
into Danton's mouth, the ones about crawling into one's bed at night and every
morning out of it. How does it go? Something about the wearisome business of
pulling on one's shirt and putting one's legs into the same britches every day.
Now why should that particular speech have embedded itself in my memory?
Why, after all this long time should I remember the sudden, sharp shock that
those words originally produced in me? I should have long ago been habituated
to the climate of failure but the intimations of future despair conjured up by
that prosaic image was like a blow between the eyes. I couldn't have been more
than fourteen or fifteen when I read *Danton's Death* and Buchner was only five
years older than that when he wrote it. Incredible! Who would have thought
that a young man could have so much death in him?

From the 1930s, all through to the early 1970s, I plunged headlong into each
day like a swimmer intent on racing the tide. So many interesting things to do,
so much work to be done; so many people to meet, friends to be made, enemies
to be fought; so many encounters, conversations, declarations of intent, experiments, agreements and disagreements; so much love, passion, hatred; so many
discoveries, places to see, books to read, plays to be written, mountains to be
climbed, rocks to be scaled, ideas to be investigated, problems to be solved; so
many planes and trains to catch, schedules to be drawn up, songs to be sung; so
many performances, concerts, lectures, seminars, festivals.

And there were the words, the new words to be taken in the mouth and savoured, dissolved on the tongue, sucked or crunched between the teeth, pouched in the cheek like gob-stoppers or licked to the smooth, brown nut kernel like sugared almonds; the jewelled and shining words of poets, the blazing words of political struggle, the endlessly uncoiling words of argument.

But time? Urgency, yes. I have rushed breathlessly through the last two scenes of *The Other Animals* and I am eager to begin work on *The Travellers*. No real sense of time passing, however, just an insatiable appetite for new things, new work, a kind of greed for creative activity. Revision? I'm in a hurry. I'll get around to it some time, perhaps. One of these days when I've run out of ideas for new plays and new songs I'll gather up all my past work and go through it with a pair of scissors and cut out all the badly written junk. But for the time being . . .

Ten years later I was still chasing my own tail, trying to catch up with all the things I wanted to do. I'm still busy trying to discover a truly authentic way of presenting working-class speech and revolutionary ideas in a dramatic form. Not, however, in the theatre. I have temporarily abandoned the theatre for folk-song. Temporarily? It's thirty-six years since I began studying the techniques of folk creation. Thirty-six years! And ten years since I became aware of my mortality and time passing and all the things left undone. Which came first, the chicken of time or the egg of mortality? Does it really matter? What is really important is that there is so little time left and so many things left undone, so many things left unsaid, unwritten; so many questions unanswered, so many problems unsolved.

As I roved out one bright May morning . . . Yes, it was a bright May morning but I hadn't roved out. At that time we had a house on the Black Esk in Dumfriesshire and I was in the barn chopping wood when that strang unmercifull tyrand suddenly appeared at my shoulder saying, 'Here's a scythe and there's a dart that hae pierced mony a gallant heart.' Ay, and mine too, he pierced mine too, the bastard!

I managed to remain upright until I reached the kitchen and then I was in the car with Peggy making that wild ride to Moffat Cottage Hospital. Hurtling round the bends of Rangecastle Hill and Fenton Heights to Boreland and over Fingland Fell and Wamphraygate, by Poldean and Dumcrieff to Moffat. A half-hour journey made in twelve minutes. A stricken heart. I can feel it now under the tender area of flesh, the zone of vulnerability, the madly racing heart trying to escape from its cage of flesh and bone. Quiet, old mole! Oh Jesus, how much time left? I thought there would be time to . . . Should I begin tidying up all those plays and things that need revising or should I embark on a new work? A play, perhaps, to show whether I have really benefited from studying the techniques of folk creation. And, of course, I want to continue singing and writing songs. Touring is no longer a good idea and even holiday trips abroad can be hazardous. Those miserable three days of intensive care in Venice! Spectral nurses (nuns?) gliding through the ward with urine bottles, priestesses bearing libations. To whom? Priapus? Persephone? Alas, my sojourn in that *ospedale* has distorted my vision of Venice forever. Time was I could look at the Grand Canal and see it overlaid with the vision of Canaletto and Guardi but not any more. Now I see, hovering in the background, Goya's black mural of *Saturn Devouring One of His Sons.* Massachusetts General Hospital (which I visited after passing out in Burlington, Vermont) has fewer nightmare memories for me, though I am conscious of a rise in my blood pressure whenever I am in the vicinity of Boston or Cambridge. And I was fond of Corsica, more than fond, until that morning in Patrimonio when breathing became so difficult and once again Peg was racing me over wild mountain roads through Frecciasca, Poggio, the Col de Teghime and down the D81 past the burning municipal tip where red kites soar in and out of the drifting, stinking amber-tinted smoke, to the *hôpital* at Bastia.

Nevertheless, while there is strength for creation, creation must be risked, as Chris once said. In any case, isn't it better to knock off while executing a new piece of work than to do so in the middle of cleaning up an old one? So here goes: a new play, *The Shipmaster,* set in the last days of sail and dealing with a sea captain who cannot accept the coming of the steam-driven ship, a closely-worked metaphor for the passing of *laissez-faire* capitalism. Quite the best thing I have ever done.

And then more touring, more recording, more frequent attacks of angina, less walking. The mountains still beckon, but I turn away. I find it painful to walk more than a hundred yards or so at a time and hills, even the gentlest hills, are beyond me. I am worried by the extra strain this puts on Peggy. She is uncomplaining but the strain is beginning to etch wrinkles on her face. I have been forbidden to drive. Peggy is threatening to buy a chauffeur's cap. Up until now I have been able to deal with illness, with gout for example, which crept up on me twenty years ago; with diverticular disease, with hiatus hernia. But heart malfunction – that is a different kettle of fish. You feel so vulnerable, such a pawn in the game played by your body.

So I have reached the point in my life when I am suddenly conscious of time passing and of the possibility of dying. I cannot claim that I sit down and ponder the imponderables or that I am afraid of dying. But I am frequently halted in my tracks by the thought of leaving so much work unfinished (and unstarted) and so many things left unsaid. Should I sit down and write five letters to my five children, declaring my love, advising, admonishing and instructing them on how I think a good life should be led? I fear that, in spite of my good intentions, I would strike a maudlin note or, by trying to avoid such, adopt a stilted or patronising tone. Then again, letters from the dead are such an obvious literary device, the kind of trick used by authors of stiff-upper-lip adventure stories. But my mind keeps coming back to Peggy. We have lived in each other's minds for more than thirty years, shared work, ideas, love . . . so when I think of dying it is not my pain I fear but hers. Guilt. That is what I fear: guilt at the prospect of leaving her with the problems of having to begin a new life.

Death, like life, has been the subject of countless aphorisms, proverbs and witticisms. As far as I am concerned, death is a cop-out. Swift observed that:

> The death of a private man is generally of so little importance to the world that it cannot be a thing of great importance to itself. And yet I do not observe from the practice of mankind that either philosophy or nature have sufficiently armed us against the fears which attend it.

The *importance* lies in the effects of death and not in death itself. It is the desolation which you sow in the heart of the ones you love, that and the anticipation of death, the feeling of uncertainty and doubt which accompanies so many decisions. I find myself these days hesitating before buying a new pair of shoes or a shirt. Will I be around long enough to make them worth the price? And is it being over-optimistic to plan a concert for six months from now, or two months from now or . . . Each spring I am filled with elation at the thought of having cheated death once again and each autumn I feast my eyes on the turning of the leaves and wander whether I'll live to see the trees reborn. Why do I think I will die during the winter months?

But it's not all guilt and decisions. There is regret. I shall regret leaving Peggy, my children, my friends, my comrades. Yes, and in spite of its imperfections I shall regret leaving the world, in spite of the grabbers and spoilers, the Thatchers and Tebbits, the ageing schoolboys with thinning hair, the plump and with-it yuppies, the wide boys and girls and all the plunderers of the common wealth.

I have read and heard tell of men and women who have learned to enjoy their old age (that, at any rate, is their claim). Are they being completely truthful? I enjoyed walking over wild moors and mountains for eight and ten hours at a stretch. I can't do that any more. I enjoyed writing against the clock for weeks at a time. I can't do that any more. Five hours at my typewriter and I am exhausted. I enjoyed spells of hard physical work alternating with intensive learning and teaching programmes. I can't do that any more. I enjoyed long and loud arguments about politics, theatre and folk-song. I can't risk that any more. Try and keep calm, said the doctor. And I enjoyed frequent and sustained bouts of love-making and I can . . . well, at seventy-four the spirit is still willing but the flesh, at times, finds it difficult to rise to the occasion. So what is there left to enjoy? You're exaggerating again, says Peggy. Well, yes . . . a little. I still enjoy my reduced hours at the typewriter, I still enjoy writing songs and singing them. It's the moderation bit I find difficult to accept. Moderation was never one of my strong points.

To work, then. I have a file of notes made more than a year ago for a play, a comedy with a cast of three women and one man. A comedy about nuclear energy. Working out the characters of three young women should be an interesting exercise. Come to think of it, *that* is the play. The actual plot can take care of itself. It's certainly amusing enough, a little too neat and tidy perhaps, but a little roughing up will take care of that. I reckon I could write it in three or four weeks or even less. And yet I hesitate. For one thing, I have another fat file for a project I have had in mind for a couple of years, an LP each side of which consists of a single band of twenty-five minutes continuous play. The theme: a road journey from Cape Wrath to London told through eight or nine songs, one leading into the other, dealing with the devastation of Britain caused by Thatcher's vandals. A kind of *Pilgrim's Progress* (or do I mean *Inferno?*) in which I could ring the changes in time and rhythm, in mode, pitch and mood. I already have drafts of three of the songs, very rough but full of ideas. Even so I think it would take longer than writing the play. It would cost a good deal more, too, between £8,000 and £10,000 to produce a limited edition of 2,000 copies. A difficult decision made more difficult by the fact that I'm in arrears with my plan to write a new political song every fortnight. I hate over-singing songs and new ones are desperately needed. Perhaps I should tackle those first and then write the play. If I managed to get into a good work-schedule I could probably finish the lot before the end of December '89. That's pre-supposing that I finish this damned book in the next couple of weeks. If it hadn't been for Alan Lomax . . .

It was Alan who talked me into writing about myself. We were having dinner in the New York Chelsea Hotel when he broached the subject, as he has done every time we met over the last ten years. He wanted a book – perhaps not *this* book but a book about growing up in one of the classic slums of the old world. On this occasion he was more insistent than usual and I capitulated. I have kept my promise and experienced much pleasure in doing so. If I have contradicted myself anywhere herein then I will call on Jonathan Swift to speak on my behalf:

> If a man would register all his opinions upon Love, Politicks, Religion, Learning, &c., beginning from his Youth, and so on to Old Age, what a bundle of Inconsistencies and Contradictions would appear at last.

Epilogue

Seventy-four years! Can it really be seventy-four years? What happened to all the time between being a young man of twenty, thirty, forty . . . fifty and an old dodderer of seventy-four? Yes, even at fifty and sixty I was still capable of climbing mountains – slowly, perhaps, but I was climbing, after a fashion. Difficult to accept that you are no longer able to run for a bus. Jesus! Times when for days at a stretch you went loping, hour after hour, over wave-like heather-crested ridges of black peat, swinging sure-footed in zig-zagging leaps from rock to rock and crag to crag down cloughs and gullies, through corries and bogs and over upland terraces of bent and tussock-grass. Wheee-e-e-e!

And the work! The coming and going, the hithering and yonning; three, four or sometimes five clubs in a week, or two concerts and a club or two, shared platforms or just the two of us. Two one-hour stints, not including encores, with Peg ringing the changes on instruments. Brilliant opening with 'Sweet Willie' or 'The Boston Burglar' with the notes of the five-string banjo rippling crisp and clear and 'Little wat ye wha's coming' ringing out low and challenging in Glasgow, Huddersfield, Cambridge, Kilmarnock, York, Lancaster, Bournemouth and the wind it did blow high and the wind it did blow loud and it waved all their petticoats to and Nelson, Aberdeen, Milan, Como, Cymbran, Chichester, Manchester city at the sign of the Plough, there lives a molecatcher and I can't tell you how Hamburg, Lugano, Baden-Baden, Seattle, St Louis, the king sits in Dunfermline toon a-drinking at the wine and San Francisco, Whitstable, Washington, D. C., Sydney, Stockport, Stockholm, Melbourne, Wollongong, Vancouver, Montreal, Saskatoon, Leigh-on-Sea. Hard travelling!

And one morning you wake up to discover that old age has come visiting in the night. Well, it's not really as sudden as all that; all the same, it's a bit of a shock (in fact, it's a hell of a shock) to find out that you can't get to the top of Suilven without feeling that your heart is about to stop beating or that your thighs refuse to obey you after an hour's easy walking. A dignified old age! Who coined that old chestnut and who are they kidding? What's dignified about shuffling your way into oblivion? I should like to be left with enough energy to depart this world screaming and kicking. That's how most of us come into it, so it would be nice to balance things out, a satisfying symmetry (I resist the urge to make a pun here). And no flowers please, by request.

But everyone, Dad, isn't the same. I mean, look at . . . what's his name? All those famous (or notorious) public figures, statesmen, politicians, dignitaries of the church. Evolution's fucking failures, lad. Fat schoolboys grown old, thin ones grown mean and vicious. They were always mean, lass, and they were born old, they were old in the womb and fossilised on contact with the air. We have grown so accustomed to these dreadful death masks that we no longer notice them. It isn't that they have stayed young-looking, it's that they haven't changed over the years. They've retained their unformed looks, their unfinished appearance. The box – the abominable, ubiquitous box – has made them familiar to us all. Talking heads, endlessly talking, saying-nothing beads. A gallery of smooth grotesques, chattering, chittering, turkey-gobbling, spittle-spattering, grimacing grotesques peddling worn-out phrases, limp clichés and unctuous lies as if they had arrived gift-wrapped from God himself. Lean forward just a little and look straight into the camera with open-eyed earnestness. Try and soften your mouth a little, a bit less shark-like. Now for that piercing glance of magnum-sized honesty. Splendid! Give it to the bastards! Make with the quiet but firm voice, let the screen drip with it, drool them into submission. Drive the hordes back to the 18th century. Beat them over the head with catch phrases. Deaden their responses with double-talk, lay down a barrage of *at this moment in time*, fire volleys of *at the present moments*, and bombard them with *at the end of the day*. Let gobbledegook reign.

We are being 'trampled to death by geese' (Kierkegaard). They are tame geese and horribly vocal. Their shrill gabble is turning us into zombies.

> Death by the needle
> Death by the pill;
> If horse don't kill you
> Then the TV will.

Tell me, Mister MacColl, MacCool, MacGhoul, do you not feel . . . (Do I not feel! Jesus! Do I not feel!) Surrounded, shadowy figures on the rim of the light . . . shadows, faces. Long, serious faces of new breed of inquisitors. No mere band of preaching friars, these. Sparkus Optatus juggling balls of white fire, impassive, mercy-less. How now, Hieronymo! Good father Bernadus Guidonis, prior of the artificial eye, prioring and peering through a glass darkly at our unmasking, our peeling off, our ritual flaying. A dry cough reminds us that Innocent III is poised with camera two. Wave of hand and sharp clack of clapper-bawd while Boniface V bends bonny head over notepad. A moment when only whirr of cameras is heard. Now what? Indrawn breath as dreaded Conrad of Marburg prepares to chartel me. What, is it to be the stoccado, the knife or the boot in the kidneys? Or the rapier, the passada, a most desperate thrust, believe it!

Epilogue

Tell me, says the voice, twisting and insinuating itself through the shadows and the brief pause is filled with anticipatory relish, *do you not feel bitter when you look back and see how all your efforts have come to nothing?* Let's call a spade a spade, the voice implies, no longer wheedling, gently flattering or heavy with sympathy. A harsher tone now, boring in with a blunt needle calculated to evoke involuntary exclamations as nerves are bruisingly explored. Tell me, Mister MacColl . . .

Bitterness. Because the political party of which I had been a supporter for most of my life was now almost defunct? Because the theatre which I had helped to create was now little more than a memory (and a memory accredited to someone else at that)? Because the folk revival to which I had devoted years of my life had now lost its impetus? Bitterness? Should I feel bitter because autumn gives way to winter and spring to summer? So the party I had served was moribund; but the ideas and concepts which had given rise to it are still as alive as ever they were. And has there ever been such a desperate need for a revolutionary party as there is today? The Communist Party's star may have waned over Britain, but in the minds of men and women communists there is still an attainable dream. Oh, the upwardly mobile cacodemics may talk airily of reforming Marxism ('it's really a very useful tool') of adapting it to 'the modern world', of altering its cloth-cap image and with a little judicious editing here and there *The Communist Manifesto* might easily take its place on the coffee table with *Vogue* and *Private Eye*. And how about a limited edition of *Das Kapital,* hand-printed on handmade paper, as a collector's item in a streamlined 20th-century consumer's paradise?

Marx, old chap, didn't foresee the kind of developments which have taken place in society. Did he not? Everything is changed; the world of the final decades of the 20th century is very different from the world of 1848. What's so different? Capitalism is still the same, only more so. The bastards have accumulated more of the earth's wealth, they are more ruthless, more rapacious, but they are still capitalists. They still live by profit, by exploitation of men, women and children, rape of the earth's resources, of the environment. Their greed is as limitless as the universe. And the poor – they are still with us, are they not? Indeed, there are many more of them now and the gap between rich and poor gets ever wider. Now entire countries, continents even, experience famine for years on end. And there is the same inexorable drive to war that there has always been, wars of enormous magnitude. And the class war is still waged with ever-increasing ferocity, a ferocity which makes the struggles of former times seem puny.

Yes, there have been changes, cosmetic ones. A touch of lipstick here, a smudge of eye-shadow there. Christ! Are those snakes peeping through the holes of the hair-net? Ah, but you have to admit the terminology has changed. Agreed, society has borrowed from primitive magic and employs euphemisms for things like unemployment in the hope that a refusal to name something will make that something go away. Perhaps I should feel bitter because the party had left me no room for surprise. It said that unemployment was a natural corollary of capitalism, that economic crisis was a cyclical phenomenon with a measurable periodicity. It said that power, and with it the world's resources, would fall into fewer and fewer hands and that as the rich became richer the poor would become poorer. They said that when the ruling class could no longer hold the workers in subjection with mere promises, they would resort to force, to fascism, and fascism would lead to war. They were right on every count. So I should feel bitter because I had belonged to a party which had been so clear-sighted? My years in the communist movement had accustomed me to evaluating experience as part of a great historical design into which was being fed more and more information. On a smaller scale, but no less significant were my attempts to correlate everything I saw, did, felt and read into a single intelligible entity which, in its turn, would become part of the greater historical design.

Thinking! Suddenly becoming aware that all those myriads of brain-cells have become activated, are combining to create order out of chaos, are helping me to explain the world! And the Communist Party has been my university. For those who have been conditioned by the media to think of communists as Moscow-manipulated automata, as fanatical robots carrying out the orders of the Politbureau or as innocent simpletons blindly obeying the diktats of sinister political commissars, let me say this: in the years that I was a member of the party I had the opportunity of meeting hundreds, possibly thousands of party members; they ranged from functionaries who had grown grey in the working-class struggle, men and women who measured out their lives in meetings, discussions, conferences, congresses, whose days and nights were spent in arranging the printing and distribution of leaflets, in organising political education classes, in fund-raising activities, in sales of pamphlets, the party newspaper and all the small but important tasks of a small but important party. There were honey-tongued miners from South Wales and argumentative ones from Durham and Fifeshire, women from the weaving-sheds of Colne and Barnoldswick, from the spinning-mills of Oldham and Duckinfield. There were schoolteachers and seamen, firemen, dockers, clerks, engineers, typists, unemployed, poets, novelists, painters, architects, plasterers, bricklayers, musicians and actors. They were bright, dull, phlegmatic, mercurial, quiet, boisterous, loquacious, taciturn, gregarious, retiring and . . . I am tempted to say that they were just like anyone else but it wouldn't be true. They were more dedicated than most people, in many instances more selfless, more aware of the world around them and more determined to change it. There were, of course, some who were later to prove traitors to the working-class cause and one or two who were Special Branch *agents provocateurs*. And there were the bores, the pompous representatives of this or that committee. There were even a few stupid ones, but then I guess that all political parties have those. Where, for instance, would the Tories be without their dafties, their little bureaucrats, their would-be 'important' officials? But I don't think I have ever met so many profoundly alive human beings, so many interesting people as those in the communist movement.

Epilogue

And why should I feel bitter because the theatre I had helped to create was no longer in existence? If actors became bitter every time a theatre folded they would be one of the most disillusioned groups of people on this earth. Of all the arts, the theatre is the most ephemeral, so why should I feel bitter because it continues to be like itself? I worked in the theatre for some twenty-five years, seven of which were spent touring with Theatre Workshop. During that time I learned a great deal about people and about myself. I lived in a state of great excitement alternating between optimism and despair. In short, I lived to the full. I acted, wrote plays, saw those plays performed by one of the most highly trained companies in Britain, won praise from Bernard Shaw, Sean O'Casey, Hugh MacDiarmid, et al. I enjoyed those seven years and would not have missed them for anything. Should I feel bitter because at the end of that time the theatre's path diverged from mine?

And the folk revival. Almost finished, said the man with the microphone, supposedly interviewing me. It was a premature pronouncement. But even if the revival had disappeared without a trace there would be no reason for bitterness. Regret yes, but bitterness? Why? For what? For having played an important part in creating such a movement? For having helped to cover the country with a network of clubs where young people could gather and make music? For having initiated the radio-ballads and proved that the techniques of folk creation could be applied to the mass media? For having helped to bring our national heritage of song to the notice of hundreds of thousands of people? Bitterness?

And would you say you have enjoyed your life, Mister MacColl? That's the kind of question interviewers fire at you when they think you may not be available for questioning much longer. At forty or fifty it is assumed that you will go on living forever, so they don't ask such questions. But at seventy, the inquisitor gets a whiff of newly turned earth or, out of the corner of his eye, catches a glimpse of a coffin sliding through the swing-doors of the antechamber into the incinerator.

Enjoyed my life? I have lived it, sometimes well, sometimes badly. In retrospect, now joining in this game of *perhapsIwon'tbeheremuchlonger*, I will say yes. I enjoyed some of it and found most of it interesting, though at the time I was so involved in living that I never stopped to ask myself whether or not I was enjoying it. It was my good fortune to grow up in a working-class community, to pass my formative years in the bosom of a politically conscious family. They provided me with riches that have sustained me throughout my life. From my mother I learned fortitude and perseverance; through my father I learned to love learning and that love has continued to enrich my days. Enjoy my life? I was blessed with a modicum of talent and was fortunate in finding ways in which it could be exercised. I found work which fulfilled me in the political struggle, in theatre and in song.

It was in the political arena that I first experienced the tremendous feeling of happiness which comes from working with others for a common purpose.

Epilogue

And other kinds of happiness too; painful walking pushing with tired muscles the leaden weight of flesh and bone hour after hour until suddenly tiredness is dissipated, gone, and muscles rejoice as legs, feet, rock and heather combine in a symbiotic ecstasy. Another peak, and another and another. Rucksack filled with air, wings on seven-league boots, blow winds and crack your cheeks! And then again, the happiness which comes with sudden recognition of something which has been there all the time but unnoticed like suddenly hearing things in an actor's voice which you had ignored before. An overpowering feeling of . . . what? Love? Yes, it is a kind of love. Dance class where Laban or Jean is trying to teach us the vocabulary of a new kind of body language. One afternoon in the recording studio when a difficult sequence in a radio-ballad suddenly came together. Concerts when Peggy and I sit side by side and probe each other's minds with songs. Yes, it is love, a soaring of the spirit, a thing complete in itself, without past or future. Not like the love you feel for your children; that love is rarely free of the feeling of poignancy and regret that the moment will not last forever, that they will grow old and may be crushed under the burdens that the world waits to heap upon them, that disappointments may dull the light in their eyes. Children! My five children, Hamish, Neill, Kirsty, Calum and Kitty. Five links of bone and flesh and blood binding me to a past in which they had no being, to a future in which I will have no being. Strange is the love you have for your children. It creeps into your life furtively like a stray cat unsure of its welcome, and then suddenly it has occupied every cell of your being. From this time on you are never completely free of the knowledge that five living extensions of yourself are loose in a hostile world and that you are five times more vulnerable than you ever were before. Your eyes seem to function differently when you look at your children; you see them as a painter sees a canvas he is working on. You look at your child's face and, in the space of a blink, you see innumerable versions of that face each signifying a different stage of development. Past and future, past and future. A sudden gesture, a turn of the head when be is unconscious of being observed; her profile as she passes by a window; actions blinding you with love and the sharp pinch of terror at the thought of time passing.

What is it that prevents us from trying to explain to our children the kind of love we feel for them? Are we afraid of burdening them with feelings too heavy for them to carry or are we just too lazy or too preoccupied with the mundane business of getting through each day without mishap? I would like to think that my children had some idea of the depth of my love for them, but I doubt that they will. Did I know what my parents felt for me? I knew they were there as a kind of background to all my other preoccupations. If I thought of love at all it was as if it was a warm overcoat which could be worn when the weather was cold and tossed aside in the summer. Still, it would be good if . . . perhaps parental love is a one-way emotion; maybe it must always be left to gnaw, unseen, at our vitals. I think it's easier for men and women to express their love for each other.

Epilogue

During my adolescence I was in love with women, with all women, with the idea of women, women corporeal, women spiritual, women pictorial and women in the flesh (particularly in the flesh, the beautiful, smooth, warm flesh), women described in prose, in poems, depicted in oils, water-colours, engravings, lithographs, carved in wood, modelled in plaster, clay, basalt, alabaster, bronze, steel and the lost-wax method. Some I worshipped from afar, others eyeball to eyeball. Some I knew for a week, a month, or three or four months. I married three of those I loved. Joan in the brash days of youth when together we set out on a great voyage of discovery into what we thought were the uncharted oceans of modern theatre. Jean, who bore me a son, Hamish, and a daughter, Kirsty. She was a dancer, a magnificent teacher who fired us all with the desire to encompass space. It was because of her efforts that Theatre Workshop, during its touring days, achieved a standard of movement which would not have disgraced a company of dancers.

Peggy was my America, my new found land. I met her in the fullness of my life and because of her it has remained full ever since. And what is it in her that moves me so profoundly? Her talent, her honesty, her understanding, her generosity of spirit, her instinct for what is good in people, her warmth, her appetite for life? Perhaps her greatest virtue lies in being able to be herself and, at the same time, to be an amalgam of femaleness. For in her I find something of all women, a special kind of perceptiveness, a wholesomeness for which words like mental, physical, cerebral, visceral, spiritual are inadequate. With my children, on the other hand, it is the part of them which is unique that engages my attention. Perhaps it is this inability on the part of parents to see more than one facet of their children at one time which creates misunderstandings between the generations, a problem not of lack of communication but of defective vision.

Time is running out on you and, apart from MacDiarmid, you haven't touched on any of the famous men and women you have . . . I mean, all those working men and women you have talked about, worthy people, no doubt, but not exactly noteworthy. Mr . . . er . . . you see, I have already forgotten their names. If they had ever been in the news or appeared in front of a camera . . . the general public tends to be more interested in people who have made their mark, so to speak. Short-sighted perhaps, but you must blame the public. They have a debased taste. And who debased it? Who destroyed their palates with gigantic doses of sugar and deafened them with the dreadful inanities of countless quiz-masters? Not the point, Mister MacfuckingColl. Vee are ticressink! Seriously, though – making one's mark is, at the end of the day, at this moment in time . . .

Jock Sinclair made his mark on those who knew him and not like an overfed spaniel pissing at every lamp-post either. He made his mark. If you had heard him recite 'Tam o' Shanter' you would have remembered it all your life, as I have done. More than half-a-century has passed since I heard him recite 'Holy Willie's Prayer' and I can still remember every pause, every inflection and the mocking glint in his eyes. And my Auntie Mag, she made her mark, hurling abuse at Mrs Cray and Mrs John Bull, a scene as memorable as the description of the enraged Polyphemus hurling rocks at the fleeing Ulysses. Sometimes I hear echoes of the impassioned voices of old timers arguing the pros and cons of the strategy of a forgotten struggle; or the measured periods of a Tillbrook peroration at the Workers' Arts Club: *Not Hobbes, my friend, but Immanuel Kant, the true philosopher of republicanism.* Men who have really made their mark. Joe Davis running like a wingless bird at a limestone wall while reciting passages from Vachel Lindsay's *Congo* or from James Joyce or Swinburn. Bob Goodman belting out Pastor Katz's sermon to the Wain Stones . . . 'there's a man there picking his nose in the house of God . . . ' Myer Bobker, Old Genge, Dick France, Hughie Graeme, Jack Evans (the Wagner of Trafford Road), Lazar (four-a-pie and one-of-'ash) Goldman. And Nellie Wallace of the flashing eyes and Blondie and Mrs Godwin and Pisser Arkroyd and all the others who made their mark, their blazing mark on the slum that I grew up in. They left their mark on me and in me. I can still remember the things they said, the way they looked and that is more than can be said for the vanishing ghosts of last night's celebrities, the heroes and heroines of countless situation-comedies, the boxed sets of family dramas, the pop stars endlessly miming themselves and each other, and the easily forgettable pronouncements of easy-mix pundits and politicians whose celebrity is fading even as I write.

And there's Bruce . . . tak'-your-glasses-wi'-ye Bruce. Willie's-gane-to-Melville-Castle Bruce. I-would-I-were-where-Helen-lies Bruce, an unfadeable laddie droonin' himsel' in pisspale ale and whiles whisperin' tales o' improbable deals, scams and ploys of stupendous magnitude and outrageous, misfortunate and unprofitable stings. Come, Bruce, tak' aff your dram and tae hell wi' a' they wersh, nice-gabbit, peelie-wally, mimmou'ed, slack-arsed craturs. My committed friend, allergic tae committees wi' their moot points and points of order and scarcely a pint in sight. And yet he's a man o' sense, ay, and sensibility tae, coupled (he was aye fond o' coupling) wi' a riotous imagination and wi' the words to gie it form and substance. And wha could ask for mair than that o' a friend? Well, mebbe I could ask for Ian tae, for the twa o' them mak's a hale, complete . . . man? World? A wee universe perhaps? Nonsense! Each of them is complete within himself, more than complete when they are swollen with argument. How I enjoy hearing Bruce's Fifeshire roar battling with Ian's West Country growl. They agree and disagree, belabouring each other with insults, curses, jibes, derision. For fuck's sake, Bruce!

Ian's a bricklayer, the archetypal bricky, the journeyman craftsman. Can read buildings, structures, foundations, ruins, the way you or I might read a book. Now there's a beautiful bit of brickwork, three hundred years old, a credit to the long-dead bastard who laid it. Beautiful. Ian's a mate of the long-dead bastard and all the other long-dead bastards who left their mark on cities, towns, villages, hamlets. A mate among mates with the masons, brickies, joiners and hod-carriers who built the pyramids, the Acropolis, Rome, Thebes, the retaining walls for the hanging gardens of Babylon. Get him and our friend

Epilogue

Glen Kitzenberger together and they could rebuild the world and improve on the original. Glen's a carpenter who has the same kind of tender relationship to wood that Ian has to brick. In downtown San Francisco he points out a curving wall that is the work of his hands. In Berkeley it's the floors in a school, in a vineyard brewery it is a spiral staircase. Ian, you two should be mates. But California's a long way off. It is! It is! Ah well, one day, perhaps. Come to think of it, we have many good friends in California. There's Debby and Steve Weiner, for instance. Now, if the world's going to be rebuilt they've just got to be in on it. Debby's an architectural historian, would be useful in an advisory capacity while Steve could act as adjudicator in the Bruce-Ian skirmishes. They're (D & S) a beautifully contrasted couple, or should I say that they complement each other. Debby is a sunny young woman, bubbling with good humour, while Steve has a nicely tempered sense of irony which has the effect of spot-focusing his most laconic observations.

Then there's Charles Laird (X chromosome fragile site Xq 270) of Seattle, our friend and window into the minuscule universe of genetics. Like Ian and Glen, he's a craftsman, a builder who labours at the bonding of ideas the way Ian bonds bricks. He erects theories into elegant structures the way Glen erects webs of oak and pine and hickory. And like all of them – Bruce, Ian, Glen, Debby, Steve, he possesses a built-in enthusiasm for living, for knowing. And like all of them he is filled with a kind of tenderness for his fellow humans. And Alan, forbye, my friend these forty years, and Howard my Goorneyish Sganarelle, my dowie knicht of the waefu' countenance . . . wi' him I shared a dream for mair than hauf a century. And Nellie', a braw fechter a' the days I kent ye. And Chris, beloved Chris, wha hewed poems oot o' every stane in Scotland and sent them wingin' oot ower a' the mapamound. Deid noo wi' Sydney wha's gane to jine his Eurydice i' the skuggie airt. Phyllis McGhee, serving boisterous, bawdy, political talk as she serves breakfast in her Dublin guest house. Bob, Lazar, Alec, Blondy, Joe, Myer . . . a' deid. C'wa, Peggy, lass, gie me your hand.

But would you say you have enjoyed your life, Mister . . . er . . .? have I? Well, I have loved and been loved. I love and am loved. I have been engaged throughout my life in work that I love. I wanted to write plays and I did so. I wanted to work in a theatre which I had helped to create and I did so. I wanted to write songs and sing and I have done that too. How many people are given the chance of fulfilling their desires? I have been wonderfully fortunate in the men and women I have known, in my friends and in those I have loved. I have been involved in lifelong love affairs with Shakespeare and Ben Jonson, Burns and Dunbar, Balzac and Aristophanes. I have had the thrill and satisfaction of taking part in working-class struggle. I have climbed rocks and mountains, walked through heather and seen my feet raise a red cloud of pollen. I have made love in the velvet darkness of a Bulgarian night heavy with the scent of roses, walked in the Corsican *maquis* drunk on the pungent smell of aromatic herbs. I have strolled in the desert at the hour when the cold night and the hot day have still not decided who shall rule.

Epilogue

In the meantime the world goes creaking along. Like me, it seems to be somewhat stiff in the joints these days and not quite sure that it's going to be here next week. And the friends of my youth – so many of them are gone, as are many friends of my later years.

> Death has done piteously devour
> Joseph of Spiddle, singeris flooer,
> Bert and gentle Alf, all three,
> Timor mortis conturbat me.
>
> Bertrand o' Maine he has brocht doon,
> And auld Moses o' New York toon;
> Vance Randolph embraced has he,
> Timor mortis conturbat me.

But the songs are still here – the beautiful, gentle, harsh, ironic, good-natured, lusty, bawdy, exquisite, passionately beautiful songs of the people. Let us hope that they continue to survive, that the kind of women and men who gave birth to them will survive, that the world which gave birth to us all will survive. I'll drink to that!

January 1989

Key to references [A] to [Z] within notes

Web resources and archives

[A] Peggy Seeger's website: http://www.peggyseeger.com

[B] The Working Class Movement Library: http://www.wcml.org.uk

[C] The British Library Sound Archive, 96 Euston Road, London NW1 2DB: http://www.bl.uk/nsa

[D] Ewan MacColl and Peggy Seeger archive, housed in Ruskin College Library, Oxford, UK: http://www.ruskin.ac.uk

[E] The Charles Parker Archive: http://www.birmingham.gov.uk/charlesparkerarchive.bcc

[F] The Charles Parker Archive Trust: http://www.cpatrust.org.uk/

Life history / general biography

[G] Orr, M. and O'Rourke, M., *Parsley, Sage and Politics: The Lives and Music of Peggy Seeger and Ewan MacColl* (1985) available as a 3-CD set from http://www.peggyseeger.com/Listen-buy

[H] Harker, B., *Class Act: The Cultural and Political Life of Ewan MacColl* (Pluto Press 2007)

[I] Littlewood, J., *Joan's Book: Joan Littlewood's Peculiar History as She Tells It* (Minerva 1994)

[J] MacColl, E. (1808–1898), *The English Poetical Works of Evan MacColl: Poems and Songs* (Hunter, Rose & Co. Edinburgh 1885)

Salford local history and children's street games

[K] MacColl, E. and Behan, D., *Streets of Song: Childhood Memories of City Streets from Glasgow, Salford and Dublin* (12T41 Topic Records 1959). The recording is available as a digital download or custom CD from Smithsonian Folkways http://www.folkways.si.edu/ under the title *The Singing Streets: Childhood Memories of Ireland and Scotland* (FW08501)

[L] Opie, I. and P., *The Lore & Language of Schoolchildren* (Oxford 1959)

[M] Opie, I. and P., *The Singing Game* (Oxford 1985)

[N] Roberts, R., *The Classic Slum: Salford Life in the First Quarter of the Century* (Manchester University Press 1971)

Key to references [A] to [Z] within notes

Theatre and politics*

[O] Goorney, H., *The Theatre Workshop Story* (Eyre Methuen Ltd 1981)

[P] Goorney, H. and MacColl, E., *Agit-prop to Theatre Workshop: Political Playscripts 1930–50* (Manchester University Press 1986)

[Q] Samuel, R., MacColl, E. and Cosgrove, S., *Theatres of the Left 1880–1935: Workers' Theatre Movements in Britain and America* (Routledge & Kegan Paul 1985)

Travellers

[R] MacColl, E. and Seeger, P., *Travellers' Songs from England and Scotland* (Routledge & Kegan Paul 1977)

[S] MacColl, E. and Seeger, P., *Till Doomsday in the Afternoon: The Folklore of a Family of Scots Travellers, the Stewarts of Blairgowrie* (Manchester University Press 1986)

Radio ballads

[T] MacColl, E. and Seeger, P., *I'm A Freeborn Man and Other Original Radio Ballads and Songs of British Workingmen, Gypsies, Prizefighters, Teenagers – and Contemporary Songs of Struggle And Conscience* (Oak Publications 1968)

[U] Cox, P., *Set into Song: Ewan MacColl, Charles Parker, Peggy Seeger and the Radio Ballads* (Labatie Books 2008); http://www.setintosong.co.uk/; see also http://www.ewanmaccoll.com

Songbooks

[V] Compiled by Peggy Seeger, *The Essential Ewan MacColl Songbook: Sixty Years of Songmaking* (Oak Publications 2001): http://www.peggyseeger.com/listen-buy

[W] Compiled by Peggy Seeger, *The Peggy Seeger Songbook: Forty Years of Songmaking* (Oak Publications 1998)

[X] Seeger, P. (ed) *The New City Songster*, 21 volumes (microfiche copies from http://www.lexisnexis.com/academic/catalog/2006pdfs/PopCulture.pdf) featuring songwriters from all over the English-speaking world, compiled by Peggy between 1968 and 1987; http://www.wcml.org.uk/ search: New City Songster

[Y] MacColl, E. and Seeger, P., *The Singing Island: A Collection of English and Scots Folksongs* (Belwin-Mills Music 1960)

[Z] MacColl, E. *Personal Choice* (Workers' Music Association 1953) contains several of the traditional songs which Ewan learnt from his father, William Miller. See http://www.wcml.org.uk/ search: Personal Choice

---

* 'Theatre Workshop – Joan Littlewood' has been the subject of recent works by Robert Leach (University of Exeter Press 2006), Nadine Holdsworth (Routledge 2006) and Murray Melvin, Editor (Oberon Books Ltd 2006)

Notes

Introduction

1 'A journeyman' is a tradesman or craftsman who has completed an apprenticeship. He would normally be employed by a master craftsman but, unlike 'an apprentice', would not be bound to the master for a fixed term.
2 Jean Newlove, a Laban-trained dancer, met and married Ewan MacColl when she became Theatre Workshop's choreographer and movement teacher. She was the second of Ewan's three wives and bore him two children: Hamish MacColl, and the extremely talented singer and songwriter Kirsty MacColl, who died in an accident on December 18 2001.
3 See [H] Chapter 4: Browned Off.
4 See [U].

Chapter 1 Early Days and Hogmanay

1 Zeppelins were rigid airships, named after their inventor and used as bombers during World War I from January 1915 until 1917, when fighter planes became effective in shooting them down.
2 Audio recordings of Betsy Miller are held at [C] [D] and [E].
3 See [Z] or listen to Ewan's *Songs of Robert Burns* (FOLKWAYS FW 8758) available from Smithsonian Folkways http://www.folkways.si.edu/ as a digital download or custom CD.

Chapter 2 One in Three Million

1 See [Q] Part 6: Ewan's father was out on strike for 11 months at this time.
2 See [I]. Joan Littlewood was Ewan MacColl's first wife.

Chapter 3 Front Doors and Back Entries

1 See [N] Chapters 1 'Class Structure'; 2 'Possessions'; 3 'Manners and Morals'.
2 See [L] Chapter 12 'Children's Calendar – May Day'. The song also features in *A Ragged Schooling* by Robert Roberts (Manchester University Press 1976) Chapter 6 The Food of Love.

Notes

3 See [N] Chapter 5 – the common scene, which reports on the mass strikes of June 1911 involving seamen, firemen and dockers.
4 See [M] for variants of '*Poor Mary/Jenny/Nellie/Sally*' or listen to [K] for Ewan's sung version of '*Poor Mary*'. See [N]: Chapter 8 – culture, and other circle and hopping games played in Salford.
5 See [N] Chapter 5 'Food, Drink and Physic'.

Chapter 4 Unnatural Habitat

1 See *A Ragged Schooling* by Robert Roberts (Manchester University Press 1976)

Chapter 5 Lodgers and Friends

1 'Eppie Morrie' (Child 223) is on MacColl/Seeger's *Popular Scottish Songs* FW 8757

Chapter 6 The Gang

1 See [M] for more on ring games: chapters V 'Wedding Rings'; XIV 'Calls of Friendship'; XVI 'Static Circles'; and XVII 'Eccentric Circles'.
2 See [L] for tongue-twisting rhymes and nonsense rigmaroles: Chapter 2 'Just For Fun'.
3 The Miller Street Boys were a rival gang. See [Y] song 5 'Raid 'Em' for mention of other gangs (the boys of Percy Street/Unwin Square/Hanky Park) or listen to [K].
4 See [L] for more on tests, Chapter 8 – code of oral legislation and initiation rites, and Chapter 13 – occasional customs.
5 See [L] Chapter 12 – children's calendar, and Chapter 18 – pranks, including door knocking and bell ringing.
6 *Lancashire – Manchester & Salford 1927 Kelly's Directory – Alphabetical List of Residents with addresses and occupations* (63BTR Back To Roots UK Data CD http://www. backtoroots.co.uk) locates 'Miller William, moulder' at 37 Coburg Street. However, most of the residents profiled in *Journeyman* date from earlier years in Ewan's childhood. Visit the Microfilm Unit (Manchester Archives and Local Studies) at Manchester Central Library (http://www.manchcstcr.gov.uk/libraries/arls) where Slater's and Kelly's Directories for this period can be viewed free of charge.

Chapter 8 Happy Days

1 We learn in [Q] Chapter 6 that Ewan went to Grecian Street elementary school. In what he calls 'the big school' there were about eight or nine hundred pupils. A large proportion of these were poverty-stricken Jews whose parents were generally from Russia, Poland, Hungary and Romania.
2 Also in [Q] Chapter 6 Ewan acknowledges Mr Rushworth's influence in fostering his interest in literature, as well as mentioning Miss Tate's hatred of the working class.

Chapter 12 Big City Big Georgie

1 See [Q] Chapter 6 for more about Ewan's induction into The Young Communist League.
2 [Q] Chapter 6 also includes a short profile of Joe Davis.

Notes

Chapter 13 Politics, Purience and Fresh Air

1 Ewan's song 'The Manchester Rambler' is quoted in Dr Pat Rickwood's *The Story of Access in the Peak District* (a Peak National Park Publication 1982) as 'probably the best thing that came out of the Kinder Mass Trespass demonstration of 1932'. Ewan was with the marchers as Press Officer of the campaign. See [J] for the songs and poems containing descriptions of natural scenery by Ewan's Scottish Muse, the 19th-century poet Evan MacColl. The lyrics of Ewan's 'The Manchester Rambler' and 'The Joy of Living' draw from his love and knowledge of poetry as well as his direct appreciation of hills and mountains.

Chapter 14 New Comrades

1 Also quoted in [Q] (page 220).
2 In [Q] Chapter 6, Ewan also describes his role in running factory newspapers like the *Salford Docker*, the *Crossley Motor* and the *Ward and Goldstone's Spark*.

Chapter 16 Theatre of Action

1 See playscript in [P] for Bluemenfeld's English adaptation of *Newsboy*; see [Q] for the 1934 American version of *Newsboy* (adapted for American League against War and Fascism by Gregory Novikov from the poem by V.J. Jerome); see [O] Chapter 1 for extracts from Ewan's production of *Newsboy*.
2 See [P] for the playscript: *John Bullion*.
3 See [P] for the playscript: *Waiting for Lefty* (1935) as well as comments on the play's impact.

Chapter 17 Living in London

1 *Draw The Fires* was a drama dealing with the revolt of the German navy during the Sparticist period in Germany. See [Q] page 249.
2 See [Q] page 252 for more on *Miracle at Verdun*.

Chapter 18 Megaphones to Microphones

1 See [V] page 378 for a summary of Ewan's radio work (from 1933 onwards).

Chapter 19 Theatre Workshop

1 These productions are described in [O]. See also [U] page 375 for a Theatre Chronology and list of Ewan's dramatic works.
2 See [P] for the playscript: *Uranium 235*.
3 See [P] for the playscript: *Johnny Noble*.

Chapter 20 On the Road

1 See [P] for the playscript: *The Other Animals*.

Notes

Chapter 21 Enter Alan Lomax

1 See [O].
2 See *The Land Where The Blues Began* by Alan Lomax (Minerva 1994) and *America Over The Water* by Shirley Collins (SAF Publishing 2006).
3 See [V].

Chapter 22 Into The Folk Revival

1 'Ballads and Blues' was a loose coalition of like-minded jazz and folk musicians that emerged from the BBC's 1953 radio series (6 feature programmes) of the same name. 'Ballads and Blues' was re-launched as a Folk Club, with mention of 'skiffle' dropped, on 24 November 1957 at the already familiar Princess Louise Pub in High Holborn. See [H] Chapter 6.
2 The 20th-century classical composer Ralph Vaughan Williams who, together with A.L. Lloyd, edited *The Penguin Book of English Folk Songs* (Penguin Books 1959)
3 A reference to the rift between MacColl and Seeger and members of the *English Folk Dance and Song Society* (based in Cecil Sharp House) for whom 'heritage' was not so centred on social justice and class struggle.
4 For more about The Critics Group, see [V] page 386 Appendix III, [U] Chapter 21 'Ballads of Accounting' pages 236–243, [H] pages 184–217.
5 See [V] page 382. Transcripts for the sketches, which Ewan wrote for The Festival of Fools, are in the Ruskin Archive [D]. There is also a video recording (originally made in 16mm ciné, but copied to VHS and DVD) of the 1970 Festival, performed live at The Singers' Club. Excerpts from a studio recording of the 1968 Festival are included on [G] available for purchase as audio-cassettes or CDs.
6 See [U].

Chapter 23 Radio Ballads

1 See http://www.ewanmaccoll.com. For a list of all The Radio Ballad songs 1957–1964 See [V] page 379. See [U] for a 2008 book dedicated to the making of the MacColl/Parker/Seeger Radio Ballads.
2 Sam Larner can be heard singing and speaking on *Now Is The Time For Fishing* (TSCD511 TOPIC 1999 / FW3507 Smithsonian Folkways).
3 *Journeyman* does not do justice to Ewan and Peggy's coverage of The Travelling People. See [R] for their collection of Travellers' Songs and [S] for a study of Romany and the cant as well as a treasury of tales, jokes, riddles and children's songs.

Chapter 24 Singing and Song-Writing

1 See [X]. Between 1968 and 1987 Peggy edited 21 volumes of *The New City Songster*.
2 'Lamkin' is on set 3 of The Long Harvest: http://www.camscomusic.com.
3 'Tamlin' is recorded on 'Cold Snap' FW 8765 (see below).

Notes

Chapter 25 Joy of Living

1 These political songs (1977–1986) were originally recorded on LPs on MacColl/ Seeger's own 'Blackthorne Records' Label. They are now available from Smithsonian Folkways http://www.folkways.si.edu/ as digital downloads or Custom CDs: e.g. *Cold Snap* FW 8765, *Hot Blast* FW 8710, *Kilroy Was Here* FW 8562. Some are also on the 2 CD Set – Ewan MacColl *Antiquities* (1998 Snapper Music/ issued under license from Cooking Vinyl).

2 'Four Minute Warning' concludes *Kilroy Was Here* FW 8562. See [W] for full lyrics and music.

3 The 2 CD Set, Ewan MacColl *Antiquities*, contains some of these.

4 *Daddy, What Did You Do In The Strike* (audio-cassette Blackthorne BS1, produced in collaboration with the NUM) a musical documentary of the 1984 miners' strike in 6 songs.

5 'The Joy of Living' is the final track both on the 2 CD Set, Ewan MacColl *Antiquities* and on *Black and White, Ewan MacColl, The Definitive Collection* (Cooking Vinyl 1990 COOKCD 038).

Index

agitprop 165, 168–9, 195–6, 202–6, 208–12, 350, 356
    see also Critics Group; plays; politics; theatre; theatre groups
Armitage, Alf 205, 212
Armstrong, Alec 182–3, 188–90, 194, 205
atomic energy *see* nuclear energy
Australia 10–11, 14–15

Balls, Ronnie 310
Baker, Laurence 169–70
Behan, Brendan 282
books of lasting influence on EM 9, 18, 42, 99, 108–11, 124–5, 134–7, 150, 153, 165, 197, 361, 364–5
Bowen, Bunny 237
Brandes, Ruth 238, 242
Bray, Jim 314
Brecht, Bertholt 209, 352–3
Bridson, D.G. 227–8
Britten, Benjamin 282
Brockway, Fenner 40
Bronson, Bertrand 335
Broonzy, Bill 266, 346
Burke, Harry 172–4
Burns, Robert 16, 65–6, 110–11, 158

Christie, Isabelle (EM's grandmother on mother's side) 5, 9
classical music 119, 201, 273–5
Coleman, Fritzroy 267, 277
Colyer, Ken 264–7
Cox, Harry 281
Cox, Peter xiii, 377
Critics Group 296–300, 331
    Festival of Fools 299
    St George and the Dragon (mumming play) 299
    see also agitprop; theatre

Daly, Brian 314
Davidson, Bill 238
Davis, Joe 165–6, 373

death 17, 30–1, 66–8
    EM's view of 361, 363–4
    illnesses of EM xii, 25–6, 41–2, 99, 107, 362–3
    rituals of, in Salford 47, 86–7
    songs about 268, 337–40, 358–60

Edwards, Alf 267, 312–14
Eisler, Hans 209, 352–3
Engels, Friedrich 140, 181, 232
Ennis, Seamus 262, 280
Ethel (Welsh cook) 101, 127–8

family
    see Christie, Isabelle; Hendry (various); Littlewood, Joan; Logan (various); MacColl (various); Miller (various); Newlove, Jean; Seeger, Peggy; Stratton, Elizabeth; Stewart, Jimmie
folk music and song writing 261–6, 272–6
folk music and song writing (*cont.*)
    EM's background in 35, 159, 346–7
    EM's work with Peggy Seeger in 266–72, 277–9, 283–94, 296–360
    revival of 277–300, 328–41, 370
    see also radio ballads; songs
France, Dick 23, 186, 192–5
Friedman, Mr 143, 146

Germany 157, 166, 232–3
Goodman, Bob 164–6, 171, 183–5, 198, 373
Goorney, Howard 237, 242, 244, 260, 374

Harding, Archie 206, 224–30
Heanan, Joe 170–4
Heaney, Joe 300
Henderson, Hamish 258, 262, 264, 357
Hendry (relatives on EM's mother's side) 7–11, 14
    see also Logan, (various); Miller, Betsy née Hendry (EM's mother)

Illingworth, Nelson 247
Ireland and the Irish 112, 305
Italy 233

Index

jazz music 56, 188

Kennedy, Peter 262

Laban, Rudolph 247
Larner, Sam 307–9, 312, 349
Lenin, Vladimir 19, 110, 140
libraries
  Manchester New Central Library 197
  Manchester Reference Library (Piccadilly)
    196–7
  Peel Park Library 28–9, 131–3, 135–7
  see also books of lasting influence on EM
Lind, Kerstin 238
Littlewood, Joan (EM's first wife) x, 31, 206–12,
    213–23, 239, 241, 243, 372
  see also theatre; theatre groups, Theatre of
    Action / Theatre Union / Theatre
    Workshop
Lloyd, A.L. (Bert) 262, 266, 269, 271, 280–2,
    329–30
lodgers (of influence on EM during childhood
    and adolescence) 60–4, 140–1, 152–3,
    157–61
Logan, John (EM's cousin) 4, 20, 54–9
Logan, Mag(gie), née Hendry (EM's aunt) 4, 10,
    14, 20–1, 27–8, 32, 48–9, 54
Logan, Nancy (EM's cousin's cousin) 58–9
Logan, Tammy (EM's uncle) 20, 27–8, 32
Lomax, Alan 261–3, 269–70, 301, 330, 365 *see
    also* folk music; television, Ballads and
    Blues (TV series)

MacColl, Calum (younger son of EM and Peggy
    Seeger) 15, 371
MacColl, Hamish (son of EM and Jean Newlove)
    15, 250, 271, 371–2
MacColl, Kirsty (daughter of EM and Jean
    Newlove) xii, 371–2
MacColl, Kitty (daughter of EM and Peggy
    Seeger) xiii, 371
MacColl, Neill (older son of EM and Peggy
    Seeger) 371
MacDiarmid, Hugh (pseud. of Christopher
    Grieve) 31, 250, 272, 275–6, 282
MacLean, John 13–14
MacNeice, Louis 305
Marx, Karl 144, 259, 368
Maxton, Jimmy 40
Meana, Louis 241
Miller (aunts, uncles and grandfather on EM's
    father's side) 7–12, 22, 222, *see also* Miller,
    Will (EM's father)
Miller, Betsy, née Hendry (EM's mother)
  childhood and early working life of 5–10, 12
  marriage 14
  relationship with son 4–5, 32, 122–3, 133–4,
    147–8
  Salford days and later 3–4, 19–22, 30–1, 47–9,
    98, 174
  see also Salford – work

Miller, Will (EM's father) 11–15, 21, 24–31, 45,
    52–3, 98, 107–8
  attempted suicide 29–30
  illnesses 11, 15, 25
  relationship with son 12–13, 15–17, 29–31
    as singer 16, 18–21, 60–1, 66–8
  see also Salford – unemployment; Salford
    – work

Newlove, Jean (EM's second wife) ix, 247, 372
  children (*see* MacColl, Hamish; MacColl,
    Kirsty
  dance and theatre (*see* Theatre Groups, Theatre
    Workshop)
nuclear energy and weapons 239, 354–5, 364–5,
    see also plays (by EM), *Uranium 235*

Old Genge 186, 192

Parker, Charles 300, 301–27
  see also Radio Ballads
Patterson, Meg 121–3
Percy/Jack/Bill (editor) 148–51
Petrie, May 123–5
plays (by EM)
  Blitz Song 260
  Flying Doctor 238–40, 255–7, 259
  Good Soldier Schweijk, The (adapted from
    Jaroslav Hašek's novel) 233, 237, 259
  Hell is What You Make It 260
  John Bullion (also by Joan Littlewood) 210
  Johnny Noble (ballad-opera) 239, 245, 255–6,
    264, 344
  Landscape with Chimneys 253, 260, 268
  Last Edition 233
  Operation Olive Branch 249, 258–60
  Other Animals, The 249, 255, 258, 261
  Rogues Gallery 260
  Shipmaster, The xi, 363
  So Long at the Fair 259, 261
  Travellers, The 250, 255–7, 261
  'Uranium 235' 239, 244–5, 251, 255, 260,
    266
plays (by others: also performed in theatre groups
    to which EM belonged)
  Blood Wedding, The 267–8, 344
  Draw the Fires 233
  Fuente Ovejuna 233, 237
  Gentle People, The 249
  *Love of Don Perlimplin for Belisa in her Garden,
    The* 241–2, 259
  Lysistrata 233, 237, 247
  Miracle at Verdun 222–3
  Newsboy 206, 209–10
  Proposal, The 249
  Ragged Trousered Philanthropists, The 152
  Rent Interest and Profit (agit-prop sketch) 169,
    202
  Singing Jailbirds, The 152
  Waiting for Lefty 210
  see also agitprop; theatre; theatre groups

Index

poems
  'Death and Doctor Hornbrook' 110–11
  'Fire Sermon, The' 208
  'Mask of Anarchy' 208
  'Red Front, The' 208
  'Stowaway, The' 162
  'Strange Funeral at Braddock' 205
  'Timor Mortis Conturbat Me' 361, 375
  'Walker, The' 204–5
  'When War was declared on Russia' 6
  see also MacDiarmid, Hugh; MacNeice, Louis
politics and union work
  of EM 23–4, 110, 141, 191–6, 231–3, 350,
    356–8
  of EM's father 13–14, 16, 19, 23–4, 26, 40,
    106, 174
  apartheid 357–8
  blacklists 28, 127
  class system 33–4, 57, 283–4, 306–7, 329–30
politics and union work (cont.)
  Communist Party 62, 140, 166–7, 185–7
    EM's belief in 329, 368–9
    EM censured by 210–12
    EM's work for 177, 180–2
    Young Communist League 24, 152–5, 157,
      182
  demonstrations 191–6, 330–1
  General Strike (1926), 19, 26
  imperialism 83–4, 112, 132, 181–2
  Independent Labour Party 40
  International Union of Revolutionary Theatres
    203–4
  May Day 38–40
  trade unions 13–14, 16, 19, 26, 107, 186
  Workers' Art Club 65, 154, 185
  Workers Theatre Movement 203, 208–9
  see also agitprop; Salford – unemployment
Prix d'Italia 305
Pudney, John 226–9
Puscy, Marion 230

radio 206, 224–31, 266–7, 269, 301–27, 331,
  333–4, 345, 348–9
  see also Bridson, D.G.; Harding, Archie; Prix
    d'Italia; Pudney, John; Pusey, Marion;
    radio ballads; Tunnel (documentary)
radio ballads
  Ballad of John Axon, The 301–5, 313, 316, 319
  Big Hewer, The 317–19
  Body Blow, The 320–1
  Fight Game, The 323–4
  On the Edge 321–3
  Singing the Fishing 307–17
  Song of a Road 305–7, 316, 320
  Travelling People, The 324–5
  see also folk music and song writing; Parker,
    Charles; Seeger, Peggy
Raffles, Gerry 237, 260
'Rastignac' (law student and library acquaintance)
  197–200
Redgrave, Michael 256

religion 53, 99, 137, 280
  Jews and Judaism 99, 109, 113–15, 140
Rouget, Gilbert 262

Salford – adult neighbours
  Caldwell, Mrs 24–5, 87–8
  Caldwell, Arthur 24–5, 30, 36, 87–8, 128
  Callender, Mr 48–9
  Drummond, George 18, 43, 88
  Drummond, Mary 17, 34, 42–4, 87–9
  Fenton, Mr (and daughters) 99–100
  Godwin, Mrs 44, 96
  Innes, Mr & Mrs 85–6, 88
  Ollerenshaw, Mrs 71
  Sinclair, Jock 21, 28, 64–8, 372
  Strickland, Mrs 71, 91
Salford – childhood friends
  Barlow, Stanley 53–4, 103, 110, 129
  Drummond, Alfred (Killus) 34, 42, 44, 75–6,
    78, 80–1, 92–3, 95, 131
  Evans, Horace 53–4, 164
  Glover, Harry 101–2
  Godwin, Tolly 70, 73, 75, 78, 80, 92–4, 96,
    98–9, 133
  Patterson, Dave & Meg 121–4
  Ryan, Dennis 112–13
  Schneider, Izzy 110, 113–15, 122–3, 126, 129
  Tattesall, 'Snotty' 8
Salford – schooling 4–5, 32, 51–3, 105–19,
  125–6, 130
Salford – schoolteachers
  Betancourt, Mr 118–19
  Driscoll, Mr 51–2
  Ellerby, Mr 105, 113, 118, 130
  Gale, Mr 109, 114, 125–6
  Little, Mr 112–15
  Pitt, Miss 118–19, 125
  Pratt, Miss 144–6
  Rushwood, Mr 109–12, 125
  Shield, Mr 115–17, 128
  Small, Mr 83–4
  Tate, Miss 106–9, 112, 116, 128
  Thomas, Mickey 52–3
Salford – street life
  burial clubs 47, 86–7
  celebrations 19–22, 36–40, 45–6
  cinema 42–3, 96, 126
  games and rituals 40–1, 69–73, 76–7, 100, 109,
    126
    'bottling' 142–3
    cigarette cards 72–3, 102
    'monkey parade' 57
  gangs 41, 73–83, 93–4, 120–1
  hawkers and vendors 46–7, 49
  holidays and excursions 43–5, 54–6, 166,
    174–7, 188, 201
    Blackpool 44
  knocking-up 85–6
Salford – unemployment
  EM 130–9, 140–1, 147, 150–1, 163, 191
  EM's father 27–9, 127, 135–6, 153, 169

Index

Salford – work
  EM 141–51, 169–74, 189–91
  EM's father 11–15, 22, 26–7
  EM's mother 27, 84, 127–8
Scase, David 238
Scotland
  Hogmanay 19–22
  'Kailyard' (school of Scottish fiction); kaleyard (cabbage patch) 276
Seeger, Peggy (EM's third wife)
  children see MacColl, Calum; MacColl, Kitty; MacColl, Neill
  collaboration on radio ballads 303–5, 309, 312, 315–17, 319, 322–5
  in concerts 277–9, 283–7, 291–2, 330, 337, 347–8, 355, 357–8
  Critics Group 296–300
  life with EM 269–72, 319, 362–3, 372
  see also folk music; radio ballads; songs
skiffle music 265–6
Smith, H. Verity 238
songs (by EM)
  'Champion at Keepin' 'em Rolling' 344
  'Come Live with Me' 353–4
  'Disc of Sun' 356–7
  'First Time Ever, The' 347–8
  'Forward Unemployed!' 343
  'Go Down You Murderers' 268
  'Island, The' 358
  'Joy of Living' 358–60
  'LBJ Looks After Me' 356
  'Legal-Illegal' 350
  'Love for Love' 351–2
  'Manchester Rambler, The' 343
  'Nuclear Means Jobs' 345–5
  'Wonder Boy' 356
songs (by Peggy Seeger)
  'Four Minute Warning' 354
songs (revolutionary)
  'Auf Auf Zum Kampf' 353
  'Red Airmen, The' 352
  'Shock Brigade, The' 352
songs (traditional ballads and others)
  'Awa' ye wee daft article' 21
  'Bonnie Earl of Murray' 297–8
  'Came ye over frae France?' 345–6
  'De'il's Awa' Wi' th' Exciseman' 67
  'Eppie Morrie' 67
  'Haughs of Cromdale, The' 350–1
  'If it Wasn't Quite a Mile' 20
  'I'm Sitting on the Stile Mary' 18
  'Laird o' Macintosh, The' 351
  'Lamkin' 337–340
  'Lang hae we pairted been' 67
  'On the Croft' 36
  'Poor Mary sat a-weepin' ' 41

'Salford May song' 38
'Tan Lin' 340
'This is No' My Ain Hoose' 351
'Wee Drappie o't' 55
'We're off for Canaan's shore' 55
Ye Banks and Braes o' Bonnie Doon' 31
see also folk music
Soviet Union 212, 221–2, 352–3
  Moscow School of Cinema and Theatre 212
Spain 233
Stanislavski, Konstantin 297, 337
Stewart, Jimmie (EM's cousin) 7
Stratton, Elizabeth (EM's grandmother on father's side) 11
street life (see Salford – street life)
Sweden 249–50

Taplow, Miss 144–6
television 369, 331
  Ballads and Blues (TV series) 264, 266–7
Thatcher, Margaret 357
theatre 109, 217, 219, 221–2, 231–2, 299–300, 365–5
  EM's classes in 217, 219, 221–2
  folk theatre 299–300
  see also plays; theatre groups
theatre groups
  Clarion Players 141, 152, 165, 168
  Red Megaphones 168–9, 195–6, 202–6, 222, 267
  Theatre of Action 205–8, 210–12, 222, 343
  Theatre Union 223, 233, 267–8, 343–4
  Theatre Workshop
    EM's break from 258–60, 370
    EM's writings for 239, 250, 253, 258–61, 266–8
    formation of 237–40
    in Stratford East 259–60, 266
    Shakespeare, William (adaptations and productions) 255, 257
    tours by 240–61, 266
  see also Critics Group; plays; theatre, folk theatre

Tunney, Paddy 300
Tunnel (documentary) 206, 227–8
Turner, Bruce 314–15
Turner, Pearl 237–8

Vietnam 331, 356–7

Wilson, Harold 356
Wanamaker, Sam 255–6
Williams, Rosalie 237
Wylie, Sanny 23, 28, 60